A Photographic History of
INFANTRY WARFARE
1939-1945

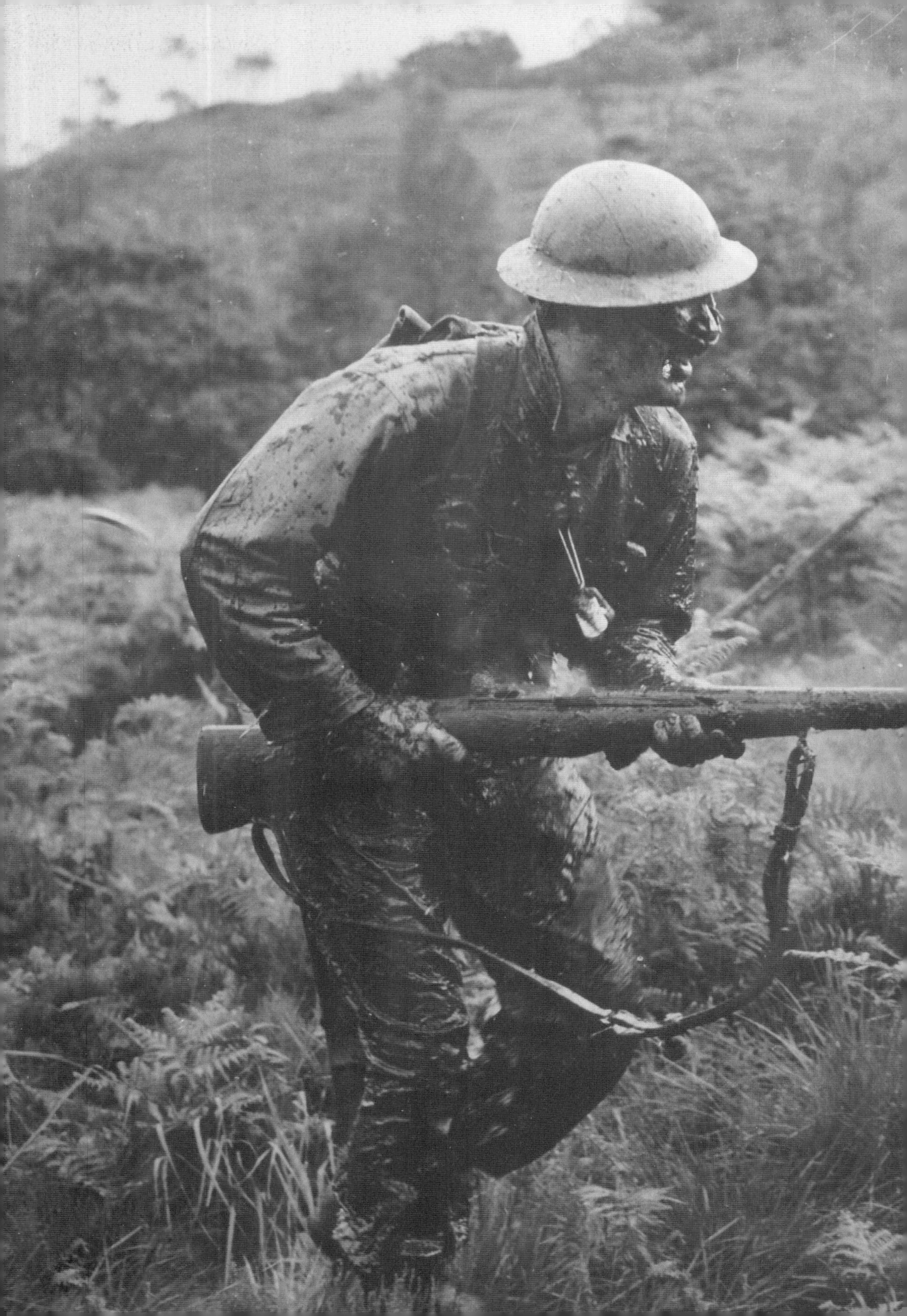

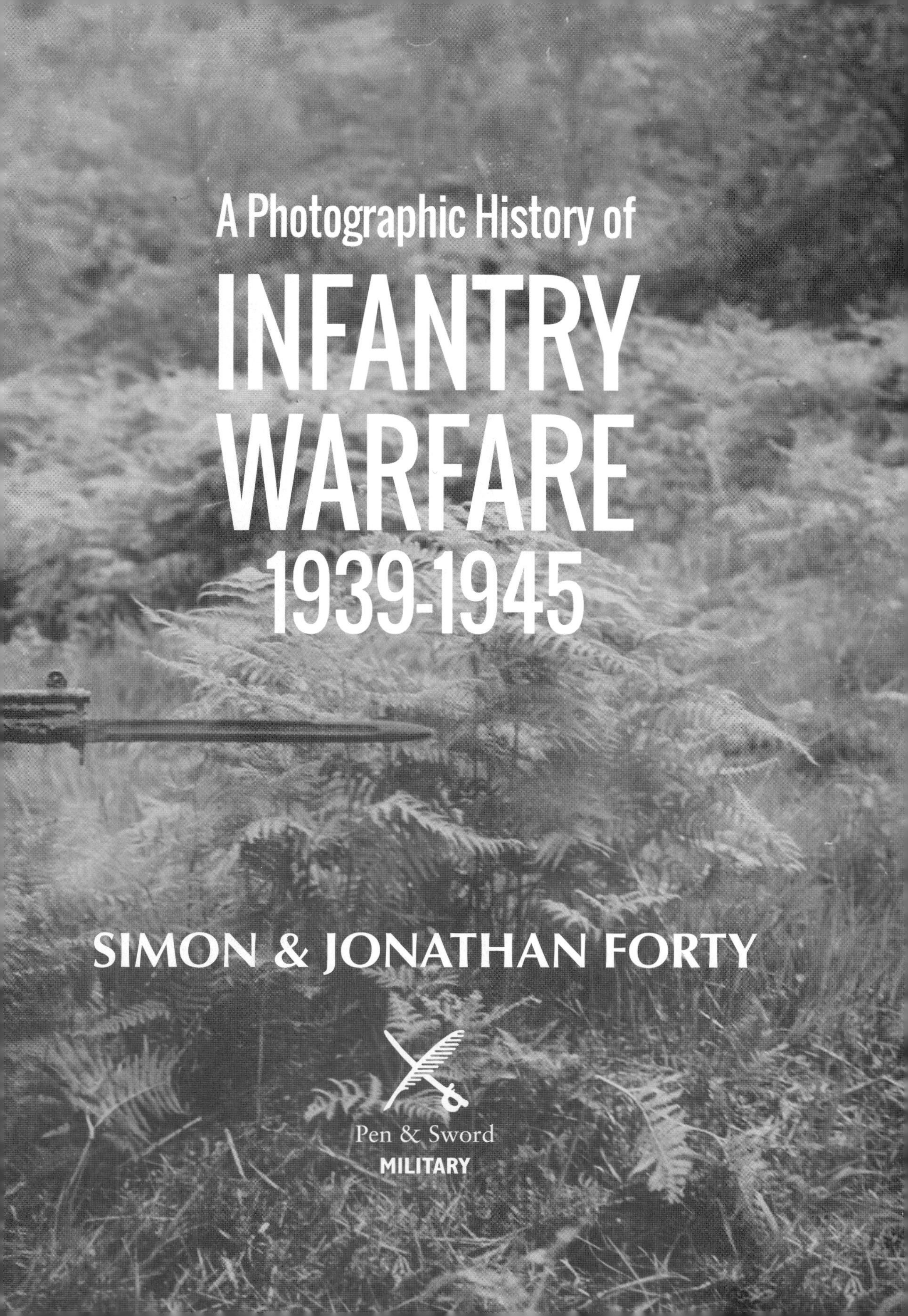

A Photographic History of

INFANTRY WARFARE 1939-1945

SIMON & JONATHAN FORTY

Pen & Sword
MILITARY

First published in Great Britain in 2021 by
Pen & Sword Military
an imprint of
Pen & Sword Books Ltd,
47 Church Street,
Barnsley,
South Yorkshire.
S70 2AS

A CIP record for this book is available from the British Library.

ISBN 978-1-52677-6822

The right of Simon and Jonathan Forty to be identified as Authors of this Work has been asserted by him in accordance with the Copyright, Designs and Patents Act 1988.

Printed and bound by CPI UK

Pen & Sword Books Ltd incorporates the Imprints of Pen & Sword Aviation, Pen & Sword Maritime, Pen & Sword Military, Wharncliffe Local History, Pen & Sword Select, Pen & Sword Military Classics and Leo Cooper.

For a complete list of Pen & Sword titles please contact
Pen & Sword Books Limited
47 Church Street, Barnsley, South Yorkshire, S70 2AS, England
E-mail: enquiries@pen-and-sword.co.uk
Website: www.pen-and-sword.co.uk

Acknowledgements

The text includes a number of directly quoted or edited excerpts from a number of works which are identified in the text and covered in the Bibliography. Many of these documents came via the excellent online resources of the Ike Skelton Combined Arms Research Library (CARL) Digital Library. Please note that some of these excerpts are contemporary and produced based on intelligence available at the time: there will be some, understandable, inaccuracies.

The photographs came from a number of sources including the US National Archives and Records Administration, in College Park, MD, the Library and Archives of Canada, the SA-Kuva Finnish archive, Hungarian archives, Narodowe Archiwum Cyfrowe, Battlefield Historian and the collection of our late father, George Forty. Thanks, too, to Richard Charlton Taylor, Leo Marriott and the late Martin Warren for their help and valuable contributions including photos and editorial comments. The individual photo credits are provided at the end of the book: if we have made mistakes here, please point them out to us via the publisher.

There are a number of websites that proved invaluable for help with captions and information. In particular we'd like to reference the US Center of Military History for high quality histories and access to technical manuals and https://durhamlightinfantry1920-46.weebly.com for fascinating detail about the DLI.

Finally, thanks to Rupert Harding of Pen & Sword for being such an understanding editor and for pointing out a number of inaccuracies.

Page 2: US Ranger training in Scotland.

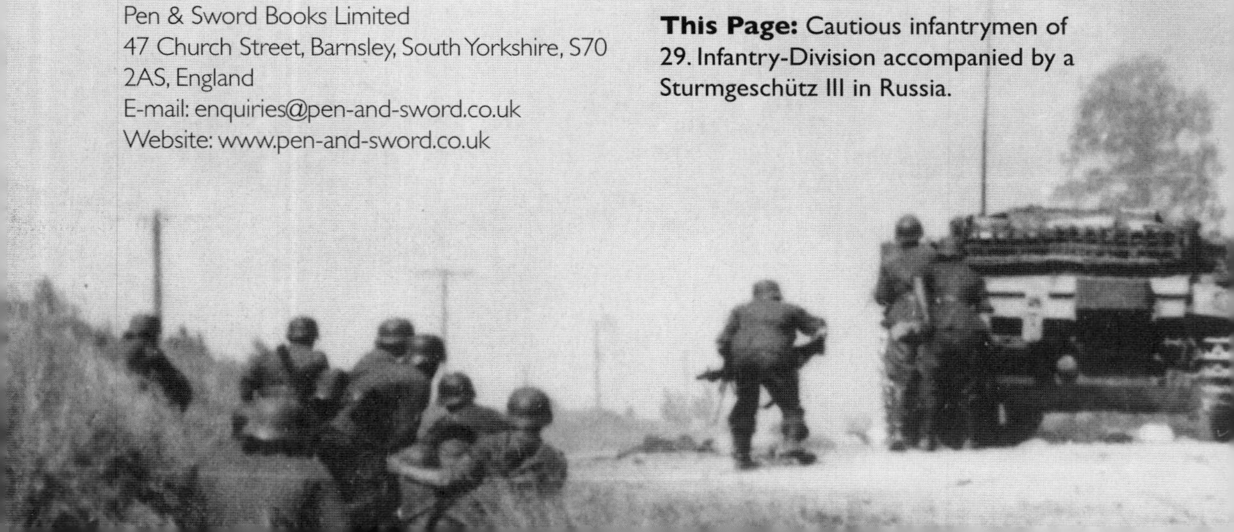

This Page: Cautious infantrymen of 29. Infantry-Division accompanied by a Sturmgeschütz III in Russia.

Contents

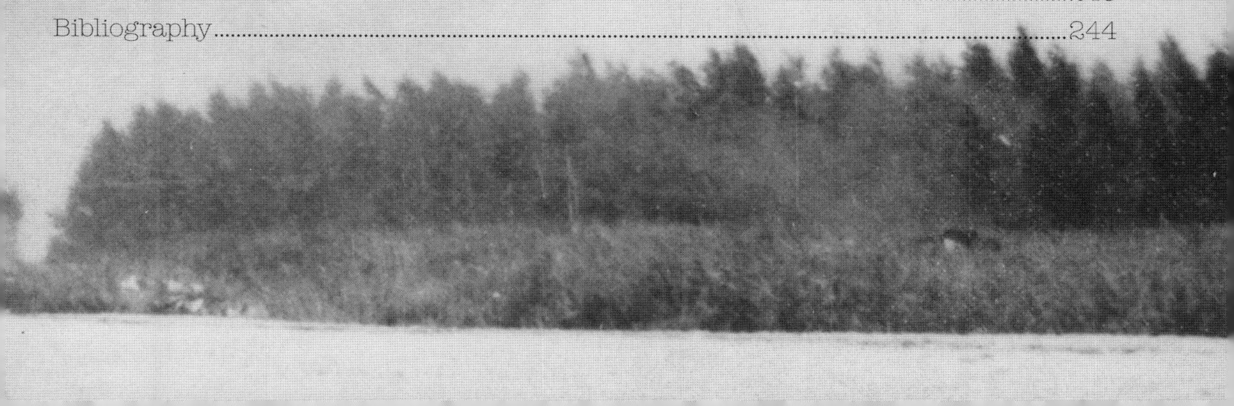

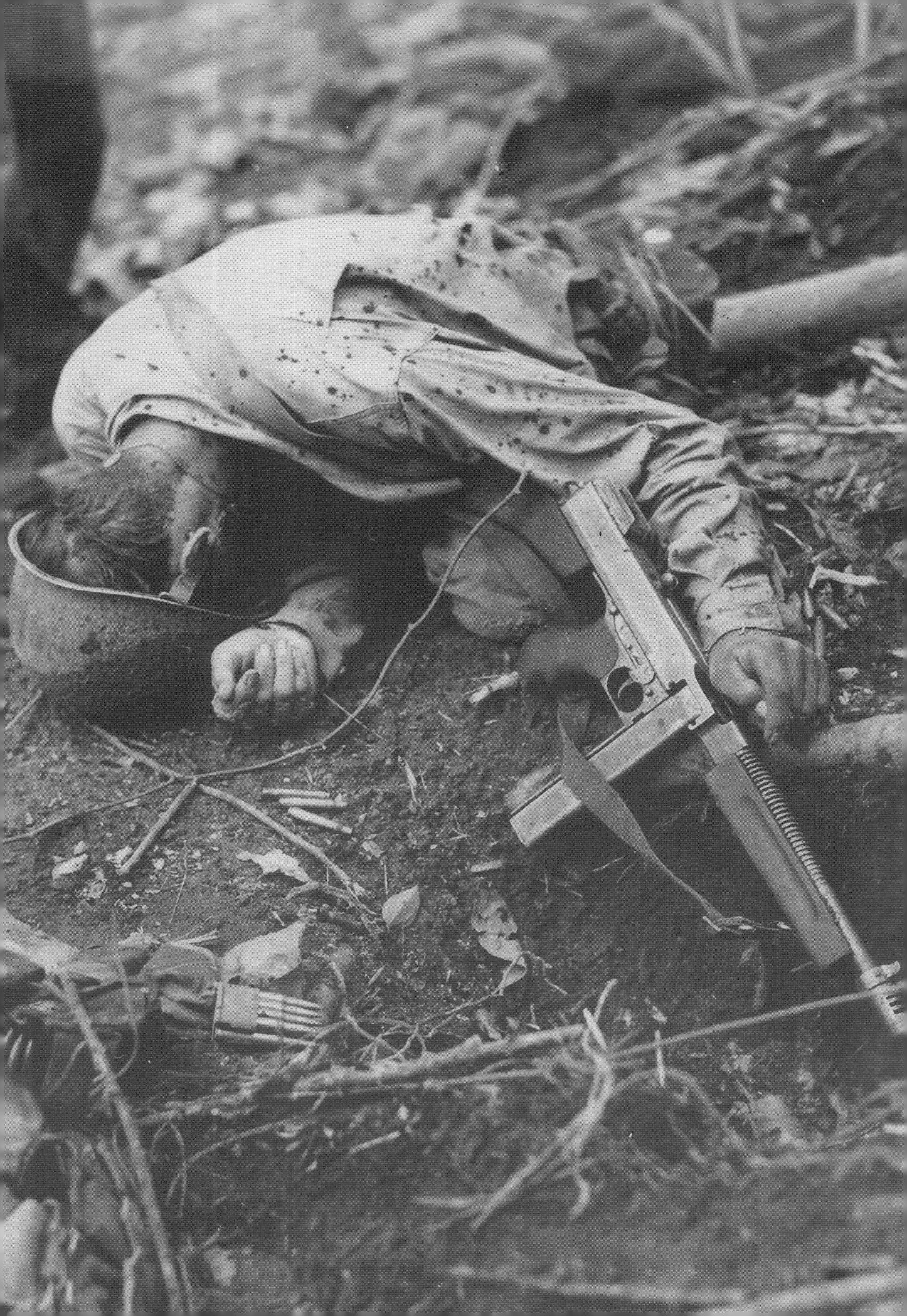

Preface

All too often, books about war in general – and World War II specifically – analyse weapons: whose tanks, machine guns or rifles were the biggest and the best. That's one reason why books on German tanks outsell most other military titles: black-suited men with silver death's head insignia looking out of big tanks named after big cats. Emphasised by Hollywood, where plucky heroes can be winged, roll a cigarette one-handed and plug the enemy with a never-ending supply of ammunition, the war-time national stereotypes are reinforced: Germans are always organised, Italians always cowards, Brits always enthusiastic amateurs who drink tea and Americans are cowboys in khaki. Victory is glorious and eventually goes to the men in white hats.

In reality, of course, everything is more nuanced. The Germans certainly were organised, but didn't have enough suitable cold weather clothing outside Moscow in 1941. The Italians fought with great courage alongside the Germans in Africa and Russia and were often left in the lurch by their Allies. Brits – and the many Imperial and Commonwealth troops who served with them – did, indeed, drink tea but they also landed gliders with pinpoint accuracy at Bénouville and fought the hard yards in the Reichswald. And Americans really were the Seventh Cavalry, who helped save the day even if they did so reluctantly, with rather less elan than Hollywood would like, and were often more suspicious of their Allies than their enemies.

Victory did, indeed, go to the men in white hats but at great cost. The suffering – particularly to civilians – showed that there were no noncombatants in the areas that the war was fought. And of all the arms that saw battle between 1939 and 1945, it was the infantry who had the hardest lot, suffering the highest casualties and the worst conditions. From the frozen north to the Sahara, the jungles of Asia to the rain-soaked Saar, infantrymen fought not just the enemy but anything the elements could throw at them.

This mainly photographic survey seeks to highlight the key points of the infantryman's war, referencing contemporary literature to show the equipment and tactics that were employed. It is in series with books on armour and artillery

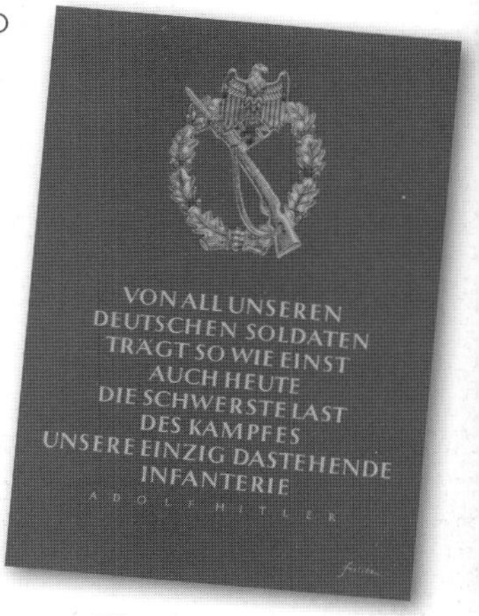
VON ALL UNSEREN
DEUTSCHEN SOLDATEN
TRÄGT SO WIE EINST
AUCH HEUTE
DIE SCHWERSTE LAST
DES KAMPFES
UNSERE EINZIG DASTEHENDE
INFANTERIE
ADOLF HITLER

Above: Third Reich propaganda poster. A quote from Hitler: 'Of all our German soldiers, the heaviest burden of the battle – today as in the past – falls on our unparallelled infantry.'

Opposite: The infantryman's war was bloody. Few could stomach the experience of battle for extended periods of time. Patton thought around 200 days was the maximum.

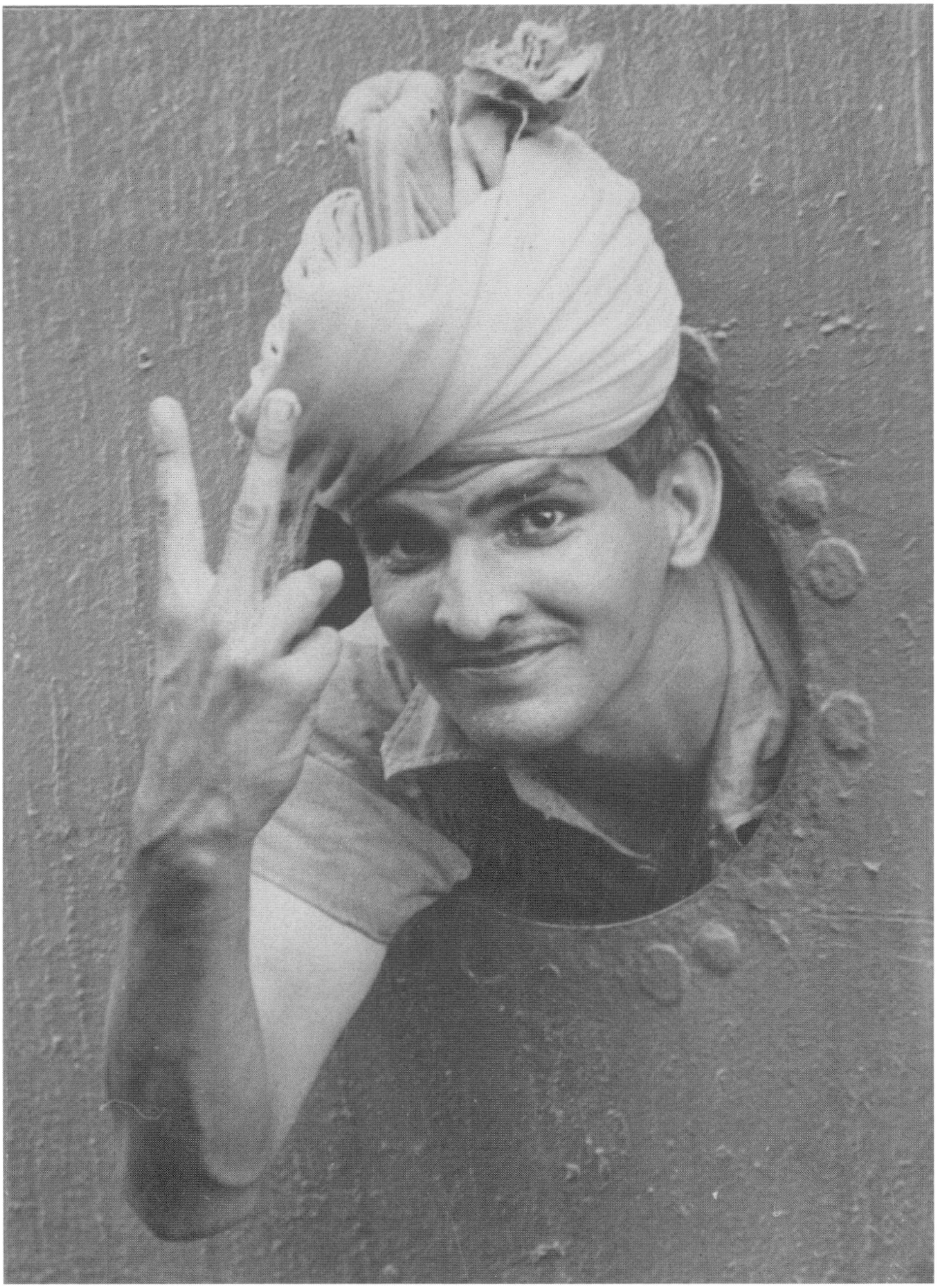

V for Victory. Not every Indian was prepared to fight for the British Empire, but 2.5 million did – 87,000 giving their lives. Some 40 percent of those who fought against the Axis powers were Muslim. India came out of the war with an agreement by the British to oversee independence – which was achieved in 1947.

Introduction

The infantryman has always had the most uncomfortable seat in the house. Young, often seen as being less intelligent than others who were whisked off to become pilots and navigators, gunners or signallers, the infantry endured the hardest conditions and heaviest casualties. From the frozen north of Norway to the hot sands of the African desert, infantrymen had to do the dirty work: get close enough to see the whites of the enemy's eyes and then kill them.

The war to end all wars had shown what modern warfare was like: World War II followed suit. The weapons might have been a little more modern and sophisticated but the end product was the same: massive armies, huge casualties and enormous destruction. The overall death toll in World War II – some 80 million – eclipsed any other war. The deaths sustained just by the Soviet Union, around 25 million, were more than the 20 million who died during World War I. Around half the deaths in 1914–18 – 10 million – were military. In World War II, that number was around 25 million, more than double that of the Great War but a reduction in overall percentage terms: aerial bombing, the Nazis' programmes of genocide, combined with their and the Japanese callousness towards PoWs and civilian populations, led to an extraordinary number of civilians killed between 1937, when Japan invaded China, and 1945 when two atomic bombs saved the lives of thousands of American and Japanese infantrymen.

Of the land forces' casualties, the infantry bore the brunt. In the western democracies the percentage of infantrymen in the armed forces had dropped since World War I but it was the infantry who saw the most lethal combat and, therefore, sustained the highest losses. Because of this, the infantry – understandably – was the least popular of the arms when it came to recruiting. Often young, not always well trained, infantrymen were on average shorter, less intelligent and much more likely to die. The best had been siphoned off to become airborne troops or, in the case of the United States, joined the US Marine Corps. Around 16 million Americans served during the war and 407,316 made the ultimate sacrifice (around 2.5 percent). Of these, 35 percent were infantrymen.

The story was slightly different for the British for whom the burden of service was spread amongst not only Britain but its empire and Commonwealth. These supplied major assistance – usually willingly, although some of the African and Indian troops were certainly less willing and, as the Japanese territorial expansion neared Australia, troops

British Commandos on Walcheren. The bloody battles to clear the Scheldt took hard fighting by Canadian, British and – at one point – American troops. The fortress island of Walcheren was flooded when RAF bombers breached the dykes but the coastal batteries of the Atlantic Wall took a heavy toll of the supporting gunships.

from that country were less involved in Europe. Nearly 18 million British Empire and Commonwealth troops in all branches of service saw action in the war: 580,497 died (around 3 percent). In Europe, Britain's main assistance came from the Canadians, whose First Army fought alongside Second British Army in 21st Army Group. The butcher's bill in 1944 was so big that the British Army had to break up units to make up the numbers of infantrymen it needed and the Canadians had to move its forces from Italy to the Netherlands – Operation Goldflake. The fighting in Normandy, the Channel coast, the Scheldt, Rhineland and the northern Netherlands was brutal with high infantry casualties.

If the western democracies worried about their problems with conscription, infantry numbers and the high body count, the levels were very different in the armed forces of the dictators. To begin with, the military death tolls were considerably higher: one in three Germans (of 18 million) and Russians (of 35 million); one in four Japanese (of 8.5 million); one in ten Italians (of 3.5 million) died. For the Germans and Japanese, living in militaristic societies, war and sacrifice were part of their upbringing. The propaganda worked as well: even in 1945 many German soldiers still believed in ultimate victory. They had been comprehensively indoctrinated to believe in their *Führer*, their race and their cause. Japanese soldiers often preferred suicide to surrender and isolated individuals kept fighting long after the war finished; the last official 'holdout', Teruo Nakamura, surrendering in 1974, 29 years after the war ended. All that being said, it wasn't just indoctrination that kept the infantry of the dictators in the field. There were many more disciplinary deaths in the armies of the dictators than in those of the Allies: figures are debated but between 10,000 and 50,000 Germans were executed during the war and most of them were deserters. The concept of *Sippenhaft* – kin liability – allowed the German authorities to pressurise its soldiers by threatening their families should they not perform as ordered.

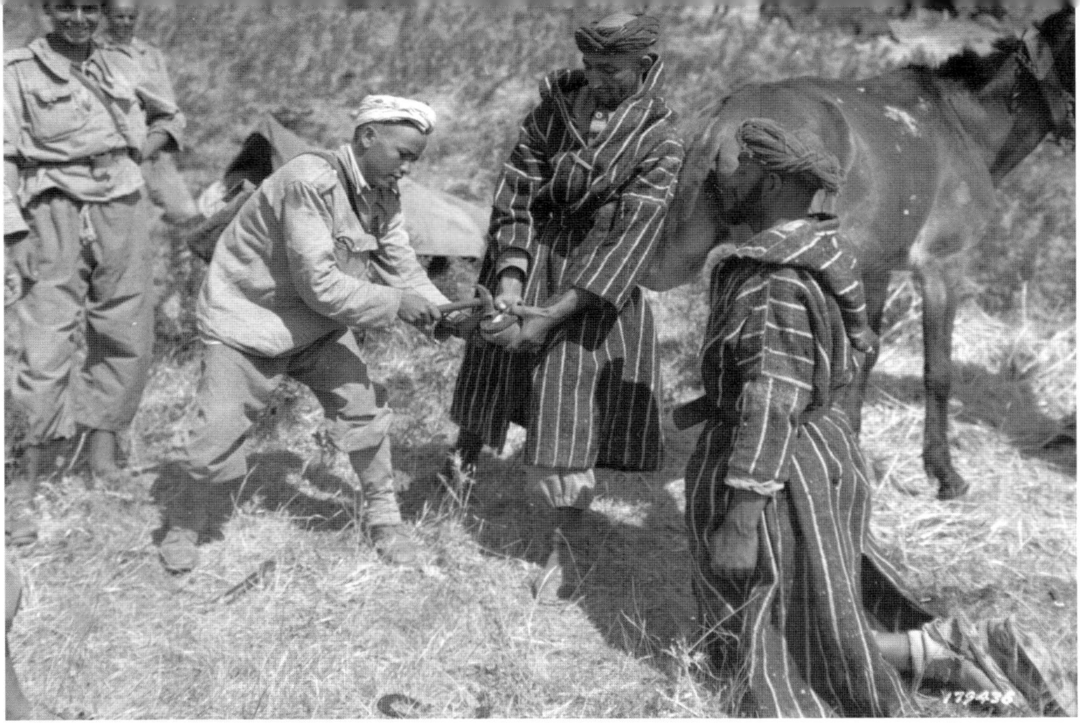

Above and Below: French forces made heavy use of the Armée d'Afrique whose colonial contingents – particularly the Moroccan Goums (**Above**) – gained an unwelcome reputation for brutality in Sicily, Italy and France itself, as they fought from their landings around Saint-Tropez to Strasbourg and over the Rhine into Germany. However, as Maj Toby Taylor mentions in his memoirs, they were first-class fighters and the advances after Cassino fell were in great part down to the Goums who, as he put it, 'put the fright into the Germans.' The French forces in the latter stages of the war were equipped with US equipment (as here, **Below**, in the Saar) and fought with skill both under their own (First (French) Army under General Jean de Lattre de Tassigny) and American control (General Philippe Leclerc's 2e Division Blindée).

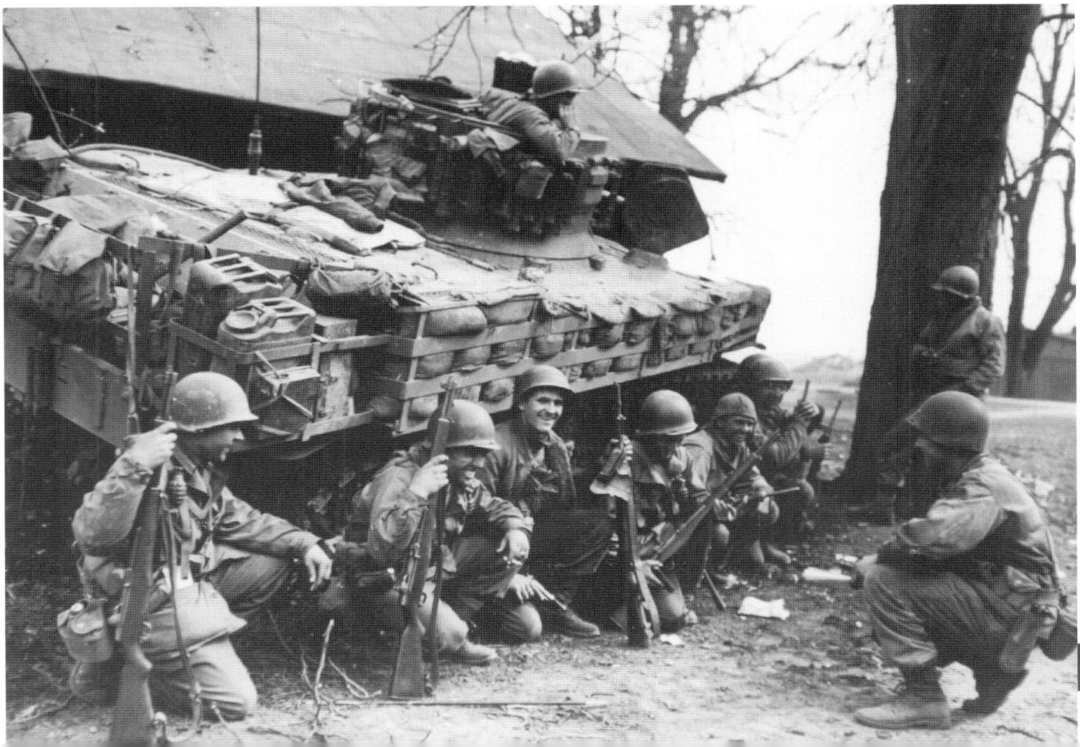

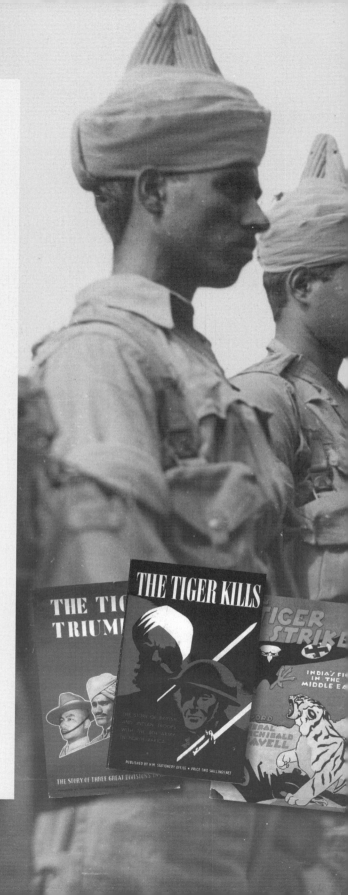

British Empire Infantry Divisions

The debt owed by the British for the military assistance from the Empire and Commonwealth is substantial.

- Eighth Army in late 1941 had four infantry divisions on strength. Only one – the 70th – was British. The others were 2nd New Zealand, 4th Indian and 1st South African, and the Australian 9th was defending Tobruk. At El Alamein there were seven infantry divisions – three British (44th, 50th, 51st) and four from the empire: 9th Australian; 2nd New Zealand; 1st South African; and 4th Indian.
- On D-Day, British Second Army in Normandy was supported by Canadian troops: the nine British (6th Airborne, 3rd, 15th, 43rd, 49th, 50th, 51st, 53rd and 59th Infantry) were joined by two Canadian (2nd and 3rd Infantry) divisions.
- In Italy in 1944, 15th Army Group – Fifth (US) and Eighth (BR) Armies – had 18 infantry divisions: six US, four British (1st, 4th, 46th and 56th), three Indian (4th, 8th and 10th), two Polish (3rd Carpathian and 5th Kresowa) and one each from Brazil, Canada (1st) and New Zealand (2nd).
- In India and Burma XIV Army and British forces in the subcontinent included Indian (5th, 7th, 17th, 19th, 20th, 23rd, 25th and 26th) and African – 11th (East African) and 81st and 82nd (West African) – infantry divisions who served alongside the British (2nd and 36th).

THE TIGER KILLS
THE STORY OF THREE GREAT DIVISIONS

Right: Books on the exploits of the Indian troops in North and East Africa, (1942) with the Eighth Army (1944) and in Italy (1946).

Main photo: There were many Indian troops at the fall of both Singapore and Hong Kong. These are mostly Punjabis and southern Indians, standing at attention prior to inspection.

Right: Private Seidu Issalia, Gold Coast Regiment, Royal West African Frontier Force, received the military medal for bravery in the East African campaign. On 4 January 1941, while acting as runner to his platoon commander, he was shot through the groin while taking a message. Despite his wounds, he crawled on and delivered the message and then crawled back to his platoon commander to inform him that his mission had been accomplished.

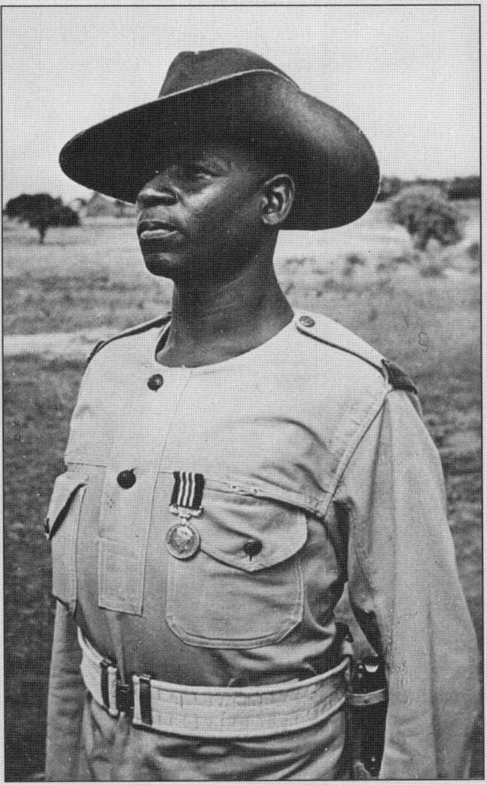

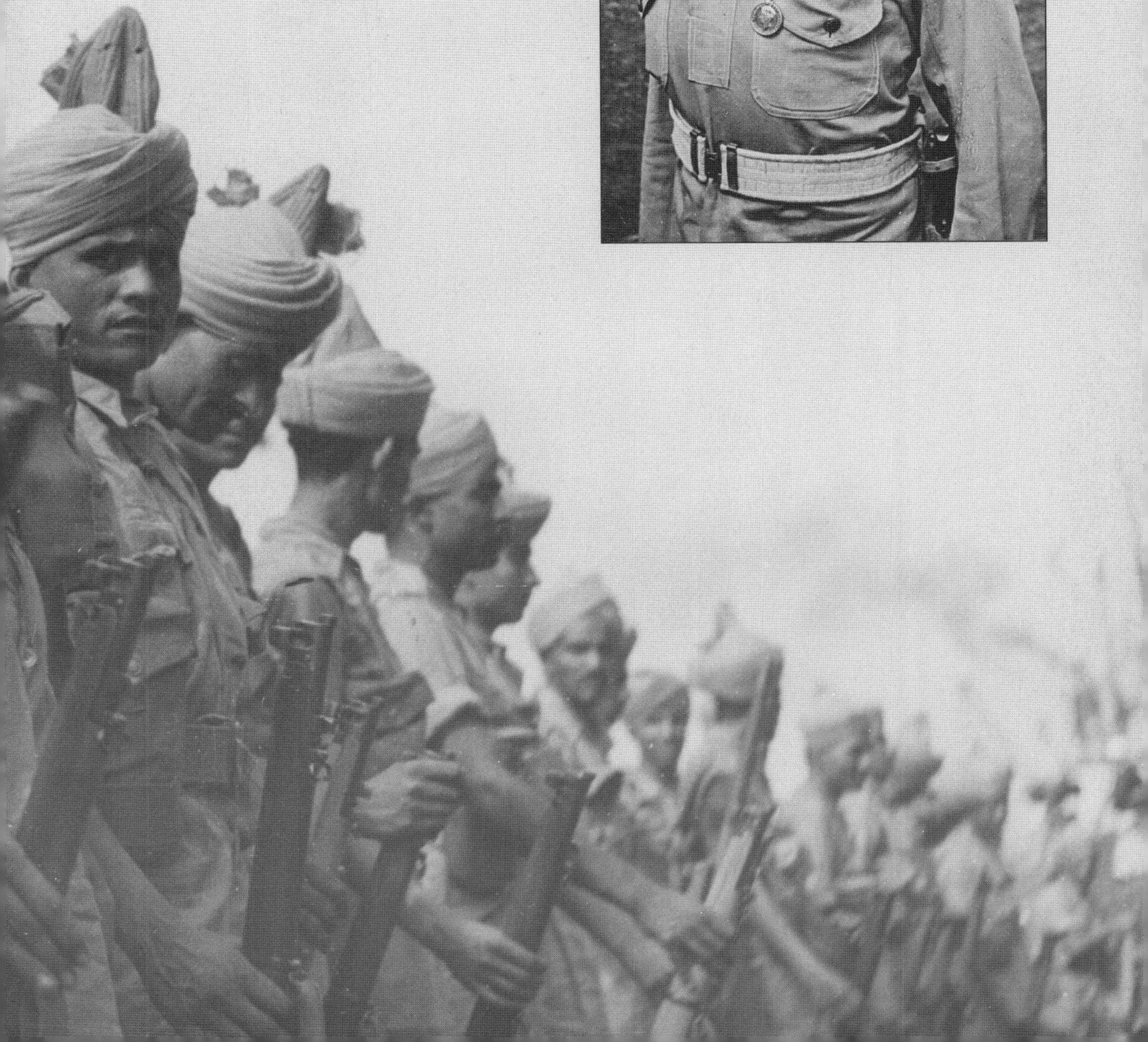

Japan – always held up as a race that preferred suicide to dishonour – has kept hidden the murky story about executions of its soldiers for desertion: over 5,000 in southeast Asia and many, many more in China. Most of these men were simply refusing to fight to the bitter end or killed by sadistic officers. By recording them as *tekizen toubou* (fleeing in the face of the enemy) and burning the records as the Allies closed in, the Japanese authorities were able both to hide the guilty and also perpetuate the misery of the families of the men they dishonoured. Russia, too, was very different to its democratic allies. On top of the purges and other political deaths, executions for desertion and other offences stood at, S.N. Mikhalev suggests, 135,000 – more than the total wartime number of US infantrymen who died in action (118,376).

Infantry casualties are discussed in more detail later but this grisly preamble sets the scene for this book. On the side of the western Allies, the unpopularity of the role of infantryman – and the high percentage of deaths – contributed to shortages in rifle regiments when it mattered during 1944. This certainly had an effect on the tactics they employed and the use – some have suggested overuse – of artillery rather than aggressive infantry attacks. One wartime British infantry officer put it more baldly: 'If I had to order my men to use their rifles I knew I hadn't got the level of artillery barrage correct.' This all too understandable approach was certainly not accepted practice elsewhere. German General Gehr von Schweppenburg said in July 1944: 'The British and Canadian troops were magnificent … However ... the command ... was not making the best use of them. The command seemed slow and rather pedestrian. It seems that the Allied intention was to wear down their enemy with their enormous material superiority. It will never be known whether Montgomery had received private instruction from his Government to avoid for the British troops another bloodbath such as they had suffered in the First World War on the Somme and at Passchendaele.' The astute von Schweppenburg had got it in one – although he was completely wrong in terms of casualty figures. Fennell notes that the battle of Normandy led to 2,354 Allied casualties a day. At Passchendaele the British and Canadian figure was 2,121 a day.

Men of the Royal 22e Régiment near Cattolica, Italy, 24–25 November 1944. Until Operation Goldflake took them to join their fellow-countrymen in the Netherlands, there were as many as 76,000 Canadians fighting in Italy.

German Infantry

On the German side, the number of men available for service was high until attrition ate away at the available cadre. The population of Germany in 1938 was 68 million: this rose to 78 million after Hitler's prewar territorial annexations – Austria, for example, providing immediately five incomplete divisions (two infantry, two mountain and one armoured). The German Army at the start of full mobilisation in 1939 comprised 51 divisions and two brigades of which 42 were infantry (including 4 motorised and 3 mountain). That's a total of 3,737,000 men in the army (not all trained) and 35,000 in the *SS-Verfügungs-truppen* (the combat arm of the SS that formed the basis for the Waffen-SS). This figure would peak in 1943 with 6,550,000 men and 450,000 SS in spite of massive casualty figures that year: 448,600 dead and 343,600 missing or PoW.

The future warriors of the Reich had started young. When war began the *Hitlerjugend* (Hitler Youth) had 8 million members, many of them fanatically imbued with National Socialist principles. Almost the first thing the Nazis did when they took power was to control education. Hitler's view was outlined in *Mein Kampf*:

'First of all, the brains of the young people must not generally be burdened with subjects of which ninety-five per cent are useless to them and are therefore forgotten again. The curriculum of the primary and secondary schools presents an odd mixture at the present time. In many branches of study the subject matter to be learned has become so enormous that only a very small fraction of it can be remembered later on, and indeed only a very small fraction of this whole mass of knowledge can be used. On the other hand, what is learned is insufficient for anybody who wishes to specialize in any certain branch for the purpose of earning his daily bread. Take, for example, the average civil servant who has passed through the Gymnasium or High School, and ask him at the age of thirty or forty how much he has retained of the knowledge that was crammed into him with so much pains. ...

'The young boy or girl who is of German nationality and is a subject of the German State is bound to complete the period of school education which is obligatory for every German. Thereby he submits to the system of training which will make him conscious of his race and a member of the folk-community. Then he has to fulfil all those requirements laid down by the State in regard to physical training after he has left school; and finally he enters the army. The training in the army is of a general kind. It must be given to each individual German and will render him competent to fulfil the physical and mental requirements of military service. The rights of citizenship shall be conferred on every young man whose health and character have been certified as good, after having completed his period of military service.'

Give me a child and I will give you the man. Indoctrination, military education, service in the militaristic labour corps (the *Reichsarbeitsdienst*) prepared young men for war and the infantry was promoted – as Hitler said in a 1941 speech: '*Über allem steht die deutsche*

Right: The Nazis made sure that they controlled education and youth movements. Outside school, all boys were expected to join the Hitler Youth. It had been set up in 1923, and under Baldur von Shirach grew to 26,000 by 1930. When the Nazi membership became the only accepted youth movement. The others were banned and their members forced to join the Hitler Youth. For example, the 600,000 members of the Lutheran *Evangelische Jugend* (Evangelical Youth) were incorporated into the Hitler Youth in 1934.

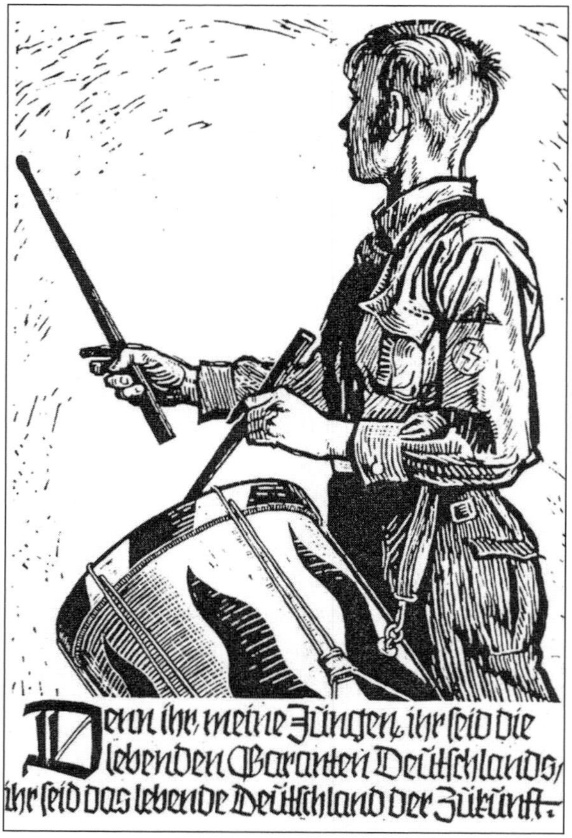
Denn ihr, meine Jungen, ihr seid die lebenden Garanten Deutschlands, ihr seid das lebende Deutschland der Zukunft.

Below: The *Reichsarbeitsdienst* (Reich labour service) was the next step up the ladder towards adulthood and conscription. The RAD was run on military lines. Not part of the *Wehrmacht*, the RAD provided young men with six-months of drill, training and hardening-up before they started their time in the armed forces. All RAD training was conducted away from home; personnel lived in barracks and, from 1934, wore a uniform,

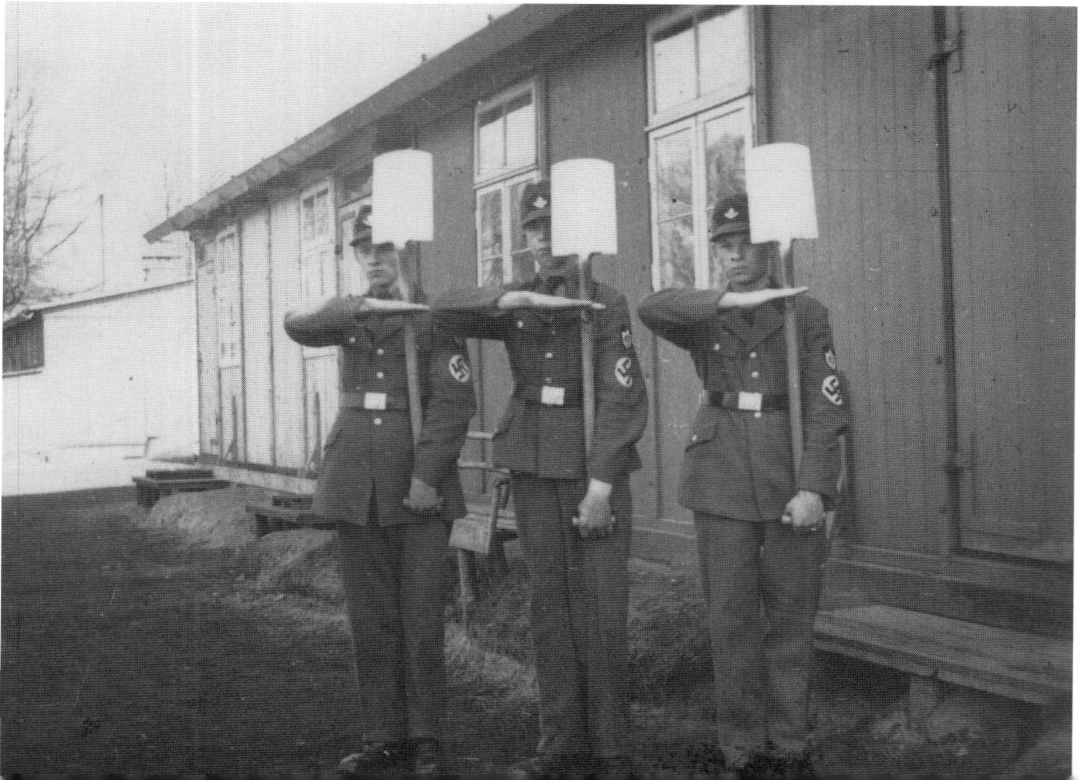

Infanterie' (Above all stands the German infantry). This militaristic society was able to take Europe by storm and reach the gates of Moscow before being beaten back, with the weather playing as much of a role as the defenders. The Germans paid a heavy price for their attack on the Soviet Union. The army lost the cream of its infantry in the bitter winters of 1941 and 1942. That the German Army was able to hold out for so long after the reverses at Stalingrad and in North Africa, particularly after the Allies invaded first Italy and then France, was a reflection on its training, indoctrination, unrivalled defensive abilities and sheer bravery – and fear of execution. But however brave its soldiers, the German Army had lost its honour and its moral compass, cooperating with the SS-*Einsatzgruppen* (the mobile death squads responsible for the murder of those the Nazis thought were undesirable), it was complicit with the brutality of the ethnic cleansing and partisan warfare of the Eastern Front.

The US *Handbook on the German Army* reported in 1945:

'The German soldier who faces the Allies on the home fronts in 1945 is a very different type from the members of the Army of 1939 which Hitler called "an Army such as the world has never seen." The German soldier is one of several different types depending on whether he is a veteran of four or five years, or a new recruit. The veteran of many fronts and many retreats is a prematurely aged, war weary cynic, either discouraged and disillusioned or too stupefied to have any thought of his own. Yet he is a seasoned campaigner, most likely a non-commissioned officer, and performs his duties with the highest degree of efficiency.

'The new recruit, except in some crack SS units, is either too young or too old and often in poor health. He has been poorly trained for lack of time but, if too young, he makes up for this by a fanaticism bordering on madness. If too old, he is driven by the fear of what his propagandists have told him will happen to the Fatherland in case of an Allied victory, and even more by the fear of what he has been told will happen to him and his family if he does not carry out orders exactly as given. Thus even the old and sick perform, to a certain point, with the courage of despair.

'The German High Command has been particularly successful in placing the various types of men where they best fit, and in selecting those to serve as cannon fodder, who are told to hold out to the last man, while every effort is made to preserve the elite units, which now are almost entirely part of the Waffen-SS. The German soldier in these units is in a preferred category and is the backbone of the German Armed Forces. He is pledged never to surrender and has no moral code except allegiance to his organization. There is no limit to his ruthlessness.

'The mentality of the German soldier of 1945 is the final result of that policy of militarism which, even in the 19th century, caused a famous German general to recommend that soldiers should be trained to ask of their superiors: "Master, order us where we may die." '

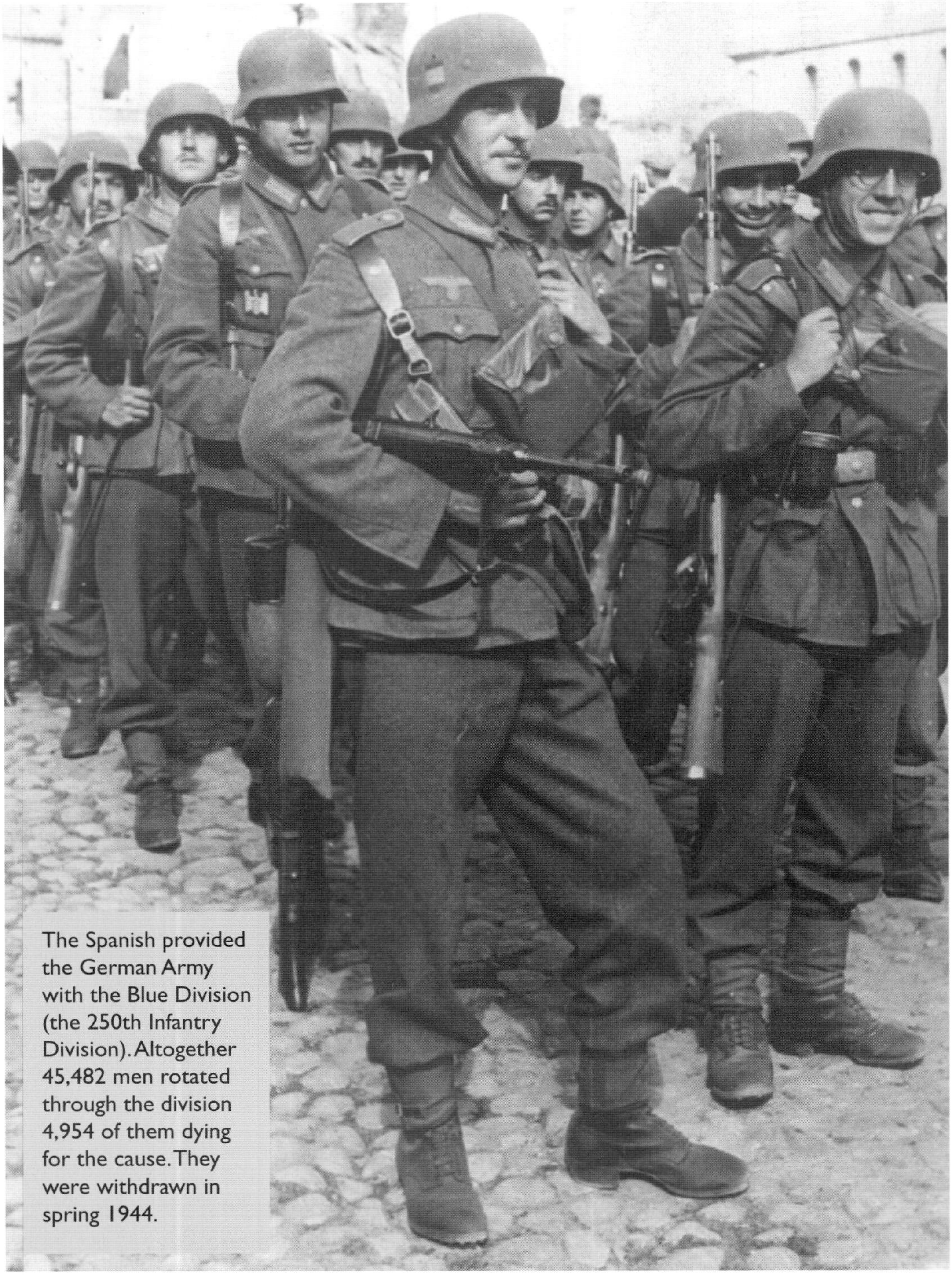

The Spanish provided the German Army with the Blue Division (the 250th Infantry Division). Altogether 45,482 men rotated through the division 4,954 of them dying for the cause. They were withdrawn in spring 1944.

The Nazis expected the Russians to collapse in front of their invasion. Initially, they did, but they held the Germans in the winter of 1941–42 and then, in spite of their losses, won a three-year-long war of attrition. The Red Army was assisted by Partisans – this party seen in Belorussia is armed with a Russian 7.62 mm DP MG (right) and a captured German MG34 (left).

Russian Infantry

The largest army and the largest employers of infantry were the Russians. The German view of their adversaries was summed up in *Peculiarities of Russian Warfare*, which was prepared by a committee of former German generals and general staff corps officers at the EUCOM Historical Division Interrogation Enclosure, Neustadt, Germany, in late 1947 and early 1948. These are some of the comments on the Russian infantrymen:

'No one who belongs to the Western sphere of culture will ever be able to understand the Russian completely, or to analyze the character and soul of this Asiatic who has grown up on the far side of the border of Europe. The Russian is unfathomable. He swings from one extreme to the other without our being able to recognize the reasons for his behavior. It is possible to predict from experience how practically every other soldier in the world will behave in a given situation – but never the Russian. The characteristics of the Russian soldier, like his vast country, are strange and full of contradictions. There were units which one day repulsed a strong German attack with exemplary bravery, and on the next folded up completely. There were others which one day lost their nerve when the first shells exploded, and on the next allowed themselves, man by man, literally to be cut to pieces. The Russian is generally impervious to crises, but he can also be very sensitive to them. He has no fear of a threat to his flanks, but at

the same time he can be most touchy about the flanks. He disregards all the old established rules of tactics, but he clings to the absolute letter of his own precepts.

'The key to this odd behavior can be found in the character of the Russian soldier, who, as a fighter, possesses neither the perception nor the ability to think independently. He is subject to moods which for us are incomprehensible; he acts instinctively. As a soldier, the Russian is primitive and unassuming, brave by virtue of natural inclination, but morosely vegetating in a group. These characteristics make the Russian in many respects an adversary superior to the self-confident and demanding soldiers of other armies. The latter can, and must, by their physical and mental qualities, achieve not merely equality, but superiority, so that they may stand up successfully against the Russian soldier.

'Disregard for human beings and contempt of death are other characteristics of the Russian soldier that are incomprehensible to us in such a degree. The Russian soldier climbs with complete indifference and cold-bloodedness over the bodies of hundreds of fallen comrades, in order to take up the attack on the same spot. With the same apathy he works all day long burying his dead comrades after the battle. He looks toward his own death with the same resignation. Even severe wounds impress him comparatively little. For instance, a Russian who was sitting upright at the side of the street, in spite of the fact that both his lower legs were shot away, asked with a friendly smile for a cigarette. The Russian soldier endures cold and heat, hunger and thirst, dampness and mud, sickness and vermin, with the same equanimity. With his simple and primitive nature, all sorts of hardships cause but few reflexes within his soul. His emotions run the gamut from animal ferocity to the utmost kindliness; odious and cruel in a group, he is friendly and ready to help as an individual.

'There can be no doubt that the sum of these most diverse characteristics makes

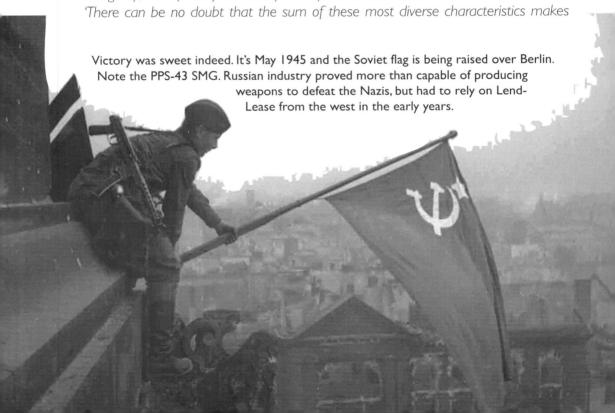

Victory was sweet indeed. It's May 1945 and the Soviet flag is being raised over Berlin. Note the PPS-43 SMG. Russian industry proved more than capable of producing weapons to defeat the Nazis, but had to rely on Lend-Lease from the west in the early years.

the Russian a superior soldier, who, under the direction of an understanding leader, becomes a dangerous opponent. It would be a serious error to underestimate the Russian soldier, even though he does not quite fit into the picture of modern warfare and up-to-date fighters. The strength of the Western soldier is conscious action, controlled by his own mind, which accomplishes wonders. Being able to act on one's own, the consciousness which accompanies the impulse, is not to be found in the Russian. But the fact must not be ignored that a change is taking place also in this respect. Even the difference between the Russian units in World War I and those in World War II was considerable. . . .

'In line with the awakening of the Russian soldier, another determining factor has been introduced into the Army by the political commissar—unqualified obedience. Carried out to the last word, it has made the raw mass of soldiers into a first-rate fighting machine. Systematic training, drill, disregard of one's own life, the natural inclination of the Russian soldier toward uncompromising subordination, and, not least of all, the unmistakable disciplinary powers available to the commissar, are the foundations of this ironclad obedience. In this connection, it must also be remembered that Russia is an autocratically ruled state with an absolute Füzhrerprinzip, demanding and, in case of necessity, compelling the complete subordination of the individual. That blind obedience of the masses is the triumph of Communism, the mainspring of the Army, and the basic explanation of its successes. Armies with a less strict concept of obedience and discipline might very easily come out second best in a contest with these troops. As an example, in the attack the Russian fought unto death. Despite our most thorough defensive measures he would continue to go forward, completely disregarding losses. He was generally not subject to panic. For example, in the break-through of the fortifications before Bryansk in October 1941, enemy bunkers, which had long since been bypassed and which for days lay far behind our front, continued to be held when every hope of relief had vanished. Directly after the crossing of the Bug in July 1941, the fortifications which had been cleared of the enemy by the 167th Infantry Division were occupied a few days later by groups of stragglers, and subsequently had to be painstakingly retaken by a division which followed in the rear. An underground room in the heart of the citadel of Brest-Litovsk held out for many days against the 45th Infantry Division in spite of the employment of Stukas and the heaviest types of special guns.

'During the winter campaign of 1941, a Russian regiment was surrounded, in the woods along the Volkhov, and, because of the weakness of our forces, had to be starved out. After one week our reconnaissance patrols met with the same resistance as on the first day; after another week only a few prisoners were taken, the majority having fought their way through to their own troops in spite of close encirclement. According to the prisoners, the Russians subsisted during those weeks on a few pieces of frozen bread, leaves and pine needles – which they chewed – and some cigarettes. It had never occurred to anyone to throw in the sponge because of hunger, and the cold (-31°F) had not affected them. From a purely physical point of view only the Russian is capable of such a feat.'

Italian Infantry

In the past, in the English-speaking world it was very easy to concentrate on the battles fought by the western Allies. Today, the Eastern Front is recognised as the place that the Nazis bled themselves dry. The huge battlefields of the east, the dramatic climate and the aid of the western Allies helped the Soviets survive and the Germans learn what Napoleon had learnt before him. While analysing these battles, it's important to remember the contribution Italy and Germany's other, smaller allies made to their cause. As James Sandkovich identifies, 'Eighty thousand Italians would lose their lives across the Soviet Union; a figure four times as large as the number of Germans who died in North Africa. In the theatre where Italy's survival was to be determined, German support was kept to the absolute minimum to prevent total collapse.'

Simon Gonsalves emphasises the point:

'Anglo-Saxon historiography not only overlooks the Italian role in the war, but Germany's other "minor" allies as well. The Third Reich's survival was dependent on the immense effort made by all of the nations that fought beside it. Without the combat troops, logistical support, and occupation forces provided by her allies, Germany could not have fought for so long in as many theatres as it did. German "arrogance, indifference, and ineptitude" concerning their allies led to horrific loss of life. Forty-six non-German divisions from Allied Axis Armies were wiped out at Stalingrad alone. Without the contributions of Italy, Bulgaria, Hungary, Romania, and Finland, Germany's collapse would have come much earlier.'

It's a point well made. The Italian infantryman – and the Italian army was predominantly infantry – has had a bad press. Easy to ridicule, scapegoated by the Germans to hide their own deficiencies, their fall from grace is always written with the power of the Roman Empire in the back of the writer's mind: *sic transit gloria mundi*. In reality the popular trope is misconceived and bears little truth. It's the same in World War I when the Italian Army proved immensely resilient– some 600,000 Italian soldiers died, most of them defending their country from the attacks of the Triple Alliance, whose forces outnumbered them. Brilliantly at Monte Grappa in October 1917, then again with British and French help on the Piave in June 1918 and at Vittorio Veneto in October 1918, the Italians overcame their adversaries to earn their place at Versailles.

Allied propaganda promoted the idea of Italian ineptitude in World War II – and the Italian cause wasn't helped by its early war failure against the British in North Africa. Their mainly infantry-based army had proved no match to a modern force whose armour (at the time the Matilda was 'Queen of the Desert') proved highly effective against the Italian tankettes and M11/39s. – and gave the British a false sense of capability. Nevertheless, it is incorrect to assume that all Italian hardware was poor – much of it saw use by the Germans after the Italian armistice. It was when Italy surrendered that it became obvious

After the poor display during Operation Compass, when Wavell's 36,000 Western Defence Force routed Graziani's Tenth Army, the Italian Army was often ridiculed by the British Press. In fact, the Axis forces in Africa were mainly Italian and they fought there and, later, in Russia with grit and determination, but not always the best logistical administration.

just how much help they had provided the Germans. In the Desert War, there were always more Italians than Germans. The Italians assisted Germany by holding Allied forces in place. As soon as they surrendered the Germans had to defend Italy and the Balkans with over 50 divisions – around 18 percent of their overall forces. The Germans were overwhelmed in 1944 after Italy's surrender when they could have done with any defenders that were available. However, the invasion of France might have happened sooner had the Allies not been tied up in the desert and Mediterranean.

The Pacific War

On the other side of the world, the Pacific War saw the two most dominant economic powers in the theatre fight a war of succession over territories long controlled by the European empires – British, Dutch and French. After years of success, that had seen territories taken from Russia and Germany and the annexation of Korea, the Japanese invaded Manchuria in 1931 and then, in 1937, China itself. By December 1941 they felt strong enough to attack the weakened British Empire and launch a pre-emptive strike on the United States.

The territorial gains the Japanese had made since taking Formosa from China in 1895 were wiped out completely over the next three years. The Japanese soldier lost the aura

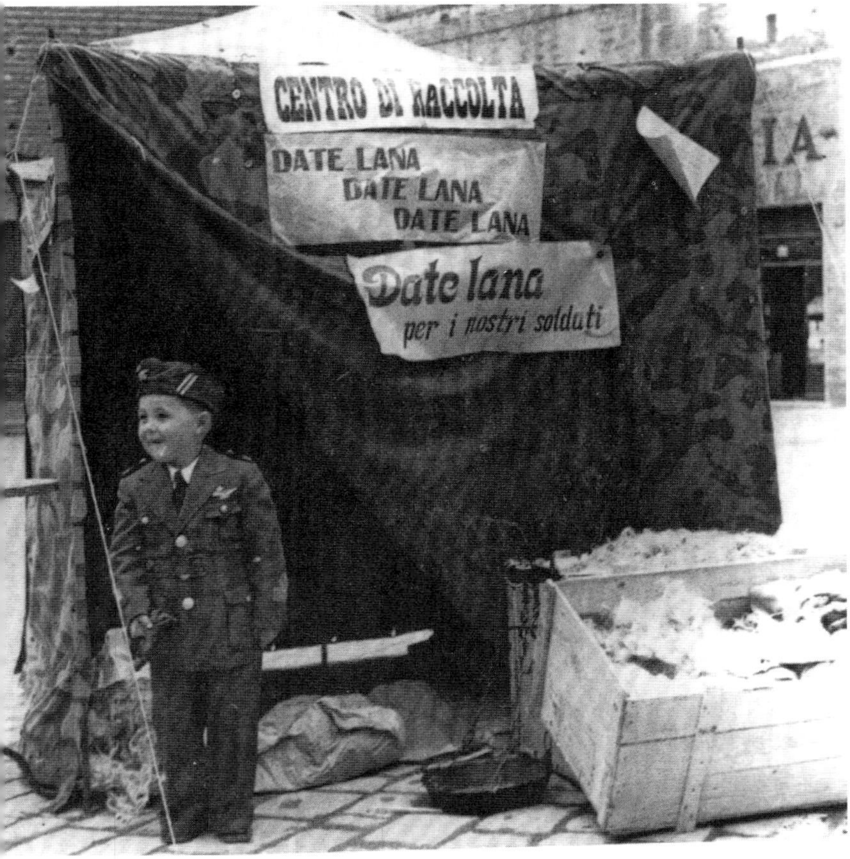
CENTRO DI RACCOLTA
DATE LANA
DATE LANA
DATE LANA
Date lana
per i nostri soldati

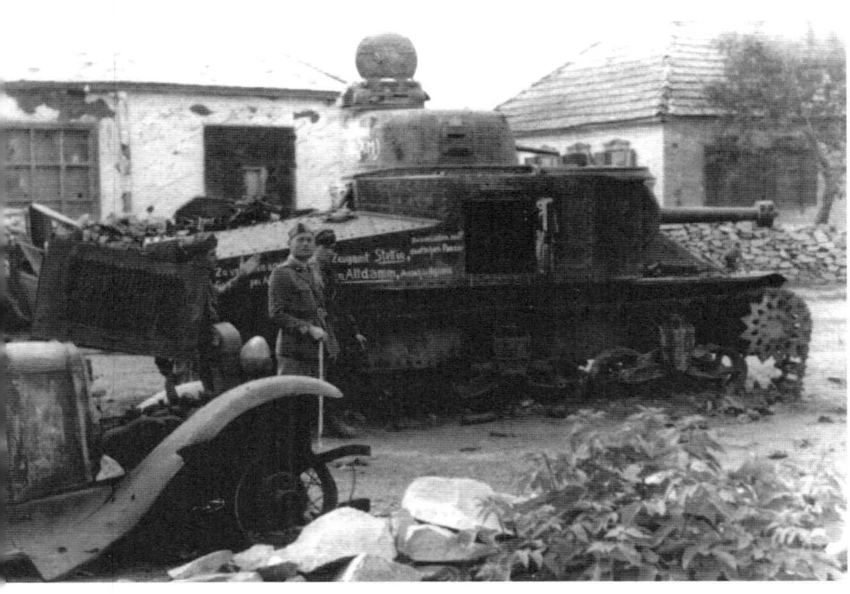

Left: All sides called on their public to help with the war effort. In Britain it was metal railings and aluminium cooking pots; in the US, war bonds; in Italy, as here, wool for uniforms.

Below left: The Ukraine, 1942. Italian soldiers examine a knocked out Russian Lend-Lease M3 medium. The US supplied Russia with nearly 1,400 of them. The Western Allies – mainly the US – supplied the Russians with some 17.5 million tons of military equipment, vehicles, industrial supplies, and food.

Above right: The Italian Army in Russia swelled to reach around 235,000 in 1942. Mainly infantry, poorly equipped, official losses were put at 114,500. Some 60,000 entered Soviet captivity and only 10,085 prisoners were repatriated between 1945 and 1954. These are Bersaglieri, light troops but probably the best Italian units.

Right: Generaloberst Ewald von Kleist and an Italian officer at Dnepropetrovsk in September 1941. Von Kleist died in captivity in Russia.

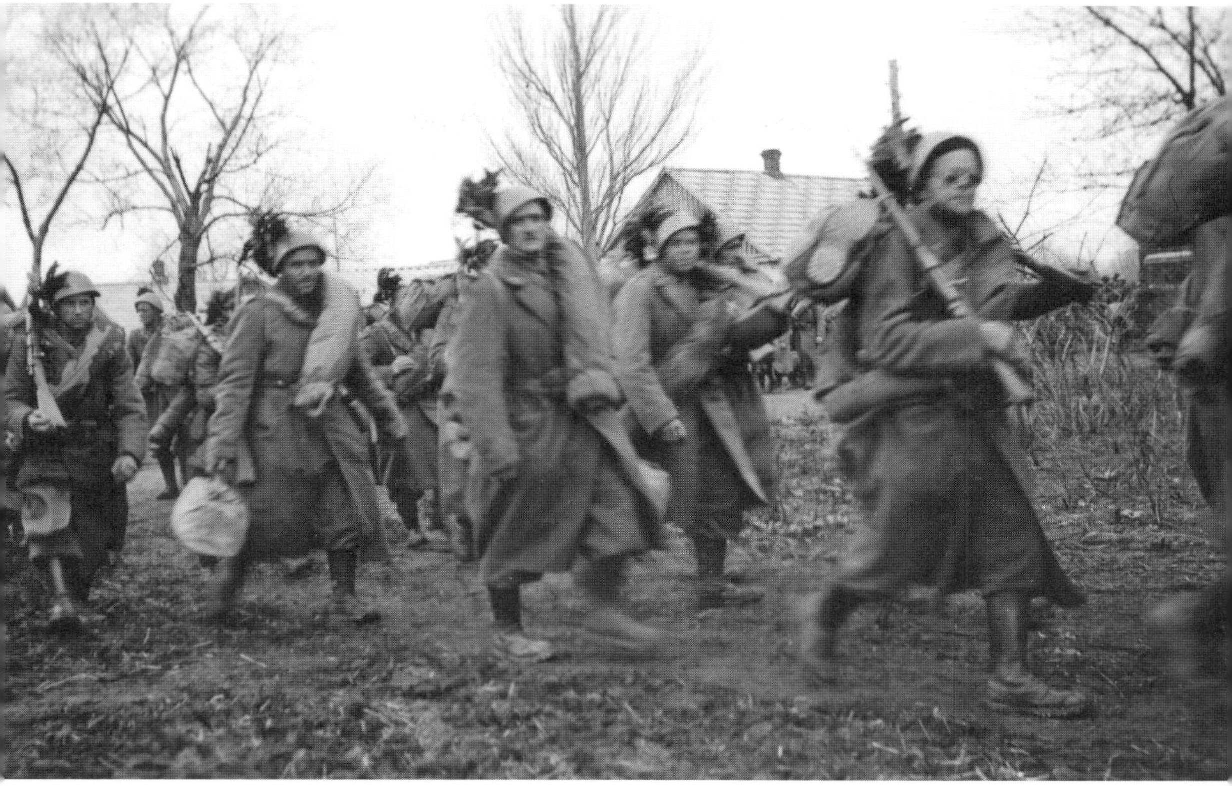

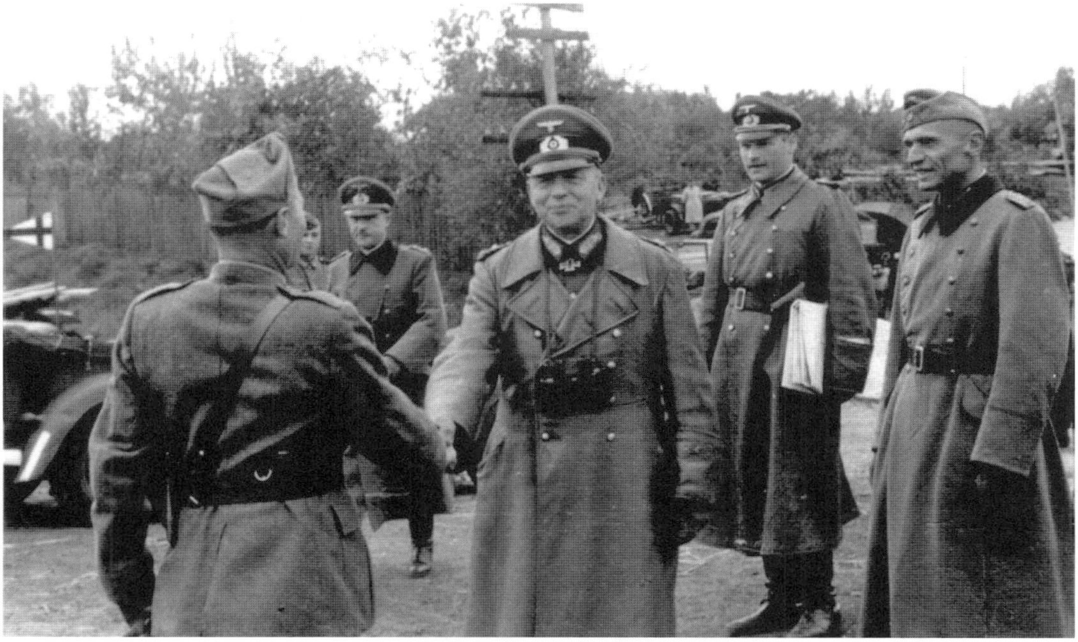

of invincibility he had won in his early campaigns. As the 1944 *Soldier's Guide to the Japanese Army* says:

'For years the Japanese were taken lightly as military antagonists, and the confidence of the Western World in its disdainful appraisal of their military and naval capabilities seemed justified by the Japanese failure to achieve decisive victory in the Chinese war. Then, following the outbreak of the war with the United States and Britain, a succession of speedy and apparently easy victories stimulated the rise of the legend of the invincibility of the Japanese soldier. He allegedly was unconquerable in jungle terrain; his fanatical, death-courting charges and last-ditch defenses were broadcast until popular repute invested the Japanese soldier with almost superhuman attributes.

Several years of combat experience against the Japanese have replaced such fanciful notions by more realistic evaluation. While the military capabilities of the Japanese soldier still are appreciated, it is now realized that he has pronounced weaknesses. As a soldier his good qualities are not innate but are the result of careful training and preparation for specific tactical situations. Hence an accurate appraisal of the Japanese soldier must give adequate attention to the Japanese system of military training and show its effect on his physical, mental, and temperamental characteristics. . . .

'Military indoctrination of Japanese boys begins in early childhood, and semimilitary instruction is given in the primary schools by the teachers when the pupils reach their eighth year.

The speed and ferocity of the Japanese attack on British Imperial possessions saw the British pushed back into India. Hong Kong, Singapore, Rangoon: the great cities of empire fell to the 'bicycle Blitzkrieg'. One by one the Pacific island chains fell and the Japanese threatened Australia before being held in New Guinea – in a campaign that killed around 216,000 Australian, American and Japanese servicemen.

Compulsory military training is continued in part-time youth schools for those who go into industrial employment after primary school. In middle and higher schools military instruction is given by army officers, and similar programs are conducted in colleges and universities. When Japanese conscripts reach induction age they have had a considerable amount of military training. . . .'

'In combat the Japanese soldier is strong and hardy. On the offensive he is determined and willing to sustain sacrificial losses without flinching. When committed to an assault plan, Japanese troops adhere to it unremittingly even when severe casualties would dictate the need for abandonment or modification of the plan. The boldness and courage of the individual Japanese soldier are at their zenith when he is with his fellows, and when his group enjoys advantages of terrain or firepower. He is an expert at camouflage and delights in deceptions and ruses. Japanese troops obey orders well, and their training and discipline are well exemplified in night operations. On the defense they are brave and determined; their discipline is good and fire control excellent. In prepared positions the resistance of Japanese soldiers often has been fanatical in its tenacity.'

In China, the uneasy alliance between the Nationalists under Chiang Kai-shek and the Communists under Mao Tse-Tung – once the Japanese were beaten they'd continue the civil war that had started in the late 1920s – combined with great assistance from the west pushed the Japanese out. In Manchuria and Korea, the Soviets fought a lightning war in 1945 over an area the size of Europe against Japanese forces weakened by re-deployment to fight in the Pacific Theatre. In India, Burma and Malaya the mainly Indian Fourteenth Army under Bill Slim held and finally demolished the Japanese forces. And, of course, the United States' island-hopping campaign in the Pacific, which has attracted most of the postwar interest, saw amphibious warfare project military power to cut off Japan's island possessions one by one. This was combined arms' warfare, with naval and air power used to help the US Army and Marine Corps landings as infantry took the brunt of the land action.

The Western Allies

Neither Britain nor America entered the war with alacrity, remembering all too well the carnage of 1914–18. In Britain there was a real disgust with war that makes the policy of appeasement, understandable especially from the safety of over 70 years of relative peace. In the United States there were other considerations: dislike of Britain's imperial strength and position in the world; a large population with a German and Scandinavian heritage; isolationism helped by the problems of the Great Depression – it took declarations of war by the Japanese and the Nazis to finally allow Roosevelt to throw the American hat into the ring. When he did so, the balance of fortune swung very much in favour of the Allies, even if it took a while for this to become obvious. Britain's

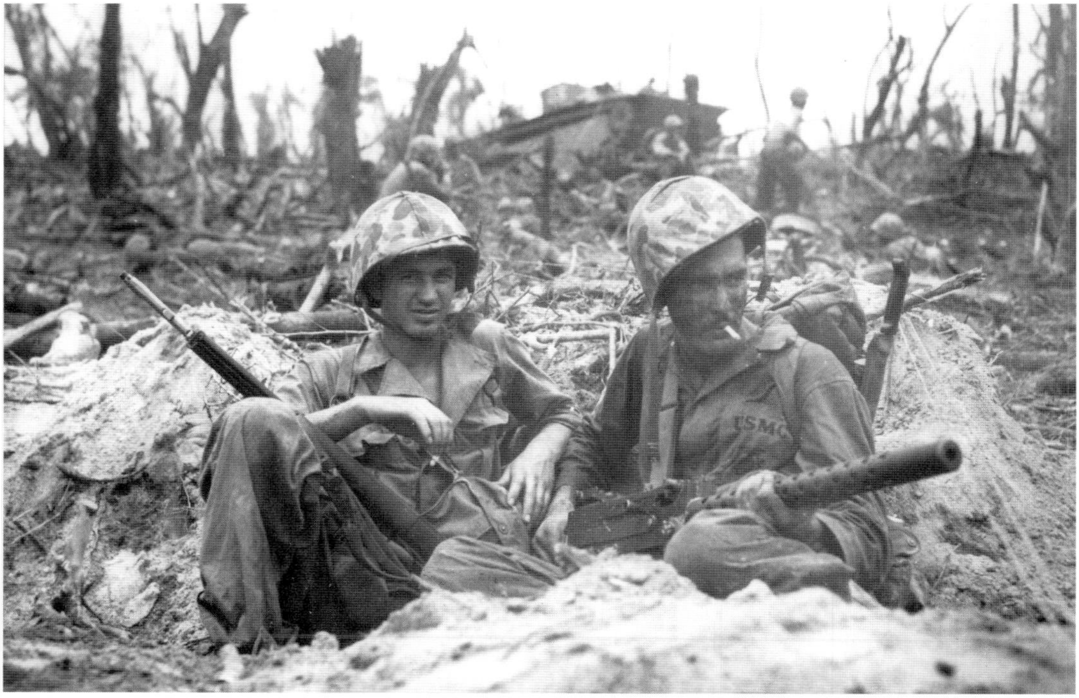

Above: Should the island of Peleliu have been bypassed? Possibly. It wasn't and 2,336 US Marines and US Army men died, along with nearly 11,000 Japanese. The battles lasted from 15 September to 27 November 1944. Note the .30cal machine gun (right).

Below: Over 25,000 men died on Iwo Jima: 6,821 Americans and over 18,000 Japanese. This marine was shot by a Japanese sniper. Close to the Japanese mainland, the fighting here and on Okinawa persuaded the American commanders that an attack on Japan itself would lead to huge casualties and that the atom bomb would be a better option.

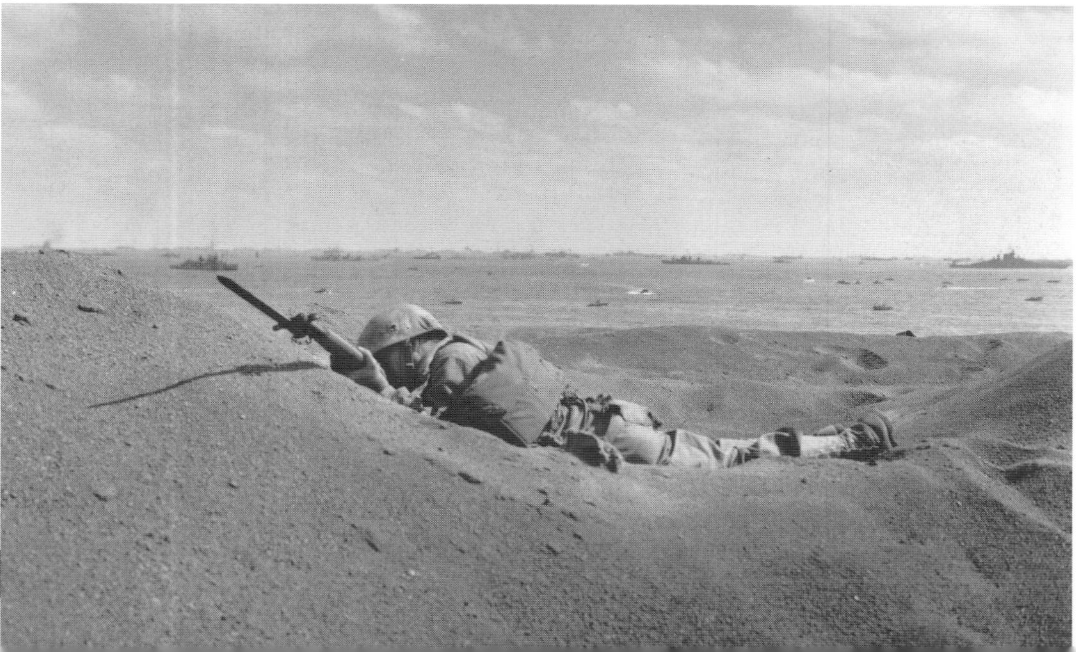

position at the end of 1941 was parlous, its forces having been defeated all over the globe. From 1942, however, two men stepped in and stopped the rot: Generals Bernard Law Montgomery and William Slim.

Slim defeated the Japanese on land, held India and crushed the invading army by teaching the Commonwealth forces to fight in the jungle. The United States did the same in the island-hopping battles that saw massive air and sea power channelled into a series of bloody amphibious operations that ended in nuclear holocaust. Japan, hit by two nuclear weapons, its territories invaded by a huge Soviet army, collapsed.

The other key British general, Monty turned round Eighth Army's – and Britain's – fortunes almost single-handedly. After Alamein criticisms may have been voiced about the speed of his actions – usually by armchair critics with little understanding of all the issues involved – but the results speak for themselves.

1942 also saw the United States forces enter combat. They had to learn sharp lessons but soon – assisted by their powerful industrial capability – became the dominant force in the Western alliance. By 1945, by force of arms, they had earned the right to be the leaders of the Free World. Their chosen supreme commander – Dwight D. Eisenhower – had shown the diplomatic abilities that would win him two presidential terms of office. American generals – Bradley, Patton, Simpson, Devers in the west and MacArthur in the Pacific – had joined the pantheon of great leaders. The Germans may have lost the war on the Eastern Front, but they lost the cream of their troops in the west. The citizen armies of Britain, its Empire and Commonwealth, and the United States, had become effective at all-arms combat with its infantry time and again leading the way.

The devastation of Nagasaki on 9 August 1945 killed 40,000. The second atomic weapon and the Soviet attack on Manchukuo forced Emperor Hirohito to step in and order the surrender. There would be an attempted coup before the emperor broadcast the surrender to the people of Japan.

LEADERSHIP

(From *Special Series No. 3 German Military Training,* 17 September 1941)

The Germans fully realize the importance of character as a basis for successful combat leadership. Their teachings on military leadership remind officers constantly of their responsibility to lead by example and self-discipline.

A book called *Company Commander* says:

The company commander is a living example to every man in his organization. To be an officer means to set an example for the men. The officer must be his soldier's incarnation of soldiery, his model. If the German officer is inspired by this mission, the best and deepest qualities of his soul will be awakened; his life's aim will be fulfilled if he succeeds, through knowledge, demeanor, and conviction, in forcing his troops to follow him. This is the manly purpose for which it is worthwhile to stake life in order to win life.

In Germany, the road to the rank of officer is open to every capable soldier; the destination can be reached only by efficiency in time of war and by actions in the face of the enemy.

The real authority of an officer is recreated daily by his entire attitude; the ancient proverb applies – "earn it in order to possess it." The more his men are convinced that the authority of his rank is deserved through moral worth, the stronger will be the influence of the officer's personality. No one should expect that rank attained by promotion will give to his position authority sufficiently high for him to relax his effort, in the belief that the objective has been reached. Real authority is not dependent upon shoulder straps, stars, and badges; it depends only on efficiency and worth.

The German military bible for company officers is the *Truppenführung* (Manual of Troop Leadership). This book gives their basic tactical and combat doctrine, and has plenty to say on the moral aspects of leadership. The following are some quotations:

- *War is the severest test of spiritual and physical strength. In war, character outweighs intellect.*
- *Many stand forth on the field of battle, who in peace would remain unnoticed.*
- *The officer is a leader and a teacher. Besides his knowledge of men and his sense of justice, he must be distinguished by his superior knowledge and experience, his earnestness, his self control, and his courage.*
- *The example and personal conduct of officers and noncommissioned officers are of decisive influence on the troops. The officer who, in the face of the enemy, is cold-blooded, decisive, and courageous inspires his troops onward. The officer must, likewise, find the way to the hearts of his subordinates and gain their trust through an understanding of their feelings and thoughts, and through never-ceasing care of their needs.*
- *Mutual trust is the surest basis of discipline in necessity and danger.*
- *We apply simple methods to our leadership. You will find that our lower units are so trained that many in them beside the leader are capable of taking command. It is the responsibility of senior officers to assist their juniors in training for the next higher grade.*
- *Leaders must live with their troops, participating in their dangers, their wants, their joys, their sorrows. Only in this way can they estimate the battle worth and the requirements of the troops.*
- *Man is not responsible for himself alone, but also for his comrades. He who can do more, who has greater capacity of accomplishment, must instruct the inexperienced and weaker. From such conduct the feeling of real comradeship develops, which is just as important between the leaders and the men as between the men themselves.*

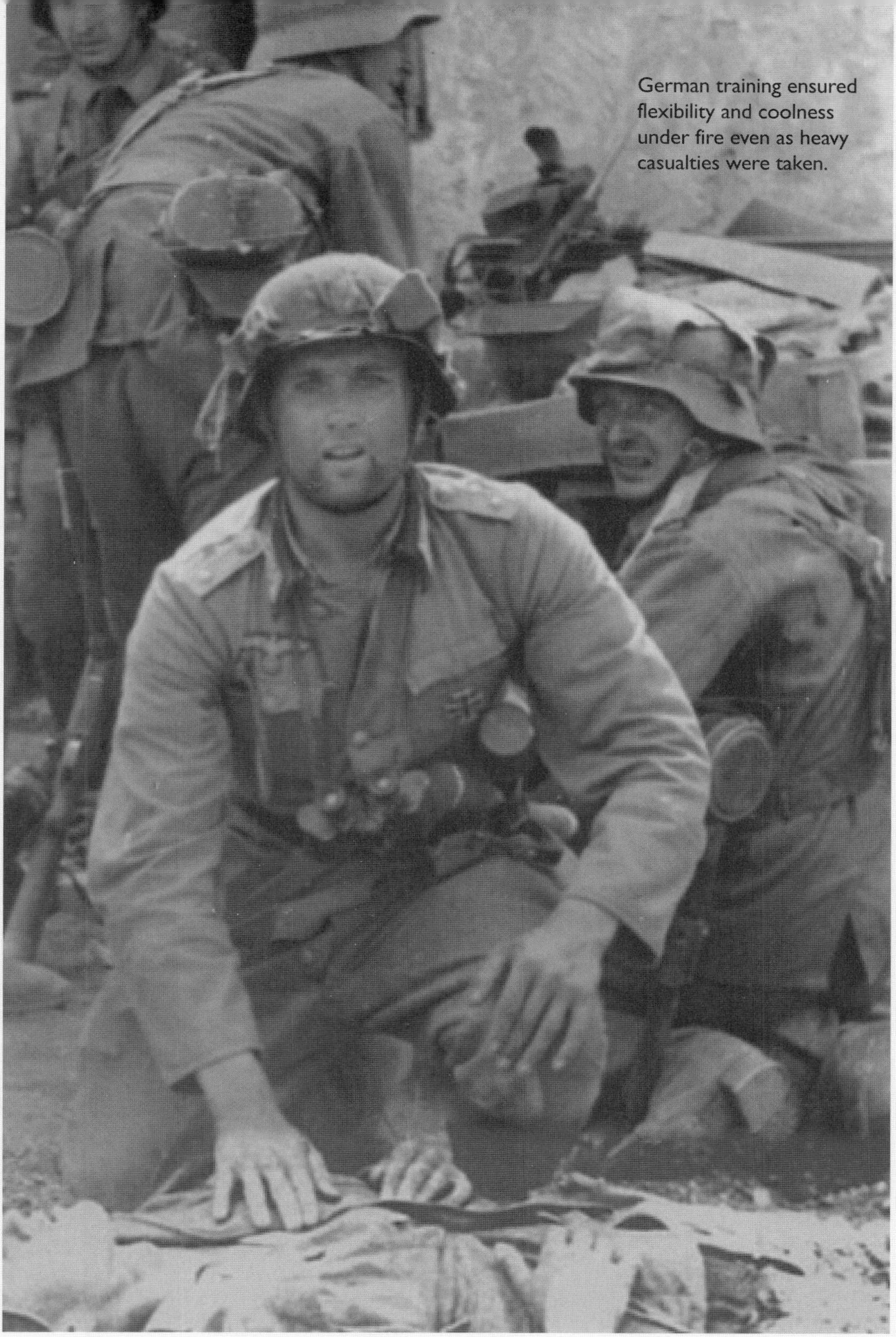

German training ensured flexibility and coolness under fire even as heavy casualties were taken.

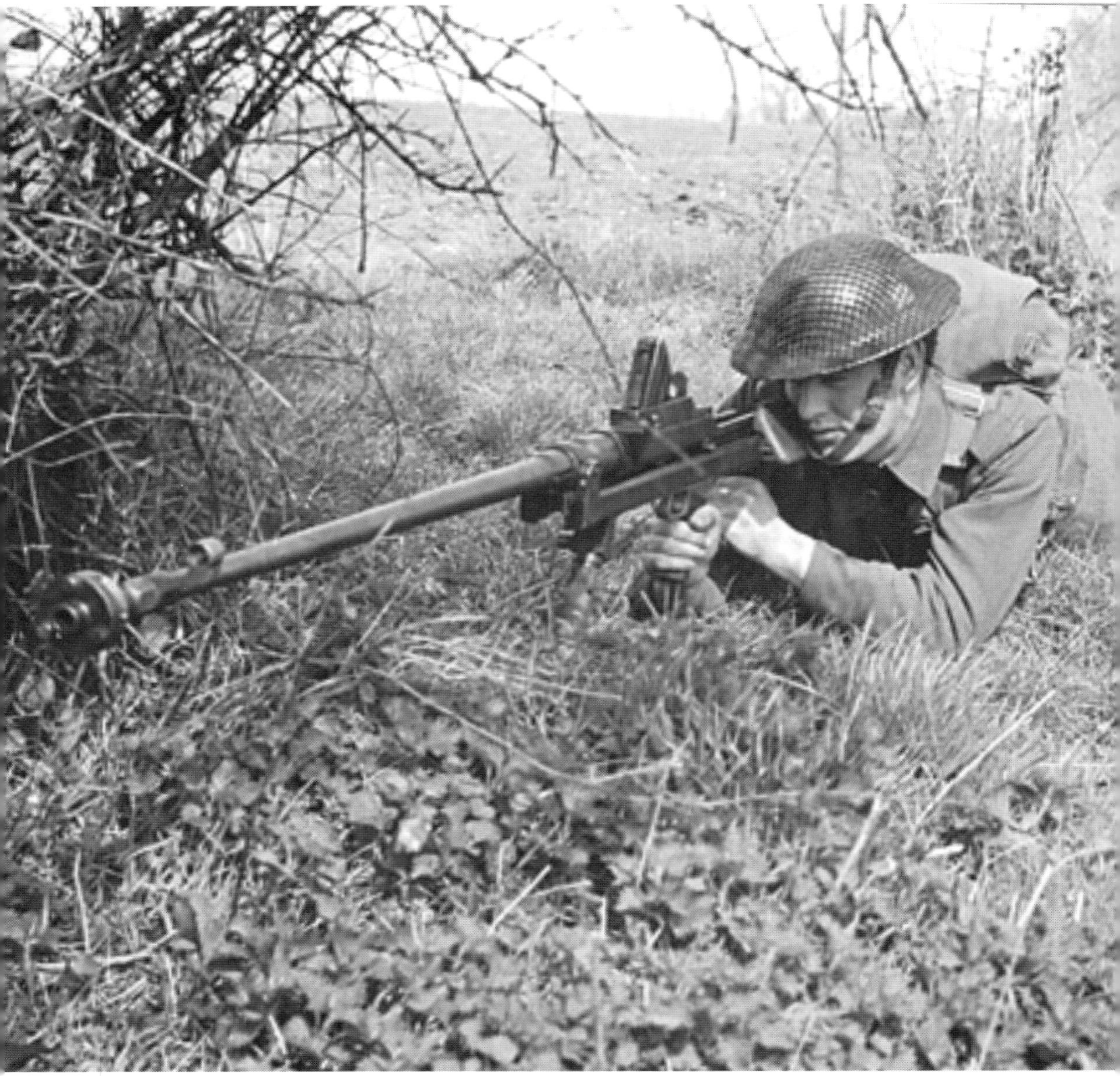

It quickly became apparent that better anti-tank guns would be needed than the rifles developed as World War I ended. The British Boys (as seen here) and German *Panzerbüchse* 38 and 39 gave way to heavier and heavier guns – Rommel, for example, made use of the Flak 8.8cm in the ground role as had been pioneered in the Spanish Civil War. As the anti-tank guns got bigger and bigger, so they became more cumbersome for the infantry. Later in the war the first of the rockets came in with the Bazooka, the *Panzerschreck* and the PIAT before the next wave – the *Panzerfaust* – completely changed the face of anti-tank warfare: light, one-time-use weapons meant any infantry unit could go tank-hunting.

1 Mechanisation

The British Mark I tank arrived on the battlefield in 1916. This fighting vehicle combined armour, firepower and mobility (in the form of caterpillar tracks) to overcome the stalemate of the Western Front. It could cross no-man's land with relative impunity and destroy fortifications, barbed wire and trenches. The stalemate on the Western Front was broken; tanks changed the shape of the battlefield.

One aspect of armoured warfare became immediately apparent – the need for weapons to stop the tanks. The initial German counter to the threat was artillery and mortar fire but results soon showed that while concentrated shelling could damage or incapacitate a tank, it rarely destroyed it. Artillery and mortars are indirect fire weapons: their crews cannot see the target. What was needed was a weapon that could be aimed directly at the target line-of-sight, and one that had a flat trajectory. The drawback, of course, was that this also exposed the weapon to return fire.

The Germans had experimented with a blunt-ended bullet with more propellant added to the cartridge. When the blunt end hit the armour it caused spalling – metal fragments breaking off on the inside, flying around maiming and sometimes killing crewmen. However, it wasn't popular with those who fired it because of the short range, damage to the rifle and potential injury to the rifleman.

The alternative was the armour-piercing 7.92mm K bullet fired from the Kar98, the standard infantry rifle. The SmK (*Spitzgeschoss mit Kern*) had a standard steel core and the SmKh (h = *hart* = hard) saw the steel core replaced by tungsten carbide. The hardened cores were designed to pierce sniper plates and gun shields. These K bullets could disable a tank by destroying the optics or penetrating the vision slits; some armour penetration was also possible to the earlier tanks. However, armour plate improved and with the arrival of the British Mark IV the 7.92mm K bullet became obsolete. What was needed was a heavier-calibre high-velocity anti-tank rifle – it would be some time before Germany or the Allies realised that tanks were the future and rifles wouldn't be sufficient to stop them.

Known as T-Gewehr 13 anti-tank rifle – and nicknamed *Elefanten Buchsen* (elephant gun) – this was the first dedicated anti-tank rifle and a new type of firearm. It had a pistol grip and was fired using a removable bipod. It was designed to target systems and tank crew through concentrated fire against vision ports, optics, fuel tanks and weapon systems. One major defect was the huge blunt force to the firer. It could penetrate 22mm (1.25in) at 100m and was used in groups by specially raised and trained anti-tank detachments to maximise damage to the target. It was fired from the prone position often from trenches or shell holes.

Some 25 years later, after having seen the tank dominate the battlefield, anti-tank guns became a major element of the infantryman's weaponry. Most countries' military doctrine did not see their tanks' main function as killing other tanks: they were designed to break through enemy lines and play havoc in the relatively unguarded rear areas. The antitank gun was the main infantry counter to tanks – and there was a continuous race between the improving armour protection of the tank and the improving punch of the antitank guns as 37mm, 2pdr and 50mm gave way to the 6pdr, 75mm and then the heavyweights: the 17pdr and 88mm weapons. From the start the Germans had made use of the flexibility of their Flak 18 antiaircraft gun as a tank killer. However, as well as fixed antitank guns – although they would continue to be an important infantry weapon – other armoured vehicles, dubbed tank destroyers, were designed to kill the tanks. In American doctrine this idea was taken to the extreme and tank destroyers were supposed to be held in reserve awaiting their chance en masse to counter an armoured breakthrough. The Germans had a range of them, from the Marder to the mighty Ferdinand or Jagdpanther.

However, as the war progressed two forms of infantry antitank weapon were developed that, once again, gave the solo infantryman a real chance of closing with the armoured enemy—the bazooka and the *Panzerfaust*. These man-portable anti-tank weapons gave the infantry an inexpensive, lightweight alternative to the increasingly heavy antitank guns (such as the British 17pdr or German 8.8cm PaK 43). All sides developed them – the American bazooka, the British PIAT and the German *Panzerschreck* (8.8cm *Raketenpanzerbüchse* 43). 289,000 of all variants of the latter were built and it proved very successful. But in many ways the *Panzerfaust* was a more significant step forward. The *Panzerfaust* 60 reached full production in 1944 when 400,000 were produced each month. A higher velocity was achieved by increasing the diameter of the tube and increased propellant. The sights were improved with apertures from 30m to 80m, as was the squeeze trigger. Virtually anyone could use them and their HESH warheads could kill most AFVs. Postwar, the recoilless rifle and LAW – light antitank weapon – would become the infantryman's last resort against tanks that got past friendly armour and aircraft.

*　　*　　*

Between the wars the viability of mechanised warfare was much debated. It was definitely helped by the growth of industrial capability, civilian use of petrol-driven transport and the development of its accompanying infrastructure. However, for nations exhausted

The Finns were equipped with *Panzerfaust* while allies of the Germans during the Continuation War of 1941–44. This photograph shows men of Infantry Regiment 12 inspecting a Soviet T-34 tank destroyed during the critical Battle of Tali-Ihantala. This took place in northern Vyborg between 25 June and 9 July 1944. Finnish success – due in no small part to its excellent artillery – helped Finland maintain its independence at war's end.

Tankgewehr M1918 tank-hunting rifle
Type: Bolt-action, breech-loading, single-shot, man-portable 13mm anti-tank rifle
Number produced: 15,000–16,000 from May 1918 – a remarkable achievement from design to production (1917–18 to end of war)
Weight: 15.9kg (35lb); 18.5kg (41lb) with bipod
Overall length: 169mm (5ft 6in)
Projectile: 13mm x 92mm (.525in x 3.75in) TuF (for use against *Tank und Flieger* – tanks and aircraft) round weighing 51.5g (0.11lb)
Effective range: 500m (547.5yd)
Crew: Two – rifleman and No 2 with extra ammunition. In practice the team also had a protection group armed with Kar98s and the French Chauchat LMG

Panzerfaust 60
Type: Man-portable, fire-and-forgot, recoilless
Number produced: Over 6.5 million of all models 1943–5
Weight: 6.25kg (13.8lb)
Overall length: 1m (3ft 3in)
Projectile: Shaped charge 200mm penetration
Effective range: from c30m for *Panzerfaust* 30 or *Panzerfaust Klein* to 100m for *Panzerfaust* 100
Crew: 1 – anyone could fire it. Little training required

The Russians had two effective anti-tank rifles, the single-shot PTRD-41, as here, designed by Degtyaryov and its semi-automatic counterpart designed by Simonov, the PTRS-41 which was a little more problematic to use (it jammed easily). These were used throughout the war, in quantity, with special tactics against the German tanks.

by the previous war – particularly the French, British and American victors – and concerned with their own conservative military requirements it remained for the most part theoretical, a topic for the specialist proponents of mobile warfare.

The French turned toward defence and built the Maginot Line. The Americans retreated into isolationism. The British had an empire to police and, having decided that war in Europe was unlikely, paid little attention to the armed forces until it was almost too late. From 1919 the British government based its policies on its Ten-Year Rule: that the British Empire would not get engaged in a major war during the next ten years. This directive was perpetuated until 1932 when it became obvious that this was probably not the case in both Europe and the Far East.

The military theorists – two of the most important being British Maj-Gen John Fuller and Sir Basil Liddell Hart – discussed armoured warfare. It was realised that to keep an attacking force together all parts of it must be at least motorised (which required a road network), but preferably mechanised (with tracks and armour for rough ground and combat) and so along with tank development came heavier armoured cars, lorries, carriers and half-tracks with which to transport infantry and other supporting arms along with their weapons. All nations began the gradual mechanisation of their armed forces, but without fully grasping the necessity for further reorganisation that such a complicated highly mobile structure would require. So although there were many new tracked or all-wheel drive vehicles and a few attempts at combining different kinds of formations, the lack of incentive, finance and road-testing during real combat along with the conservative nature of higher commands precluded any sustained serious development.

Then came the Spanish Civil War (1936–39) and all the nations sat up and took notice. Both sides had their international sponsors, and – helped by the Russians and Germans – the Nationalists and Republicans fought the first modern war with substantial air and armour components. The shockwaves went around the world and mechanisation became the order of the day. It was the Germans who had progressed farthest by the

GERMAN PANZERS AGAINST POLAND 1939

1. Panzer Division	309
2. Panzer Division	322
3. Panzer Division	391
4. Panzer Division	341
5. Panzer Division	335
10. Panzer Division	150
Panzer Division Kempf	164
1. Light Division/6. Panzer Division	226
2. Light Division/7. Panzer Division	85
3. Light Division/8. Panzer Division	80
4. Light Division/9. Panzer Division	62
Panzer Regiment 25	225

Blitzkrieg didn't involve large numbers of heavyweight tanks. For the attack on Poland, 1. Panzer-Division had 93 PzKpfw Is, a tank never intended for combat and only armed with machine guns, 122 PzKpfw IIs, a mere 26 PzKpfw IIIs, 56 PzKpfw IVs and 12 *Panzerbefehlswagen* (command tanks) – hardly an armoured spearhead. Jentz, Thomas: *Panzertruppen – The Complete Guide to the Creation & Combat Employment of Germany's Tank Force 1933–1942*

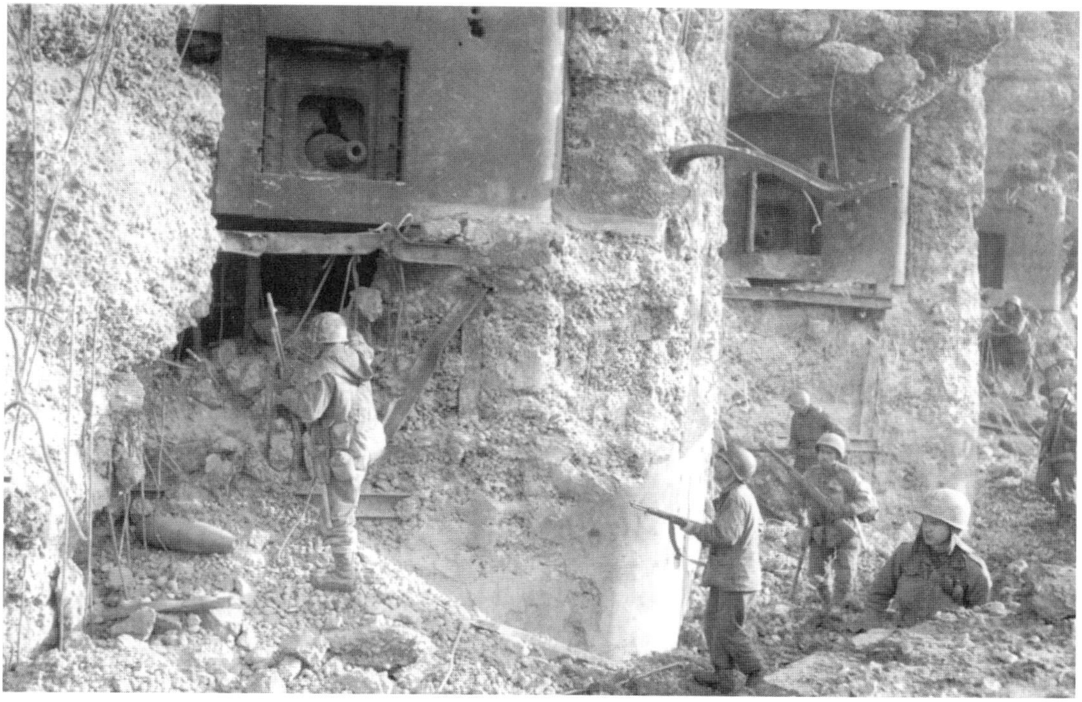

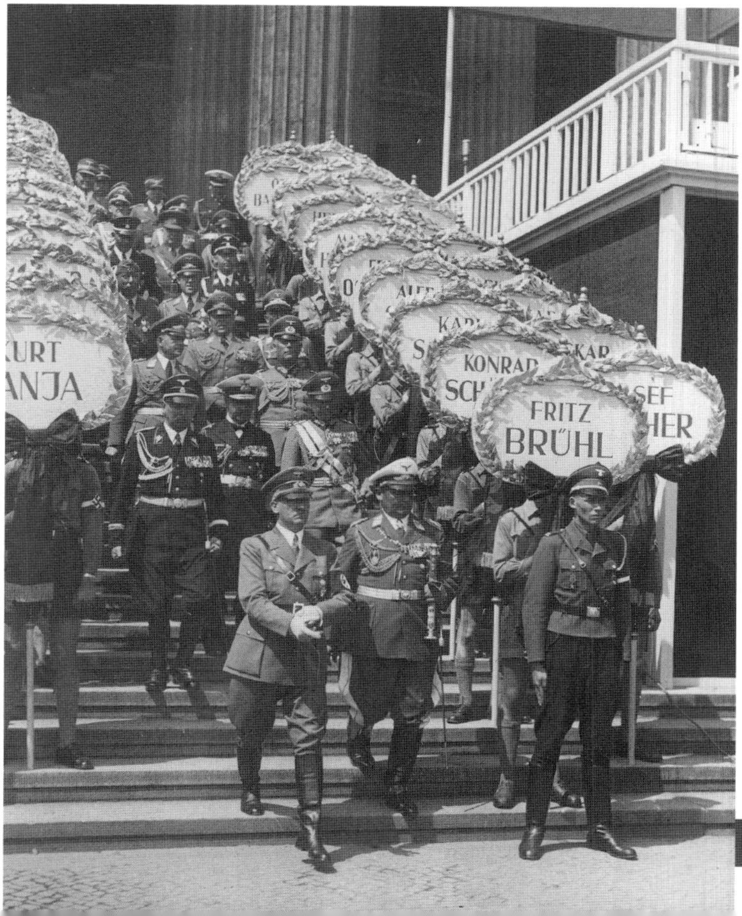
KURT
FRITZ
BRÜHL

Above: Fixed defences were popular between the wars and fortified lines were built by the Czechs, Germans and, of course, the French – the Maginot Line. Some of these impressive concrete structures saw a great deal of fighting during the war – the Atlantic Wall, of course, the Westwall and, mainly around Alsace, the Maginot where some forts changed hands three times in 1944–45.

Right: Nazi bigwigs – Hitler and Goering at the front – remember those lost in Spain (named on the placards). The war proved a useful testing ground for tactics and weapons

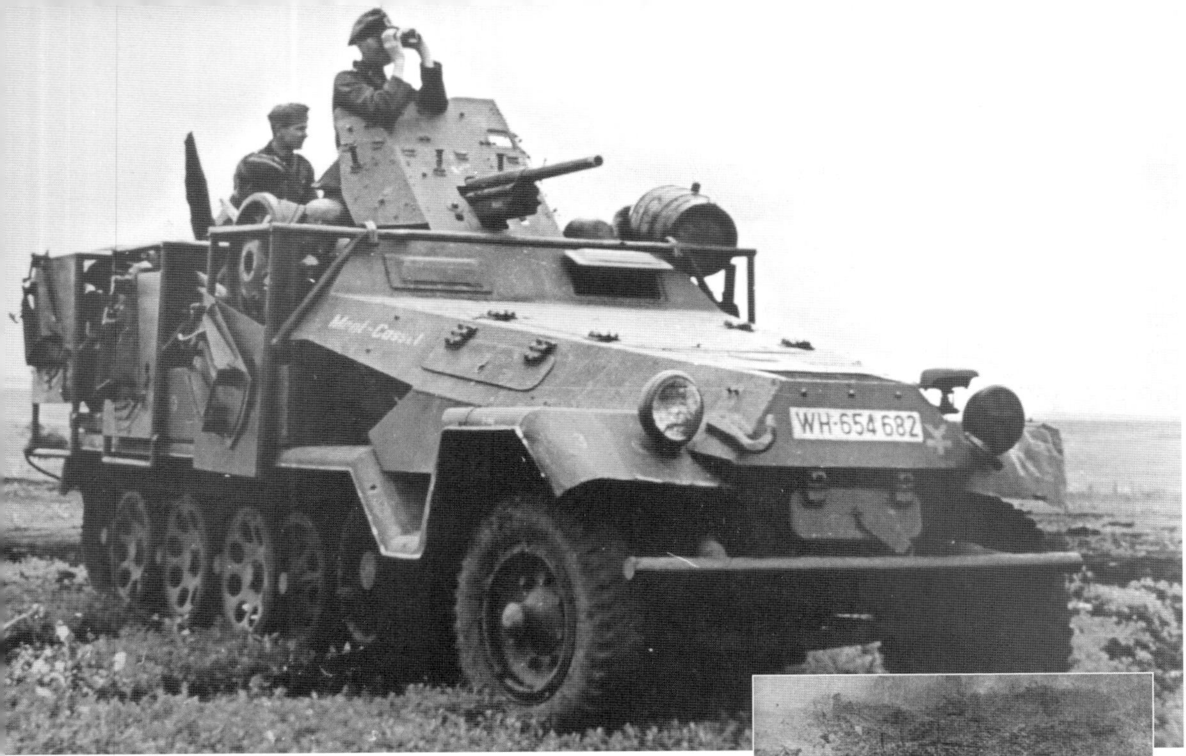
WH-654 682

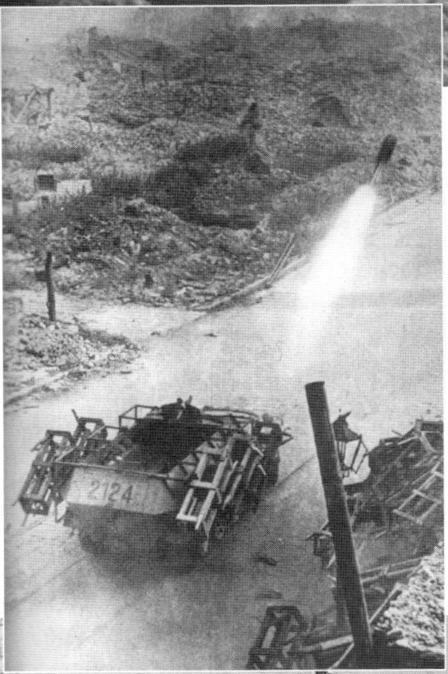
2124

Above and Right: The SdKfz 251 could carry 12 men but was also produced in a range of variants and variations that included the 251/9 with a 7.5cm KwK 37 L/24 and 251/10 with a 3.7cm PaK to give anti-tank capability. This 251/10 has the attachments for *Wurfrahmen* rockets. Two sorts were fired: 32cm napalm and 28cm HE. The range was 2,300m.

Below: An SdKfz 7 of the Royal Hungarian Army towing a road trailer, Hungary 1944. Used as a gun tower, the SdKfz 7 was also used as the platform for various anti-aircraft guns including the 7/1 with a 2cm Flakvierling 38 L/65 quadruple mounting and the 7/2 with a 3.7cm weapon.

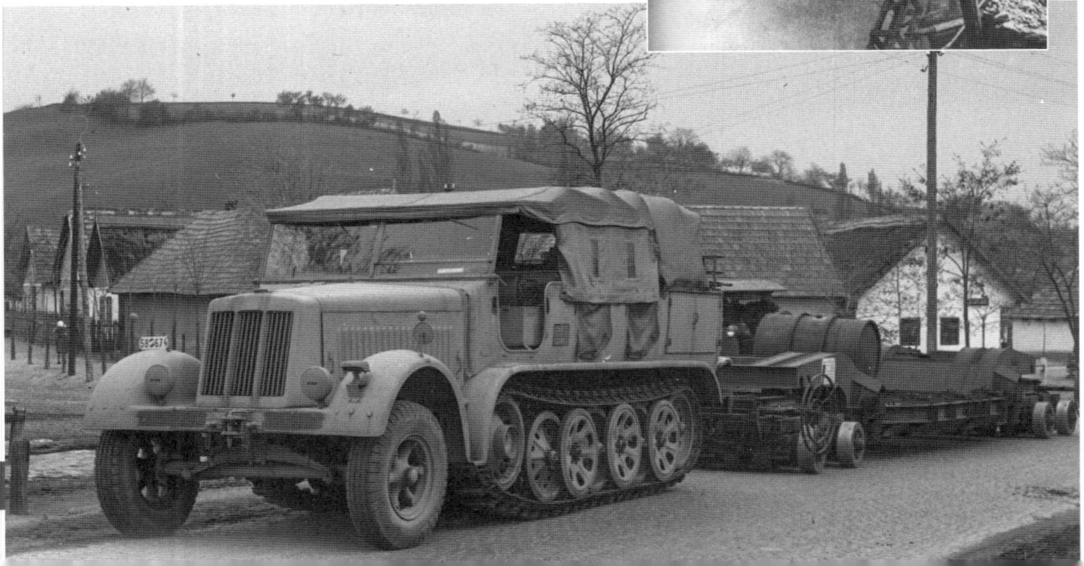

start of fresh hostilities, with the successful creation of Panzer divisions equipped mainly with the light PzKpfw I and II. The Panzer division also had two *Schützen* battalions (they would be renamed Panzergrenadiers in 1941) and a motorcycle battalion.

These nascent formations marked a new level of combined all-arms warfare whose initial results took the Germans themselves by surprise. Enabled through the unique circumstances of a secret reconstruction of the German Army, allowing input and initiative from radical theorists, and the arrival of an excited *Führer* on the scene, the subsequent secret rearming and intense wargaming with primitive resources began the evolution of a more highly mobile stand-alone all arms battlegroup. These Panzer divisions came equipped with their own supporting infantry, artillery, anti-tank, reconnaissance and engineer units that were transported in a variety of half-tracks, armoured cars and motorcycles which could just about keep up with the tanks over rough terrain and thus maintain attack momentum. The infantry used half-tracks, under the nomenclature *Sonderkraftfahrzeug* (special motor vehicle) that had an open-top armoured superstructure, truck type wheels for steering at the front, with caterpillar tracks behind spreading the weight and making it manoeuvrable over rough terrain. There were eventually many variants carrying different weapon systems as well as command, communications and ambulance versions. The early SdKfz 250 was used by reconnaissance units and could carry six men, but the prime infantry-carrying half-track used throughout the war was the SdKfz 251 series (also known as Hanomags after their main manufacturer). Slope-armoured, it carried a crew of 12 including the driver, platoon commander, and ten Panzergrenadiers and their equipment, had a top speed of 50kph and was armed with one or two M42 machine guns.

Although the new mobile armoured divisions had an enormous impact on the battlefield they were by no means representative of the German Army as a whole. In 1939, 80 percent of its divisions were entirely reliant on the older forms of troop transport. Trains and trucks were used when the infrastructure was available, but otherwise the infantry

The SdKfz 8 was used as an artillery tractor (as here) but could also be used as an infantry personnel carrier. Note the pintle-mounted MG34.

GERMAN ARMY DIVISIONS USED FROM THE INVASION OF POLAND TO NORTH AFRICA

Divisions used against Poland
Armeegruppe Nord (inc reserves)
Panzer Divisions: Kempf, 3 and 10; Panzer Lehr
  Regiment
Infantry Divisions: 1, 3, 11, 12, 21, 23, 32, 50, 61, 73,
  106–208, 217, 218, 228
Infantry Divisions (mot): 2, 20
Infantry Brigades: Netze, Lötzen, Goldap
Cavalry Brigades: 1

Armeegruppe Süd (inc reserves)
Panzer Divisions: 1, 2, 4, 5
Infantry Divisions: 4, 7, 8, 10, 14, 17–19, 24, 27, 28,
  30, 31, 44–46, 62, 68, 213, 221, 239
Infantry Divisions (mot): 13, 29
Light Divisions: 1, 2, 3, 4
Gebirgsjäger (Mountain) Divisions: 1, 2, 3
SS-Leibstandarte Adolf Hitler (motorised regiment)
  attached to 17. Inf Div
SS-Germania (motorised regiment)

Slovak Army Bernolak
Infantry Divisions: 1, 2, 20

Divisions used against the Denmark and Norway
Group XXI
Infantry Divisions: 69, 163, 170, 181, 196, 198, 214
Gebirgsjäger Divisions: 2, 3
Motor Rifle Brigade: 11

Divisions used against the Low Countries and France
OKH Reserve
Infantry Divisions: 5, 15, 25, 34, 45, 50, 81, 88, 96,
  205, 211, 267, 290–295

Armeegruppe A
Panzer Divisions: 1, 2, 5–8, 10
Infantry Divisions: 2–6, 8, 9, 10, 12, 13, 15–17, 21,
  23–29, 32, 34, 36, 52, 58, 62, 68, 71, 73, 76, 87,
  211, 251, 263, 267
Infantry Divisions (mot): 2, 13, 29
Gebirgsjäger Divisions: 1
Infantry Regiment: Grossdeutschland

Armeegruppe B
Infantry Divisions: 4, 7, 15, 31, 33, 205, 207, 208,
  211, 225, 227, 253, 254, 256, 269, 526
Cavalry Division: 1
SS Adolf Hitler Regiment
SS Der Führer Regiment
SS Verfügungstruppe

Flieger (Airmobile/Para) Division: 7
Luftlande (Airlanding) Division: 22

Armeegruppe C
Infantry Divisions: 60, 75, 79, 93, 95, 167, 168, 197,
  198, 213, 215, 218, 221, 239, 246, 252, 257, 258,
  262, 268, 554–557
Gebirgsjäger Divisions: 6

Divisions used in Invasion of Yugoslavia
Second Armee
Panzer Divisions: 6, 14
Infantry Divisions: 79, 101 (leichte), 125, 132, 183
Infantry Divisions (mot): 16
Gebirgsjäger Divisions: 1st
Division zbV (Frontier Guard): 538

Twelfth Armee
Panzer Divisions: 9; LSSAH
Infantry Divisions: 73
Infantry Divisions (mot): SS-Das Reich
Infantry Regiment (mot): Grossdeutschland

First Panzergruppe
Panzer Divisions: 5, 11
Infantry Divisions: 294
Infantry Divisions (mot): 60
Gebirgsjäger Divisions: 4

Divisions used in Invasion of Greece
Panzer Divisions: 2, 9, 16 (on Belgian-Turkish border),
  LSSAH Regt
Infantry Divisions: 72, 73, 50, 125, 164
Gebirgs Divisions: 5, 6

Divisions used in Invasion of Crete
Flieger (Airmobile/Para) Division: 7
Gebirgs Divisions: 5
Luftlande (Airlanding) Sturmregiment

German Divisions used in North Africa
1941
Afrika Korps: 15. Panzer Division, 5. Leichte Division

January 1942
Afrika Korps: 15. and 21. Panzer Divisions
90. Leichte Division

February 1943
Fifth Panzerarmee
Afrika Korps: 15. and 21. Panzer Divisions
164. Leichte Division
Ramcke Fallschirmjäger (Para) Brigade

So much for mechanisation. The German Army was a huge user of horses with all the associated problems – not least, feeding and caring for them. The plus points were that, in extremis, you could eat them as happened, for example, during the battle of Stalingrad. They could also keep moving when a motor vehicle bogged down – although the *rasputitsa* was often too much for any transport.

marched to combat, with its weapons pulled by horse-drawn transport. Even by 1943 out of over 300 German divisions only 52 were mechanised or motorised (see table opposite).

It was the same for the Allies, although the British and Americans were at least motorised, the British the most of all. Apart from various lorries, they also had their Universal carrier – a small, open-topped armoured vehicle that had only tracks and was steered like a tank,. It was used extensively by all Allied forces other than the US. First made in 1935, production by 1939 had focused on two main versions (a Bren carrier and a scout) and by the war's end over 110,000 had been built. Simple, easy to maintain, reliable and fast, each infantry battalion had 26 carriers and they were used for everything – carrying troops, heavy weapons and ammunition, reconnaissance, communications and as ad hoc ambulances and general runabouts. Other later versions mounted 3-inch or 4.2-inch mortars, Vickers or Browning machine guns, PIATs and even a flame thrower.

The US at first produced the M2 half-track, which was based on an older French design. Made to carry a dozen men, it mounted a .50-calibre machine gun, had a road

Continued on p. 46.

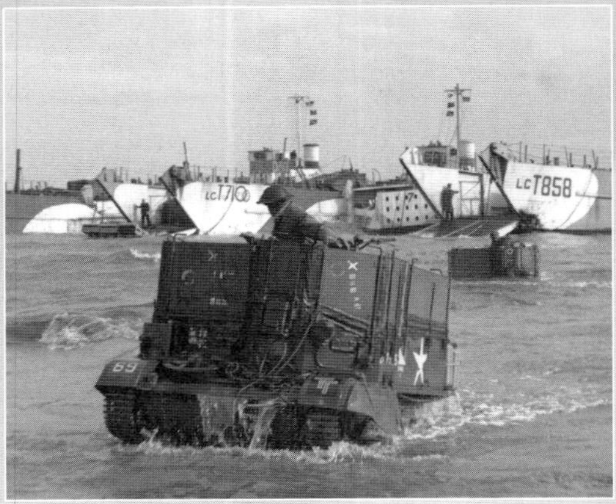

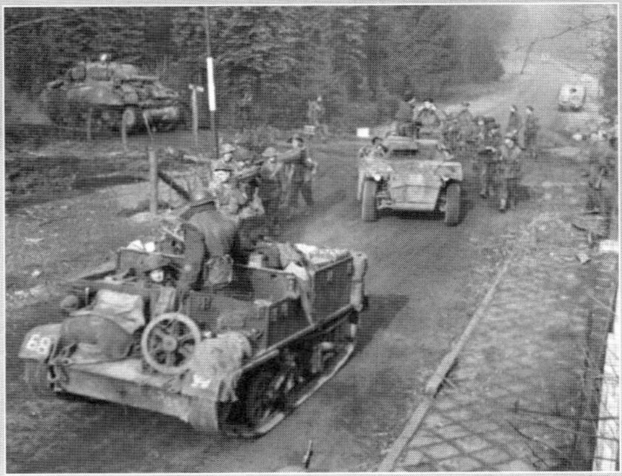

The British Universal carrier was a maid-of-all-work that was used as a scout vehicle, artillery tractor, ammunition carrier or weapons' platform – with Boys anti-tank rifles, Vickers MMGs (**Opposite, Above** – note 50th Inf Div TT sign) or mortars . They could be waterproofed with a screen (**Above left**) and while they were vulnerable to air-bursting artillery, they provided excellent all-terrain mobility from North Africa to Russia. Produced in huge numbers – nearly 30,000 Universal carriers were manufactured in Canada alone, and 5,000 Windsors (the Canadian version) – it has a claim to being the most manufactured armoured vehicle in history.

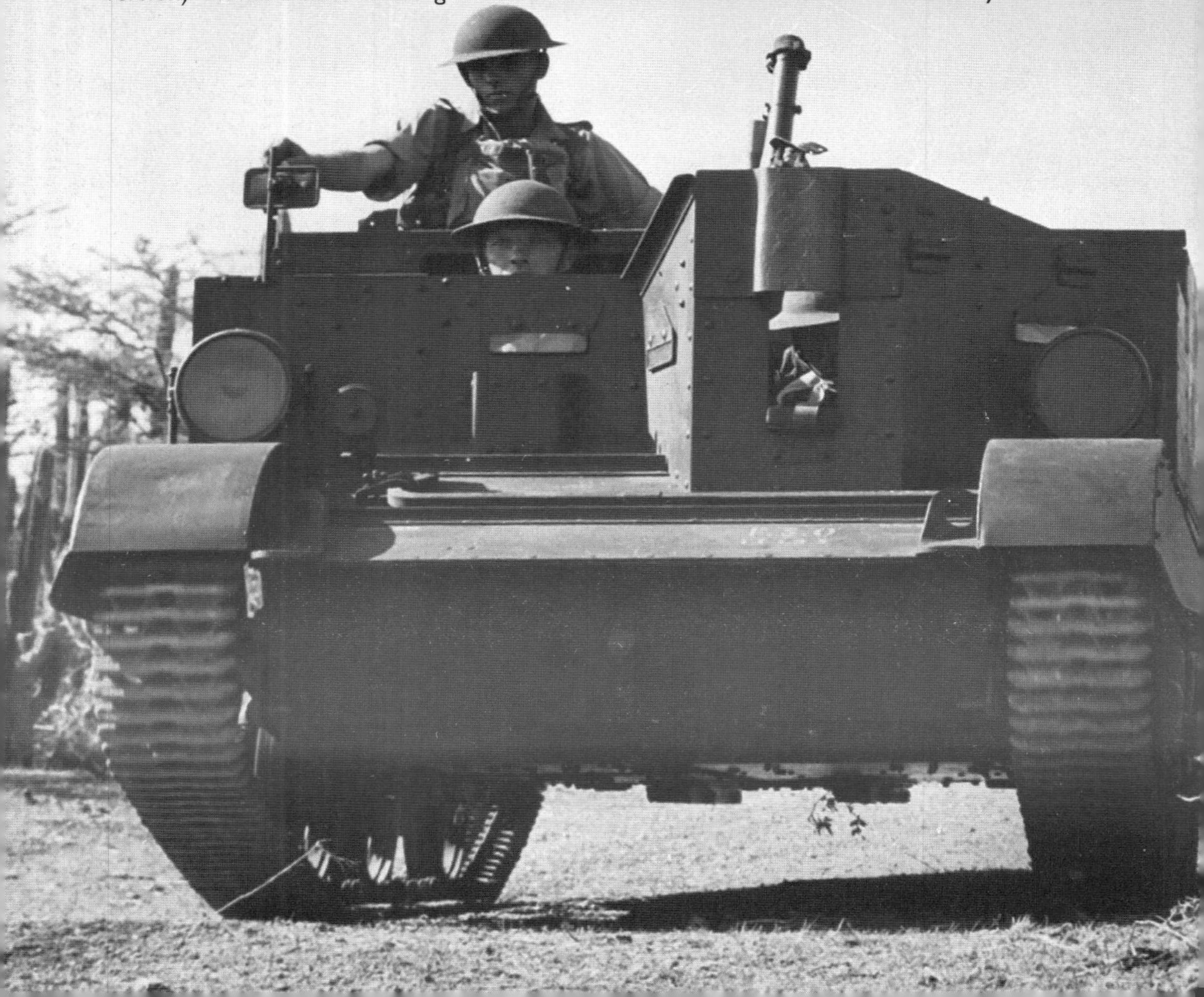

Opposite, Inset right: A Universal carrier and Humber scout car of 43rd (Wessex) Division during the British advance on Goch, 17 February 1945.

Main photo: A Universal carrier of 2nd Bn, Shropshire Light Infantry in Curaçao in 1940.

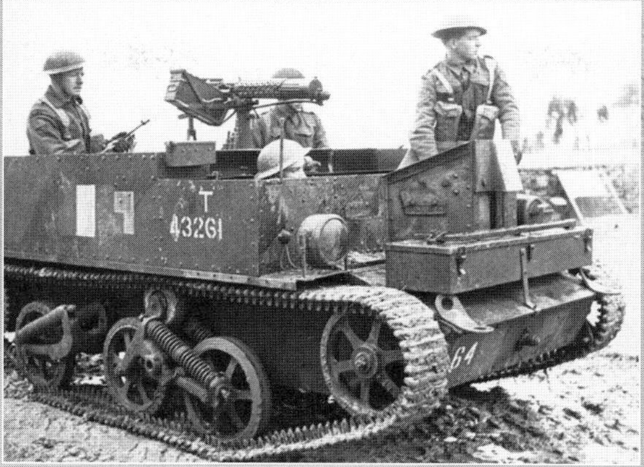

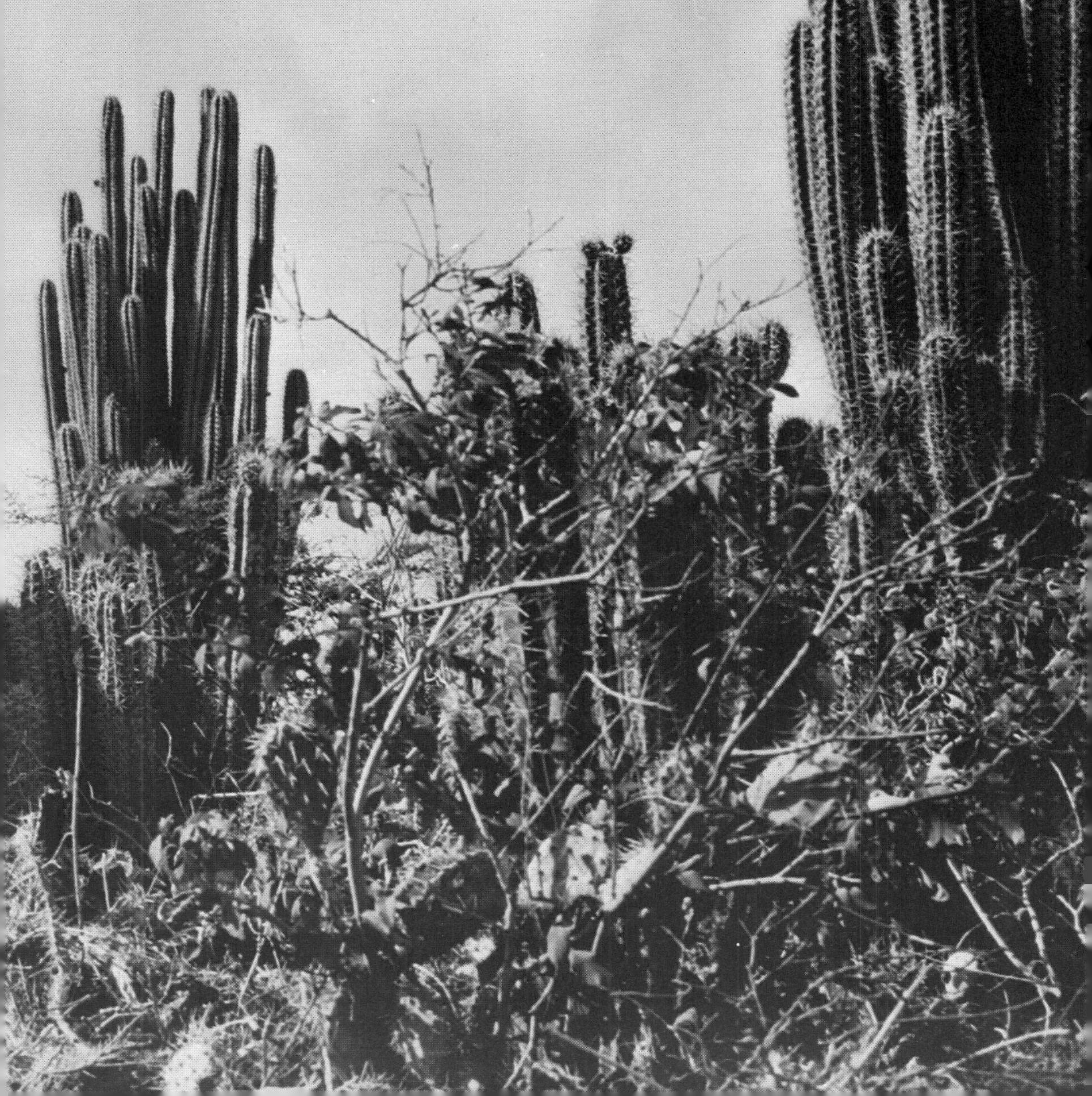

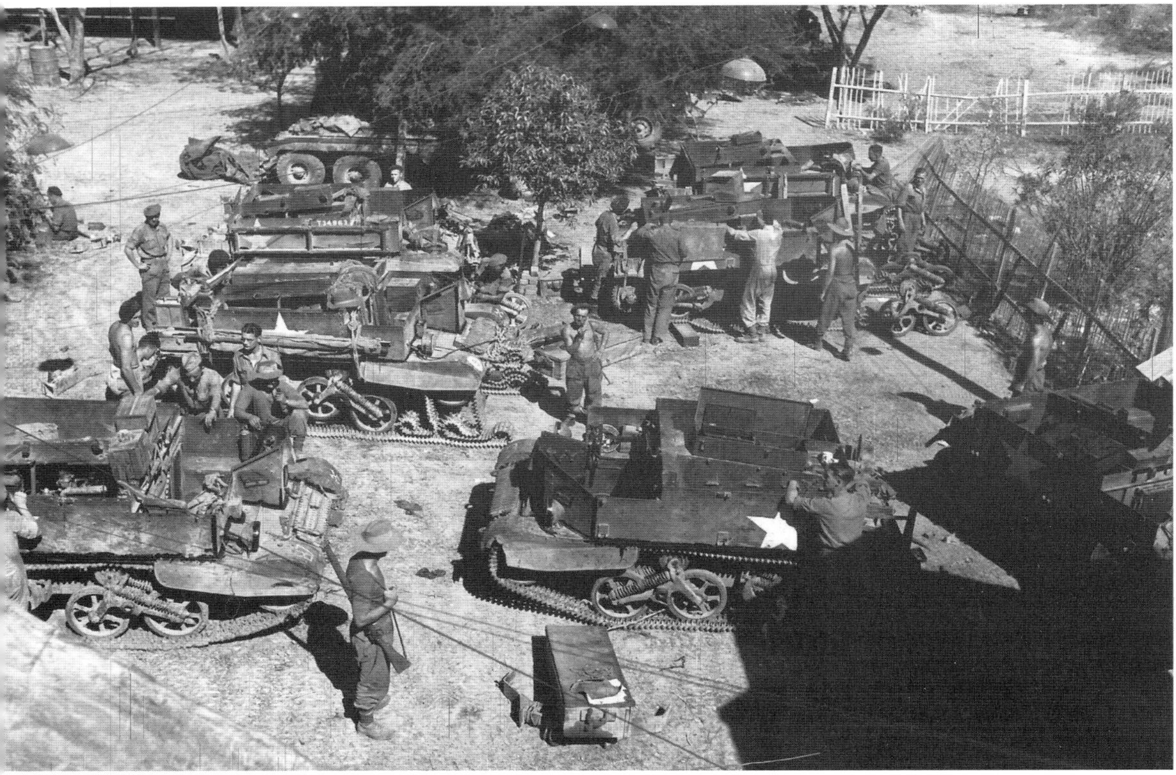

The success of the Universal carrier led to the production of many different versions of the original design and similar vehicles such as the Loyd, Windsor and, postwar, the Oxford Carrier. The Americans were asked to come up with a version that would remedy some of the issues that showed up in service – these included weak rear axles and tracks

Continued on next page

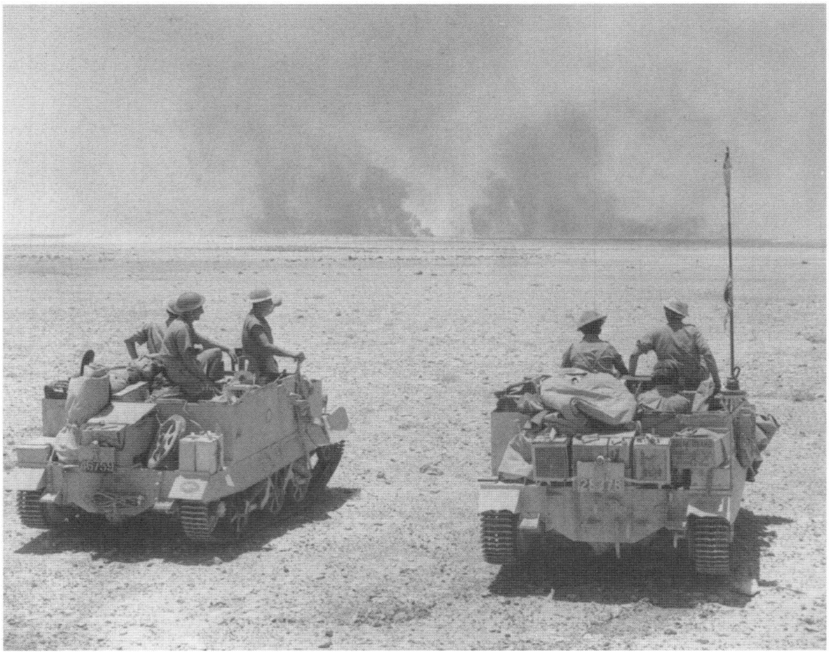

that gave out under load, a steering system that needed regular realignment, heavy use of brake pads, and lack of engine power – particularly when towing the 6pdr. Ford USA's reworking – the T16 (**Opposite, Above**) – took a long time to reach the front (arriving in 1944). It had an extra roadwheel but wasn't popular with the British until an improved T16E2 Mk II was produced with altered bogie units that smoothed out the ride.

Opposite, Below: Many – but not all – carriers had radios. These are from 9th Rifle Bde seen in 1942 during the Gazala battles. Typical of the Desert War both are carrying heavy loads.

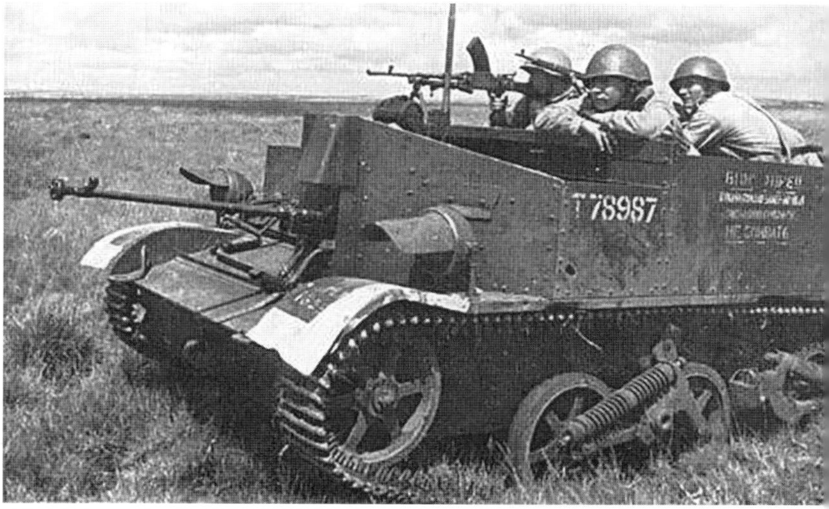
T78987

Above right: Lend-Lease carrier in Russian use (note also Boys anti-tank and Bren guns).

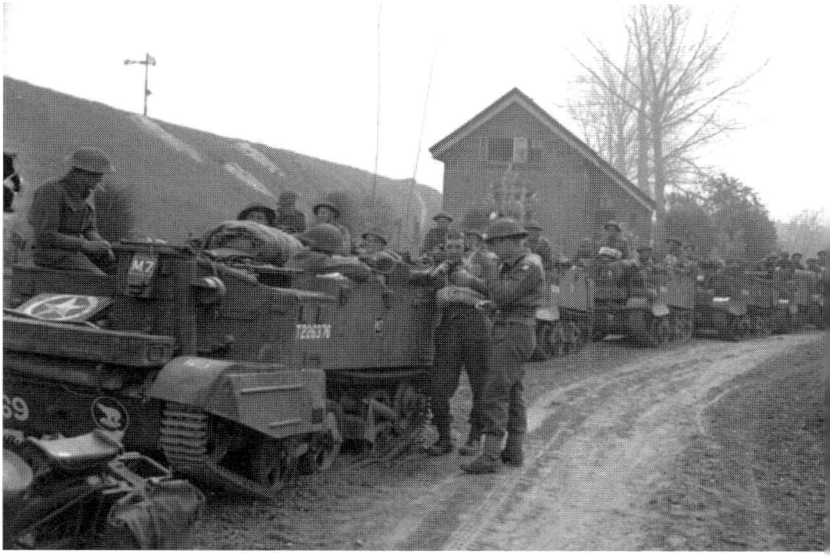
M7

Centre right: The Polar Bears (British 49th West Riding Division) fought with First Canadian Army for much of 1944 and 1945. Here carriers wait to cross the Ijssel to attack Arnhem, March 1945.

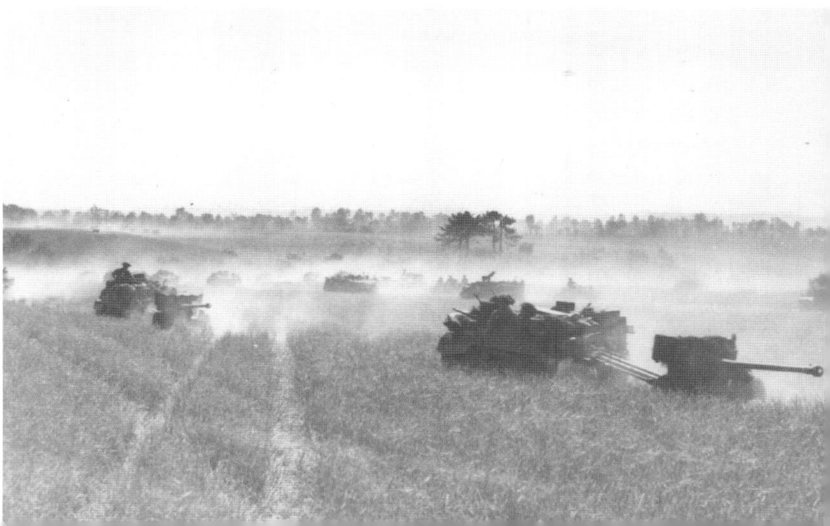

Below right: Vehicles of Canadian 3rd Infantry Division moving through during Operation Tractable, 14 August 1944. The carriers in the foreground, are towing 6pdr anti-tank guns.

The famous US Army range of 6x6 2½-ton trucks performed many roles and saw service with many of the Allies during the war and on into the postwar period. The main version was the GMC CCKW – the Jimmy – well over 550,000 of which were built. Another 200,000 plus were built by Studebaker and REO many of which went for Lend-Lease. Here a Jimmy is used as an artillery tractor to tow a 105mm howitzer along an Algerian beach after the Operation Torch landings in North Africa. Troopships can be seen in the background.

speed of 76kph and was used primarily as an ammunition carrier for the 105mm howitzer and for transporting machine gun squads. The M3 was developed at the same time as the M2. The M3 would become ubiquitous for US forces and was provided to almost all the Allies, including the Soviets, with some 50,000 produced in a variety of designs. Larger than its predecessor, it had an added rear door and extra seating and was equipped with two M1919s and an M2HB Browning.

All these half-tracks were open-topped and were primarily designed to swiftly de-liver and drop infantry rather than as fighting platforms, even though with their armour and MGs they often ended up being used as such, especially the German Hanomags. They were also important for their ability to transport or tow heavier weapons such as antitank and light artillery pieces that were so vital to beef up the infantry's punch. Their open superstructure allowed for greater situational awareness and easy dismount as well as letting troops fire from their positions inside their compartment, but at the same time

Continued on p. 50.

Right: The American M2 and M3 halftracks – the former designed for use as an artillery tractor, the latter as an infantry carrier – proved hardy and mobile vehicles that enabled armoured infantry to keep pace with the tanks and enter combat without the encumbrance of heavy gear that could be left in the carrier. They were usually to be seen covered with personal equipment – bed rolls, duffel bags and the like, as here – and numerous machine guns. This is an updated M3A1 (**Above**) and has a Browning M2HB mounted in an M32 ring mount above the front right-hand seat, mineracks extending down the length of its sides and two .30cals. Its seen as part of Seventh US Army entering Geisselhardt northeast of Stuttgart. The .50cal MG in its ring mount is shown well in this view (**Below**) of an M2A1 in Aachen on 14 October 1944. Its gun crew is unlimbering the 57mm anti-tank gun. Note the armoured gunshields stored in the side mine racks.

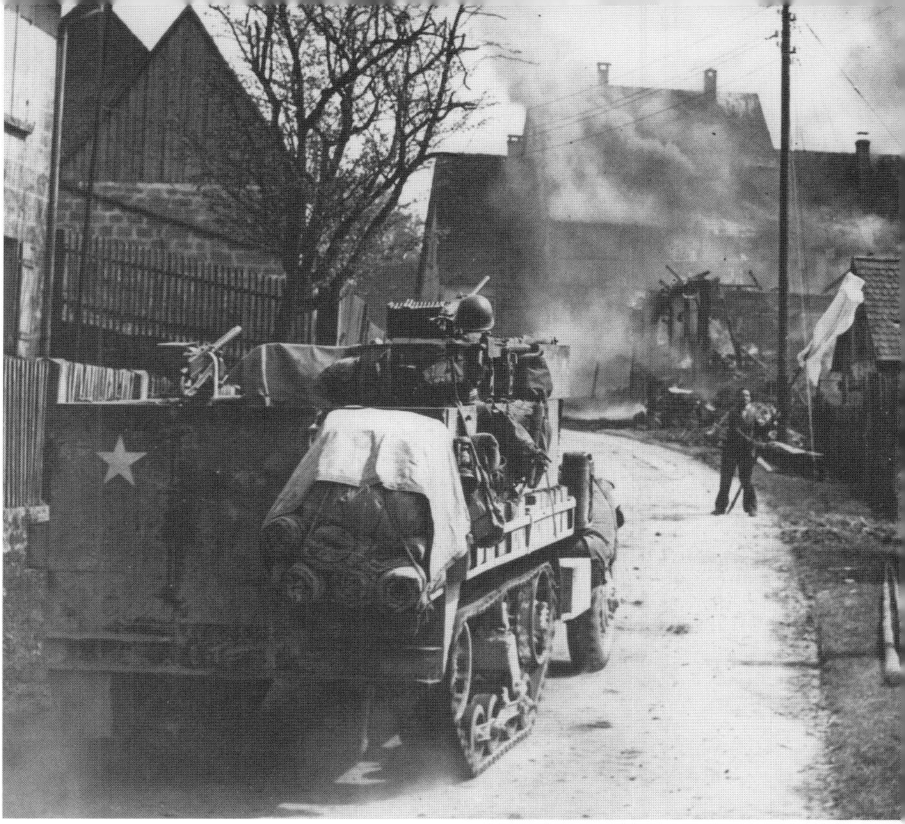

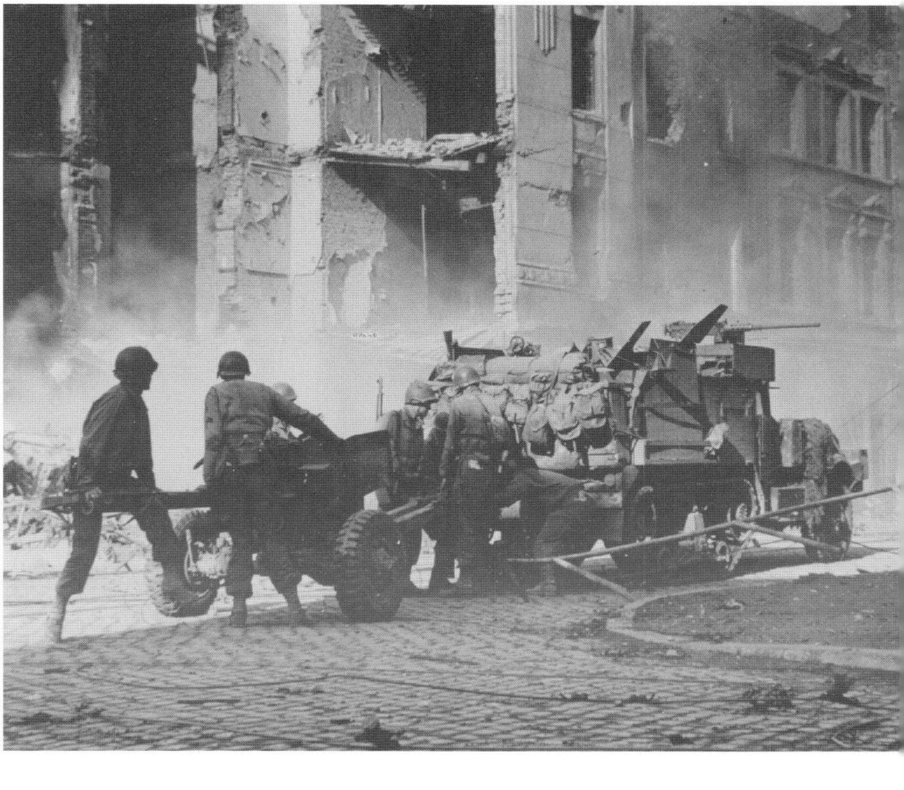

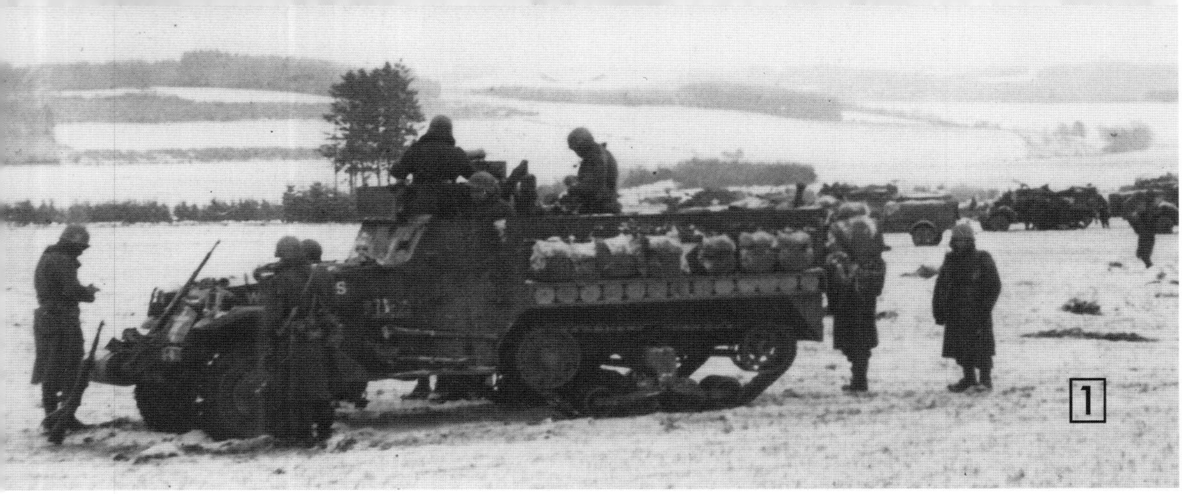
1

1 Another classic view of an M3A1. This one is outside Bastogne at the end of 1944 as 11th Armoured Division awaits its next action. With a top speed of around 45mph and a seating capacity of 13, the halftracks served the armoured infantry well, although they were criticised for poor armour and less mobility than tanks. Tests between them and German Hanomags showed the latter to have less carrying capacity because of the armour arrangement, problems with the maintenance of the overlapping wheels and reduced mobility because the front axle wasn't powered.

2 A photograph that shows well the mobility of the US Army. It's taken on 20 December 1944. The Germans have attacked in the Ardennes and reinforcements are being rushed to the front (the halftracks on the right are heading to Bastogne) while inessentials and artillery are moved away from the threatened town. The speed of the American reaction ensured that Eisenhower was able to rush his reserves – the elite 82nd and 101st Infantry Divisions – to two of the hotspots: the 101st held Bastogne while the 82nd stopped the 1st SS-Panzer Division *Leibstandarte*'s northern attack.

3 The Willy's Jeep was versatile, produced in huge numbers and helped win the war. It was more like a small truck than a car. It gave a rough ride – particularly if you were in the back, had a high centre of gravity and pulled viciously to the left when braking. But it could also tow a 105mm howitzer at 20mph if it had to. 640,000 examples were built during the war and it was truly ubiquitous.

4 One of the many Jeeps that crashed with fatal consequences, generally after a rollover, this one at Kettering, England, 25 January 1943.

5 The Dodge WC 57 Command Car – you can tell they were good, Patton had one – was one of a range of four-wheel-drive vehicles produced by the company for the US military. Dodge built 337,500 4WD units and the WC 57 evolved into the postwar Power Wagon.

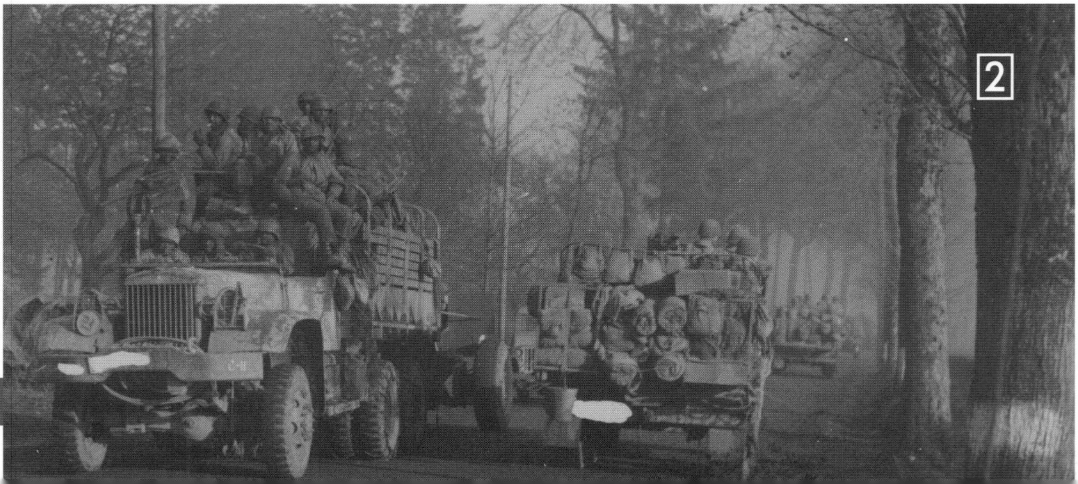
2

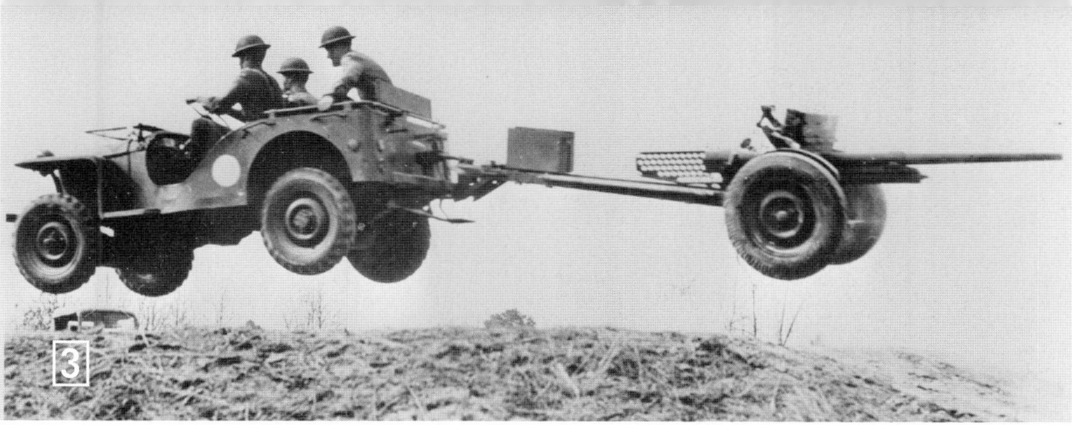
3

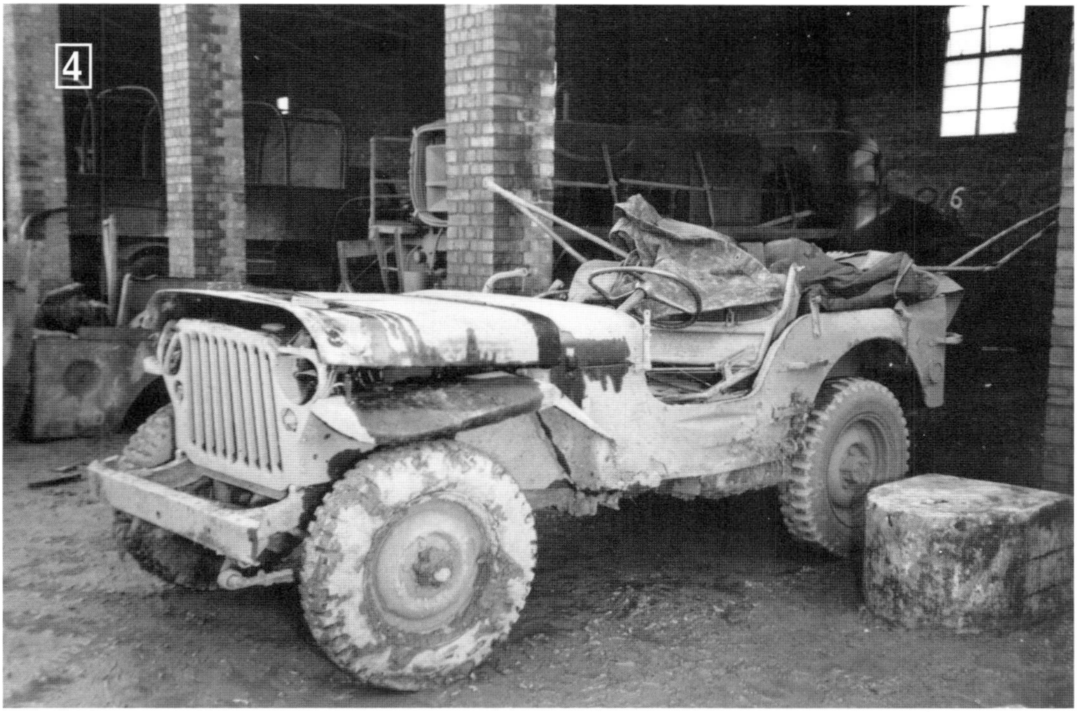
4

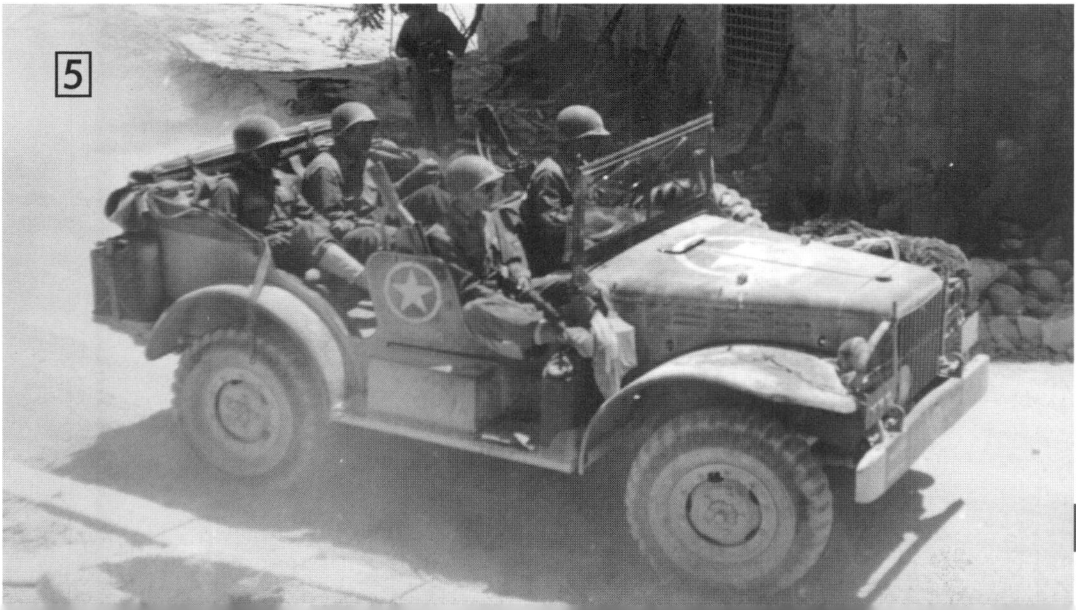
5

they were vulnerable to aerial attack, snipers, grenades and plunging fire from mortars and artillery. Besides this, such mechanised vehicles could never be produced in sufficient quantity to transport the entire infantry component of any Allied or Axis army and so nations also used a wide selection of lorries and trucks. Constrained from obtaining vital raw materials by the Allied blockade, the ability to fully motorise – let alone mechanise – the infantry was never a realistic possibility for the Germans. Their 1942 redesignation and formation of the mixed mechanised and motorised Panzergrenadiers concentrated dwindling supplies of vehicles to favoured elite regiments.

For the Allies it was a different matter. The USA and Canada's combined industrial capacity was added to the British and Soviet efforts to easily outweigh German output and its original organisational advantage. Having lost virtually all the BEF's frontline equipment at Dunkirk, the British automotive industry began producing a variety of such vehicles, including lorries from AEC (Matador), Albion (CX22S and FT15N), Austin (K2/Y, K5), Bedford (MW, OXD and QL), Leyland (Hippos 1 & 2, Lynx and Retriever), Morris

Continued on p. 54.

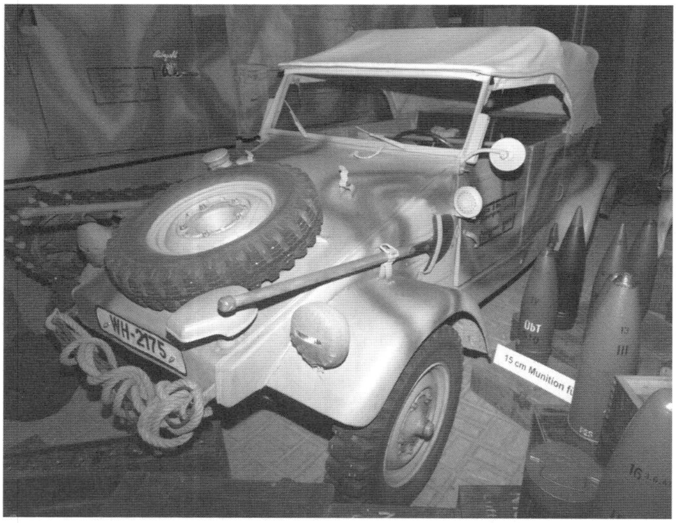
WH-2175

Left: The German Kübelwagen wasn't really equivalent to a Jeep, although the two are often compared. It was longer than the Jeep but lighter and only had two-wheel drive, wasn't suitable for towing or the addition of a radio but was a brilliant staff car with a comfortable ride, and a reliable air-cooled engine that worked well in hot and cold conditions. 50,435 were built by VW with few modifications over the span of the war.

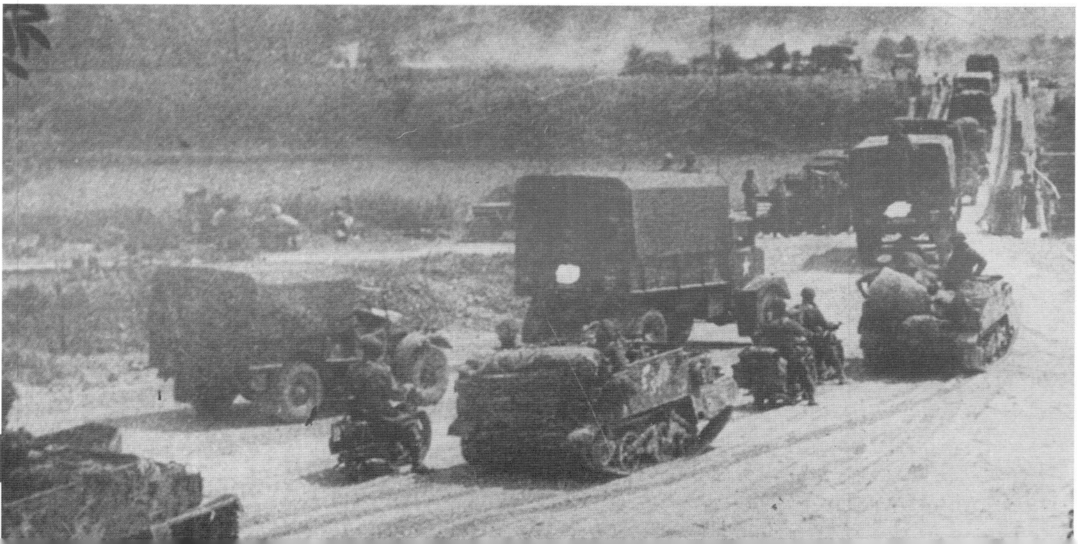

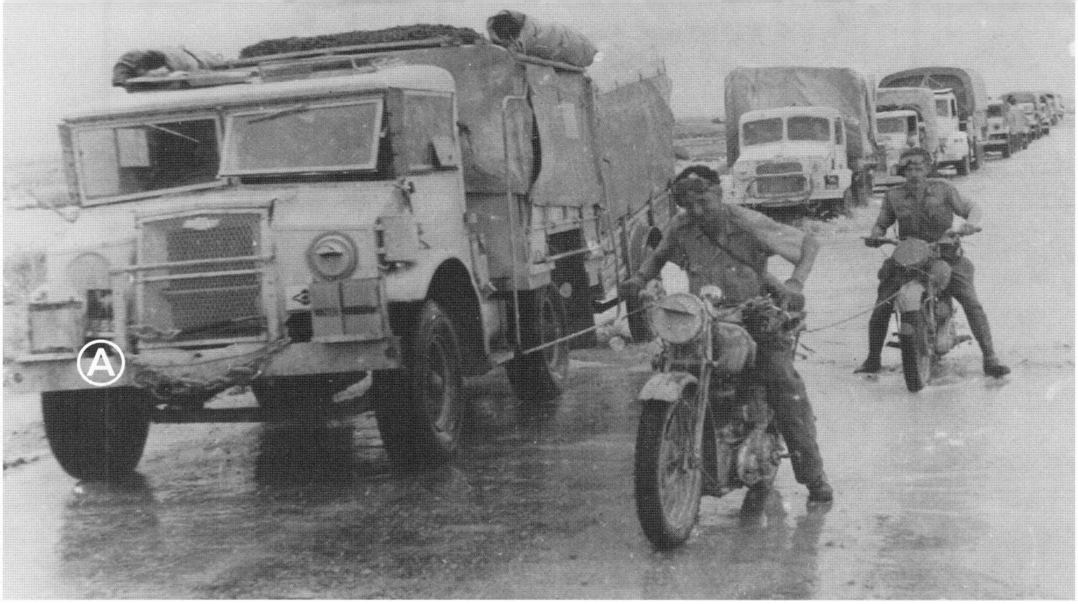
A

Mechanised forces needed to be able to contend with a range of temperatures and climates in a war that spread around the globe: dusty summer conditions in France (**Opposite, Below**) as British forces cross the Canal de Caen in August 1944; rain (**Above**) and sweltering heat (**Below**) in the desert. British manufacturers couldn't hope to provide Imperial forces with sufficient vehicles by themselves. Luckily, there was plenty of capacity both in the Commonwealth and also the United States. Note the GHQ Middle East vehicle markings (a camel at A) on the Chevrolet CMP hauling a trailer (**Above**). The CMPs had a range of bodies – GS, ambulance, troop carrier, wireless, etc.

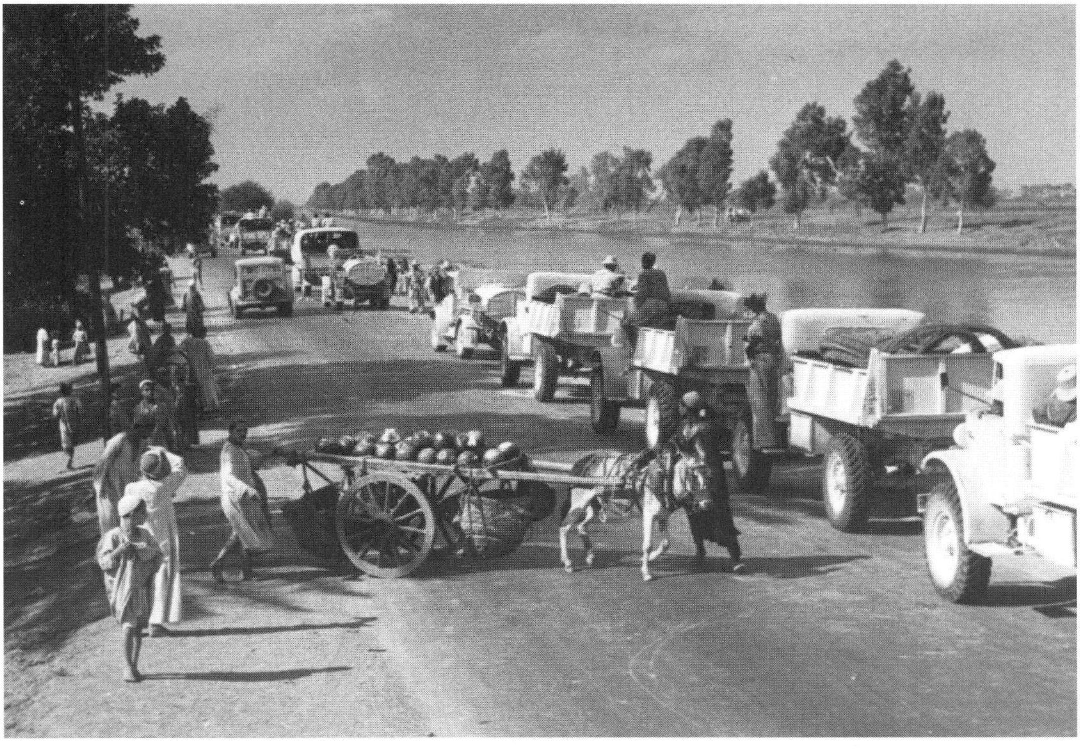

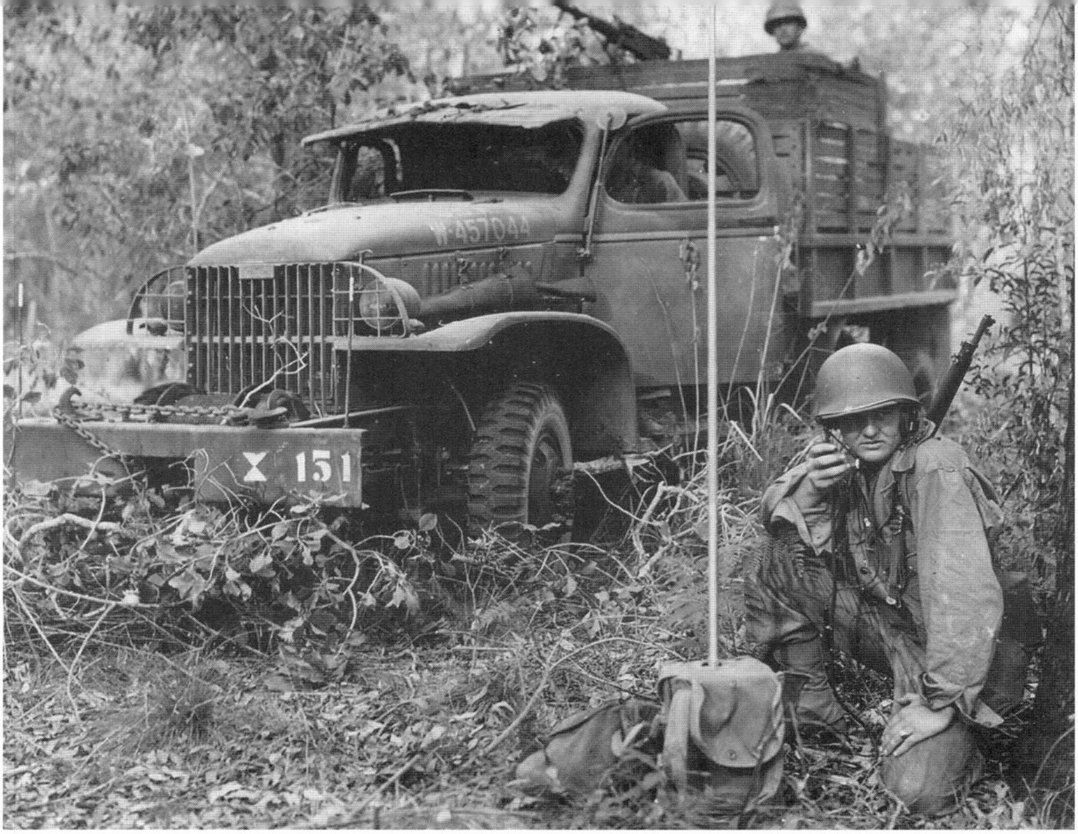
W-457044
X 151

Above: A pretty portrait of a GMC CCKW 2½-ton 6x6 cargo truck. It's got a winch, an enclosed cab and pintle-mounted .30cal MG – one in four manufactured had a ring mount over the co-driver's position. The Jimmy – know postwar as the Deuce – was only phased out in the 1950s.

Below: Men of 180th Infantry Regiment (45th (US) Inf Div) pass through Lioni, 26 September 1943. The use of trucks to move infantry about helped mobility, but there were consequences as pointed out in a letter to the Seventh Army historian by the CO of 253rd Infantry: 'Considerable facility was developed in the use of organic and attached units' transportation in shuttling foot troops. However, as the period wore on two disadvantages of this practice developed: (1) constant use and some necessary overloading of vehicles increased greatly maintenance requirements on vehicles and underlined the need for assistant truck drivers for all vehicles; (2) supply needs tended to suffer as trucks were used to haul personnel.'

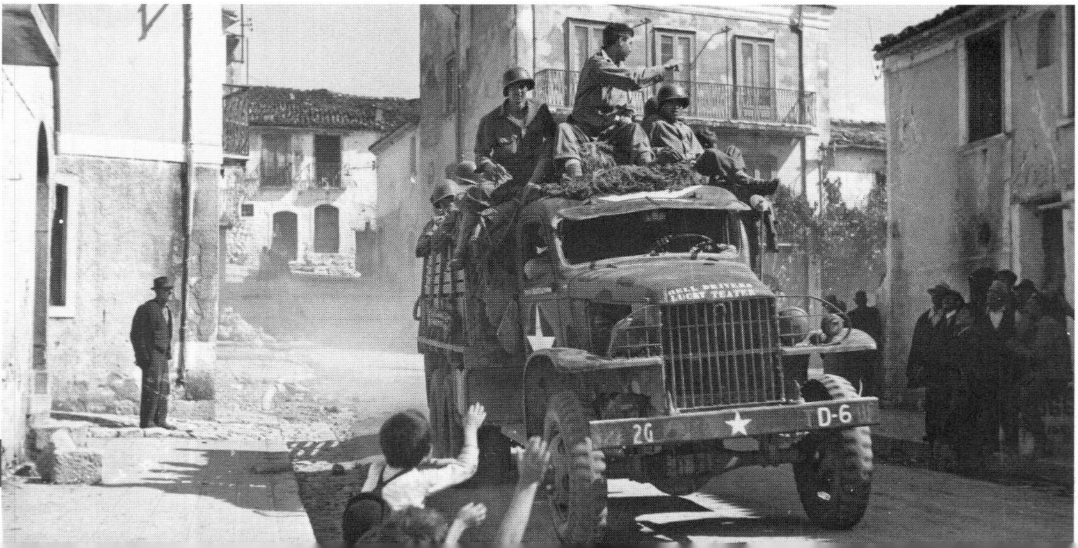
2G
D-6

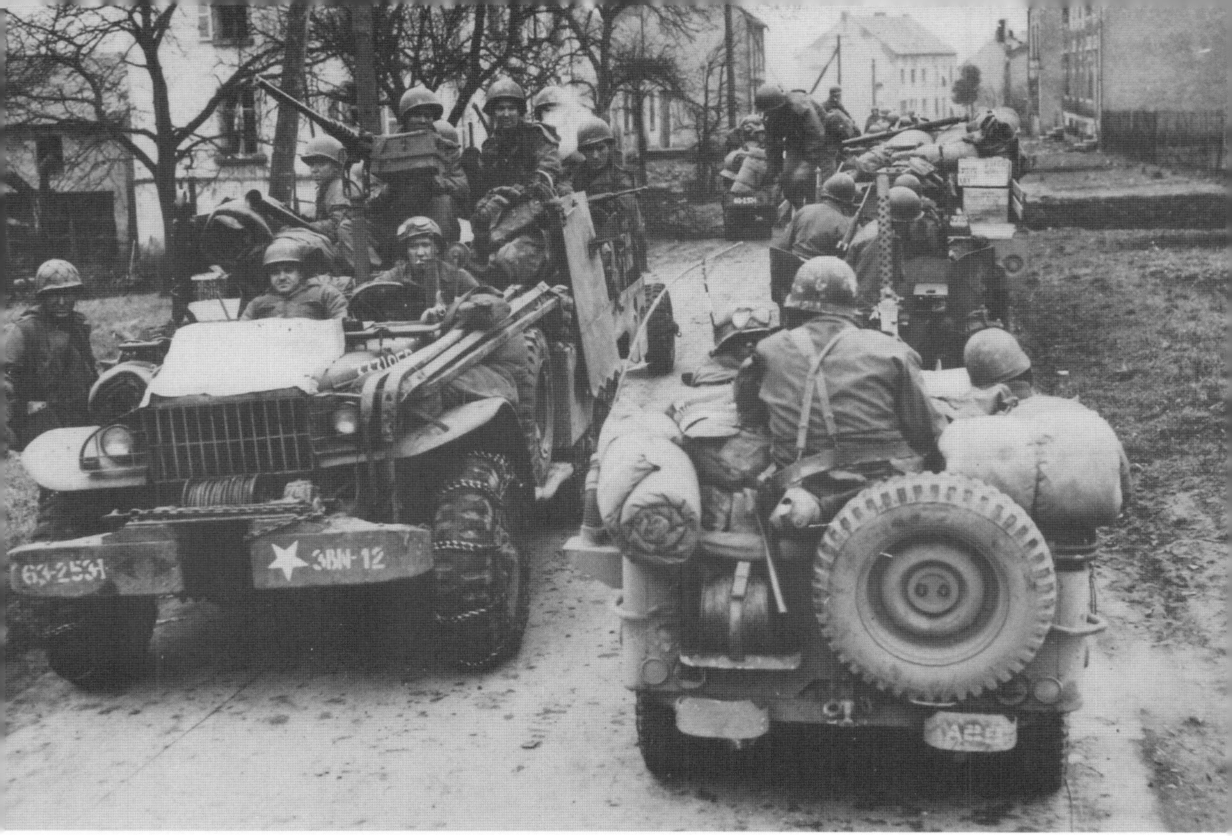

Above: Vehicles of the 253rd Infantry (63rd Inf Div) near the River Saar in 1945. The Jimmy on the left has its canopy bars stowed alongside the driver. Note snow chains, pintle-mounted .50cal Browning M2HB, lack of cab and – attached to the side of the truck – the armoured shield for the 57mm anti-tank gun it's towing.

Below: General Motors Canada developed the C15TA Armoured Truck on the chassis of the Chevrolet CMP C15. It was used by British and Canadian units as an APC and ambulance. It could carry two crew and eight passengers at 40mph thanks to a GMC 6-cylinder 100hp gasoline engine.

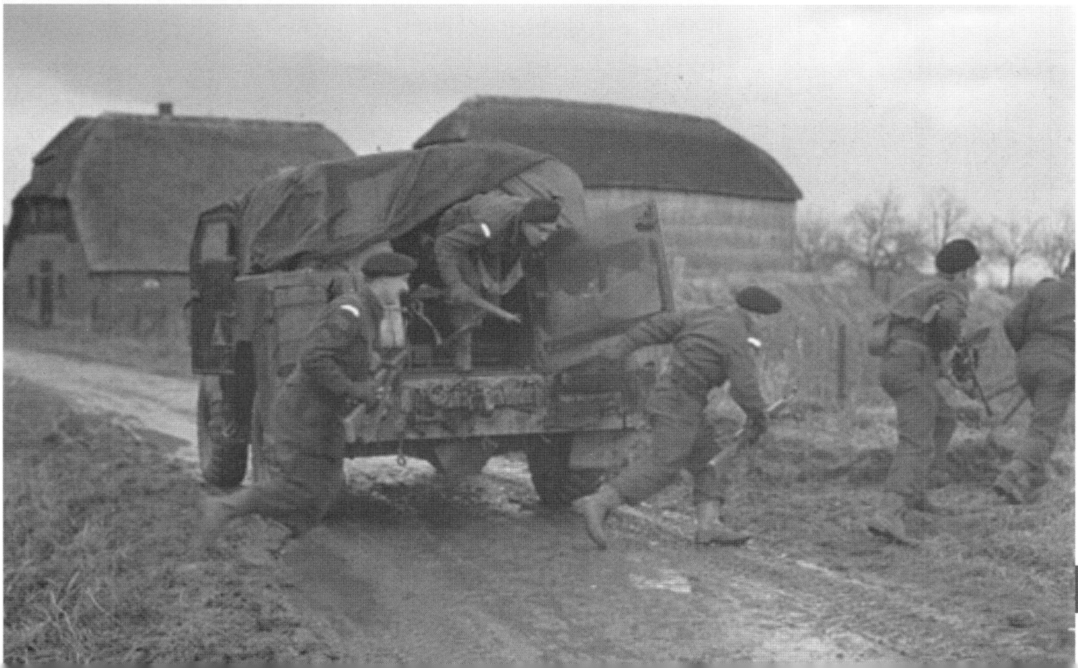

(PU, C9 and 15 cwt) and Thorneycroft (Nubian and Tartar). The British were also helped to re-equip by the US, who supplied huge amounts of equipment, including Chevrolet, Chrysler, Dodge, Ford and GMC trucks in various combinations. They were also aided by an outstanding industrial effort from Canada, whose CMP trucks were produced in huge numbers and many combinations with carrying capacities of 800–3,000lb – the latter 4x4 variant being the most numerous. Versatile, rugged and easy to produce, CMPs accounted for nearly two-thirds of all military trucks of all types built in Canada during the war and were supplied to all Allies.

With various Allied nations producing a wide variety of vehicles and the German propensity to reuse enemy equipment, photographs of all forces on the move at that time show the random nature of a particular unit's vehicles. As the war progressed Allied industrial production enabled all troops to be motorised or mechanised, whereas the Germans struggled to maintain production, with shortages of raw materials and the destruction of factories through intense aerial bombing.

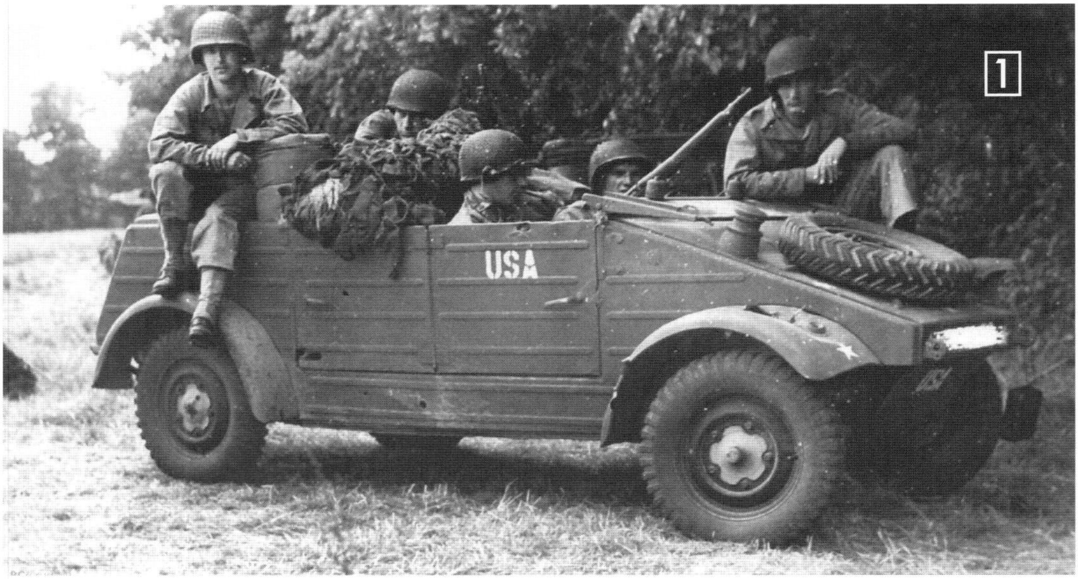
1
USA

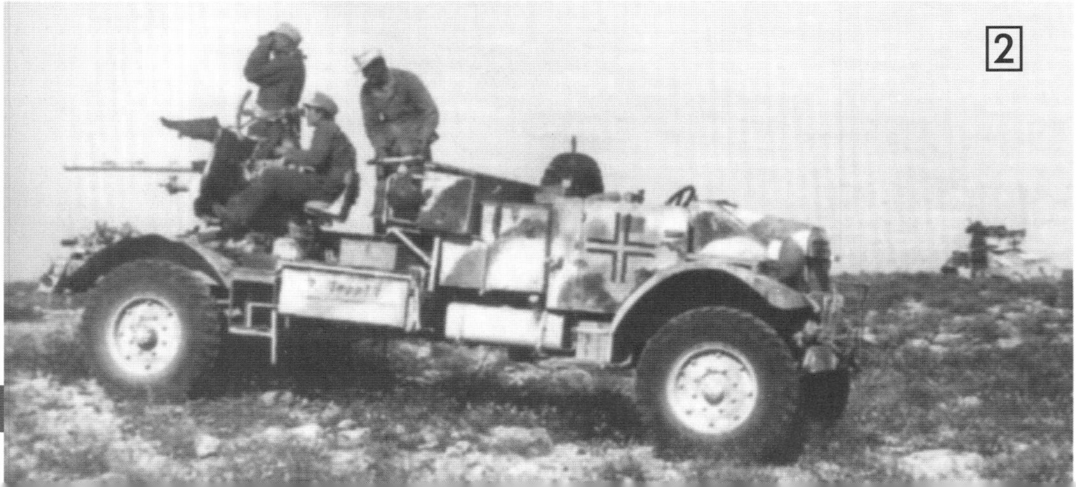
2

1 and 2 Both sides made use of captured equipment – the Germans, in particular, thanks to the number of British vehicles captured at Dunkirk in 1940 and the materiel it took from the countries it conquered. Here, a Kübelwagen under new ownership (**1**) and a British CMP Ford F60L (**2**) with a portee QF 2pdr anti-tank gun. The Germans have renamed their booty 'Sepp'.

3 There's a difference between making use of a tank to speed travel – particularly of interest if you're a footslogger walking from Poland to Moscow – and travelling into battle on top of a tank. To maintain the speed of an advance or a pursuit, infantrymen of every nationality hitched a ride. Here, soldiers of the 18th SS-Freiwillige-Panzergrenadier-Division Horst Wessel on the back of a StuG 40 Ausf G in Slovakia, December 1944.

4 A 2nd Armd Div M4A1 carries infantry from 2/291st Inf (75th (US) Div) before attack on Frandeux 27 December 1944.

5 Infantry boarding M5 light tanks. In Italy, 'The employment of the two arms in this manner was found especially useful in mopping up strong points of resistance in order to assist forward the main advance. In some instances tank-borne infantry was carried into action for other missions, notably for consolidating ground taken by the armour, and in certain phases of pursuit. This practice gave the advantage of getting the riflemen forward rapidly, and it was also effective as a means of bringing up quickly the heavy weapons needed to support the consolidation.'

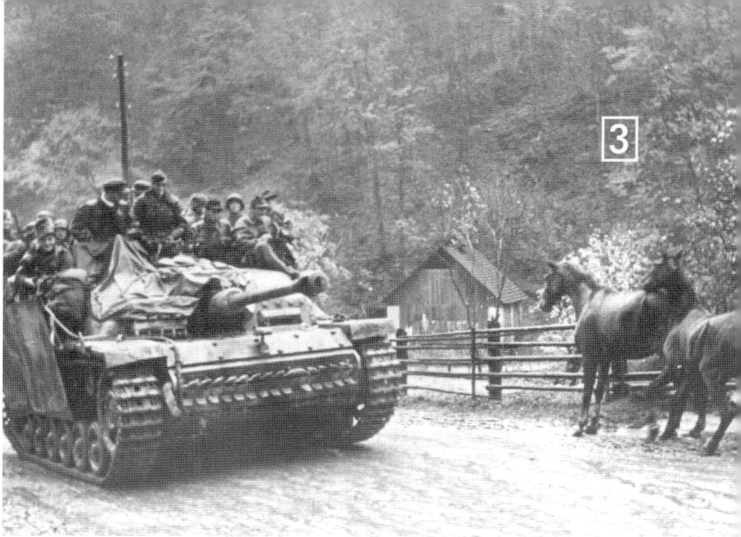
3

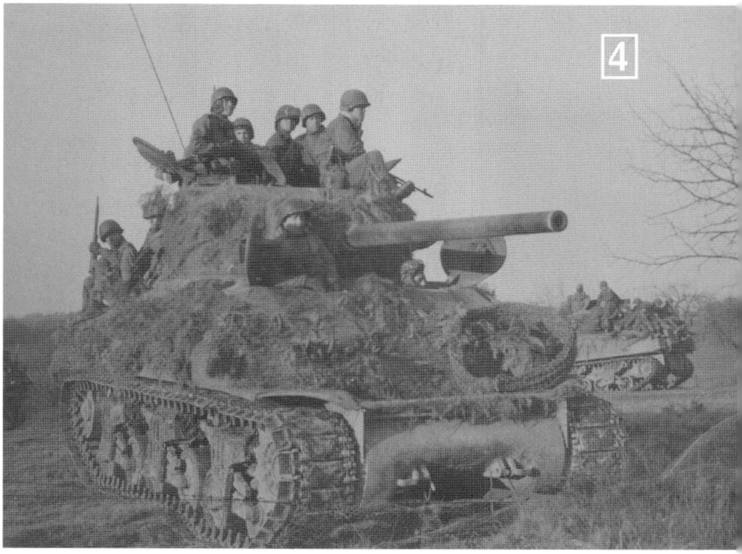
4

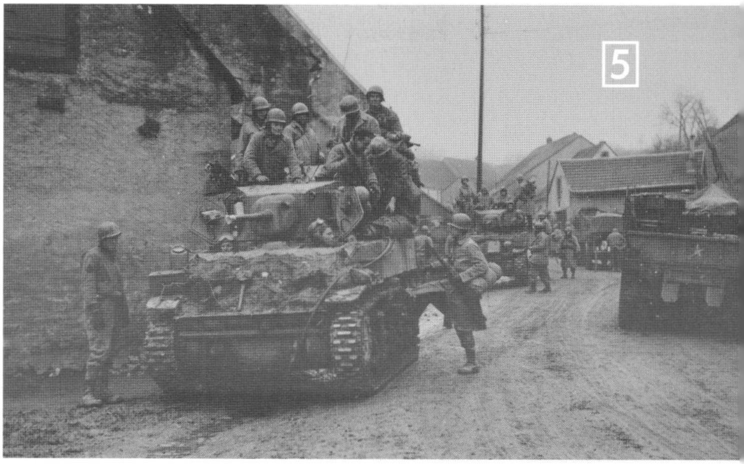
5

INFANTRY-TANK COOPERATION

(excerpts from *Lessons From The Italian Campaign, Intelligence Bulletin* Vol II No 12, August 1944)

Reports and comments on battle experience from the Army level down to the battalions and companies have all stressed the need of greater cooperation between infantry and armor as a major lesson of the campaign. This lesson has been applicable to the elements of the armored division, and to the infantry divisions and separate tank battalions alike. One outstanding conclusion has been drawn: that for all practical purposes there is no real difference between the armored infantry and the foot troops of the normal infantry division. ...Thorough understanding of the plan of action on the part of both infantry and tank commanders in an operation employing the two arms is paramount to success. In most situations involving elements of the infantry division and attached separate tank battalions, the responsibility for insuring this understanding often rests with the infantry commander. ... During the last operation (from the time of the breakthrough at Anzio to the capture of Rome), it was found that combined infantry-tank training cannot be stressed too much. The recent training of this regiment with the armored elements of the Division have proved to be the greatest value.

The cost-effective method of employment of the infantry and tanks was found to be a strong assault wave of medium tanks in the advance, followed at 100–200yd by the infantry closely supported by light tanks in immediate contact. Previous experience had shown that the leading tanks often bypassed concealed infantry and automatic weapons which would wait until the armor had passed and then attack the following infantry. Without immediate armored support, the infantry would be stopped with losses. The presence of the light tanks with the following infantry gave the needed support and means of dealing with such islands of resistance and strong points left in the wake of the leading tank waves. In breaking the defenses surrounding the Anzio Beachhead and in subsequent operations. It was found that the best troop arrangement for a force of this type was a company of medium tanks, a battalion of infantry, and a company of light tanks.

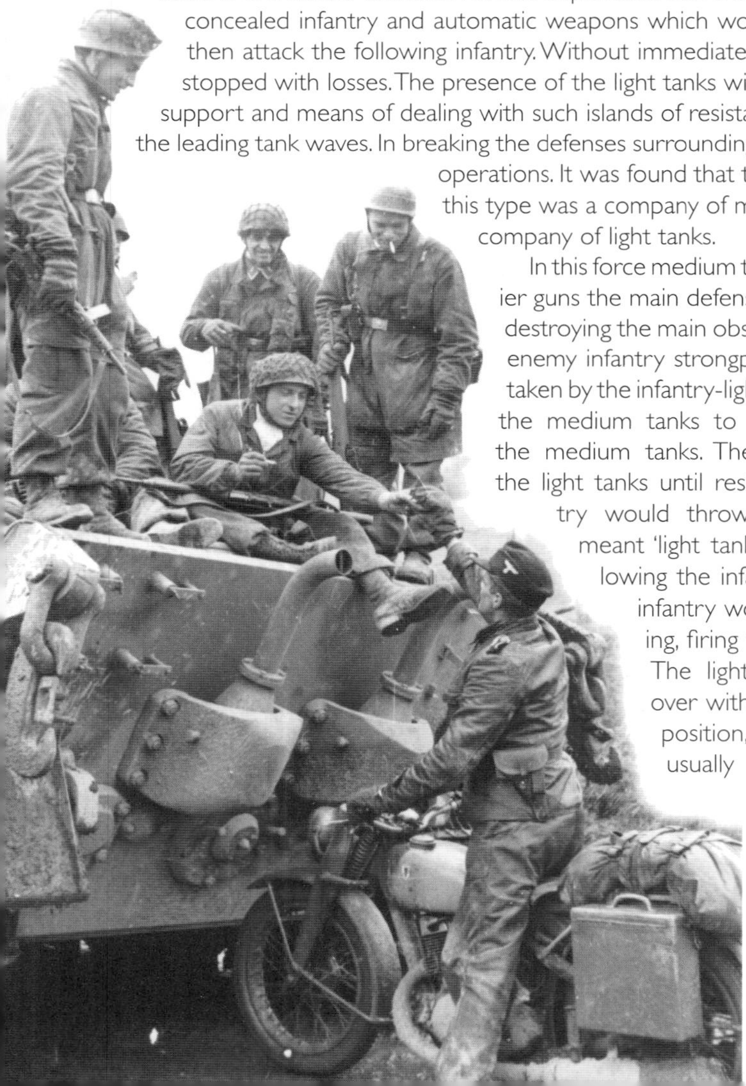

In this force medium tanks preceded, destroying with their heavier guns the main defenses. As the medium tanks moved forward destroying the main obstacles of the defense, they bypassed many enemy infantry strongpoints. These strongpoints would then be taken by the infantry-light tank team following immediately behind the medium tanks to take advantage of the shock effect of the medium tanks. The infantry moved forward followed by the light tanks until resistance was met. At this time the infantry would throw out a green smoke grenade which meant 'light tank help wanted here.' The light tanks following the infantry would move to this point, and the infantry would designate the target by signal, pointing, firing tracer ammunition, or by a combination. The light tanks then would work the position over with MG and 37mm fire and move into the position, followed closely by the infantry, who usually had only to mop up and collect the prisoners. Casualties, particularly among the infantry, were very light through this effective use of the medium tank-infantry-light tank team.

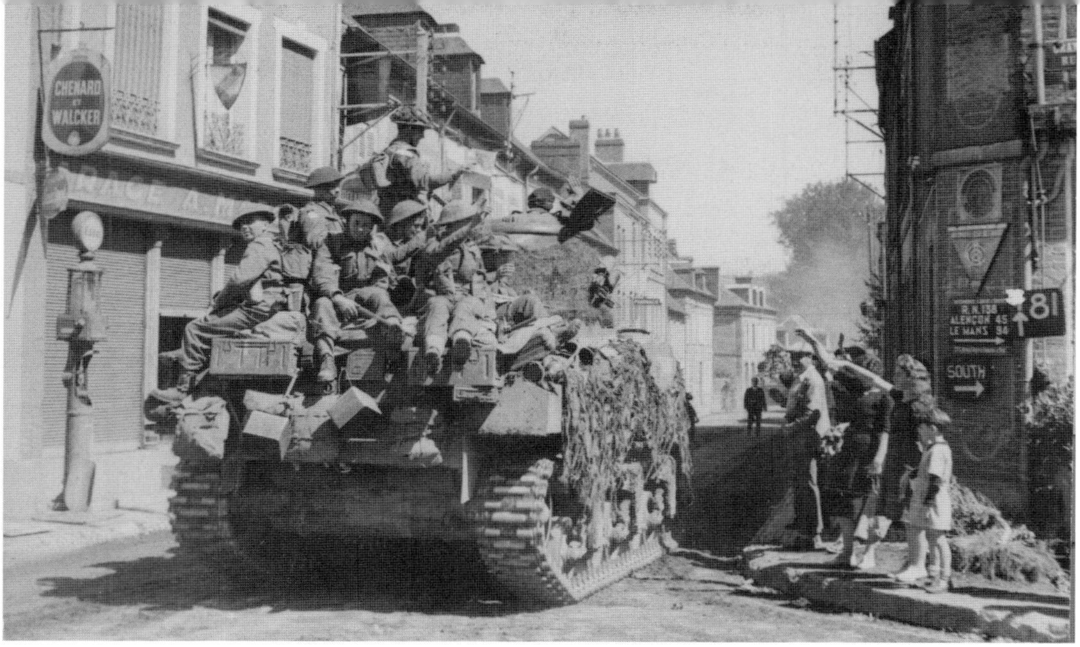
CHENARD ET WALCKER
ALENCON 45
LE MANS 34
81
SOUTH

Opposite: Classic Battle of the Bulge photograph showing Fallschirmjäger of II./FJR 9 aboard a Königstiger of Kampfgruppe Peiper. The progress of these huge Panzers during the advance can only be described as stately.

Above: The German Army has broken and is streaming back through France. The Allies are in hot pursuit. The 'great swan' has begun and within a few days British troops will be on the outskirts of Antwerp. 'One general disadvantage noted in the employment of infantry carried on tanks was the difficulty of reorganization after dismounting and deployment. Proper squad and platoon organization and control could not be maintained while the riflemen were carried forward on the tanks; consequently after dismounting and deployment for action, some reorganization was required.'

Right: Another hot pursuit – paratroops of the 513rd PIR, 17th (US) Airborne Division, on board Churchills of British 6th Guards Tank Brigade enter Munster. The Guards ended up near Lübeck on the Baltic Sea.

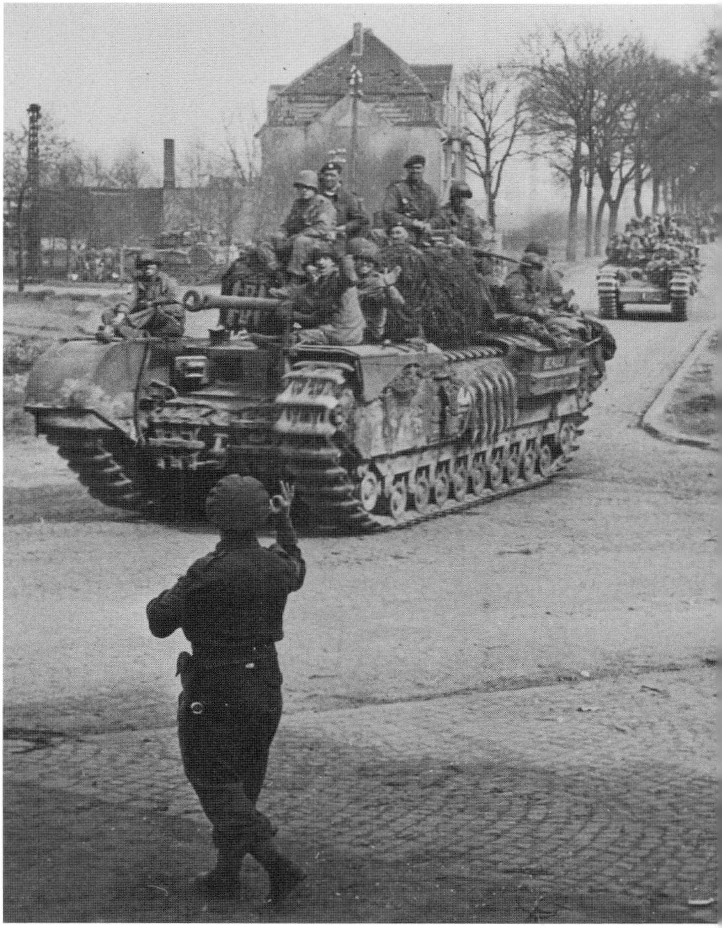

USE OF TANKS WITH INFANTRY

(edited excerpts from *Intelligence Bulletin*, Vol. II, No. 4: December 1943)

The correct and incorrect ways of using infantry with tanks, according to the German Army view, are summarized in an enemy document recently acquired. In this document the Germans list the correct and incorrect methods side by side, an arrangement which is also followed in this section, for the convenience of the reader. The document is of special value and interest, not only because the column headed "Right" indicates procedures approved by the enemy, but because there are implications, in the column headed "Wrong," of certain errors that German units may have made from time to time.

Wrong		*Right*
A. ATTACK		
Attack not thoroughly discussed in advance.	(1)	Thorough discussions of reconnaissance and terrain will take place. Riflemen and tanks will maneuver jointly as much as possible, in advance.
Inadequate coordination between armored and artillery units.	(2)	The mission of protecting armored elements not yet discovered by hostile forces will be distributed among artillery. (Flanks will be screened by smoke.)
Failure of armored cars and tanks to maneuver jointly in advance.	(3)	Armored cars used for observation will maneuver with tanks before an intended attack.
Distribution of too many tanks in proportion to infantry used in the attack.	(4)	Tanks not intended for use in an attack will be kept outside the range of hostile fire
Tanks deployed and distributed among small units.	(5)	For effective results, available tanks—at least an entire company—will be combined for the assault.
The use of tanks in unreconnoitered terrain when speed is essential.	(6)	Terrain must be reconnoitered, especially when an attack at great speed is contemplated. Facilities for mine clearance must be at hand. If a tank detonates a mine, the remaining tanks must halt while the minefield is reconnoitered. After this, the minefield must either be cleared or bypassed.
All tank commanders absent on reconnaissance.	(7)	A number of tank commanders must always remain with the company.
Tanks launched without a clear statement of their mission.	(8)	The mission of tanks will be widely understood.
When a sector full of tank obstacles has been taken, tanks are ordered to cross this sector in front of the riflemen.	(9)	Riflemen cross the sector first and create passages, while the tanks provide covering fire from positions on slopes.
Tanks advance so rapidly that riflemen are unable to follow.	(10)	Tanks advance only a short distance at a time. Riflemen advance with the tanks.
When two successive objectives have been taken, tanks ignore the possible presence of hostile forces in areas between these objectives, even though an attack on still another objective is not contemplated at the moment.	(11)	When two successive objectives have been taken, the entire area between them must be made secure by means of tanks, artillery, assault guns or antitank guns, and heavy weapons
Tanks within sight of positioned hostile tanks advance without benefit of covering fire.	(12)	Responsibility for covering fire is divided among artillery or heavy antitank guns. If these are not available, PzKpfw IIIs and PzKpfw IVs provide protection.
Tanks are ordered to hold a captured position, even though heavy weapons are available for this purpose.	(13)	As soon as an objective has been taken, tanks are withdrawn and are kept in readiness for use as an attacking reserve or in the preparation of a new attack.

Wrong		_Right_
Riflemen and light machine guns remain under cover during own attack.	(14)	Riflemen and machine guns cover the antitank riflemen, who have the mission of destroying hostile tanks which may attempt to by pass.
Tanks take up positions so close to hostile forces that early discovery is inevitable.	(15)	If possible, tanks take up positions outside the range of hostile artillery fire. Tanks which are compelled to take up positions in the vicinity of hostile forces do so as late as possible, so that the hostile forces will not have time to adopt effective countermeasures.
Tanks remain inactive when a mission has been completed.	(16)	When a mission has been completed, tanks promptly receive orders as to what they are to do next.

B. DEFENCE

Distribution of tanks along the entire front.	(1)	All available tanks are kept together so that during an enemy attack prompt action can be taken against an advantageous point. Tanks, assault guns, and heavy antitank guns must be kept at a distance while firing positions are being prepared.
Subordination of tanks to small infantry units for the purpose of static defense.	(2)	When tanks have fulfilled their task they are withdrawn behind the main line of resistance, and are kept in readiness for further action.
After repulsing an attack, tanks remain in the positions from which they last fired.	(3)	After repulsing an attack, tanks move to alternate positions as soon as heavy arms or riflemen have taken over the responsibility of delivering covering fire.
As hostile tanks approach, own tanks advance, having failed to take up advantageous firing positions beforehand.	(4)	A firing front is created at a tactically advantageous point in the area against which the attack is directed. Tanks deliver surprise fire— from positions on reverse slopes, if possible.
Tanks which have no armor-piercing weapons are sent into battle against hostile tanks.	(5)	Tanks without armor-piercing weapons are kept back, and are used for antiaircraft protection, as well as in establishing communications and in supplying ammunition.
When hostile tanks approach, German riflemen and their heavy arms remain under cover, and leave the fighting against tanks with infantry to own tanks, assault guns, and antitank guns exclusively.	(6)	All arms take part in defense against hostile tanks. Infantry accompanying the tanks are kept somewhat apart , however, so that tanks, assault guns, and antitank guns are free to engage the hostile tanks.
All available tank reserves are compelled to remain out of action because of minor defects.	(7)	Repairs will be arranged in such a manner that a number of tanks are always ready for action.
Tanks which must remain in forward positions do not dig in, and thereby constitute targets for hostile artillery.	(8)	Tanks which are within range of hostile observation must be dug in as fast as possible. In winter, they must be hidden behind snow walls.

C. NOTES ON USE OF AMMUNITION

When only a few hostile tanks attack, fire is opened early.	(1)	When only a few enemy tanks attack, it is best to wait until they are within a favorable distance and then destroy them with as few rounds as possible.
Against a superior number of tanks, fire is opened at close range.	(2)	Fire is opened early on a superior number of tanks, to force them to change direction. High-explosive shells are used at first. Since this early opening of fire gives away own positions, new positions must be taken up.
PzKpfw IVs will fire hollowcharge ammunition at ranges of more than 750 yards.	(3)	Tanks which are short of 75 mm armor-piercing shells must allow a hostile force to approach to a position within a range of 750 yards.

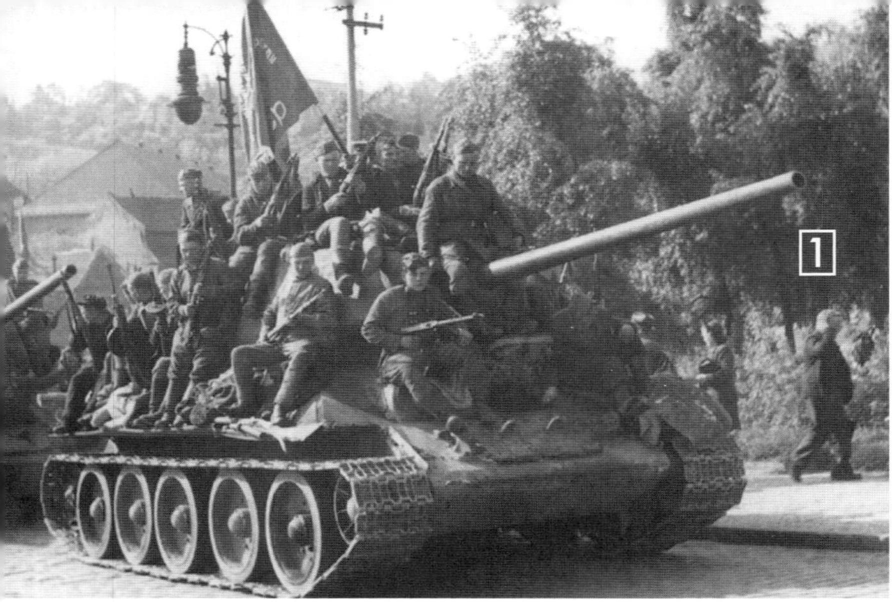
1

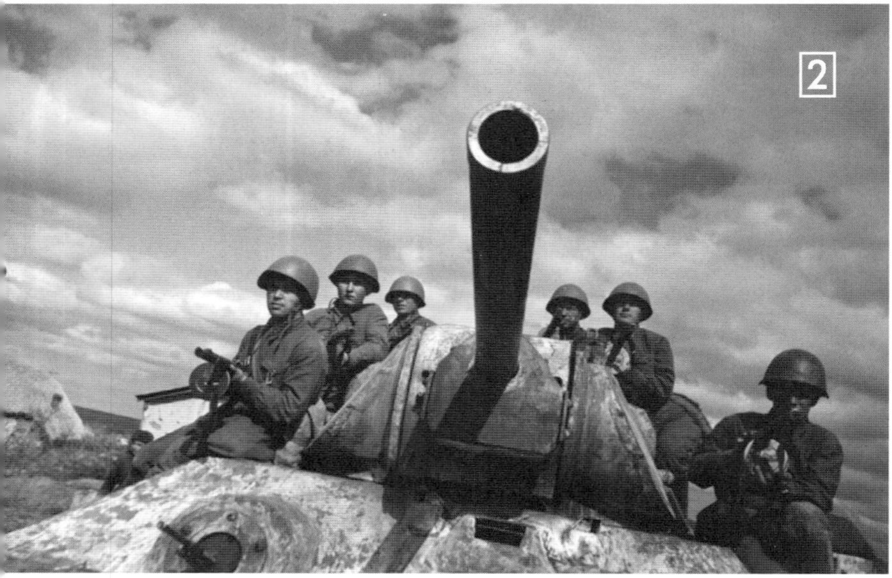
2

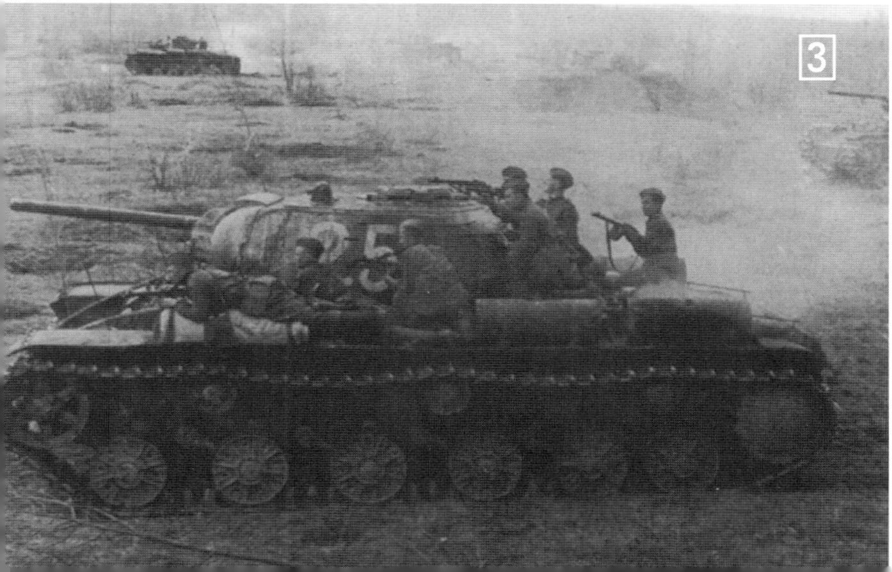
3

During the Spanish Civil War, Russian infantry started to ride into battle on the back of tanks. While many other countries' infantry would hitch a lift with a tank unit, it was unusual for the infantry to actually ride into battle like this. The Russian *tankovyy desant* teams, however, had rope handholds attached to the tanks and the tactic was far from unusual, dangerous though it was.

1 T-34/85 of the 55th Guards Tank Brigade enters Prague.

2 Soviet infantry on a T-34/76 of the 5th Guards Tank Brigade during the Kharkov Offensive Operation in May 1942.

3 KV-1S heavy tanks from the 6th Guards Tank Regiment with 'tank desant' teams during an attack on North Caucasus Front, 1943.

The APC as we know it started when Canadian Lt Gen Guy Simonds, commander of II Canadian Corps had 72 M7 Priest SP guns turned into APCs for use in Operation

Continued on next page.

Totalize. The Canadians had sustained high casualties in the battles around Caen, and needed a new approach. The APCs worked well and became a fixture for 21st Army operations thereafter.

4 Here a 'Defrocked Priest' transports men of 1st Black Watch, one of the leading units in the operation.

5 Entry of the 4th Can Armd Div into Delden on 4 April 1945. The vehicle is a converted Priest used as an armoured command post. There's a Ram Kangaroo behind it.

6 The official history of the REME identifies the changes to the M7: 'This involved the removal of the 105mm. Howitzer and various stowage bins; repositioning of the wireless set; blanking off the gap left by the removal of the howitzer and mantlet; and increasing the armour and hull sides to the level of the front superstructure. Suitable store protection and accommodation for the infantry to be carried was added, with facilities for mounting and dismounting, and the vehicles when converted carried twenty in addition to a crew of two.'

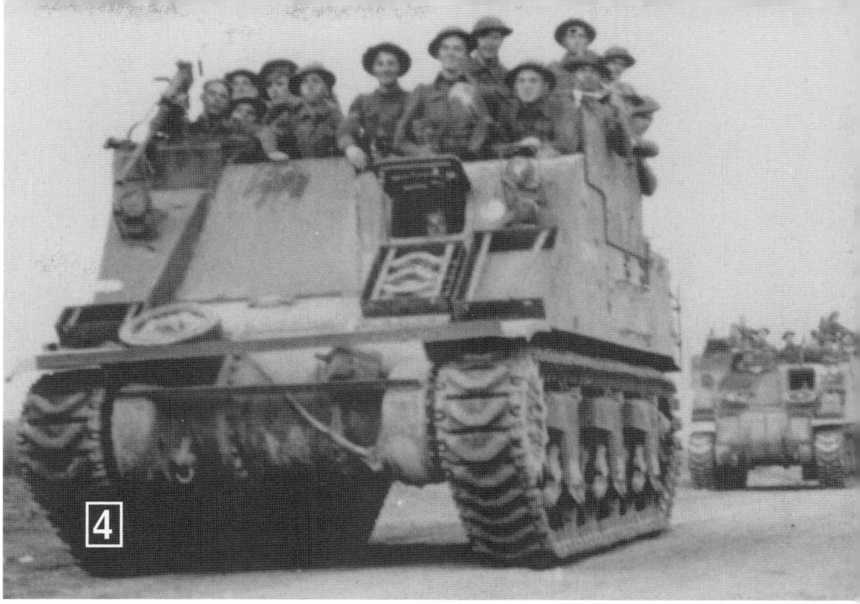
4

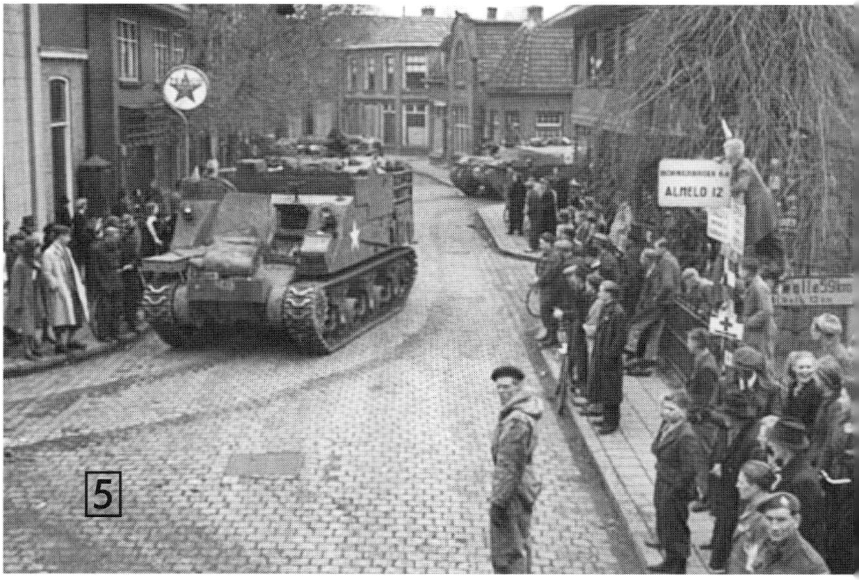
5
ALMELO 12

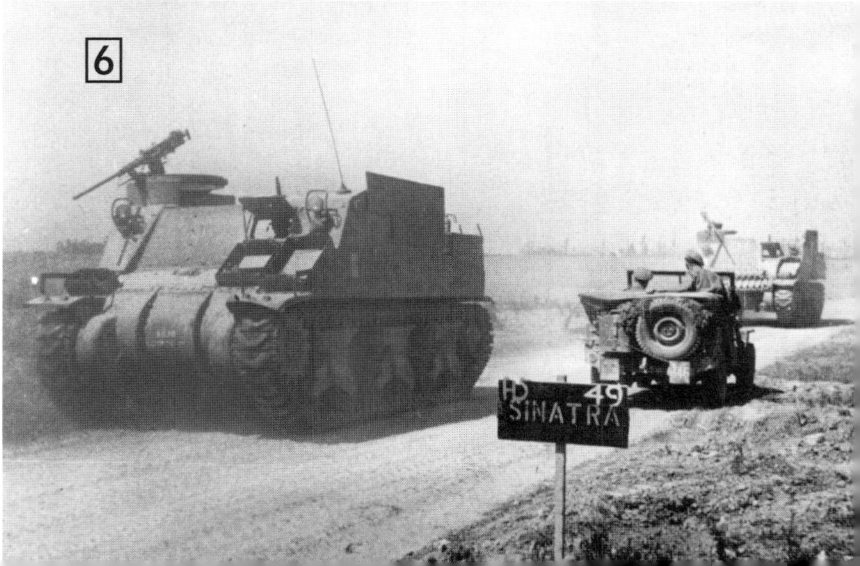
6
HD 49
SINATRA

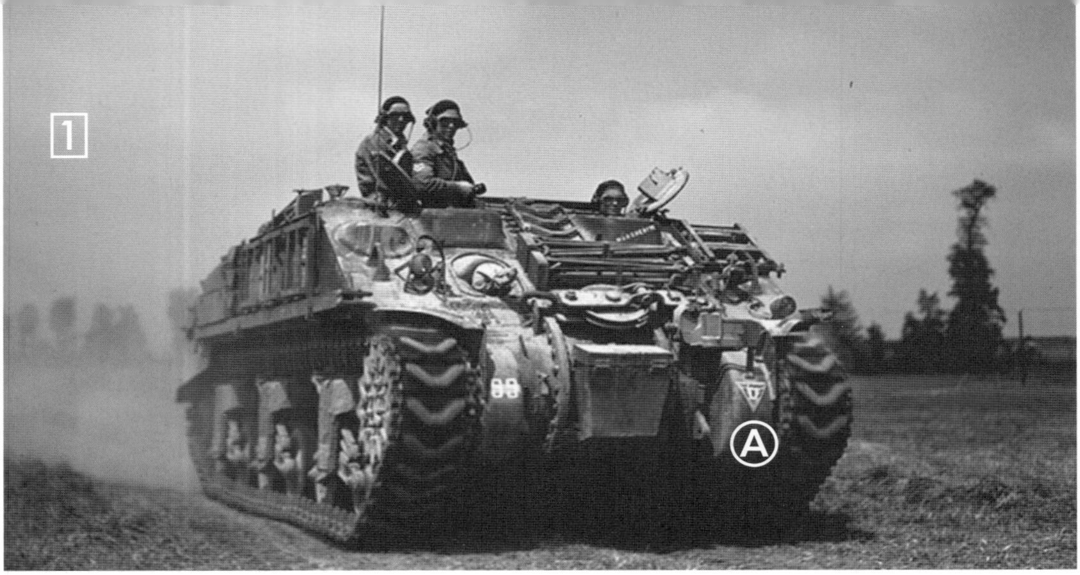
1
A

1 The 'Defrocked Priests' were a good starting point, but a more mobile and protected platform was created by modifying Shermans (as here) or Canadian Ram (**3**) tanks. The turrets and associated equipment were removed, allowing 8–12 fully laden troops to be carried. This meant that a section of three carriers could carry a rifle platoon; a troop of 12 could lift a rifle company and HQ; and a squadron of 53 carriers could lift an infantry battalion and its HQ. The Kangaroo's crew was two men. There's a preserved example at Mill in the Netherlands, commemorating the 1st Canadian Armoured Carrier Regiment, a title conferred on 1 January 1945. Previously, two units had been created: the 1st Canadian and the British 49th Armoured Personnel Carrier Regiments under 79th Armoured Division (whose insignia can be seen at **A**). The concept may not have been completely original – Stuart Kangaroos had been used, primarily as artillery tractors, in the desert, but there's no doubting their effectiveness.

2 Kangaroo crews on the Kleve–Calcar road during Operation Veritable. The area had been taken by the Canadian Royal Hamilton Light Infantry on 19 February 1945. Seven of the carriers had been knocked out in the attack. These are conversions of the Ram Mk II without the machine-gun turret (see opposite) at the co-driver's position.

3 Troops of 4th Bn, Dorsetshire Regt (130th Inf Bde) on the outskirts of Ochtrup, Germany, 3 April 1945 in a Kangaroo of A Sqn, 49th APC Regt. They are advancing eastwards from the Rhine bridgehead. Note the machine-gun turret at the co-driver's position in this Ram Mk II conversion.

4 Men of British 49th APC Regiment (one-time 49th RTR) with their Kangaroo outside Kranenburg. Note the Kangaroo insignia at **B**.

5 Priest conversion outside Conselice, Italy, 1945. Between October 1944 and April 1945, 102 Priests and 75 Shermans IIIs were converted by South African workshops in Roma and REME workshops at Ancona – 52 M7s in 18 days and 25 Shermans in 9 days.

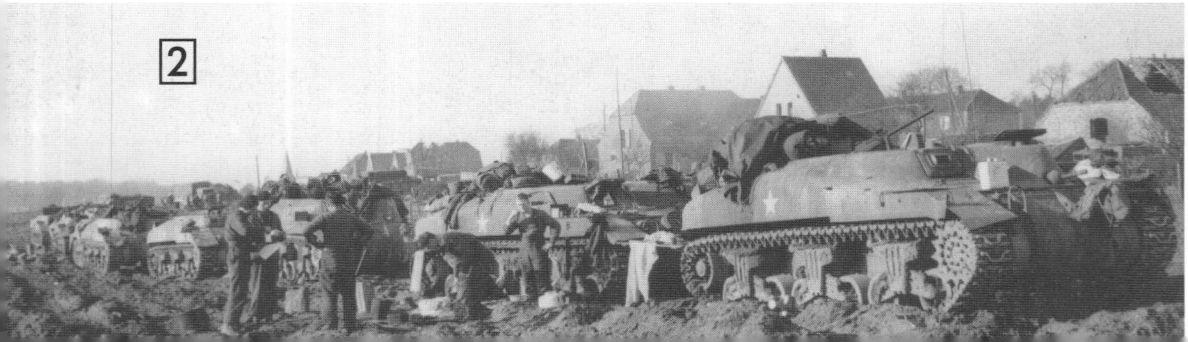
2

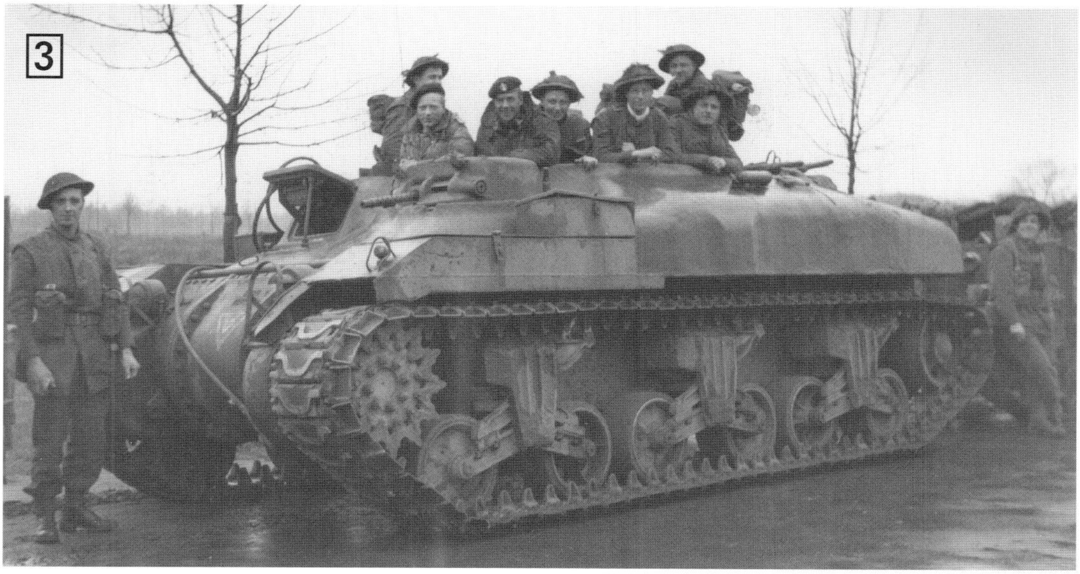
3

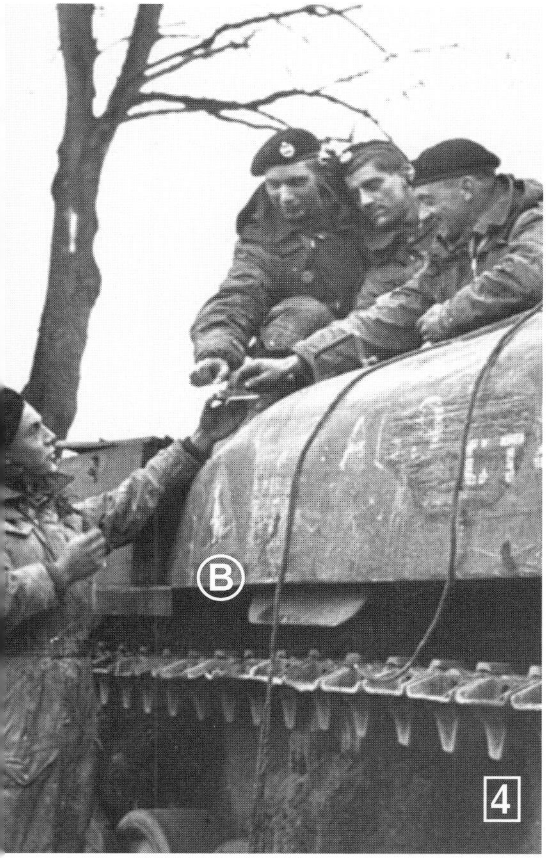
B
4

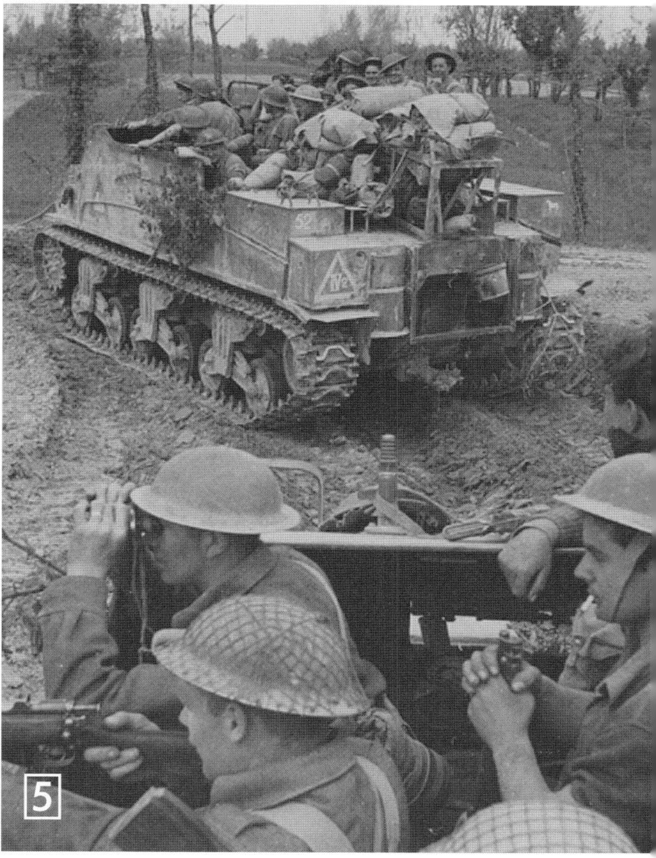
5

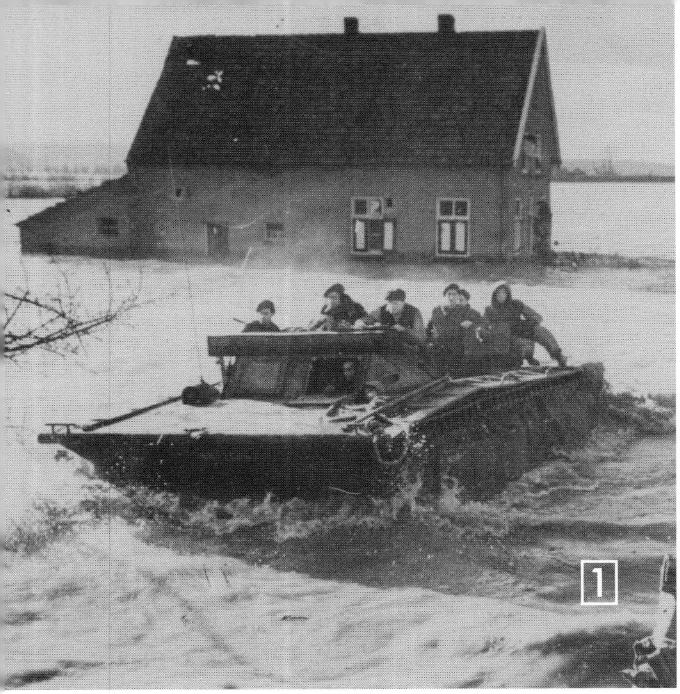
1

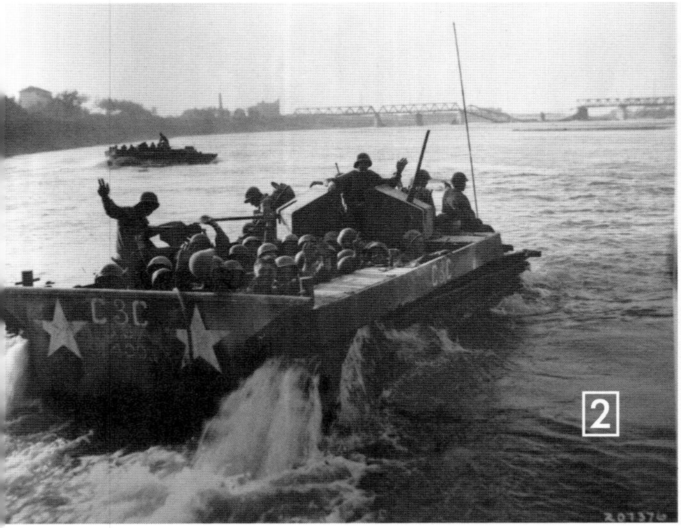
C3C
2

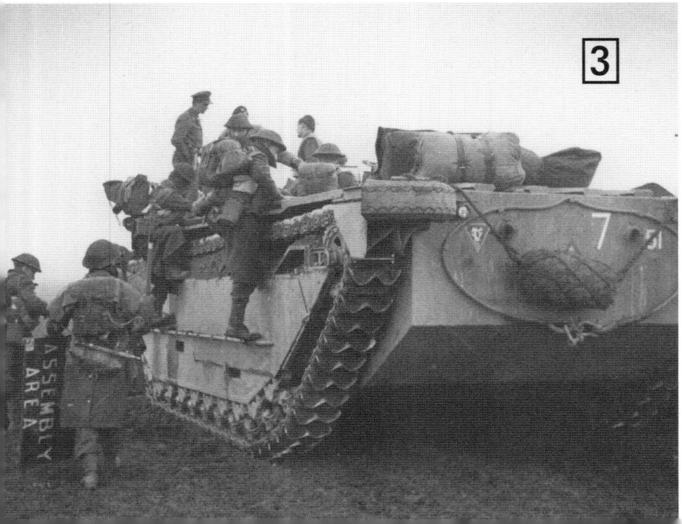
3
ASSEMBLY AREA

1 LVTs were used extensively in Europe in the latter parts of the war – particularly in the fighting around the Scheldt and Rhineland. The British called them Buffaloes and 200 had been delivered by the end of 1943. By the time of the Rhine crossing 600 were available. This one is seen east of Nijmegen on 21 February 1945 as it rescues Canadian soldiers from inundated countryside where they had been marooned by floods caused by the Germans breaking dykes.

2 LVTs were also used to cross the River Po in Italy. Here, 351st Infantry Regiment, (88th (US) Inf Div) cross near Ostiglia on 24 April 1945.

3 Men of 15th (Scottish) Division board Buffaloes to be ferried across the Rhine. Note the 79th Armoured Division insignia on the back.

4 It's the start of Operation Veritable, 8 February 1945 and a combination of factors – mainly heavy rain and broken dykes – have flooded the Waal. 79th Armoured Division has the answer – 115 Buffaloes. Here men of the Canadian North Shore Regiment mount up to lead the attack of Canadian 3rd Infantry Division's 8th Brigade.

5 Another of the war winners, the DUKW had the drivetrain of the GMC CCKW and a boat-shaped body. The name derives from the GMC numbering method: D for 1942 design, U for utility, K for all-wheel drive and W for tandem rear axles). Over 21,000 were built and it first saw service during the invasion of Sicily. It more than paid its way during the landings in Sicily and Italy before performing brilliantly during the Normandy landings. Photo shows a DUKW carrying a 57mm anti-tank gun in the south of France during the landings.

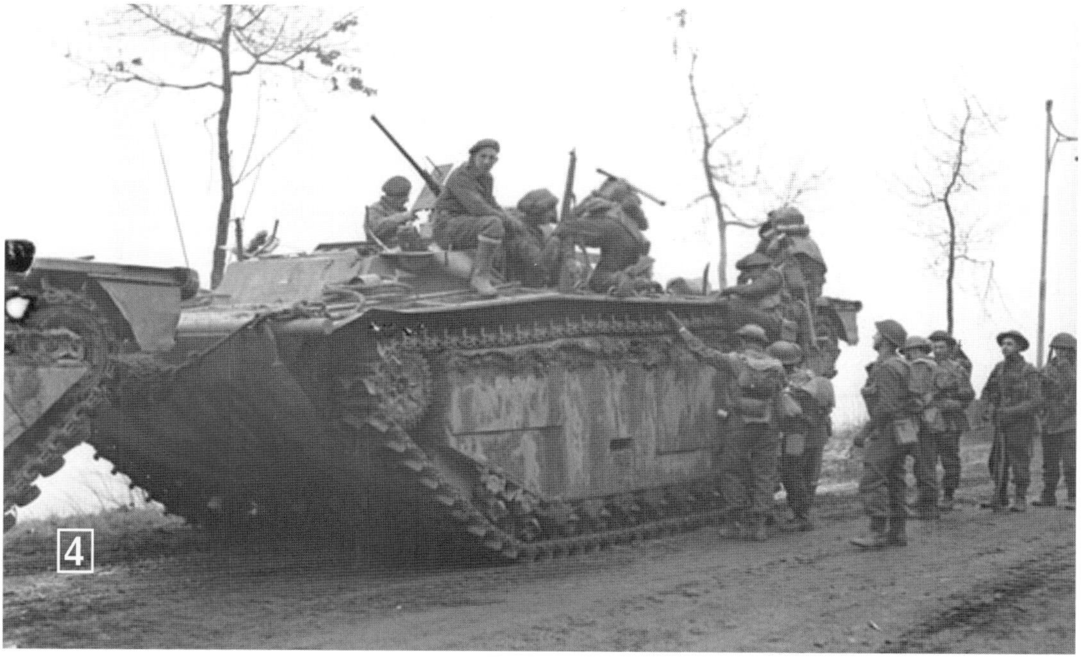

4

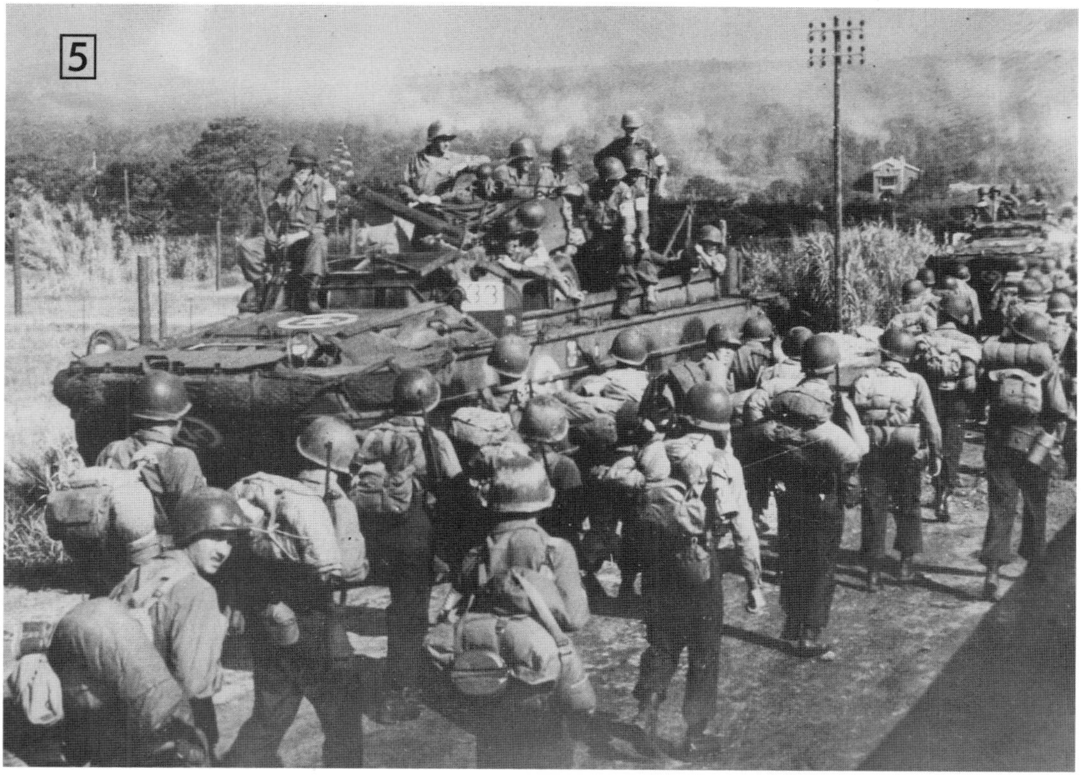

5

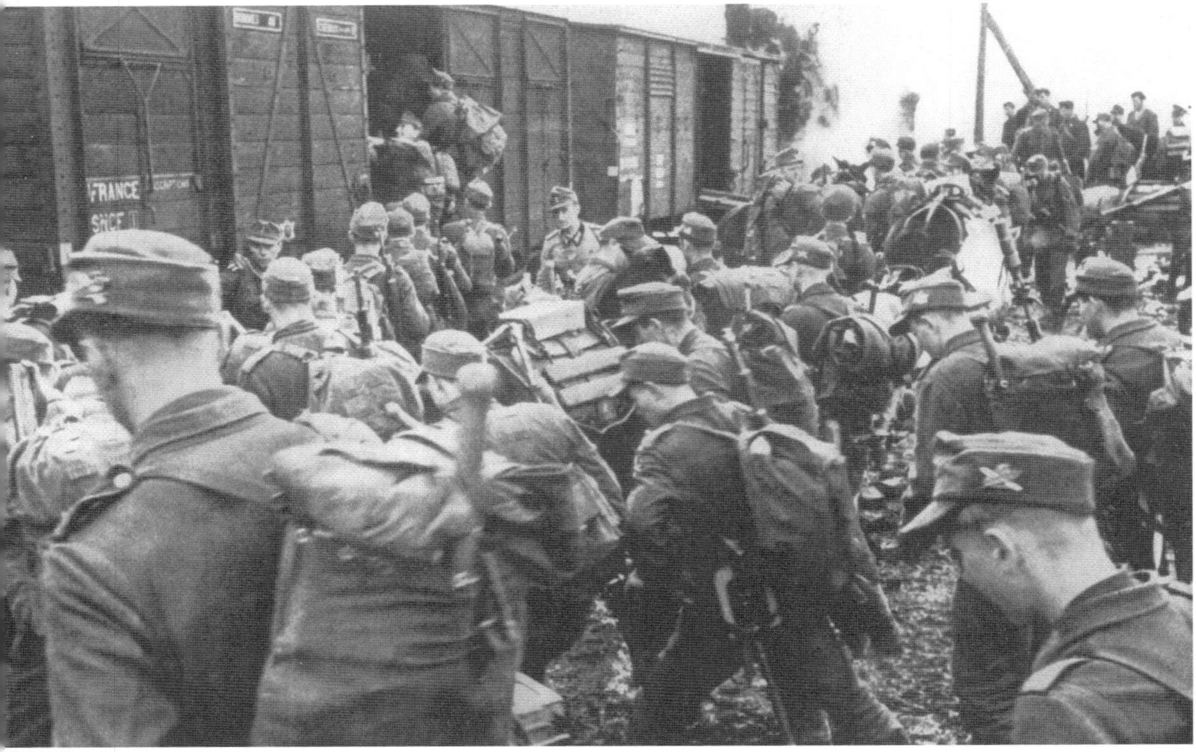
FRANCE

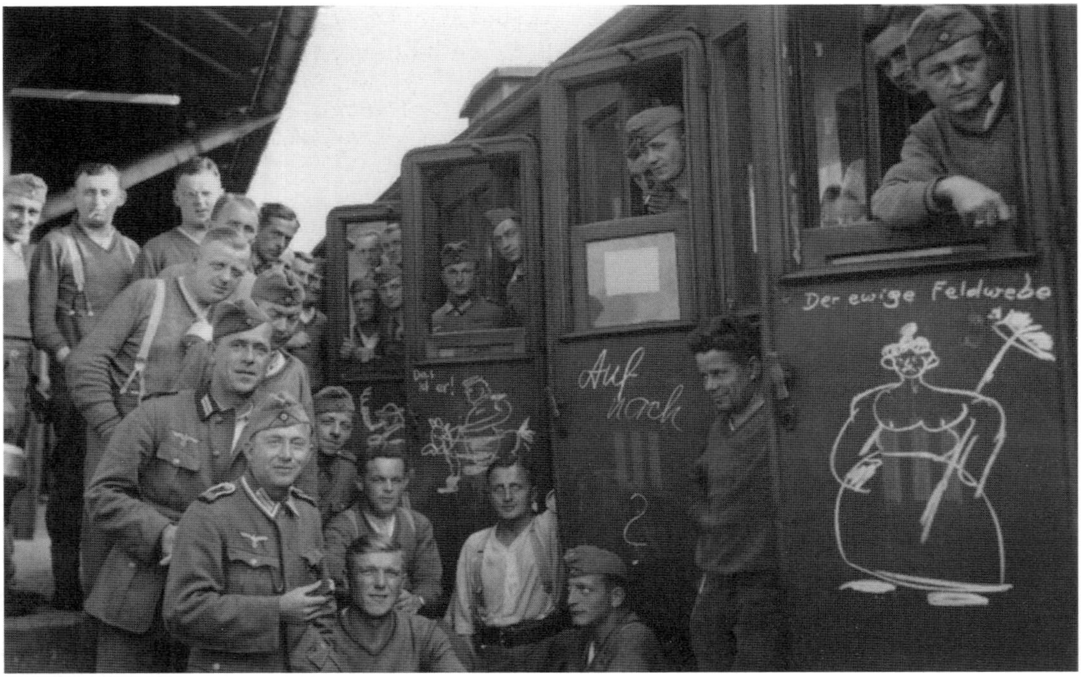
Der ewige Feldwebe
Auf nach

Railways were hugely important during World War II moving troops, munitions and materiel. Targets for air forces of both sides, nevertheless they allowed Germany to do as it had done in the Great War – concentrate forces quickly by using internal lines of communication.

Above left: German Gebirgsjäger board a French train.

Below left: *Das ist er!* (This is it!), *Auf nach?* (Where next?), *Der ewige Feldwebel* (The Eternal Sergeant) – and another German troop train.

Right: American troops reached Britain by troopship and were then transported from the ports to their camps by train. It would be their first taste of Britain and there was some attempt to greet them in a friendly way – doughnuts on the journey would have helped.

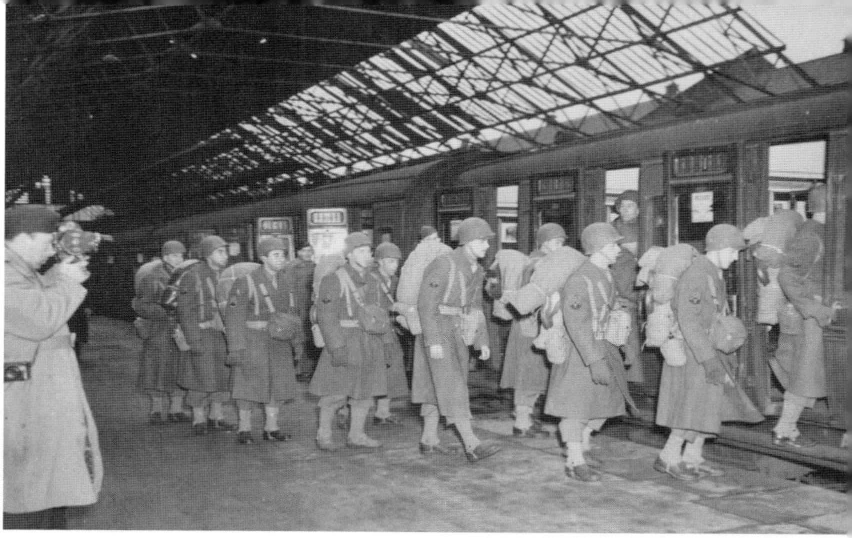

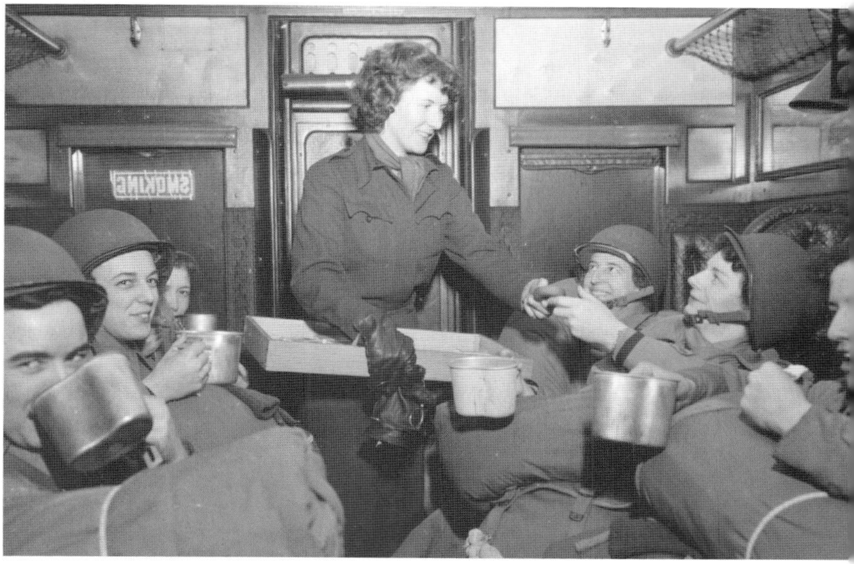

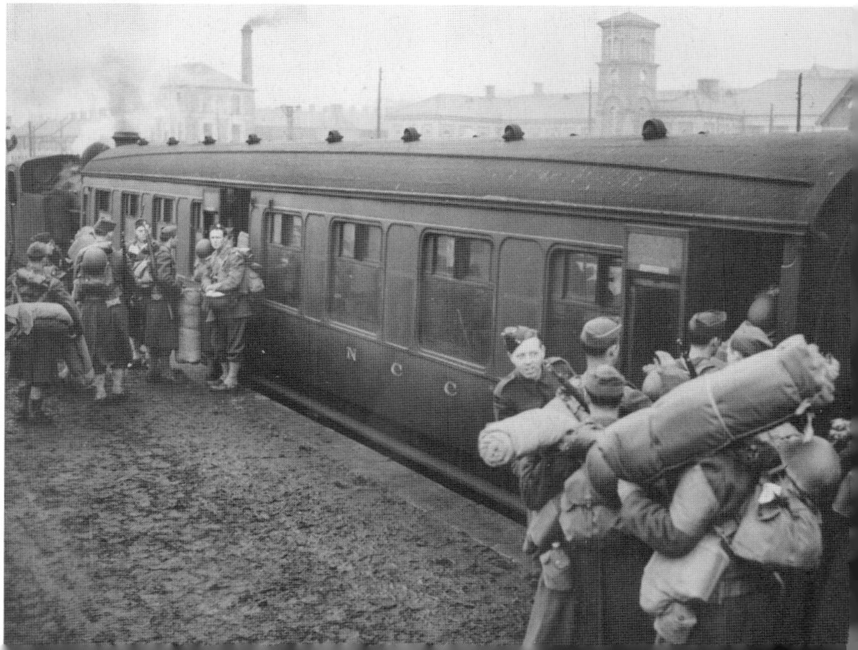
N C C

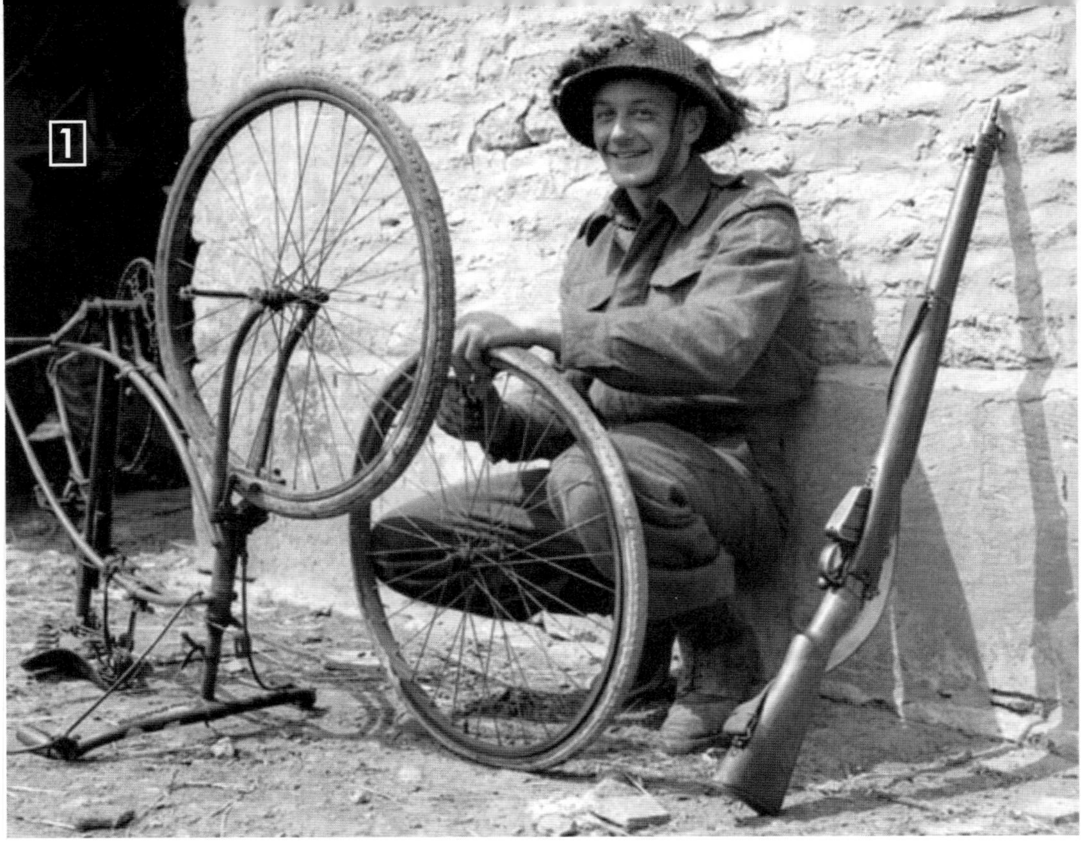

The Western Allies didn't make as much use of pushbikes in 1944–45 as the Axis infantry had done at the start of the war – and at relevant moments throughout: some of the troops that held up the British Paras at Arnhem were cavalry. The Japanese used them extensively during the Malayan campaign. British and Canadian follow-up troops were issued with them so that, as they arrived in Normandy, they could speed towards their alloted places in the line. In reality, they weren't used to any great degree and the locals gratefully liberated them. Photos show: **1** A Canadian rifleman repairs a puncture in Normandy; **2** Bikes in landing craft in England; **3** A German bicycle patrol in Italy enjoys a tow from a Kübelwagen; **4 and 5** German bicycle troops in Russia; **6** Re-enactor showing original bike with *Panzerfaust* attachments.

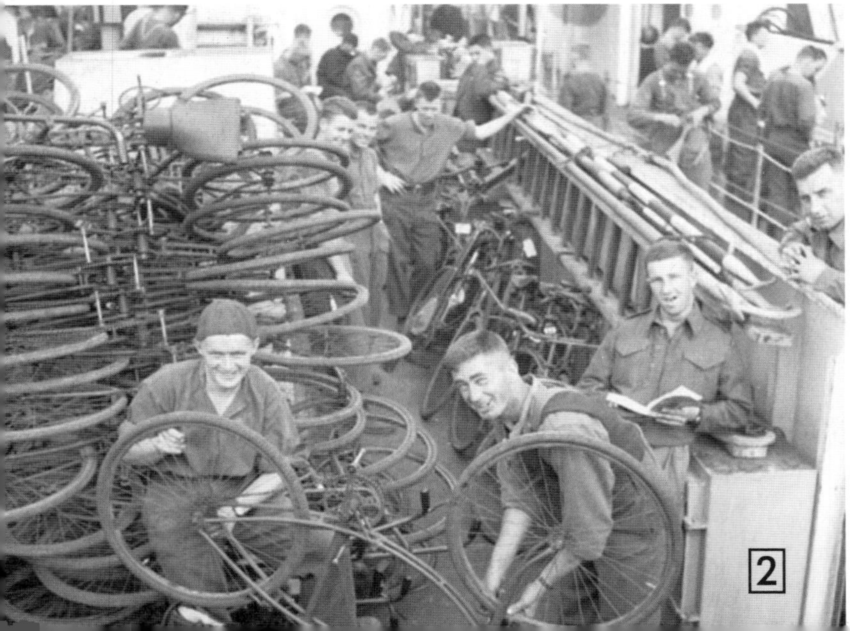

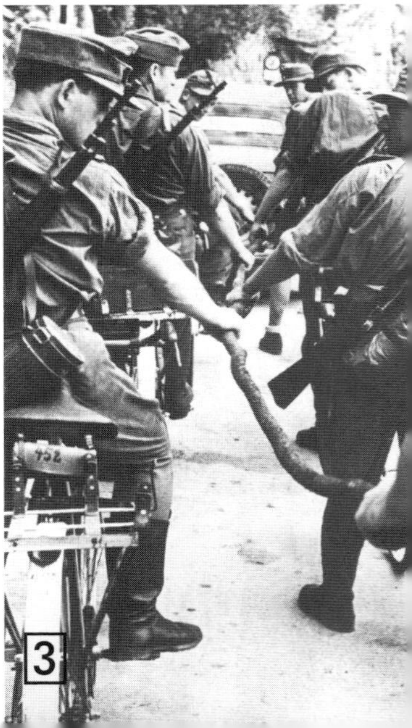

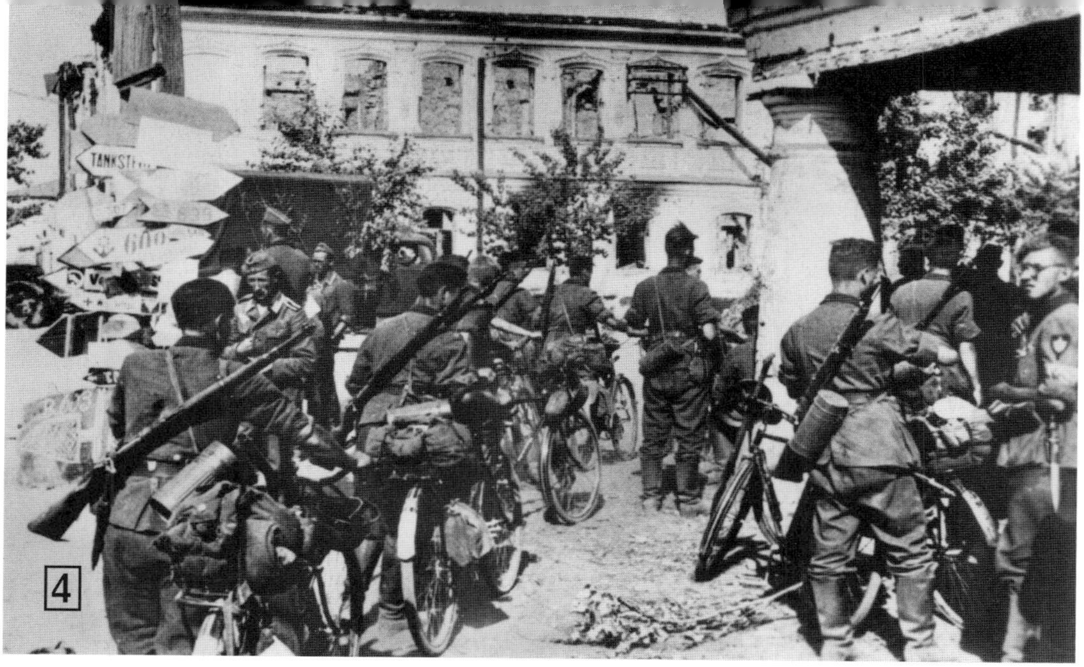
4

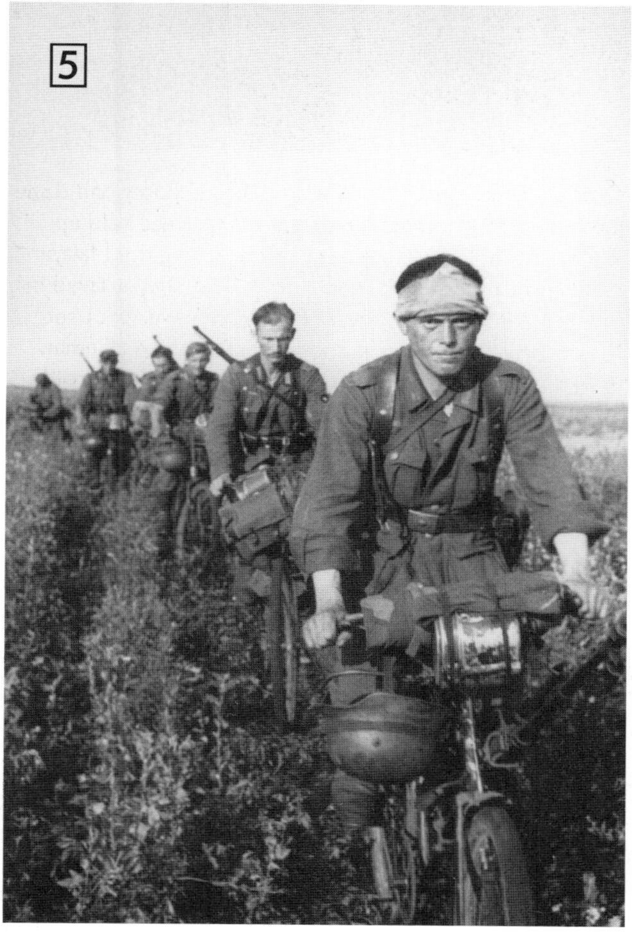
5

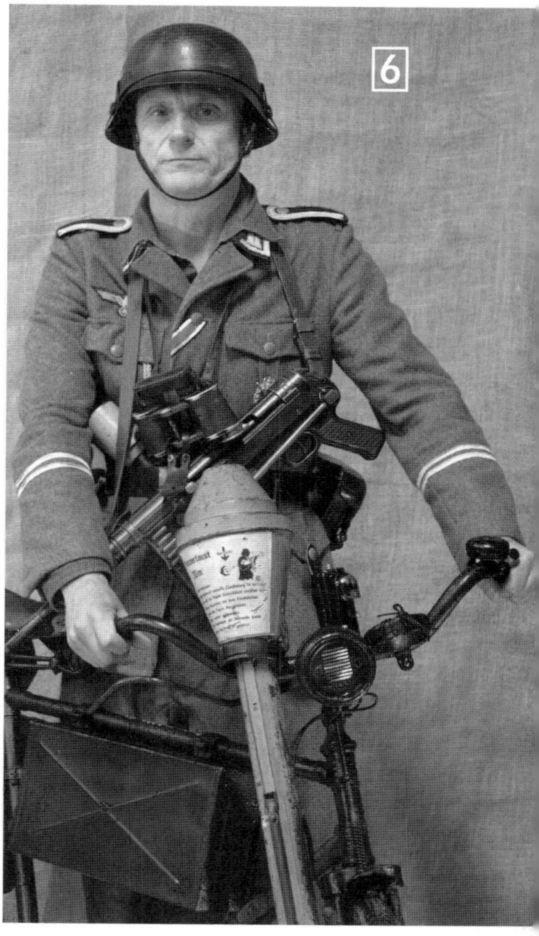
6

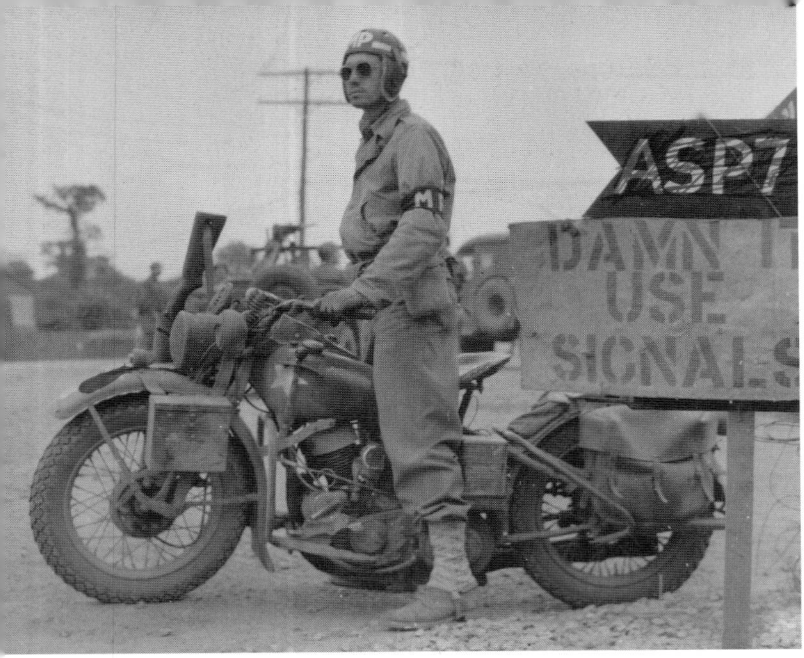
ASP7
USE

Motorcycles provided a combination of qualities which made them indispensable to armies at a time when communications were still relatively primitive. They ranged from the robust versions used by motorcycle troops, the MPs and couriers to the folding air-portable lightweights issued to the paratroops.

Above left: American MP on traffic control astride one of the ubiquitous Harley Davidson WLAs. Note the scabbard for the M1A carbine in front of the right-side handlebar.

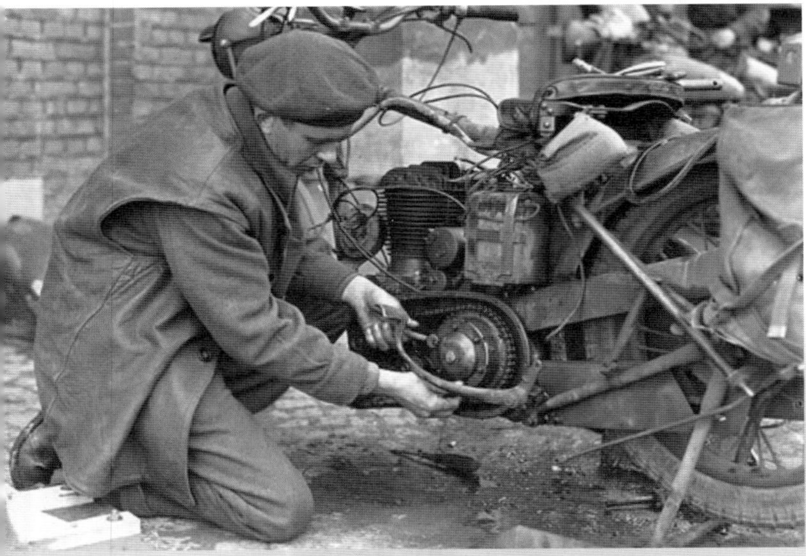

Centre left: Norton produced around 100,000 motorcycles for the military during the war. Most were a 500cc single-cylinder side-valve four-stroke – the 16H that was used as a general workhorse. Even though the Norton 16H was known for its solidity, like all motorcycles of the time, it still needed regular maintenance. Here, a craftsman of the 11th Infantry Brigade Workshop, RCEME, adjusts the clutch on such a machine.

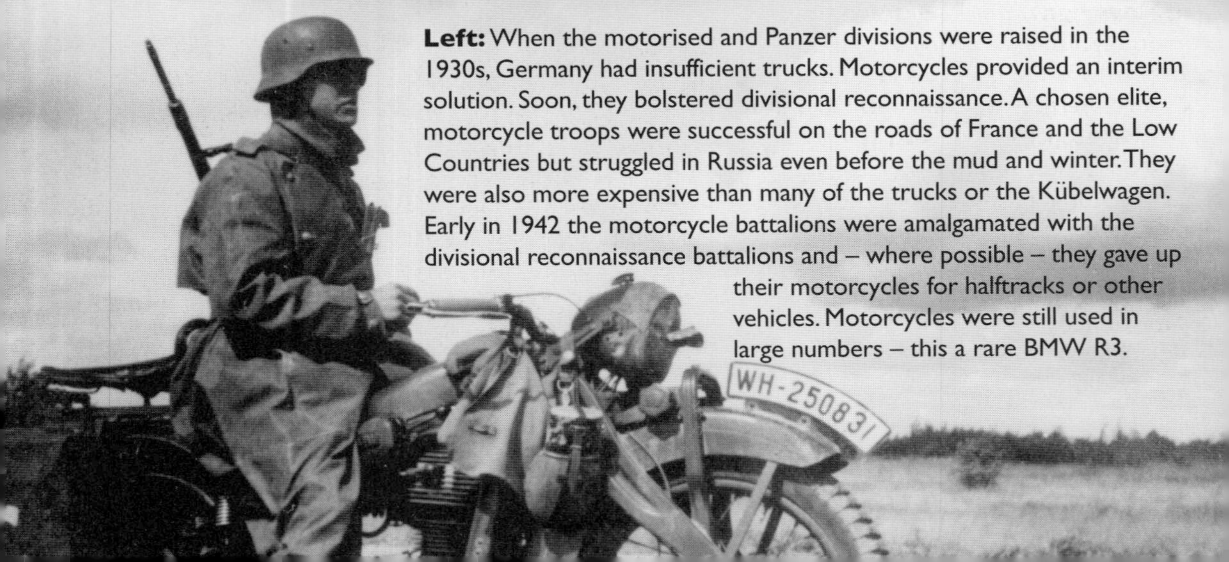
WH-250831

Left: When the motorised and Panzer divisions were raised in the 1930s, Germany had insufficient trucks. Motorcycles provided an interim solution. Soon, they bolstered divisional reconnaissance. A chosen elite, motorcycle troops were successful on the roads of France and the Low Countries but struggled in Russia even before the mud and winter. They were also more expensive than many of the trucks or the Kübelwagen. Early in 1942 the motorcycle battalions were amalgamated with the divisional reconnaissance battalions and – where possible – they gave up their motorcycles for halftracks or other vehicles. Motorcycles were still used in large numbers – this a rare BMW R3.

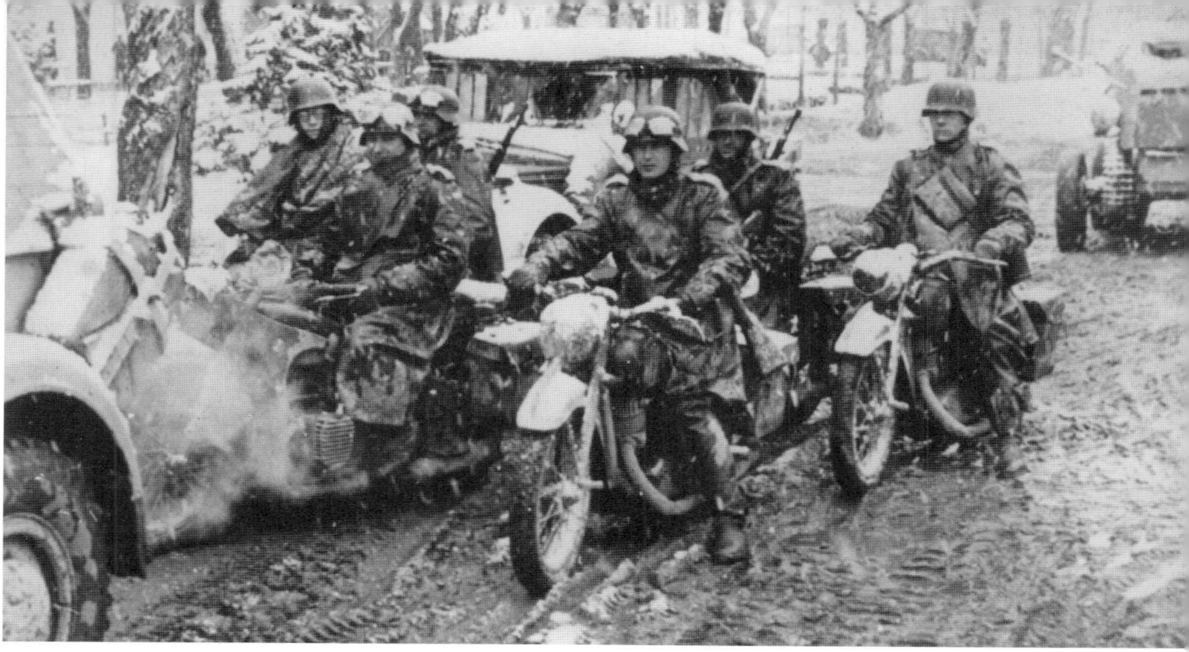

Above and Right: Essential for a wide range of duties – from carrying dispatches to fast-moving patrol work – German motorcycles came from several different providers included BMW, Zundapp, DKW, NSU and Victoria. A large number of these machines had sidecars which were manufactured by Zundapp, BMW, Stoye, Royal and Steib. The shaft-driven Zundapp KS750 and BMW R75 were unusual in having their third wheels powered, which made them far better than most of the competition when crossing rough terrain. These photos show German motorcycle troops in Serbia in April (**Above**) and Russia on 23 December 1941 (**Right**).

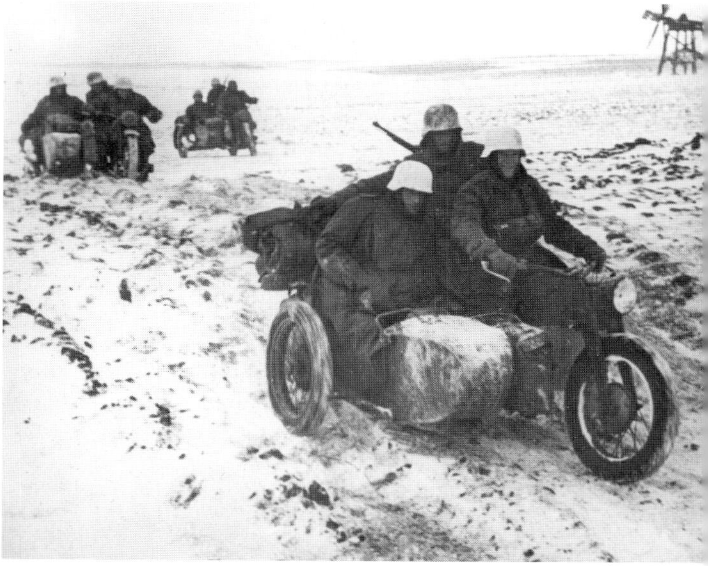

Below right: British and American motorcyclists didn't have quite as many problems as the Germans in Russia. France, Germany and the Low Countries had a reasonable main road system and the winter of 1944–45 – while the coldest for some years – was nowhere near as difficult in the west as it was in the east. Here, dispatch riders on an American Harley WLA and a British Norton 16H.

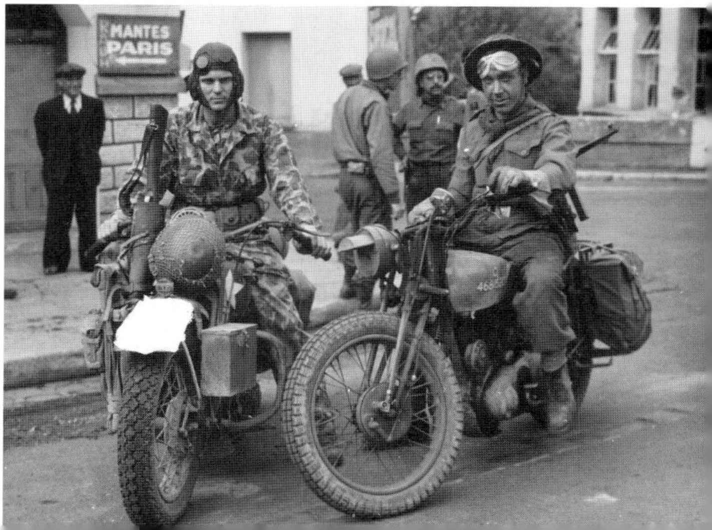
MANTES
PARIS

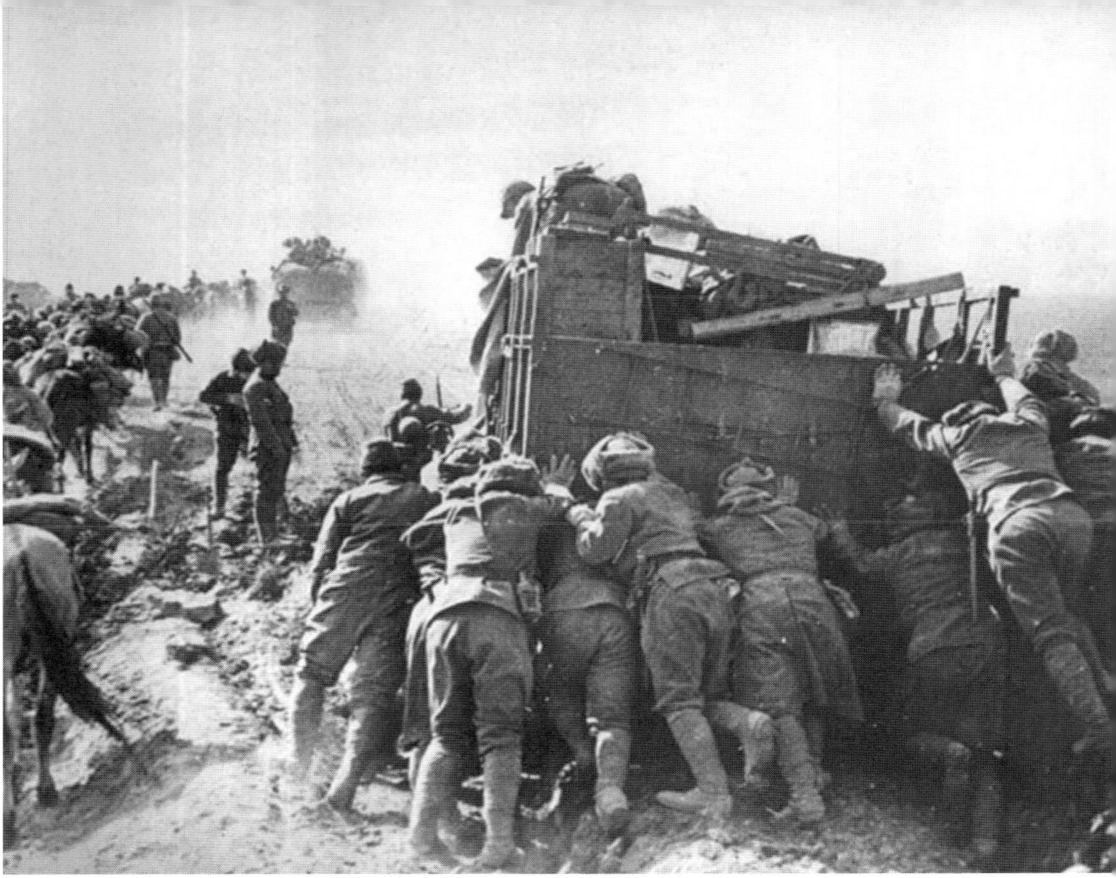

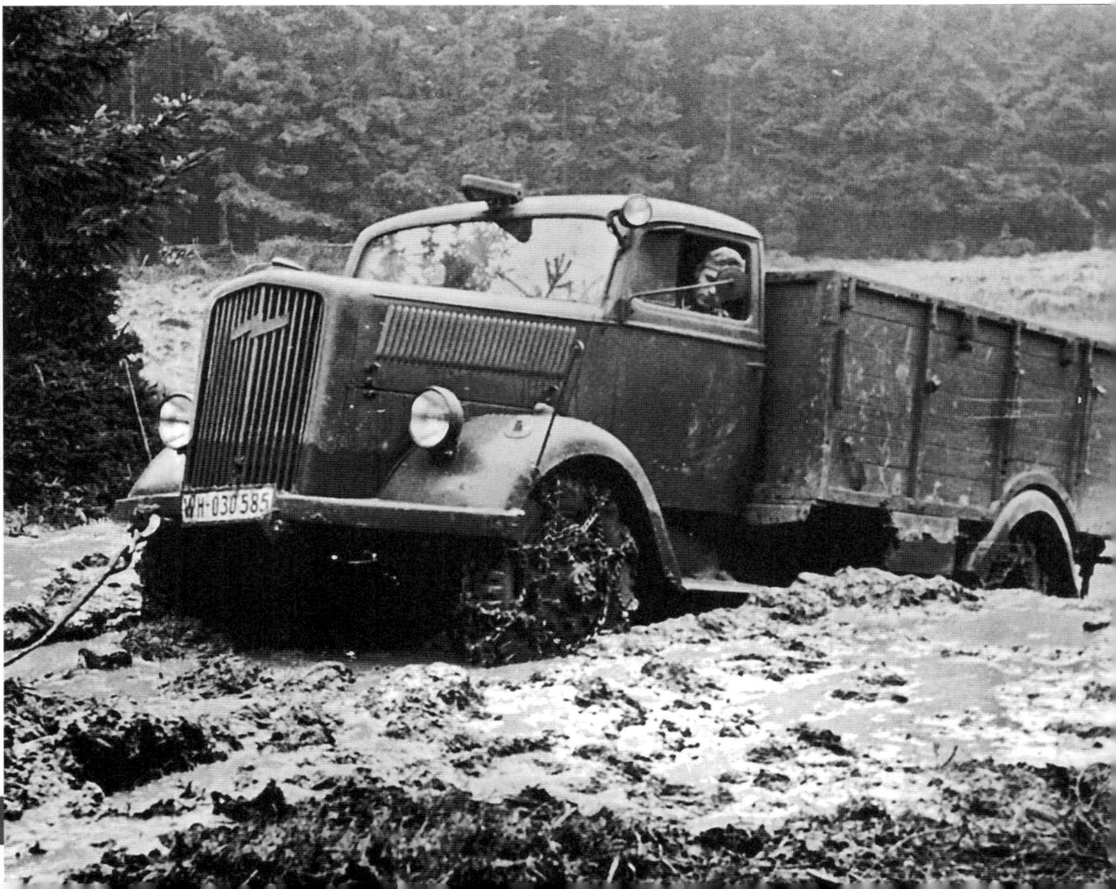
WH-030 585

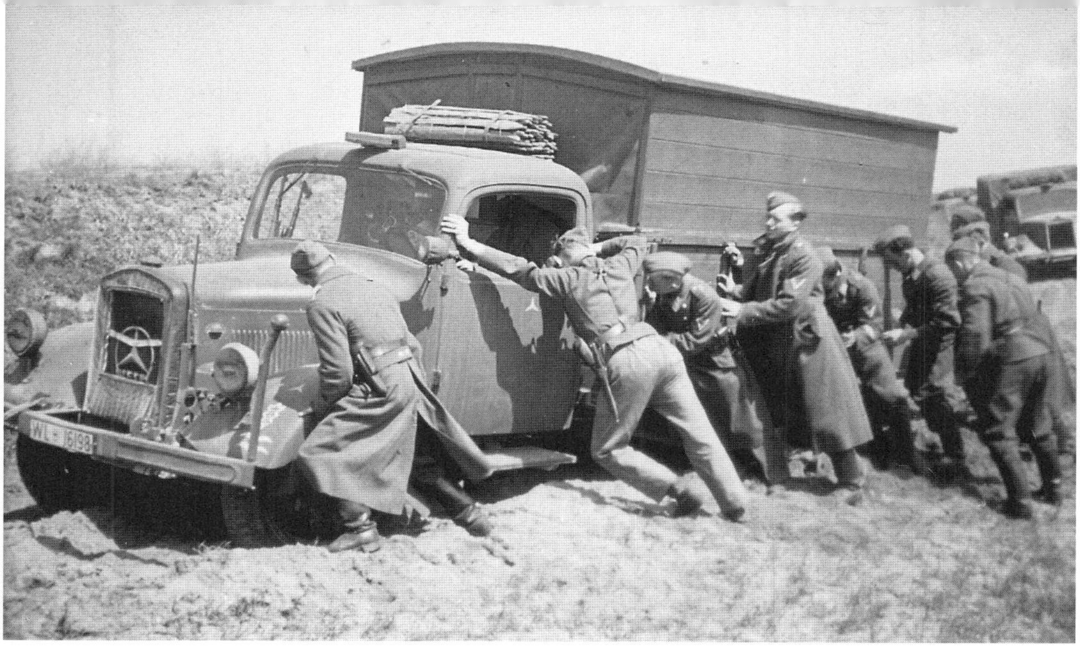

The road conditions in eastern Europe and elsewhere (the Japanese in Manchuria **Opposite, Above**) in 1939–45 were nowhere near the quality they are today. Farm tracks, unmetalled surfaces, green lanes – off the main roads it was difficult to find routes of the necessary quality to carry armies, heavy weapons, supplies, ammunition and armoured vehicles. Apart from the obvious problems caused by snow and freezing, just as happened to Napoleon – whose invasion started two days later than Hitler's – the campaign became bogged down as early and unseasonal snow melted and brought the *rasputitsa*, the literal translation of which is 'unmade road season'. Wheel chains didn't help this three-ton Opel Blitz (**Opposite, Below**) when the mud was this deep. Of course, when the mud dried the ruts damaged suspensions and transmissions. The desert, too, posed its own problems as shown by this Mercedes-Benz L3000 (**Above**).

Below: Tracks helped – to a point. There are worried looks from the crew in the back of the SdKfz 10 at the PaK 40 they are pulling through the floods. The *leichter Zugkraftwagen* 1-ton SdKfz 10 was a useful troop carrier that could also pull light artillery pieces – such as the 2cm Flak 30 and 38, various PaK anti-tank guns and the 7.5cm and 15cm infantry guns.

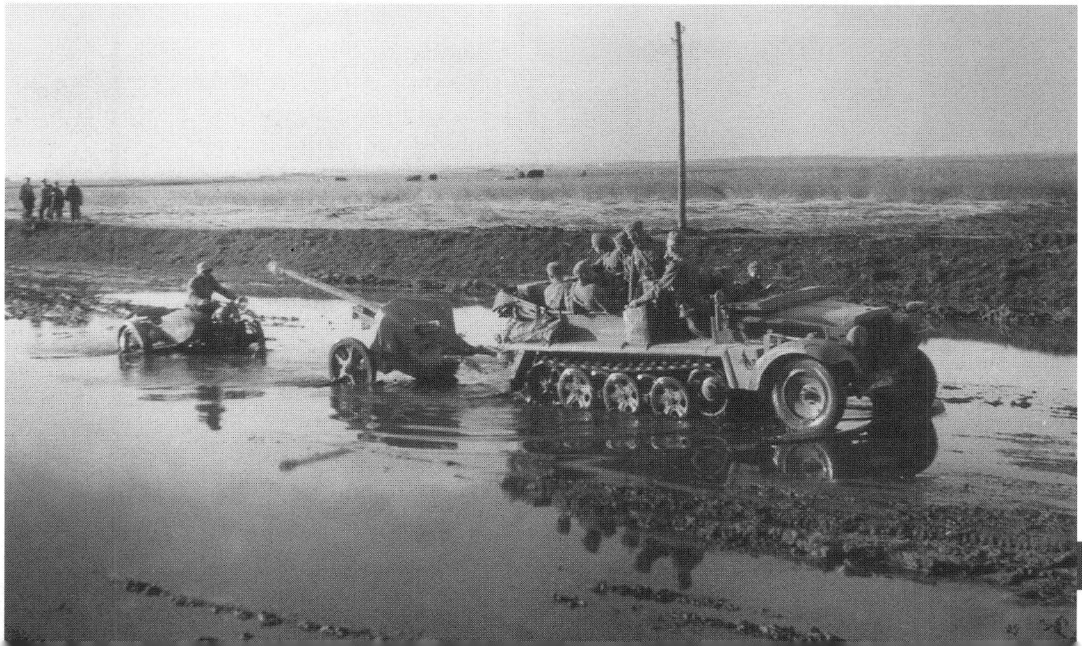

1 German supply train in the Norwegian mountains on 31 May 1940. The Poles and French inflicted a number of reverses on the German invaders, but the morale and skill of the German infantry won through in the end. The Germans used nearly 3 million horses and mules during the war and they were most effective in the mountains.

2 It's 31 October 1941. Winter is on its way and the German Army isn't ready for the hell that awaits it. There is little suitable cold weather clothing or preparations for the engines. Operation Typhoon – the thrust to Moscow – is less than 100 miles from the Russian capital. On 2 December it will be within 25 miles. On 27 November 1941, Eduard Wagner, the Quartermaster General of the German Army, reported that 'We are at the end of our resources in both personnel and material. We are about to be confronted with the dangers of deep winter.'

3 The Kuban area on the Black Sea saw both sides using camels for transportation.

4 SS-Panzergrenadiers – possibly 11. SS-Freiwilligen-Panzergrenadier-Division 'Nordland' who fought Tito's men – cross a mountain stream in pursuit of Yugoslav partisans. One of the soldiers carries a MG34 machine gun with a drum magazine, next to a pack mule with supplies.

5 Resupply in the Italian mountains. A mule train from the CP of US 157th Infantry Regt (45th Infantry Division) heads towards the 3rd Battalion with a load of 5gal cans of water, K rations, and other supplies. In the valley below, the town of Pozzuli north of Naples, 20 December 1943. The US Army made extensive use of pack animals when applicable – such as in the winter of 1944–45, when the 10th Mountain Division used more than 14,000 mules as it fought through the North Apennines and the Po Valley.

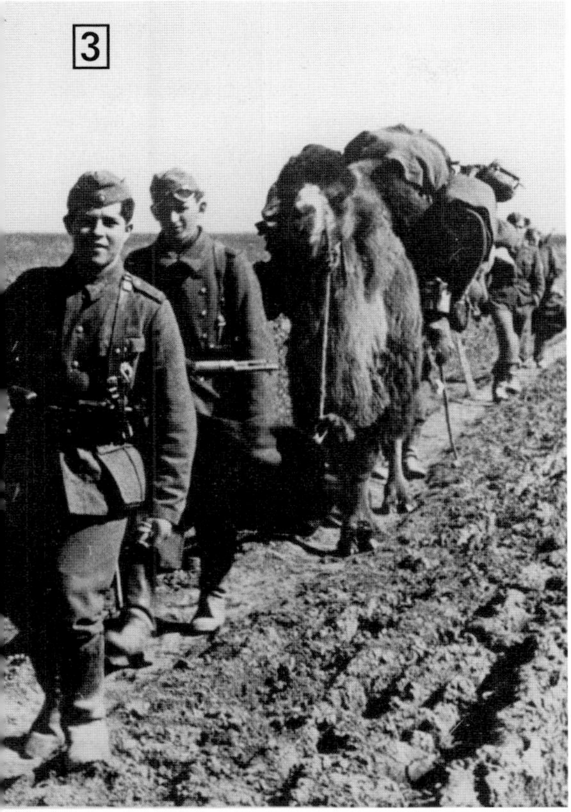
3

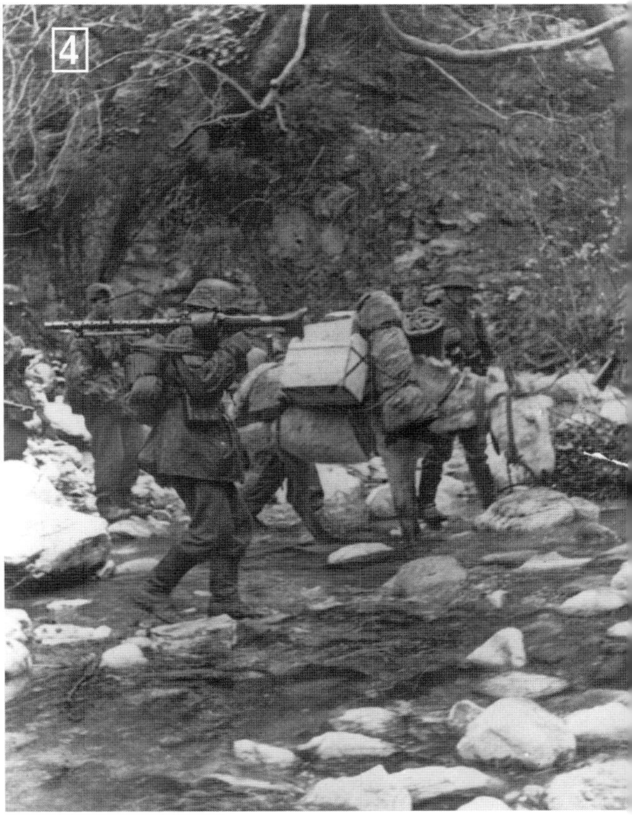
4

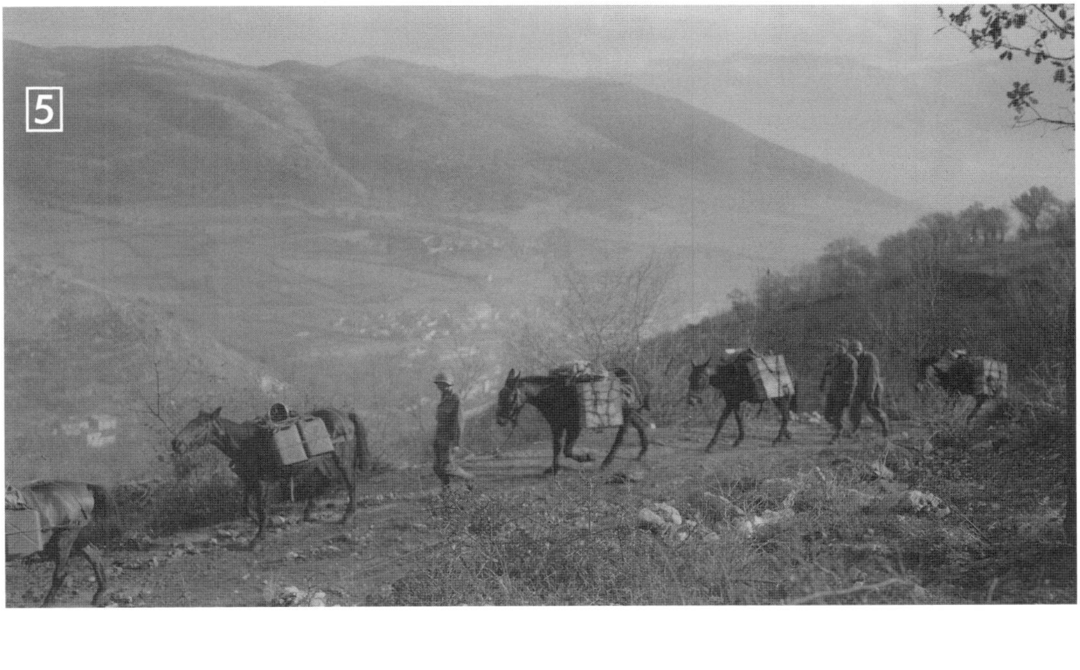
5

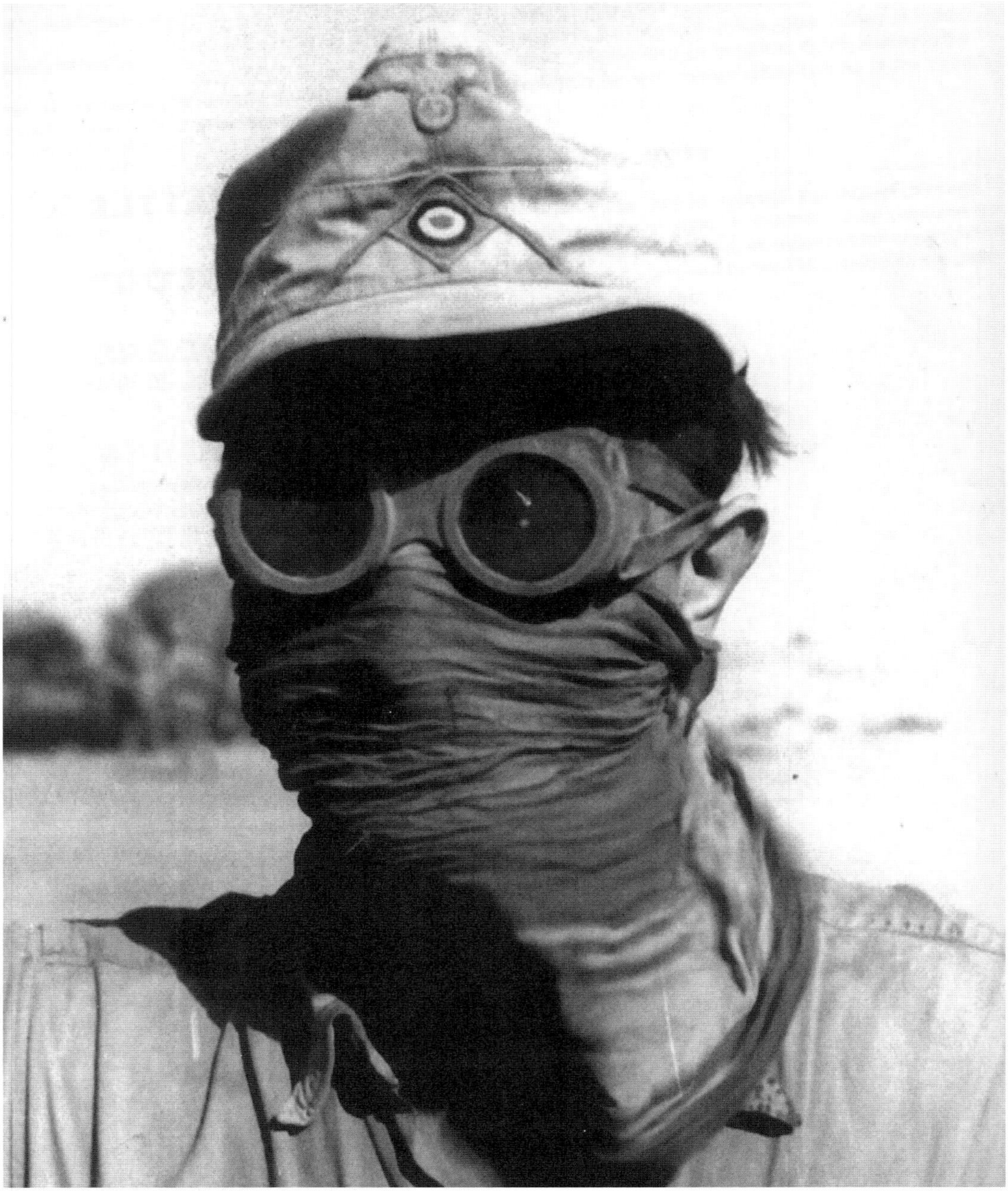

You need protection from the sand in the desert: this Afrika Korps soldier has Zeiss Umbral sand-sun goggles, a scarf and, of course, his tropical cap – with its sun-bleached appearance (often deliberately so), scarlet lining, side ventilation holes and inverted V soutache in suitable *Waffenfarbe* (the infantry's was white; *Panzergrenadier* silver and *Gebirgsjäger* light green). The soutache was officially discontinued from September 1942 although it continued to be used.

2 The Extremes: Desert, Jungle and Snow

In the desert interior about 10km from the coast, the vibration of the air makes accurate observation over 1km practically impossible. The light shimmers and plays tricks. Mirages – often looking like sheets of water – appear and all contours become blurred, with only a few elevations standing out like islands. Infantry in the desert are constantly exposed to the effects of sand and dust, in the long columns that transport them to combat as well as in battle itself. Because of the dust thrown up by vehicles, movement on the ground is impossible to conceal and it is difficult to differentiate between friend and foe from the air. In the day, the problems are sand, dust, heat and searing light; at night, the freezing cold. Sand gets into the works of weapons and engines, making maintenance and protection vital. Distances become difficult to judge in almost featureless terrain.

The desert war was a mechanised war. Mobility was key and thus supply lines and supplies (transported, buried and camouflaged) became even more important factors in planning and maintaining momentum. The interdiction of both sides' resupply convoys – the importance of Malta as a supply base and a centre of air operations, and the British control and use of the Suez Canal were vital factors in the campaign.

Tactically, that parts of the desert were more easily traversed by motor vehicles made it a war of big advances and enveloping movements, but it also made it difficult to hold ground and critical to dig in properly. The danger of enemy tanks breaking through the front made it necessary to develop all-around defensive positions that saw a huge increase in the use of antitank mines. Against motorised or armoured opponents, static troops could only hold their own in elaborately prepared defences – the British called them 'boxes'.

The area suitable for military operations was confined to the relatively narrow strip along the coast and the southern desert zone, both more favourable for rapid movement than the rocky steppe-like north. All soldiers in the desert were equipped with a pair of dust goggles. There were special air filters (often placed inside) for all motor vehicles, including tanks. In combat, the water consumption was generally so limited that the men even had to go without washing almost entirely. Each man usually received a canteen in the morning filled with coffee or tea, which had to last the whole day. Normally no water was used to clean vehicles and equipment. However, no great lack of water developed because the fighting was always in the coastal area and in numerous places there were sufficient supplies of fresh water to take care of the basic needs of the troops.

As a result of their empire, the British were most experienced in desert conditions and some of their clothing and equipment was much sought after. Although their armour was deficient, their motor vehicles were superior to those of the Germans, with adapted aircraft tyres, higher ground clearance and lower bodies. Pocket compasses were indispensable and were issued to each man. The compasses used by the British, in which the dials floated on oil, were better than their German counterparts and British maps were also considered a particularly valuable prize when captured. The normal British battledress (BD) was clearly too hot for day wear in the Middle and Far East, but desert nights were often bitterly cold once the sun had set, as were numerous mountainous areas of Tunisia. Thus BD was worn on occasions and greatcoats, sheepskin coats and the like were widely used. A new Khaki Drill (KD) was adopted. KD was evolved by the British Army in India, using lighter cloths and Indian cottons to make tunics, shirts, long trousers and shorts, to be worn with boots or shoes and puttees. In the 1930s KD also incorporated British Aertex fabric in its bush shirts and jackets and by 1939 British troops wore pale tan KD shorts or trousers with long sleeved Aertex shirts and jackets with pleated chest pockets and scalloped flaps, lower bellows pockets which were also flapped, rank epaulettes, long sleeves with a buttoning cuff and a matching waist belt and brass buckle. One of the most unpopular of the tropical items were the KD shorts with extra deep turnups, worn either buttoned up or let down to be bound round the ankles with special threaded white tapes, thus eliminating the need to wear KD trousers. They were a disaster when issued early on in North Africa and did not last long, being known as 'Bombay Bloomers'. By and large KD kit worked well in the desert and later in the Mediterranean theatre's summer.

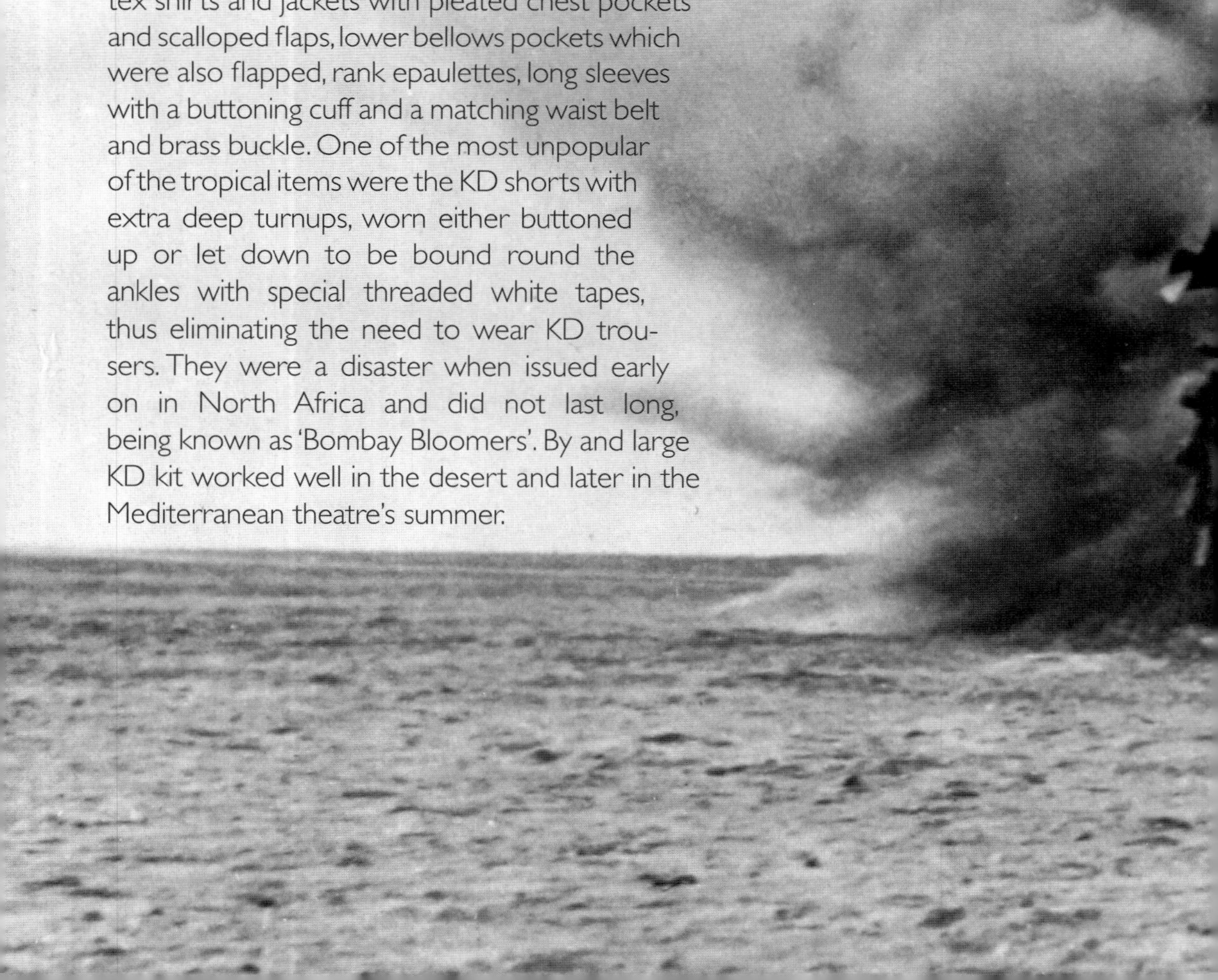

In the desert many officers took to wearing hard-wearing corduroy trousers and desert boots – suede with crepe rubber soles universally known as 'Brothel Creepers'.

The German 1940 *Tropenanzug* was the work of the Hamburg Tropical Institute. Made from a watertight linen, in the style of the former German colonial forces, it had defects. It was too stiff, did not give adequate protection against heat or cold and in the

British troops wearing KD and standard 1937 webbing take shelter behind a knocked out PzKpfw III in a posed photo.

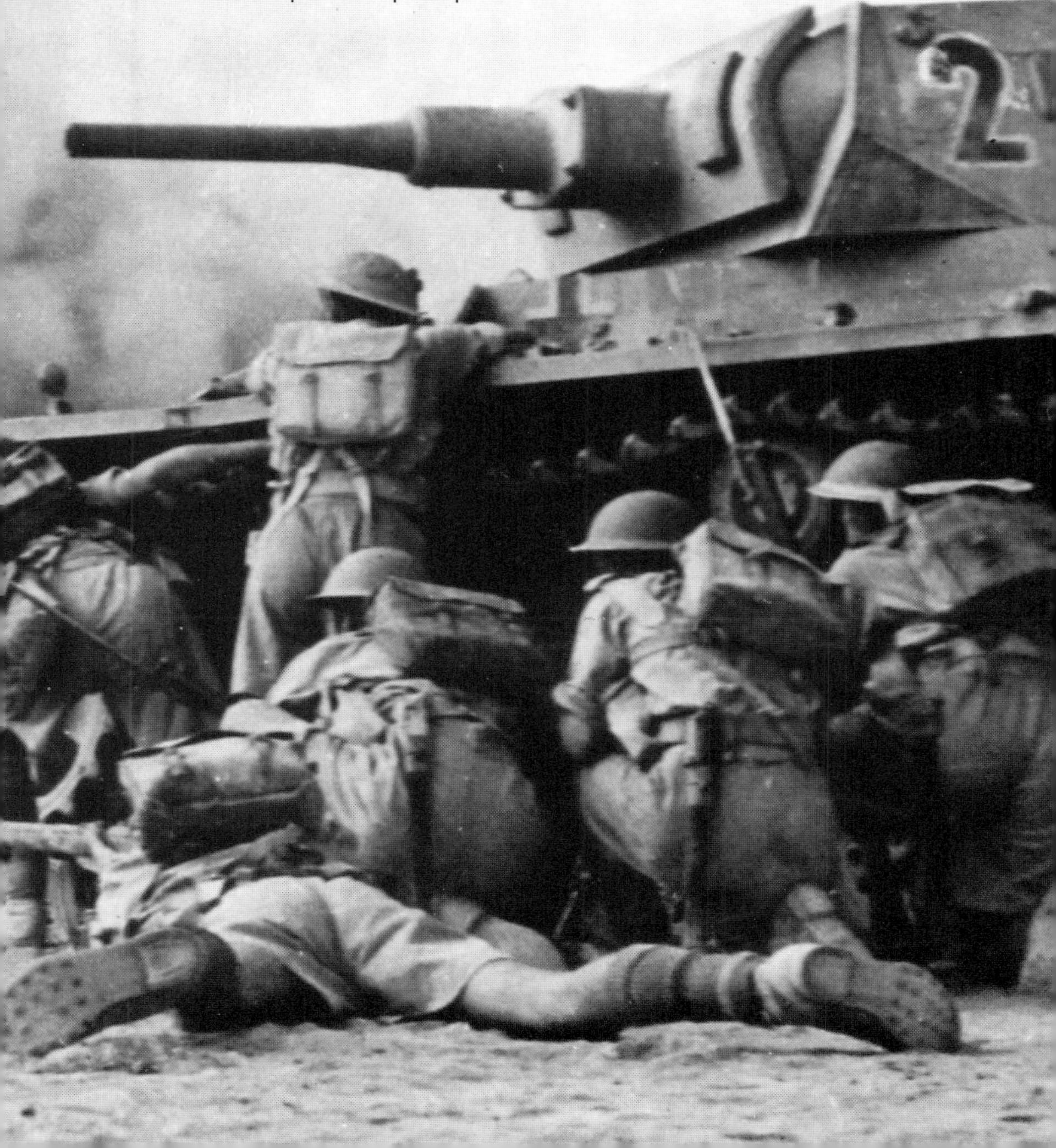

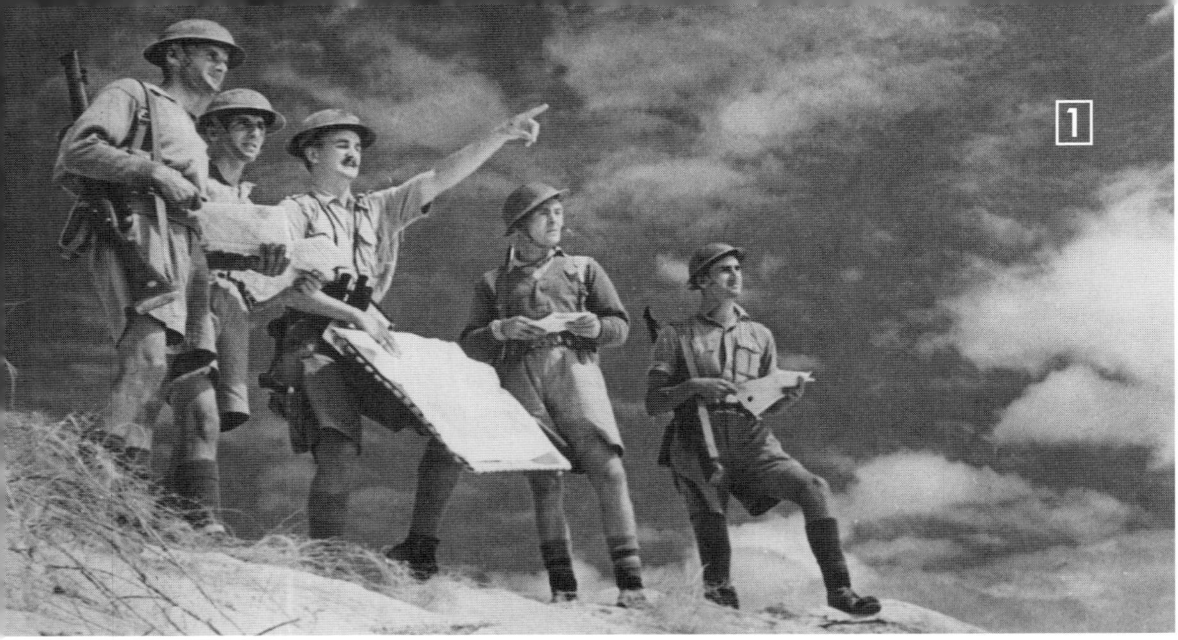
1

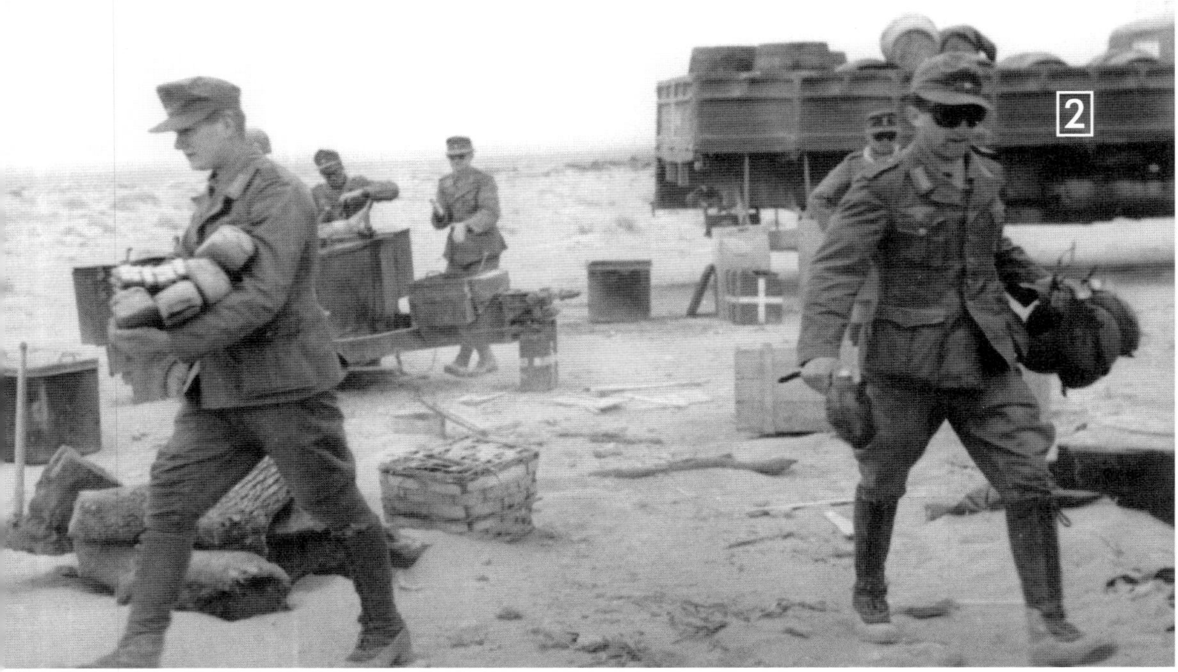
2

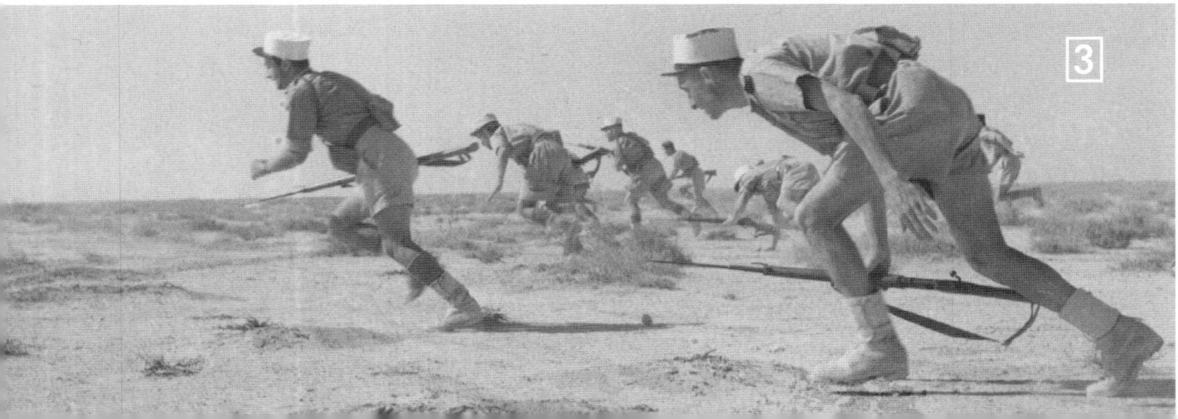
3

1 It's a truism everywhere, but even more applicable in the sandy wastes of the desert, soldiers need to be able to map read. The British maps were only as good as those who used them. This is a British military map-reading class undergoing instruction in November 1941.

2 Bread supplies for the Afrika Korps. Note the early pattern (pleated pockets and scalloped flaps) tunic and breeches along with long canvas/leather boots. Both were overtaken by later issue equipment, which faded in the sun.

3 French troops from the 1st Free French Brigade with their distinctive white-covered 1939 Kepis.

4 Classic view of Australian troops in the desert – shorts, Mk II Brodie helmets, officer with revolver and long-bladed bayonets.

early mornings absorbed moisture from the dew so that it became intolerably uncomfortable. The British tropical uniforms, in contrast, were excellent. Large quantities of them were captured at the fall of Tobruk and worn, the Germans especially liking the shorts and trousers. High boots restricted circulation, so were either cut down or replaced by lace-up shoes with cloth tongues. The shorts issued to the troops were not supposed to be worn in the front lines or during combat, since they left bare legs exposed to injury by thorns and stones, and such injuries healed slowly. The original breeches also proved unpopular and were soon replaced.

The olive-drab caps with wide visors, however, were well-regarded, especially when bleached in the sun (or by using other means) giving the wearer the look of an old African hand. The tropical helmets that were issued were entirely useless in combat and could be used only in rear areas. The German troops often painted their steel helmets – when they wore them – or wore white covers. The tropical coats issued, which were made from a thick woollen material, were good, but the English ones, which were fur-lined and reached only to the knees, were better. Owing to the stiff material from which it was made, the German tropical shirts were inferior to the British types. With the exception of footwear no leather was used in any clothing, being replaced by thick linen.

Plagued by flies, fighting at times in 50°C, frozen by night – the lot of the infantry was a difficult one and perhaps explains the undoubted respect and often chivalrous behaviour exhibited by both sides when it came to prisoners and medical facilities.

GERMAN HEALTH PAMPHLET FOR NORTH AFRICA

This pamphlet was given to soldiers entering the North African desert campaign.

The climate of the country is quite different from that of your homeland. The days in summer are hot and sunny, in winter, warm; the nights, on the other hand, are cool in summer, in winter, very cold. Throughout the entire country, water is very scarce. The German soldier must, first of all, accustom himself to the climatic peculiarities. The population of the country has different customs, ways of living, and practices, than our people. They have a different religion. Do not disregard all this in association with the people of the country. You will get on much easier. There are illnesses there which we do not have in Germany. You must, therefore, know the dangers which threaten you in this particular country.

Observe the following:

(1) Water
The virus of many different kinds of diseases can come from the water of this country. Therefore, never drink unboiled water, also do not rinse out your mouth with it, as long as your superior officers do not designate the water pure! Boil your water! It is best to drink tea or coffee and use the portable filter apparatus. It makes all fresh water potable! Drink no mineral water and no lemonade as long as it has not been expressly designated as harmless by your superior. Ice in restaurants and ice-cooled drinks, which are offered for sale on the streets, are not prepared under sanitary conditions and, therefore, are harmful to your health; avoid them, even if you are extremely thirsty. Do not wash yourself in dirty water, do not bathe in streams, lakes, ponds, pools. Bathing in the sea is permitted. Do not bathe when in an overheated condition.

(2) Nutrition
You will receive the best food from your unit. Do not eat raw meat. Never drink unboiled milk, especially not goat milk! Wash all fruit in purified water or peel it before eating. Do not buy quarters or halves of melons when they are offered by street merchants. Buy only whole, uncut melons. Do not pick up any food from the ground, especially meat, fish, and sausage; in the heat, foodstuffs perish quickly and contaminate! Protect your rations from flies. They carry disease.

(3) Dress
Always wear a stomach band. You protect yourself against catching cold. Always wear your sun helmet out of doors during the heat of the day. Otherwise, wear your field cap. It serves no purpose and is harmful to the health to run about in warm countries with the upper part of the body naked. It is a mistake to believe that one is cooled off in that manner. When the air-temperature is greater than 38°C (100°F) the wind has a heating effect on the skin.

(4) Bivouac
Avoid particularly the dwellings of natives. Before you take up quarters in houses or barracks, clean the area thoroughly. Excrement and refuse are the breeding places of flies, and these carry to food-stuffs or direct to people the germs of dangerous illnesses (especially dysentery). Therefore, latrines must be free from flies. The trench-latrine serves the purpose.

(5) Vermin
Besides flies there are body lice, ticks, mosquitoes, snakes, and scorpions in this country. Mosquitoes are carriers of fevers, and malaria. Combat the mosquitoes in the morning and in the evening in your barracks

by continuously killing them. If you burn a light in your barracks, keep the windows closed when possible; mosquitoes are attracted by burning lights. Use your mosquito net when you go to bed. Be careful, however, that when you lie under your mosquito net that there are no mosquitoes in the net and that the net is carefully tucked in under the bed and no openings are left for mosquitoes to enter.

If you have body lice, report it immediately: body lice and ticks carry spotted fever and relapsing fever, and both are serious illnesses. The snakes in this country are poisonous. They hide themselves in the sand. Scorpions are often found under loose rocks. Therefore, do not run about with bare feet and naked legs. Inspect your sleeping-bag daily for snakes and scorpions. Shake out your boots before putting them on. They are a favorite hiding-place for scorpions. It is frequently maintained that a drink of liquor is beneficial after you have suffered a snake bite. This is foolishness. Alcohol, under such circumstances, is harmful.

If you should be bitten by a snake, apply a tourniquet directly above the wound on the side toward the heart. The pressure applied to the tourniquet should not be great enough to cause the wounded part to swell and turn blue. With a disinfected razor blade, make a cross-like incision at the wound. Each cut should be at most about 1 inch long and not deeper than 1.25cm (0.5in). Allow the wound to bleed for 3 minutes; sucking the poison from the open wound is frequently recommended. This should be undertaken only by one who has no open sores or cavities in his mouth. With the blunt side of the disinfected razor blade, rub several potassium permanganate crystals into the wound; bind the wound and remove the tourniquet. Then report to the unit surgeon or medical officer immediately.

(6) Venereal Diseases
Women who solicit freely are usually infected. You should visit those houses only which are approved by the military authorities. Always use a condom. Follow orders, and take a prophylaxis after having exposed yourself.

(7) Concerning Animals
Dogs and cats are frequently carriers of diseases, e.g., rabies, serious worm and blood diseases. Do not handle dogs, cats, or monkeys.

(8) Vaccinations
The vaccinations prescribed by the military authorities protect you from serious diseases. The unvaccinated person not only endangers himself, but the lives of his comrades as well!

(9) Prevention of Malaria
Do not hesitate to take tablets to prevent malaria, when they must be taken! You do not know the danger to which you and your comrades are exposed.

(10) Skin Irritation
Roter Hund (Red dog) is an annoying skin irritation, which is caused by excessive heat and attended by extreme perspiration. Frequent bathing in warm water and lathering with medicinal soap (when available) is the best protection. If you have *roter Hund*, lather yourself with medicinal soap, and allow the lather to remain on your skin for 15 minutes. Blot yourself dry--do not rub. Dry yourself especially carefully in those parts where the conformation of the body causes skin wrinkles and between the toes.

(11) Slight Injuries
If you receive a slight wound on the calf of your leg from a thorn, or from striking against a sharp rock or from insect stings, apply a sterile bandage. If you allow such apparently trivial wounds to go unattended, they can develop into annoying and slowly healing sores.

Infantry in the Jungle

From above, tropical and semitropical jungle looks lush, green and beautiful. Up close, in its dense forests, swamps and marshes, it is one of the toughest and most extreme environments on earth in which to live and fight – a nightmare of incessant moisture and malevolent insect and reptile life. It's all monsoon rains, malarial mosquitoes, snakes and scorpions, ticks that carry lethal scrub typhus and amoebic dysentery, leeches that penetrate the tightest clothes to suck blood and lung fly whose vicious bite hardens into a large septic lump. Wounds fester in the heat and take a long time to heal.

Many more casualties arose from the difficult conditions encountered than from the enemy. Such terrain precluded the use of large-scale formations and tended to break up and isolate units, who had to operate alone for long periods, supplied by air drop. Most jungle fighting takes place at close range, with raids, ambushes, sniping, mines and boobytraps. Evasion, concealment and camouflage become critical. Bases are only temporary hidden bunkers and tunnels; movement and operations are often carried out at night. This fragmented, guerilla-style warfare called for greater independence among smaller self-contained infantry units that were beefed up with a few extra men and more firepower. Both in equipment and tactics, the Allies steadily learnt and improved, while the Japanese continued to rely on their close-quarter ferocity and fanaticism, but also operated at night whenever possible. They usually had a squad of about 15 men. It would contain two two-man teams, one for an MG (Type 11, 96 or 99), the other a light 50mm mortar, a designated sniper and a rifle grenade launcher, while the rest of the squad carried Arisaka 6.5mm (later 7.7mm) rifles or Nambu 8mm semi-automatic pistols.

The Japanese wore their *Bousyo-i* tropical cotton uniform, originally in tan or light khaki. It was later superseded by versions in medium to dark green. The jacket had an open collar and buttoned side-vent flaps below the armpits with pleated internal pockets with flaps. Trousers could be full-length or threequarter but troops also wore knee-length shorts with a lightweight cotton shirt which had three front buttons, threequarter length sleeves and patch breast-pockets with flaps. Officers wore a short or long-sleeved lightweight white tropical shirt with the green trousers, or a green tropical tunic with the shirt collar outside and folded over the outer tunic collar. Rather than the leather packs of World War I, a large-scale replacement programme saw a linoleum-like material of rubberised fabric, or canvas, or cotton duck substituted for leather. In general, belts, ammunition pouches, instrument cases, holsters, and the like were of rubberised fabric while bandoliers and packs were of canvas or cotton duck.

The British had a section of ten men armed with .303 SMLEs (they would eventually develop a shorter, lighter version the No. 5 Jungle Carbine), 9mm Mk II Stens and the American M2 Carbine, augmented by a Bren gun, for which everyone carried a few ammo clips. (They did not issue mortars to sections, but there was a 2in mortar at

1 Japanese tropical uniform with loose shorts. All components are the same flat-green hue. These include tabi, light wrap puttees, breeches, muslin shirt, coat, and cap. It's very comfortable, but it is too light to provide protection against mosquitoes and to sustain even normal jungle wear. The pack normally contains extra shoes, socks, and breech clout. Towel, soap, and other toilet articles are carried, as well as a first-aid packet and a sewing kit. A shelter half is used as a ground sheet, or to roll up in. It makes an excellent poncho and, because of its superior rain-shedding quality, Japanese soldiers prefer it to the issue raincoat.

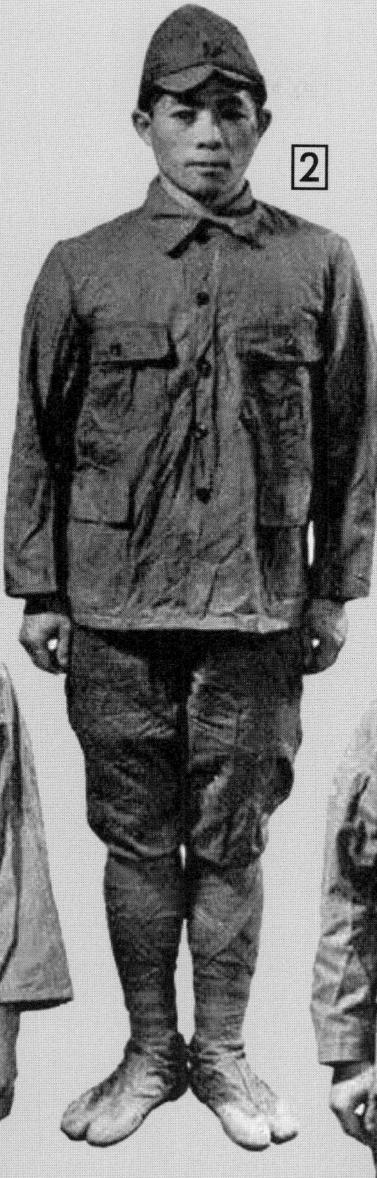

2

2 Japanese lightweight uniform – note the split-toed *tabi* footwear.

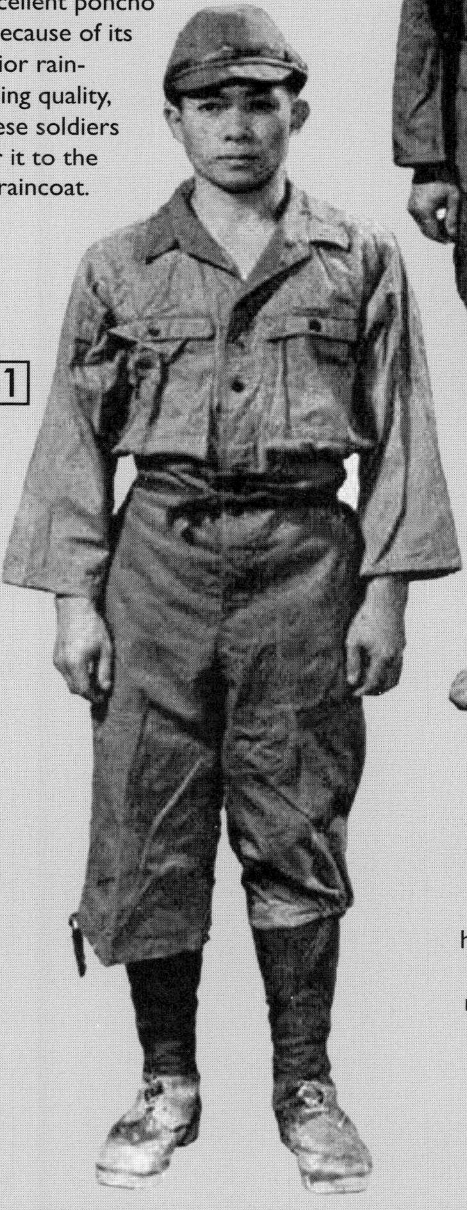

1

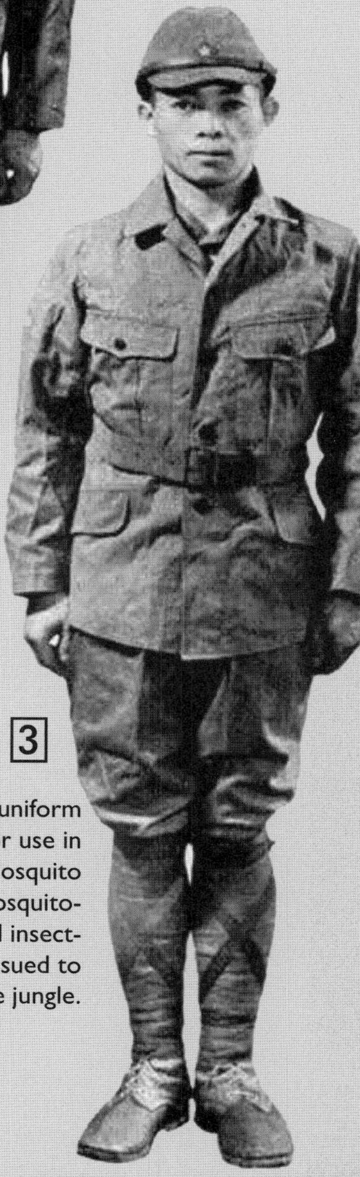

3

3 Japanese tropical uniform with putees for use in mosquito areas. Mosquito headnets and bars, mosquito-proof gloves, and insect-repellent were also issued to troops in the jungle.

Clothing and Personal Equipment issued in the Japanese Army

Helmet, steel	1
Cap, cloth, khaki, peaked	1
Trousers, drill, long, pairs	2
Tunics, drill	2
Shirts, cotton khaki	2
Underwear, cotton sets	2
Socks, cotton pairs	2
Shoes, split-toe, rubber, pairs (*Tabi*)	1
Boots, leather, pairs	1
Shelter half, khaki, waterproof	1
Puttees, pairs	1
Pack	1
Haversack	1
Hold-all, canvas (see **Below**)	1
Mess tin	1
Belt, leather	1
Pouches, leather	3
Water bottle	1
Gloves, mosquito, pairs	1
Head mask, mosquito	1
Respirator	1
First aid field dressing	1

Above Right: Enlisted man in M98 full field uniform, with all insignia removed.

Opposite: Japanese jungle troops detrucking. Note the travelling position of the steel helmets. (When caps are worn, the steel helmet is secured over the mess kit.)

Right: Instead of the pack a canvas hold-all is sometimes used – a piece of light canvas with carrying straps at each end. When rolled it can be carried across the back, slanting diagonally upwards from left to right. The hold-all serves as a combat pack and usually includes overcoat or blanket, shelter half and tent poles and pins.

(1) Pack strap cross knot
(2) Main pack strap knot
(3) Canteen strap
(4) Haversack strap
(5) Bayonet
(6) Tent section
(7) Overcoat
(8) Tent and overcoat are folded in four equal parts
(9) Haversack
(10) Canteen

1
2
3
4
5
6
7
8
9
10

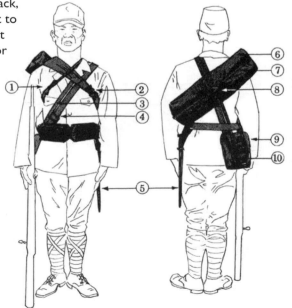

platoon level.) The Americans had a dozen men in their basic rifle squad, most armed with semi-automatic M1 Garand rifles, while one man carried a fully automatic BAR (Browning Automatic Rifle) that fired the same ammo as the M1 and replaced the less penetrative Thompson submachine gun. The M1903A4 sniper rifle and M19191 Browning machine gun were other options. Still heavier support weapons, including the M1A1 bazooka, 60mm M2 mortar and M2 flamethrower became increasingly available.

As the war and the Allies progressed, custom-made guerilla units were formed for operation behind the Japanese lines – the Chindits, Merill's Maurauders and Carlson's Raiders. All jungle troops also carried machetes, extra explosives and grenades and used mules to carry light howitzers and mortars as well as their supplies.

In the damp jungles of the Far East the British KD required a redesign – the resulting 'Jungle Green' (JG) was more than just a dyed version of KD. After much research the 1943 JG consisted of an Aertex blouse and hard wearing drill trousers, but the blouse was soon dismissed by the troops as being too light, uncomfortable and impractical, with a tendency to ride up even more readily than the original wool BD blouse. Where possible it was replaced by a longer, four-pocket JG Aertex bush shirt, or the more comfortable and popular two-pocket Indian wool (flannel) shirt. Headgear – such as slouch hats – was issued for jungle wear, but as in the Middle East most soldiers wore their normal regimental hats, berets, or in action, steel helmets. Other necessary clothing items such as long stockings, hose tops, thin vests and pants etc, were issued to all ranks as necessary.

The Americans wore a one-piece reversible (green/brown) camouflage jungle suit made of herringbone twill with a long front zipper for cooling and featuring two large expanding pockets on the chest and two on the hips. It was nicknamed the 'frog skin' suit by the troops who found it generally too heavy, hot and uncomfortable. At the same time the USMC produced a two-piece jungle suit in the same printed reversible camouflage

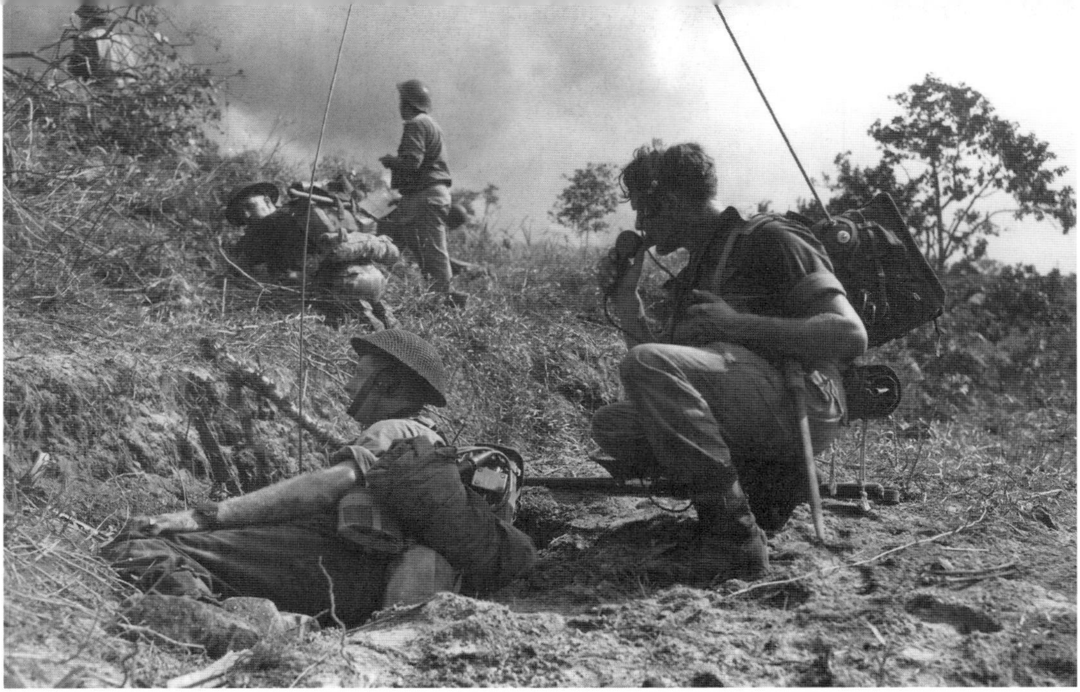

Above: The landings on Borneo in July 1945 saw Australians take control of the island with naval and aerial support from US assets. Photo shows an Australian FOO calling down artillery support.

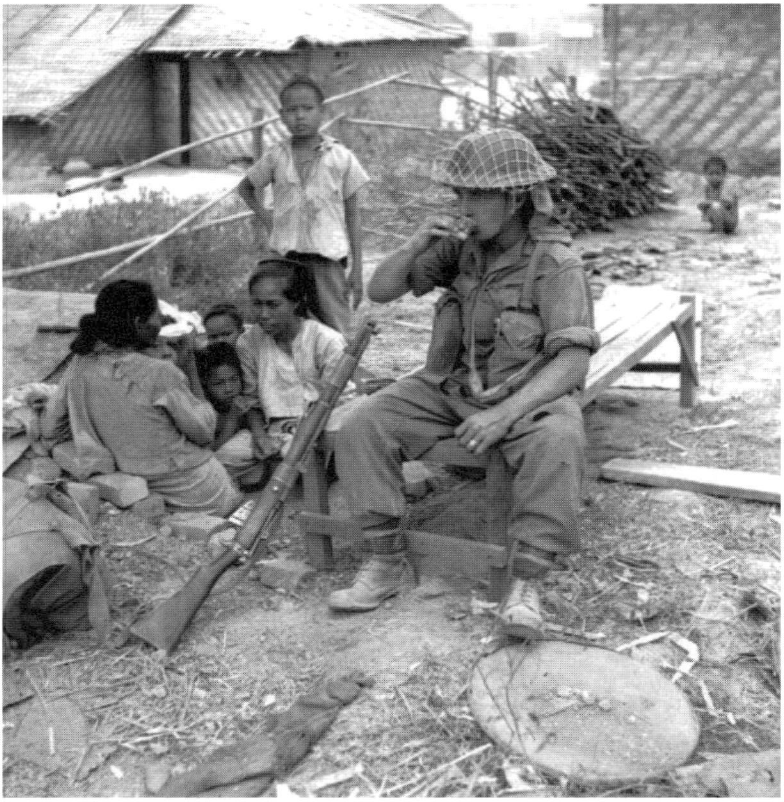

Left: The XIV Army campaign in Central Burma in the spring of 1945 was dependent on air support – the British needed 7,000 sorties by transport aircraft every day for logistical support – and there were times when the USAAF side of the equation proved tricky. In the end, it didn't matter and XIV Army achieved its objectives, partly by converting some infantry units (Indian 5th and 17th Divisions) to mechanized and some to air-portable. Operation Extended Capital destroyed the Japanese and first Meiktila and then Rangoon fell. This photograph is in Meiktila in March 1945.

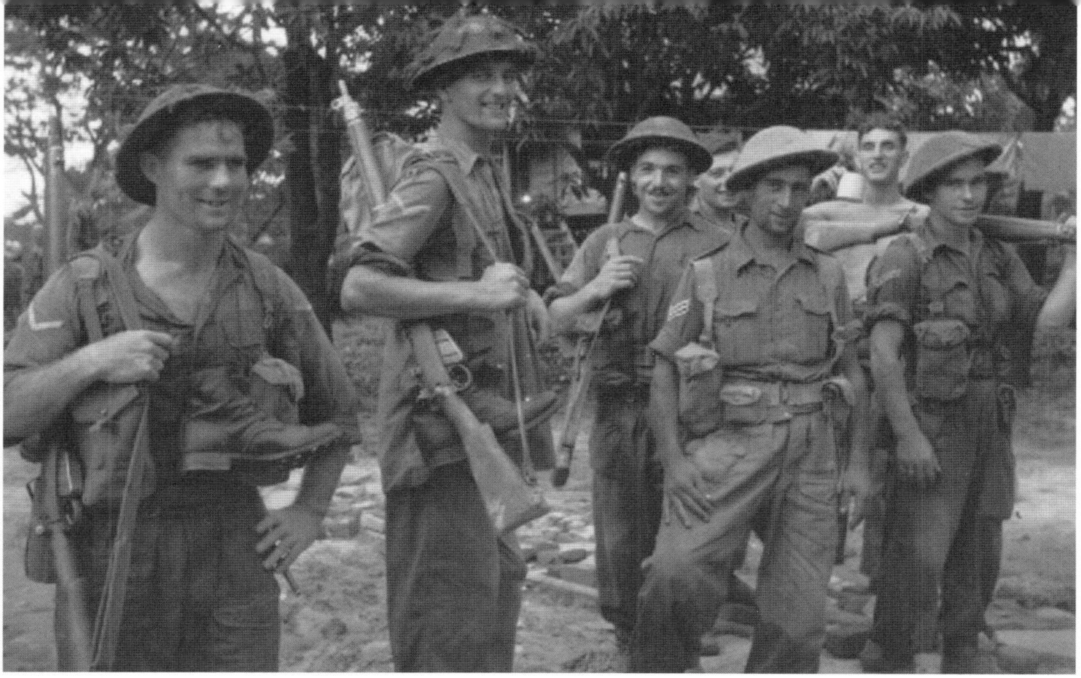

Above: British troops in 1937 webbing and JG in the Sittang Bend area, 1 August 1945. An overwhelming British victory, Japanese Thirty-third Army attempted to break out and join other retreating Japanese formations. They lost 14,000 men, over half dead, for a loss to the British forces of only 95 killed and 322 wounded.

Below: Over 250,000 Gurkhas served in 40 battalions with British and Indian forces during World War II. The Gurkha brigade fought effectively in Burma as they did in every theatre – they won over 2,700 gallantry awards. This early war photo shows 9th Gurkhas training in Malaya in 1941.

herringbone twill (HBT) material used by the Army. The jacket had a single chest pocket on the left and a single skirt pocket on the right and there were two patch pockets on each side of the loose fitting trousers which were closed with pressure snaps instead of buttons. Camouflaged helmet covers were made from the same HBT material.

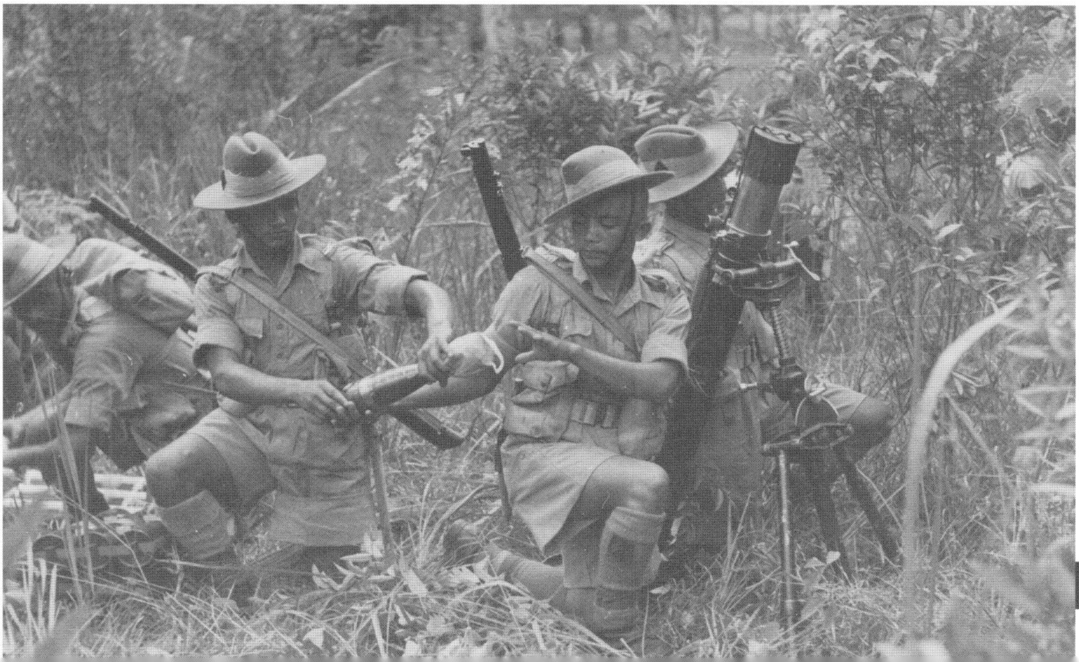

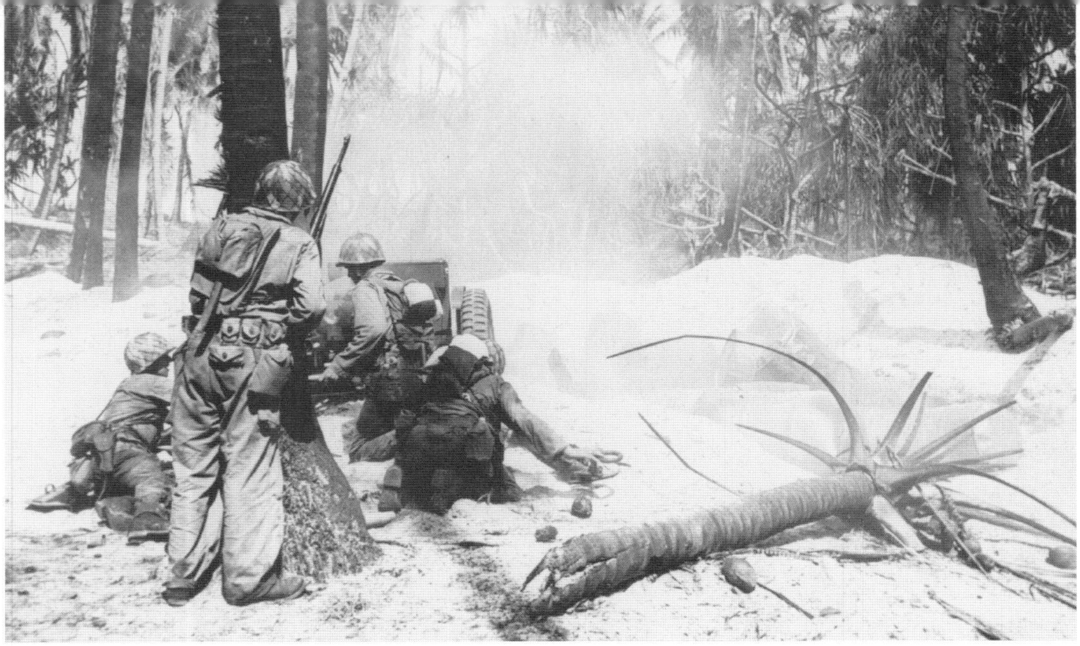

Above: Men of US 7th Infantry Division attack a Japanese pillbox on Kwajalein Atoll on 31 January 1944. Note the standing man's belt with ammo pouches for his M1 rifle, the water bottle and hanging First Aid pouch containing a field dressing and sulfa powder.

Below: Marine Sgt John Wisbur Bartlett Sr fires his Thompson SMG during the Battle of Okinawa. The man next to him carries a BAR. Note Bartlett's canvas leggings into which the dungaree trouser legs have been bloused, and the camouflaged helmet covers both men are using.

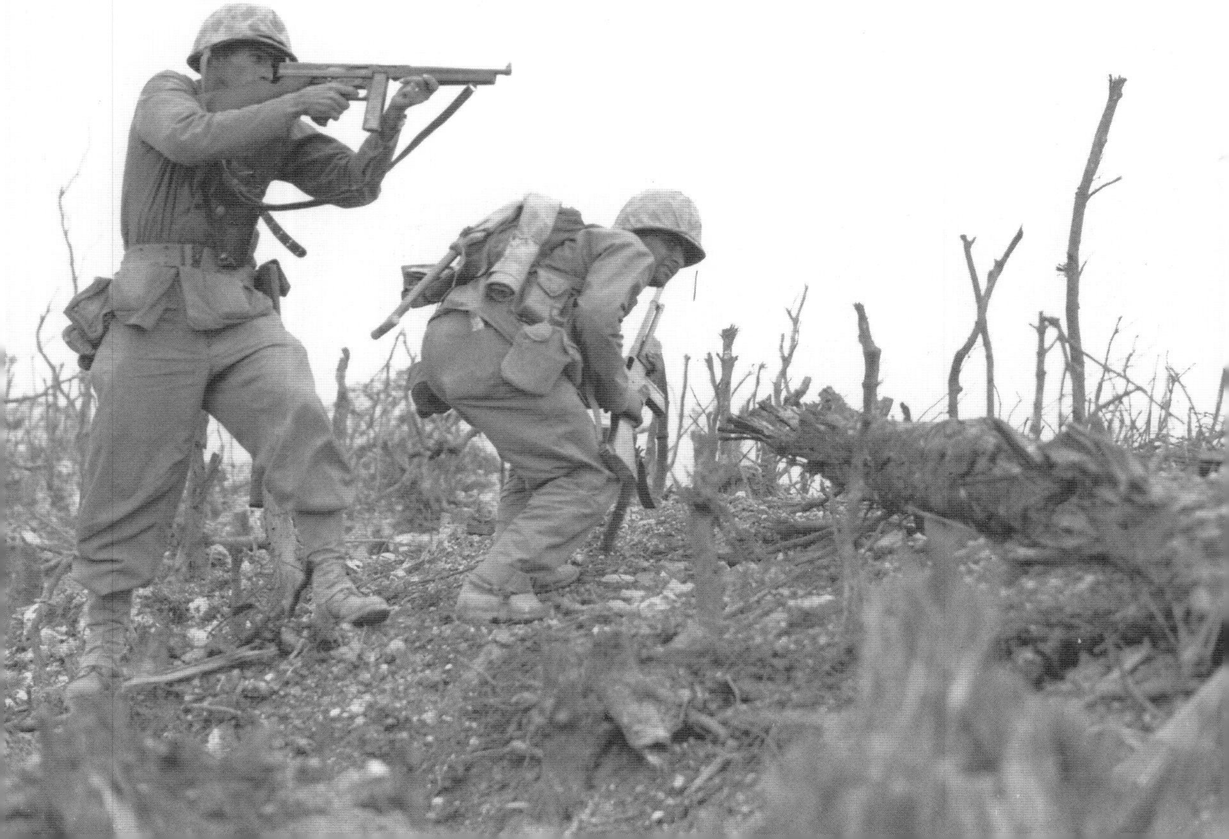

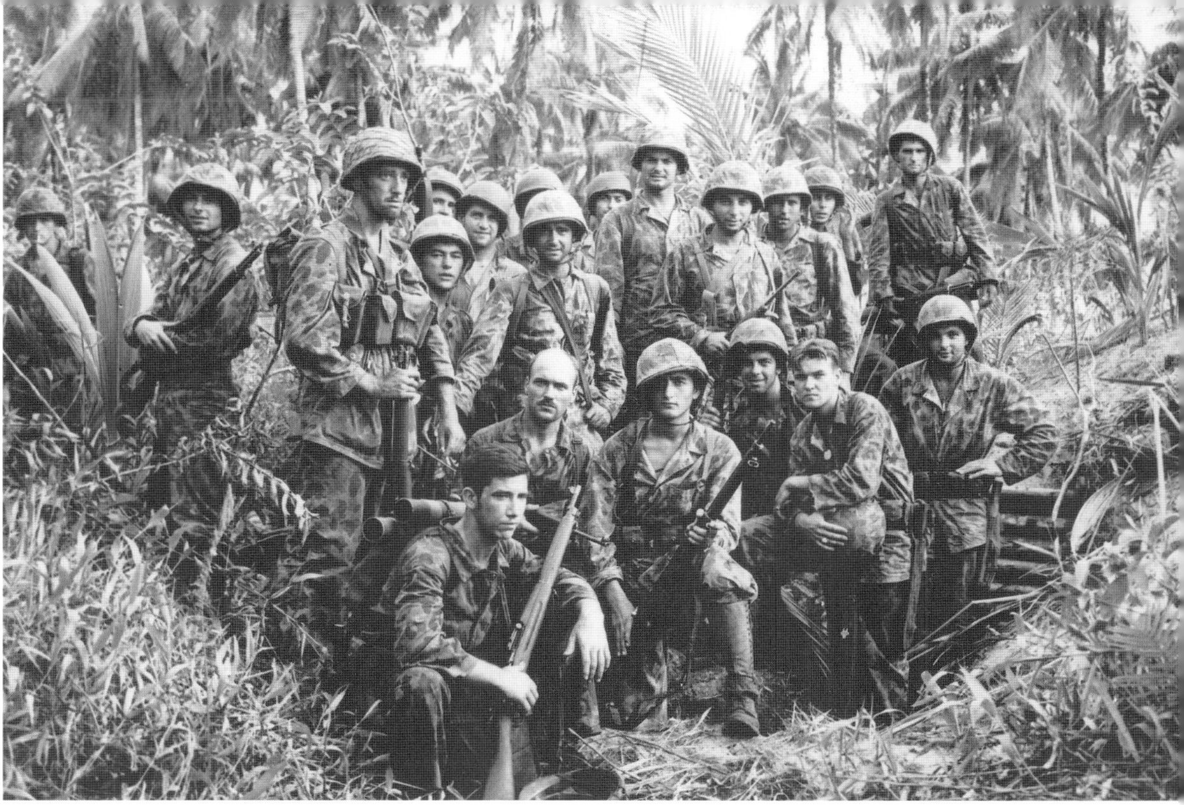

Above: Four Marine Raider battalions served operationally during the war. This is the 2nd Battalion – 'Carlson's Raiders' – seen in front of a Japanese pillbox on Bougainville. Note both Springfields and Garands carried, the tubular rifle grenade containers on the back of the man in the foreground and the machetes.

Below: Making sure they keep their weapons dry, the first wave of US troops wade a stream on 9 January 1945. Kamikaze aircraft couldn't halt the assault by Sixth US Army. Over 200,000 Japanese and well over 100,000 civilians died in the ensuing battles.

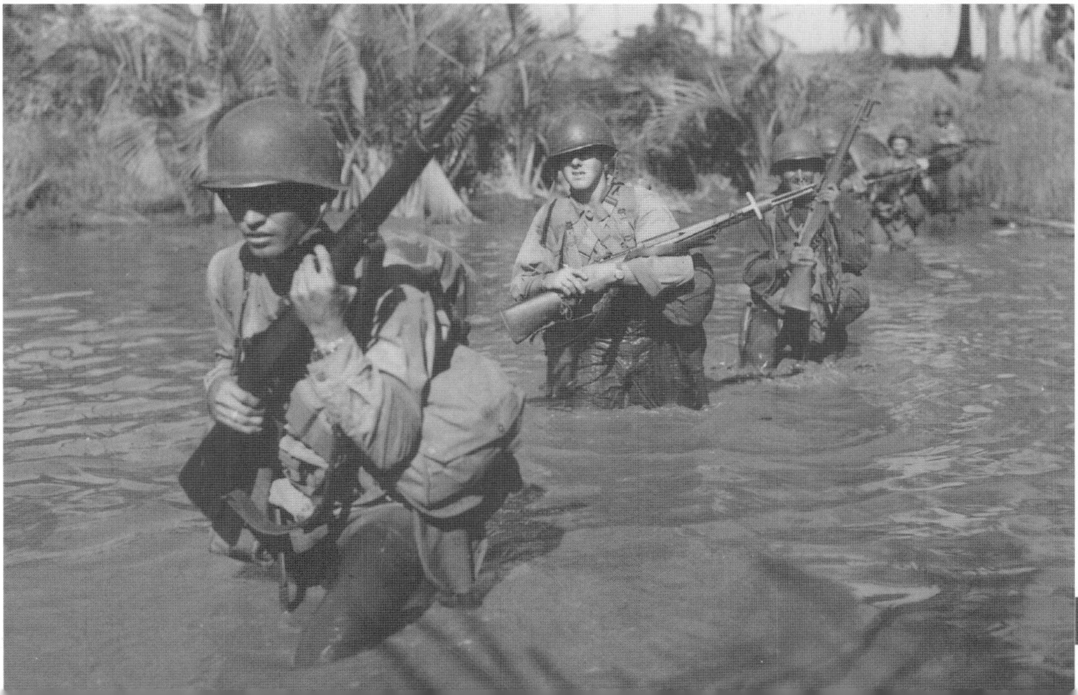

Above: Canadian troops arrive in Hong Kong. There were nearly 2,000 Canadians in the garrison when it fell to the Japanese in December 1941.

Above: The Japanese rolled up the British and Commonwealth troops in Malaya and Burma but were held by Slim's XIV Army, seen crossing the Irrawaddy at Katha, 18 January 1945.

NOTES ON OPERATIONS IN MALAYA

(Tactical & Technical Trends No 15 of 31 December 1942)

'One of the reasons for our failure in the Malayan Campaign was that, we were mentally and physically surprised by actual conditions of jungle fighting.' After arriving at this conclusion, British GHQ India issued a long report containing an analysis of the difficulties faced by the British troops in Malaya, suggestions for overcoming them in future campaigns, and, finally, suggestions for specialized training of troops to fight in the jungle.

In this campaign, as in others, bombs and machine-gun fire from enemy aircraft had an unduly detrimental effect on the morale of the troops unless they were allowed to engage them with small-arms fire. The material effect of such firing is relatively unimportant compared with the morale effect, which is enormous.

The jungle growth in Malaya falls into two categories: primary jungle, which is natural vegetation that has not been touched; and secondary jungle, which consists of terrain cleared of primary jungle but subsequently overgrown by very dense underbrush. In the first type, visibility is usually from 20 to 30 yards, and on the tops of hills the foliage is quite thin. Travel through this type of vegetation is not too difficult and requires only a small amount of cutting. Secondary jungle, on the other hand, requires heavy labor to cut through the ferns and brambles; it is found on the sides of roads and the banks of rivers, often giving the impression that the primary jungle beyond it is also impassable.

In Malaya, as in nearly all jungle country, there are a small number of open areas, in this case, the tin mines. However, little use could be made of the effective fields of fire, since these areas were nearly always outflanked.

The British comments emphasize a striking similarity between jungle warfare and night operations, in that both favor the offensive. The extremely limited visibility, the small fields of fire, and the impossibility of securing effective artillery support all hinder the defenders and favor the attackers.

a. Difficulties of Jungle Warfare

One of the most significant features of jungle fighting was found to be the unusual amount of fatigue which troops felt in this type of warfare. Called upon to march long distances without the aid of their motor transport, often isolated from supplies and support, and subjected to the enervating climate and difficult terrain of the jungle, soldiers were much more susceptible to fatigue than usual.

Morale, too, was affected by conditions not encountered in normal types of warfare. Tactical situations often appeared much worse than they were, since control of subordinate units was frequently lost in the dense jungle where communications presented unusual difficulties. It was found that rumors were even more prevalent than usual among groups of soldiers, and this, also, was at least partially due to difficulties with communications. The British believe that greater efforts must be made to maintain communications, not only for command purposes but also to support morale, by keeping all the small groups informed of the local, and so far as possible, the general situation.

b. Japanese Offensive Tactics

The Japanese invariably advanced on as broad a front as possible, making use of all available communications (roads, railways, rivers, and the sea) as well as sending their infantry through the jungle. In attacking, they would nearly always undertake to contain the forward defenses and then make an envelopment. The British stated that nearly every time that light holding attacks were made against their forward positions, they could be sure of an impending encirclement. It was also noted, however, that when the British flanks were effectively secured, the Japanese did not hesitate to make a frontal attack aimed at infiltration and penetration. Such tactics obviously emphasize the necessity for allotting the minimum number of troops to the strategic defense of vital areas and retaining the maximum number for counterattack. They also emphasize the vital necessity of maintaining control of these reserves through proper communications.

It is interesting to note that the Japanese ordinarily launch two encircling attacks in depth, the first to a depth of 1,000 yards, and the second to a depth of about 5 miles. These figures apply to a Japanese regiment. Ordinarily, when contact was made at about 0800, the first encircling attack came almost immediately and the second sometime in the early afternoon. The first, shallow attack was not considered dangerous by the British and in some actions the Japanese omitted this preliminary and concentrated on the larger encirclement. During these attacks, the Japanese employed a holding detachment against the British front lines.

c. Artillery

The jungle did much to limit the effectiveness of artillery, but where it could be employed it caused the Japanese a great deal of trouble. Captured reports nearly always referred to British artillery in terms of the greatest respect. The best type of artillery fire was found to be a rolling barrage laid astride a road on a front of 300 to 400 yards.

d. Tanks

Since the few tanks that were used were confined to the roads, the problems of antitank units were greatly reduced. Often as many as 30 to 50 tanks participated in one attack, but they were usually easily ambushed. Although the fronts were not vulnerable to the 2-pounder, they could nearly always be knocked out by a hit on the side or the rear.

e. Communications

Individual runners were the most satisfactory. Visual signal devices were practically useless, and there was seldom time or material to lay wire. Some use was made, however, of civilian communication facilities. When this was done, the exchanges had to be carefully guarded and supervised by military personnel, since the local operators could not be depended upon. In the few cases where wire was laid, it functioned satisfactorily, and was not so vulnerable to enemy bombing and artillery fire as it would have been in more open terrain. The range of radio was greatly reduced by the jungle, and it seldom worked at night. Small walkie-talkies were the most valuable form of radio and lent themselves particularly well to the operations of small groups. Code was almost never used below division headquarters, for runners took less time than coding and decoding.

f. Personnel Vehicles

Tracked carriers and armored cars were effectively used where the road net was satisfactory. The carriers, however, in addition to being vulnerable to armor-piercing ammunition, were also inviting targets for grenades dropped from trees, a favorite Japanese trick. Wire netting over the tops of carriers would have been an effective method of neutralizing this danger. The light machine gun on the carriers had the advantage of height and was almost never removed and used on the ground. The armored car, although even more road-bound than the tracked carrier, had the advantage of operating silently and could, therefore, be used in mobile surprise attacks. It also had heavier and better armor, making it less vulnerable than the carrier. In the withdrawal these armored cars were usually the last to go, for they were particularly suited for ambushing the enemy.

g. British Suggestions for Offensive Tactics

In jungle warfare the advantages accruing to the attackers are so great that the British believe the careful working out of a tactical plan should be subordinated to seizing and maintaining the initiative. This does not mean that thorough grounding in tactics and techniques of small groups, and of the individual soldier should be minimized, but rather that 'the essence of the encounter battle (meeting engagement) is that it must be fought automatically by all officers and men according to a battle procedure...constantly practiced and applied to all types of ground.'

As a result of these observations this report suggested the following tactics to British troops:

The success of the encircling attack lies in its speed. To attempt this, highly trained jungle troops, capable of quick cross-country movement and well-trained in map reading, are employed to seize a part of the road from the enemy. This initial seizure is simply to establish control before the beginning of the main attack, which will be made against the rear of the enemy defenses. This main attacking force may be divided into three detachments: (a) the initial striking force which secures a strip of road (not more than 400 to 600 yards should be necessary for a battalion attack); (b) a second force which attacks the enemy's rear immediately upon seizure of the road; (c) a reserve which may be used either to exploit the action of the second force or to relieve the first if the latter has lost too heavily in its initial encounter.

The success of such an attack is dependent primarily upon supplies and speed, for there can rarely be assistance from supporting arms. Consequently, the point selected for the attack in the enemy's rear should provide good cover for the unsupported infantry.

In the jungle the frontal attack is normally made on a narrow front, astride a road. It is designed to exploit the fact that all control is concentrated along the road, and is executed with a relatively narrow artillery barrage, usually extending about 200 yards on either side of the road. One of its advantages is that it allows for greater use of artillery. The use of tanks will be effective only if the enemy is insufficiently supplied with antitank guns, and if the attacking infantry follows very closely behind the tanks.

To achieve the best results the British believe that this attack should be combined with infiltration on the flanks of the main attack. These infiltrating detachments should be given objectives well to the enemy's rear, such as bridges or ammunition dumps.

h. Defensive Tactics

The defense, as stated, is inevitably hampered in jungle warfare. In the face of greatly superior enemy forces, when it is not possible to seize the initiative at once, the object must be a system of defense which will kill the maximum number of the enemy, but above all which will maintain the defending forces as a unit Only by maintaining control is there any hope of reducing the enemy's numbers to the point where a counterattack can be launched. The static defense is as worthless in the jungle as in the desert, and the British now believe, for example, that the only way to hold a position for a prearranged number of days is to meet the enemy sufficiently far forward so that the delaying actions will last for the number of days desired. To apply these tactics requires troops of the highest caliber, for their morale will inevitably suffer in a series of even short withdrawals, and the tendency will be for smaller units to withdraw before they are ordered to do so.

Since control of the roads is the objective of both the forces, defense must take the form of a series of zones of resistance located in depth down the road. In successful defensive actions in Malaya, battalion depth was about 2 miles and regimental depth up to 6 miles. Above all, the enemy must not be allowed to get completely in the rear of the defensive positions. Company defense areas are about 300 yards in diameter; and within platoons, squad defense areas should be about 100 yards apart. Squads themselves are usually dispersed in two or three groups, 30 yards from one another.

In order to conduct a defense successfully, normal Japanese tactics must be studied. The Japanese usually make initial contact on a road, with the objective of finding and containing the front line troops, as a preliminary to encirclement Since this initial contact is made with considerable speed and at the expense of ordinary security measures, their leading formations are particularly vulnerable to ambush. A normal Japanese leading detachment would consist principally of a group of four or five bicyclists, followed at several hundred yards by another group of 60 or more bicyclists. After the forward group is allowed to pass, a successfully camouflaged ambush should be able to wipe out the large group following. Another type of ambush for these forward Japanese troops might consist of placing fairly strong, well-camouflaged forces on the flanks of a road, some distance in front of the other friendly positions. The Japanese are allowed to make contact, and to bring up their troops for the holding attack and subsequent encirclement; they may then be struck from the rear by the forward troops on the flank.

i. Counterattacks

The Malaya fighting indicated that in the jungle immediate rather than deliberate counterattacks were required. Counterattacks were invariably unsuccessful when ordered by higher command since the situation had nearly always changed, usually for the worse, by the time the attack was launched. On the other hand, immediate counterattacks by reserves of forward units were nearly always successful. One general type of counterattack proposed for the future is as follows:

When the enemy makes contact, the leading defending battalion immediately withdraws. The enemy is then allowed to push forward to a bridge, village, or other vital feature. At this point a surprise frontal attack is made. This method has the advantage of not breaking up the main body to place counterattacking units on a flank.

j. Patrols

The British believe that in the jungle, fighting patrols, rather than mere observation patrols are always desirable. Patrols should aim to kill as many of the enemy as possible, giving information to their commander by 'reporting by fire.' This is based on the belief that events move so quickly in the jungle that a patrol which waits to report enemy movements on its return will invariably be giving stale and incorrect information. Patrols should also be considered as one of the best means of locating and disorganizing enemy encirclements during the approach march. Finally, the British believed that only small patrols can achieve the requisite mobility, and they recommend a patrol of one leader and two others.

Fighting in the Snow

The German military was not prepared for the pitiless Russian winter. They were expecting a quick victory following the invasion of the USSR in June 1941. This failed, with the advances stalled around the outskirts of Moscow by October 1941. With the loss of two-thirds of their motorised transport there were serious logistical problems getting supplies to the various fronts; one being the supply of warm clothing. Combat in the depths of the Russian winter was brutal, with temperatures falling to -30 or even -40°C, freezing German armour and equipment but, most of all, the soldiers, who had not been properly equipped to fight a winter campaign. Instead they had to wear every item of clothing in as many layers as they could with added coats, blankets and improvised coverings in an attempt to cope. Soviet kit was prized when they could capture it or loot it from prisoners and corpses. Meanwhile, in the hiatus caused by the cold during the first winter outside Moscow in 1941, fresh Russian divisions came from the Ural Mountains – snow specialists, used to operating in freezing conditions. For the Red Army frostbite was a punishable offence, as proper winter equipment was officially issued. This consisted of long woollen underpants and vest, a thickly quilted woollen jacket and trousers – *telogreikas* ('bodywarmers' with the slang name of *vatniks*) – a *Ushanka* faux fur cap with ear flaps, fur-lined mittens with trigger finger slits and Valenki boots made from layers of beaten felt soled in leather or worn with galoshes. There was also a short mid-thigh length suede leather sheepskin and fur-lined coat – the *Polushubok* – worn by officers. It was warmer than a trenchcoat but not as bulky as the *vatnik*.

The German *Taschenbuch der Winterkrieg* (Winter Warfare Manual) was published on 5 August 1942 and was based on the experiences of the first two winters of the war in Russia. Essentially, it looks at the two vital problems of winter warfare: mobility and shelter. The handbook emphasizes the importance of the systematic preparation and disposition of forces for combat, the need to cut roads and trails and light mobile patrols (if possible, on skis), suggesting that experience has shown that a circular trail around billets and bivouacs is the most effective security measure [**Left**].

Reconnaissance patrol operating in direction of enemy
Inner security track
Track for messengers
Outer security track

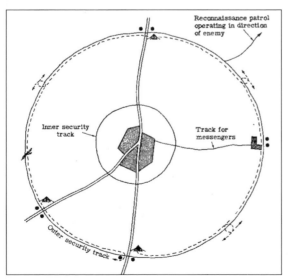

The problem in Russia was that the settlements were few and far between, and often useless anyway for the quartering of troops.

'The dearth of settlements and combat requirements frequently make it necessary to be completely independent of permanent billets. On the other hand, frequent bivouacking may impair the combat efficiency of the unit.

Especially careful security measures are required when in bivouac. The site of a bivouac should be camouflaged as much as possible, and should be difficult to approach by the enemy. Nearness to protecting sectors is therefore generally advisable. In addition to aggressive reconnaissance and security measures, the construction of field fortifications (and, above all, of obstacles) guarantees the safety and unmolested quartering of the unit. Small units, especially patrols, can best provide security for themselves in terrain which cannot be reconnoitered easily.

'Sentries must be well camouflaged to avoid revealing the bivouac. Low temperatures or biting wind will make it necessary to relieve them frequently, but care must be taken to maintain continuity of observation and to prevent the enemy from drawing definite conclusions concerning the posting of security forces. Weapons and skis must be kept within easy reach.

'Aside from tactical requirements, the selection of the bivouac site must depend on protection against dampness, wind, and cold; and nearness to a supply of wood and lumber is desirable. Low ground, depressions, and valleys usually have lower temperatures than their surroundings. Snowdrifts around hollows and accumulations on the lee side of elevations may be used in the construction of snow caves. Areas free of snow are exposed to the wind and are not suitable for bivouacs. Wooded areas are warmer than open fields and conceal the glow of fires. Fir trees which are not too high, with branches that extend down to the snow, afford good shelter possibilities for smaller units which are heavily snowed in. Work on the bivouac must begin immediately after the halt so that the men may stay warm. Extra time spent on construction shortens the time available for rest but ensures greater relaxation and warmth later.'

It looks cold and all they've got are scarves, caps and overcoats. Care of weapons in the cold was essential: 'When firing, do not permit the hot parts of the weapons to come in contact with snow. When changing hot barrels, do not lay them in the snow, or they will warp. Take care that neither snow nor water enters the muzzle or bolt; otherwise the barrel may swell or burst while firing'.

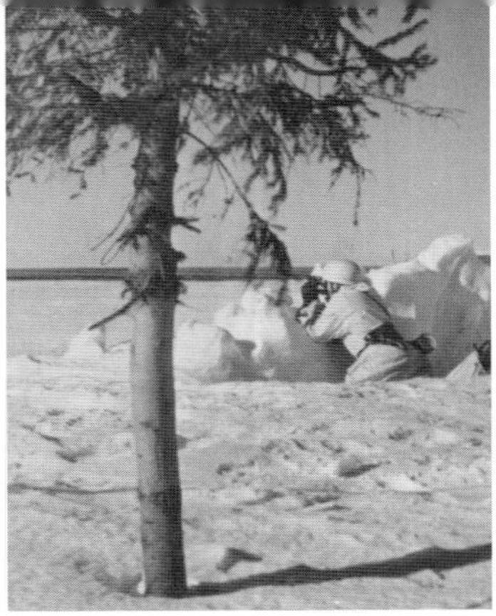
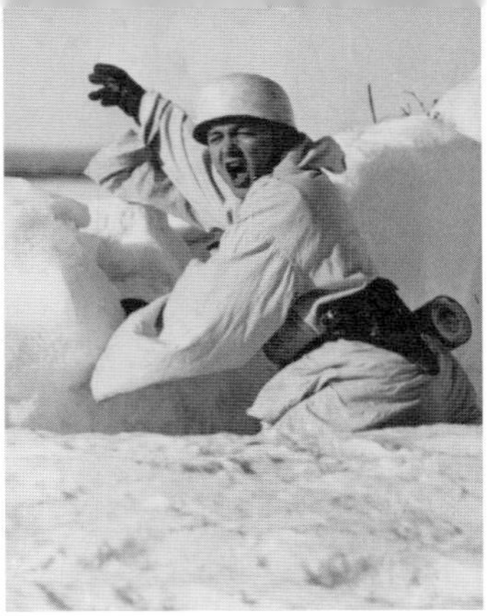
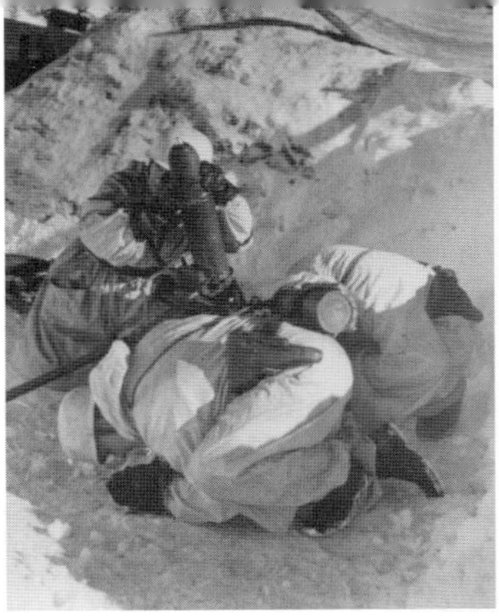
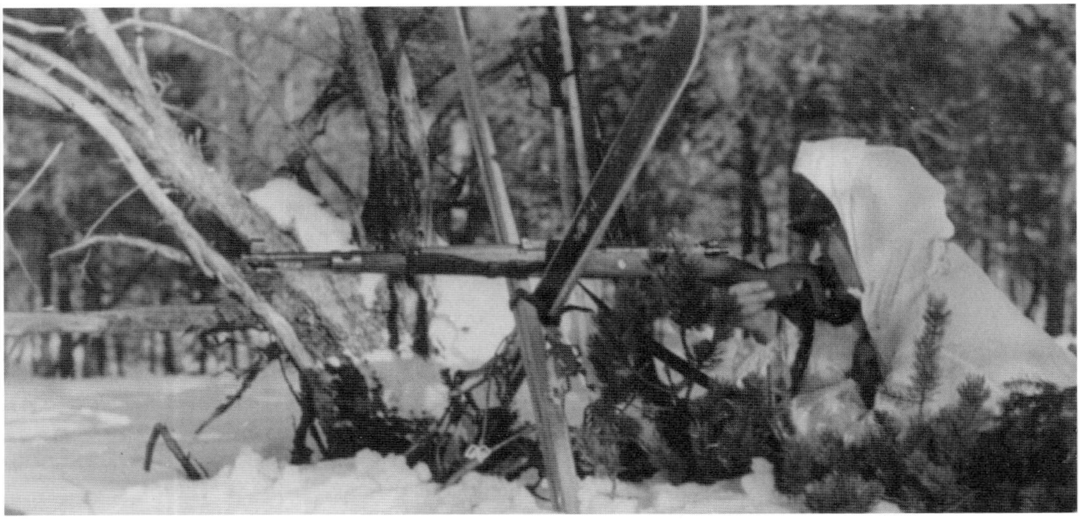

Top: Snow-camouflaged mortar team. Note Fallschirmjäger helmets.

Above: Using skis as a bipod – this German sharpshooter is seen in the far north near Kandalaksha.

Right: Artwork by Franz Renk showing a field-made sheepskin coat as often worn on the Eastern Front. The Russian December 1941 winter counteroffensive started with the temperature -26°C and the snow was more than a metre deep. Three days later one of Second Panzer Army's corps had suffered 1,500 frostbite cases, 350 requiring amputations and a 'serious crisis in confidence had broken out among the troops and the NCOs.' (Glantz 2001.)

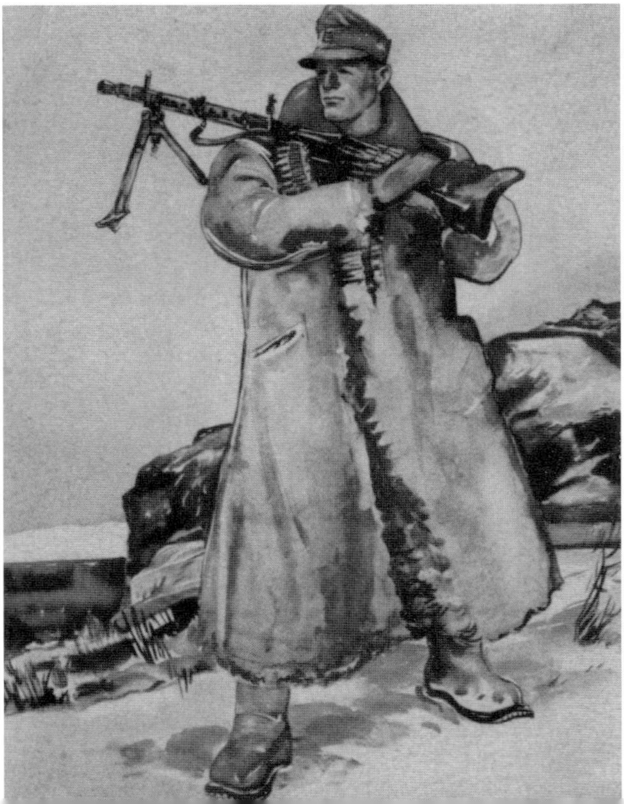

The ill-equipped German troops suffered huge numbers of casualties to frostbite – making captured Russian clothing and footwear a valuable commodity. If none were around then anything available was used to insulate clothing and footwear. The standard German leather marching boots were useless as they conducted cold directly to the feet.

The *Winter Warfare Manual* says this about winter clothes:

'A prerequisite for sufficient protection against the cold is the correct fitting of all clothing. Tight clothes impede the circulation of the blood, which might lead to frostbite.

'The field cap (Feldmütze) should be large enough to be worn over the knitted woollen muffler, and its flap should cover the back of the head and ears. The field blouse (Feldbluse) should be roomy enough to wear over the sweater and twill jacket. Motorcyclists and motorcycle riflemen must be able to wear a knitted woollen sweater in addition to sweater 36 [an issue garment]. If a man wears the knitted turtle-neck sweater, the collar of the field blouse must be wide enough so that the turtle-neck will fit between the neck and the detachable collar band. Sleeve-straps should be buttoned. Field jackets must be long enough to protect the waist and kidneys. Riding breeches should not stop blood circulation in the calf, and they must allow the knees sufficient freedom of movement.

'The pleat in the back of the regulation overcoat must be worn open, otherwise the coat will be too tight to afford protection against the cold. Overcoats for mounted men should be long. surcoats and protective topcoats, which are designed to be worn over the regulation overcoat, should be long and roomy.

'Sweater 36 and the knitted woollen sweater should cover the waist and the kidneys. The sleeves should be long enough to keep the wrists warm. In extremely cold weather the steel helmet should be worn over the field cap and the knitted woollen cap. The ears must not come in contact with the metal of the helmet. Footgear should be large enough to permit the toes to move freely when, in addition to inner soles, two pairs of socks or one pair of socks and one pair of foot cloths [**Below**] are worn. [The Russians used them too, *portyanki*.]

'An especially effective measure for protecting the feet is to wear paper between two pairs

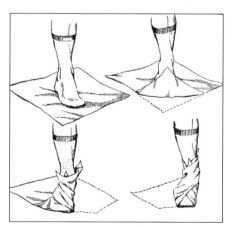

of socks, and another layer of paper or foot cloths over the top pair of socks. All wrinkles must be smoothed out. If ski boots are worn, a piece of cloth should be sewed over the heels of the socks in order to prevent wear at that point.

'Boot leather can be kept from freezing by covering the shoes or boots with the foot of a sock or a casing made of fur or similar material.

'Clean underwear will keep the soldier warmer than underwear which has been worn for a long time. Therefore, all laundry facilities should be used. Special protective measures for the genitals should be taken *if the weather is very cold or the wind very strong. . . .*

'Use the natives to manufacture straw shoes. Motorcyclists should put layers of newspaper between the shirt and sweater to protect the chest from the wind. Wrap several layers of newspaper around the knees as protection against the cold, inserting them between the drawers and the outer knee-length stockings.

'The sleeve straps of the field blouse should be buttoned or tied, and gloves should be drawn over the sleeves. Put paper, hay, or straw loosely in boot tops. . . .

'Even during a temporary halt the troops should take time out to mend and clean their clothes. Particular attention should be devoted to drying wet clothes and, above all, footgear. Do not let boots or shoes dry near a fire or burning stove.'

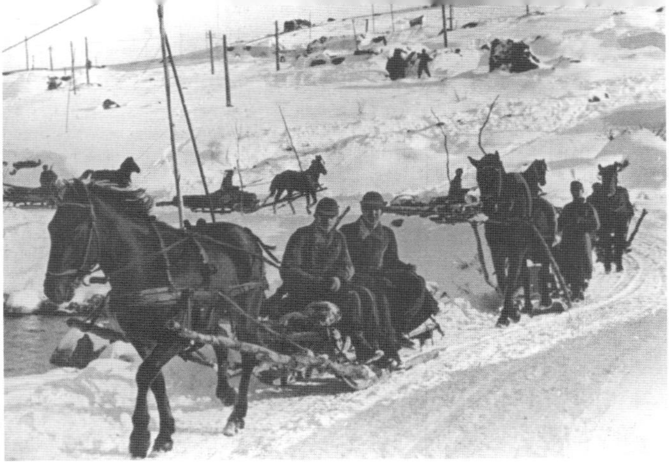

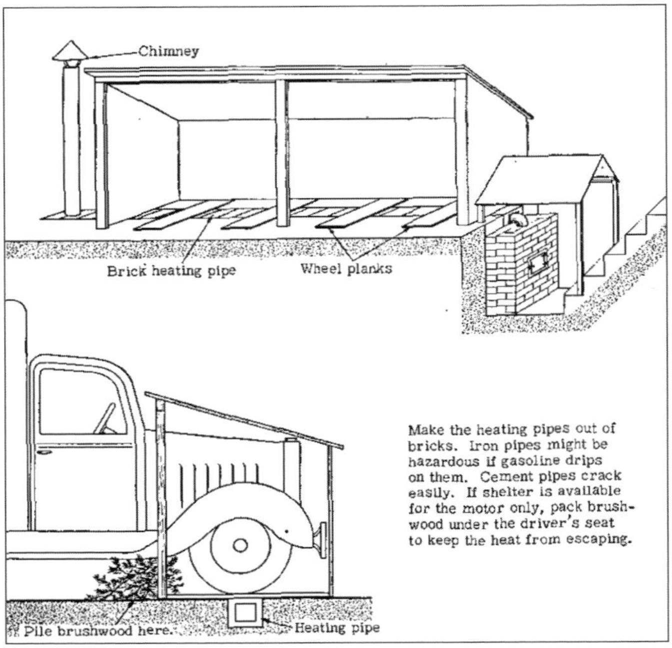
Chimney
Brick heating pipe
Wheel planks
Pile brushwood here.
Heating pipe

Make the heating pipes out of bricks. Iron pipes might be hazardous if gasoline drips on them. Cement pipes crack easily. If shelter is available for the motor only, pack brushwood under the driver's seat to keep the heat from escaping.

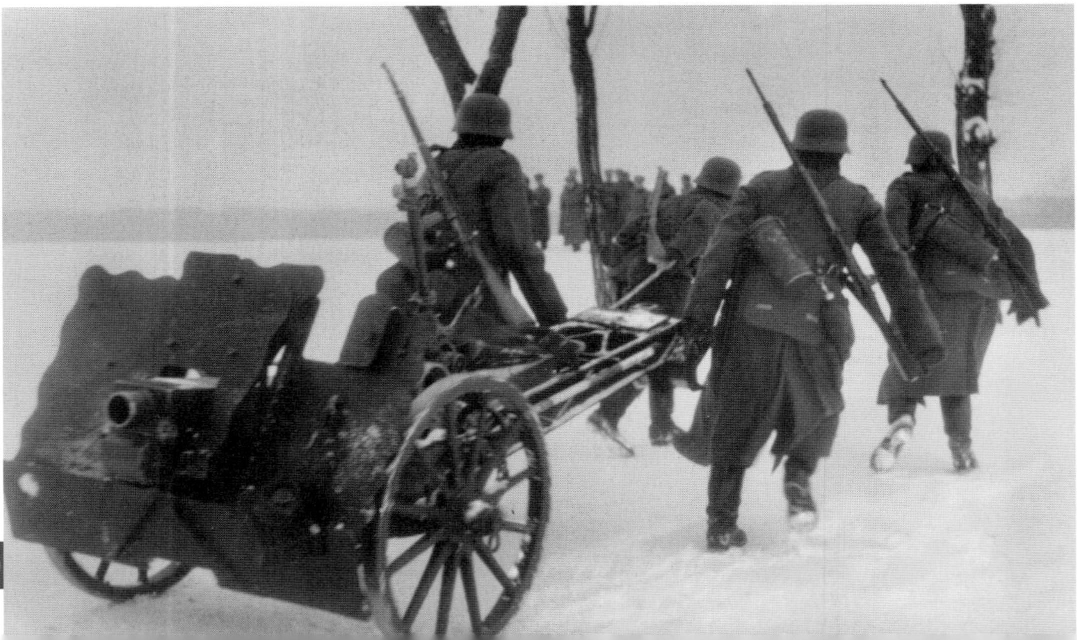

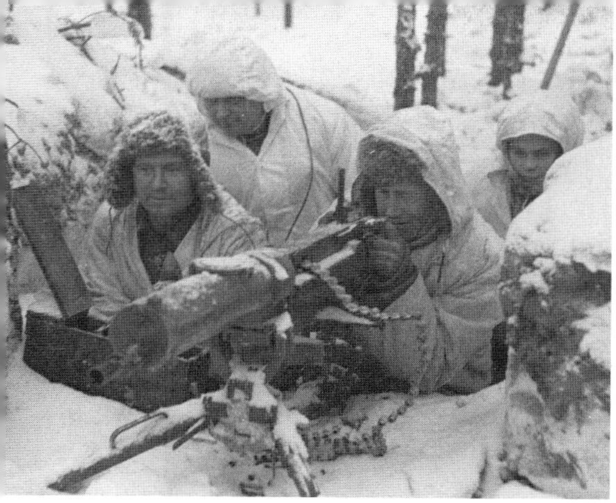

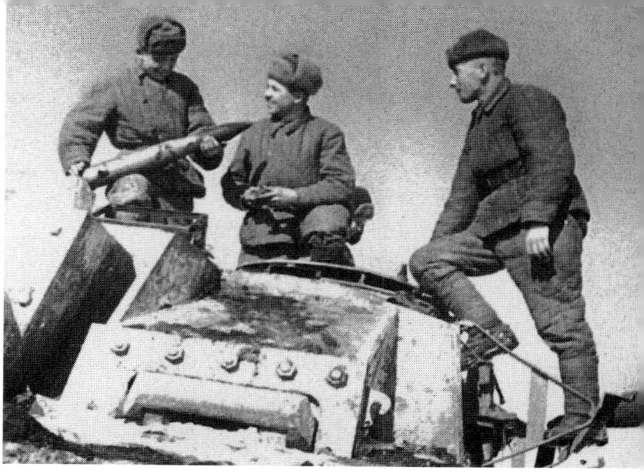

Opposite: Transport problems in the snow. Glantz mentions, 'Troops could not tow the guns out of their emplacements. The motors of some vehicles would not start; the grease on the bearing and in transmissions in others froze while they were running.' Vehicles and guns had to be abandoned, supplies were running short, and, all the while, Red Army ski battalions harassed the Germans. The German Winter Warfare manual has a section on hand sledges, akjas (see p.105) and horse-drawn sledges (**Above**) which are used to cut trails as well as transport men and materiel. Keeping engines turning over or warm enough to start when required (**Centre**) was a problem. In the end, much of the infantry equipment was hauled by hand (**Below**).

Above left: The Finns were masters of the terrain and the weather, and had tactics to cope with both. Initially in 1939, they were able to combat the Russian strength in numbers. Russian capabilities improved markedly when specialists were brought from Siberia in late 1941. Here, a Finnish Maxim machine gun team on exercise.

Above right: Russian cold weather gear included *telogreika* and *vatnie sharovari* (padded jacket and trousers) and *valenki* compressed felt boots. These soldiers of the 3rd Ukrainian Front are on a captured StuG III Ausf G.

Below: 'The possibilities for employment of ski troops depend to a high degree on their state of training. The ski unit must be specially trained before it may be committed. The more advanced the training, the harder may be the tasks assigned to the unit.

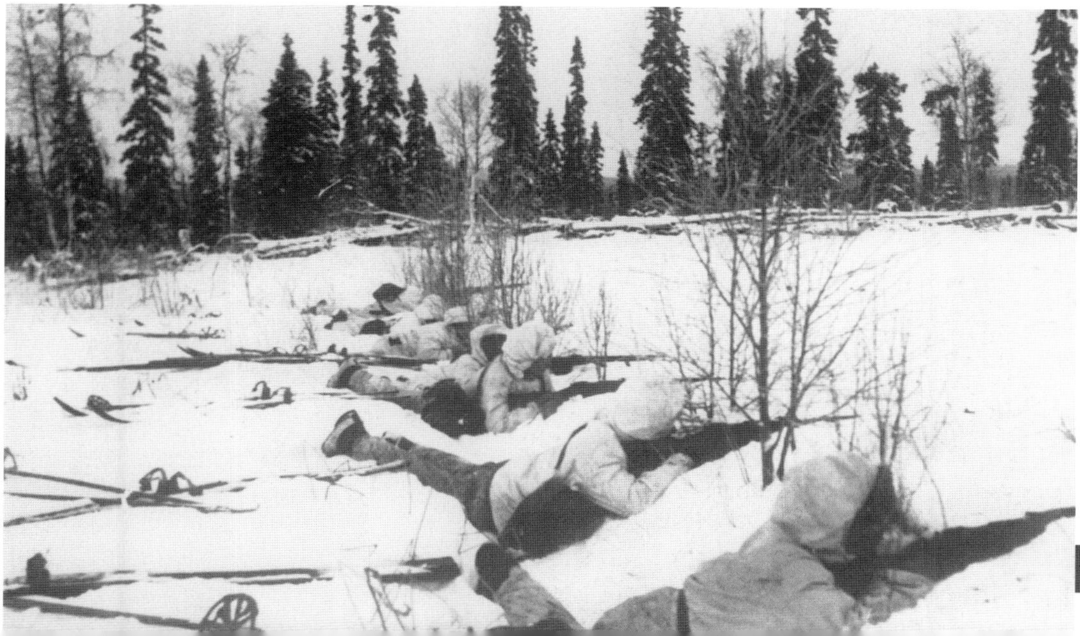

The Destruction of the Soviet 44th Motorized Rifle Division

(This section is based closely on and quotes from Dr Allen F. Chew (1981))

On 30 November 1939 the Red Army invaded Finland. In spite of tactical surprise and huge superiority in men, artillery and armor, Soviet forces suffered severe reverses. As Dr Alan Chew argues, 'the Finns were prepared for combat in snow at subzero temperatures; the invaders were not. It was almost that simple.'

The Red Army commanders anticipated a lengthy struggle and a stubborn defence but Stalin ignored advice and rushed into the invasion without adequate preparation. This miscalculation is dramatically illustrated by the annihilation of the Soviet 44th Motorized Rifle Division in January 1940 by a well-trained and well-equipped, if numerically inferior, force prepared for the environment – dense coniferous forests, few and widely separated roads – and the climate – extreme cold.

The central prong of the Soviet Ninth Army's offensive saw the 163rd Rifle Division capture Suomussalmi on 7 December but, important for the defence, it was delayed as Finnish reinforcements were hurried to the front.

By Christmas the Finnish forces – now organised as the 9th Division – totalled 11,500 men, with three infantry regiments: JR27 (Lt Col Johan Mgkiniemi), JR65 (Lt Col Karl Mandelin) and JR64 (Lt Col Frans Fagernäs). Importantly, the regimental commanders and the division commander, Col Hjalmar Siilasvuo, had fought together in German 27th Jäger Battalion in World War I and in the Finnish civil war of 1918.

On 27 December Colonel Siilasvuo counterattacked, and two days of fierce fighting saw the Russians fleeing in disorder towards the frontier through snow that was at least three feet deep. Temperatures reached -40°F as daylight lasted only about five hours.

Soviet Ninth Army sent 44th Motorized Rifle Division (Kombrig – Brigade Commander – Alexei Vinogradov) as reinforcement along the road from Raate to Suomussalmi. Ukrainians unfamiliar with northern woods, they were spotted by Finnish air reconnaissance (Siilasvuo had one aircraft at hand) from 13 December, and the Finns knew that they had to avoid the two Russian units linking up.

Colonel Siilasvuo had prepared for this eventuality. On 11 December he had set up a roadblock made up of JR27's two infantry companies reinforced by additional mortars and guns. Using initiative and cross-country mobility, JR27 was able to hold up the 44th Division whose vehicles, including about 50 tanks, couldn't move off the road into the pine forest, and whose infantry were similarly restricted because they couldn't use the skis they had.

In contrast, the Finns – experienced skiers – kept the 44th Division under constant surveillance, and were able to harass it night and day all along the 20 miles between the roadblock and the border thanks to the foresight of Col Siilasvuo who had prepared improvised winter roads to facilitate these flank attacks.

On New Year's Eve the destruction of the Soviet division started when the Finns probed around Haukila farm from the south, where it met the largest concentration of the 44th Division – a reinforced regiment and most of the tanks and artillery strongly entrenched in a two-mile area just east of the roadblock.

On 1 January a reconnaissance unit reported the enemy in the Eskola area, about 1.5 miles south of the Raate road. Using the winter road along Lake Pärsämönselkä, first a light battalion was sent to stop the Soviets pushing farther south, and then Task Forces Kari and Fagernäs, skied to positions from which they would later launch coordinated flank attacks. Maj Kaarle Kari's three battalions bivouacked near Mäkelä; Lt Col Fagernäs' two battalions near Heikkilä. Company Lavi continued to Vänkä, just south of Raate.

Camping was possible, in spite of cold, thanks to the Finnish Army tents, easily transported on akhio sledges which could also be used to haul mortars, heavy machine guns, and supplies and to evacuate the wounded. The tents were heated by wood-burning stoves, slept 20 men and using fieldcraft and experience gained from their work as lumberjacks, ensured comfort and safety. On the other side, many of the Russians, whose division had come from Kiev, unused to the climate and with inadequate clothing and equipment, froze to death.

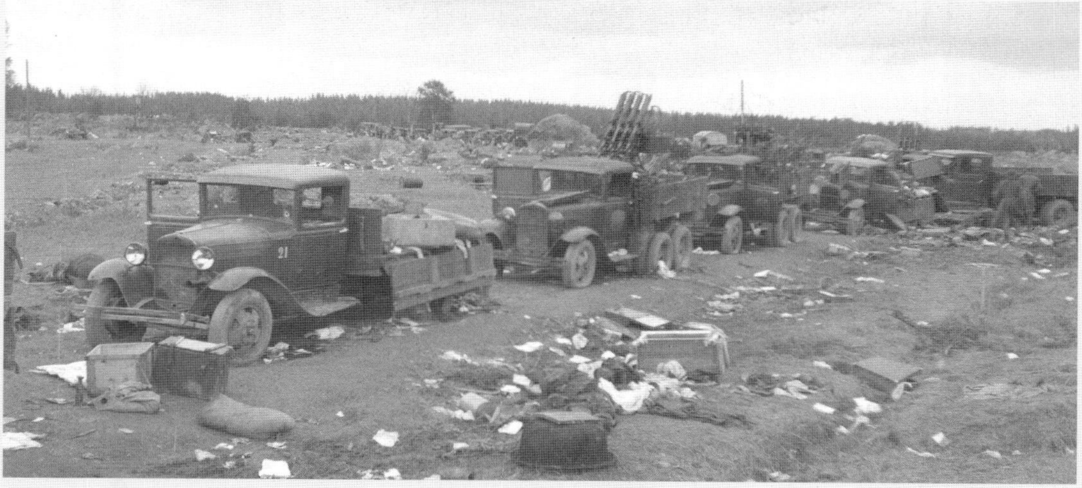

Above: Remains of a Russian column on Porlammi Road seen on 2 September 1941 after a battle that destroyed the Russian 43rd Rifle Division. The Red Army lost 7,000 killed, 1,000 wounded and 9,000 captured, the Finns lost 700 dead.

Below: A Finnish ski patrol armed with Moisin-Nagant M91 rifles and a Suomi KP/-31 SMG.

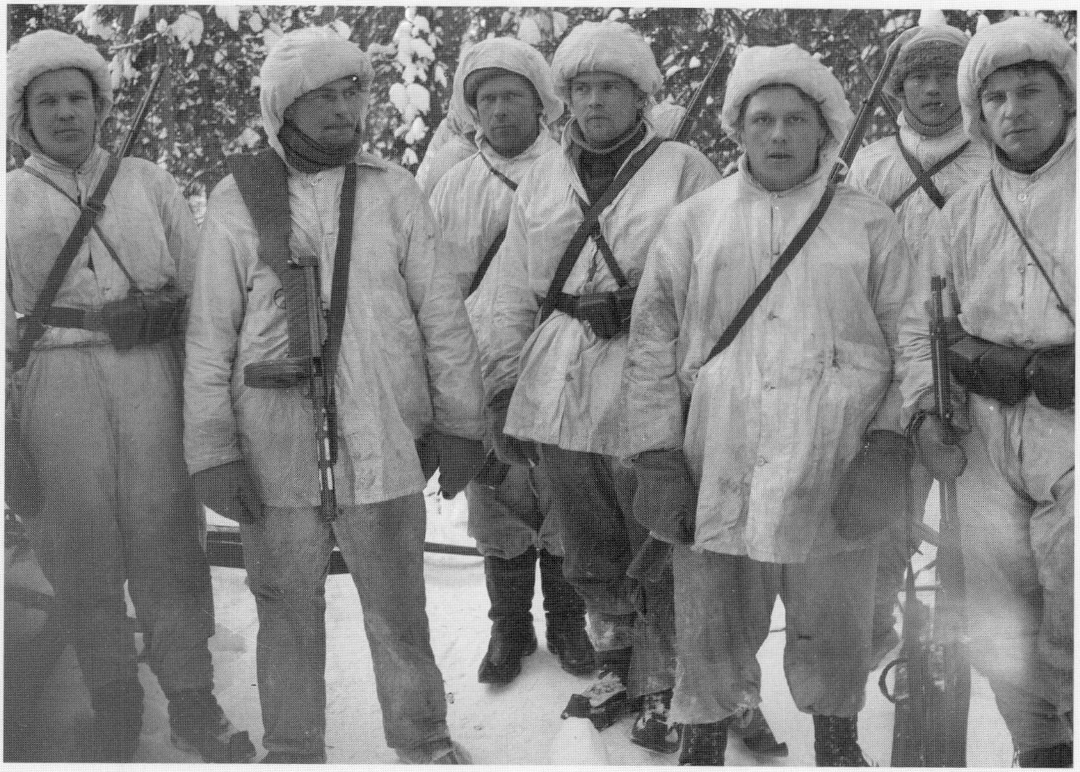

The Russian torment got worse when II/JR27 (Capt Eino Lassila) attacked on the night of 1 January, using skis to travel silently and pulling machine guns and ammunition on sledges. They did more than attack. An attached engineer platoon set up roadblocks by felling trees and mining them. Fortune also favoured them. They hit a section of Soviet artillery rather than infantry and tore them to shreds. As they fought, the Finns extended the winter road up to the battle lines and by 07:00 on 2nd the Finnish attackers had two antitank guns, perfectly timed to negate an armoured counterattack and knock out seven Soviet tanks, whose hulks contributed to the roadblock.

A key advantage the Finns had was in the provision of food and warmth: hot meals, tea, warm tents. The Russians were cold and hungry – more so after the Finns had targeted their field kitchens (all 55 were eventually destroyed or captured).

Between the afternoon of 2 January and the evening of the 6th, the Finns harried the Russians, cutting the road in a number of places and blowing the Purasjoki River bridge near Likoharju.

The decisive battles occurred on 6 January as the 44th Division tried desperately to fight its way out to the east, but was cut into smaller and smaller fragments. Late in the evening Vinogradov authorised a retreat that had been underway in many sectors for hours. This is not to say that the fighting stopped. The Russians were still trying to fight their way through to the east on 7 January, and mopping-up continued for several days, as the Finns hunted down half-frozen stragglers in the woods along the entire length of the Raate road and to the north.

The Finns captured 43 tanks, 70 field guns, 278 trucks, cars, and tractors, some 300 machine guns, 6,060 rifles, 1,170 live horses, and modern communication equipment which was especially prized. A conservative Finnish estimate put the combined Russian losses (the 163rd and 44th Divisions, plus the 3rd NKVD Regiment that tried to effect a rescue) at 22,500 men. Counting killed, wounded, and missing, Finnish losses were approximately 2,700 (only about 12 percent of these casualties were frostbite cases).

Key winter combat skills demonstrated in the battle were:

- Skis: Finnish ski patrols kept their road-bound enemy under continuous surveillance, whereas the Russians remained ignorant of the Finnish strength and dispositions.
- Improvised roads: in terrain where trucks fitted with snowplows could not get through, the simple method of compacting snow with a series of horse-drawn sleds was quite effective.
- Specialized training and equipment: sleeping on pine boughs in heated tents kept the Finns comfortable while their opponents were literally freezing to death a few hundred yards away.
- Planning: the Finns accelerated their enemy's debilitation by firing on his campfires and destroying his field kitchens. The Russians had reason to regret the folly of launching their invasion without thorough preparations to cope with the environment, but they were not the last to make that costly mistake.

Right: Hostilities between Russia and Finland – the Continuation War – ceased on 5 September 1944. and the Germans were forced to leave the country. The Finns were still equipped with much German equipment (as this 20mm of II/5. Light Anti-aircraft Battery) but had to turn its weapons on its erstwhile allies.

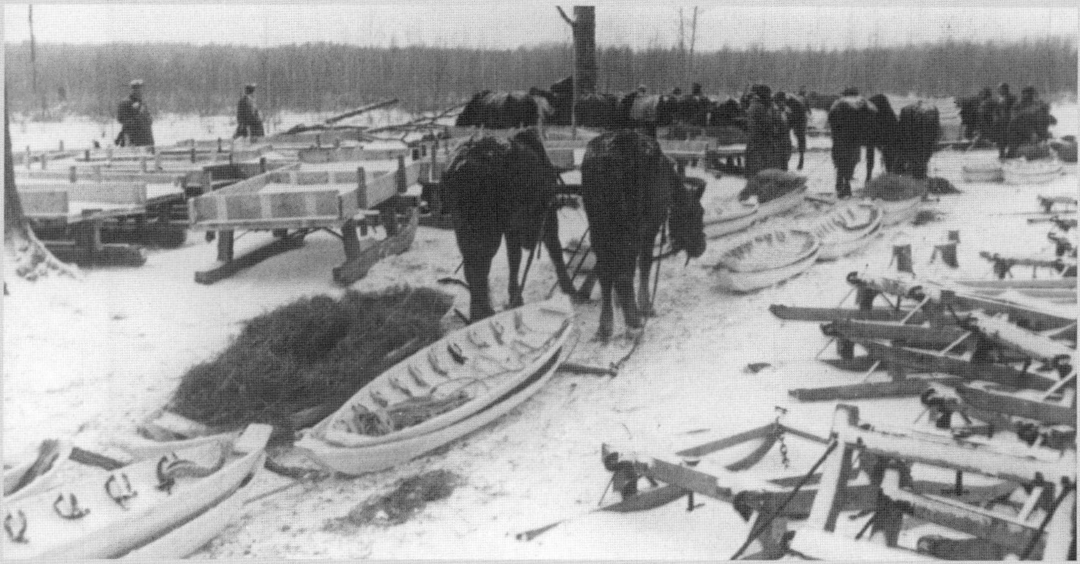

Akja had many functions. The weapons version was made of pinewood, open at the rear, but with a detachable board stern piece. The weapon's akja is used to transport light weapons and ammunition. There are two rings, one fastened to the front and one to the rear, for the towing and braking ropes. The weapons akja can be hauled by one to three skiers, depending on the load. The boat akja has the same shape as the weapon's akja, but it is closed on all sides. It is used to transport signal equipment, ammunition, hand grenades, mines, food carriers, radio equipment, heavy mortars, flamethrowers, etc. It may also be used for the evacuation of wounded.

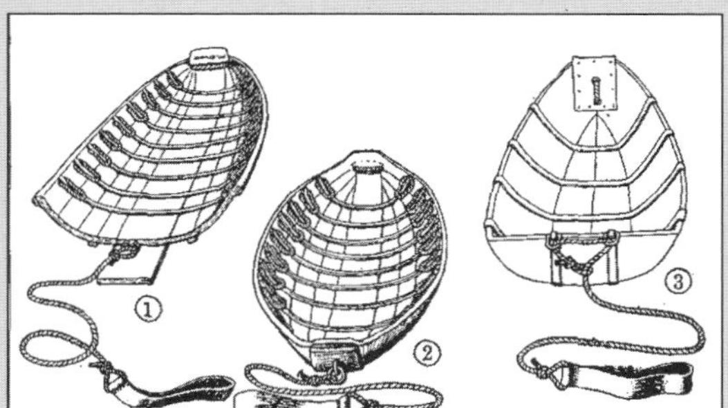
①
②
③

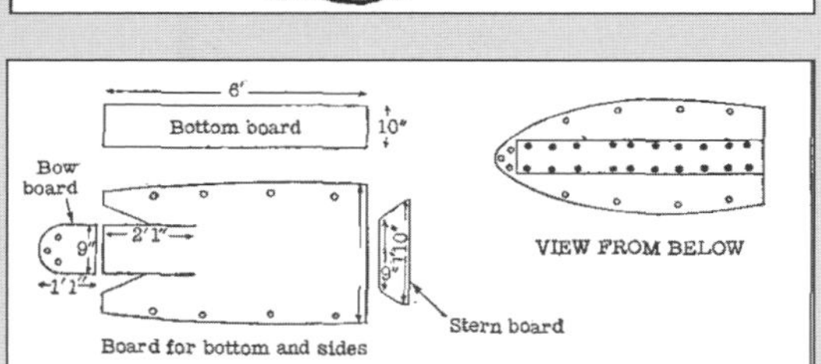
6'
Bottom board
10"
Bow board
2'1"
9"
1'1"
1'10"
Board for bottom and sides
Stern board
VIEW FROM BELOW

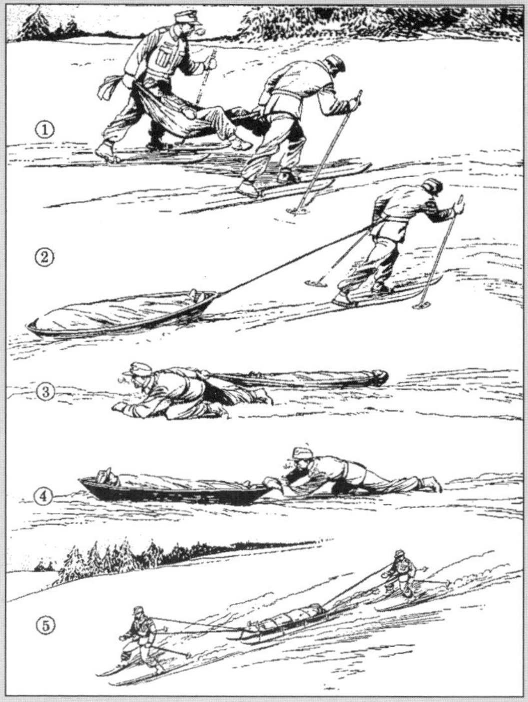
①
②
③
④
⑤

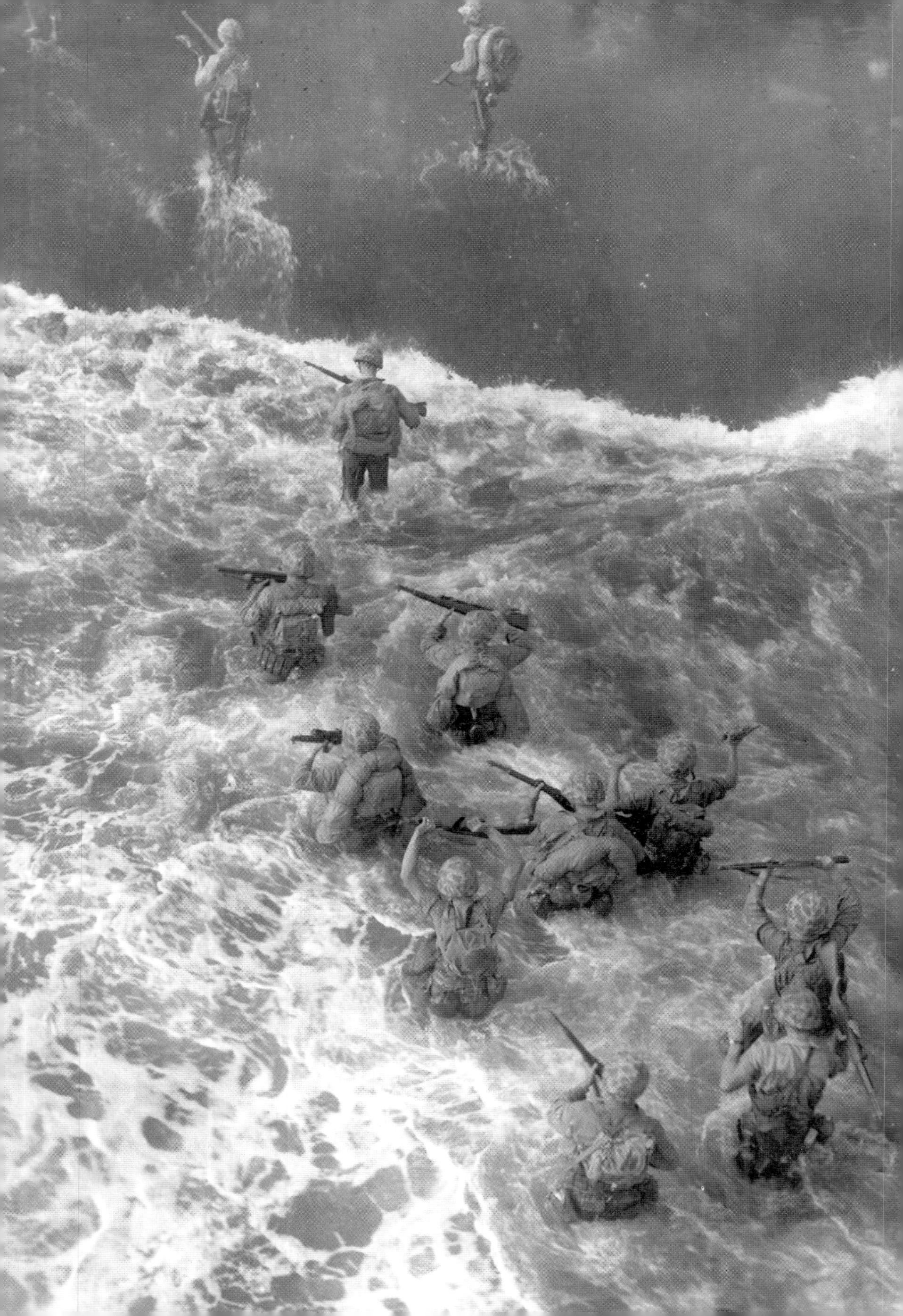

3 Amphibious Operations

Amphibious warfare attained a high level of operational development during World War II. Worldwide, four main amphibious operational doctrines were devised: by the Japanese, the British, the U.S. Marine Corps and General MacArthur in the Southwest Pacific Area (SWPA).

Developed prewar, the Japanese emphasised surprise, speed and aggression. They targeted weak spots and used night attacks. Once ashore, their mantra was mobility and this meant the Japanese always kept their opponents guessing where they'd be. The Malayan campaign is a good example of this. A smaller Japanese force, Lt Gen Tomoyuki Yamashita's 25th Army, conquered the entire 700-mile Malay Peninsula in 70 days thanks to good planning, speed – particularly the use of bicycles – and the defenders' failure to destroy military facilities, especially airfields and the Churchill stores. Without these Japanese logistics would have become an issue.

The keys to Allied amphibious doctrine in the ETO/MTO were (1) landing with minimal casualties by exploiting German weak spots, targeting poorly defended beaches and using deception; (2) surprise – landing in the dark after only short, heavyweight bombardment; (3) airborne assault of key positions to be held until seaborne forces arrived; (4) specialist equipment such as the DD Shermans and 79th Armoured Division's 'funnies'; (5) digging in and preparing a defensive cocoon, making use of the firepower of offshore warships to help break up enemy counterattacks; (6) capturing a port – but not until after the initial assault (because of the experience of Dieppe).

American doctrine in the Pacific split into that practised by the USMC and the slightly different approach from General Douglas MacArthur. The USMC's doctrine used an 'overwhelming combined-arms frontal assault' on the small islands and atolls. This required firepower, shock power and aggressive infantry tactics after extended bombardments of enemy positions. Armour – both land-based and amphibious – was

Continued on p.110.

Struggling through the surf, US Marines land on Cape Gloucester, 26 December 1943. Having started the war with little or no amphibious capability, the Allies in general – and the US forces specifically – built up a range of equipment and procedures for this sort of operation. Cape Gloucester wasn't the toughest battle the Marines would have but, nevertheless, 310 died and around 1,000 were wounded in fighting that lasted until 16 January 1944.

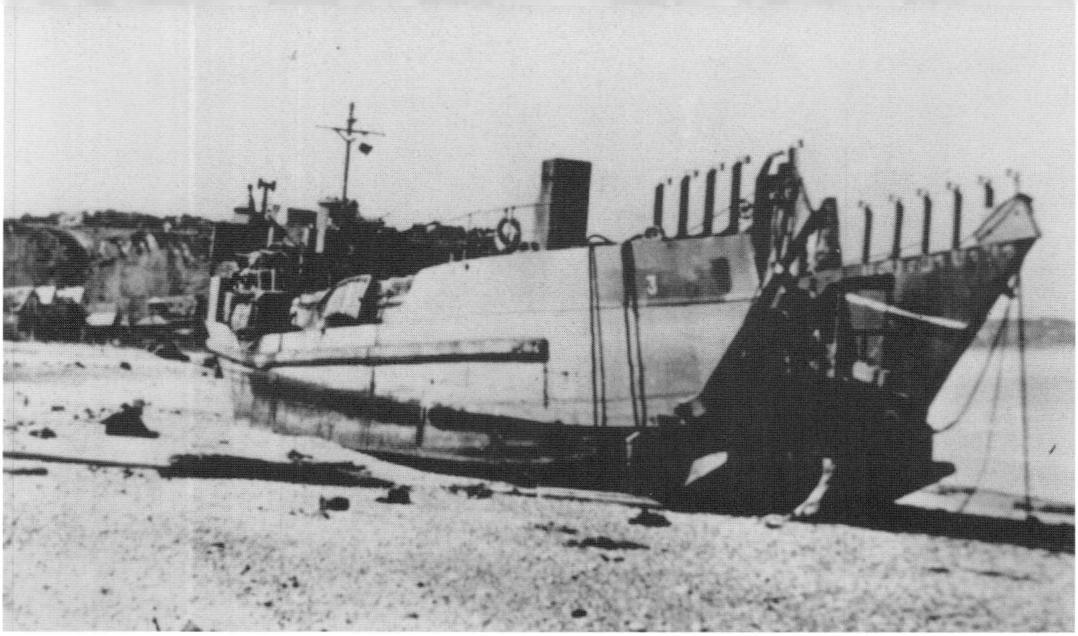

The attack on Dieppe in 1942 was a disaster. Of the 5,000 Canadians who took part, 3,367 were killed, wounded or taken prisoner. The equipment used in the attack – particularly the Churchill tanks – didn't impress the opposition. There were reasons for the attack: the RAF wanted to bring the Luftwaffe to battle; the Russians wanted the Allies to relieve pressure in the east with an attack in the west; the Canadians, in the UK from before Dunkirk, wanted some action; and the Americans were pushing for a cross-Channel action as soon as possible. However, with RAF Bomber Command not taking part and the RN not supplying any capital ships, the assault went in without a bombardment.

Above: An abandoned landing craft on the pebbly beach which caused real problems for the tanks.

Below: German troops look at the chaos. Note the early exhaust pipes to waterproof the Churchills. Only 27 of the 58 Churchills landed, and they didn't provide a significant punch to the attack. Their armour protection was good – of the 27 none were penetrated and 15 reached the seawall – but their 2pdr and 6pdr guns were ineffective. Because of this, the infantry suffered badly.

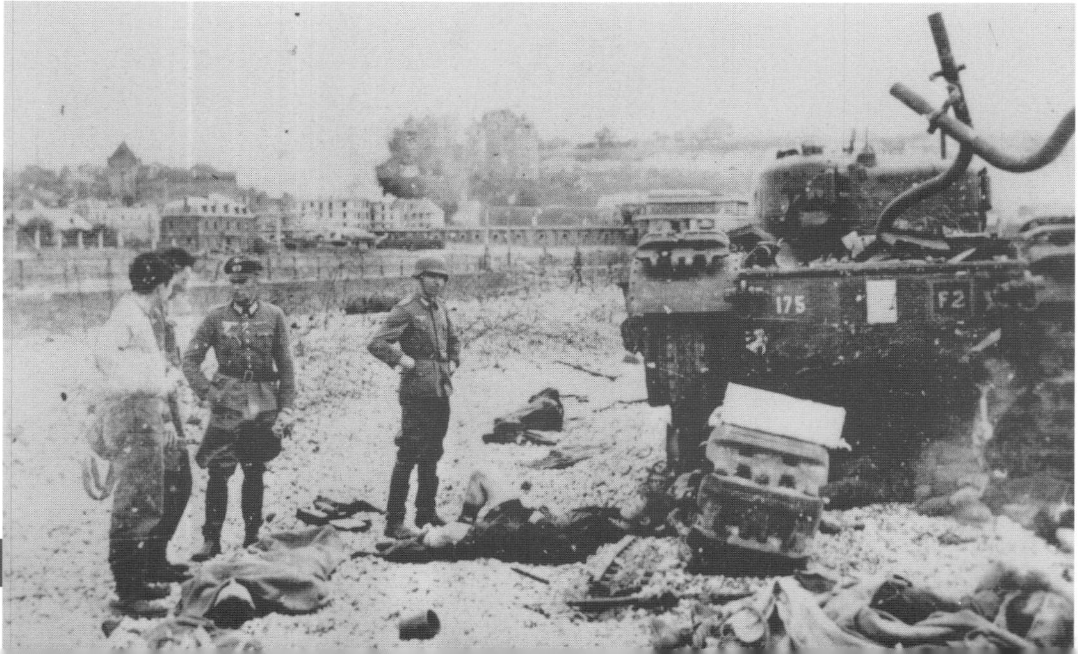
175
F2

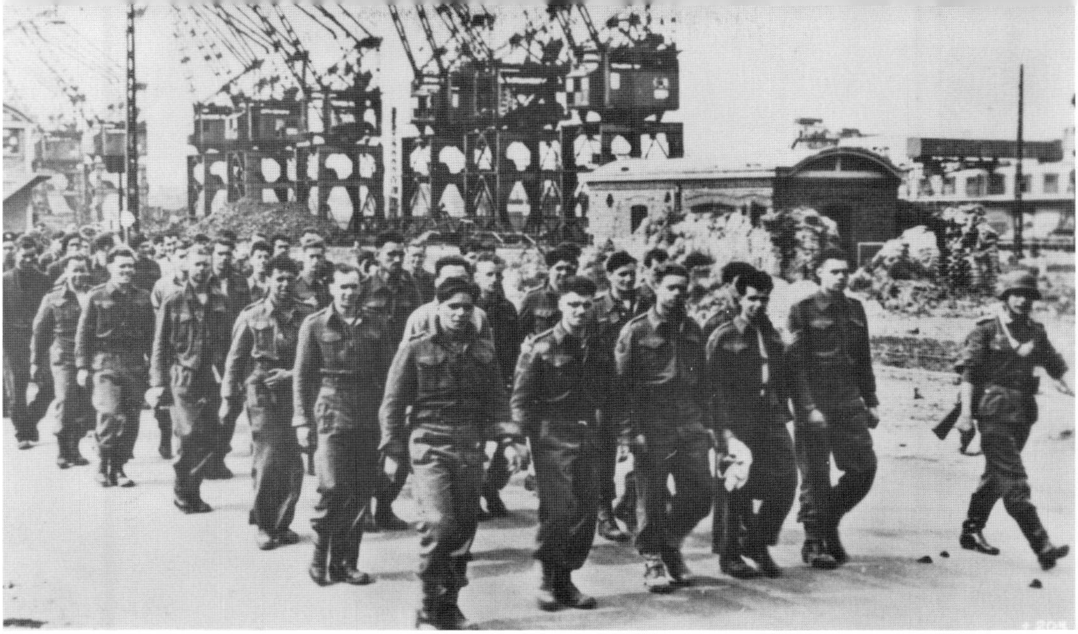

Above: Canadian soldiers are marched away from Dieppe to a PoW camp.

Below: The Germans made two significant amphibious landings during the war. The first was in Norway. The Germans didn't expect to be opposed and, consequently, lost the heavy cruiser *Blücher*, carrying invasion troops, to the torpedoes and guns of Oscarsborg Fortress. The Germans were able to land troops along the west coast and, helped by air power, withstand Allied attacks. The strategic situation was changed by events to the south and the Allies evacuated. A year later, just as Operation Barbarossa was due to start, the Germans invaded Crete to secure their flank. The majority of the German troops were landed by air and such was the level of *Fallschirmjäger* casualties that Hitler decided that they ought not be air-dropped again and should be used as ground troops in future. There were a couple of attempts to land 5th *Gebirgsjäger* by sea, one of which ended with the convoy being intercepted and there were heavy casualties. The bulk of the *Gebirgsjäger* were delivered by aircraft. They are seen here waiting to board the Ju52s. There was another seaborne landing by a brigade of Italian 50th Infantry Division Regina on 28 May which was unopposed by the Royal Navy.

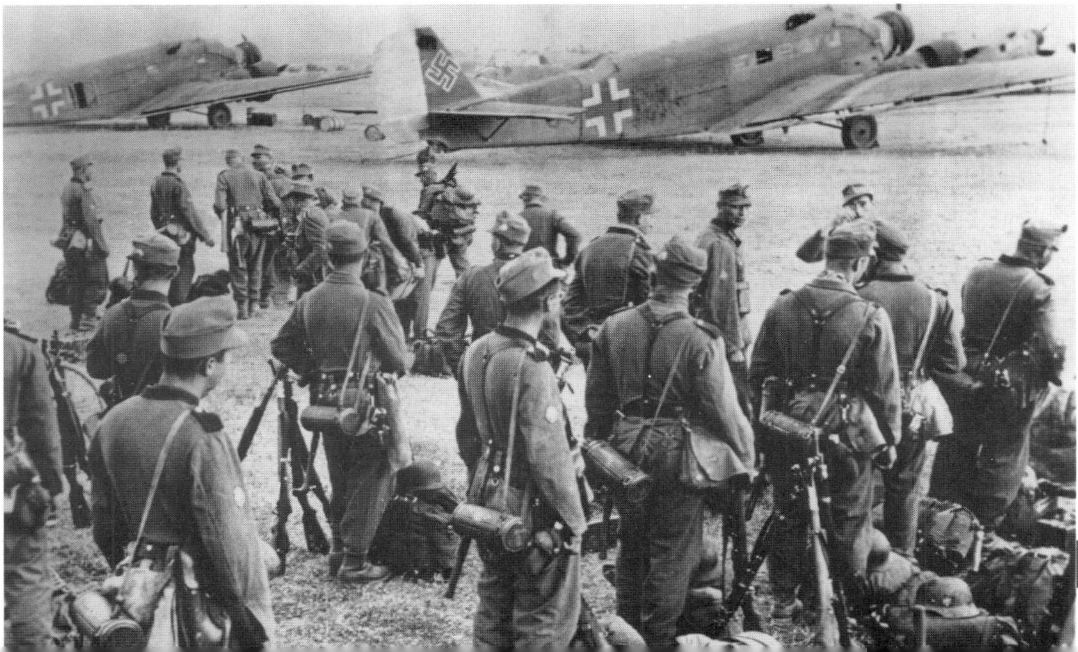

Casualty rates of landing forces for WW2 amphibious operations

Operation (By)	Date	Codename	Casualties	Landing force	Casualty %
Crete (GER)	20.05.41	Merkur (Mercury)	6,700	22,000	30
Malaya (JAP)	8.12.41	E	9,800	60,000	16
Philippines (JAP)	10.12.42	M	12,000	79,000	15
Timor (JAP)	20.02.42	H	500	5,900	8
Guadalcanal (US)	7.08.42	Watchtower	6,200	81,000	8
Algeria (US/UK)	8.11.42	Torch	1,500	107,000	1
Sicily (US/UK/CAN)	9.07.43	Husky	22,800	478,000	5
Salerno (US/UK)	9.09.43	Avalanche	12,000	115,000	10
Tarawa (US)	20.11.43	Galvanic	3,300	18,000	18
Anzio (US/UK)	22.01.44	Shingle	23,200	110,000	21
Hollandia (US)	22.04.44	Reckless	4,000	80,000	5
Normandy (US/UK/CAN)	6.06.44	Overlord	208,800	750,000	28
Saipan (US)	15.06.44	Forager	16,500	78,000	21
Guam (US)	21.07.44	Forager	7,800	54,900	14
Tinian (US)	24.07.44	Forager	2,200	17,400	13
Riviera (US/UK/FR)	15.08.44	Dragoon	13,600	250,000	5
Peleliu (US)	15.09.44	Stalemate	8,700	28,500	31
Leyte (US)	20.10.44	King II	15,600	257,800	6
Iwo Jima (US)	19.02.45	Detachment	26,000	87,000	30
Okinawa (US)	1.04.45	Iceberg	59,400	290,000	21

This revealing table shows the casualty rates for the war's major amphibious operations, covering the landing force from its initial assault and through the operational pause that happens as the lodgement is secured. Rates of 30 percent or thereabouts are very high – roughly the equivalent percentage of Russian casualties at Stalingrad. The losses for Crete (discussed on p.111) led to the Germans discontinuing major airborne operations. The Japanese benefited from the unpreparedness of the defenders, and the tactical skill and aggression of the attacks.

used wherever possible. Because the operations were so far from land, the logistics were primarily sea-based until airfields could be captured.

In the SWPA, MacArthur's approach was determined by scarcity of resources, such as naval firepower. MacArthur, therefore, searched out enemy weak points in landings spread over a big enough distance to stretch defensive configurations – and captured a port or airfield as soon as possible.

Defensive strategies against amphibious operations can be distilled into three categories: forward, mobile and in-depth. Forward means the seashore. Defenders tried to push the attackers into the sea. This approach required strong defensive positions and good artillery backup: think Omaha. Mobile defence countered landings by a massed counterattack – Salerno and Anzio are good examples. But the arguments about the approach proved divisive – particularly in Normandy where the Germans couldn't decide how to use or where to place their armoured reserves.

In-depth defence removed naval warship support from the equation, but allowed

Operation Torch brought the Americans into the Desert War and saw the first of the full-scale set-piece amphibious operations in the west that culminated in the D-Day landings. Three landing sites − centred on Casablanca in Morocco (Western Task Force) and, in Algeria, Oran (Center) and Algiers (Eastern) − saw US and Allied forces land in North Africa. The Western Task Force sailed direct from the United States and the other two from the UK, as did the aircraft dropping US paratroops. The landings were successful but were too far from Tunisia to have an immediate bearing on the Desert War. It did allow the American forces to be blooded, equipment and command structures to be tested, and future operations benefited from the lessons learned. Photo shows US Rangers at Oran.

a lodgement. The Japanese used this approach on Iwo Jima and Okinawa, for example, seeking to bleed the Americans dry and, therefore, stop or delay an attack on Japan itself.

Minor amphibious operations began in earnest following the Nazi conquest of mainland Europe. In 1940 the British Combined Operations HQ, coordinated offensive actions against the enemy with its ultimate goal to train and enable large-scale amphibious invasions of occupied Europe. They began with 'pinprick' raids to gather information, annoy the Germans and boost the country's morale. These were undertaken by the newly formed Small Scale Raiding Force (62 Cdo). The SSRF was in turn absorbed by the newly formed Commandos as they expanded and went on to launch ever larger assaults. 1942 saw successful raids that captured secret radar equipment (Bruneval, February) and destroyed the only dry-dock in France capable of taking the *Tirpitz* (St Nazaire, March), but also the failure of the biggest raid to date, on the port of Dieppe in August (see pp. 108–109).

After Dieppe, Combined Operations now implemented a colossal, long-term training programme for all three armed services: mass troop embarkation, sailing landing craft in convoy, using new types of specialist craft, beach landing, supplies and support. Infantry, as well as marines, commandos, pilots, sailors and RNVR personnel all took part.

Another significant area of change was in the craft used for the mission. Before the war no landing craft had existed, but soon the UK and US developed many different

Continued on p.115

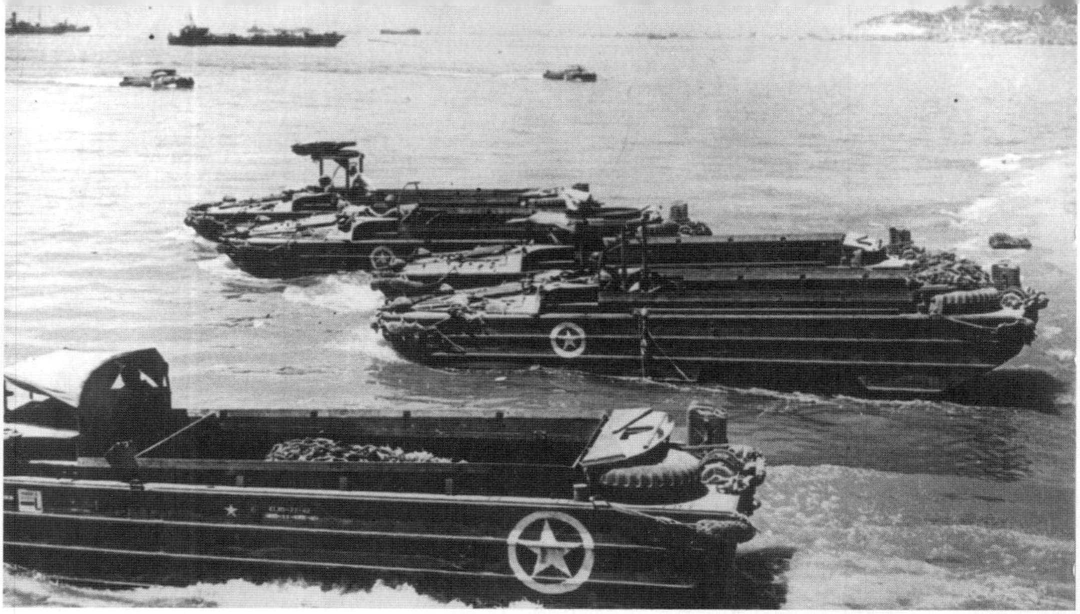

Above: The landings in Sicily. One major success of Operation Husky was the first use of the DUKW. They proved efficient, easy to use and just what was needed. They were indispensable in Normandy and future Allied amphibious operations.

Below: The British landed to the west of Syracuse. In the aftermath of the landings, emptying ships of supplies is hard work. This human chain is hefting ammunion. Behind, SP artillery – an M7 mounting a 105mm gun.

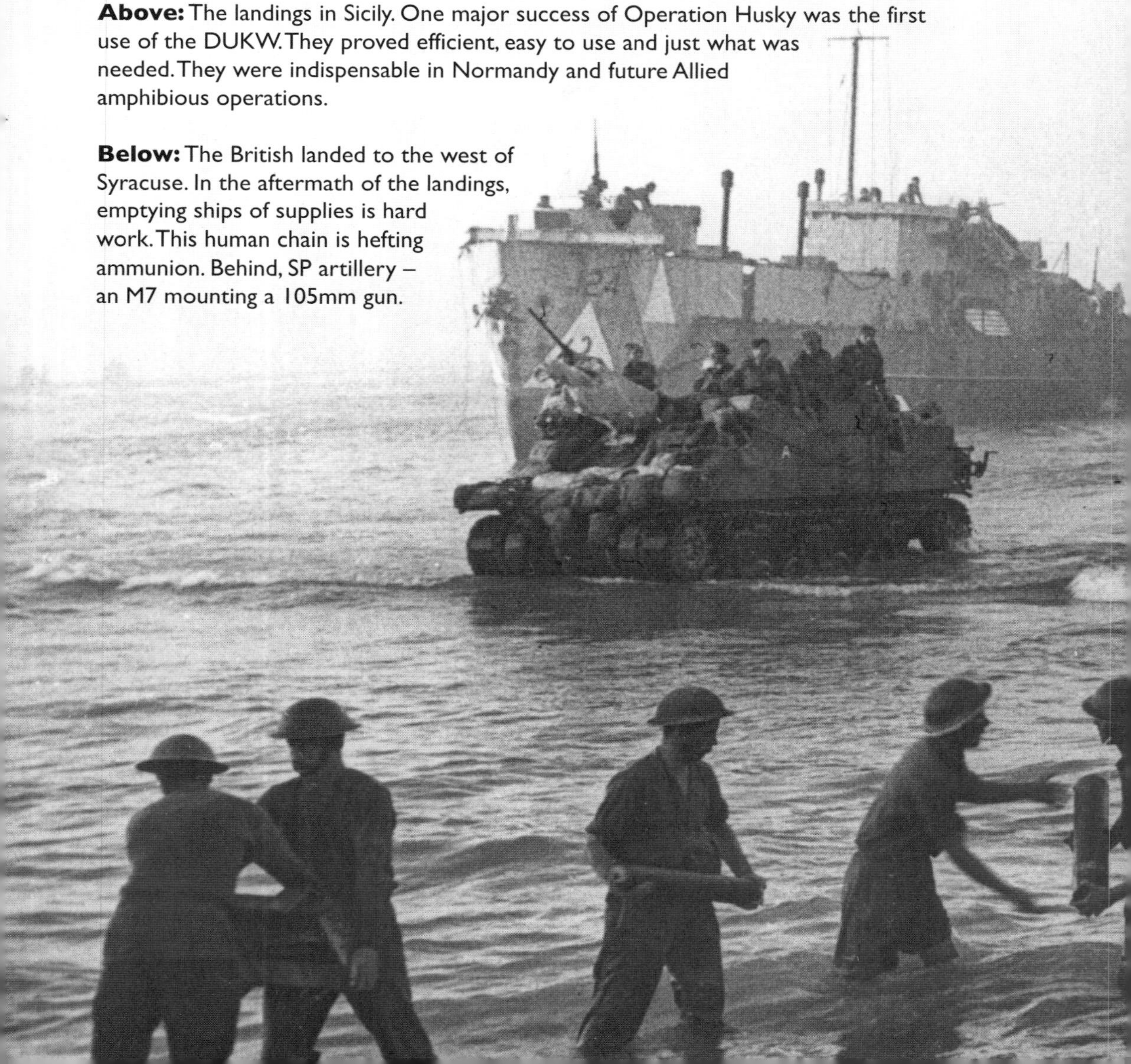

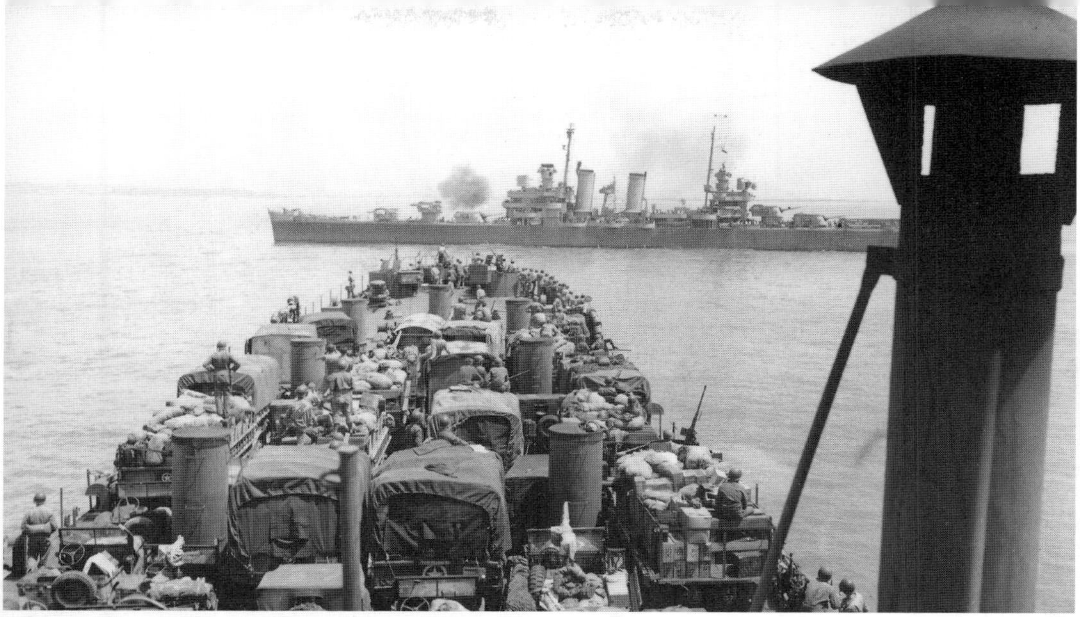

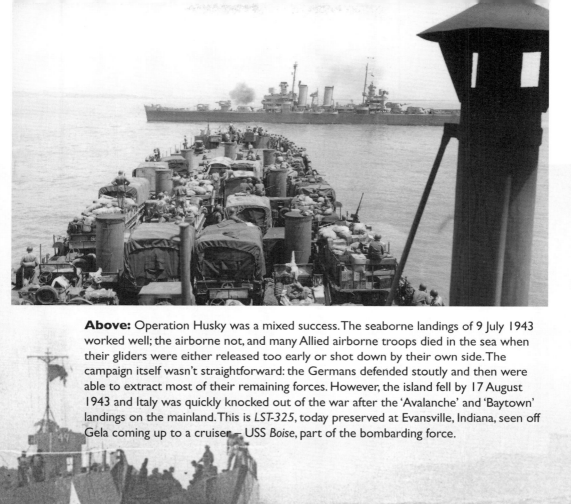

Above: Operation Husky was a mixed success. The seaborne landings of 9 July 1943 worked well; the airborne not, and many Allied airborne troops died in the sea when their gliders were either released too early or shot down by their own side. The campaign itself wasn't straightforward: the Germans defended stoutly and then were able to extract most of their remaining forces. However, the island fell by 17 August 1943 and Italy was quickly knocked out of the war after the 'Avalanche' and 'Baytown' landings on the mainland. This is *LST-325*, today preserved at Evansville, Indiana, seen off Gela coming up to a cruiser – USS *Boise*, part of the bombarding force.

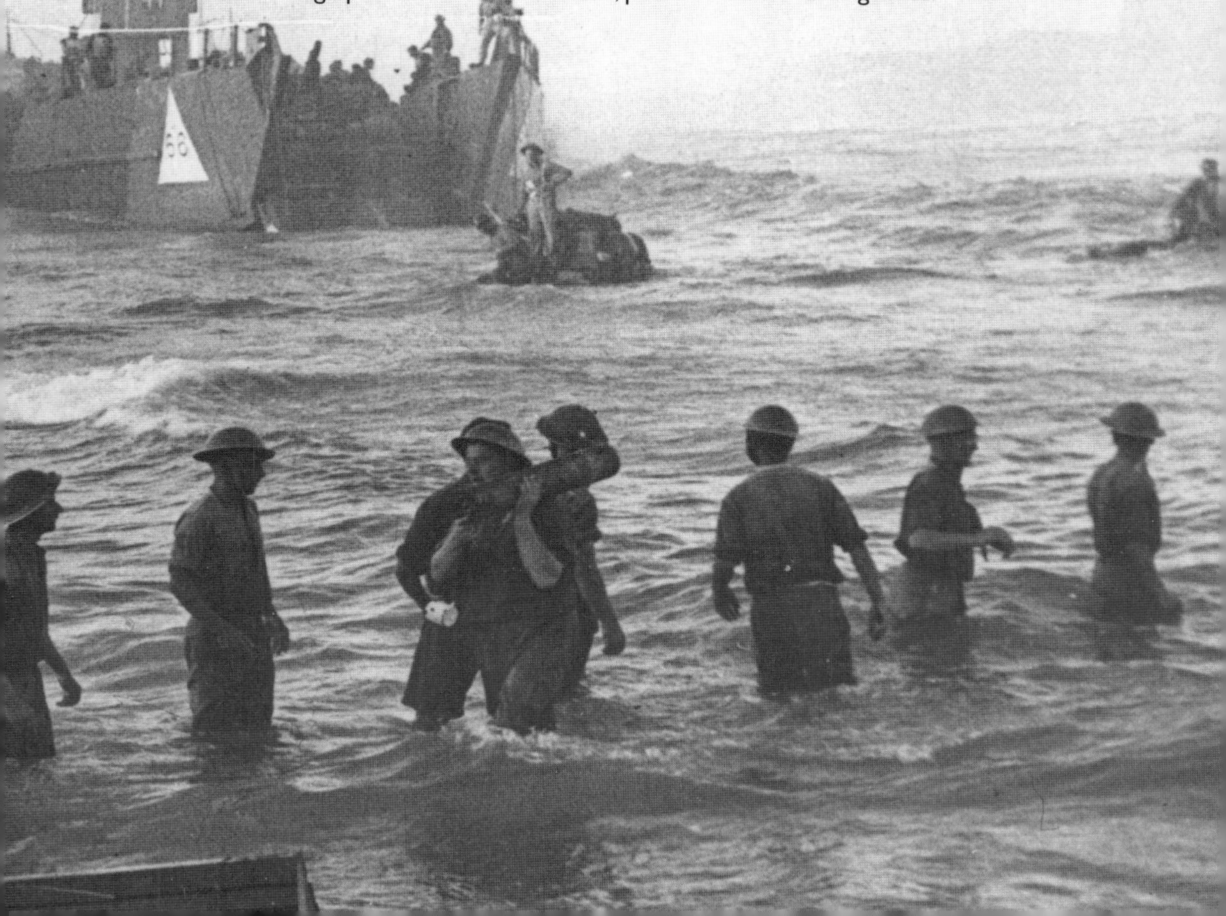

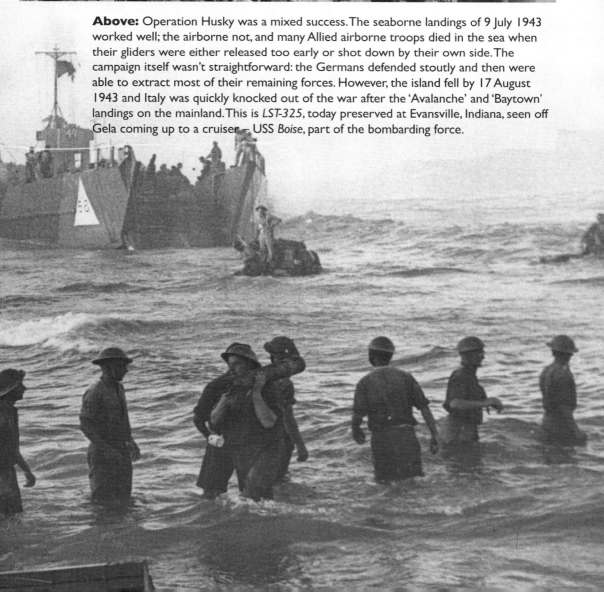

Above: The Salerno landings started well on 9 September 1943, but the strategic concept of landing the British 300 miles further south (Operation Baytown) proved a mistake. Hampered by clever demolitions and mining, British Eighth Army arrived only in the nick of time after counterattacks had almost driven US Fifth Army back into the sea. Here, on D-Day, the 143rd Infantry Regimental Combat Team dashes onto the beach at Salerno.

Below: The under-strength landings at Anzio on 22 January 1944 also showed up problems with Allied strategy. They surprised the Germans, but having landed successfully the troops dug in rather than advancing and gave time for German commander, *Generalfeldmarschall* Albert Kesselring, to bring his reserves into play. Held within a tight perimeter, bombarded by everything from infantry guns to the railway gun 'Anzio Annie' some 15 miles inland, the Allies held on until Operation Diadem broke through the Gustav Line. As the Germans streamed back in retreat, US Fifth Army commander Mark Clark ordered Lucien Truscott to go for Rome rather than attempt to cut off the German retreat. The possibility of ending the war in Italy quickly disappeared. Here, LSTs unload stores onto the quayside in the harbour at Anzio. Once they broke out, the 'German infantry was organized in small, mobile rearguard groups. The composition and strength of these groups ... consisted of motorized infantry or infantry in half-track vehicles – equipped with a high proportion of light machine guns, in either case – and often included support by tanks or self-propelled guns. Each rearguard included an engineer component, and sometimes a battery from the divisional artillery regiment. The basis of the rearguard is an infantry company. An infantry battalion fighting a rearguard action normally sends only one of its rifle companies at a time on active missions. The three rifle companies are used in rotation, as long as their strength remains approximately equal. The following elements support the company (or companies, if the terrain makes it necessary to employ more than one): two or more antitank guns from the regimental antitank company, and half the heavy support weapons allotted to the entire rear guard – that is, tanks, SP guns, infantry guns, and gun howitzers. In country favorable to them, these reinforced infantry companies have proved capable of holding up a sizable Allied force on a fairly wide front.' (*Intelligence Bulletin* Vol II No 12, August 1944.)

designs to land infantry, tanks, and supplies, and huge well-decked landing ships transported the smaller craft to target coastlines. Less than three months after Dieppe, on 8–16 November came the Anglo-American 'Torch' landings in North Africa. An Allied fleet of 350 warships and 500 transports carrying some 107,000 (mostly American) troops was divided into three main task forces that launched successful assaults and seized key ports in Casablanca, Oran and Algiers before advancing eastwards into Tunisia.

Next came Sicily – the largest amphibious landing of the war in terms of its area and the number of men put ashore on the first day. Over 3,000 ships carried 180,000 troops, thousands of vehicles and 600 tanks, landed at multiple sites supported by 4,000 aircraft, including a paratrooper and glider assault group with 137 gliders and 400 transports. The weather, always critical, caused many mishaps and there were costly mistakes. A category 7 gale scattered the air armada causing various friendly fire incidents, while hundreds of paratroopers in heavy kit jumped too soon and others in gliders were released too early so all were drowned at sea.

Despite this, 'Husky' was a tactical and strategic success. The planning and logistics had evolved and much improved since 'Torch'. Men and materials were managed at the landing sites by appointed beachmasters, helped by new kit such as the DUKW. There was improved waterproofing of vehicles and recovery for any that became stranded or broken down and better organisation of the infantry's ultimate objective, to head for, take and hold any high ground overlooking the beach in order to secure the landing sites. When Hitler realised the scale of the 'Husky' he cancelled a planned offensive in Russia and transferred reinforcements to Sicily. Although ultimately to no avail, with the terrain favouring defence the Germans were able to make a tidy withdrawal of most their forces to the Italian mainland.

The three-pronged invasion of the Italian mainland began on 3 September with XIII Corps of Eighth Army landings at various points on the eastern coast of Calabria ('Baytown') led to the hoped-for collapse of Mussolini's government at about the same time the main invasion at Salerno ('Avalanche') began. Another opportunistic operation ('Slapstick') was launched simultaneously 130 miles away.

'Avalanche' saw US Fifth Army, comprising US VI Corps and British X Corps landed on a 35-mile front without a preparatory bombardment. The landings were violently opposed and the fierce counterattacks almost succeeded in overwhelming the beachhead. Intense naval bombardments and heavy air support repeatedly saved the operation, until Eighth Army arrived from the south.

On 22 January 1944, another smaller landing took place at Anzio on the west coast 25 miles south of Rome and 70 miles behind enemy lines, in an attempt to circumvent the Gustav Line. 1st British and 3rd US Divisions landed successfully but were contained in their beachhead for months by determined German counterattacks until finally reinforced to seven divisions, they managed to break out on 23 May 1944.

Continued on p.119.

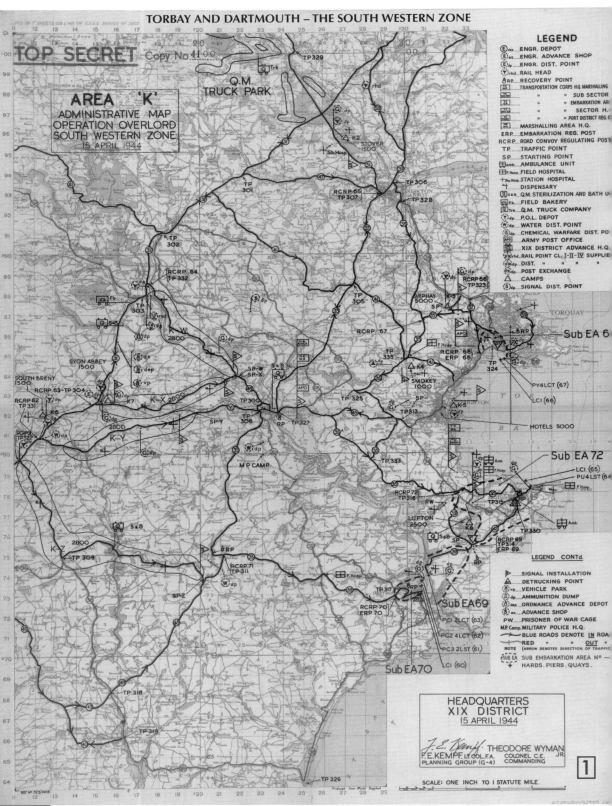

TORBAY AND DARTMOUTH – THE SOUTH WESTERN ZONE

TOP SECRET   Copy No. 41

AREA 'K'
ADMINISTRATIVE MAP
OPERATION OVERLORD
SOUTH WESTERN ZONE
15 APRIL 1944

Q.M. TRUCK PARK

LEGEND

Edep	...	ENGR. DEPOT
Eas	...	ENGR. ADVANCE SHOP
Edp	...	ENGR. DIST. POINT
Yrhd	...	RAIL HEAD
RP	...	RECOVERY POINT
		TRANSPORTATION CORPS HQ MARSHALLING
		" SUB SECTOR
		" EMBARKATION AR
		" SECTOR H.Q
		" PORT DISTRICT REG. O
		MARSHALLING AREA H.Q.
ERP	...	EMBARKATION REG. POST
RCRP	...	ROAD CONVOY REGULATING POST
TP	...	TRAFFIC POINT
SP	...	STARTING POINT
amb	...	AMBULANCE UNIT
F.Hosp	...	FIELD HOSPITAL
Sta.Hosp	...	STATION HOSPITAL
	...	DISPENSARY
S&b	...	Q.M. STERILIZATION AND BATH U
Fb	...	FIELD BAKERY
Trk	...	Q.M. TRUCK COMPANY
Ydp	...	P.O.L. DEPOT
Wdp	...	WATER DIST. POINT
	...	CHEMICAL WARFARE DIST. PO
APO	...	ARMY POST OFFICE
	...	XIX DISTRICT ADVANCE H.Q.
	...	RAIL POINT CL. I-II-IV SUPPLIE
Edp	...	DIST.
PX	...	POST EXCHANGE
△	...	CAMPS
Sdp	...	SIGNAL DIST. POINT

LEGEND CONTd.

	SIGNAL INSTALLATION
	DETRUCKING POINT
vp	VEHICLE PARK
dp	AMMUNITION DUMP
dp	ORDNANCE ADVANCE DEPOT
as	ADVANCE SHOP
PW	PRISONER OF WAR CAGE
M.P. Camp	MILITARY POLICE H.Q.
	BLUE ROADS DENOTE IN ROA
	RED OUT
NOTE	(ARROW DENOTES DIRECTION OF TRAFFIC
SUB EA	SUB EMBARKATION AREA No —
	HARDS, PIERS, QUAYS.

HEADQUARTERS
XIX DISTRICT
15 APRIL 1944

F.E. KEMPF LT. COL. F.A.   THEODORE WYMAN JR.
PLANNING GROUP (G-4)   COLONEL C.E. COMMANDING

SCALE: ONE INCH TO 1 STATUTE MILE

1

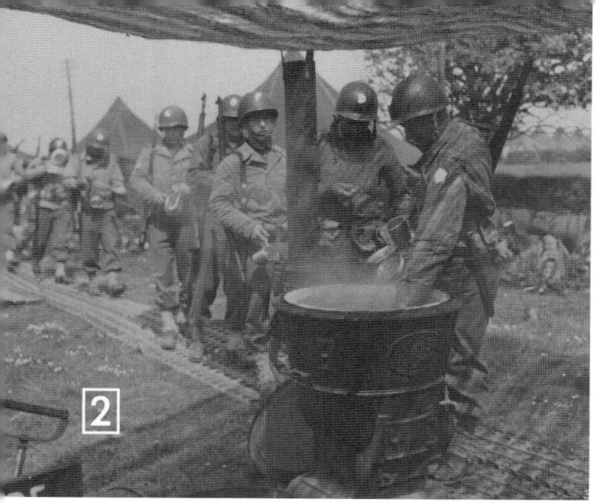

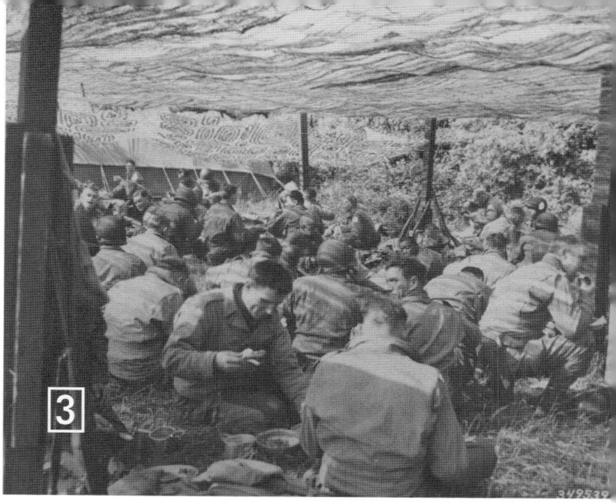

Normandy was the most important of all the Allied landing operations. Five beaches, a huge armada of vessels from battleships to landing craft, aerial paratroop and glider operations – altogether five infantry and three airborne divisions took part with a panoply of special forces, armour and assault troops. Over 150,000 men landed and the planning for the assault, follow-up and logistics took months. The infantry's role is exemplified here and on pages 120–121. **1** Map showing the area from Torquay to Dartmouth, the road routes, embarkation points and various camps. **2 and 3** The troops waiting in their sealed camps where they made their final preparations before (**4–6**) boarding ship. (**4** LSAs were used by British and Canadian troops as well as the US Rangers at Pointe du Hoc; **5** the major part of the US assault force was launched from Portland. In the foreground an M15A1 CGMC with a 37mm cannon above two .50cal machine guns; **6** US 4th Infantry Division and 101st Airborne sea echelon onboard an LCT (Mk 6) which later beached at Utah.

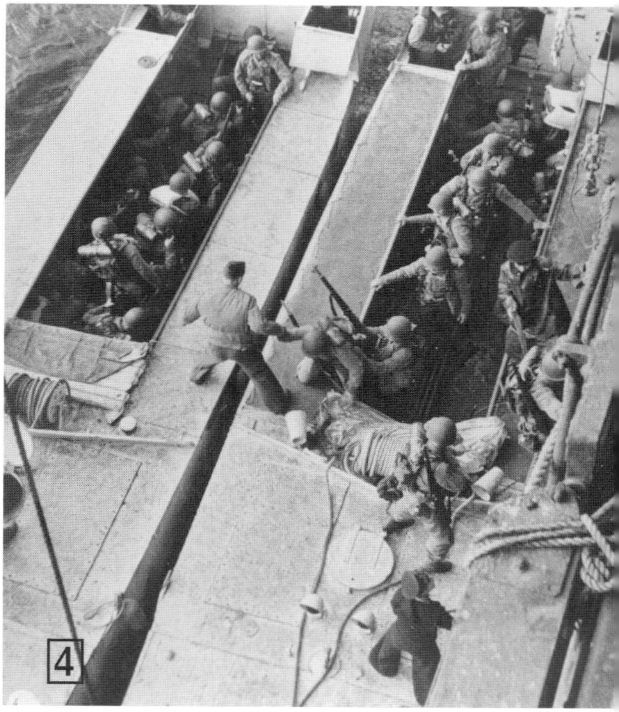

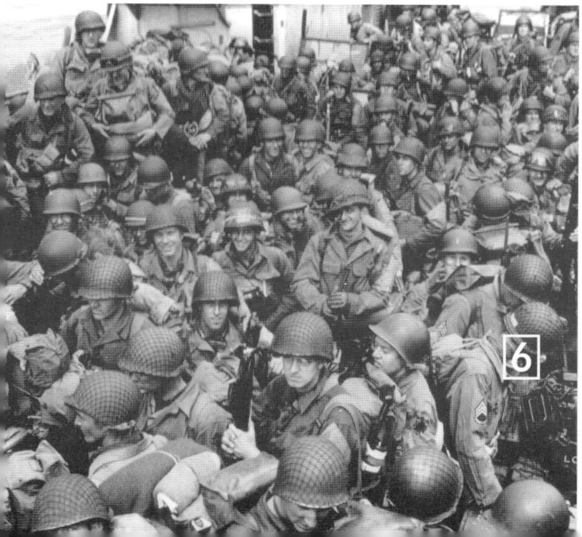

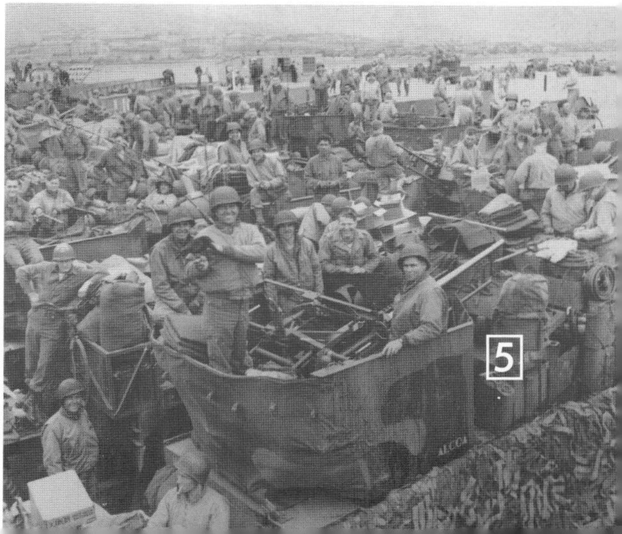

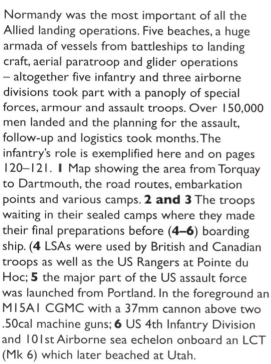

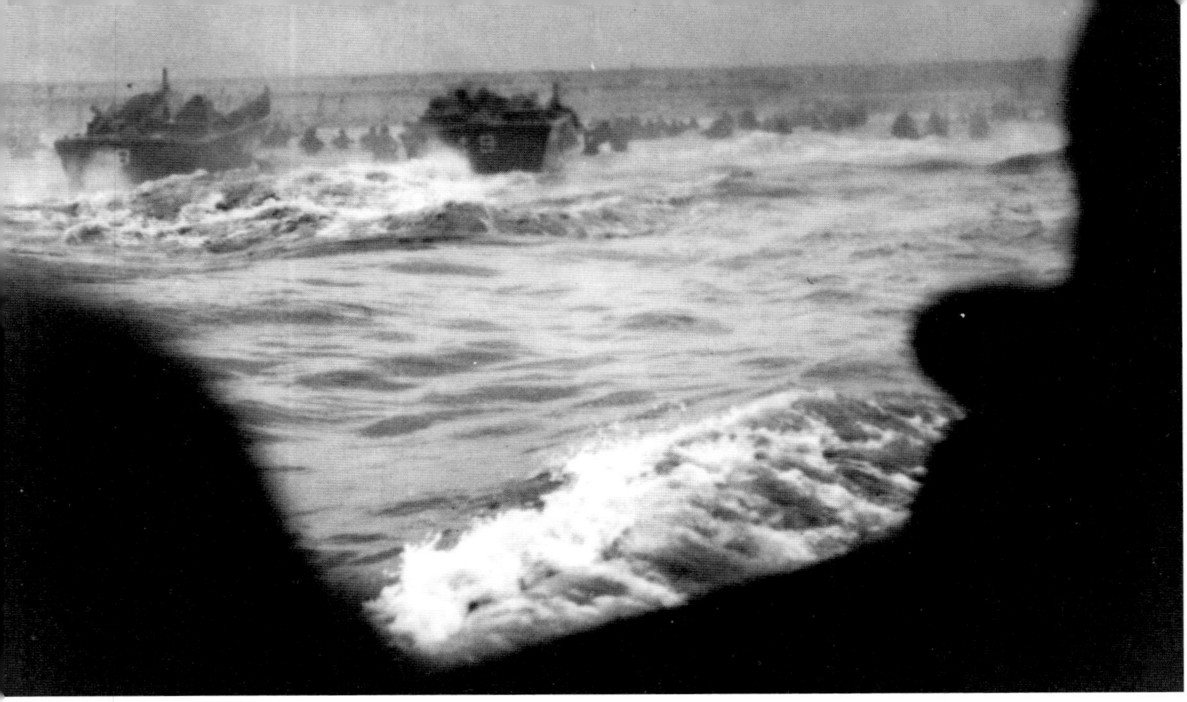

Above: LCVPs from US Coast Guard attack transport USS *Samuel Chase* approach the Easy Red sector of Omaha Beach. They carry 16th Infantry (1st Infantry Division). Looming above them are the bluffs that will peg them onto the beach. They are defended by dug in and bunkered guns which have been carefully ranged-in, minefields, barbed wire and strongpoints. It doesn't matter how much training you have had, when you hit the beach you will probably be sick as a dog from the choppy sea, terrified by the carnage that surrounds you and it will take real courage even to get off the landing craft.

Below: Once the shoreline has quietened down, the heavy lift starts. LSTs and freighters begin bringing vehicles – from tanks to trucks – as well as the logistical requirements to keep an army fed and watered, their vehicles full of gas and their ammunition stocks high.

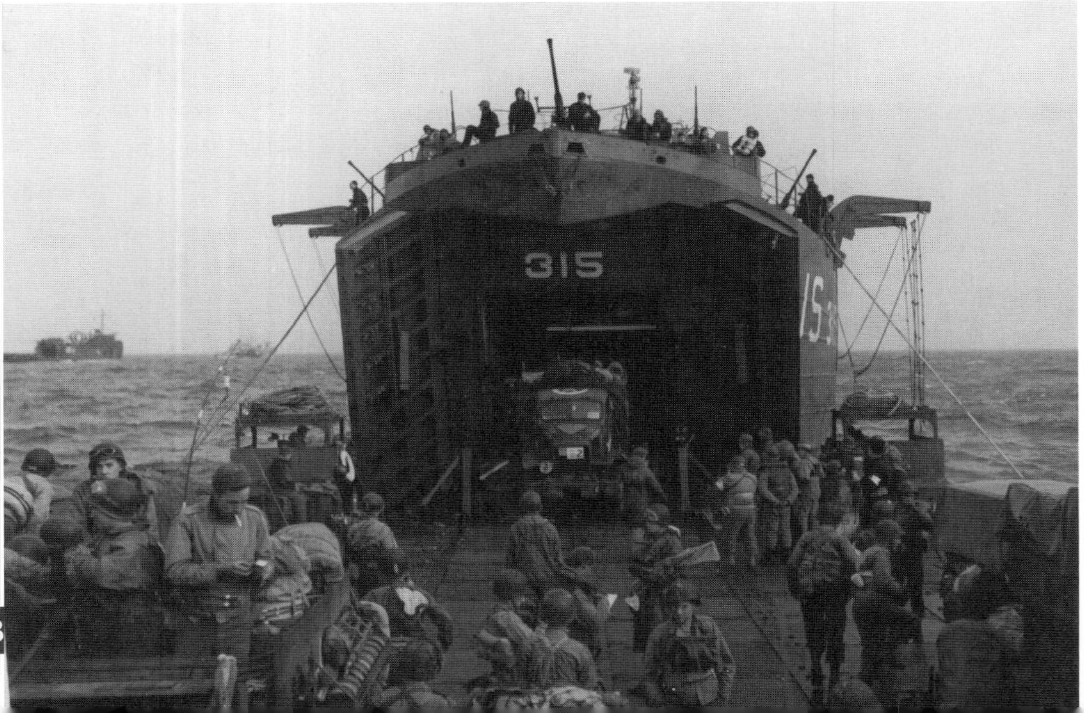
315

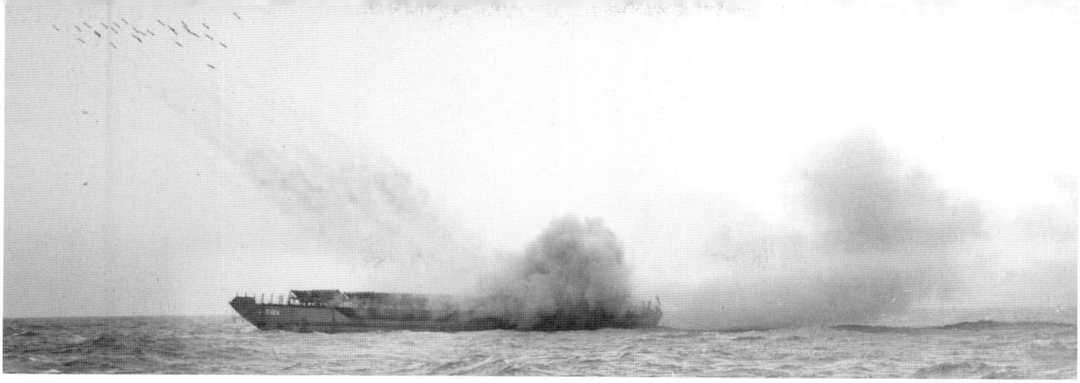

Above: Testing a rocket-firing LCT(R) in Portsmouth Harbour. These ships were converted from British Mk 2 and Mk 3 LCTs and were equipped to fire over 1,000 RP-3 60lb rockets. LCT(R)s were fitted with Type 970 rangefinding radars but they weren't the most accurate of artillery – those fired at Omaha went over the heads of the German defenders on the bluffs. The rockets were fired in ten salvos of 120 and each had the blast of a 6-inch shell without the penetrative power. It took less than 1min 30sec to fire them and they obliterated an area of 400 yards x 100 yards deep.

Below: One of the best-remembered landmarks in Bernières, today it's called Canada House (**A**). Note the SBG assault bridge (**B**) in place on the seawall. The photo was taken around midday on 6 June as the Stormont, Dundas and Glengarry Highlanders, part of the reserve 9th Inf Bde, came ashore. Canada House was liberated by the Queen's Own Rifles of Canada, but at the cost of over 100 casualties.

The most important amphibious landing of the war took place in Normandy on 6 June 1944. The landings, the battle for Normandy and the subsequent break out proved a complete vindication of the Allies' attack strategy and highlighted the problems with the Germans' forward defence. The vaunted Atlantic Wall was quickly breached without the anticipated losses. The thousands of tons of reinforced concrete that had taken up so much time and expense to produce and utilise, and the thousands of defenders in place from the Arctic Circle to the Atlantic coast of Spain were all proved pointless, as Allied ingenuity and bravery first achieved a lodgement, then sustained it, drawing the German reserves into two months of attritional struggle that they couldn't afford. The arguments between Rommel and Geyr Von Schweppenburg about the location and use of the German Panzer reserves ended up with the bulk of the German tanks stuck in a defensive role unable to drive the attackers back into the sea.

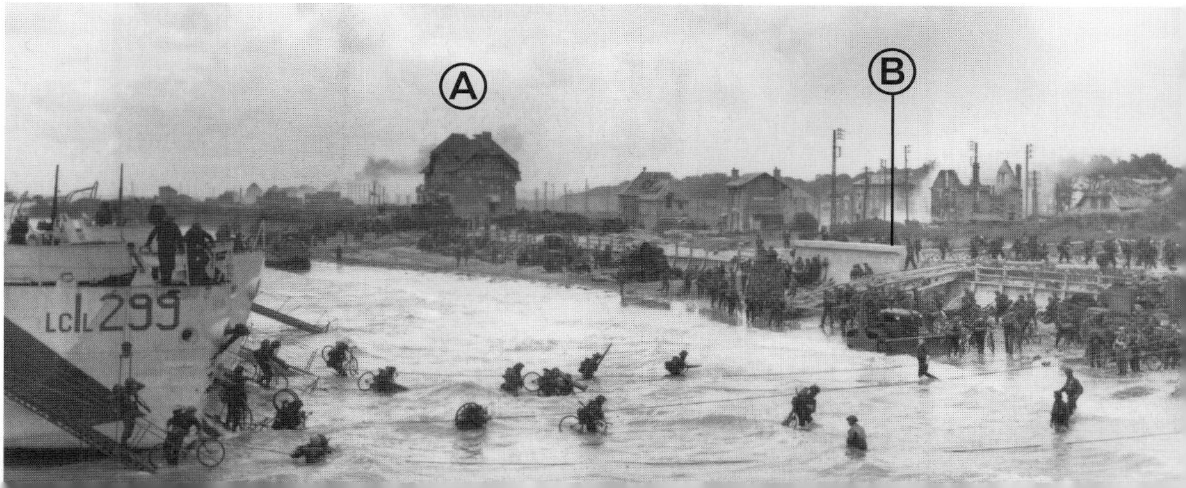
A
B
LCIL 299

The Pacific

As Operation Avalanche had amply demonstrated, World War II amphibious assaults depended upon naval gunfire and air support to compensate for the lack of heavy weapons amongst the beach landing forces. In the central Pacific naval gunfire was the decisive advantage possessed by the US forces. Battleships formed bombardment groups for virtually every major amphibious assault, sometimes firing for up to a fortnight before and also during the operation itself.

In the southwest Pacific, with the US Seventh Fleet suffering from a lack of aircraft carriers and battleships, amphibious operations were concentrated against enemy weak points followed by the capture of a port or airfield to enable an increase in the flow of supplies. Multiple landings over a broad front were also used to prevent the Japanese from being able to concentrate their forces. US Marines spearheaded many of these attacks and helped train the US Army divisions that also participated.

Guadalcanal was the first island assaulted. A ferocious six-month land, sea and air battle was a precursor of what was to follow over the coming years showing plainly the logistical challenges, difficult jungle terrain, atrocious weather and a fanatical enemy who fought to the death. After the Solomons came the Gilberts (Tarawa and Makin) where the landing forces had to disembark and negotiate reefs and lagoons while being raked with enfilading fire. Through all this the US stoically persevered, learning and improving their techniques with each landing. With their huge industrial capacity and inventiveness they developed a logistic resupply and support chain that was second to none, with a brilliant series of vehicles and landing ships that overcame each obstacle. These included LSTs that carried LVTs in their enormous holds. These amphibious tractors – nicknamed Amtracs (see pp. 124–25) – mutated from ship to shore cargo-landing vehicles to become armoured assault vehicles carrying the first wave to the beachhead, armed with

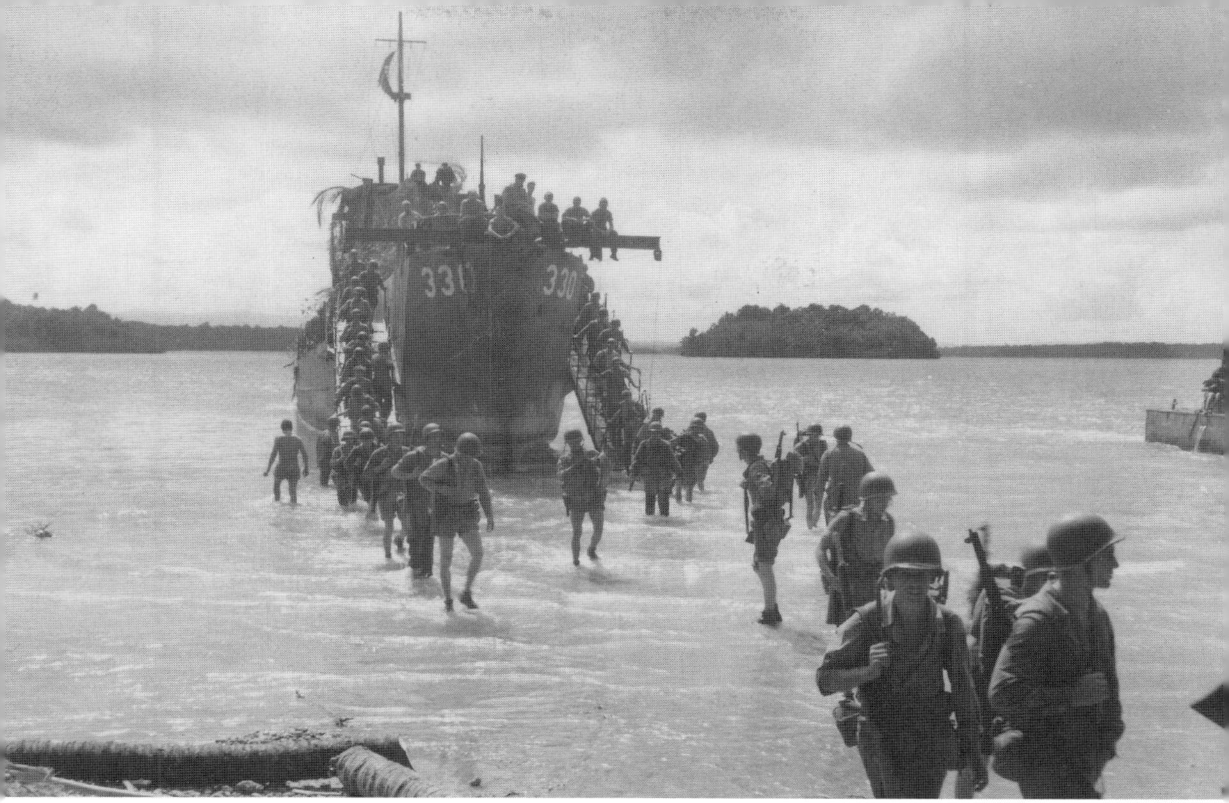
331
330

Opposite: It's 23 July 1943. In the Med the Allies are fighting on Sicily. In the Pacific *LCI-69* is near Rendova Island, New Georgia. The arrival of the new LCIs and LSTs made a big difference to operations in the Pacific. Operation Toenails – the invasion of the New Georgias – included LCI(L) Flotilla Five which boasted 26 LCIs, each 158ft 6in long with a beam of 23ft 3in and capable of carrying 180 troops. Note the 20mm cannon armament – there were four Oerlikons, one forward, one amidships and two aft.

Above: Reinforcements for New Georgia make their way down the ramps from *LCI-331* on a good day: the sea isn't rough and there's no enemy gunfire.

Right: An obvious target for Japanese air attack – accounting for the bristling anti-aircraft armament – the Operation Globetrotter invasion fleet heads for Sansapor, Dutch New Guinea, July 1944.

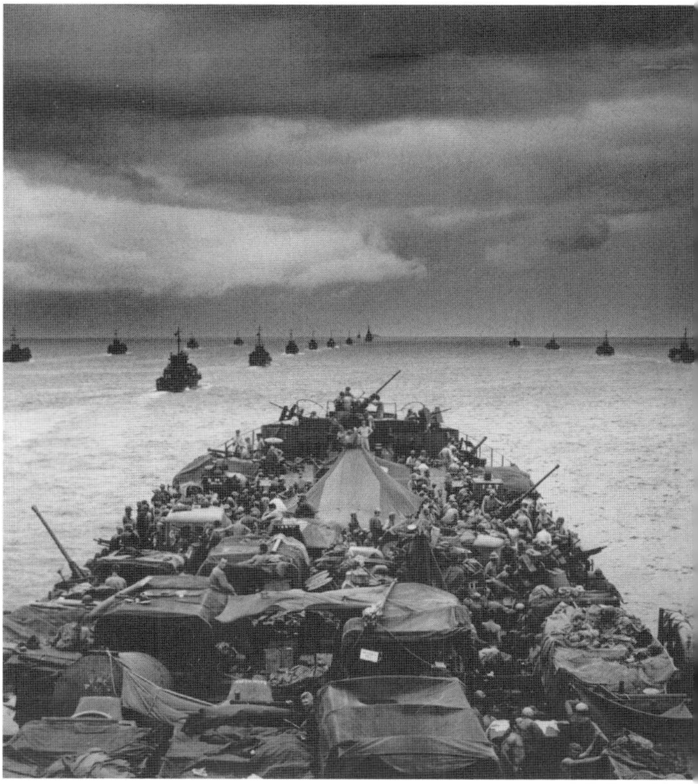

guns, howitzers or flamethrowers, while the DUKW transported supplies, equipment, artillery and ammunition from the ships. With such specialised equipment the techniques for cracking each island's defences evolved during the Pacific island-hopping campaign as the Americans edged ever closer to the Japanese home islands. After New Guinea, the Marshall Islands, the Marianas (Saipan, Guam and Tinian), Iwo Jima, and finally Okinawa, the US steeled itself to complete obliteration of the enemy through overwhelming firepower as the only solution to diehard fanaticism. Faced with such a refusal to surrender it is not surprising that America chose to save its own troops' lives and use nuclear weapons

The amphibious landings in the Pacific are particularly notable for the distances involved. Often supplied by a ship-borne logistic chain thousands of miles long, the US forces honed the art of amphibious warfare to perfection – but it still needed bodies on the line as the casualty figures in the table on p. 110 show.

Below: D-Day, Saipan, 15 June 1944 – one of the major battles of the Pacific War begins as 8,000 US Marines are delivered to the beaches by 300 LVTs. The fighting lasted until 9 July. A final Banzai charge on 7 July saw 4,300 Japanese and 2,000 US die. The butcher's bill was huge: some 29,000 Japanese and nearly 3,000 American troops were killed.

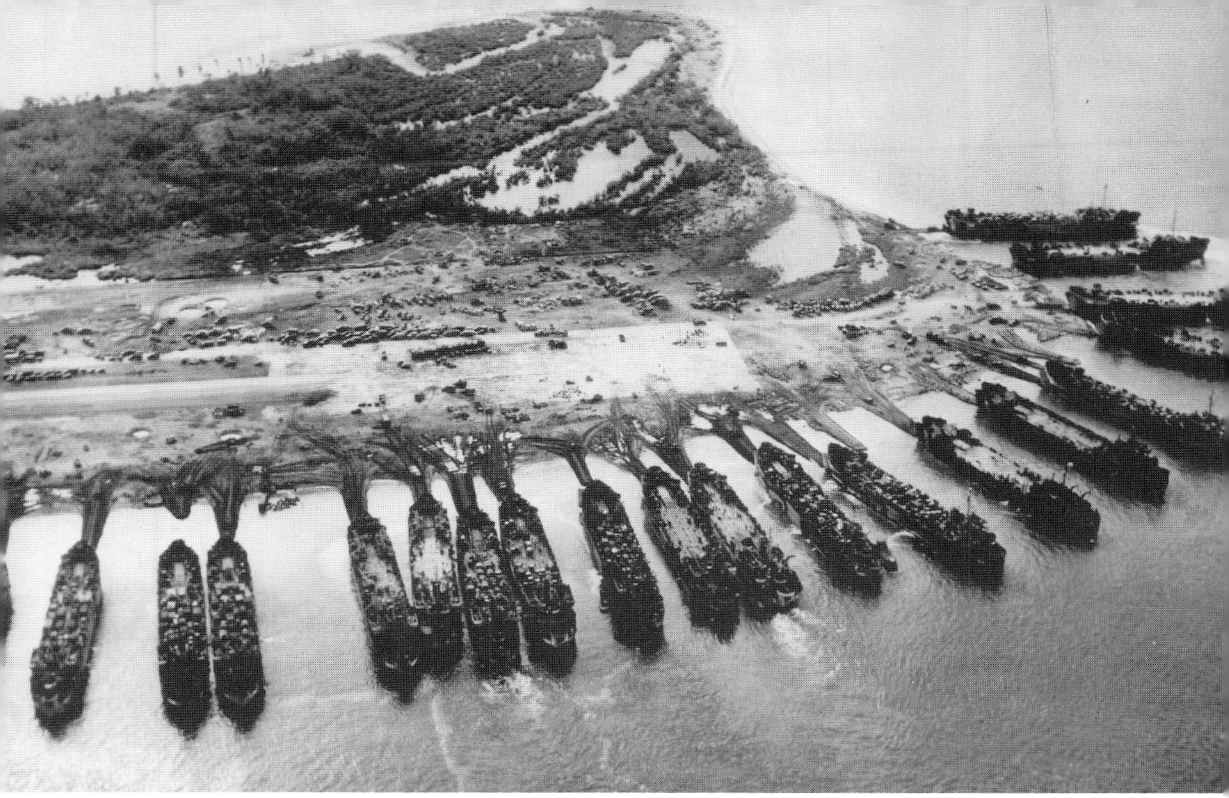

Above: LSTs disgorge men and equipment on Leyte in the Philippines. The Japanese had taken the islands in 1942; on 17 October 1944 the Americans returned. The fighting lasted until 25 December. Over 3,500 Americans lost their lives. 49,000 Japanese died, many from starvation.

Below: Operation Oboe – the Australian landings on Borneo between 1 May and final victory on 15 August 1945 – ended in the battle for Balikpapan, when the Allies' overwhelming superiority in numbers and equipment saw over 2,000 Japanese killed for the loss of 229 Australians.

Below right: Bit by bit the Philippines were taken back from the Japanese. The fighting for Corregidor and Caballo islands took place between 16 and 26 February.

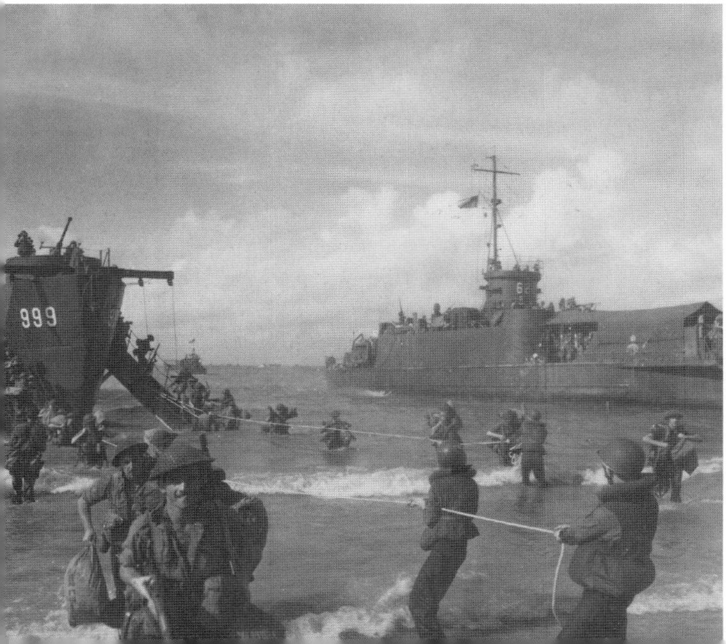
999

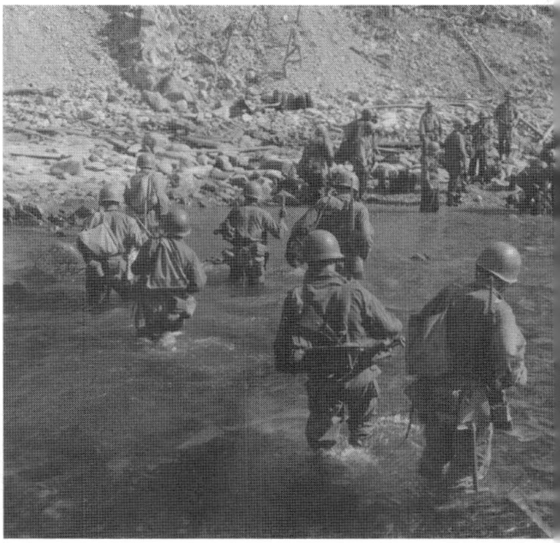

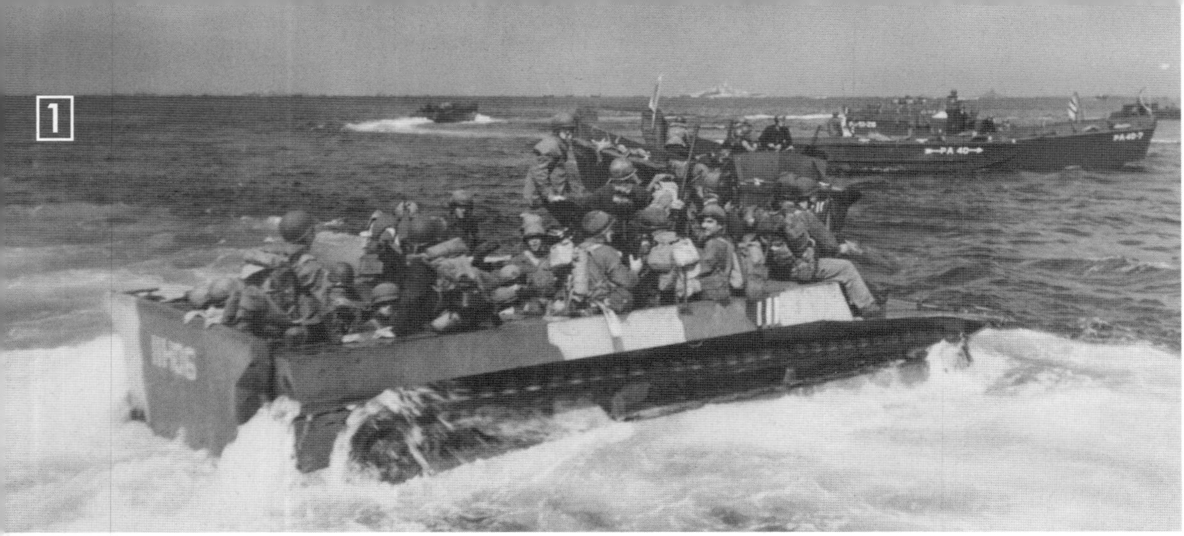
1

1 The LVT (landing vehicle tracked) series first came into use for ship-to-shore haulage using the unarmoured LVT1 and 2s in 1941–43. After Tarawa an armoured version – the LVT(A)1 with a turret-mounted 37mm – was hurried into service in 1944. Here 7th Infantry head towards the beach at Okinawa.

2 LVT2s heading towards Tinian on 24 July 1944. Nearly 3,000 were produced and this version saw the most action. Note twin MG positions with armoured shields at the bow.

3 The 37mm of the LVT(A)1 proved too small and so the 75mm howitzer that had armed the M8 GMC was used to create the LVT(A)4. These carried 100 rounds of 75mm ammo and had an open top clearly seen here. (**A**) A32, an LVT(A)4, is seen on Iwo Jima with the distinctive bump of Mt Suribachi in the background. In total 1,890 of these were built, seeing action first at Saipan. Behind A32 are (**B**) an LVT2 which had no ramp and from which the passengers had to exit over the side and two (marked **C** and **D**) LVT4s with rear ramps. Note the gunshields (not always employed) on the machine guns.

4 The turreted version were known as Amtanks, the unturreted as Amtrac/Amtracks or Alligators. Here, LVT(A)4s head towards Peleliu in September 1944.

5 LVT2s approch Saipan on 15 June 1944. The battle was fought by 2nd and 4th Marine and 27th Infantry Divisions. Over 29,000 Japanese soldiers and civilians died in the fighting which finished on 9 July.

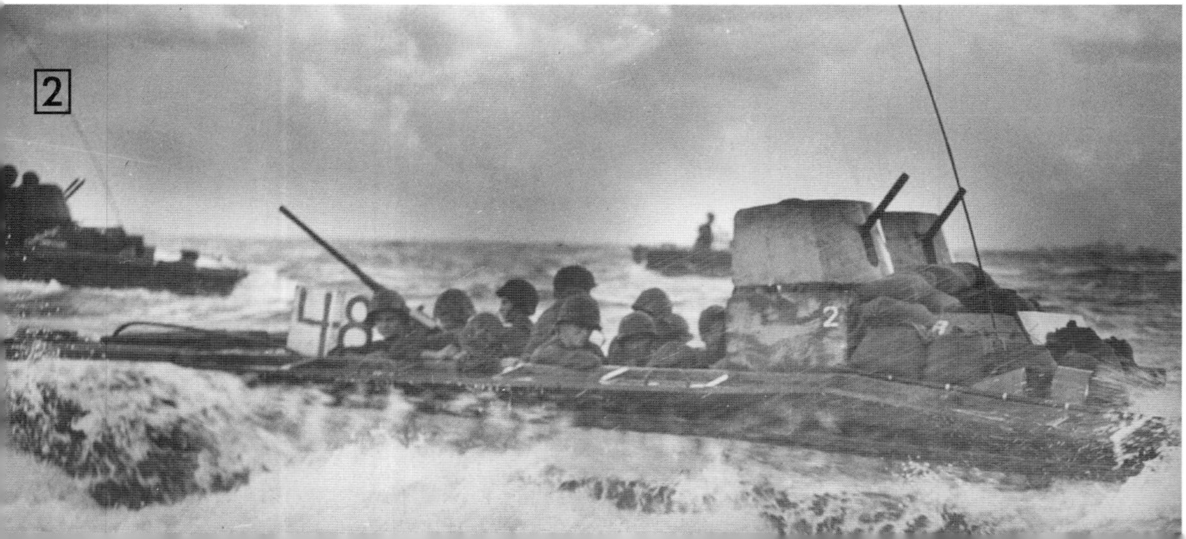
2
48

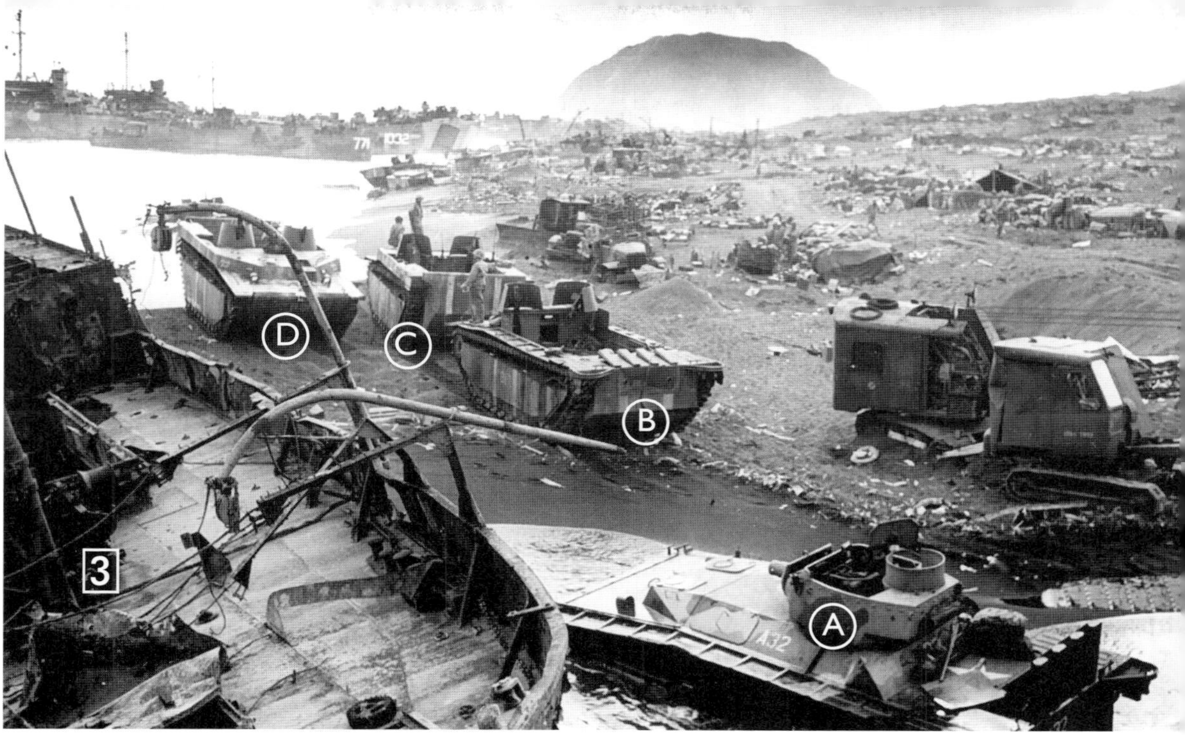
3
D
C
B
A
A32

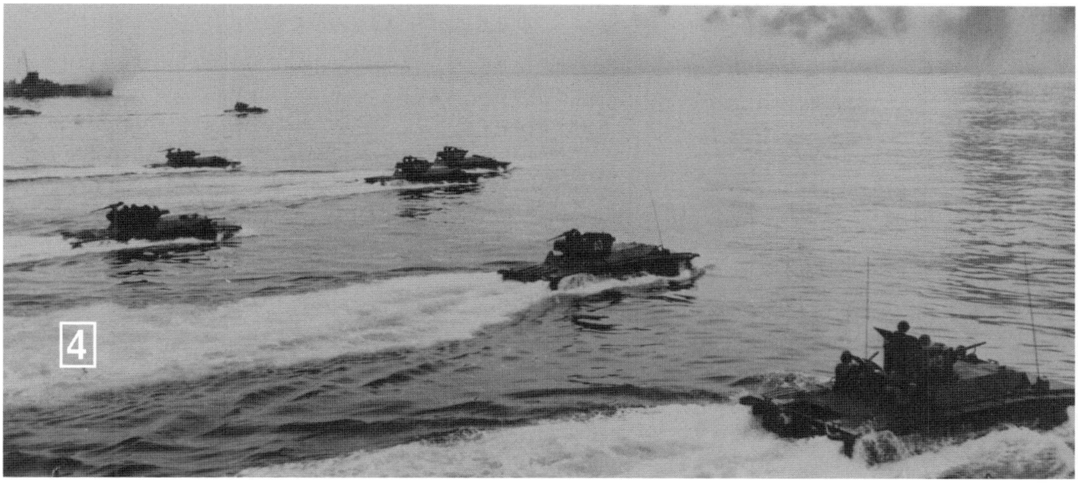
4

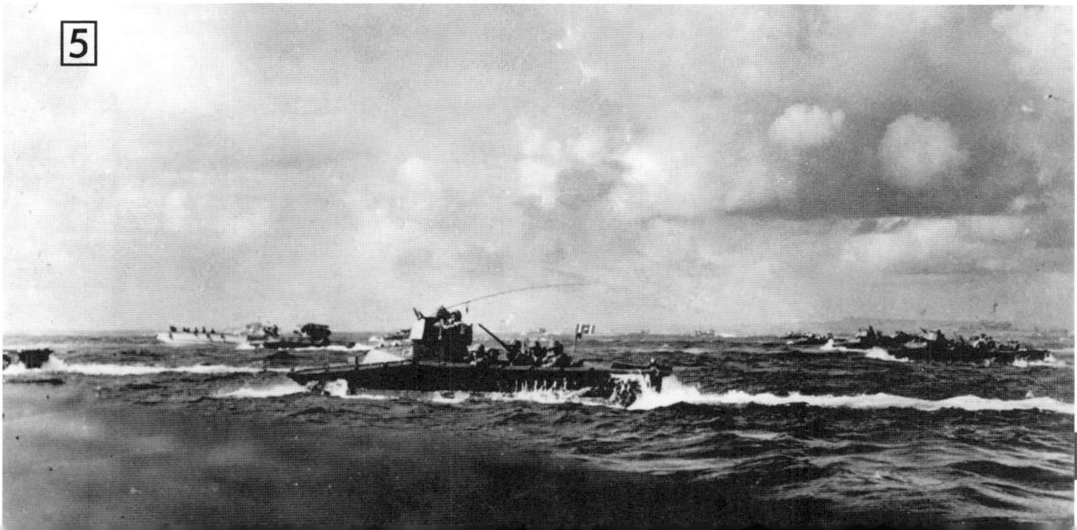
5

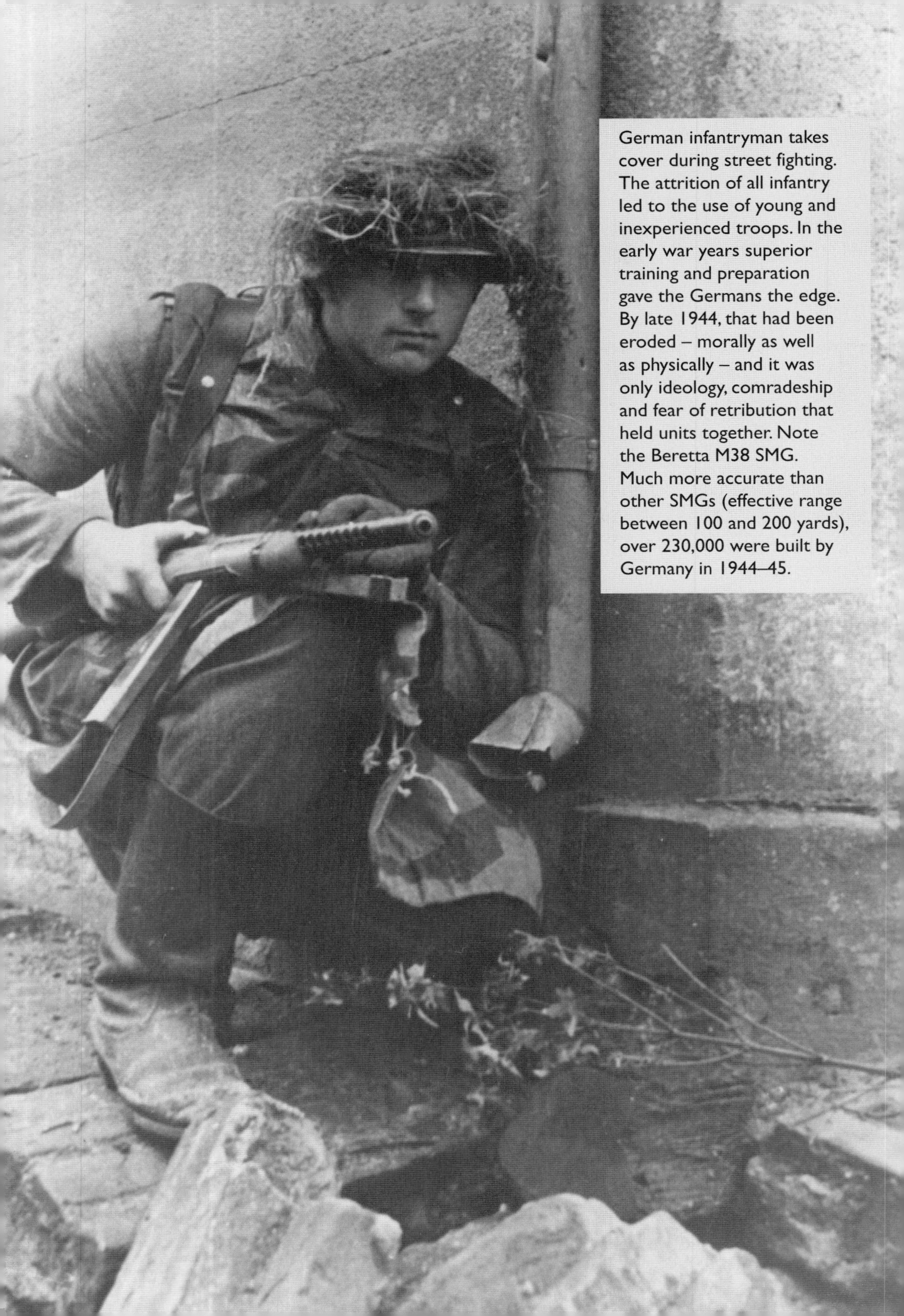

German infantryman takes cover during street fighting. The attrition of all infantry led to the use of young and inexperienced troops. In the early war years superior training and preparation gave the Germans the edge. By late 1944, that had been eroded – morally as well as physically – and it was only ideology, comradeship and fear of retribution that held units together. Note the Beretta M38 SMG. Much more accurate than other SMGs (effective range between 100 and 200 yards), over 230,000 were built by Germany in 1944–45.

4 Casualties

The course of the action in northwest Europe is well known. From the successful invasion of Normandy in June 1944 to the complete annihilation of the *Wehrmacht* as a fighting force and total surrender in May 1945, the Allies bested the Nazi forces and regime. Better logistics, air supremacy, overwhelming might: many factors contributed to this victory. The Allied infantry was at the forefront – but it was hard fighting and the casualty rates were extremely high. Rather than looking generically at the casualty rates, the opening part of this chapter concentrates on a single US Army unit: the 28th Infantry Division. The information is based on an eye-opening thesis by Maj Jeffrey P. Holt from 1982, along with the *Annual Report of Medical Department Activities* by the 28th's Divisional Surgeon, Lt Col Larry W. Weest. Together they highlight the problems faced by the Allied armies in Northwest Europe whose citizen soldiers battled not just with the enemy but against cold, disease and combat – unnatural conditions for civilised people to contend with.

The 28th Infantry Division, a National Guard unit immortalised by the photographs of its men on the Champs Élysées in liberated Paris on 29 August 1944 (see next page), was involved directly in three of the hardest battles fought by American soldiers in northwest Europe: the Hürtgen Forest, the Battle of the Bulge and clearing the Colmar Pocket – all of them in harsh weather conditions that contributed considerably to the casualty count. During its two weeks in the Hürtgen, the 28th had more than 750 reported cases of trench foot. During the four months of combat from October to February, the division suffered around 20,000 casualties. The 28th's statistics also include 2,247 of its men captured by the enemy. These casualty figures tested the division, the US Army's replacement system and, ultimately, its performance.

The division's manpower issues started before the division left the United States, the earliest concerning the quality of manpower available. Many of its officers were over 40; competition between US Army, USN and USMC for high-quality personnel saw the ground combat units lose out time and time again – something that improved during the war, but too late to help the 28th in the early years. Before 1944, Holt identifies, '43.6% of the recruits assigned to the infantry scored in the lowest two mental categories of the Army General Classification Test. This compares unfavorably to the Army Air Force (AAF) which had only 20.3% in the lowest categories, and to the Army Service Forces

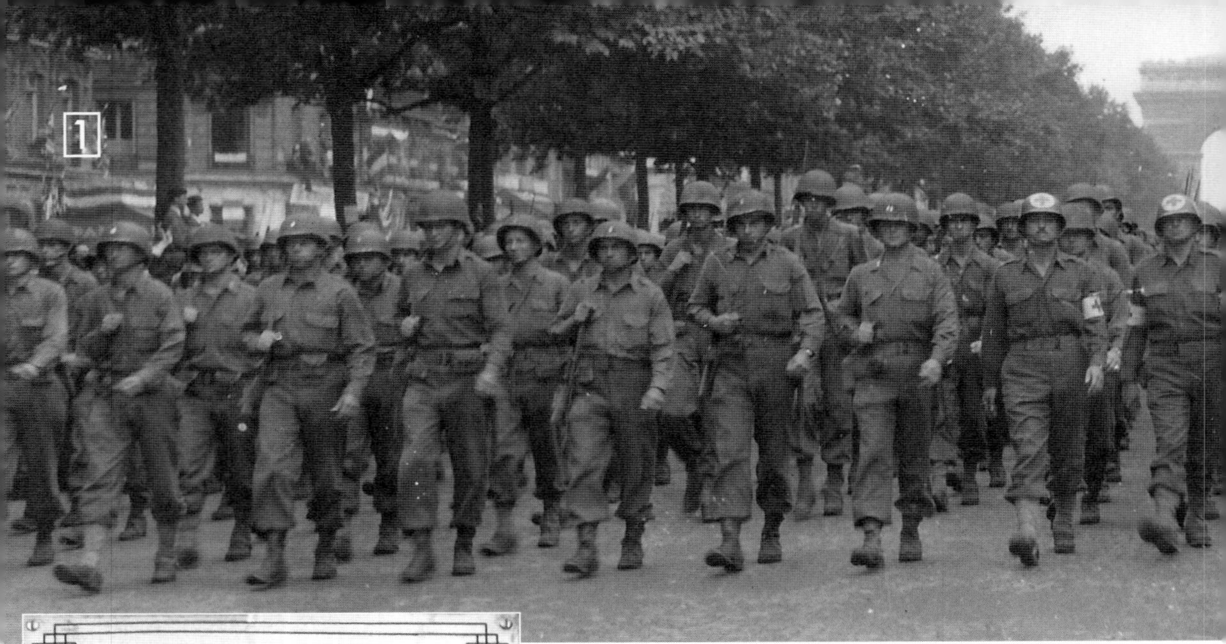

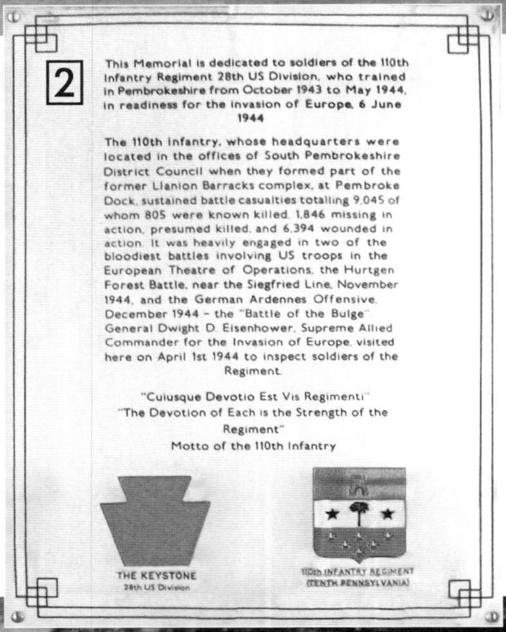
This Memorial is dedicated to soldiers of the 110th Infantry Regiment 28th US Division, who trained in Pembrokeshire from October 1943 to May 1944, in readiness for the invasion of Europe, 6 June 1944
The 110th Infantry, whose headquarters were located in the offices of South Pembrokeshire District Council when they formed part of the former Llanion Barracks complex, at Pembroke Dock, sustained battle casualties totalling 9,045 of whom 805 were known killed, 1,846 missing in action, presumed killed, and 6,394 wounded in action. It was heavily engaged in two of the bloodiest battles involving US troops in the European Theatre of Operations, the Hurtgen Forest Battle, near the Siegfried Line, November 1944, and the German Ardennes Offensive, December 1944 – the "Battle of the Bulge". General Dwight D. Eisenhower, Supreme Allied Commander for the Invasion of Europe, visited here on April 1st 1944 to inspect soldiers of the Regiment.
"Cuiusque Devotio Est Vis Regimenti"
"The Devotion of Each is the Strength of the Regiment"
Motto of the 110th Infantry
THE KEYSTONE
28th US Division
110th INFANTRY REGIMENT
(TENTH PENNSYLVANIA)

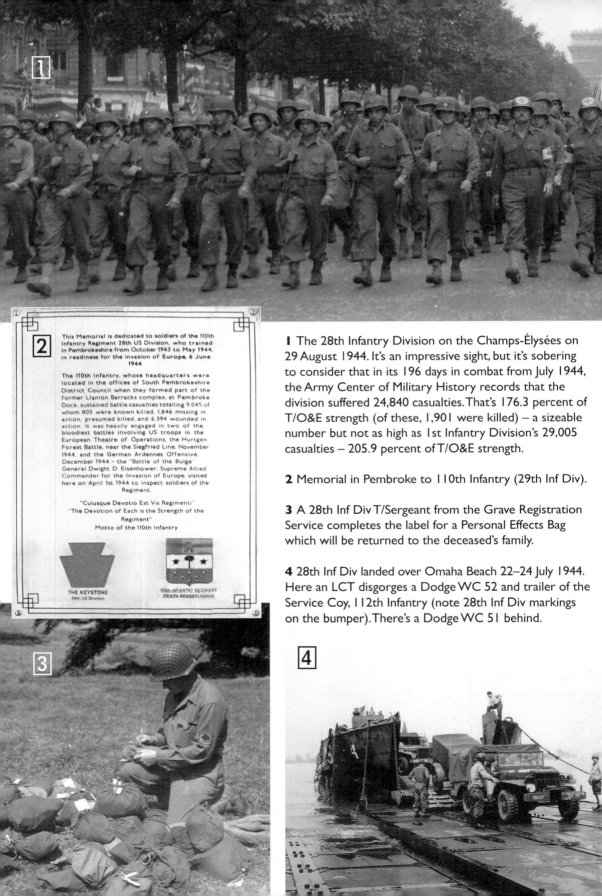

1 The 28th Infantry Division on the Champs-Élysées on 29 August 1944. It's an impressive sight, but it's sobering to consider that in its 196 days in combat from July 1944, the Army Center of Military History records that the division suffered 24,840 casualties. That's 176.3 percent of T/O&E strength (of these, 1,901 were killed) – a sizeable number but not as high as 1st Infantry Division's 29,005 casualties – 205.9 percent of T/O&E strength.

2 Memorial in Pembroke to 110th Infantry (29th Inf Div).

3 A 28th Inf Div T/Sergeant from the Grave Registration Service completes the label for a Personal Effects Bag which will be returned to the deceased's family.

4 28th Inf Div landed over Omaha Beach 22–24 July 1944. Here an LCT disgorges a Dodge WC 52 and trailer of the Service Coy, 112th Infantry (note 28th Inf Div markings on the bumper). There's a Dodge WC 51 behind.

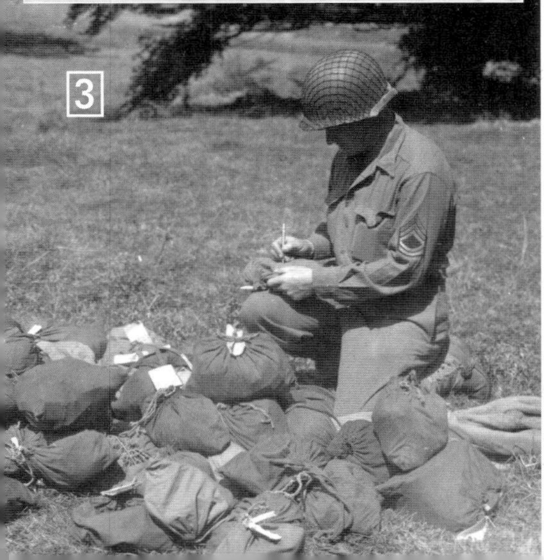

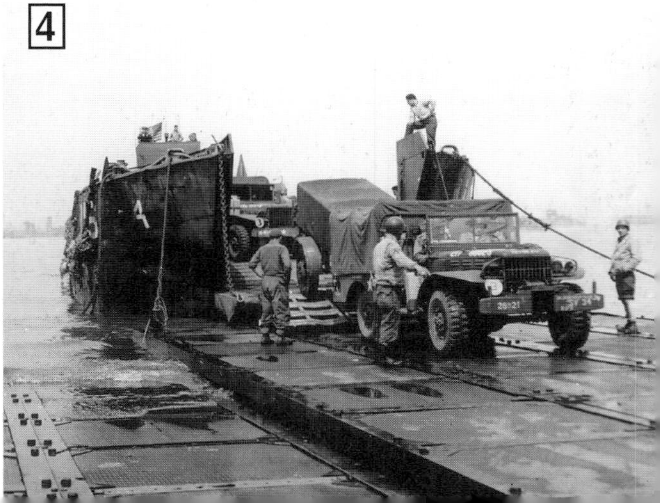

(ASF) which averaged less than 30%. In the highest two categories the differences were equally pronounced. Only 27% of the infantry was in the upper categories, compared to 42% and 52% in the AAF and ASF respectively. Infantry recruits were also likely to have less education, be shorter and weigh less than recruits in the ASF or AAF. There were numerous reasons for such disparities. Some were deliberate acts of policy while others were the result of flaws in the system.'

Federalized for active service on 17 February 1941, the division was 9,000 men below its authorised strength and when it received replacements they were draftees. The division – itself far from trained – had to handle induction training for the trainees. And as these men became fit for duty, the army suddenly decided they were needed elsewhere. Holt: 'from January through June of 1942, the 28-ID experienced the following losses in personnel: 2,000 volunteers for flight training, 2,500 soldiers departed for Officer Candidate School, 1,000 left to serve as cadre for a new infantry division, 1,500 became replacements for the 45-ID and 400 volunteered for airborne training.' During this period, on top of manpower changes, the organisation of the division changed from 'square' – two infantry brigades of two regiments – to 'triangular' with three regiments of three battalions each. Divisional manpower dropped by 7,000 and they gained 1,400 vehicles. It was only after it reached England – in mid-October 1943 – that things settled down sufficiently to allow proper training. The key defects of this were the lack of armour/infantry integration and the fact that in July it was catapulted into the bocage country for which the army as a whole was not well-prepared. So displeased with the division's performance was First Army commander Gen Omar Bradley that he replaced both commander and assistant commander: James E. Wharton came in as commander for Lloyd D. Brown – and then, by an extraordinarily unlucky quirk of fate, 24 hours later Wharton was killed by a German sniper. Norman D. Cota, who had performed so well with 29th Division on D-Day, was brought in to replace him.

Nevertheless, the division was beginning to come to terms with combat and the casualties that brought: 2,000 by the end of August. As 80 percent of these were infantry, that meant 30 percent of the riflemen in the division had been lost and many of those were the leaders. Luckily, for a few weeks after the Falaise Gap was closed, the Germans were in disarray and the Allies were able to recover – but they had to do it on the move. Between its Paris parade and 13 September the 28th advanced to the German border and the Siegfried Line. Once there, once again the fighting was fierce: initial gains were thrown back by violent counterattacks. The American troops, who – along with all the Allies in the heady weeks after the collapse of German resistance in Normandy – had thought the war was over bar the shouting, found themselves in a second battle of attrition. By 17 September, after a week of heavy fighting, the 28th had suffered over 1,900 battle casualties – and 830 non-battle casualties, a figure that increased to nearly 1,000 by the end of the month. The number of battle fatigue casualties increased, among them Pvt Eddie D. Slovik, the only American soldier to be court-martialled and executed for desertion in the war; indeed, the only one since the Civil War – 24-year-old Slovik would be the only execution of 21,000 American soldiers found guilty of desertion.

During September and October the division tried to bed in 3,352 replacements. This was not an easy process – as Holt identifies: 'Leaders criticized not only the quality that

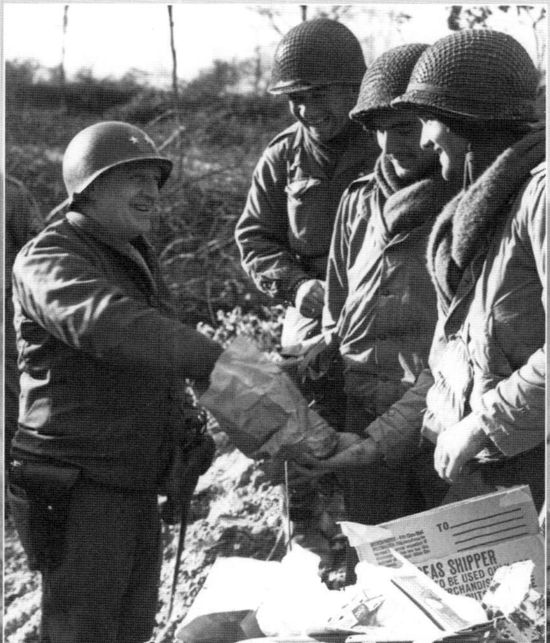

Left: Gen Norman Cota took over 28th Infantry Division but the unit struggled in the Hürtgen Forest. As was usually the case, high casualties and low morale led to increasing battle fatigue cases.

Below: The Hürtgen Forest – Maj Gen James Gavin would later say, 'For us the Hürtgen was one of the most costly, most unproductive, and most ill-advised battles that our army has ever fought.'

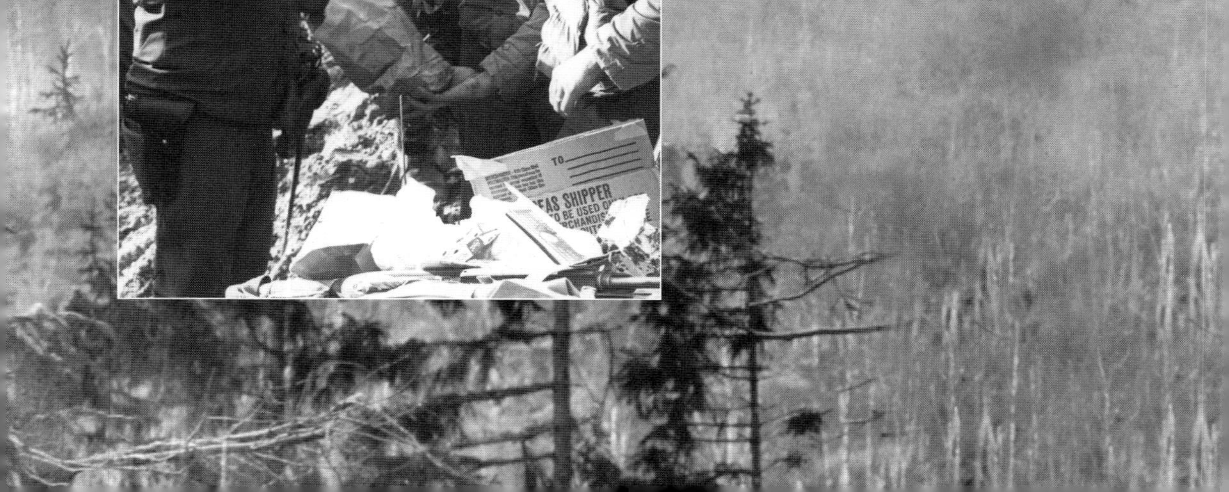

resulted from the hasty conversion of non-infantry personnel to combat riflemen, but also that of trained infantry replacements as well. As a result, most units had to concentrate precious training time on individual soldier skills. More complex unit skills were hard to develop and almost impossible to sustain in this environment. This created a vicious cycle that led to excessive casualties and poor unit performance. The health and morale of soldiers were also bound to suffer in such a turbulent system.'

It was taking up to five months to process a soldier from completion of basic training in the United States to a unit in Europe. Understandably, during this time his physical conditioning worsened. He was then thrown into the mincing machine at the front where infantry soldiers – particularly replacements – had a low expectancy of surviving injury or disease. Unsurprisingly, this included battle fatigue. There were minimal rest and recreation opportunities even when out of the line – the best facilities were the American Red Cross caravans – and the preparation for 28th's battles in the Hürtgen Forest was in a quiet sector around Elsenborn where they still suffered 59 dead, 519 wounded and 433 non-battle casualties and had to put up with awful weather. The divisional surgeon recorded: 'Upon reaching Siegfried Line a new phase of combat began. The Divisional units became fixed in their positions and the previously moderate weather was replaced by continual cold and rain. The men were subjected to almost incessant pounding by artillery as well as the weather.'

On 25 October the 28th were trucked to Roetgen in Germany where they relieved 9th Infantry Division. The 9th had suffered grievously in their time in the Hürtgen: over 4,000 casualties – see the table on p. 136. (Indeed, the 9th's wartime statistics also make unpleasant reading: 264 days in combat, 2,905 dead, 33,864 – 240.4 of T/O&E.)

Continued on p. 134.

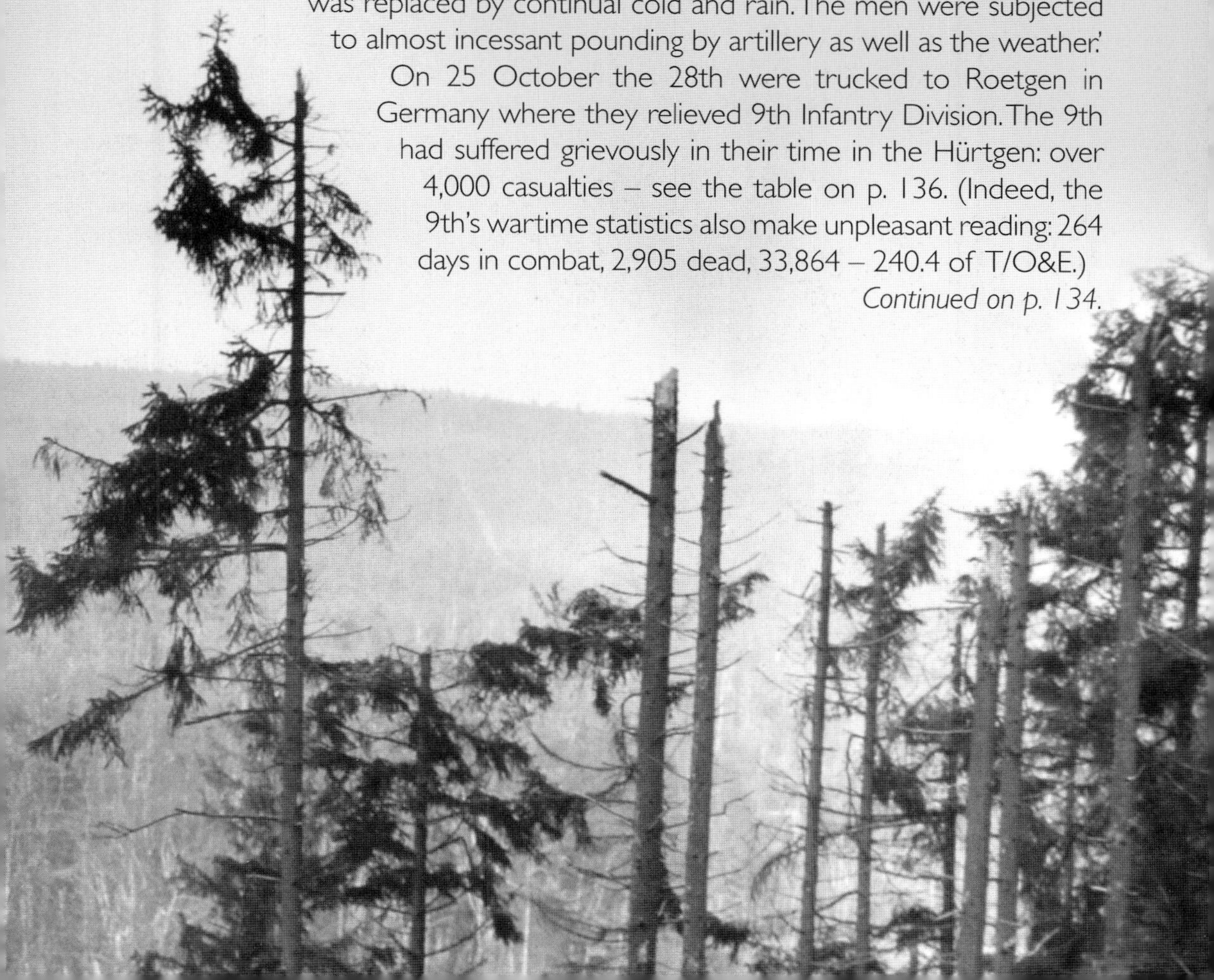

Combat Lesson No 7: Replacement Orientation
(edited excerpts)

Replacement Instruction – the Wrong Kind

A Lieutenant comments on his ominous introduction to front-line existence:

'On my way to the front as an officer replacement, I met several individuals who had come back from the line. Invariably they recounted to me their hair-raising experiences – their outfits had been "wiped out," or "pinned down for days"; "officers didn't have a dog's chance of survival," etc. One platoon sergeant went statistical on me; he said his platoon had lost 16 officers in one 2-week period. I expected confidently that I would be blown to bits within 15 minutes after my arrival at the front.

'Later experience has shown me that enlisted men who come in as replacements are subjected to similar morale-breaking tales. I have tried to get my old men to give the new replacement a break by being careful not to exaggerate their battle experiences or in any way distort the picture of front-line existence. Give the new men a common-sense introduction to the combat zone and there will be fewer men going on sick call before an attack.'

Noncoms and privates of Company 'K,' 11th Infantry, ETO, draw attention to the same problem:

'Our replacements come to us filled with tenseness and dread caused by stories they have heard in the rear. Special instructors from the front should be used at replacement centers to talk the new men out of this un-necessary panic. Of course, the soundest remedy is to have the replacements occupy a defensive position for a time, but even then the kind of treatment they are given upon arrival at the front makes a big difference in the amount of good they will do their new outfit.'

Replacement troops prepare to move up. Omar Bradley said, 'Early in the campaign, replacements were filtered directly into their squads, fresh from the "repple depples." [replacement depots] Casualties among them greatly exceeded those of battlewise veterans on the line. Many went into the lines at night and perished before the morning. ... By fall of 1944 we had reorganized this procedure and replacements were being indoctrinated by division before being committed into the line.' He continued, 'Among U.S. troops the replacement depots soon developed an infamous reputation for callousness and inefficiency.'

– the Right Kind

Poor orientation of replacements may seriously affect the fighting ability and survival chances of the men themselves and may also endanger the unit with whom they first serve. For these reasons, leaders of platoons, squads, and companies should find out exactly what orientation and training have been given the men and should provide essential orientation 'on the spot' in so far as is practicable before sending them into combat. If a divisional training plan similar to that described below is in operation, the problem of inducting new men into the smaller units is much simplified, and lower-unit orientation can be modified accordingly.

This effective training system is described by the Chief of Staff, 83rd Division, ETO:

'Our division has received thousands of replacements since its first combat experience in Normandy. More than 90 per cent of these replacements have been infantry. Many of the replacements came into the division lacking confidence in their ability and paralyzed by apprehension engendered by loose talk before and upon their arrival.

'Some time ago we started a course of instruction for our replacements. It lasts 2.5 days and is conducted by battle-experienced personnel. Particular emphasis is placed upon the following points:

'a. How to live in a foxhole. This includes construction of the foxhole and information on preserving health and maintaining bodily cleanliness under combat conditions.

'b. Development of an aggressive attitude. We emphasize particularly their better chances for survival if they avoid being pinned down.

'c. Use of the fragmentation grenade, antitank grenade, and bazooka. We give about 25 percent of the replacements a chance to fire the grenade and bazooka; all of them observe the effectiveness of these weapons.

'Throughout the course, the men are trained in groups of 12. They are later assigned to organizations by these same groups so that each man always has some acquaintances when he joins his combat unit.

'We have found that this course of instruction gives the replacements much greater self-confidence; it 'debunks' the notions they have picked up at the rear. The course has definitely improved not only the morale but also the fighting ability of our replacements. We expect to continue the plan for all replacements who come to this division.'

Common Failings

Says a successful Third Army Rifle Company Commander, ETO:

'The following failings are common among replacements. They must be strictly and promptly eliminated if excessive casualties are to be avoided and combat efficiency obtained:

- Lack of ordinary discipline (saying "Yeah" instead of "Yes, sir," etc.).
- Jumping at the sound of every outgoing or incoming artillery shell.
- Unwillingness to use the rifle. (Many have been told never to fire without direct orders for fear of revealing positions.)
- Lack of pride in self, organization, work.
- Poor physical condition.
- A tendency to bunch together when in danger.
- Freezing under fire.
- Slovenliness in care of equipment.
- Lack of skill with rifle and other infantry weapons.
- Fear of the night.
- Ignorance of squad formations.
- Ignorance of field sanitation and of personal hygiene in combat areas.'

9th Infantry Division Casualties as Reported by the Division Surgeon, 15 June–31 December 1944

	KIA	WIA	Disease	Battle injury	Exhaustion	Total
15 June–1 July	390	2,900	824	220	165	4,499
July	172	3,570	973	448	557	5,720
August	376	2,125	1,232	438	30	4,201
September	218	2,111	1,224	398	176	4,127
October	384	2,510	1,877	600	323	5,694
November	82	753	1,962	516	52	3,365
December	197	907	1,663	541	117	3,425
Total	1,819	14,876	9,755	3,161	1,420	31,031

The 28th was only 250 short of its official complement when the fighting began, but soon there were heavy casualties. Indeed, the 28th's figures were even worse than that of the 9th: 16 M10 Tank Destroyers, 31 Sherman medium tanks, and scores of machine guns, antitank guns, mortars, and many other material losses. It wasn't all a one-sided exchange, the Germans lost 2,000 killed, 913 taken prisoner, and 15 tanks destroyed.

It had all started so well! A huge artillery barrage on 2 November had cleared the way and within 48 hours 3rd Battalion, 112th Infantry Regiment, had taken Schmidt, something the 9th hadn't done in two weeks. Sending tanks forward to support them against the inevitable German counter-attack, however, proved difficult. The notorious Kall Trail was narrow, crumbling into steep ravines and mined. Only three Shermans of the 707th Tank Battalion reached the village by 4 November when the Germans – elements of 89th Infantry and 116th Panzer Divisions – counterattacked. In spite of the tanks, panic ensued and the 28th started to splinter. Three companies broke and ran: around 200 becoming PoWs. Desperate attempts to send reinforcements came to naught as the Germans infiltrated the Kall Trail. It was cut for a period but six more Shermans and nine M10s of the 893rd TD Battalion helped nearby Kommerscheidt hold until the 9th, before it, too, fell. In the meantime, another panic had seen Vossenack fall on the 6th. Of the more than 2,000 GIs who had advanced east of the Kall, only around 300 returned.

What had caused such a debacle? A mixture of terrain, weather and inexperienced troops added to poor command decisions that expected the units to hold in the face of artillery and tank attacks. Holt refers to Gen G.S. Patton's view on the staying power of infantrymen. 'He believed that an infantry unit was capable of about 60 hours of fighting. Beyond that point it was too exhausted to continue.' This was particularly true as the veterans became casualties and replacements took their place.

The 28th Division's losses were substantial: the 112th Regiment had seen 167 killed, 719 wounded, 431 missing and 544 non-battle casualties – 2,093 of the original 3,000. The

THE SECOND ATTACK ON SCHMIDT
28TH DIVISION
2-9 November 1944
U.S. LINE AM 2 NOV
GROUND GAINED AND LOST BY U.S.
U.S. LINE 9 NOV
ROADBLOCK
AXIS OF MAIN U.S. ATTACKS
GERMAN COUNTERATTACKS
WEST WALL PILLBOXES
(GERMAN 275TH DIVISION UNITS NOT SHOWN)
Contour Interval 50 meters
MILES
KILOMETERS
Hürtgen
HÜRTGEN
FOREST
Brandenberg
Bergstein
Vossenack
Kommerscheidt
Schmidt
Harscheidt
GERMAN COUNTERATTACK AM, 4 NOV

division had 6,184 casualties – 45 percent of its original strength – of which 750 were from trench foot. One in three officers – 249 of 828 – were casualties including a regimental commander, and three of the nine battalion commanders.

It was no secret that a serious shortage of infantry replacements was looming – the War Department had been directing conservation of manpower from late 1943 onward, and began conversion programmes to produce infantry replacements. It issued a formal directive in May 1944 that required theatres to establish manpower conservation programmes. When push came to shove, Patton converted service troops to riflemen. Omar Bradley discusses the problem in *A Soldier's Story*, highlighting the stress that the Hürtgen Forest battles had placed on the US forces. 'In December,' he wrote, 'the average division attacked with but three quarters of its rifle strength ... [on] December 15 G-1 reported the 12th Army Group short 17,000 riflemen among its 31 divisions on the line.'

He went on, 'Within five short weeks the winter attack had cost us 64,000 casualties ... And as if this were not already strain enough on the bankrupt replacement system, trenchfoot added almost 12,000 more. ... At the very moment when we needed them most, too many men were being diverted to the Pacific.'

On 14 November the 28th Division moved to the east of Bastogne to recuperate. Things had to get better! Certainly, the manpower improved: by end-December replacements had almost completely filled the ranks. Many of them, however, weren't infantrymen and had to receive basic footslogger training with the division. Nonetheless, the Army Specialized Training Program had kicked in by this time and the quality of the replacements had started to improve. Set up at the end of 1942, this programme was offered at 227 universities in the United States. The requirements for joining were fierce and attempted to take the cleverest enlisted soldiers and prepare them to become officers. When the replacement crisis arrived, the program was ended and its 70,000 trainees were

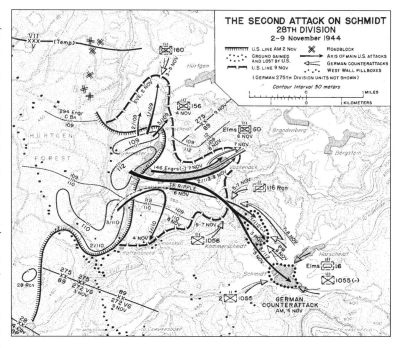

put into the replacement system. Famous names who were involved in the programme included Mel Brooks, Robert Dole, Henry Kissinger, Gore Vidal and Kurt Vonnegut.

In the Ardennes, the 28th had a large sector to defend – a frontage of 25 miles that meant the division had to defend from isolated positions rather than a continuous line. When, on 16 December the quiet Luxembourg–Belgian front became the epicentre of a major German counterattack, 28th Infantry Division bore the brunt of the attack, and did so with great bravery and effective defence. For three days they delayed the Germans, 109th and 112th Infantry on the shoulders of the attack, the latter winning a Presidential Unit Citation. The 110th fought as a number of units, the final stand at Clervaux holding up the Germans for long enough to allow the 101st Airborne to secure Bastogne. The 110th incurred 2,500 casualties; some of the survivors were able to escape to the west where they continued the fight. They were luckier than the 106th (US) Infantry Division whose 422nd and 423rd Regiments were surrounded and forced to surrender. The Germans gained over 6,000 PoWs.

The performance of 28th Infantry Division had been exemplary in spite of the high casualties, and the many replacements necessitated by the losses in the Hürtgen Forest. Its recent experiences helped it in the aftermath of the battles in the Ardennes. It was able to bed in new replacements and move south to Alsace where it was in time for the third of its testing campaigns.

At the start of the battle to close the Colmar Pocket in January 1945, the 28th was moved from the Ardennes, travelling by train. The plan was to use the division defensively as they were 'capable of only limited action.' Of course, it didn't work out like that and the 28th had to go into battle in awful weather – intially, it was very cold (-20°C) with deep snow lying on the ground. As the thaw set in, everywhere became a mudbath. They fought their way through to Colmar, the 109th Infantry Regiment, led by Col James Rudder who had commanded 2nd Rangers at Pointe du Hoc on D-Day, reaching the outskirts before diplomatically allowing the French 5th Armoured Division take the city. The 28th would have one final action – moving back north on 23 February, attacking across the Ahr River in Germany on 6 March before being placed in defensive positions. It had endured 196 days of combat since 27 July 1944 and sustained 16,752 casualties.

Clervaux stood directly on the XLVII Panzerkorps route towards Bastogne. A handful of 28th Inf Div soldiers, led by Capt John Aitken, supported by B/2nd Tank Bn, 9th Armd Div, were besieged by the German 2. Panzer Division on 17 December. Every hour of delay helped the defenders of Bastogne.

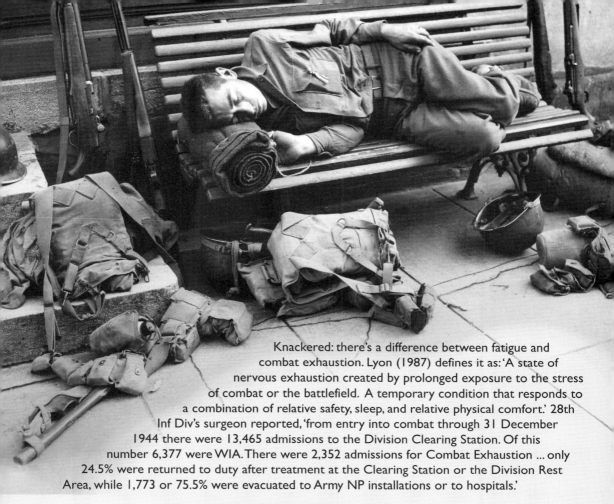

Knackered: there's a difference between fatigue and combat exhaustion. Lyon (1987) defines it as: 'A state of nervous exhaustion created by prolonged exposure to the stress of combat or the battlefield. A temporary condition that responds to a combination of relative safety, sleep, and relative physical comfort.' 28th Inf Div's surgeon reported, 'from entry into combat through 31 December 1944 there were 13,465 admissions to the Division Clearing Station. Of this number 6,377 were WIA. There were 2,352 admissions for Combat Exhaustion ... only 24.5% were returned to duty after treatment at the Clearing Station or the Division Rest Area, while 1,773 or 75.5% were evacuated to Army NP installations or to hospitals.'

Key Causes of Battlefield Stress

(edited excerpts from Maj Robert M. Lyon (1987))

- **Fatigue:** General Patton said, 'Fatigue makes cowards of us all.' A survey of infantrymen in four different divisions in Italy during a relatively quiet period in April 1945 indicated that even during the best of times nearly one third of the soldiers averaged four hours or less of sleep out of each twenty-four hours while they were in the line.
- **Physical discomfort:** Exposure to cold, heat, and wet; constant dirtiness; and vermin wears a man's resistance down increasing his susceptibility to a mental, as well as physical, breakdown. Henri Barbusse said, 'Dampness rusts men like rifles, more slowly but more deeply.'
- **Separation:** The separation of a soldier from home, family, friends, and women and the possibility that he may never see them again creates stress.
- **Isolation:** The battlefield is the loneliest place in the world creating a strong need for company.
- **Fear:** The threat to life, limb, and health versus the obligation to perform one's duty creates an inner conflict that can lead to breakdown.
- **Loss of comrades:** The experience of watching others suffer and die makes a significant contribution towards the strain of the battlefield. Data collected in World War II indicated a high correlation in units where soldiers saw close friends killed or wounded and later saw men crack up.
- **Uncertainty:** Rumors constantly inflate and deflate the expectations of soldiers.

Trench Foot

Trench foot is caused by prolonged exposure of the feet to damp, unsanitary, and cold conditions. The word trench gives the clue: while discovered before World War I it came to the fore in the trenches. It's not like frostbite. It can develop in temperatures up to 60°F in as little as 13 hours. It's worth pointing out to anyone who has suffered from athlete's foot or a similar issue, that trench foot is rather different. During World War I 75,000 British soldiers were casualties of trench foot and it led to gangrene, ulcers and amputations. Poor vascular supply may make feet numb, and they give off a decaying odor – the early stages of necrosis setting in. The high command of every army was only too well aware of the problem as is shown in this memo from Gen Patton:

MEMORANDUM (dated 21 November 1944) TO: Corps and Division Commanders.

1. The most serious menace confronting us today is not the German Army, which we have practically destroyed, but the weather which, if we do not exert ourselves, may well destroy us through the incidence of trench foot.

2. If the prevention of trench foot were impossible, I would not mention it, but prevention is perfectly practicable and is a function of command.

3. Trench foot is due primarily to two causes, both of which produce a reduction in the blood supply of the foot. The first cause is due to the feet being cold and wet, which naturally shrinks the small blood vessels. The second cause is due to reduced flow of blood to the foot due to tight socks, and/or tight shoes, and tight leggings.

4. If company officers and non-commissioned officers did their full duty, there would be no trench foot. The onus of their failure rests on you. You must see to it that the following points are brought home to all members of your command:

a. First, each man is personally responsible for the health of his feet. He has to live with them, and if, through carelessness, he becomes a victim of trench foot he may well become a cripple for life.

b. Second, company officers and non-commissioned officers must see to it that the men care for their feet.

5. This care should be exercised along the following lines:

a. Where men have arctics, they should be worn in wet and cold weather.

b. Before putting the arctics on, the shoe should be dried and two pair of dry socks worn inside it. Size of shoe must be large enough to permit this to be done without constriction. Lace shoe as loosely as possible. Same procedure applies when no arctics are available.

c. The shoe should also be treated with dubbin, particularly where the upper joins the sole. One treatment of dubbin is not sufficient; it should be repeated daily.

d. Men should carry one extra pair of socks in their helmets. This will not only keep the top of the head warm but will dry the socks.

e. Whenever opportunity affords—and certainly each night—the galoshes, shoes, and socks should be removed, and the feet massaged vigorously for at least five minutes by the watch. The men should then put on a pair of dry socks next to the foot and preferably a second pair of dry socks outside the first pair. If only one dry pair is available it should be worn next the skin.

6. Orders have been issued that all new shoes be treated with dubbin before issue. Unit supply officers are responsible to check that this is done.

7. When possible a pair of dry socks will be issued with the daily ration and the wet pair turned in for laundering and drying.

8. We are going to have weather conditions from now on until the end of the war which will be conducive to trench foot. To win the war we must conquer trench foot. You have conquered every other obstacle—I am sure you can conquer this.

Trench foot can be prevented by keeping the feet clean, warm, and dry. During World War I it was discovered that regular inspections were a key preventive measure as were buddy systems of checking and massaging. Trench foot contributed significantly to the enormous infantry casualty rates. From October 1944 to April 1945 there were more than 70,000 soldiers in the ETO hospitalized for trench foot. More than 90 percent of these casualties were infantrymen and less than 50 percent would return to combat. However, as Holt points out, this did not pertain in the British and Canadian armies who had only 205 cases. Even allowing for smaller numbers of troops it shows that the British clothing was warmer and more water resistant, its sock/boot combination more resilient. The British were also good at providing hot food – and, of course, tea – regularly.

Lt Col Larry W. Weest, 28th Infantry's Divisional Surgeon, had this to say in his *Annual Report of Medical Department Activities* of 16 February 1945:

'Due to the wet cold weather, the long cramped hours in fox-holes, and the lack of overshoes, this unit suffered hundreds of trench foot casualties. Immediate steps were taken to stem this occurrence. Galoshes were obtained but unfortunately most of them were smaller than the average soldier's size. This was remedied later. Preventive measures taken by the soldiers were preached, and various systems of supplying dry socks used. With the supply of galoshes and the teaching of prevention the rate dropped. With the introduction of shoe pacs in the later winter, frost bite was reduced to a minimum, and at this point it is usual to investigate any occurrence to determine whether lack of galoshes, or lack of preventive measures were contributory

'Sanitary methods taught by the U.S. Army are simple, practical and efficient but the average solider, in spite of instruction, will not often apply them in combat and then needs constant indoctrination. This is reasonable to the extent that his life is his main consideration. In garrison or in static situations the general sanitation is good. From the medical view point one wishes that the unit commander would, in a tactical situation, take a longer view toward sanitation and not forget it in his preoccupation with the immediate military problem. It should be possible to coordinate higher supply agencies with the sanitary and preventive measures prerequisite to a planned military operation so that items of supply, such as stoves, galoshes, winter clothing, heavy socks, rain coats etc, are readily available when the need arises. Usually requisitions are placed when the need arises and a relatively long period must elapse before these supplies can be received.'

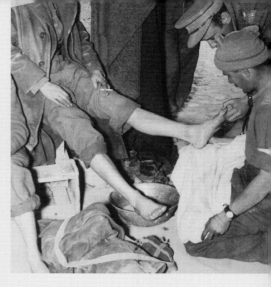

Foot inspection, Benghazi.
Feet are a problem for infantrymen. Wounds are one thing, but to lose large numbers of men through lack of sufficient care, primarily through trench foot, is like a self-inflicted wound. Studied and understood since World War I, it's surprising how much of a problem it turned out to be in 1939–45, particularly in autumn/winter 1944. 'The first thing the soldier lost, and if he was lucky the only thing, was his toenails. If the trench foot worsened, a GI's feet would turn white, then purple, until they finally turned black. If the situation reached this level, the soldier would be unable to walk. Toes were lost in some instances, and feet required amputation in the more extreme cases. If the unfortunate patient began to show the symptoms of gangrene, doctors had little option but to remove the lower leg. During the winter of 1944–45, enough men to fill the ranks of three full infantry divisions (45,000 men) moved off the front lines due to trench foot.' (Thompson, 2017.)

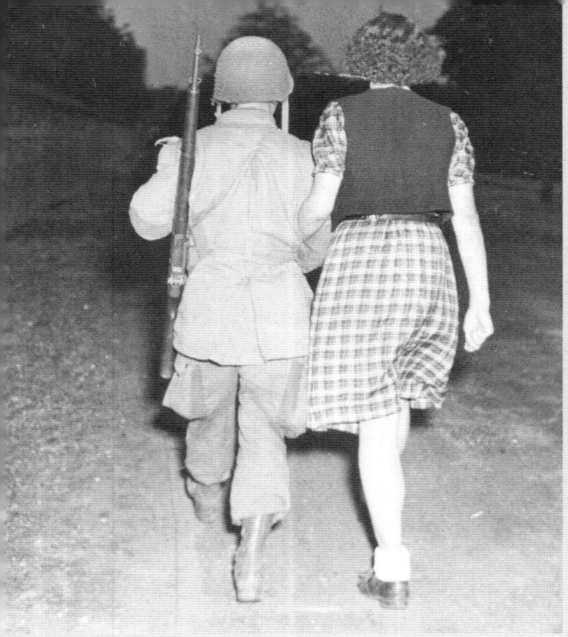

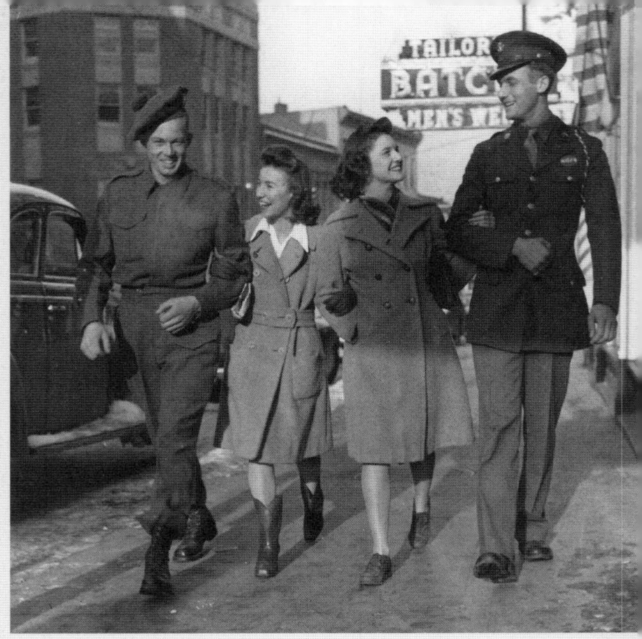
TAILOR

Above: Sex is important. In his listing of causes of battlefield stress, Lyon identifies, deprivation of sexual contact as an important element, because 'Sexual contact provides security, a feeling of value, a release for pent up emotion to include stress and in many cases a feeling of masculinity. Unfortunately this emotional reinforcement is usually denied the soldier.' Because of this, brothels were heavily used when the forces were in town and venereal disease became a significant issue.

Venereal Disease Control

(edited excerpts from Weest, 28th Inf Div surgeon's Annual Report, 1945)

'It was held the responsibility of commanders to see that Venereal Disease was held to a minimum. Generally, the rate for the year may be considered fairly low. Certainly considerable time and effort were employed in instructing troops, making "pro" stations available, issuing mechanical and chemical prophylactics, ... The biggest single contributing factor to VD is drunkenness. The average soldier in garrison will take care of himself if he is sober but when the status of inebriation dulls his faculties he is either clumsy and inefficient in the application of prophylactics or forgets about them all together.

'On the continent in addition to the factors mentioned above, one has to combat a state of mind of the soldier which is composed of the so called "last fling attitude" with release of his repressions in the towns of relaxation. Since prostitution is widespread it is possible that the number of combat days is the one dominant factor in controlling VD. Although instruction and sex education have been stressed more than ever. ... As it is the soldier often finds himself alone in a large city and easily falls prey to roving prostitutes. ... The fact that this Division has been in active combat since landing in France has minimized somewhat the dangers of too frequent sex contact. Most of our cases of VD have occurred in those troops who went on pass to Paris although occasional cases have been picked up in smaller towns and cities, and not at time during active operations. ... Certainly the many opportunities for easy sex contacts on this continent constitute a constant threat to VD control coupled with the soldiers' release of inhibition and his "tomorrow we may die" attitude.'

British forces certainly had problems with VD. By the end of the 21st Army Group campaign, Jonathan Fennell writes, 'the British had suffered 4,390 losses to VD ... [the] Canadians 7,000.' It Italy between 17 October 1943 and 31 March 1945 the Eighth Army figure was 15,140.

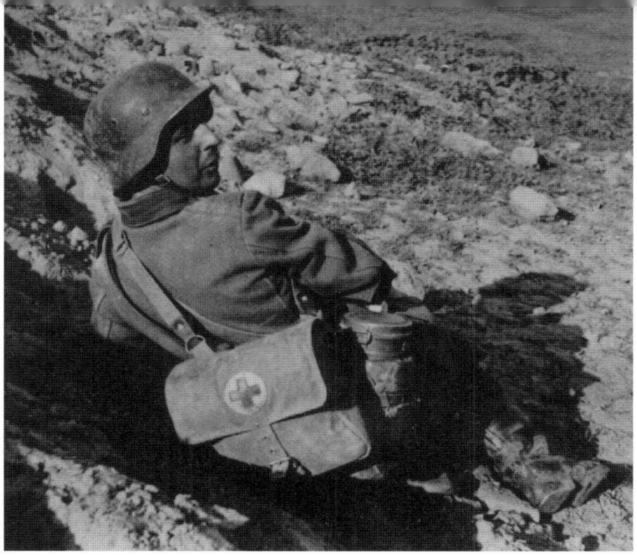

Right: German medic in Russia. Both sides had to contend with weather, long logistical distances and, if truth be told, a lack of humanity on both sides. In the Red Army, 12 percent of officer casualties July 1942–June 1943 were medics. Many of the Russian doctors and medical staff were women and during the battle of Stalingrad, the female medical orderlies had to crawl into no man's land and drag the wounded back. 'Much of their heroism was wasted by the sloppy and indifferent evacuation from the Stalingrad theatre. Many of the wounded died on the banks of the Volga while waiting to be ferried across to safety. High casualty rates were suffered by the ferry drivers and many vessels carrying wounded were sunk by enemy fire. Once evacuated, casualties had to endure poor conditions in field hospitals. Despite the presence of some of the finest Russian doctors, these were described as meat-processing factories.' (Kaplan, 2000.)

Below: Finland is blessed with many stretches of open water and so floatplanes (here Junkers K43s) were used to evacuate sick and wounded soldiers who would not otherwise have survived long land journeys over bad roads.

German Casualty Evacuation

1 Stretcher bearers or walking wounded arrive at battalion aid post from battlefield
2 Ambulance car post
3a Field dressing station
3b Lightly wounded collecting point
4 Divisional field hospital
5 Casualty collection point
6a Army field hospital
6b Army field hospital for lightly wounded
7 Hospitals in Germany or elsewhere

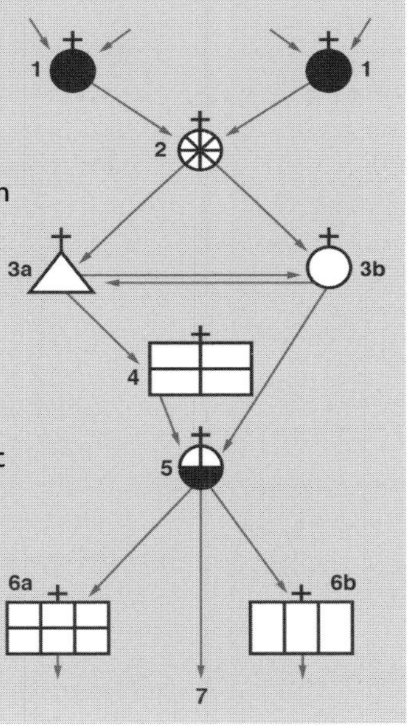
1
1
2
3a
3b
4
5
6a
6b
7

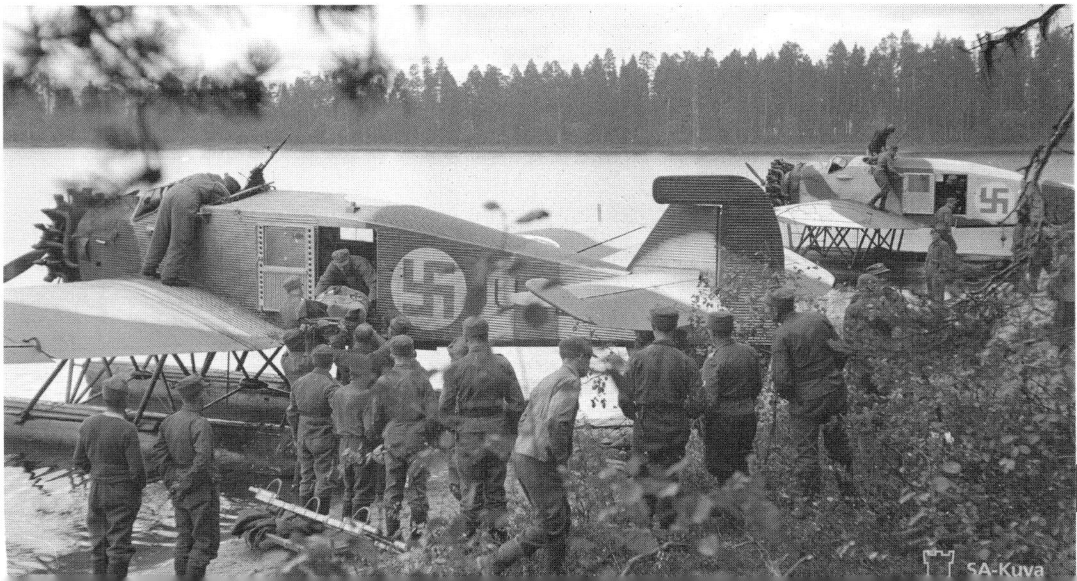
SA-Kuva

Medical Kit Examples

Red Army Medic	Japanese Medical Orderly	US Medical Private
10 ammonia ampoules	Peptic tablets (for stomach trouble)	Plaster, Adhesive, Surgical, 1-Inch by 5 Yards
10 iodine ampoules	Aspirin tablets	Scissors, Bandage
5 soft-gauze bandages	Morphine solution	Pin, Safety, Medium
20 safety pins	Tincture of iodine	Burn Injury Set, Boric Acid Ointment
5 individual first aid dressing packs	Iodoform (an antiseptic)	Eye Dressing Set
5 small aseptic bandages	Zinc oxide	Iodine Swab, 1 1/2-cc, 6 (and Metal Container)
3 scarves for bandages [triangle bandages]	Atabrin	Bandage, Gauze, Adhesive, White, 1-Inch by 3-Inch, 16
3 metal mesh sections [for splints]	Quinine sulphate	Bandage, Gauze, Compressed, White, 3-Inch by 6 Yards, 72
1 straight scissors	Benzoin	Bandage, Triangular, Compressed, White
1 folding knife	Knife, saw, etc., (to make a stretcher)	Tourniquet, Field
1 individual anti-chemical package	Adhesive plaster	Kit Component, Insert, Type 1
1 notebook	Bandage	Pencil, Lead
1 pencil	Gauze	Dressing, First-Aid, Small, White
	Scissors	Kit Component, Litter Strap
	Thermometer	Emergency Medical Tag (20 in Booklet in Duplicate)
	Boric acid	
	Rivanol solution (a disinfectant)	
	Syringe	
	Sodium bicarbonate	
	Absorbent cotton	

Above: Every army had infantry medical orderlies who, along with stretcher bearers, were picked to minister to the wounded in the field. These men had medical pouches and bags containing medical supplies such as these examples.

1 Stretcher bearers didn't just lug stretchers, they halted serious haemorrhages, applied splints and dressings, used tourniquets and gave the wounded morphia.

2 Detail from an Ernst Eigener sketch showing German stretcher bearers – *Krankenträger*. Their stretchers came in two equal-sized collapsible halves, easily carried and assembled. They also used two-wheeled carriers.

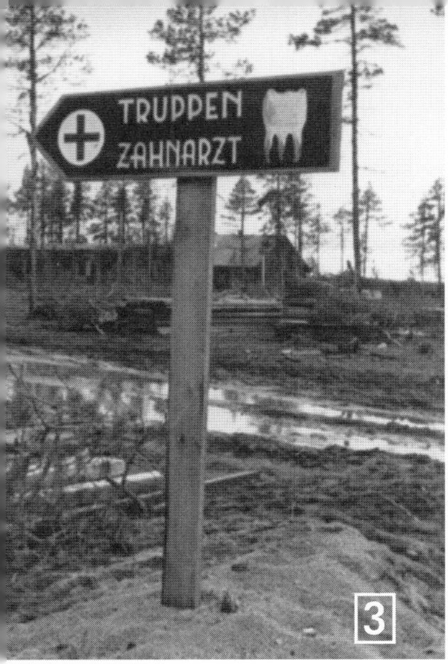
TRUPPEN
ZAHNARZT

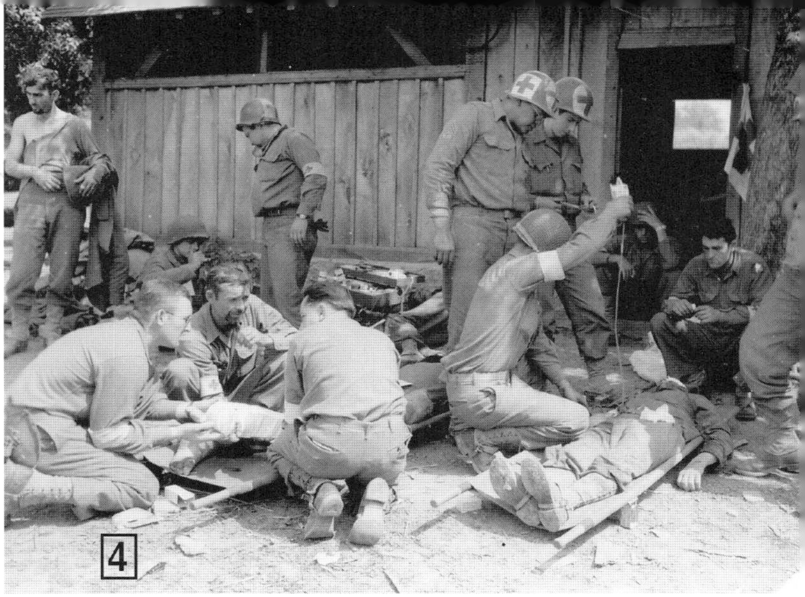

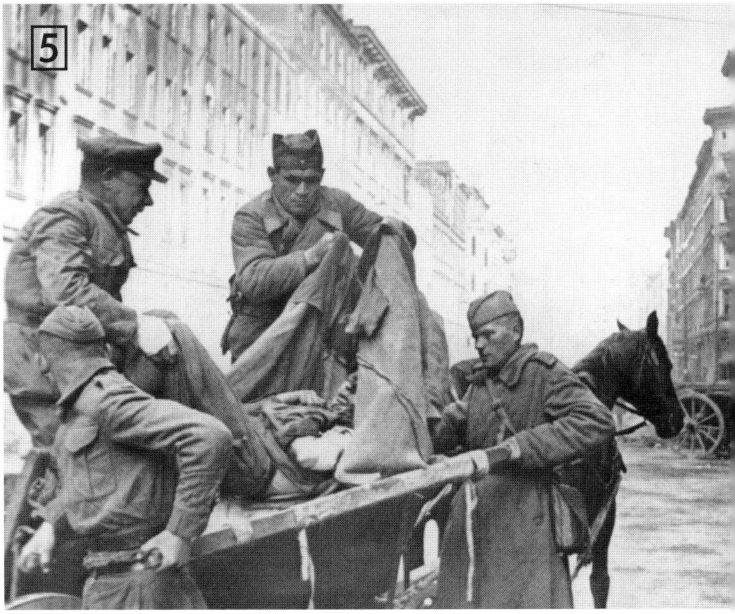

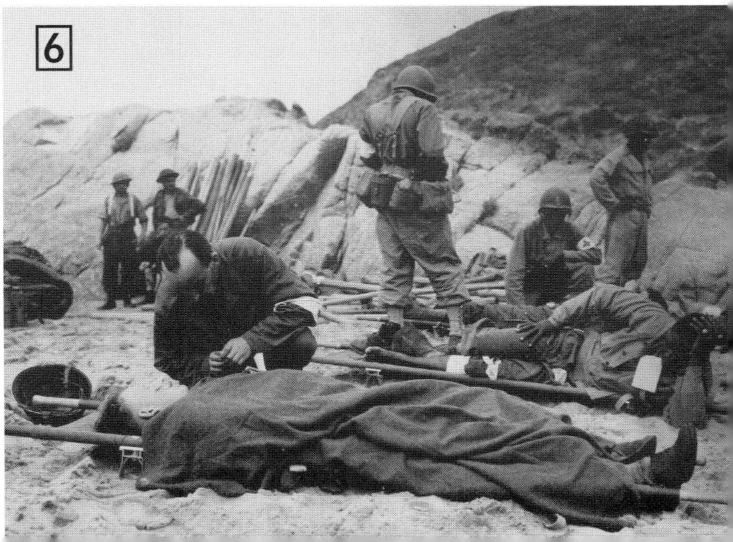

3 People forget about army dentists. At Gallipoli in 1915 by the end of July, 600 men from 1st Australian Infantry Division had been evacuated from dental disease. In 1942–45, the US military dentists did over 69 million restorations, over 16 million extractions, and made over 2.5 million full or partial dentures. The British invasion force in 1944 was equipped with one mobile dental unit for each armoured division, two for each infantry division and three for each corps.

4 Plasma mixed with sterile water and injected into the bloodstream sustained life until surgery could take place. It saved many soldiers' lives; here, men of 30th Inf Div at Mortain.

5 Conditions in the east weren't always as modern as in the west. Here, horse-drawn casualty evacuation in Russia.

6 A French chaplain gives the last rites to a French soldier on Elba, 17 June 1944. Padres and chaplains played an important role in military units, working closely with the medics.

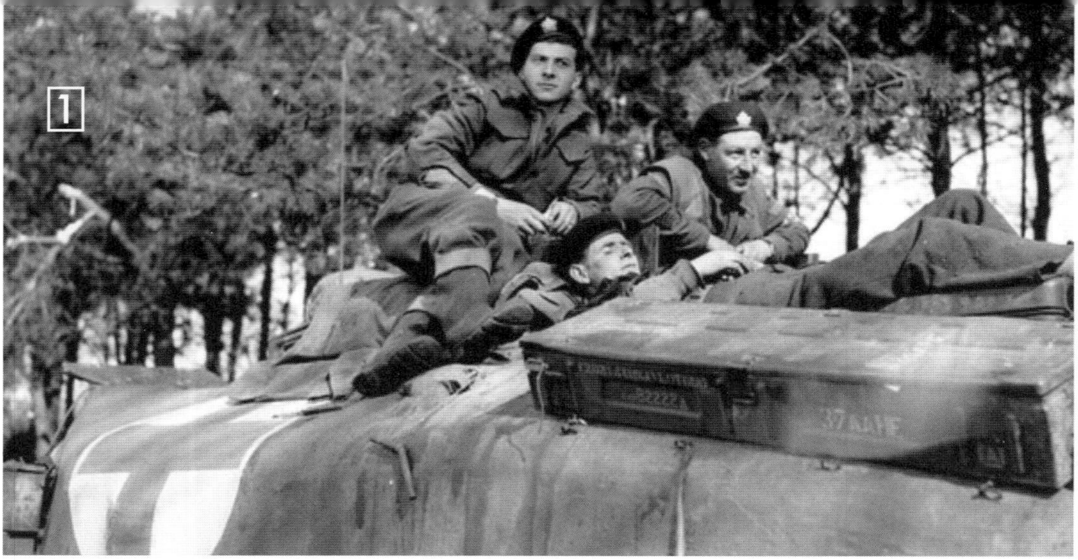
1

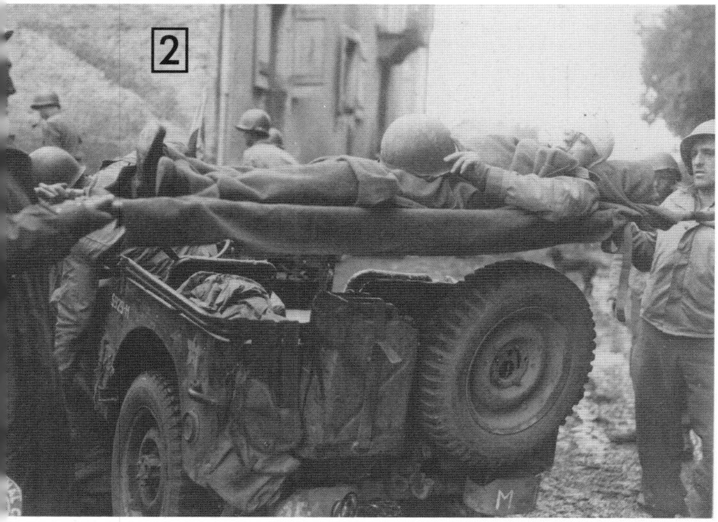
2

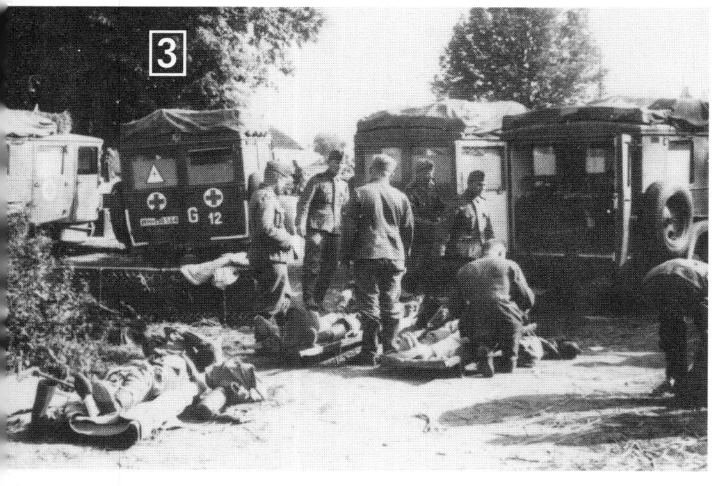
3

Casualty evacuation took many forms. Once the stretcher bearers had delivered the wounded to the battalion aid posts they were moved on by jeep, ambulance and even APCs. Being a medical orderly in an infantry unit was a dangerous profession. When 47 Cdo returned to England after its 10-week sojourn in France post-D-Day two of its 10 orderlies were dead and three wounded

1 Crew of a Ram Kangaroo used by the Fort Garry Horse as an armoured ambulance, Holten, Netherlands, 8 April 1945.

2 Villersexel, 14 September 1944 Seventh Army casualty unloaded from jeep by men of the 3rd Battalion Aid Station, 180th Inf Regt. Vehicles such as jeeps, Universal carriers and Weasels were used to carry the injured to ensure they received quick treatment.

3 German ambulances – the best known is the Opel Blitz. Adam Opel AG was bought up by GM in 1929 and was taken over by the Nazis in 1940. It built some 100,000 Blitzes as lorries, radio vehicles and ambulances.

4 Canadian soldiers who were wounded in the Normandy beachhead being carried off an LST, Southampton, 8 June 1944. The proximity of the invasion beaches to England ensured a quick return to mainland hospitals.

5 Canadian medics in Normandy, 27 June 1944. Once the lodgement on Normandy was large enough, hospitals were set up – in July Bayeux became the location for a Nos 7, 8 and 10 general hospitals (capacity 2,400), there was also No 6 (capacity 200) at Douvres. Around 35,000 men and women (over 3,500 nursing sisters) had served with RCAMC by the end of the war. They treated 83,943 Canadians and upwards of 60,000 other Allied personnel. for wounds and sickness.

6 Convalescing German soldiers pose for a group photograph. New Year 1943. There were various nursing bodies in wartime Germany – such as the German Red Cross (*Deutsches Rotes Kreuz*), freelance nurses (*freie Schwestern*) and auxiliary nurses (*Schwesternhelferinnen*) – as well as an increasing number of male nurses.

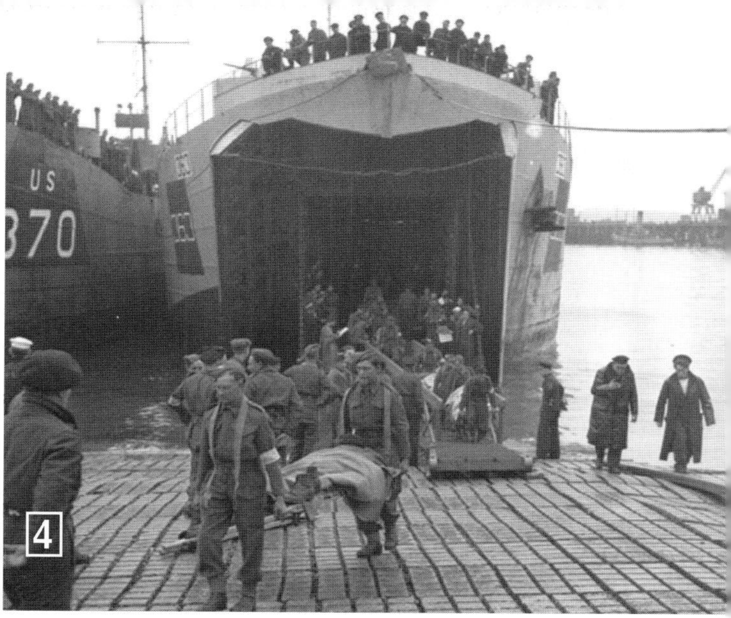
US
370

4

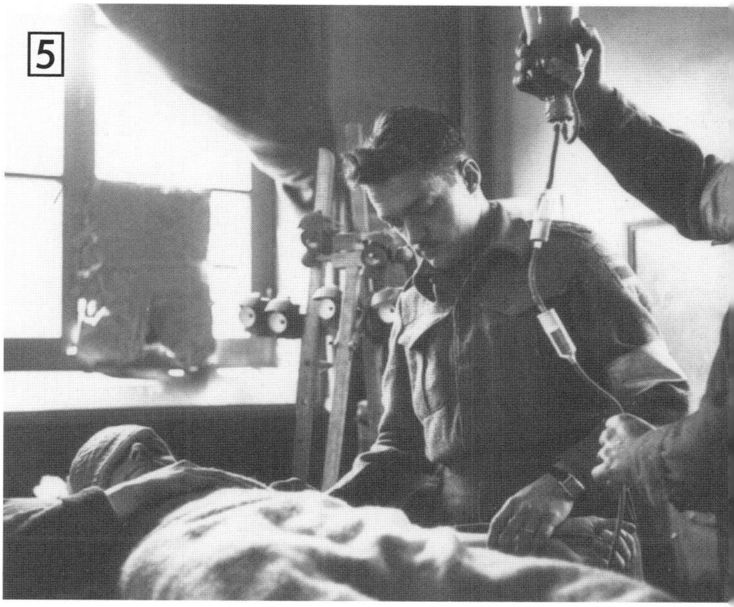

5

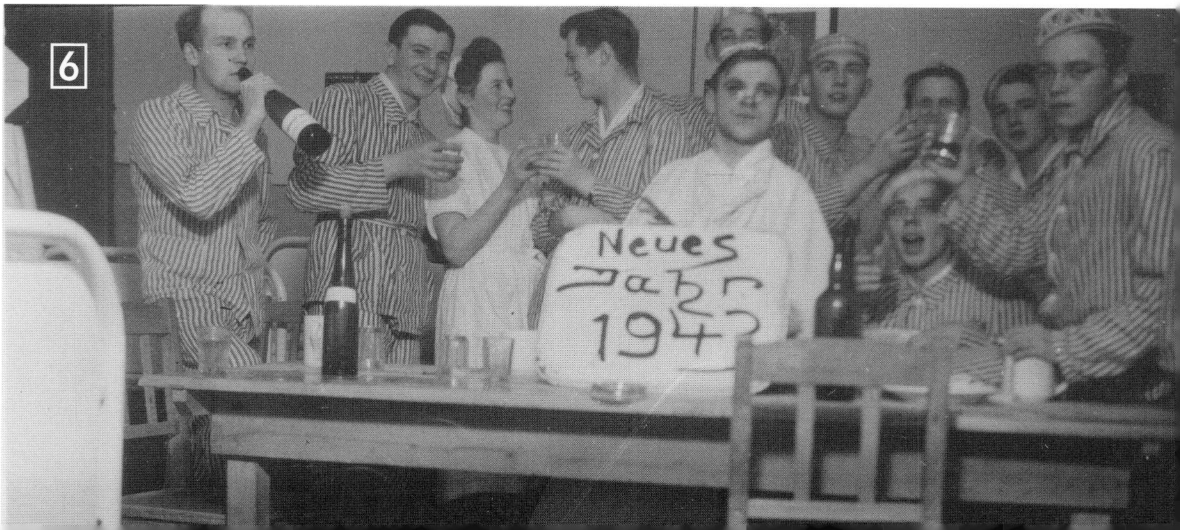
Neues

6

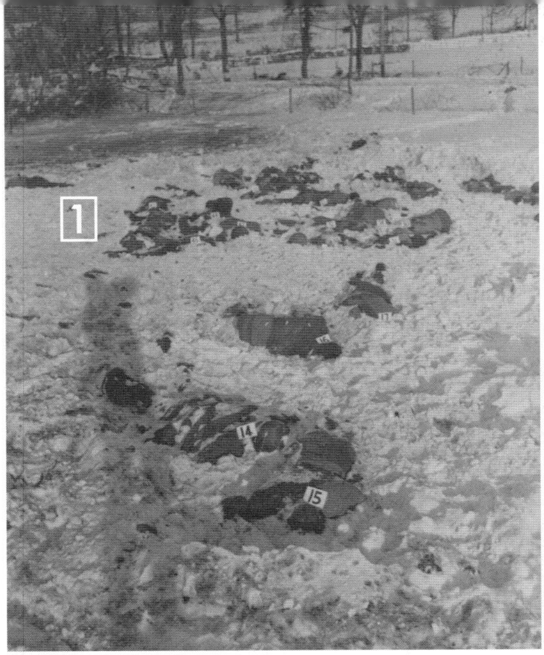
1

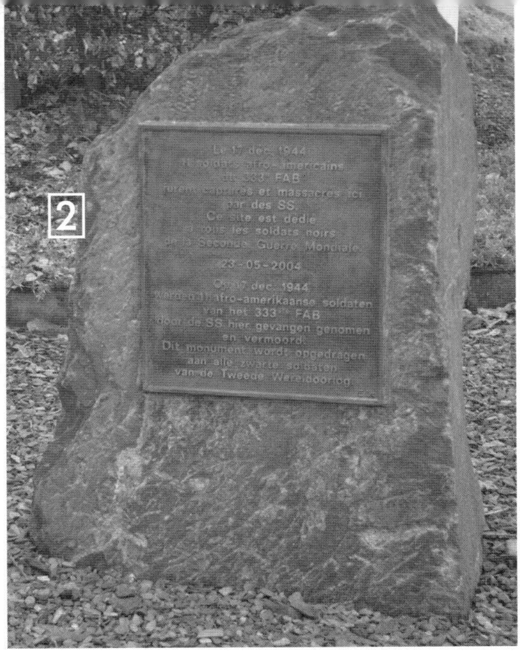
2
FAB
par des SS
Ce site est dedie
les soldats noirs
Guerre Mondiale
23-05-2004
dec 1944
afro-amerikaanse soldaten
333 FAB
SS hier gevangen genomen
en vermoord.
Dit monument wordt opgedragen
aan alle zwarte soldaten
van de Tweede Wereldoorlog

WW2 CASUALTY TOTALS ARMED FORCES

	Served	KIA/MIA	WIA	PoW/captured	% killed
British Empire and Commonwealth	17,843,000	580,497	475,000	318,000	3.3
Soviet Union	34,476,700	10,725,345	14,915,517	5,750,000	31.1
United States	16,353,639	407,316	671,846	130,201	2.5
Germany*	18,200,000	5,318,000	6,035,000	11,100,000	29.2
Imperial Japan	8,400,000	2,121,955	94,500	40,000	25.3
Italian	3,430,000	319,207–341,000	320,000	1,300,000	9.3–9.9

* incl. conscripted foreigners

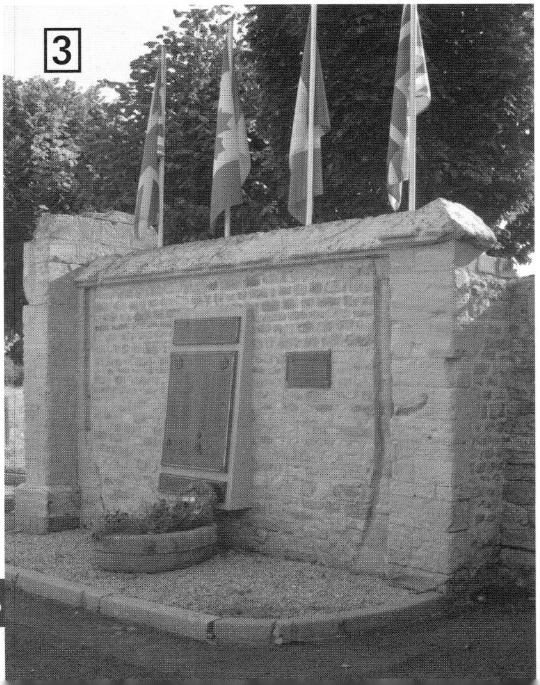
3

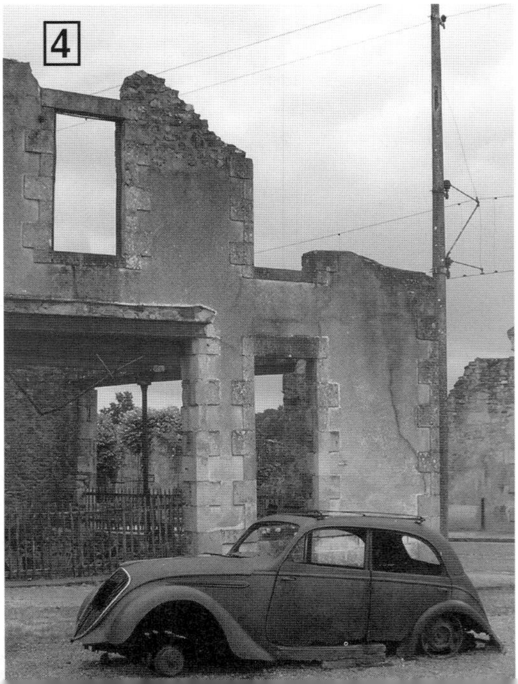
4

There are casualties of war and there are murders. The Waffen-SS was responsible for many of both. From the start they executed captured soldiers – they did so in the Polish campaign, got used to it in Russia and continued in Europe in 1944.

1 After the convoy carrying Battery B of the 285th Artillery Observation Bn was shot up near Malmédy, the survivors – 84 of them – were massacred at Baugnez crossroads, near Malmédy, eighty-four bodies were found.

2 There were other atrocities in the Ardennes. This is the memorial to the Wereth 11, artillerymen of the 333rd FA Bn, tortured and murdered by men of *Leibstandarte*'s KG Knittel.

3 Memorial to the 24 men of the Canadian Royal Winnipeg Rifles and two Green Howards who were murdered in the grounds of the Château d'Andrieu on the night of 7/8 June 1944. Nearby, Ardenne Abbey was the scene of another massacre of 23 Canadians by their *Hitlerjugend* captors. It would not be the last: troops of *Hitlerjugend* murdered as many as 156 Canadians in the following weeks.

4 Oradour-sur-Glane, the village that 2nd SS-Panzer-Division *Das Reich* infamously destroyed in retaliation for actions by the French resistance, was left untouched post-war on General de Gaulle's orders.

5 When there's so much death around you, sights that would otherwise be abhorrent to civilised people become the norm.

6 and 7 The proper treatment of the dead, memorial services and burials are important not just for soldiers and their families but nations who mourn the citizens who made the ultimate sacrifice.

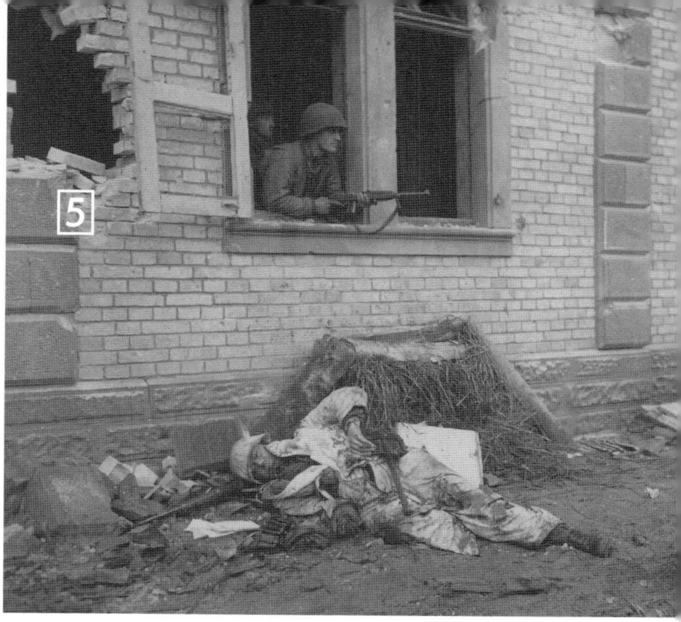
5

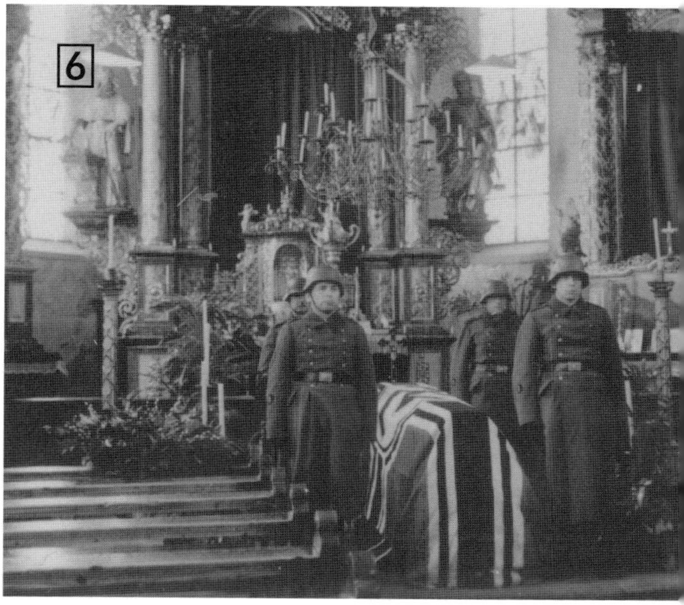
6

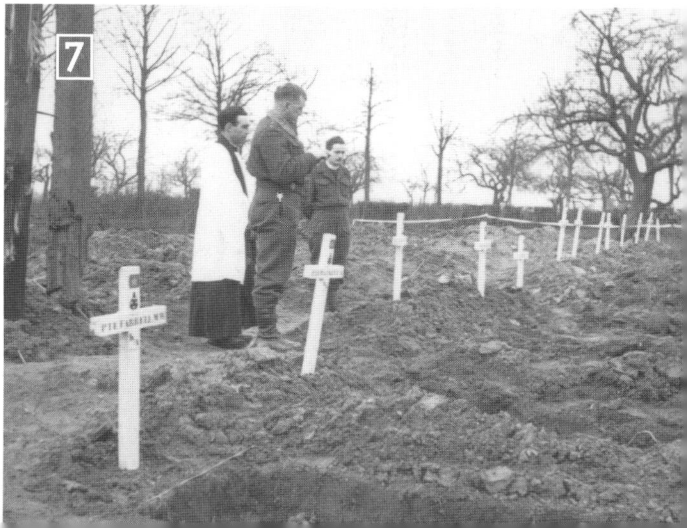
7

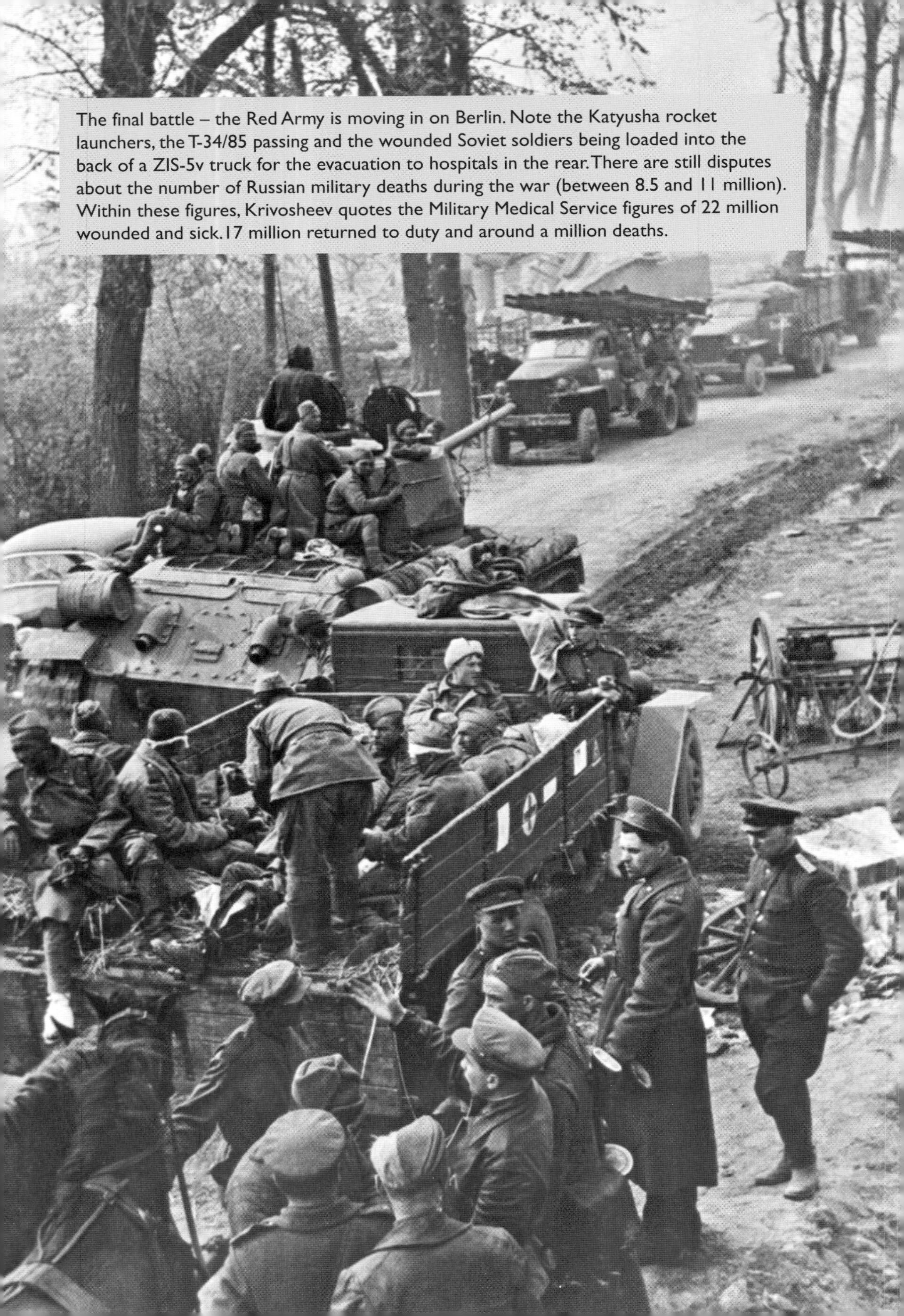

The final battle – the Red Army is moving in on Berlin. Note the Katyusha rocket launchers, the T-34/85 passing and the wounded Soviet soldiers being loaded into the back of a ZIS-5v truck for the evacuation to hospitals in the rear. There are still disputes about the number of Russian military deaths during the war (between 8.5 and 11 million). Within these figures, Krivosheev quotes the Military Medical Service figures of 22 million wounded and sick. 17 million returned to duty and around a million deaths.

5 Russia

The Eastern Front was the critical theatre of combat against the Nazis, the statistics of the fighting bewildering in size. In its vast interior, eventually, through enormous sacrifce and determination, Hitler's dreams were turned to dust. Lulled to some extent by the Molotov-Ribbentrop non-aggression pact, the Soviets – just like every other European country – had let the Germans get a head start and had a lot catching up to do. Repeatedly purged of its officers by a paranoid Stalin, equipped with much outdated weaponry, ill-trained and barely mechanised, the Red Army was in disarray when Operation Barbarossa began in June 1941, and had to endure huge losses of men and materiel that would have forced any other country to capitulate. But with the huge Russian hinterland to withdraw into and an almost endless supply of new recruits, the Soviets relocated critical industries, replaced lost armies and just like the Western Allies, learnt the new German way of warfare.

Although the intial impact of Barbarossa seemed overwhelming, in fact the invasion was fatally flawed. Riding high on their own previous successes and dismissing the enemy as inferior in every way, the Germans critically underestimated the size and length of their project and the resilience of the Soviets. They compounded this by dividing their forces in a three-pronged attack: north into the Baltic states and Leningrad, south to Ukraine and the Caucasus and centrally towards Moscow. In the end they achieved none of their goals and were outmanoeuvred and outfought by a Soviet Army that clawed itself back from the brink of destruction to fully defeat the vaunted *Wehrmacht*, aided by Soviet industry (with some critical early help from the Western Allies) that ultimately outproduced its German counterpart.

Following the initial onslaught the first Soviet attempts to halt the Germans were overstretched linear defences of rifle regiments, lacking depth, anti-tank obstacles and heavy support weapons. When such lines around Minsk and Kiev were pierced and no retreat allowed until too late, over a million prisoners were taken. Odessa and Sevastopol – supported with heavy entrenched artillery and adequately resupplied – were more tenacious and only fell after massive sustained attacks.

The true savagery of the German *Einsatzgrüppen* and the colluding *Wehrmacht* in their treatment of prisoners and civilians ensured a hardening of Soviet attitude and purpose. This was magnified by Stalin's gruesome attitude towards those who were captured, which was not far off Japanese in its contempt. NKVD regiments were often

Above: A Red Army sapper unit in Insterburg, East Prussia – today's Chernyakhovsk, in the Kaliningrad enclave. The 3rd Belorussian Front took the city on 21–22 January 1945. The soldiers are armed with PPSh-41 SMGs and carry probes to detect mines (see pp. 208–211).

Above right: The Berlin Reichstag amidst the detritus. The Russian soldier has a PPSh-41 SMG around his neck, wears a cap (*pilotka*) and carries a pack (*myeshok*). He's swapped his canteen (*flyaga*) for a German mess tin. The *myeshok* was tied shut using the shoulder strap loop.

Opposite: Victorious Russian troops in Budapest. The city survived a 50-day siege before surrendering on 13 February 1945 with great loss of civilian life (some 38,000). Note their *schapka ushanka* synthetic 'ear-flap' fur hats decorated with a metal cap star.

Eastern Front Casualties

	KIA	WIA	PoW	Died in captivity	Total dead
Soviet Union	6,829,600	13,500,000?	4–5,000,000	2–3,000,000	8–10,000,000
Poland	24,000				24,000
Romania	17,000		80,000		17,000
Bulgaria	10,000		10,000		10,000
Axis					
Germany	3,637,000	3,498,060	3,000,000	500,000	4,137,000
Italy	55,000	30,000?	70,000	27,000	82,000
Romania	226,000	243,000?	500,000	55,000	281,000
Hungary	245000	89,313	500,000	55,000	300,000
Finland	62,731	158,000	3,500	473	63,204

Sources: Krivosheev, Overmans, Ellis.

held behind the front lines to police their own troops, using deserters (and political prisoners) in penal units to clear minefields and as first-wave cannonfodder. As the war progressed, Soviet initial shortages of heavy weapons and ammunition were increasingly made good and their quality improved. Soviet defensive tactics also matured, often imitating those of their opponents. Immense anti-tank lines, minefields and interconnected trench systems were built, beefed up with bunkers and redoubts, supported by heavy artillery, armour held in mobile reserves and rugged American and Zis trucks carrying Katuyshya rocket systems. Individual units now held narrower distances of the front line, so that they could deploy in more depth with at least a second echelon. Partisans behind German lines were extensively rearmed and reorganized to attack in conjunction with conventional forces.

As Barbarossa became bogged down its imperfections and problems became more apparent. The Germans had expected a short campaign and were unprepared for the savage Russian winter, to which the Russians seemed immune. They were surprised, too, at the toughness of the Russian peasant infantry, controlled and spurred on by ruthless Commissars. Unsophisticated but experienced, used to the need to be self-sufficient, with the countryman's excellent awareness of ground, the Soviets excelled in the colossal battles within ruined urban areas where the German all-arms approach created a battlefield more suited to vicious close-quarter combat, and a rubble-strewn landscape perfect for defence. Russian infantry came equipped with the Mosin-Nagant rifle, the SVT38/40 semi-automatic rifle, the PPD-1934/38 sub-machine gun and the slim DP 1929 light machine gun with its distinctive round, flat top-mounted magazine. At Stalingrad, the bloodiest battle of the war, using small teams armed with such weapons, along with grenades, explosives and Molotov cocktails backed by close support snipers, the Russian infantry perfected the art of urban warfare, to which the Germans had given little previous thought. In defence, more integrated systems evolved, consisting of individual house strongpoints with interlocking fields of fire linked together by trench sewer and 'mousehole' tunnel systems. Unique characteristics of the Soviets included more specifically trained snipers within each unit and the continued use of anti-tank rifles long after other nations had moved on to handheld missile launchers (Bazooka, PIAT, *Panzerfaust*, etc). Though lacking the punch of these missile weapons, the Soviet anti-tank rifles nevertheless were a tool for their time. The PTRD-41 and its cousin the PTRS-41 fired 14.5mm tungsten-cored armour-piercing rounds capable of penetrating 35–40mm of armour at 300m. Both were around 7ft long with detachable barrels for two-man transportation. Mass-produced, accurate and readily available, they could pierce the weak point of tanks – their thinly armoured sides, wheels and suspension systems, roof turrets and engine louvres – as well as shoot out vital vison blocks. Used en masse as a way in which to give the infantry more defensive punch, they could be very effective. Each infantry regiment had an anti-tank company of 27 teams and there were also independent anti-tank battalions that could be assigned where necessary to further bolster an in-depth defence. Russian infantry regularly used tanks to manoeuvre around the battlefield. Using rope loops to provide

mounting handholds, these 'tank desant' teams rode into an attack before dismounting to fight on foot and protect the armour from anti-tank weapons, although sometimes platforms for their heavy weapons were attached to AFVs to enable firing on the move. Given that tanks were obvious targets this warfare was fraught with danger but in desperate times it was deemed expedient.

The increasing sophistication of Soviet defence in depth culminated in the Battle of Kursk, where the infallibility of Blitzkrieg was destroyed by deeply echeloned infantry in well-constructed defences of bunkers and trenches screened with minefields, anti-tank obstacles and layered with antitank weapons, supported by armour and artillery. They exacted an terrible toll on attacking Germans and wherever the defences were punctured operational and strategic reserves restored the situation.

Russian equipment was practical and utilitarian. Here (**1**) men take the opportunity to eat during a lull in the action. Note the helmets (*stalshelm* or *kaska*), greatcoats (*shinel*) and weapons: two PPSh-41 *Papasha* (Daddy), a DR-27 LMG on a bipod and a AVS-36 automatic rifle. (**2**) On the march they carry their rolled greatcoats wrapped into a *shatka* bedroll – their rain capes/tent halves (*plashch palatka*) will be wrapped round their *myeshok* (pack), caps (*pilotka*); note spike bayonets (*shtik*) and DR-27 LMG; (**3**) These men wear tunics (*gymnastiorka*), breeches (*sharovari*), ammo belts (*remyen*) and boots (*sapongi*). Their epaulettes carry shoulder boards (*pagoni*). The weapons are: a captured Italian Carcano M91 carbine with folding bayonet (left) and a PPS-43 (right).

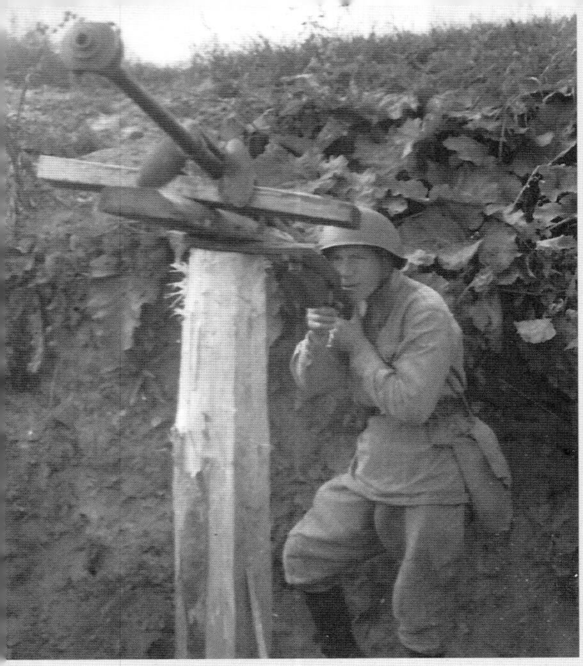
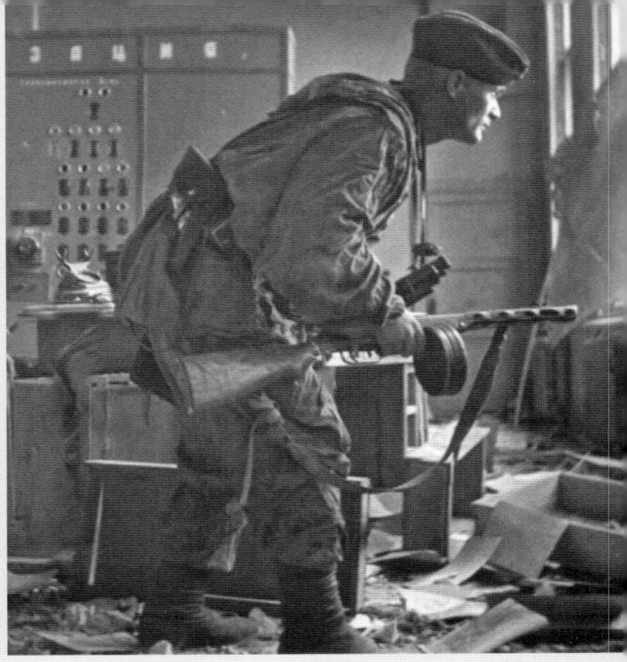

The Commissar

(from *Peculiarities of Russian Warfare*)

Probably the most controversial element in the Russian Army – even in the Soviet Union itself opinions varied concerning his usefulness, his position, and his duties. The political influence of the Party and of its representatives in the army – the commissars or (after 1942) *Politruk* [deputy commander for political affairs] – was tremendous, but their military involvement lessened. ... They came mostly from the working class, were almost without exception city people, brave, intelligent, and unscrupulous. But they also took care of the troops.

It is not true that the Russian soldier fought so well only because of fear of the commissars, under the pressure of machine guns set up behind him and manned by Politruks. A soldier who is motivated solely by fear can never have the qualities that the Russian soldier of this war displayed. Basically the Russian has no less national – as distinguished from political – ethos than the soldier of the Western armies, and with it the same source of strength.

The attitude of the common man toward the commissar was conditioned not only by fear of his power, but also by his personal exemplification of the soldier and fighter. His concern for the welfare of the troops also determined to a large extent his relationship with the men. In all the captured reports dealing with the activity of the commissars there was considerable mention made of the condition of the troops.

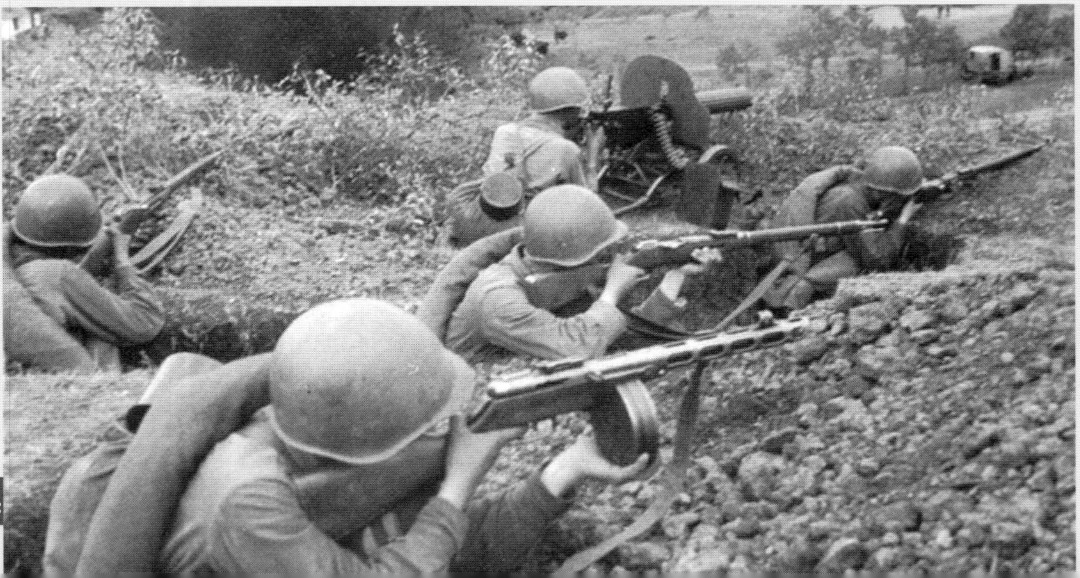

The Russian Infantryman

(from Peculiarities of Russian Warfare)

'As good as immune to seasonal and terrain difficulties, he was almost complete master of the terrain. There appeared to be no terrain obstacles for the infantryman. He was as much at home in dense forest as in swamp or trackless steppe. Difficult terrain features stopped him for only a limited time. Even the broad Russian streams were crossed quickly with the aid of the most primitive expedients. It could never be assumed that the Russian would be held back by terrain normally considered impassable. It was in just such places that his appearance, and frequently his attack, had to be expected. The infantryman could, if he chose, completely overcome terrain obstacles in a very short time. Kilometers of corduroy road were laid through marshy terrain in a few days; paths were tramped through forests covered with deep snow. Ten men abreast, with arms interlocked, and in ranks 100 deep, prepared these lanes in 15-minute reliefs of 1,000 men each. Teams of innumerable infantrymen moved guns and heavy weapons wherever they were needed. During the winter, snow caves which could be heated were constructed to furnish night shelter for men and horses.

The German conduct of delaying action, with leapfrog commitment of forces in successive positions, was not known to them. This method of fighting, requiring great mobility and high-grade leadership, was not used by the Russians. The Russians always sought only simple and complete solutions. When they decided to withdraw, they did so in one jump, and then immediately went over to active defense again.

When armored forces which had broken through chased them off the roads, the Russians disappeared into the terrain with remarkable skill. In retreating, retiring from sight, and rapidly reassembling, the Russians were past masters. Even large forces quickly covered long distances over terrain without roads or paths. Thus, in 1941, Russian rifle regiments thrown back by our armor crossing the border at Tauroggen again opposed the same panzer division south of Leningrad, after a march of eight hundred kilometers.

Opposite, Above left: PTRS-41 anti-tank rifle being utilised in the anti-aircraft role.

Opposite, Above right: 'The best weapon of the Russian infantryman was the machine pistol. It was an easily handled weapon equal to Russian winter conditions, and one which we also regarded highly. This weapon was slung around the neck and carried in front of the chest ready for immediate action. The mortar [see pp. 222–226] also proved highly valuable: the ideal weapon for terrain conditions where artillery support was impossible. At the beginning of the Eastern Campaign, Russian infantry far surpassed us in mortar equipment and in its use.' Russian recon scout, Voronezh, carrying a PPSh-41 SMG.

Opposite, Below: Red Army soldiers during the Battle of the Caucasus, 1942. Note the PM M1910 Maxim machine gun.

Above: Classic view of soldiers armed with a Degtyaryov Pekhotny DP LMG.

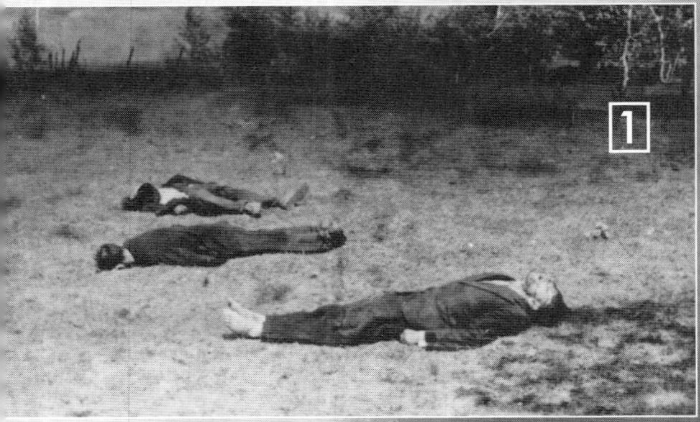
1
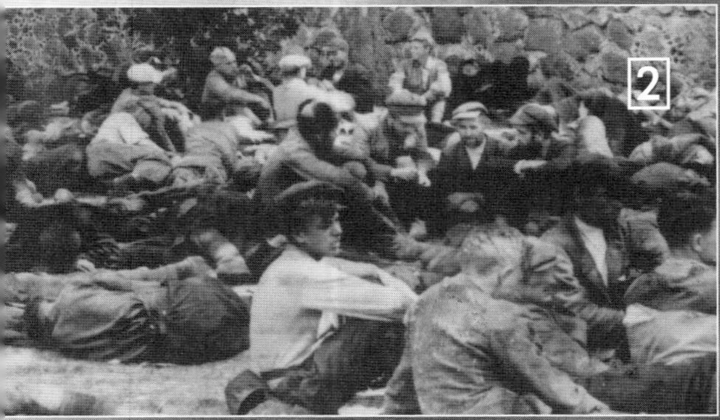
2
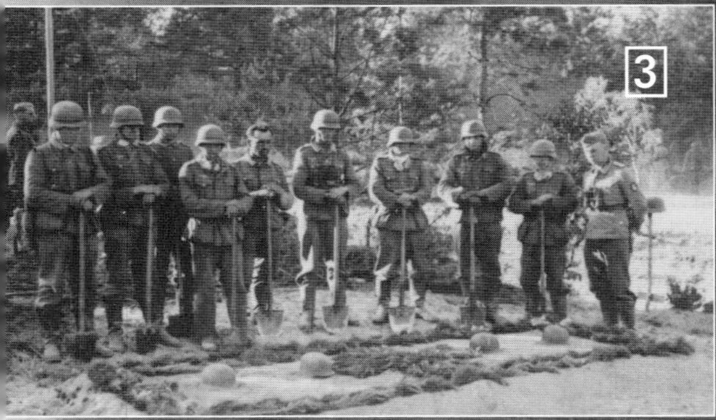
3
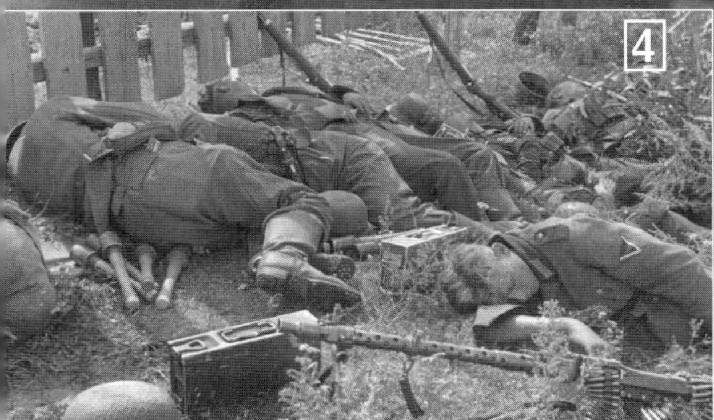
4
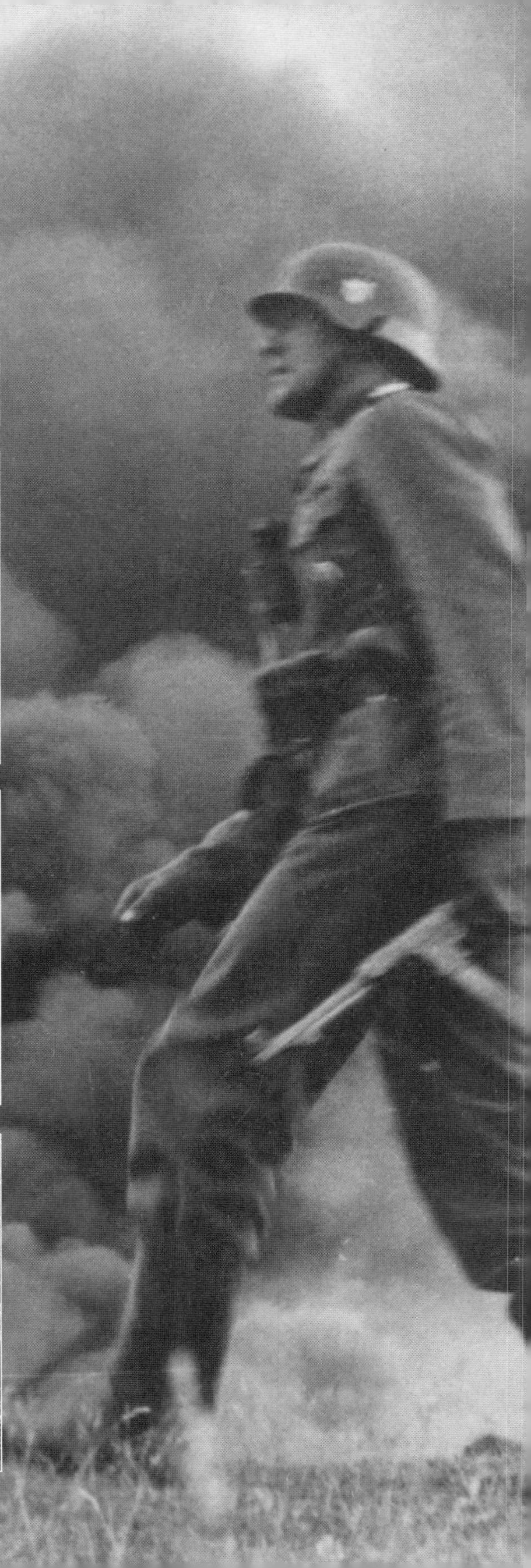

OPERATION BARBAROSSA
INFANTRY REGIMENT 15,
29. INFANTRY DIVISION (MOT)

The Falcke (Falcon) Division was raised in Wehrkreis IX in 1936 and took part in the invasions of Poland and France. The attack on Poland, while it was part of XIV Corps of the German Tenth Army and commanded by General-leutnant Joachim Lemelsen, saw the division's Infantry-Regiment 15 murder as many as 300 Polish PoWs at Ciepielyw on 8 September 1939. After its involvement in Poland, the division took part in the attack on France under Generalmajor Willibald Freiherr von Langermann und Erlencamp but it was under command of Generalmajor Walter von Boltenstern that the 29th Infantry Division moved across the Russian border on 22 June to the north of Brest-Litovsk as part of previous CO Lemelsen's XXXXVII. Army Corps (mot). It used Rollbahn 2 (the main Warsaw–Minsk highway) and then headed towards the Dnieper. By 11 July it had crossed the Dnieper, pushing through what had been left of the Stalin Line (it was abandoned in preference to the more westerly Molotov Line) near Mogilev and had reached Kopys. Next up was Smolensk. Between 15–23 July the division took the south of the city, then recrossed the Dnieper and took the north. It went on to fight at Bryansk before suffering big losses at Tula. After further fighting at Orel in early 1942, in June they advanced from Khakov to the Don and Stalingrad. The fighting in the city was heavy and between 3 September 1942 and 21 January 1943 the division was completely destroyed either in small-unit actions in the streets and houses of the city or when it was used to plug a gap in the German southern defences against Russian 64th Army. The division was reconstituted from the 345th Infantry Division, becoming the 29th Panzergrenadiers on 23 June 1943. It fought in Sicily and Italy, finally surrendering to British Eighth Army in northern Italy.

1 For all their postwar obfuscation and disclaimers the German Army was involved in the extermination of the Jews and great violence towards civilians. These are dead 'partisans'.

2 Jews rounded up by the regiment – very, very few in the areas occupied by the Germans survived the genocide.

3 The Germans lost a lot of men in 1940–41, many of them their best young NCOs and junior officers. Often these deaths would lead to a barbarous revenge against prisoners and civilians alike.

4 Grabbing some sleep while they can amongst their weapons, this German squad's MG34 and ammo boxes are well in evidence as are plenty of grenades and Kar98ks. The photograph was taken in 1941 at the start of Operation Barbarossa while the Germans were advancing at great speed.

Main photo: A squad leader passes a burning farmstead, carrying his MP40 machine pistol.

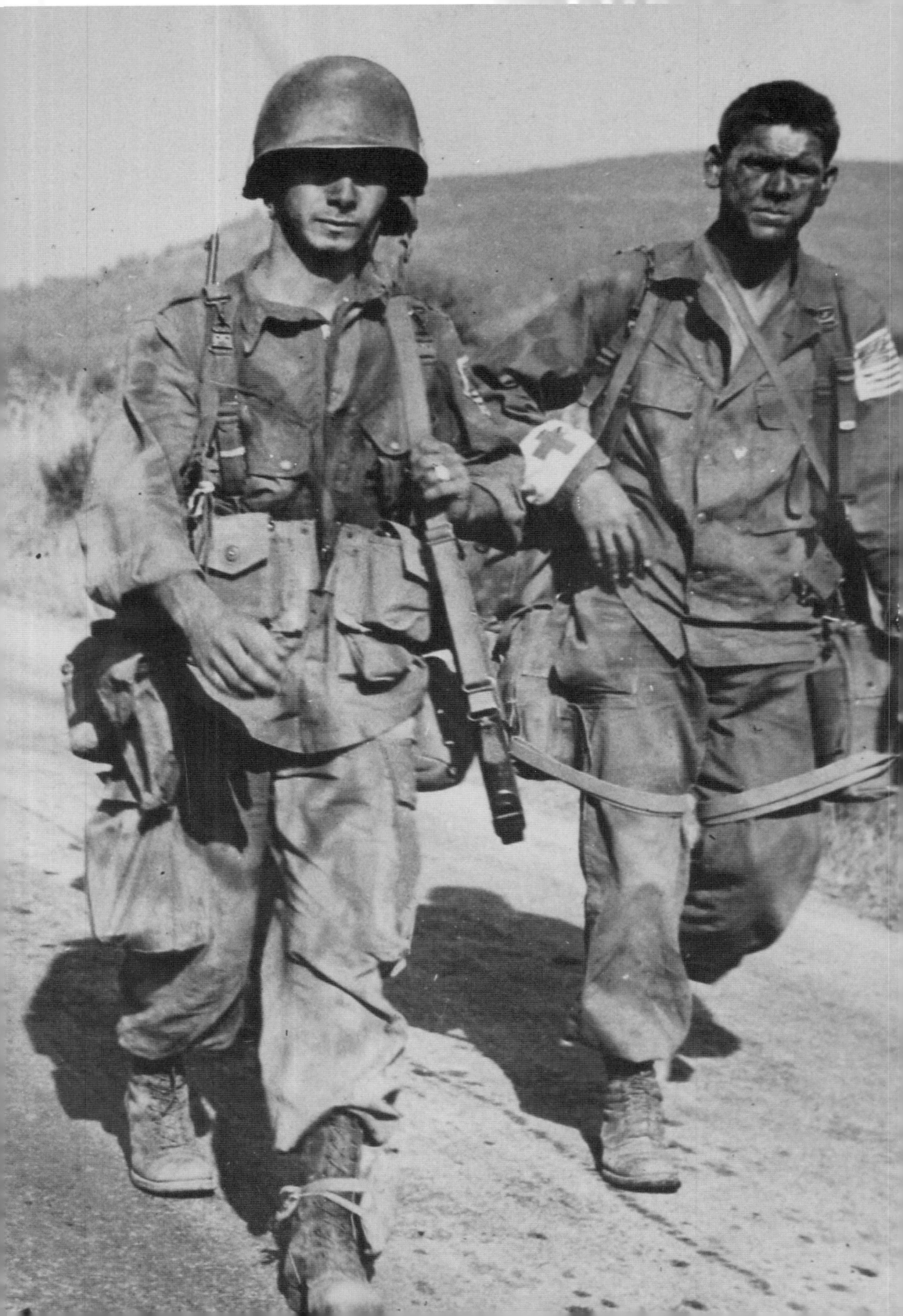

6 Northwest Europe

While huge armies clashed on the Eastern Front, in the west the battles were no less fierce, just smaller. Once the second front opened on 6 June 1944, the Germans were slowly pushed back to their prewar boundaries and then into Germany itself. They defended venomously and with great determination, fighting for every inch of territory and laying down their lives in a futile attempt to hold off the inevitable.

The attritional battle that followed the invasion saw the Americans fighting through the bocage while the British and Canadian armies held off the bulk of the German armour. The Allies never lost the initiative and the front exploded as Operation Cobra broke through at the base of the Cotentin peninsula. As Patton's Third (US) Army was pushed into the hole created by First (US) Army, the Americans were able to ride a weak counterattack at Mortain that did little more than extend a German salient into the converging Allied envelopment. The resulting pocket was, eventually, closed at Falaise and the Germans' defeat was catastrophic.

Remarkably, they were able to pull together a defence in the Netherlands and along the Westwall that – combined with frightful weather – held the Allies. The Germans took the opportunity to counterattack through the Ardennes and in Alsace. The result, after initial gains, was another stinging defeat as the Panzer spearheads ran out of fuel, lacked the bridging capabilities they needed and had no air support. And, having expended their energy, and the best of their remaining troops, all that was left was retreat and surrender.

While the battles in the west were certainly tank heavy, it was the infantrymen who sustained the most significant casualties as is discussed elsewhere. This chapter examines two main facets of the war in the west: the American slog through the bocage that required ingenuity to overcome, and the British Operation Blackcock which exemplifies late war tactics and weaponry.

Tired American paratroops from B/509th PIB near Le Muy in southern France. The Germans didn't attempt to hold the area but retreated north. The Allies weren't able to inflict a major reverse on them during a fighting retreat in which the 11. Panzer Division played an important role. The landings had, however, captured Marseille which, when cleared, was able to ensure a continuous stream of personnel and materiel to the US and French armies. After fighting their way through the Vosges, the US Sixth Army Group was poised to jump the Rhine and plunge into southern Germany but they were halted by Eisenhower. While part of the reason was his wish for a broad front, there's also a hint of personal animosity between him and Devers, the army group commander.

Busting the Bocage: American Combined Arms Operations in France, 6 June-31 July 1944

(edited excerpts from Captain Michael D. Doubler (1988))

After successfully invading France on 6 June 1944, the first task of the First (US) Army was to consolidate its lodgement in Normandy. It did this by taking the Cotentin peninsula and the major port of Cherbourg. It was then time to attack southwards against the German Seventh Army. GOC Omar Bradley had thirteen divisions in four separate corps, from west to east:

- VIII Corps (Maj Gen Troy H. Middleton) – 79th and 90th Infantry, 82nd Airborne (replaced by 8th Infantry).
- VII Corps (Maj Gen J. Lawton Collins) – the 83rd, 4th, and 9th Infantry.
- XIX Corps (Maj Gen Charles H. Corlett) – 29th, 30th, and 35th Infantry and 3rd Armored..
- V Corps (Maj Gen Leonard T. Gerow) – 1st and 2nd Infantry and 2nd Armored.

Of these divisions, a number had already seen action: the 1st, 2nd, 4th, and 9th Infantry, the 82nd Airborne, and the 2nd Armored had combat experience – but not in the bocage. The African campaign and Mediterranean Theatre where some had been blooded and the hedgerows of Britain where they had trained just didn't compare to the nightmare that awaited them in the small fields and thick hedgerows of northern Normandy. Although they were aware of the bocage, Allied planners – consumed by the minutiae of the cross-Channel invasion – hadn't expected it to cause the problems it did. 82nd Airborne's Brig Gen James M. Gavin summed up: 'Although there had been some talk in the U.K. before D-Day about the hedgerows, none of us had really appreciated how difficult they would turn out to be.'

The Germans understood the battlefield – they'd occupied it for around four years. They had prepared thoroughly for this battle carefully setting up a layered defence based around:

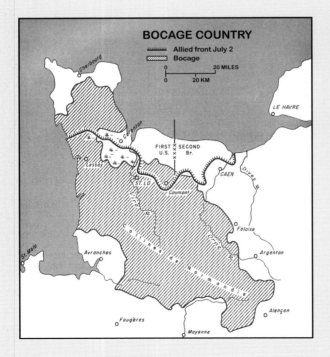

'a series of interconnected, compartmentalized fields. Small detachments defended each field and its surrounding hedgerows. Behind these forward positions, the Germans organized a defensive zone consisting of echeloned belts of prepared battle positions. Available tanks and assault guns were distributed throughout the battle zone to blunt American attacks and to support German counterattacks.

BOCAGE COUNTRY
Allied front July 2
Bocage
0
20 MILES
0
20 KM
Cherbourg
LE HAVRE
Carentan
FIRST U.S.
SECOND Br.
Lessay
ST. LO
CAEN
Dives R.
Caumont
Falaise
Orne R.
Collines de Normandie
St. Malo
Avranches
Argentan
Alençon
Fougères
Mayenne

The bocage stretched through the Cotentin peninsula south taking up most of Manche, Calvados and Orne.

The many hedgerows and enclosed fields of Normandy's bocage – a defender's paradise.

'In addition, the Germans organized each field as a defensive strongpoint and confronted the attacking Americans with a deadly mixture of direct and indirect fires. The Germans employed their direct-fire weapons to trap American infantrymen in a deadly hail of cross fire and grazing fires coming from all sides. Machine guns were the primary weapons of the German defense. At the opposite corners of each field, the Germans emplaced heavy machine guns in positions dug into the earthen embankments of the hedgerows. The purpose of the heavy machine guns was to pin down attacking infantrymen in the open, making them easy targets for small arms and preplanned indirect fires. Light machine guns and machine pistols supplemented the fire of the heavy machine guns and were emplaced in other firing positions to the front and flanks of the attackers. The Germans also used their light machine guns to place bands of grazing fire along the bases of hedgerows paralleling the American attack. The purpose of the grazing fire was to inflict casualties on American infantrymen seeking cover and concealment during their advance. Indirect fire was a key component of the German defense. Once pinned down in the open, preplanned artillery and mortar fire punished American units. German mortar fire was particularly effective, causing as much as 75 percent of all U.S. casualties during the Normandy campaign.'

There were slit trenches in the hedgerows for protection from the inevitable, quickly procured and accurate American artillery. Wire communications allowed the coordination of the defence. Snipers and booby-traps were everywhere. The infantry had *Panzerfaust*, *Panzerschreck*, a range of antitank guns – including the 88mm Pak 43 and Flak 88s used in the ground role – as well as SP guns and tanks.

The Germans criticised the Americans – as they did the British on the other side of the Normandy beachhead – for lack of aggression, poor tactics, lack of infantry-tank cooperation and dependence on artillery. Doubler quotes a German corporal in 275th Infantry Division: 'Americans use infantry cautiously. If they used it the way Russians do, they would be in Paris now.'

It's worth examining these frailties a little closer. It's true that the Allies used a lot of artillery barrages and, where possible, aerial bombardment, rather than attacking with infantry and tanks. Why shouldn't they? It wasn't a race. The Germans had chosen to fight a battle of attrition. What better way of doing so than making best use of your assets. It may have taken a bit longer but it proved effective. As far as lack of aggression is concerned, many of the Allied soldiers were seeing action for the first time in an environment suited to the defence.

The biggest criticism that can be levelled against the Allies is that it took them some time to improve their tank-infantry tactics – indeed, many would say it didn't work properly for some months to come. Part of this was down to the lack of training between the infantry divisions and their dedicated tank units – which were only assigned to their divisions a few weeks before D-Day. Doubler uses the 745th Tank Battalion as an example. It wasn't assigned to the 1st Infantry Division until 21 April, and tank companies were not attached to individual infantry regiments until they were already in combat after D-Day.

What did the Americans do about it? They showed flexibility, resourcefulness and bravery. They worked out tactics that forced them through the bocage, and while it may have taken longer to reach Saint-Lô than had been scheduled, they got there and inflicted massive casualties on the defenders. It was the Germans who lost the war of attrition in Normandy and the result was that they lost France.

Much of the American resourcefulness was based on working out the best way to clear the hedgerows so that they could bring their preponderance of armour into the battle. Dozer tanks were good, but few and far between. Explosives worked – but acquiring the amount of explosives required to clear the number of hedges involved was impossible and, anyway, using them to open gaps in hedgerows alerted the enemy to the point of attack. Various methods of attaching cutters to the front of tanks were tried, the most publicised approach was that supplied by Sergeant Curtis G. Culin. The 'Rhinos' thus formed were never quite as impressive in action as was hoped, but after Omar Bradley had espoused the cause: 'Within a week, three out of every five tanks in the breakout had been equipped with the device.' (*A Soldier's Story*). That was quick, decisive work.

Tank-infantry communications – so necessary for close cooperation – were improved. A number of interim measures involving field telephones and wire helped but the solution – as Doubler identifies – was 'interphone boxes, which were connected directly into the tanks' intercom systems, and were

COMPARATIVE STRENGTHS WW2 DIVISIONS

	INFANTRY DIVISION			ARMOURED DIVISION		
	BR	**US**	**GER**	**BR**	**US**	**GER**
Strength	18,347	14,253	12,772	14,964	10,937	14,727
Rifles	9,437	6,518	9,069	7,463	2,063	9,186
MGs – light	1,262	400	614	1,376	465	1,239
– other	40	236	102	22	404	72
Mortars – light	280	90	54	120	84	46
– med	79	54	32	60	54	16
Bazookas	436	557	108	302	607	-
A/Tk guns	110	57	22	78	54	41
Artillery – light	-	54	53	-	54	29
– med	72	12	15	48	-	26
Vehicles – motor	3,347	2,012	617	2,459	2653	2,427
– horsedrawn	-	-	1,375			
Tanks – light				44	77	-
– med				246	186	168

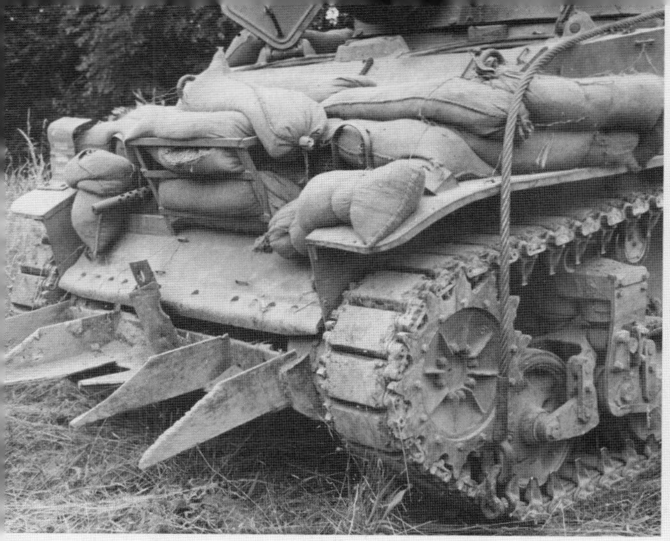

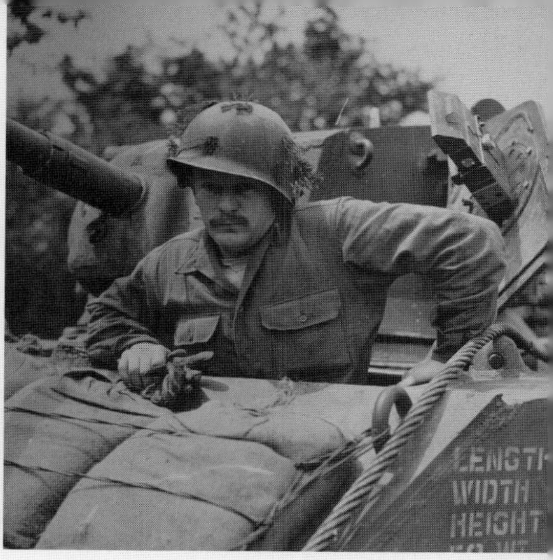

WIDTH
HEIGHT

Never quite as successful as postwar commentators would have you believe – bulldozer blades tended to be a better bet – nevertheless, creating and installing the cutters that were linked by Omar Bradley to Sgt Culin (Above right) showed resolve and creativity.

then mounted on each Sherman's back deck in empty ammunition containers. To talk with the tankers, infantrymen simply plugged a radio handset into the interphone boxes.'

As the tanks and infantry worked closely together they built up a rapport that greatly assisted operations. They were further helped by aerial observation provided by the L-4 Piper Cubs or the larger L-5 Stinson Sentinels who could direct artillery fire and provide up to the minute advice on visible German positions and actions. A surprisingly small number of these aircraft were lost over Normandy – Doubler identifies nine – and their effectiveness can be shown by the fact that the Germans (and later, in the Pacific Theatre, the Japanese) learnt to stop firing when they saw an observation aircraft as the immediate response when the observers saw muzzle flashes was a deadly accurate salvo of artillery.

Tactical developments by the units on the ground – particularly the 29th and 83rd Infantry and 2nd and 3rd Armored Divisions – provided different ways of combating the German defences and finally paid off. The main achievement was bringing the US Army's main offensive weapon – its large number of tanks – into play, whether that was though close small-unit operations with individual tanks (the infantry divisions' approach) or larger attacks using companies of tanks (the preferred approach of the armoured divisions).

Casualties were still taken: CCA 3rd Armored's attack on Villiers-Fossard after a heavy pre-attack bombardment by aircraft and artillery was successful but still incurred 401 casualties (351 from indirect fire of artillery and mortars) and CCA lost 27 of its 116 tanks to both short-range *Panzerfaust* attacks and also the longer-range anti-tank guns.

Operation Cobra – the successful breakout from the Normandy bridgehead that had been so cleverly orchestrated by Montgomery and Bradley – saw American infantry speeding into battle on top of its supporting armour mimicking the 'tank desant' teams of the Red Army. Inherently dangerous in a hostile environment as the infantry can be easily attacked by machine-gun fire, it did mean that tanks had local security when attacked by infantry.

The fighting in the bocage, its slow progress and heavy casualties in June and July 1944, is often overshadowed by the Cobra breakout. At the time – as with the British fighting around Caen – uninformed Press expectations could only be satisfied by glorious successes, but it was in the attritional fighting in Normandy that the Allies proved they had the tactical nous and strategic staying power to combat the much-vaunted German *Wehrmacht*. The stunning success of the campaign reflected this hard-won professionalism.

Operation Blackcock

Previously planned as Operation Shears, Blackcock was designed to clear the Roer Triangle. The German defence was what was left of the 183. Volksgrenadier Division (GR 330, 343, 351) and the 176. Infantry Division (GR 1218, 1219, 1220). The British attacked with three divisions: 7th Armoured, 52nd (Lowland) and 43rd (Wessex). There was substantial artillery support and many of the new specialised armoured vehicles – Crab flail tanks, Crocodile flamethrowers and Kangaroo APCs – were also available. The operation exemplifies the all-arms nature of war in northwest Europe in 1945, the importance of careful planning and the effectiveness of the specialised equipment of 79th Armoured Division. The following section looks in detail at the infantry side of 7th Armoured's first mission of the operation, codenamed Angel. The edited details come from the official 21st Army Group report on the operation and the 9th DLI War Diary covering the dates 16–21 January 1945. The operation was broken down into ten phases, as detailed below and shown on the map, and Angel was subdivided into three elements:

ANGEL: 7th Armd Div, 131 Lorried Inf Bde to:
- **I** to establish a bridgehead across the Vloed Beek and capture Dieteren;
- **II** establish a firm base in the area Schilberg–Echt;
- **III** clear Susteren from the N and assist the RE to open a Class 40 route Sittard–Schilberg.

BEAR: 7th Armd Div, 8th Armd Bde to seize Waldeucht and Koningsbosch

CROWN: 52 Div to seize Breberen–Isentbruch line including Schalbrugh

DOLPHIN: 7th Armd Div, 22 Armd Bde to seize a firm base area Monfort.

EAGLE: 52 Div to seize Haaren–Braunsrath area.

FLEECE: 52 Div to seize area Karken–Kempen–Heinsberg–Kirchoven.

GLOBE: 7th Armd Div, 22 Armd Bde destruction of all enemy in area Posterholt–St Odilienberg–Linne–Maasbracht; cover RE bridging operations up the Sittard–Schilberg road as far as the Vloed Beek; prevent enemy infiltration between the R Meuse and the Juliana Canal.

HART: 43 Div to seize area Harzelt–Langbroich–Schierwaldenrath–Putt–Waldenrath–Straeten.

JUG: 43 Div to seize area Schafhausen–Dremmen–Uetterath–Erpen.

KETTLE: 43 Div will co-operate with XIII US Corps (102nd Inf Div) in capture of Randerath spur.

OBJECTIVES AND DISPOSITIONS
8 CORPS
XIII CORPS
44 RTR
176 DIV
183 DIV
ANGEL
DOLPHIN
GLOBE
BEAR
EAGLE
CROWN
HART
JUG
KETTLE
FLEECE
SIEGFRIED LINE
7 ARMD DIV
52 (L) DIV
43 DIV
102 U.S. DIV
157 BDE
129 BDE
130 BDE
214 BDE
155 BDE
156 BDE
8 ARMD BDE
6 GDS TK BDE
6 GDS
5 RTR
2 DEVONS
1 RTR
8 H
IRB
R. ROER
R. WURM
JULIANA CANAL
RIVER MAAS
MAESEYCK
SITTARD
SUSTEREN
GEILENKIRCHEN
LINNICH
HEERLEN
MAASTRICHT
LEGEND
BRITISH & U.S DISPOSITIONS
OBJECTIVES
ENEMY DISPOSITIONS
ENEMY GUN POSITIONS

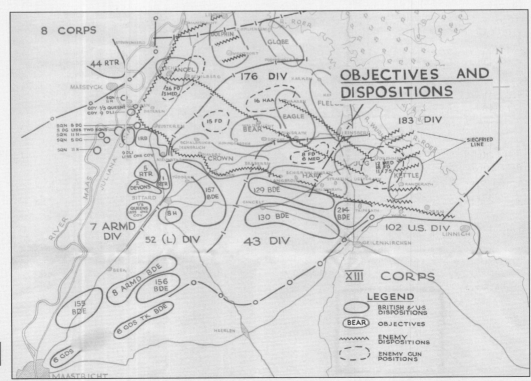

Operational narrative from the official report

[compare to 9th DLI *War Diary* on pp169–176 and see map on p. 168 for progress. Note, in report and War diary, place names, soldiers' names and units are capitalised. Capitals have been remmoved for clarity.]

It was considered essential to capture Bakenhoven, about one mile NW of Susteren, so a bridge over a small stream to the SW of the village [the Vloed Beek] could be constructed before the operation proper began, and thereby secure a proper start line for the opening assault on Dieteren.

This preliminary was successfully carried out on 15 Jan by one coy 1/5 Queens who were assisted through the minefield south of the village by flails. The enemy counter-attacked the village in some strength and severe hand-to-hand fighting ensued, but the village was firmly held in spite of fairly heavy casualties.

Task ANGEL

This was divided into three phases codenamed ANGEL I, ANGEL II, and ANGEL III, to be carried out by 131 Lorried Inf Bde with these troops:

1/5 Queens 2 Devons 9 DLI 1 RTR [Cromwell tanks] One sqn less one tp Lothian and Border Yeomanry [Flails] One sqn 141 RAC [Crocodiles]	258 Bty NY [Antitank Bty, 65th Anti-Tank Regt, RA (the Norfolk Yeomanry) M10 Achilles] Two tps 1st Cdn APC Regt [Kangaroos] One TCL [a tentacle radio unit, see p. 235]

ANGEL I

(a) This operation was due to start at 2100 hours 15 Jan. The time was so selected in order to allow the bridging of the Vloed Beek to be done during the night. However, weather conditions became so bad and a thaw having set in, it was decided at a visit of the Corps Commander to HQ 7 Armd Div during the afternoon to postpone the operation until 0730 hours the next morning.

(b) Troops: 9 DLI • One Coy 1/5 Queens (the coy in Bakenhoven) • One MMG pl 3 Coy NF [No. 3 Support Coy, Royal Northumberland Fusiliers] • One tp 258 A/Tk Bty • B Sqn Lothian and Border Yeomanry

(c) There was little opposition, except mortar fire, in the early stages and the objective, Dieteren, was secured by 1045 some 25 PoW being taken.

(d) The remainder of the day and the whole of the night 16/17 Jan was spent in constructing the all important bridges. The main one over the Vloed Beek was constructed after some 12 hours of arduous work in impossible conditions. Enemy shellfire was intense and accurate. Casualties to RE personnel were considerable and two bulldozers were knocked out. The enemy counter-attacked this site during the night from the woods to the south but were beaten off chiefly by the spirited action of one Flail tank which found itself on the north side of the Beek and had to harbour there alone all night. Eventually this bridge was destroyed by a direct hit. A new site had to be found and eventually crossings were established a few hundred yards to the SE, but not completed until some hours after first light on 17 Jan. In addition during this night the approaches to the bridge constructed south of Bakenhoven on 15 Jan became impassable and a new bridge was erected. The first two bridges on the main Sittard–Susteren road were constructed after slight enemy opposition had been successfully dealt with by the coy of 1 RB sent out to cover these crossings.

ANGEL III

(a) Owing to the difficulty in bridging the Vloed Beek, the Div Commander decided, pm 16 Jan, that ANGEL III was to take place before ANGEL II. The number of tracked vehicles involved in the latter phase made it desirable that the crossings be complete and secure before it launched. This was not the case with regard to ANGEL III and time therefore would be saved by putting this phase first.

(b) Troops: 1/5 Queens • One sqn 1 RTR • One tp 258 A/Tk Bty • Three Wasps [Flamethrowers]

(c) At 0600 hours 17 Jan, 1/5 Queens, were sent over the Vloed Beek on foot and they reached their forming-up area for the attack on Susteren, some 1,000 yards NW of this village without much enemy interference. The attack opened at 0630 hours and reached the northern outskirts without difficulty. There, they were halted by two SP guns and two tanks. This was followed by a German counter-attack of bn strength supported by tanks and SP guns. Very hard fighting ensued and the Queens were hard put to it to retain their positions but did so. The situation eased when a sqn of 1 RTR, which had been put over the Vloed Beek at a bulldozed crossing, came to their assistance about an hour later. The action to take the village continued slowly against determined opposition. By 1500 hours all except a small quarter to the SE was in our hands. Some sixty or more PoW were captured.

ANGEL II

(a) The move up for this phase started at 1045 hours 17 Jan. At this time the bridges were still not complete, but it was decided to risk putting the heavy vehicles over the bulldozed crossing which had already sufficed for the two tps of
1 RTR on their way to join 1/5 Queens.

(b) Troops: 2 Devons • 1 RTR less one sqn • One MMG pl 3 Coy NF • One tp 258 A/Tk Bty • Two tps 1 Cdn APC Regt • One sqn 141 RAC. This group was organised so that equivalent columns could be sent up from Dieteren, one on the main road Dieteren–Susteren–Schilberg and the second on the road Dieteren–Ophoven–Echt. In addition there was a third, reserve, column to be used as opportunity offered.

(c) Delayed until 1530 hours by the very bad going for the heavy vehicles and mines in the start line area. The LEFT column, on the route Dieteren–Ophoven–Echt, went well almost entirely across country. The enemy put up considerable resistance in Ophoven but this was overcome and by 1830 hours the forward coys were firmly established in the NW edge of Echt. The whole of Echt was in our hands by midnight. Meanwhile the RIGHT column, intending to move up the main Susteren–Schilberg road, was quickly held up by determined enemy opposition, NE of Susteren. The enemy held a road block where the road and railway cross, and were in some strength along the railway embankment to the south of it. Our own tanks found it impossible to manoeuvre off the road in this area, and were unable to counter the well sited enemy SP guns. Fighting continued in this area for the rest of the day, all night and well into the morning of 18 Jan.

(d) During the afternoon 5 KOSB (from 155 Inf Bde of 52 (L) Inf Div) had been placed under command 131 Inf Bde in order to clear Oudroosteren, and to take over Dieteren from 9 DLI allowing the latter to come in to Bde reserve. It was essential to clear Oudroosteren in order to protect the left flank of the Div. The task was completed by 1800 hours against slight opposition and 35 PoW were captured. The main road bridge over the Vloed Beek, south of Susteren was completed by 1700 hours and the 1/5 Queens from the north and the 1 RB from the south had linked up by 2050 hours. By 0300 hours on 18 Jan the last bridge south of Susteren was complete, and the road open to that point.

(e) During the night the reserve column, mentioned in (b) above, was sent up the left route into Echt. At 0630 hours on 18 Jan 2 Devons attacked Schilberg from Echt with the assistance of Crocodiles. Strong enemy opposition meant it was not until the afternoon that the village was cleared. 9 DLI, less one coy sent to reinforce the RIGHT column of 2 Devons in its attempt to clear the main road, had been sent up the left route to Echt, so relieving additional troops of 2 Devons for the final clearing of Schilberg and also Hingen.

(f) In order to assist the advance of the RIGHT column a two-company attack by 5 KOSB was laid on to take the enemy position on the railway embankment and Heide. This was successful by 1515 hours, the enemy withdrawing NE. The roadblock by the road and railway crossing was finally cleared at 1230 hours and the advance of the RIGHT column up the road continued, but slowly as there was continual harassing by enemy SP guns, and hastily scattered mines had to be cleared.

(g) The RIGHT column of 2 Devons eventually linked up with the rest of the unit in Schilberg during the night 18/19 Jan and the main road from Sittard was opened. This unit successfully beat off two strong enemy counter-attacks from the east and NE during the night. The enemy on both occasions consisted of some 100 infantry backed by SP guns.

9th DLI War Diary 16–21 January 1945

(note map reference numbers have been left in place but these relate to a
map too large to reproduce in this section; editor's comments in square brackets)

Gebroek 16 January

0600   Tac HQ set up in Gebroek A & B Coys moved up to Gebroek ready to go on to the FUPs [forming up points].
Bn tpt [transport] formed up in order of priority in Buchten. [Attack due for 15 January but delayed by weather.]

0730   A Coy moved up through Bakenhoven [today Baakhoven] B Coy's flails, coming out

0741   from Bakenhoven, were late in starting but B Coy got away soon after H-hour. There was slight enemy
shelling east of Bakenhoven, but not enough to cause any delay. Some of the smoke fell short, & the
southern section was held up for a while to let B Coy go ahead.

0751   B Coy reported they were near the Vloed Beek though flail progress was slow. No mines were encountered
A Coy were also delayed in getting to the first obstacle.

0805   A Coy 1/5 Queens (known as Q Coy) ordered to be ready to move.

0810   A Coy report crossing Vloed Beek – no opposition, though 1 PoW was sent back from the canal, identified
as 5 Coy, II./GR 1219 [Grenadier Regt 1219 of 176.Inf Div]. B Coy now reported they were across the Vloed
Beek; there had been some spandau fire from the right, but a DF [direct fire] task quietened it & they had
little trouble in the early stages. Q Coy were ordered to move & D Coy came forward.
A & B Coys soon crossed the flat ground between Vloed Beek & Roode Beek crossing the latter, A at
0828, B at 0825. A Coy captured intact the stone bridge at 671766 though it was prepared for demolition.

0840   Q Coy was sent up behind B Coy, & Coy 0845 were crossing the Vloed Beek.

0846   A Coy reported crossing the main road into Dieteren. B Coy reported one pl on the main road, and slight
opposition on the right.

0856   A Coy reported they were on their final objective; B Coy were moving up from the main road, & Q Coy were
now across the Roode Beek 2 more PoW came in, from 416. A/Tk Coy, 176. Div. They said that there were 60
men in Dieteren & 80 in Susteren. Bn HQ followed by C Coy, began their move from Gebroek to
Dieteren. D Coy were on their way forward to the road junc–church area.

0905   Q Coy crossed the Roode Beek, and at 0920 they reached the main road, & turned down to the concrete

0923   works near Susteren. B Coy reached their final objective in the village. A & B Coys were now mopping up in
the village, & consolidating their positions; Q Coy were moving onto their objective, & D Coy were coming
up to Dieteren, which they reached at 0955. So far the operation had been extremely successful practically
complete surprise had been gained, and there was hardly any opposition either on the Vloed Beek, where
there were a great many positions, or in Dieteren itself. A small party held out for a while at 675771, between
A & D Coys, but they were soon mopped up. A number of Germans lay up in the houses for a time, but
there was little fight left in them. PoW included the crews of two 81mm mortars (the mortars were found
at 674770) & refs of 159 Ers Bn [Ersatz-Bataillon], 176 Recce Bn, & 416 A/Tk Coy, 6 PBn [Pioneer-Bataillon],
5 Coy II./GR 1219, 1 & 2 Coys I./GR 1219.

Dieteren 16 January

1030   Tac HQ arrived in Dieteren, along with C Coy, & set up at 673767. All So far, German coys
were now in position & organising for the expected counter attack. Reactions had been slight, but while the
CO was visiting coys, shelling of B Coy area began.

1110   Some of this was the edge of a 25pdr shoot directed on a party of Germans seen between Susteren &
Dieteren, but no harm was done to B Coy. The German party was not heard of again A Coy sent in 1 offr
& 11 OR PoW [from] 1 & 2 Coys I./GR 1219.

1205   Enemy were reported from Oud Roosteren, but later messages said that

1240   11 Hussars had sent patrols over to that village. No opposition by fire or counter attack came from the
north. B Coy sent in five more PoW [from] 5/II/1219 GR. A party taking PoW to Gebroek found that a scissors
bridge had been put across the Vloed Beek, and passed word to the REs that the stone bridge at 671766
was intact. This bridge had been prepared for demolition, but wires & detonators were removed by the REs
as soon as they heard that the bridge was still there. A message was sent back to Gebroek, to call up the
A/Tk guns & other essential vehicles, as it was expected that the bridge over the Vloed Beek would soon be

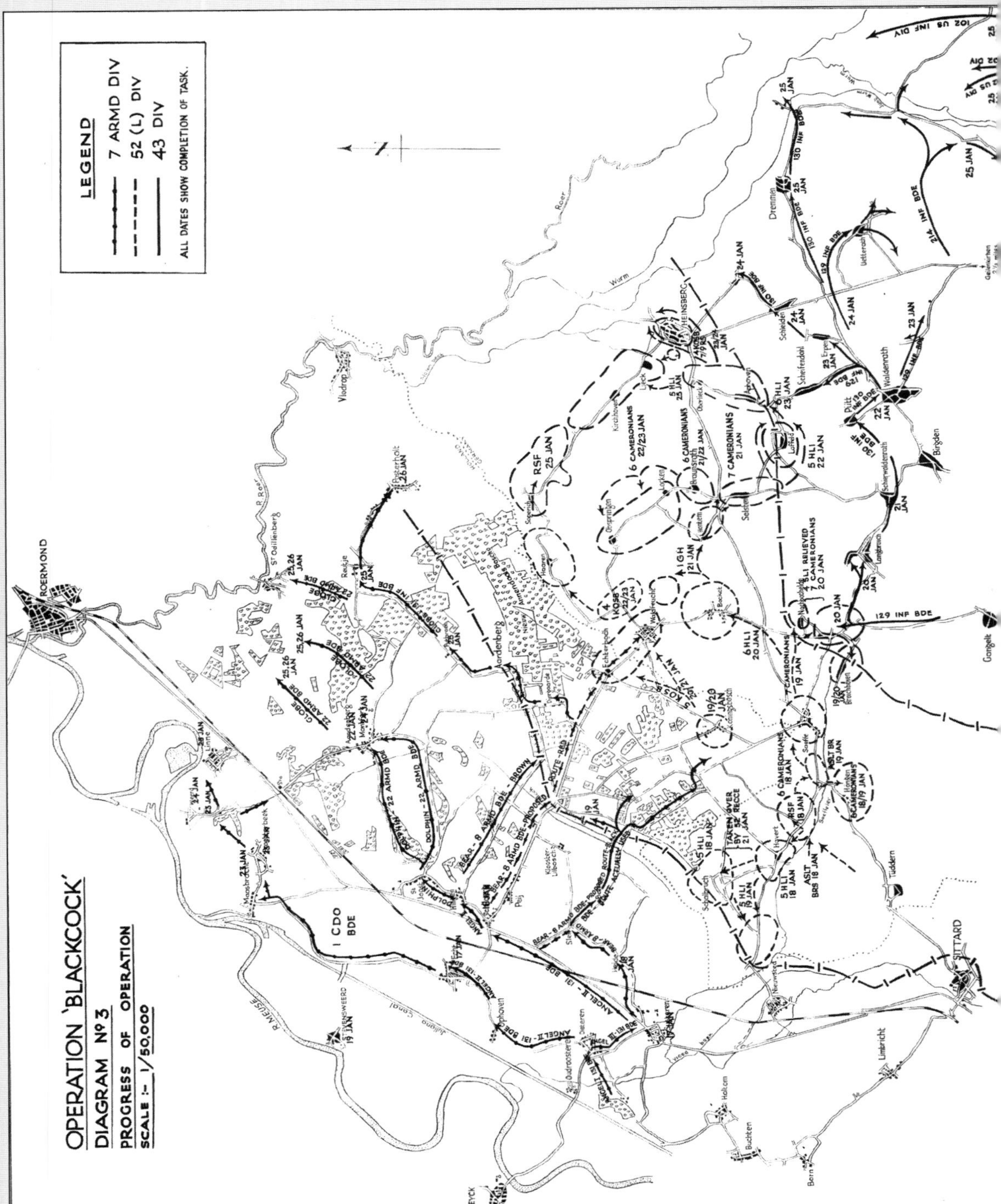
OPERATION 'BLACKCOCK'
DIAGRAM Nº 3
PROGRESS OF OPERATION
SCALE :- 1/50,000
LEGEND
7 ARMD DIV
52 (L) DIV
43 DIV
ALL DATES SHOW COMPLETION OF TASK.
ROERMOND
HEINSBERG
SITTARD
MAESEYCK
I CDO BDE
R. MEUSE
R. Roer

ready for use. During the afternoon German reaction to the occupation of Dieteren, & to the bridging, began in earnest. Dieteren itself, particularly B Co area, was heavily shelled and in spite of the constant & extremely effective arty smoke screen, which covered the bridging sites, all the open ground west of Dieteren, & much of the village itself, the canal was constantly & accurately shelled, with especial attention to the Bailey bridging site.

1445   German patrols were again reported near Oud Roosteren which was still in their hands. Shelling of the village, & stone bridge area, continued. CB [counter-battery] fire was called for, but caused no permanent improvement.

1612   All coys reported OK. Comms forward to coys were working well, comms with the outside world were less promising, as there seemed no likelihood of line getting through, and the W/T was a 22 set. During the after noon Q Coy heard movement of tracked vehs in Susteren, and there was an unconfirmed report of tks & inf at 675755

1700   moving up to 670758 75 Gren were put across the roads but nothing more

1710   was heard or seen of this column. A further recce back to the bridge was made, to de serve the possibilities of getting up essential tpt. The bridging was delayed owing to casualties, non-arrival of two lorry loads of equipment, blown up by a mine on the road out of Bakenhoven, & constant shelling. One flail crossed by the scissors bridge, and canted it over to one side. A carrier with amn bogged in the mud while approaching the scissors bridge. Shelling of Dieteren continued all evening, and D Coy suffered some casualties. The 2IC, adjutant & RSM came up from Gebroek & arranged carrying parties for a 19 set, batteries & amn. Comms with Bde grew worse, owing to failing batteries, but touch with coys was maintained. [Comms were a problem and it was only hard work by signallers that kept the forward companies in touch. Pte Thomas Foster was awarded an MM for his courage. German artillery stopped bridge building so that spare batteries and wireless sets had to be taken forward on foot. Foster made the two-mile journey seven times.] One RAOP [artillery observation officer] kept in touch with the outside world on a 33 set, & for some time this was the only rear link for the Bn.

2020   More movement was heard from Susteren & patrols were sent out by A, B & Q Coys, to provide warning of any imminent counter attack. Shelling of B Coy continued, but casualties were few.

2330   Patrol from Q Coy reported enemy in Susteren & the arty were called on to shell the village, which they did. A total of 40 PoW were captured during the day. [4]

Dieteren 17 January

0005   A tracked vehicle was heard moving towards B Coy & was shelled.

0120   A/Tk guns began to come up; two to Q Coy & one to C. More enemy movement heard on the north & NW of Susteren. During the early morning the 1/5 Queens attack on Susteren was begun and their inf & tks started crossing the canal.

0410   Tracks heard moving down the main rd Schilberg–Susteren & tks & inf were again reported on the NW outskirts of Susteren. Comms grew worse, & two coys 2 Devons were sent up to the Gebroek– Bakenhoven, to be ready to crew the canal crossing.

0800   1/5 Queens were reported into Susteren, and 6 PoW came back. The persistent reports of a German attempt to counter attack up the line of the Vloed Beek now crystallised, and a platoon of C Coy, under Capt Ashton & Lt Slee went down to a point 200 yards S of the bridge site.

0845   Meanwhile, 1/5 Queens were having trouble in Susteren, a counter attack coming in from the east, with seven tks. One of their coys had heavy casualties but brewed up one of the tks with a PIAT, & managed to hold out.

0905   C Coy patrol ran into a strong German party advancing up towards the bridge, and called for arty support, which was put down in the area 668755–669754.

0915   A PoW was captured & the arty stopped while he was sent back to tell his comrades to surrender. As they would not agree to this, fire was continued, on 668757 & then was switched 300 yards S. This was successful

0950   & the pl collected 8 PoW.

1010   The sqn of 1 RTR in support of 1/5 Queens passed through Dieteren, & went across country into Susteren, arriving in time to break up the counter attacks which were pinning down the Queens coys.

1035   C Coy pl, who had been held up by spandau posts beside the canal, went in to attack them, & were

Left and Centre left: The report commented, 'This operation showed clearly that the Germans intend to fight delaying actions in all small towns and villages which are suitable. An armoured division needs to pay as much attention to this type of fighting as does a infantry division. Such centres of resistance can sometimes be bypassed, but they will eventually have to be cleared. To clear them quickly and economically requires a carefully worked out battle drill. There must be the closest cooperation and an adequate system of communication between the inf, tanks and Crocodiles employed on such a task.' Artillery, of course, played a significant role. The report said about artillery, 'The initial planning proved sound and effective and the general regrouping plan for each phase worked well.'

Below left: As well as Pte Foster more medals awarded to 9th DLI soldiers for their actions on 16 January. At the first canal, A/Corporal Frederick Emmanuel Oliver single-handedly took on a weapons pit and was awarded a Military Medal. At the second canal, Major Anthony Geoffrey Radcliffe Noble led the attack across the canal routing the enemy. He continued to lead with 'exceptional skill and courage' in the fighting at Schilberg and was awarded the Military Cross. When the Germans counterattacked holding up bridge-building, (T)Capt Horace Wallace Ashton held off the attackers, leading an bayonet charge and directing artillery fire as necessary allowing the bridge to be built. He was awarded the Military Cross. This is the 9th DLI in Baakhoven on 16 January.

Opposite: Ram Kangaroos delivered 9th DLI to Echt. The War Diary records the death of 1 officer/13 men of 9th DLI between 16 and 21 January with 4/61 wounded and 1/43 missing.

successful in clearing up the threat to the bridge. At one time the German force had been close enough to the bridge site to destroy an armd D8 *[armoured bulldozer]* with a bazooka.

1100 1 RB *[Rifle Brigade]* reported at the canal at 674744, and a bridge begun. The Germans were still in the eastern part of Susteren, and at midday D Coy were sent down to reinforce 1/5 Queens *[who had been counterattacked]*. The afternoon was (for Dieteren), comparatively quiet. The rest of Bn HQ moved up, after some trouble in the mud round the bridges the bn. area was shelled, and the C Coy patrol, which had been sent back to the canal bank, was finally withdrawn, as the threat from the south was finished. 2 Devons, supported by 1 RTR began moving up, one column going east & then north up the main road, the second up the back road, through Ophoven, to Echt. 1/5 Queens reported that they had cleared Susteren up to the railway.

1645 CO, 5 KOSB (52 Div) came up to recce Dieteren, as they were expected to relieve us.

1830 Message from Bde; our future role likely to be assisting 2 Devons, and one coy to be at short notice to come under their command. B Coy were ordered to stand by.

1920 CO 2 Devons came to confer about the support we were to give them & provisionally arranged that one coy should be ready to join the column going up the main road, while the rest of the Bn would prob ably be required to follow up the western column to Echt. The evening and night passed quietly. Supplies & vehicles were coming up in fair quantity, and the main road was clear through Susteren. An enemy aircraft dropped two bombs in the open ground west of the village, but no damage was done.

Dieteren 18 January

The Devons advance went well on the left, & they captured Echt without much difficulty. Resistance was much stronger on the main road, where there were extensive minefields, & trees across the road. B Coy were sent to help clear the main road,

0630 & the Devons began to move across from Echt to Schilberg.

0745 D Coy returned to us from Susteren.

Echt 18 January

This morning 5 KOSB came up to take over Dieteren, & the Bn, less B Coy, moved up to Echt to relieve 2 Devons. One coy 5 KOSB passed through & occupied Oud Roosteren. Kangaroo troop carriers were sent back to pick up the Bn, & they moved up through Ophoven to an assembly area south of Echt. A & C Coys were pushed forward to the northern edge of the town, & D Coy kept in reserve, with a secondary role of covering the left flank. Patrols were sent out to the canal bank, to see if any Germans were holding out on the far side & to find out if the bridges at 678801 & 675797 were intact. Identifications in Echt were mainly 6 Coy II./GR 1219. For the first day, Echt was quiet enough & German attention was still concentrated on the efforts to open up the main road.

1700 The patrols returned from the canal bank, with the information that all bridges were destroyed, & though there were several positions along the bank, there appeared to be no German force in occupation. 2 dead Germans were found at a house near the canal, and another was killed by the patrol.

1800 Bn had suffered 28 casualties since the beginning of the operation. C Coy sent in a PoW, from 6/II/1219 GR.

2130 Interrogation of PoW at the RAP *[Regimental Aid Post]*. *[He was an]* Alsatian from 176 Fus Bn *[Fusilier-Bataillon]* said that his Bn had two Tiger Mk I tks, & five SP. 75 equipments, & believed they were the only AFVs in 176. Div. PoW from 6/II./GR 1219 said that his bn had been in the Ohe-Laak-Stevensweerd area, but that most of them had gone E. (Later confirmed. when 1 Cdo crossed into the 'island' across the Maas). Patrol sent to Gebroek 6979 reported no enemy, a piece of information required by the arty, who were intending to form a gun area round the village.

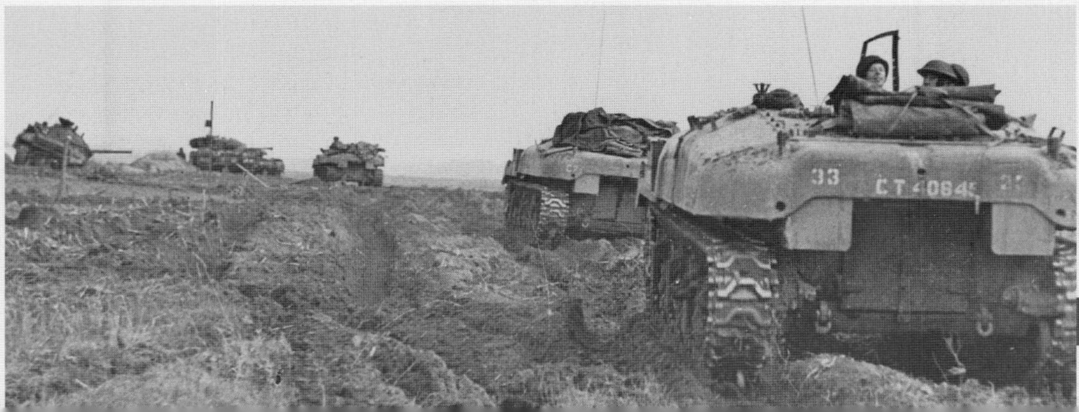
33
CT 40845

Above: Men of 9th DLI in Echt. Note lack of packs. In combat, studies by the Army showed that a load of 25lb didn't affect performance and that 50lb was the maximum for long-distance walking – unless the troops had been specifically trained or were very fit. S.L.A. Marshall suggested postwar that the figure should be 40lb but Marshall's total didn't include all the kit the British School of Infantry thought was essential (ground sheet/cape, mess tins and more ammunition). This would lead to a British postwar figure of 46lb for fighting order and 63lb for marching order.

Below: Churchill Crocodiles on the outskirts of Sint Joost. They were tardy but effective once they started flaming at 1745 on the 21st.

Echt 19 January

0220   The Devons column coming up the main road was reported to have linked up with their main body, but the road was not yet completely clear.

0800   CO went to visit 2 Devons, now in Peij, & found the main rd was clear. He was recalled for a conference at Bde (now moved up to Dieteren),

0930   where future plans were outlined. 1 RB were to clear Sint Joost, & the Bn, with 11 Hussars, was to advance on Montfort, in two columns. 2 Devons, who were to help in the clearance of Sint Joost, were somewhat weak on the ground, & D Coy were put under their comd in Peij, to cover the eastern flank, where approx. one coy of Germans was reported. 'Enemy in some strength' were also reported, in Sint Joost During the morning B & C Coys each brought in a PoW, one from 4 Coy 159 Ers Bn, the other 6 Coy II./GR 1219.

1245   O Gp [orders group] for the intended attack on Montfort. D Coy returned from 2 Devons during the evening, and Came into reserve on the eastern side of Echt, their forward posns having been taken over by B Coy. The Bn spent a quiet day & night, & the only news was of progress in the other sectors of the battle. General situation was that the main road was clear as far as the Schilberg X rds, with 2 Devons east of the X rds, 1 RB fighting in Sint Joost & 1/5 Queens east of the main rd. 8th Armd Bde were fighting in the Koningsbosch–Waldfeucht–Bocket area, with 52 Div coming up towards them from the south. 2 PoW appeared from a cellar – 8 Coy II./GR 1219.

Echt 20 January

The main interest today centred round Hingen & Sint Joost which were held in strength by a battalion from Para Regt Hubner, sent down from Roermond. This village not only covered the approaches to Montfort, but covered the main road as well, to Maasbracht & Linne. While patrols from 11 Hussars struck north from Echt & Schilberg, and parties of Commandos came over the canal into the Maasbracht area. 1 RB & 8 Hussars tried to clear Hingen & Sint Joost.

1700   By the afternoon, Hingen had been cleared, but the attack had come to a standstill, owing to the very strong resistance. A PoW said that there were about 200 men in Sint Joost & they had been ordered to hold out to the last man. It was thought that the reason for this resistance was to make time for the manning the Siegfried Line across the Roer. There were also uncon firmed reports of SP guns in the woods east of Sint Joost. Owing to the importance of Sint Joost, the Bn were ordered to provide one coy to be ready to clear the village and capture the bridge at 717809, which was needed for the advance to Montfort. C Coy were detailed for the operation, and a plan made, by which they were to bypass the village on the east, going up from the rd junc 714802 to the track bend 716805, up the track, & so to the area of the bridge, I RB providing a firm base in Hingen. During the afternoon the CO made a recce of the village, but the orders for the attack were too late to allow daylight recce by coy & pl comdrs.

Peij 20 January

2015 A 'skeleton' Tac HQ set up at 707793 beside 8 Hussars. There was some excitement about a possible counter-attack on Peij from the east, but this area was covered by 2 Devons & the threat never materialised. Hingen, Peij, & Schilberg X rds were all targets for sporadic shelling. C Coy established a 'rear link' at rd junc 714802, and the coy pushed on towards the bridge. W/T comms broke down

2315 almost immediately, and no news came back. Two stragglers returned to the rear link carrier, having lost their pl while crossing a stream, but they could give no information about the enemy.

2340 I RB reported that their rt forward coy had made contact with the left pl of C but had since lost touch.

Peij 21 January

0010 So far all seemed well, but when wireless touch was re-established 13 pl reported they were split up & needed help. B Coy were warned to get ready to move up to Peij & attack straight up the village.

0030 Sgt Wilson came back to Tac HQ with one PoW from 6 Coy Hubner Para Regt. C Coy had apparently been split up by shelling and from what was learnt later, two platoons must have been broken up & captured.

0330 Lt Slee, C Coy, came back to Tac HQ. He had been cut off from his pl & knocked out by the explosion of a 'bazooka' rocket fired at a house he was in, but was able to get away when he come round. B Coy were sent in to attack straight up the village, but their advance was slow, meeting very heavy opposition from every

0735 house & garden. Cas were heavy & they were finally halted by daylight.

0755 Fresh plans were made for clearing the village. A & D Coys supported by two sqns 8 Hussars, & two tps of Crocodiles were to attack first, & D Coy were to pass through to the bridge, as far as road bend 716812. Zero finally fixed for 1030 hrs. News during the morning was of enemy pockets east of Peij & Hingen; a few tks north of Sint Joost; and arty fire on all these targets.

1035 A Coy got way after some difficulties with Crocodiles arriving late, and moved quite well in the early part Of their advance, where the opposition was light, D Coy reported that their Crocodiles had not arrived &

1100 were told to carry on without them, and, if necessary, pick up the tp operating with A Coy.

1115 A & D Coys both advancing, A Coy meeting only slight opposition & sending back one PoW. D Coy reported that their Crocodiles had now reached them.

1147 Opposition begins to stiffen & A Coy met SA fire. At this time they were not in touch with any Crocodiles and D Coy reported that theirs would not go any further. Up to this time, none of the Crocodiles had

1220 used flame at all, and the sole support for the advance had been from the tks of 8 Hussars, who were giving fire support from the rt flank.

1240 D Coy were ordered to try & work round the left flank clear of A Coy & carry on without their Crocodiles which stayed with A Coy but in spite of all efforts, the advance again slowed down against heavy resistance. More reports came in of enemy in the north of Sint Joost,& east of Hingen & Peij.

1400 Major McCartney OC A Coy, was reported as wounded but it was later heard that he had been killed.

1430 Cas to date. A Coy 2 offr & 9 ORs, D Coy 10 ORs. The CO went up to see D Coy, to find out the possibilities of clearing the rest of the village, as the original attack was now definitely halted.

1450 More shells on Hingen, Peij & Schilberg.
The position was that A, B & D Coys had all suffered cas, & had been unable to reach the bridge because of determined enemy defence & & lack of cooperation from the Crocodiles which had never closed in to 'flaming' range. 30 men of C Coy had returned from the village & were put under comd of B Coy. Most of the rest, inc Major Anderson, were believed to be PoW.

1700 D Coy, who still had one platoon uncommitted, put in a final attack with a tp of Crocodiles in support. The Crocodiles went forward at last light & set every house on fire; D Coy followed up & and cleared

1745 up the village as far as the bend 716812. This was the end of the resistance in Sint Joost – the Crocodiles were a complete success as soon as they started operating, and broke up the determined resistance of the

Hubner Bn. Few were captured; a good many killed in the cellars, and the rest withdrew to the north. In view of the fight they had put up, D Coy expected some to return and counter-attack the village, but were proved wrong. As they were thin on the ground, D Coy drew back into positions closely covering the bridge & sent patrols up to the bend.

1750 A Coy 1 RB were now ordered up to go through D Coy & clear the rest of the village.

1830 A Coy 1 RB moved up through Hingen & contacted D Coy in the area of the bridge. Their plan was to advance slowly & take up a def posn as soon as opposition was met. D Coy patrolled up to the bend again & found nothing. Five PoW came in from 3 & 7 Coys Hubner & 176 Div Arty.

1900 A German counter-attack was thought to be forming up at 718812 but arty treatment prevented anything happening. Brigadier visited Tac HQ & discussed the possibilities of a relief by 1/5 Queens on the 22nd

Sint Joost was found completely clear & A Coy 1RB were able to move on to occupy the rd junc area

2150 716815 & Steil thus covering the starting point for the advance on Montfort.

2330 As it happened, the relief on the 22nd was to be by 2 Devons, & arrangements were made for it to begin at 0800, as all coys could get out by daylight. We were to make back to Slek, immediately south of Peij, for a short rest, taking up posn providing defence in depth & on the east flank.

COMMENTS

Operational comments from the official report

Enemy

The enemy fought well during the earlier phases of this operation and particularly so when the fresh reserves from Regt Hubner, brought south from the Roermond area, arrived on the scene. He has brought delaying actions by small bodies of inf backed by SP guns to a fine art. During 'Blackcock', owing to the great difficulty experienced by our armour of manoeuvring off the roads or tracks, everything was in his favour and he made full use of it. The wooded areas and the often surprisingly broken ground gave him the opportunities required. Working over country which he knew thoroughly, and behind his own mines, he used his SP guns boldly and to full advantage.

Close support from the RAF could not be counted upon although on good flying days many targets were successfully engaged.

It was anticipated that there might be a large percentage of exposure casualties amongst the troops. This fear, however, proved groundless and their general health remained good throughout.

Weather

The whole operation took place in severe winter conditions. This imposed considerable hardship on both men and machines. The hard frost did not entirely remain throughout and there were falls of snow, slight thaws and occasional fog to complicate operations. The roads generally remained icebound and the heavy tracked vehicles, particularly Kangaroos, found movement difficult. The road approaches to newly constructed bridges were always a problem and several bridges became damaged or blocked for short periods as a result of skidding vehicles. Off the roads movement was always a gamble. There was a thin frozen surface crust which collapsed, on account of the occasional short thaws, under the weight of heavy vehicles and bogging was frequent.

Arty

The question of over-worked FOOs requires consideration. During this operation, lasting 11 days, they were on almost constant duty the whole time. Replacement or relief is almost impossible to arrange, and although the individuals concerned worked throughout with praiseworthy enthusiasm it is questionable whether they could have continued very much longer without definite deterioration in the standard of their work.

Searchlights

These generally did good work and, except when their effect was nullified by fog, were a valuable assistance to bridge construction, maintenance and for fighting during the hours of darkness. It is essential that all lights have their own communications and not have to rely on the nearest gunner bty. In one instance a Searchlight tp was placed close to a bty for communication purposes and casualties were received by the light personnel due to enemy counter bty fire although they themselves had not used their light.

Air

(a) Support was much hampered by weather conditions but on clear days excellent results were obtained. Instances are as follows:

22 Jan: 168 sorties flown by Typhoons at eight targets with 1,000lb and 500lb bombs; also armed recces, and one target engaged by medium bombers.

23 Jan: 80 sorties flown by Typhoons at nine targets including the HQ of 176 Div; also 62 sorties by medium bombers on two targets. On this day RAF expressed gratitude to our Arty who laid 'Apple-Pie' on one target.

(b) It is to be remembered that targets within the bombline can be sometimes engaged provided precise arrangements can be made to identify the target by the use of coloured smoke, etc.

(c) There were instances of unsuitable targets being demanded, eg 'one tank in wood …' On the other hand consideration of priorities, number of sorties already flown, time of day, etc, may prohibit acceptance of what seems a most desirable target.

(d) In view of the enemy practice of evicting civilians from the cellars in non-German towns and villages, the possibility of killing numbers of civilians must be weighed against the target's military importance.

As a result of the air attacks on the non-German village of Montfort, enemy mortar fire was silenced and this road centre was completely blocked. This had been vitally important to the enemy as it enabled him to switch his SP guns to threatened points such as St Joost and Linne.

It is reliably reported, however, that civilian casualties were high.

Specialised Armd Equipment

• **Flails:** When used under snow conditions Flails can't be considered 100% efficient. Casualties to following vehicles will occur and the fact must be accepted. When the ground is ice-bound, or otherwise very hard, considerable damage to bob weights is bound to take place. In spite of these two factors the Flails proved invaluable during the operations and were widely used. It is not perhaps fully realised by the Inf how much the heavy firepower of the Flail can assist them into their objective after Flailing is completed. It was found during this operation that when Flails operate over frozen ground the weight of the tank track will so damage S mines and Schu mines as to neutralize them. If the inf walk in the tank tracks, which are easy to follow-over frosty ground or ground lightly covered with snow, they will get through without casualties.

• **Crocodiles:** During this operation Crocodiles were, in general, used as they should be and not in small packets. There was still a tendency for insufficient tying up between them and Inf and supporting tanks. It may well take three or more hours to arrange this satisfactorily but in the end it will be found time well spent. It is essential that a carefully prepared system of signals is arranged so that the Inf can let the Crocodiles know when to move on to flame the next house or group of houses, pill box, or other point of resistance. It is also essential to have a close tie up between the Crocodile which is very vulnerable, and the supporting tanks upon which it relies for its protection. Inf must learn to follow up the jet of flame immediately.

• **AVREs:** Little comment is necessary. They proved invaluable in the early stages of operations and generally proved most successful.

• **Kangaroos:** Proved most useful but it is essential to guard against over working both crews and machines. To put tps into Kangaroos when it is safe, to use TOTs or for the men to march is an incorrect use of the vehicle. To hold Kangaroos forward after the completion of the task, with the idea that another task may materialize, is uneconomical. In this operation, the command of columns which included Kangaroos, rested with either the Inf or Tank Commander and, thanks to careful preliminary planning, this arrangement worked well.

• **Weasels:** The Divs held these concentrated in a pool to be used as and when required and the vehicles were not issued out to lower formations indiscriminately. They proved a valuable source of transport reserve, and, in particular, excellent for the evacuation of casualties.

Drivers were provided by Inf bns and there is no doubt that this ad hoc arrangement discounts the full capabilities of these vehicles. In any case, drivers require some days' special training.

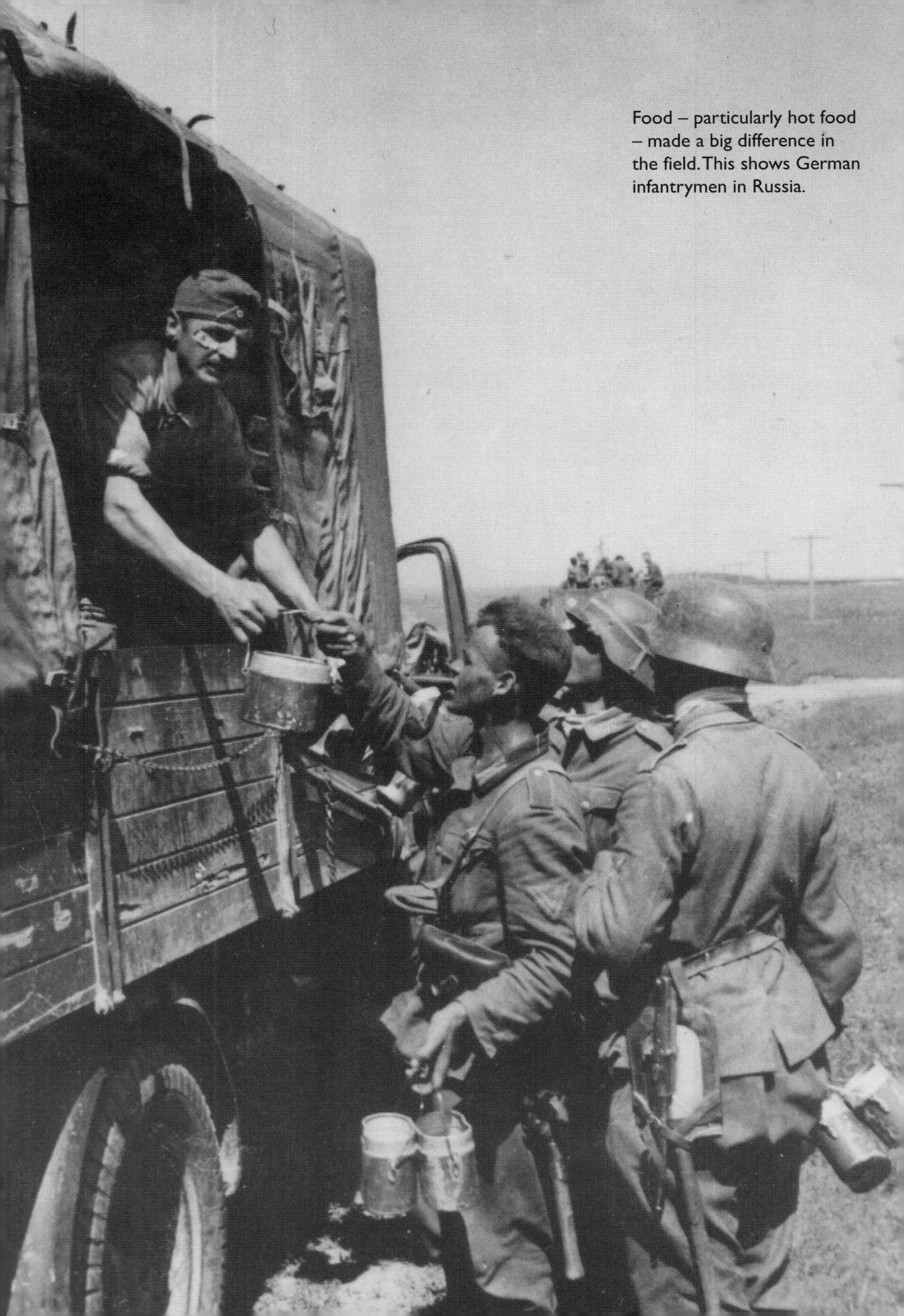

Food – particularly hot food – made a big difference in the field. This shows German infantrymen in Russia.

7 Life in the Infantry

Life as an infantryman during World War II was, of course, nasty, brutish and, often, short. It required considerable physical and mental endurance just to travel the distances they did, no matter the weather, let alone take part in battle. Postwar analysis of how many soldiers actually fired their weapons by S.L.A. Marshall – albeit flawed – nevertheless held a kernel of truth: many infantrymen either didn't fire their weapons in combat or, if they did, did so inaccurately. Some of this may have been because of religious beliefs, but most of the problems were caused by stress. Battle is not just dangerous and scary, it's unnatural. Few ordinary people can spend any length of time watching their mates get killed and killing the enemy without it affecting them. Patton thought 200 days. There was a cycle: the new recruits arrived in theatre; if they were lucky they weren't killed immediately. If they survived they gained experience and became good soldiers. Then, after fighting for some time, they became cautious – they knew the dangers and tended to avoid them. Finally, some of them stopped functioning – a lot didn't, but those that didn't were no longer quite as efficient as they had been.

Morale is a key issue when it comes to keeping soldiers in the fight and there are many things that can affect a soldier's morale for better and worse:
- unit cohesion – the strongest factor; strong leadership and a well-knit unit
- training – knowing what to do when under fire and not being thrown in the deep end
- propaganda – all sides practised it; strong leaders with the right message could counter it. A good example of a bad message: making the Japanese soldier seem to be a simian superman more at home in the jungle than the Allies
- information – particularly from home in the form of mail and newspapers
- escapism – films, theatre productions, entertainments, sex – the company of women
- normality – getting out of the line; clean clothes, baths, hot food and alcohol – something other than boxed rations
- leave – getting away from the battle area, preferably home

Morale may keep soldiers in the battle but it's not the reason why they fight. Of course, that's all very well in democracies. For those countries with dictators – or, in the case of Japan, people owing total obedience to the emperor – the soldiery didn't have a choice. Worse than that, Russian political officers and Nazi officials enforced their regime's orders at gunpoint. Thousands of German and Russian

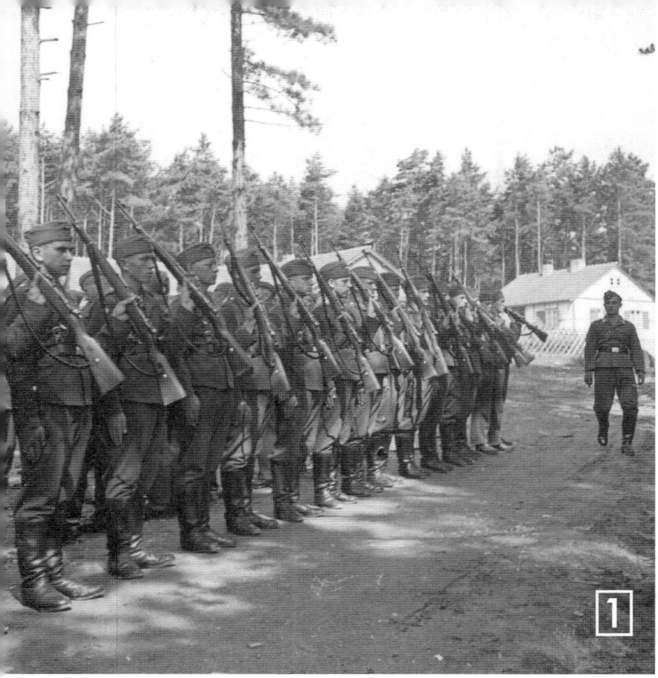
1
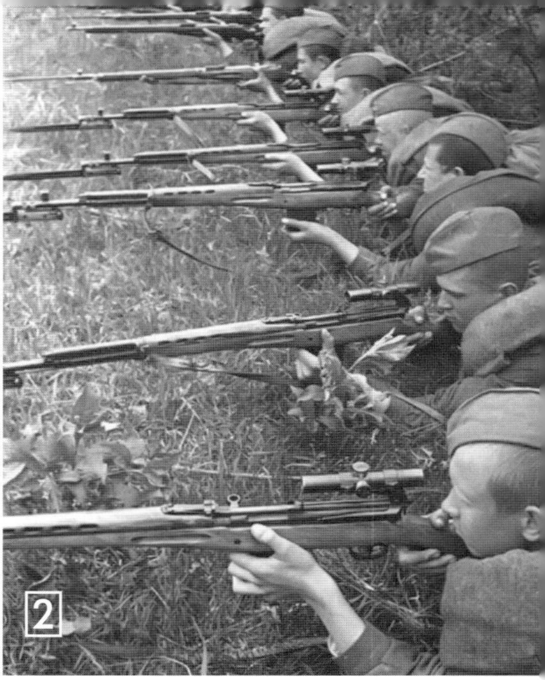
2

The main weapon of the infantryman of World War II was the rifle and learning to keep it clean, use the sights – especially telescopic sights for snipers – and use the bayonet were important parts of early training. **1** German recruits hold out their rifles for inspection. **2** Cadets of Red Army's Sniper Academy fire combat rifles with optical sights (SVT-40s) and without them (Mosin-Nagant rifles). **3** Cadets return personal weapons (Mosin-Nagant and SVT-40 rifles) to the rack after training. Note their *shatka* (rolled *shinel* greatcoats carried over the shoulder). **4 and 5** Accuracy and marksmanship were important factors in training. These are men from the RAD. **6** In the field, soldiers cleaned their weapons meticulously and regularly – particularly in jungle conditions, as here on Bougainville where men of 93rd Infantry Division clean their M1 Garand rifles, April 1944.

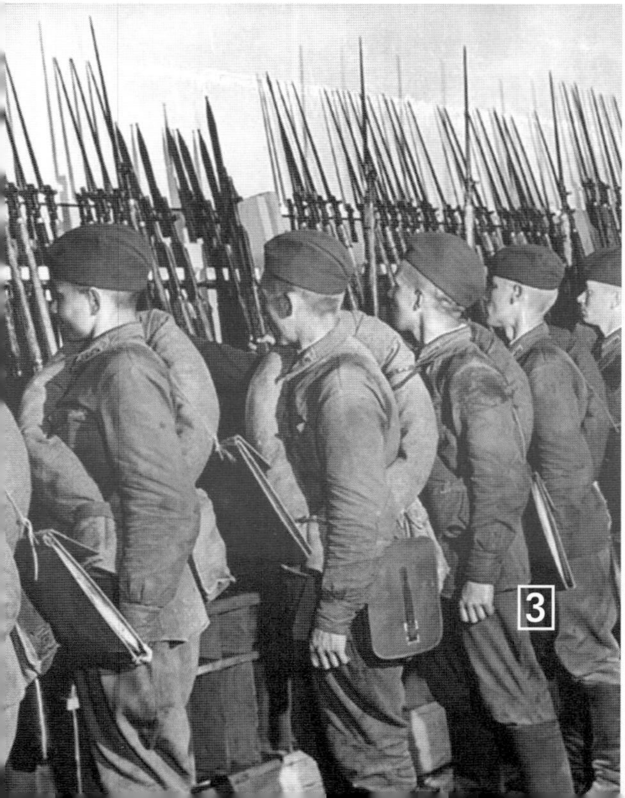
3
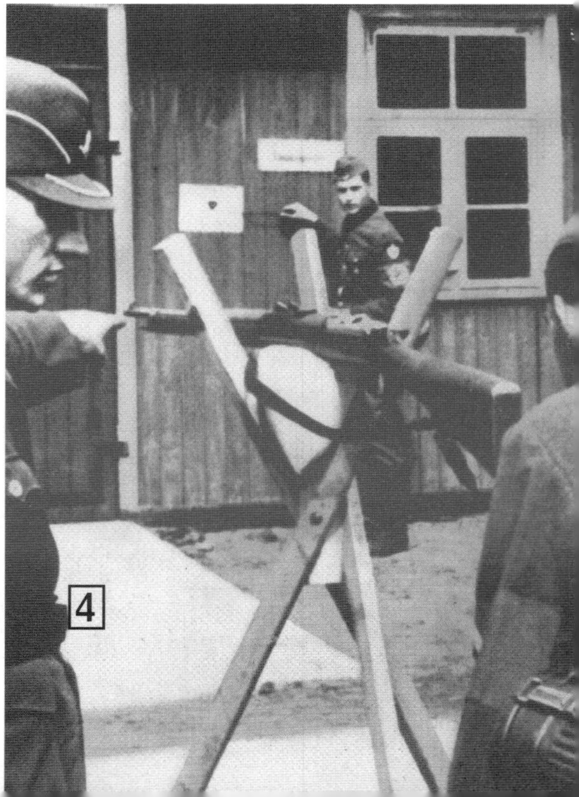
4

soldiers were executed, and the regimes pressurised families to ensure soldiers' continued commitments. For the armies of the free world, the reasons were very different. Some volunteered; some fought because they were conscripted – but their countries fought because of the aggression of their enemies who had either attacked them or an ally.

The United States entered the war because it was attacked by Japan and because Germany declared war. While its president may have been sympathetic to the British and European cause, politically it did not want to become embroiled in a second European war. It was ambivalent about helping maintain the British Empire – and would exact a high price for its assistance. The armies of the British Empire were also ambivalent about their involvement – India because it wanted independence from British rule; South Africa because the Boer lineage meant the country was split with many pro-German. What is clear is that many Commonwealth soldiers were not fighting for the preservation of the political status quo. Postwar, veterans would have a political role. Much of the British citizen army, as Jonathan Fennell details, was politicised and ended up playing an important part in the political revolution that saw Labour win the 1945 General Election. Indian and Pakistani veterans, too, played an important role in the fight for India's independence and its partition. Thoughts of home were not confined to family but to a wider political picture. These infantrymen fought for a better, and different, future.

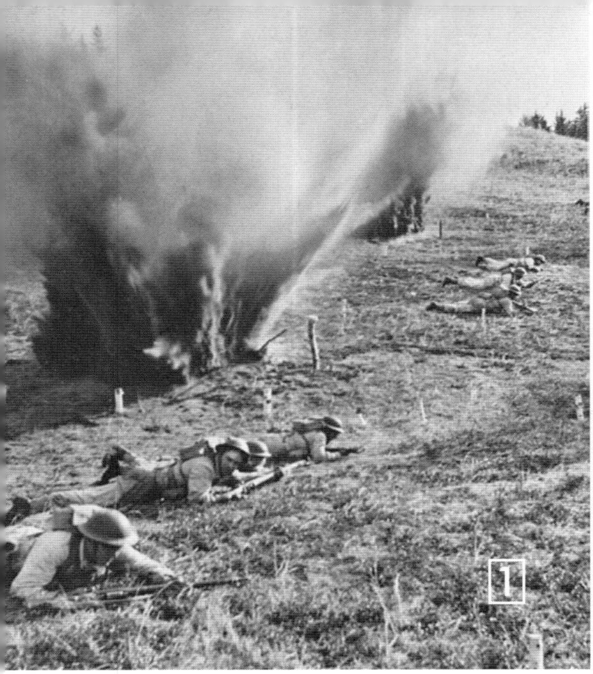
1

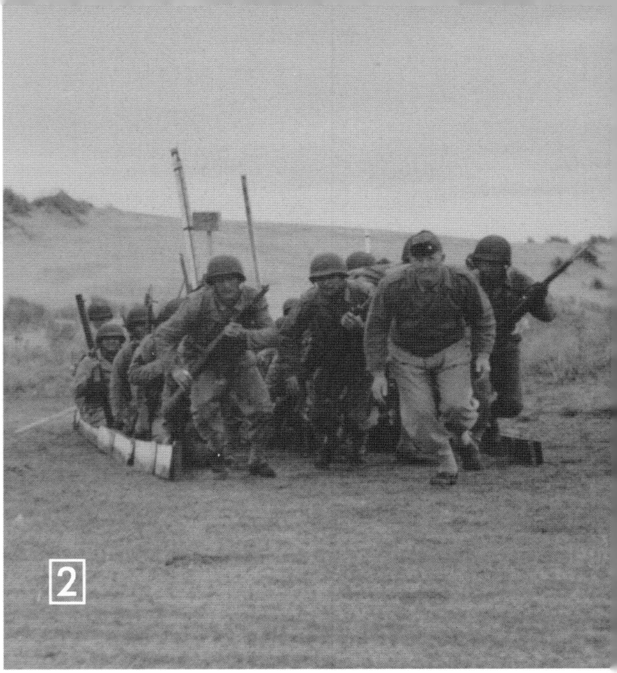
2

1 When they weren't fighting, few soldiers enjoyed long periods of rest and relaxation. They trained for their next mission, and much of that training was physically demanding, used live ammunition and could be extremely dangerous. Training accidents were frequent. This is a training exercise on Salisbury Plain, 6 February 1944.

2 The US Army Assault Training Center at Woolacombe and Braunton taught the units that would assault the beaches of Normandy. Here men learn how to leave a landing craft.

3 Training on new equipment was essential. The DUKW performed excellently from its introduction during Operation Husky thanks to the hard work in the UK beforehand.

4 A German Obergefreiter teaches a Hitler Youth teenager how to fire a *Panzerfaust*.

5 Beach training in Italy for the landings in the south of France.

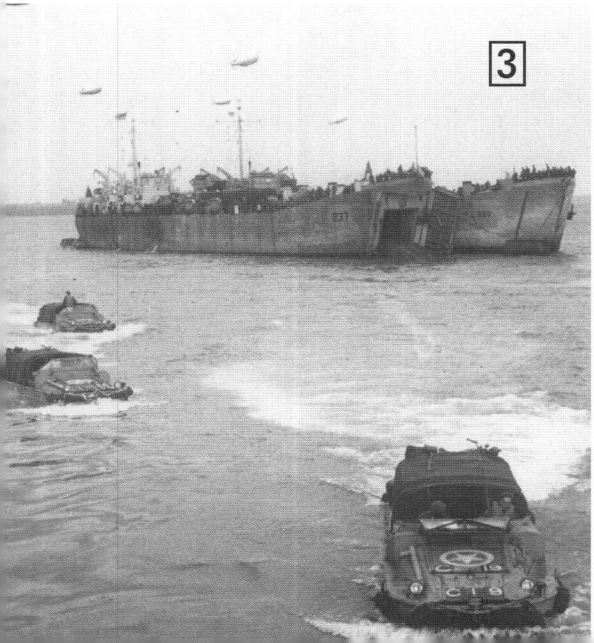
3

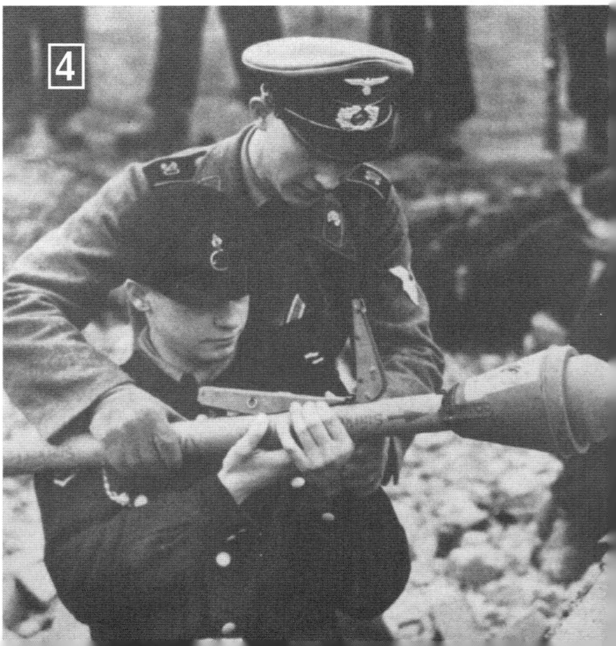
4

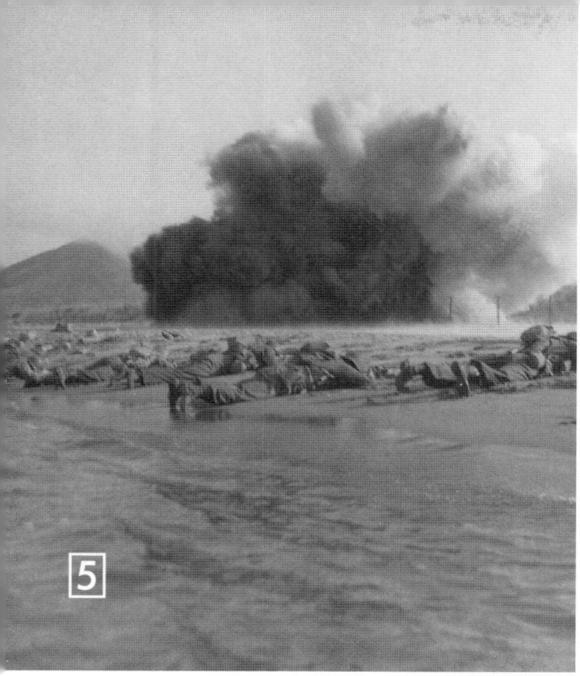
5

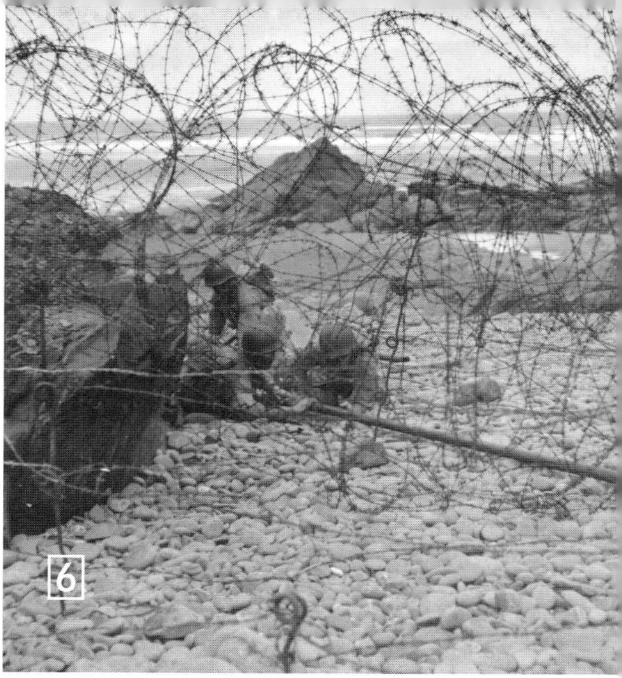
6

6 Captain McClintock a British engineer officer in the Bengal, Bombay, and Madras Sappers and Miners invented the Bangalore torpedo in 1912. Most armies used them. Here, US troops train in their use at Woolacombe.

7 German infantry training took place over a period of 16 weeks and included fire and movement, command, ballistics, heavy weapons, tactical field training – map reading, fieldcraft, camouflage – but physical fitness training was never far away with route marches carrying full pack and weapons. The training of the German infantryman was comprehensive, brutal – injuries were frequent – and discipline was harsh and, not infrequently, enforced by capital punishment.

8 Polish troops training in Scotland. Two Polish units played a big part in the battles in northwest Europe: General Stanisław Maczek's 1st Armoured Division that fought with First Canadian Army and General Władysław Anders Polish II Corps made up of men who had been released from captivity in Russia to serve in Italy.

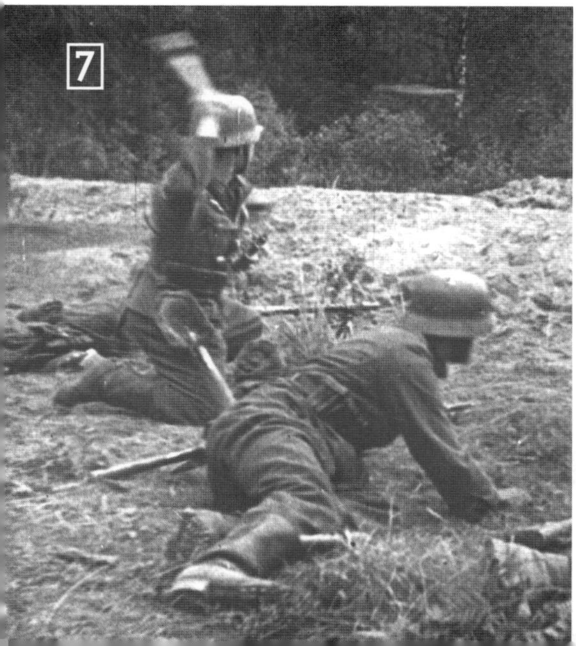
7

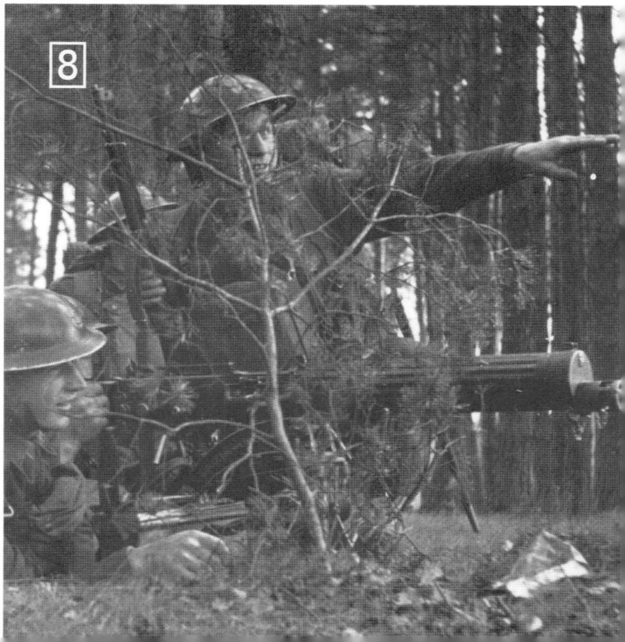
8

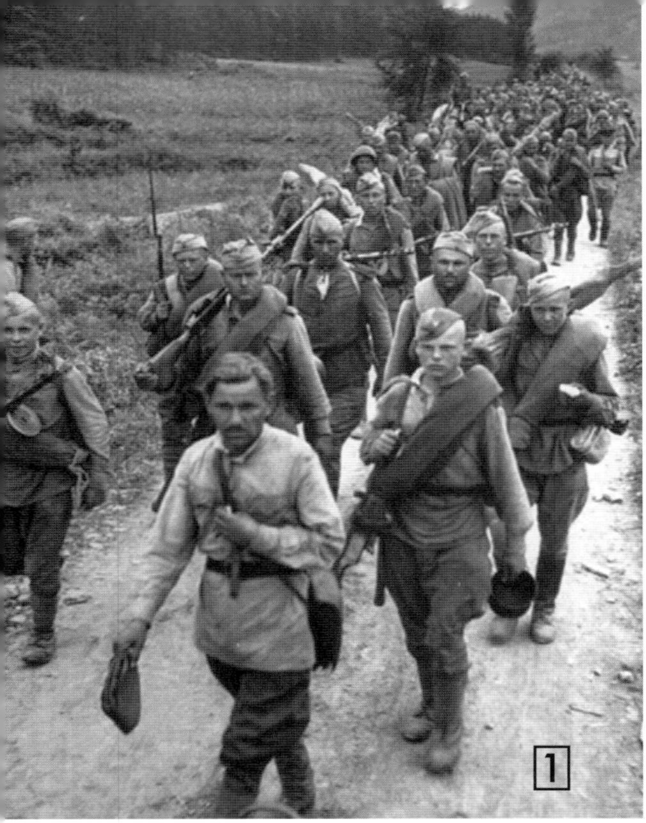
1

In the end, it didn't matter how motorised an army was, in World War II the footsloggers had to march and they covered huge distances doing so. These photographs show Russians in North Korea in October 1945 (**1**); British troops in Overloon being passed by a Churchill AVRE (**2**); US 10th Infantry Regt (5th Inf Div), having cleared the village of Nachtmanderscheid in Luxembourg, heading off in the snow. It's 24 January 1945 and the Allies are close to eradicating the Bulge (**3**); and German troops in France in 1940, knotted handkerchieves protecting their heads from the hot early summer sunshine (**4**). Monty said: 'Why does a soldier leave the protection of his trench hole in the ground and go forward in the face of shot and shell? It is because of the leader who is in front of him and his comrades who are around him. Comradeship makes a man feel warm and courageous when all his instincts tend to make him cold and afraid.'

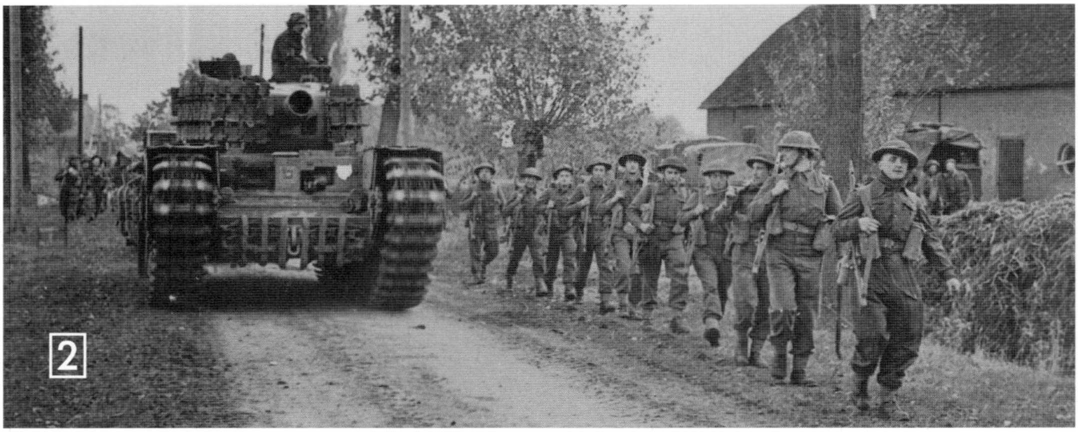
2

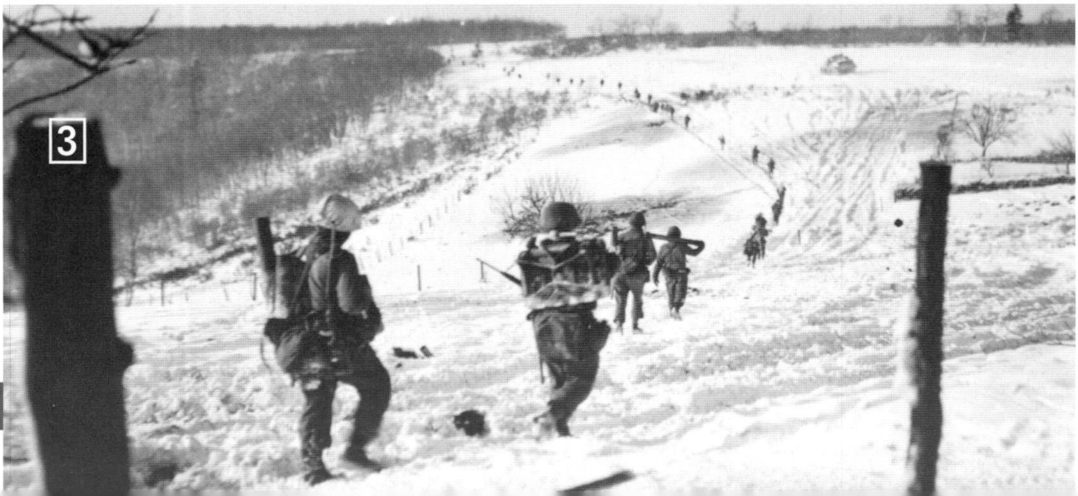
3

RATES OF MARCH

(From German Tactical Doctrine; Special Series No 8, US War Dept, 1942)

Since it is important to provide conditions which permit an even rate of march, the mixing of different sorts of troops should be avoided as much as possible. (Pack animals are one disturbing factor in maintaining an even rate of march.) On good roads and under favourable conditions the following average speeds can be accomplished:

Type of unit	Distance/hour
Foot troops	5km (3 miles)
Foot troops (small units)	6km (3.5 miles)
Mounted troops (trot and walk)	7km (4 miles)
Mounted troops (trot)	10km (6 miles)
Bicyclists	12km (7.5 miles)
Motorcyclists	40km (25 miles)
Large organizations with all weapons:	
(1) Including rest periods	4km (2.5 miles)
(2) Under stress, without rest periods	5km (3 miles)
Motorized units	30km (18 miles)

For foot troops under ordinary conditions the distance prescribed as a "buffer" between companies, or similar units, is 10 paces; for mounted troops and trains, 15 paces. Such distances do not apply, of course, when air defense depth has been ordered.

Intense heat, poor roads, snow, ice, absence of bridges, and other local conditions greatly influence the march rate and the travel distance accomplished. The rate for foot troops on a cross-country or mountainous march decreases from the normal hourly rate by as much as 2 or 3km.

When great distances must be covered rapidly, motor and rail transportation can be used to expedite marches; for distances under 150km (93 miles) the use of motor transportation is recommended. When circumstances require foot or mounted troops to make forced marches, every effort is made to assist the accomplishment. Strict march discipline is preserved, and severe measures are meted out to malingerers. The men are told why the particular march is being made, and arrangements are made for rests where refreshments such as hot coffee or tea will be served. Their packs are carried, if possible, in trains.

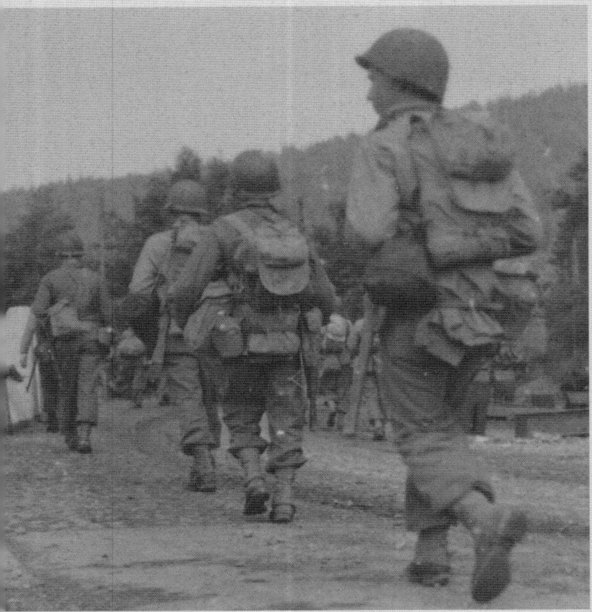

TYPICAL US RIFLEMAN'S EQUIPMENT WEIGHTS

Equipment	*Weight (lb)*
Rifle, M1 (loaded)	10.20
Sling, M1	.53
Cleaning kit, M1	.53
Cartridge belt, M1923	1.44
10 x 8-rd clips in belt	5.31
Ammo: bandolier w/6 x 8-rd clips (x2)	6.74
Bayonet, M1 w/M7 scabbard	1.56
Grenade, MK II, frag. (x2) (1.31 each)	2.62
Hatchet M1910 or saw	1.50
or Entrenching M1910 w/handle	2.25
Pistol, captured	2.00
Total equipment	**32.52**
Clothing weight (underwear/socks/long johns/shirt and trousers/cap/boots/sweater/jacket/parka/scarf/gloves/blanket/shelter half/toilet gear)	+ **30.52**
Common equipment (helmet/liner, First aid pouch, Canteen/cover/filled, M1943 entrenching tool, suspenders, pack, K-rations)	+ **18.98**
Total rifleman's load	**= 82.02**

Above: Equipment weights varied considerably depending on availability, what was lost or discarded (US soldiers were known for chucking away items during long marches), and destruction in combat or by accident. This is what the US riflemen carried.

Below: Japanese infantry show off their marching drill. Three are carrying Czech ZB vz 30 LMGs which were bought by China and produced under licence. They were also used in Manchukuo and by the Japanese when captured. The Japanese also made good use of bicycles and horses: an Imperial Japanese Army division had approximately 22,000 men and 5,800 horses.

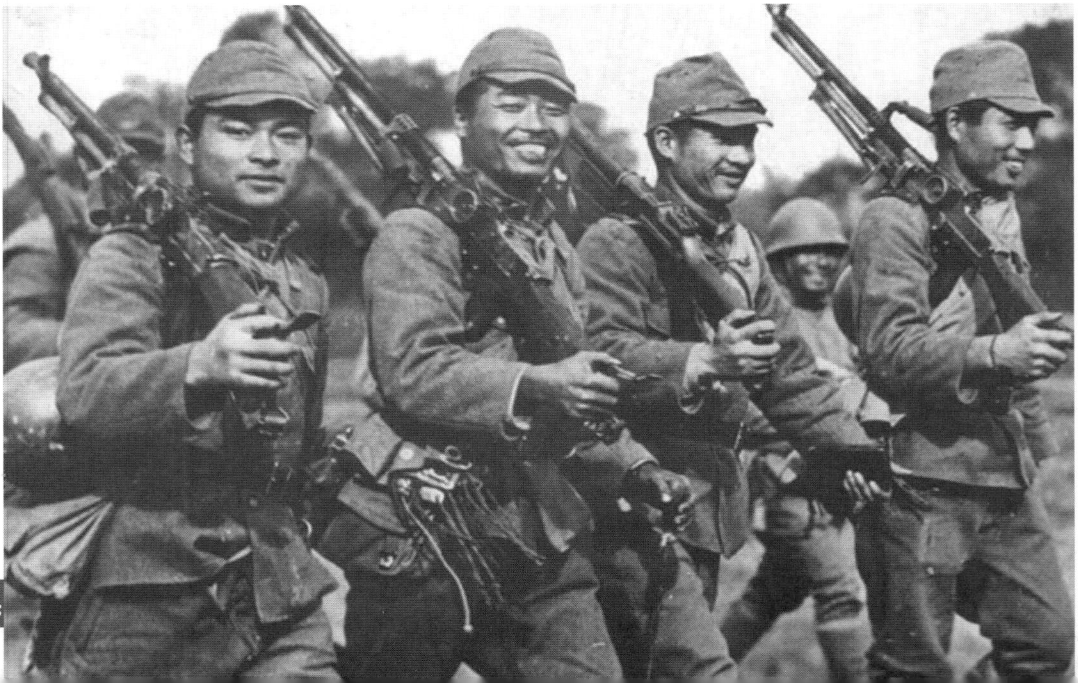

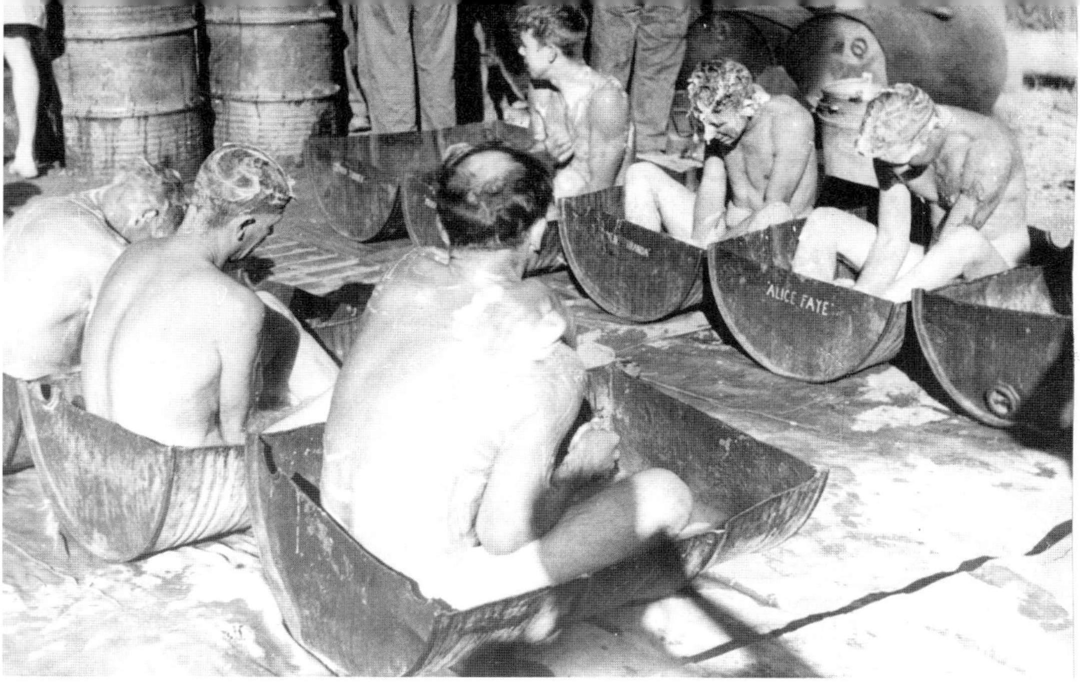
ALICE FAYE

Yes it's prosaic, but there's no doubt that ablutions and cleanliness play a large role in an infantryman's life. Self-esteem and cameraderie are pointers to unit cohesion and battle stress. The abnormal environment created by battle and fear can be eased somewhat by normality: by doing things that don't involve weapons and battle – even if that means sitting in two inches of cold water in half an oil drum, or shaving in the barbed wire of the Westwall or in the middle of a Finnish forest.

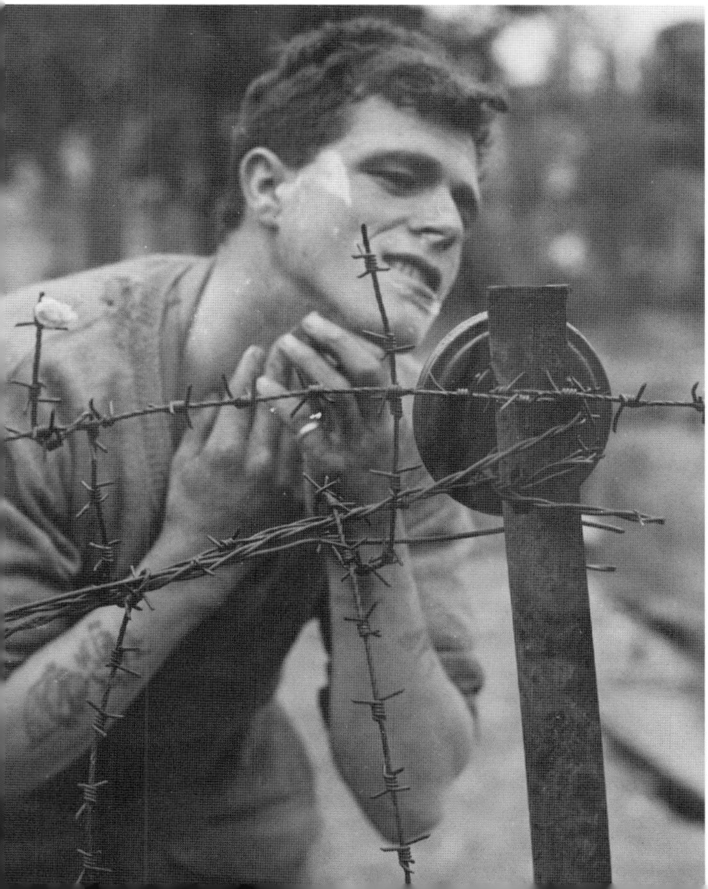

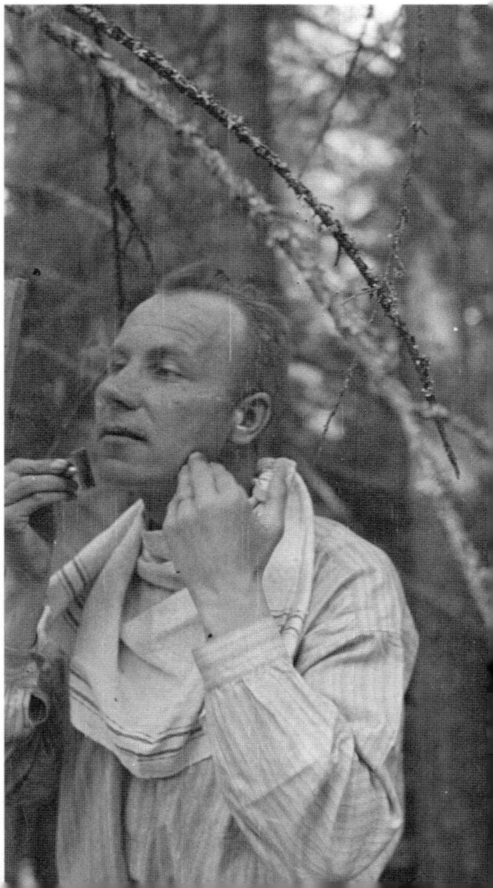

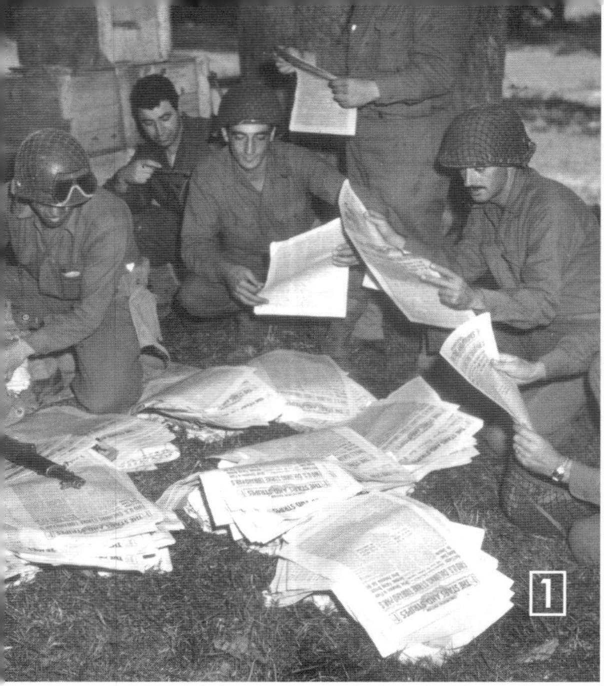
1

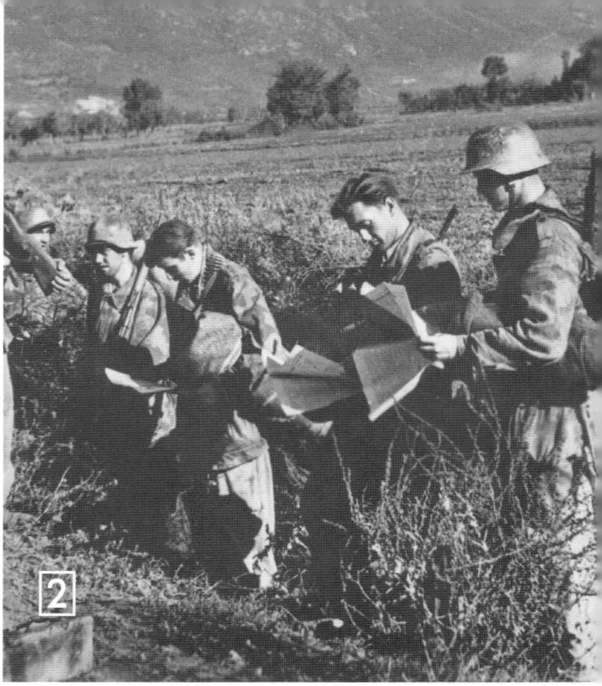
2

1, 2, 3 Newspapers – any news from home was important. Sir Michael Howard, a captain in the Coldstream Guards in Italy, said in *BAR*, 'Overall the lesson that I learned was the overwhelming importance of morale to see one through not only danger, but as important, if not indeed more so, discomfort and boredom, for they are just as difficult in terms of morale as danger. ... It was as difficult, if not more so, to maintain high morale out of the line when the unit had little to do and was uncomfortably housed rather than in sticky situations where danger itself provided its own kind of challenge. Desertion was at its highest rate in Italy among units that were out of the line and were thoroughly "browned off".'

4 As well as the official military newspapers – such as the German *Signal* or *Die Wehrmacht*, the Indian *Fauji Akhbar*, American *Stars and Stripes* or *Yank*, Canadian *Maple Leaf*, or Russian *Za Rodinu* – there were many homegrown newspapers from the *Tripoli Times* to *The Goat Island Groan*.

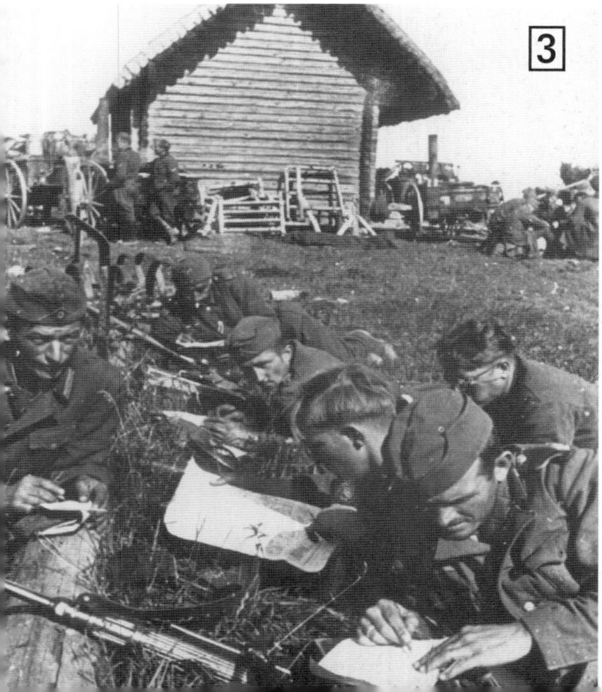
3

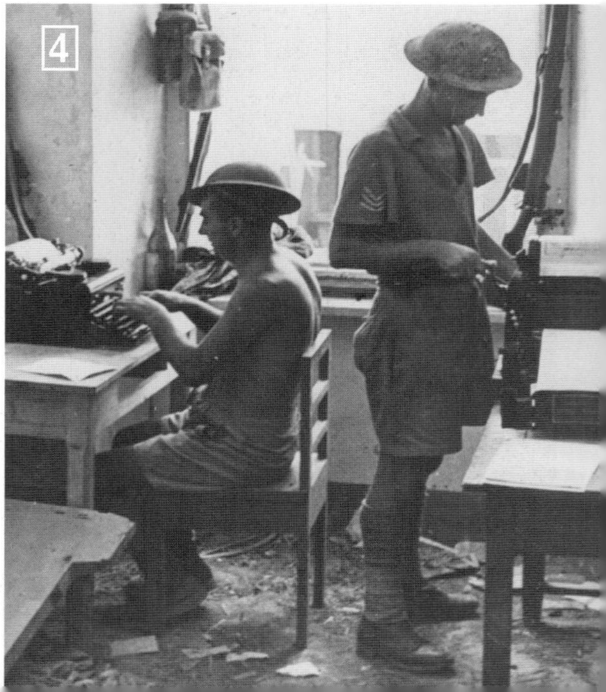
4

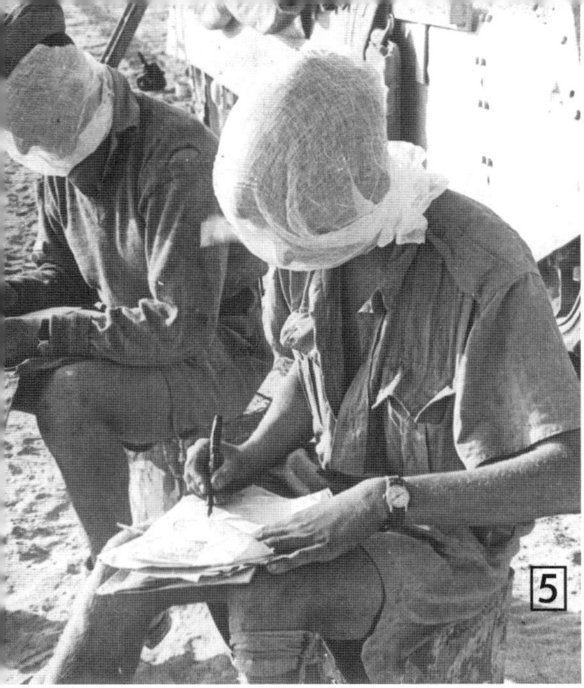
5

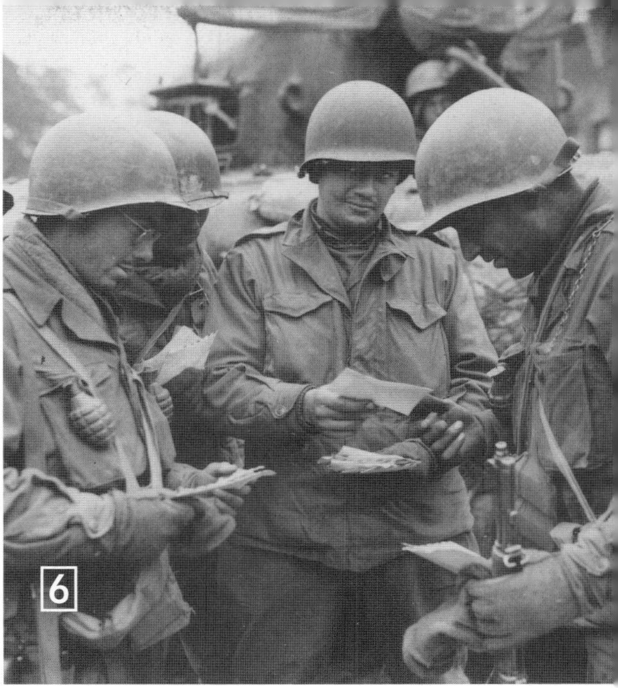
6

5–7 Letters to and from home; parcels containing everything from clothing to food; these have been important to soldiers from earliest times – there are letters from Romans in Africa asking their families for gear. Good postal systems were part of every military operation – as was censorship. Even the letters of the armies of the democracies were censored to ensure military information wasn't given out and to monitor disaffection and morale. In 1942, American servicemen benefited by the introduction of Victory Mail: personal letters went for free. The Soviet postal service – part of the People's Commissariat for Communications of the USSR – delivered up to 70 million parcels per month to the Soviet Army. The British forces' post under the Royal Engineers innovated the use of Kodak Airgraphs and air letters.

Note anti-insect headnets (**5**). For Europeans, flies, bugs and other insects made life intolerable and caused disease. Howard noted how his early war experiences were curtailed to 'ten fairly hairy days at Salerno followed by ten months out of action due to recurrent malaria.'

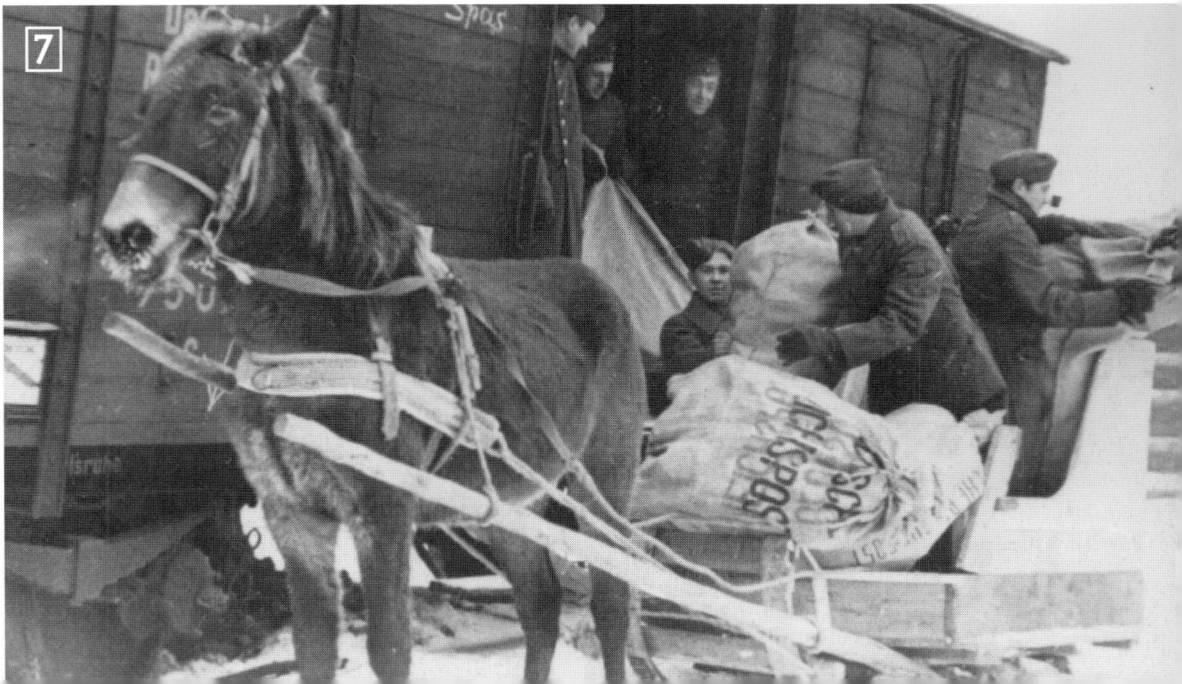
7

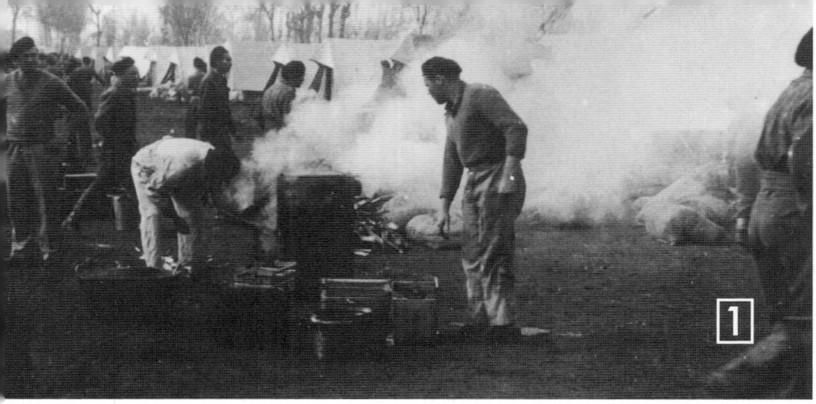
1

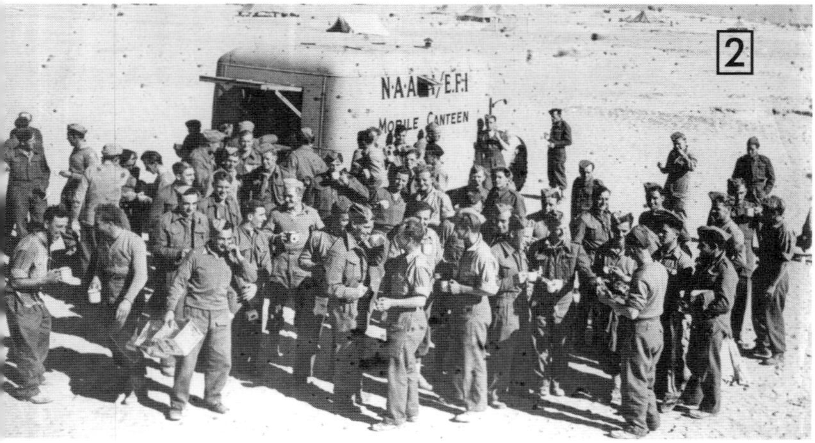
2
N·A·A·F·I / E.F.I
MOBILE CANTEEN

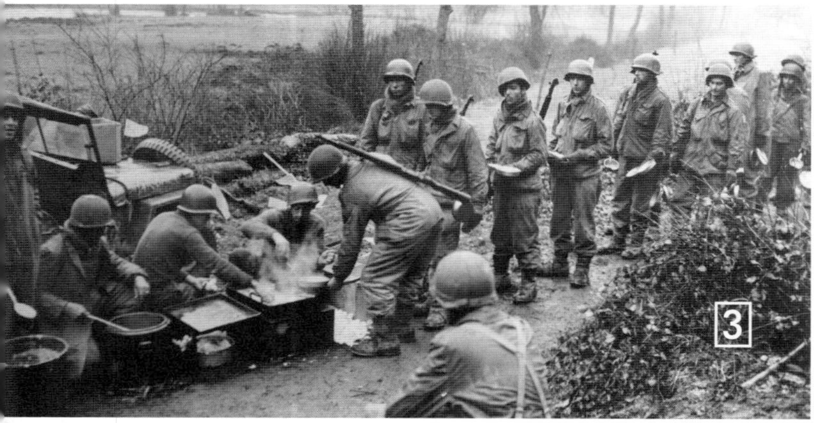
3

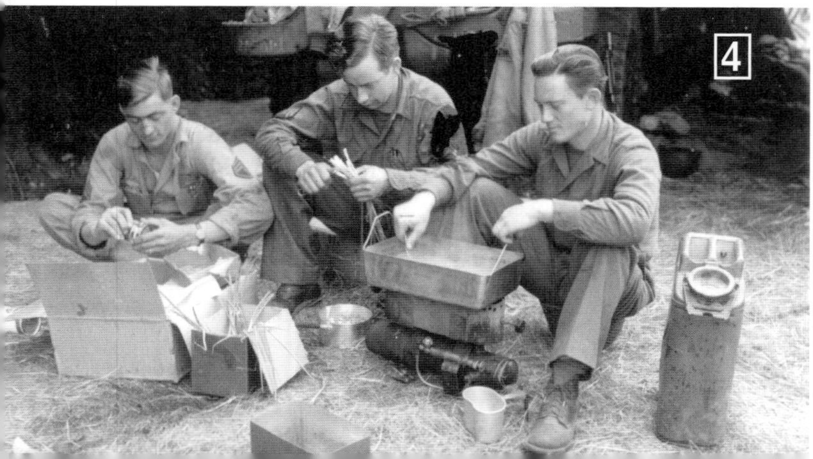
4

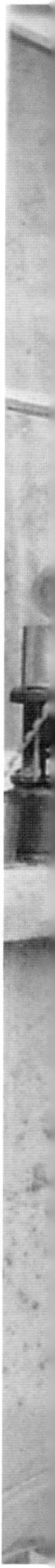

An army, we all know, moves on its stomach and the armies of World War II were no exception. Hot food, and plenty of it, was an essential adjunct to good morale.

1 and 6 Polish field kitchens in 1939 (**6**) and 1944 (**1**).

2 The NAAFI supported the troops on active service, with nearly 10,000 trading outlets. Here soldiers in the North African desert flock round a mobile canteen.

3 A chow line for A/9th Armored Infantry (US 6th Armored Division) on a wet 18 February 1945.

4 A good cook was worth his weight in any army, as was a good cooker.

5 A few US Army units in the ETO – 2nd and 30th Infantry Divs, the 17th Engineer Bn and the 41st Armd Inf Regt (US 2nd Armd Div) – were issued with HBT camouflage uniforms. Unfortunately, it was too similar to those of the Waffen-SS and led to a number of 'blue on blue' friendly fire incidents. This is Pvt Joseph De Freitos of the 41st Armd Inf Regt having lunch.

7 4th Indian Division cooks making flatbread near Cassino, 5 March 1944.

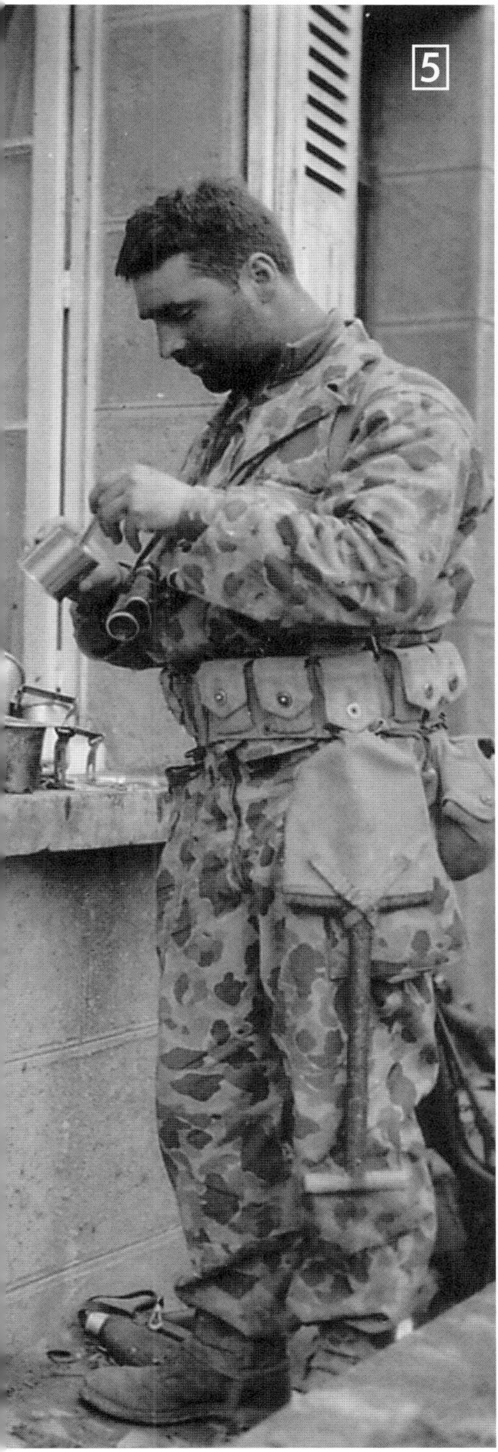
5

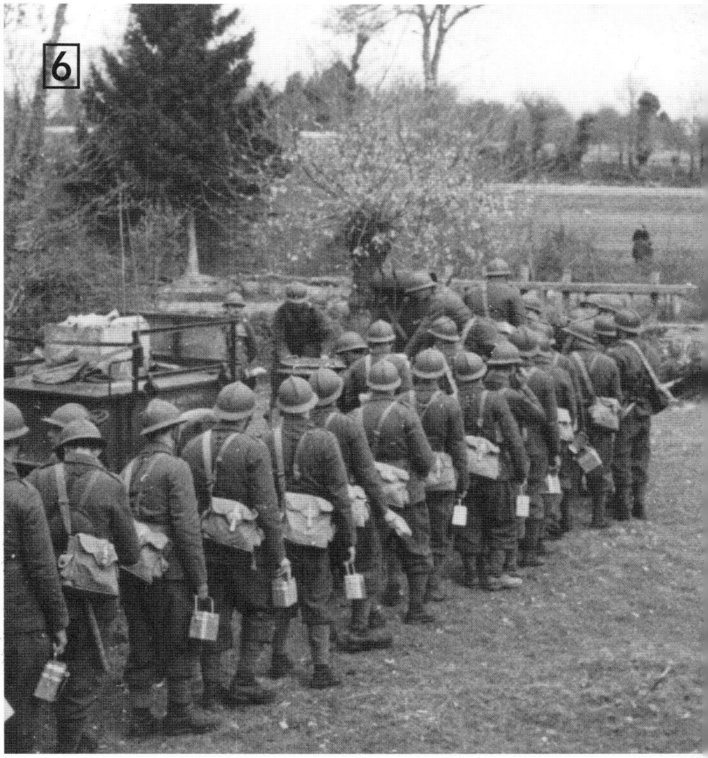
6

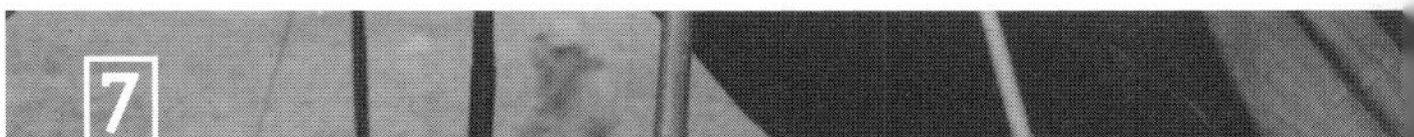
7

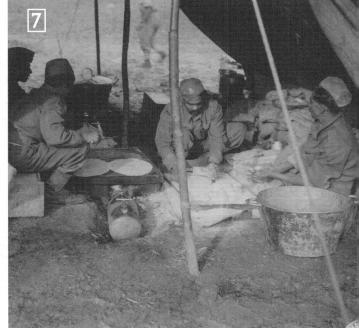

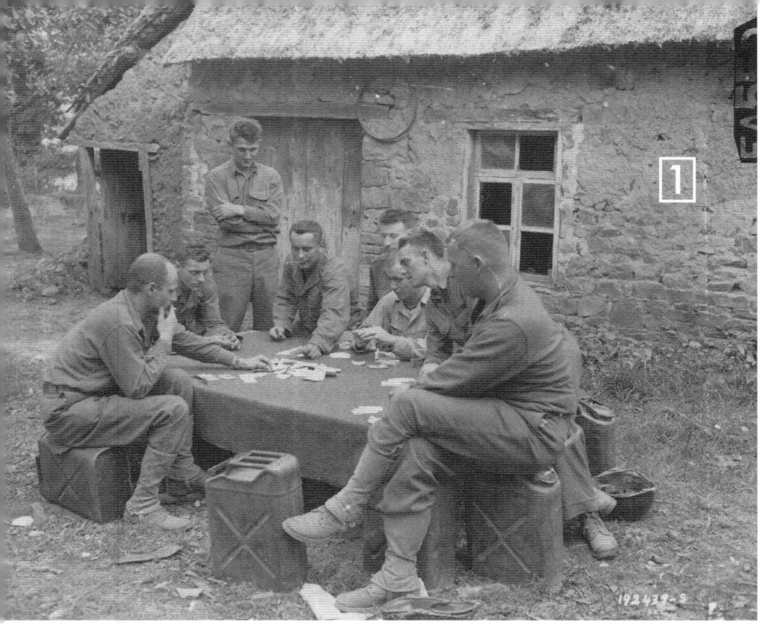
1

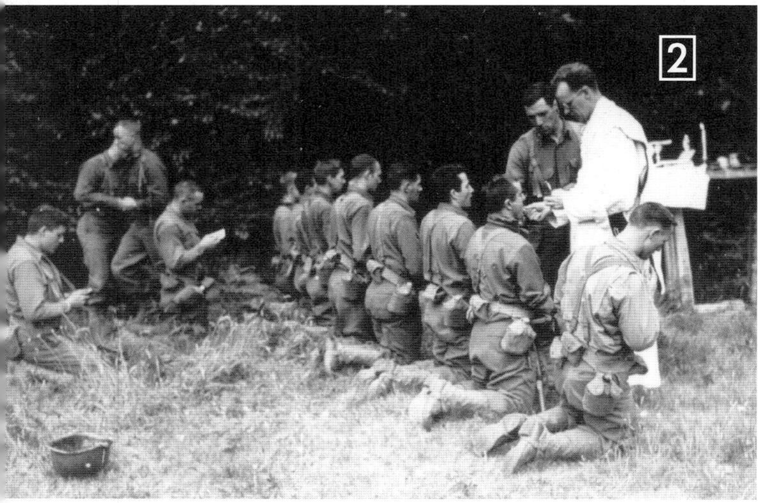
2

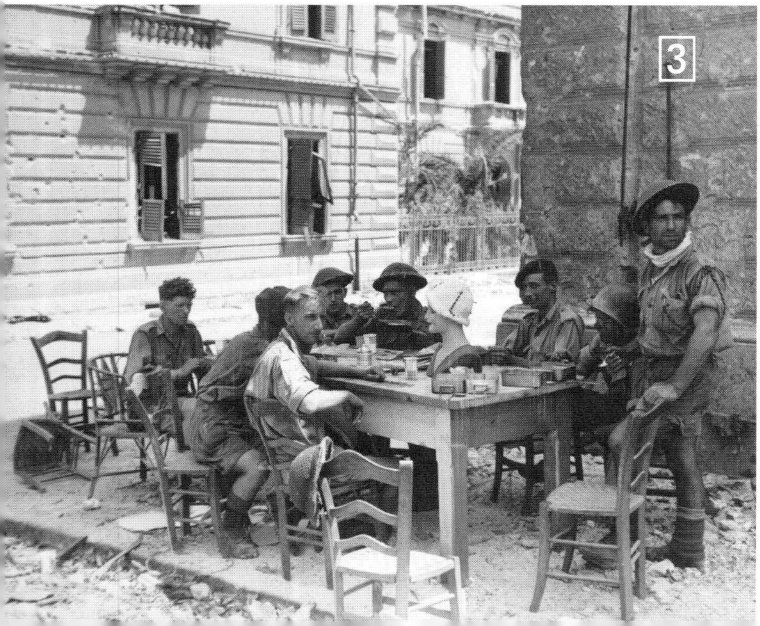
3

1 Boredom weighs heavily on soldiers. The anxiety caused by waiting to go into action builds up over extended periods and leads to battlefield stress and, ultimately, can lead to significant reduction in performance levels.

2 It is said that there are few atheists in foxholes. Certainly religion and superstition did play an important role in soldiers' lives – although the values of Christianity and the need to kill the opposition could make uncomfortable bedfellows.

3 Unit cohesion is of great importance in battle and often makes the difference between victory and defeat. The German soldiers who made life so difficult for the Allies in the last six months of the war may have been crammed with Fascist ideology, but in the end they fought for their comrades.

4 Alcohol and drugs played a big part in most soldiers' lives. Many a Russian attack was fuelled and sustained by vodka. Drugs were used increasingly, too: methamphetamines, benzedrine and dexedrine, and – of course – nicotine. Here, it's nothing stronger than gin that could be injected into oranges to supply fortifying refreshments.

5 Physical discomforts wear down human beings' resolve. Clean, vermin-free uniforms and keeping good boots in order help.

6 and 7 Hot food for the troops was essential but not always possible. Here Russian troops carry food containers forward – a dangerous occupation if snipers are about.

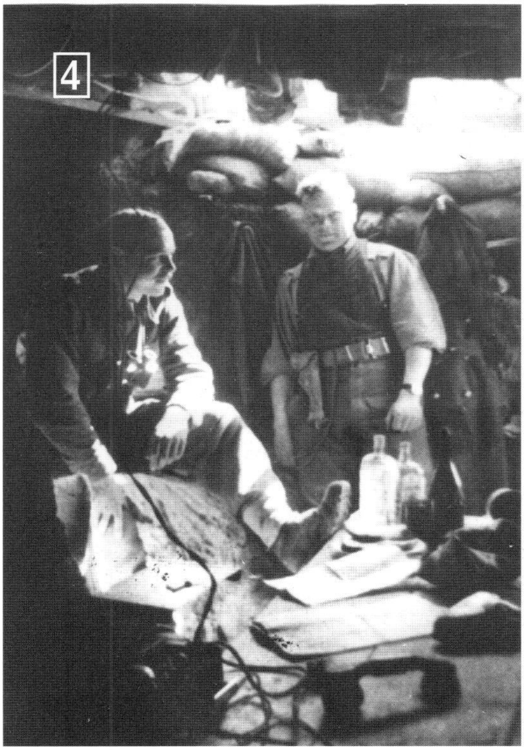
4

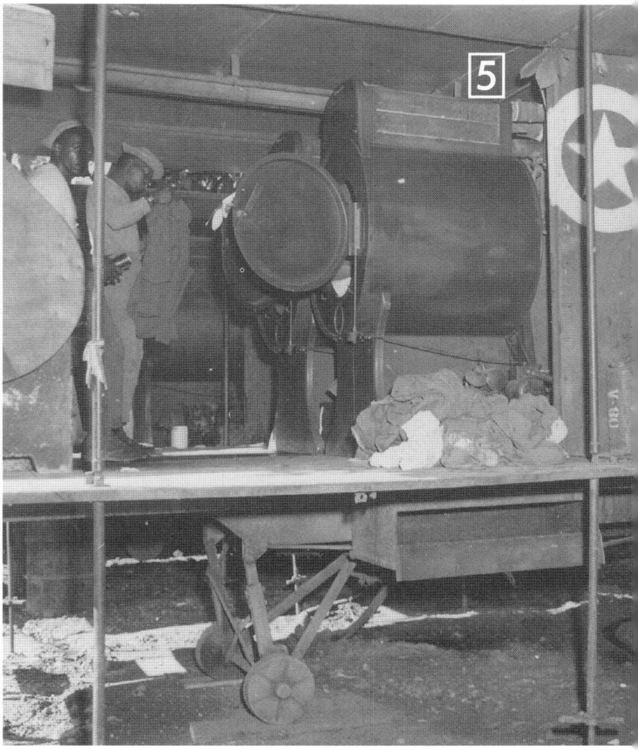
5

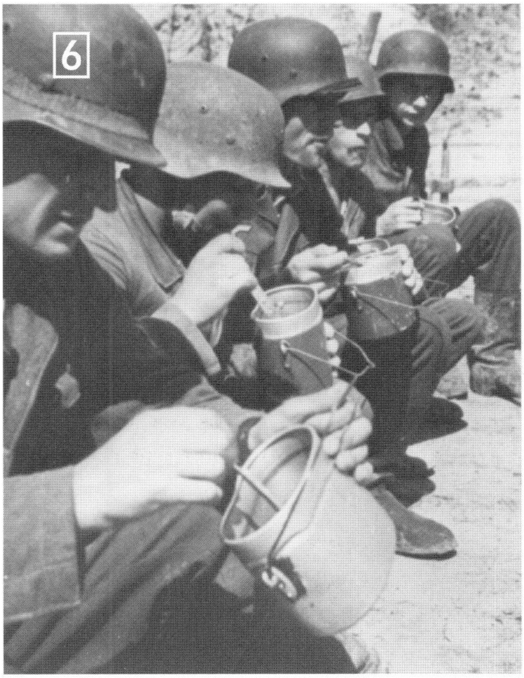
6

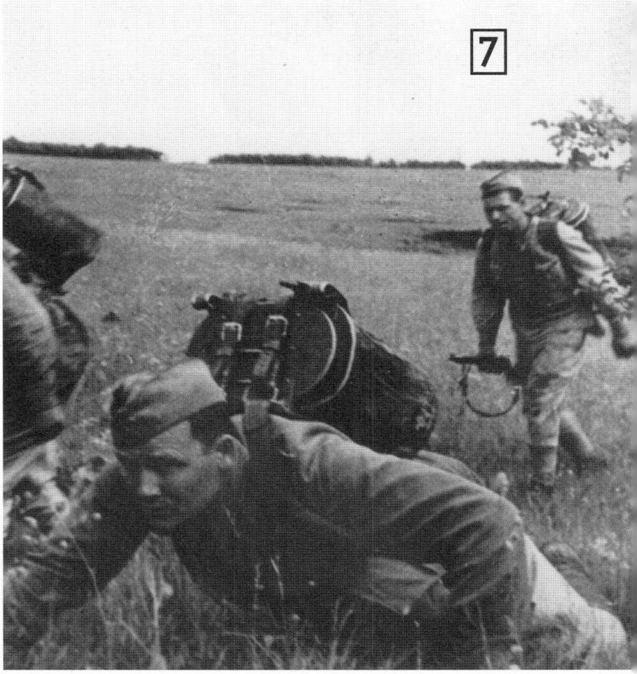
7

Appendices

1 Defensive Positions

1

2

3

1 Defensive positions, particularly the Atlantic Wall and Westwall, saw upgrades during the war as gun positions were emplaced under metres-thick concrete, fields of fire were ruthlessly created by knocking down buildings and evacuating civilians, and barbed wire thickets and minefields were laid profusely. Today, the wire has gone and the mines have been lifted but the concrete often remains.

2 Anti-tank ditches were an essential to curtail armour operations. Fascines were used to bridge them and there were also specific vehicles such as the Churchill Ark – a turretless AFV with bridging on the superstructure – or armoured bulldozers. Most infantry units would also have bridging equipment at divisional or corps level.

3: Laying wire on the Italian Front, December 1943.

4 The most important thing was to dig in to protect against artillery bombardment. Here, German infantry awaits a Soviet attack on their trenches on the Perekop isthmus. The Leutnant watches the Soviet positions through Scherenfernrohr SF14ZGi scissor binoculars.

5 'In small towns, a perimeter defense could be used. Narrow, crooked streets allowed little field of fire or observation within the town. Groups on the highest roof acted as OPs as well as antisniper and anti-infiltration security groups. In towns too large for effective perimeter defense, the outskirts were merely outposted. Platoon combat groups were organized at the principal street intersections, occupying two or three adjacent buildings.

Continued on next page.

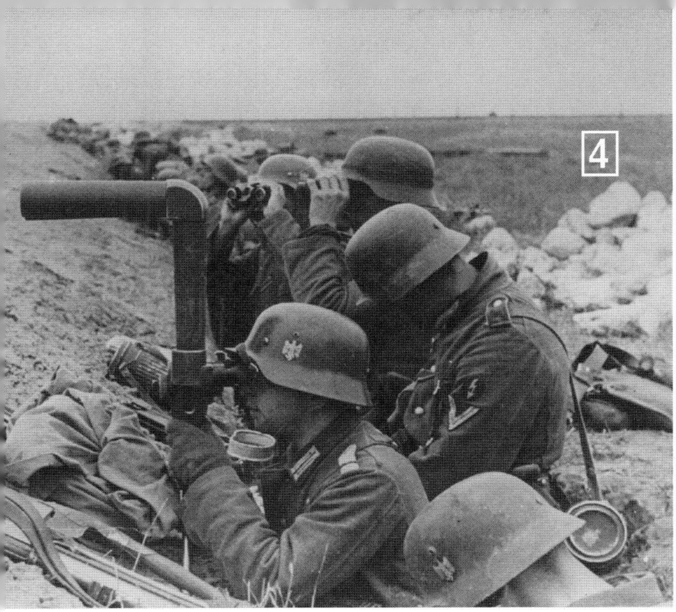
4

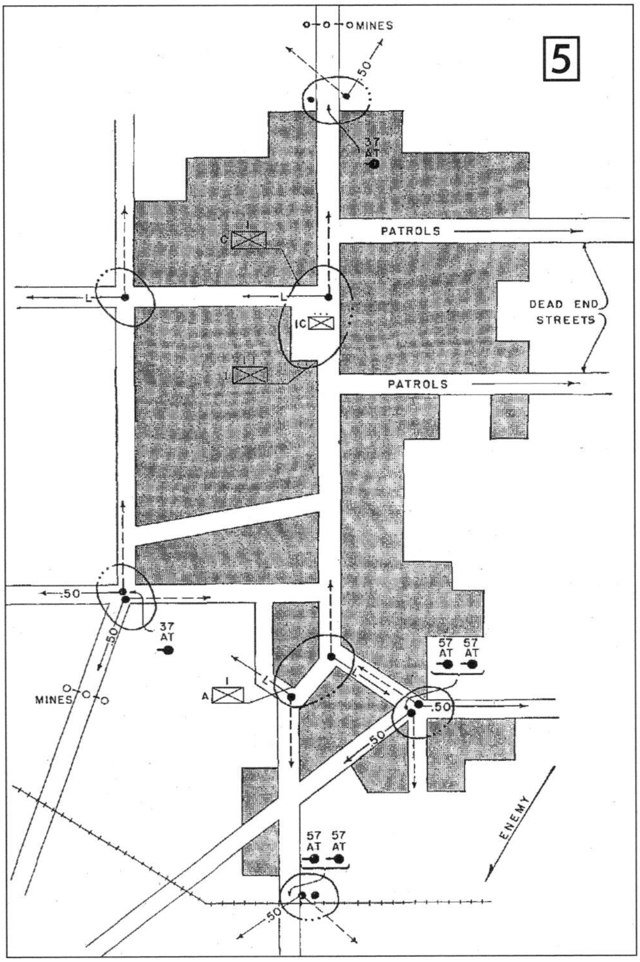
5
MINES
.50
37
AT
PATROLS
C
L
IC
DEAD END
STREETS
PATROLS
.50
.50
37
AT
57 57
AT AT
MINES
A
.50
.50
ENEMY
57 57
AT AT
.50

MGs were located to fire down the streets in all directions. In this way solid bands of grazing MG fire could cover the spaces between combat groups. Also AT guns and mines were used to block principal entrance roads. Reserve units held interior intersections, prepared to counterattack.'

The defense of a town must be prepared to meet the methods of attack which may be employed by the enemy. Since this must include the possibility of flanking attacks and encirclement, it follows that an all-around defense must be the rule. The following points, not covered in the experiences quoted above, should be borne in mind in planning the defense of a town:

1. Avoid placing principal centres of resistance close to landmarks or at edge of town where enemy adjustment of artillery or mortar fire will be facilitated. Positions either outside of or within the town should be chosen.
2. Where practicable, form salients by organizing outlying buildings to cover perimeter of town with flanking and enfilade fire.
3. In addition to a central reserve within the town, provide if possible for a concealed mobile reserve (preferably strong in armor) to be held outside the town to counter enemy flanking maneuver.
4. Wherever adjacent terrain features dominate the town they should be secured. This use of high ground may be the key to successful defense.
5. Within the town, the construction of street obstacles or barricades to impede enemy movements, and the organization of groups of buildings into strong points should be carried out as extensively as the time available will permit. (*Combat Lessons No 2.*)

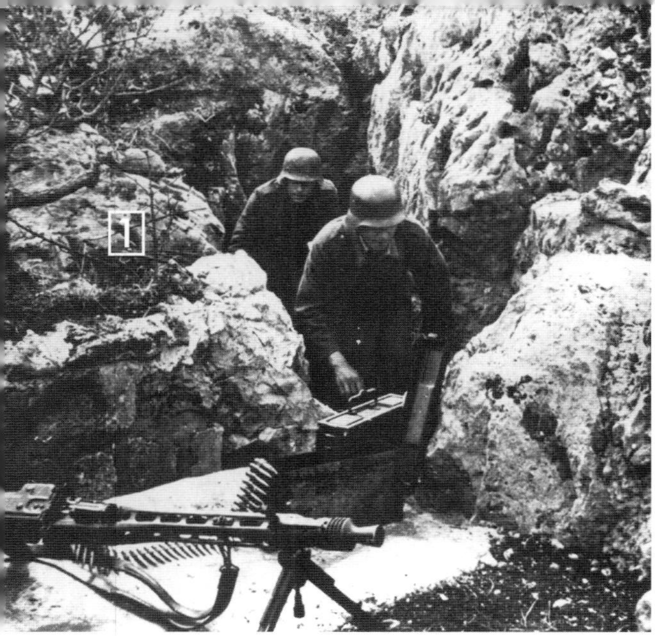

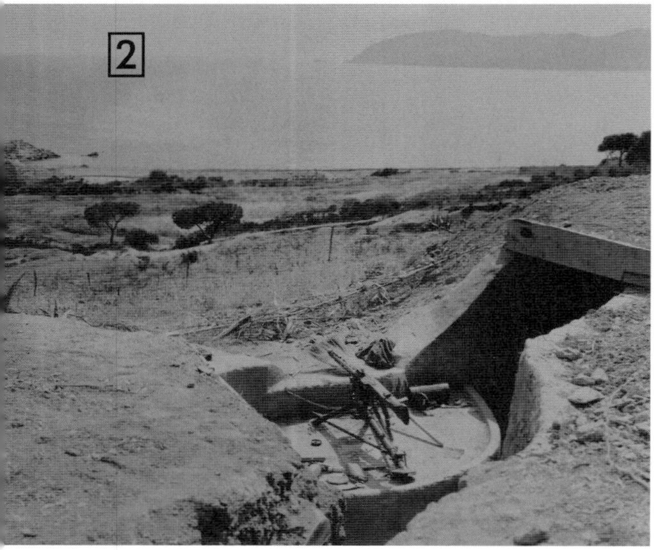

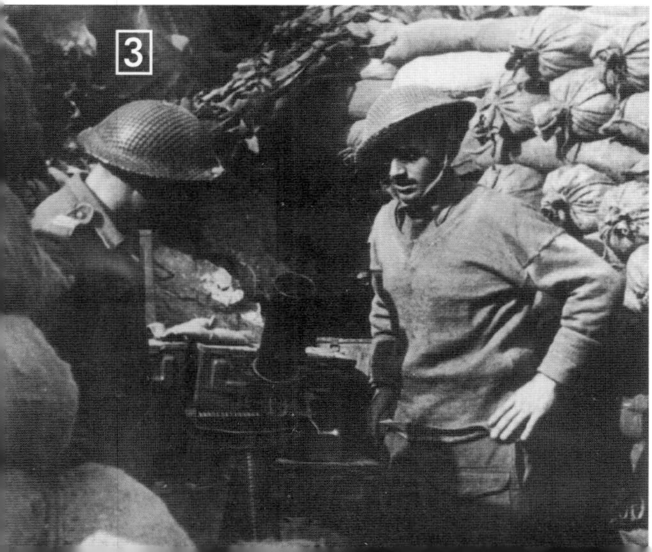

1 and 2 The Germans had had time to build strong defensive positions in the countries they had conquered in 1939–42: trenches and dugouts, often with thick concrete overhead protection; cleared fields of fire. They also had two excellent machine guns: the MG34 and 42 (as in these two photos: **1** in Italy; **2** overlooking an invasion beach on the island of Elba). Organisation Todt built many of these, often using slave or pressganged labour. 'When a line is to be held for an extended period, German infantrymen take up a series of positions screening the main line and covering a network of observation posts. As far as possible, these positions are situated on forward slopes. Listening posts and outposts usually are established, to give warning of the approach of hostile forces. If further withdrawal seems unlikely, mines and wire are used to give the forward positions additional protection. In such cases, the mines and wire are situated 50–150yd in front of the positions. Each of these positions, distributed fairly evenly over the company or platoon front, invariably holds two riflemen or two men and a light machine gun. Heavy weapons, HMGs, and mortars are sited behind the line of forward weapon positions. As a rule, the mortars are sited in pairs in the center – on reverse slopes, if possible – while the HMGs are sited on the flanks. Where the field of fire permits, a mortar section may be strengthened by a pair of HMGs. The heavy weapons remain under the battalion or company commander, depending on whether the battalion is Panzergrenadier or Grenadier. Dugouts for personnel and supplies are constructed to the rear, and are connected with the positions by communication trenches. (Whenever possible, the dugouts, too, are on reverse slopes.) It is interesting to note that the positions themselves generally are not connected with each other. Positions are lightly manned during the day – with the machine gunners usually carrying the burden of defense, while the remainder of the personnel rest in dugouts. At night, forward positions are fully manned. The screening positions are likely to be only a few hundred yards in front of what the German soldiers themselves regard as their main line of resistance (*Hauptkampflinie*). In static defense the distances between the forward positions, combat outposts, and the so-called main line of resistance are greatly shortened.' (*Intelligence Bulletin* Vol II No 12, August 1944.)

3 The Allies' positions were often less carefully constructed as they were on the attack. Sandbagged revetments took the place of concrete, as with this 3in mortar in Italy manned by the Polish 5th Kresowa Infantry Division during 1944.

4 If you can see it, we can hit it – the 8.8cm proved an excellent weapon over long distances making field of fire the crucial factor in siting the weapon, although its high silhouette meant it was always dug in, as here.

5 The Germans made great use of flooding in their defensive positions, particularly in winter when swollen river banks and dykes were burst. They also opened sluices of drainage ditches and breached dams, to ensure inundation of low-lying land.

6 Both sides dug in quickly after an assault both to help withstand quick counter-attacks and also to protect the infantry from artillery.

4

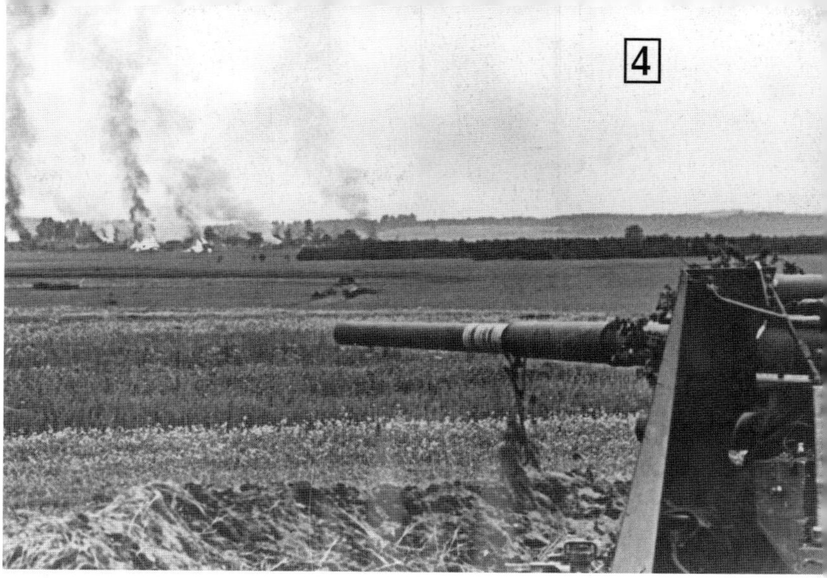

5

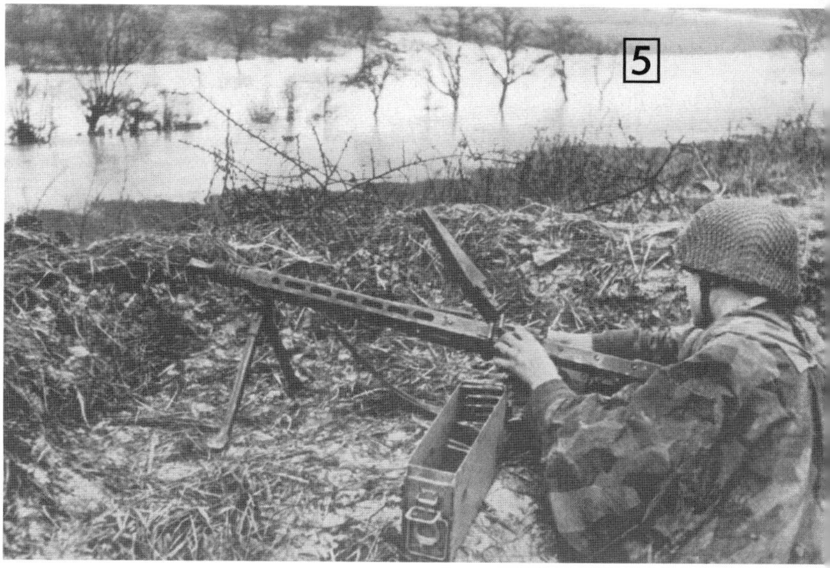

6

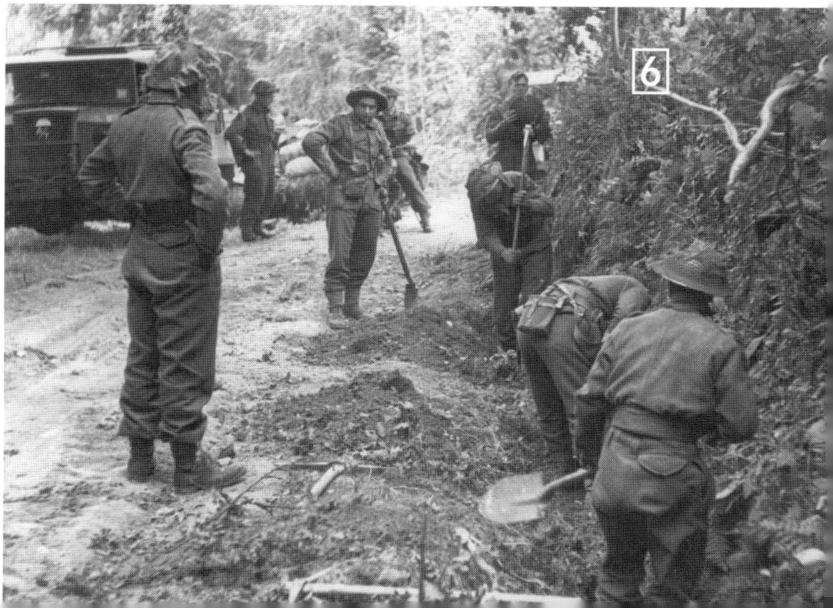

A GERMAN BATTALION DEFENSE AREA IN NORTH AFRICA

(*Tactical and Technical Trends*, No. 31 12 August 1943)

The German doctrine as applied to defense calls for the concentration of the available forces in a few, very strong islands of resistance. In contrast to the pre-1940 French 'linear' practice of setting up the defense in platoon strong-points supported by field artillery in the rear, Maj F. O. Miksche a well-known Czech military writer, pointed out in 1942 that the Germans favor the use of defense areas containing at least a rifle company, reinforced by appropriate supporting weapons, organized for all-around defense, wired-in behind minefields, and provided with their own infantry artillery. Even a battalion may be employed in one of these positions, which, when developed to their fullest extent, are self-sustaining defense areas, capable of resisting armored attack. An example of such an island of resistance will be found in the following translation of a German document entitled *Training Publication for the Installation of Battalion Defense Areas* issued by the Commander-in-Chief of the Panzer Army in Africa. A combat officer very recently returned from southern Tunisia reports that defenses of this type were met with there.

In order to strengthen the power of defense, the troops will organize defense areas which they can hold against attacks coming from any direction.

a. Dimensions

The normal battalion front in a defensive position may be from 3,500 to 4,000 yards; company defense areas (see Fig 1) are some 700yd wide by 300yd in depth, and spaced about 500yd apart.

Fig 1 Battalion defense area This lay-out is for an area on more or less level ground. In actual practice, of course, natural defense positions would be entrenched. The front-line wire, naturally, would scarcely be laid out in a straight line. Both diagrams are based on German sketches, and are notable for their simplicity. The three forward company defense areas are composed of several platoon strong-points subdivided into squad positions like the ones illustrated in Fig 2 (overleaf).

3500 yds.
Wire fence, later to be made a double-apron fence.
Minefield
Minefield
500 yds.
500 yds.
700 yds.
Company defense area
700 yds.
300 yds.
Company defense area
700 yds.
300 yds.
Company defense area
800 to 1000 yds.
Battalion CP
Company defense area with artillery

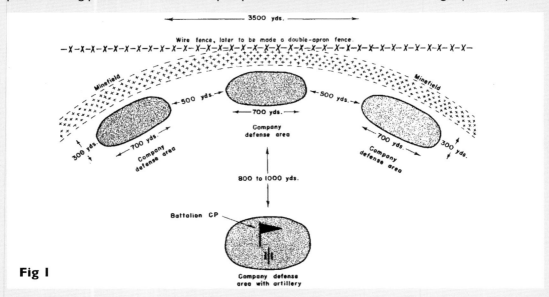

Fig 1

The 8.8cm Flak anti-aircraft gun was an efficient tank killer out to at least 3,000m. If the gunners could see a tank they could probably hit and kill it, something that made them greatly feared by their enemies – so much so that every German anti-tank gun became an 88. Rommel actually had only 86 in 1942, although this number was bolstered by using Luftwaffe versions. Obscuration caused by dust and sand was a problem that was helped by using the Scherenfernrohr SF14ZGi binoculars on a tripod. While used extensively by the artillery to measure angles of azimuth and elevation and the height of shell bursts, to establish safety zones for advancing friendly troops and lay field guns, the scissors binoculars were also used in trench warfare for observation and reconnaissance.

b. Garrison of Company Positions
A battalion sector is divided into several company defense areas. In general, a rifle company with infantry heavy weapons attached occupies each of the four sub-defense areas. The unit command posts are also to be installed within these defense areas. Artillery is stationed behind the forward company defense areas on terrain protected by the rear company defense area of the battalion sector. *[Note: Whether this artillery is composed of the infantry guns, or attached field artillery is not clear but field artillery was found in such defense areas in Tunisia. Obviously, while the lay-out is such that infantry guns could cover the forward company positions, some field guns of greater range could be used, if available.]*

c. Weapons
Weapons are distributed so as to give mutual supporting fire. Every company defense area is provided with infantry light and heavy weapons. Armor-piercing weapons, and antiaircraft guns are attached.

d. Defenses
The company defense area is to be fenced in with wire. However, platoon areas within such company areas are not to be enclosed by wire. *[Note: Perhaps sufficient wire for both inside and outside entanglements was not available as wired-in platoon areas have been encountered.]* The distance of the wire entanglements from the most forward weapons is about 50 to 100 yards.

To facilitate reconnaissance activity, narrow lanes through the wire entanglements are to be laid out on the enemy side. Wide lanes are permitted only on the flanks.

To defend the protective minefields, and wire entanglements, rifle pits, listening posts, observation posts, and weapon emplacements are installed. Dugouts are constructed for the garrison of the area.

Communication trenches are to be dug only between the firing positions or observation posts and nearby dugouts. Extensive communication trenches give the attacking enemy a chance to gain a foothold inside. In stony terrain the parapet is to be made of sandbags or stone, but trenches must first be dug deep enough into the ground (by blasting, if necessary) to prevent the position from showing above the surface.

As a matter of principle, no installations, as seen from the enemy side, must stand out above the surface of the grounds. Defended areas are not to be laid out on the crests of ridges but on the slopes *[whether forward or reverse slopes, is not made clear]*. Although the highest positions are normally the most desirable for observation and antiaircraft purposes, such installations must not be placed on forward slopes in view of the enemy, but somewhat further to the rear, masked by the crest.

Dummy positions (also for artillery and antiaircraft) are to be used for the purpose of diverting enemy artillery fire. Distance from the other positions must be great enough to protect the latter from the natural dispersion of artillery fire.

The sections of trenches inside a position must have frequent traverses or angles to reduce the splintering effect (see Fig 2). Good camouflage is the best protection against enemy fire.

Fig 2 Two layouts for a squad position, reinforced. The large number of heavy and automatic weapons is worth noting. A squad area provided with an AA/AT gun, a mortar, an HMG, a LMG all well dug in and mutually supporting, flanked by similar squad areas and reinforced with the fire of infantry cannon from the support position, make a defensive position of great power, entirely aside from the garrison's rifle and grenade fire.

Rifle pits for the protection of mine fields and obstacles, and for harassing machine gun fire.
HvMG
Ammunition
37-mm AA/AT gun
OP
AT rifle
LMG
Water tank
Ammunition
Dugout
50-mm mortar
Dugout
OP
20-mm AA/AT gun
HvMG
Dugouts
LMG
Ammunition
Ammunition
Water tank
81-mm mortar
Ammunition
Distance from weapon or dugout, to weapon at least 5 yards.
40 to 60 yds.
Necessary to have all trench sections zigzag.

Fig 2

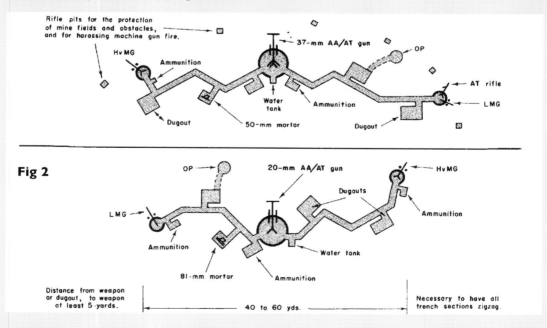

e. Transport

In rolling country, vehicles must be completely hidden from the view of the enemy. In level country, this result is obtained by keeping the vehicles well to the rear of the combat positions, and by using camouflage with nets. These nets can be improvised with open mesh wire covered with any sort of brush or camel thorn.

Comments

Such a defense area could, if necessary, be supplied from the air if ground communications were cut off. By necessity, the plan here outlined bears a superficial similarity to defensive layouts found in our own field manuals, but it should be noted that the method prescribed in the above document is based on the German theory of defense against the principal effort in a German armored attack. Such an attack combines overwhelming local superiority in men and equipment, the onset of tanks with motorized infantry and artillery following, combined with a fire from massed artillery, mortar and heavy weapons of the utmost possible violence, supported by dive-bombing. All is concentrated on a narrow front of perhaps 1,500 yards. The theory of defense assumes that the islands of resistance must allow the tanks to pass through since they can not prevent it, but do endeavor to stop by fire especially from the flank, the motorized infantry and artillery which follow behind. Cut off from their supporting infantry, the tanks are expected to be stopped by the rear elements of the defense and destroyed. A counterattack launched by the rear elements follows to eject any remaining enemy forces that retain a foothold in the defense system.

The extraordinarily wide frontage, 3,500 yards, is remarkable, as well as the wide spaces between the company defense areas — 500 yards. One commentator suggested that this defense would be far easier to pierce than our own more closely-knit system, but it must be remembered that the German plan here outlined is based on no theoretical study but upon the hardest possible school of African battle.

Another interesting feature is the concentration of heavy weapons entirely within the company defense areas.

A third feature is in the extensive use of minefields. Whether these minefields are laid by the garrison or by engineers is not made clear in the instructions, but as each German infantry company contains a group of men trained to lay and lift mines, it seems reasonable to suppose that the minefield in front of the battalion area was to be laid by the garrison. The absence of any indication of mines between the company defense areas is rather odd. It would seem logical to mine these avenues rather heavily. The failure to indicate such mining should, however, not necessarily preclude the possibility that mines might be found there. The system here illustrated would appear vulnerable to infantry attack. This, in fact, was the method used by Montgomery at Alamein, where, reversing the German practice, infantry and engineers equipped with mine detectors led the assault, behind a devastating artillery barrage. It is understood, however, that the British had a substantial superiority in both guns and tanks.

In southern Tunisia was found a rather unusual lay-out for a German platoon on the defensive. American officers report that inside the wired-in company defense areas, were wired-in platoon defense areas, laid out in a more or less Y shape. The accompanying sketch is schematic, and not to any scale, but illustrates the plan of such a position.

One branch of the Y, or the broad angle might be pointed forward, or occasionally, one branch ran over a crest with the other two limbs on the reverse slope. Automatic weapons were placed at the ends of the trenches; the trenches themselves were sometimes blasted out of the rock. Mutually supporting crossfire, of course, was provided throughout the company area.

2 Camouflage

(edited excerpts *British Infantry Training 1944 Part VIII Fieldcraft, Battle Drill, Section And Platoon Tactics*)

Object: The aims of personal concealment and use of cover are not merely protective but aggressive; they enable the attacker to work his way forward undetected and to allow surprise action by the defender who has not been located.

Camouflage (appearance) and fieldcraft (behaviour) combine to make the picture we present to the enemy. Concealment alone may prevent observation and effect surprise; if coupled with measures in another quarter which mislead the enemy's observation, surprise is the more complete. Training should aim to teach every soldier that, as well as concealing the real whereabouts of men, weapons, and defences, he must confuse the enemy's observation and waste their time by misdirecting these elsewhere. Misdirection may be purely tactical – by movement alone, or by the use of dummy figures, models, and false works, or even better, by a combination of both.

Rules:
(a) Camouflage is tactics – In training, camouflage should never be treated as a 'specialist' subject, but as part and parcel of every tactical move, for it deals with what the enemy sees of that movement.
(b) Against whom? Differing methods must be employed against a ground observer with field glasses and the observer who is harassed by fire and smoke. The reconnaissance plane at 30,000ft is a very different proposition from the-low flying fighter. Consider first who your enemy is and camouflage accordingly.
(c) The enemy the critic. Questions of camouflage are never settled indoors but only from the enemy's point of view. Criticism from this angle should be continued during training and war. On new ground old tricks may fail.

Personal concealment: Every soldier must be as inconspicuous as possible, consistent with fighting efficiency. The soldier in battle should be confident of his ability to make himself a difficult target.

Four factors (apart from movement) make the soldier easy to see:
(a) Tone. It should match the surroundings, but it is always safer to err on the dark side. In a green countryside, dull clothing and dark blanco are essential, and white skin should be darkened with camouflage cream, soot, blanco, or cocoa. Where there is snow, white sheets should be used.
(b) Shine. It catches the eye and must be completely eliminated. A dark hessian cover dulls the steel helmet and every piece of brass on equipment and weapons should be painted with a dark dull paint.
(c) Shape. The smooth dome of the steel helmet should be broken by natural garnish, which also helps to destroy the distinctive shape of the head and shoulders.
(d) Shadow. Eliminate this under the helmet by making the garnish come down below the rim.

A difficult area for concealment, particularly from aerial surveillance. This is where air superiority is a boon!

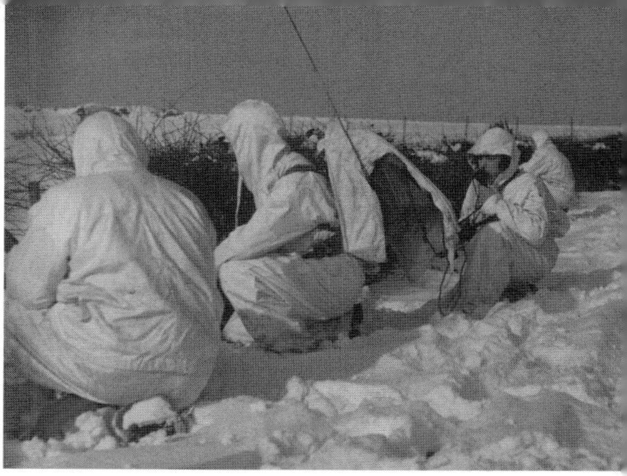

Right: Winter camouflage was pretty similar for all countries. If nothing purpose-designed was available, then white sheets were used.

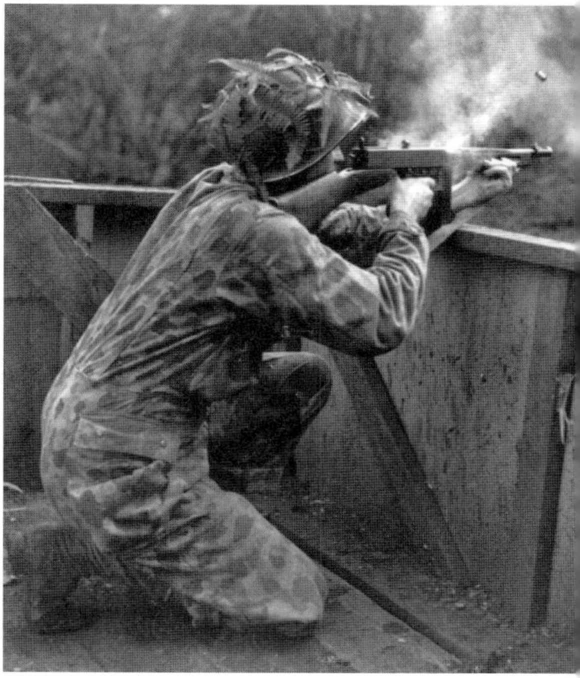

Centre right: The US forces' disruptive camouflage pattern was the M1942 frog skin or duckhunter. Primarily used by the USMC, it was five-color jungle on one side, and three-color beach on the other.

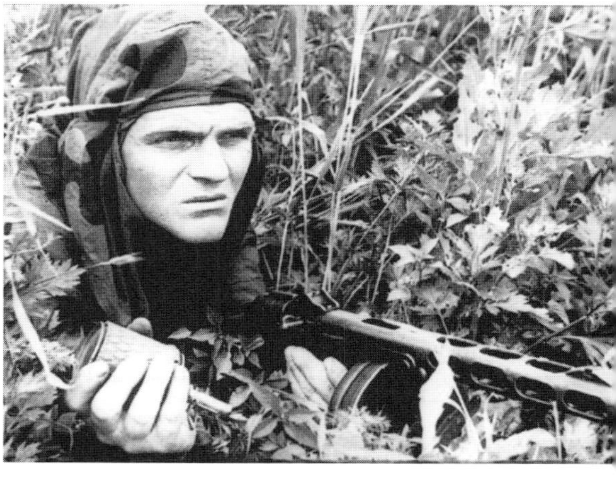

Below right: Soviet 'Amoeba' (a modern term) pattern camouflage was worn by reconnaissance troops, motorised infantry, paratroopers, assault engineers, scouts and snipers. It came in two versions: a one-piece (*maskirovochnyy kombinezon* – deception combination) and a two-piece (*maskirovochnyy kamuflirovannyy kostyum* – deceptive camouflage). 'The Russians were excellent at camouflage. With their primitive instinct they understood perfectly how to blend into their surroundings, and were trained to vanish into the ground upon even the slightest provocation. As previous examples have illustrated, they skillfully used darkness, vegetation, and bad weather for concealing their intentions. ... Artificial camouflage was another device not unknown to the Russians. Even at the beginning of the war we came across Russian troops wearing camouflage suits of bast fibers dyed green. Lying prone in the grass, these soldiers could be spotted only at a very short distance, and frequently were passed by without having been noticed at all. Reconnaissance patrols frequently wore "leaf" suits of green cloth patches, which provided excellent camouflage in the woods.' (*PoRW*)

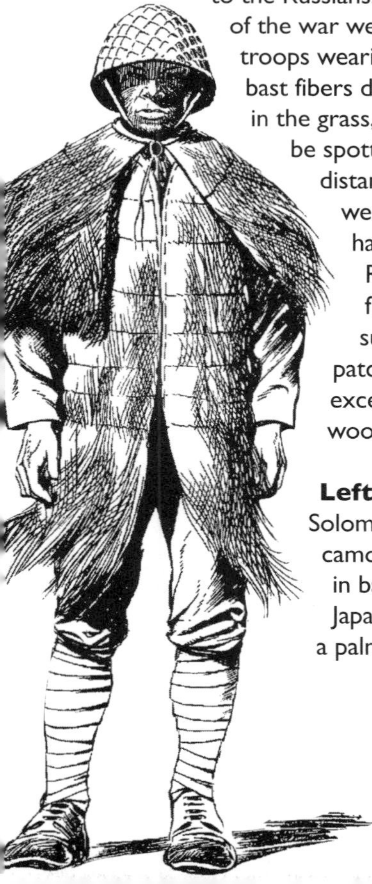

Left: Captured in the Solomons, a number of these camouflage suits were found in bales, and one was on a Japanese sniper shot out of a palm tree by US marines.

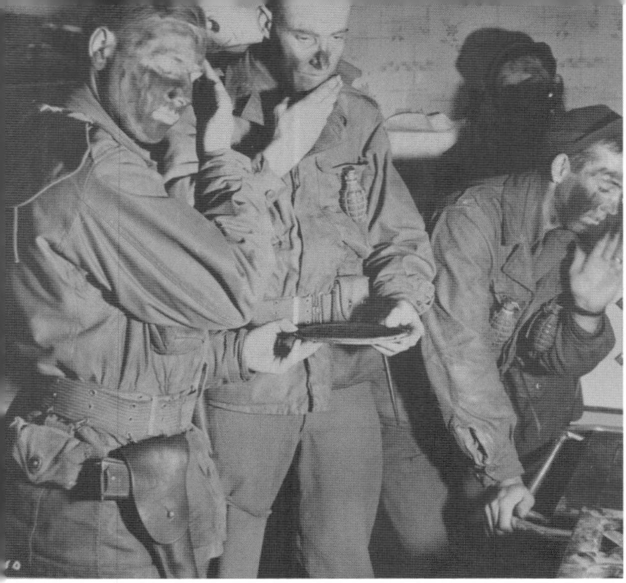

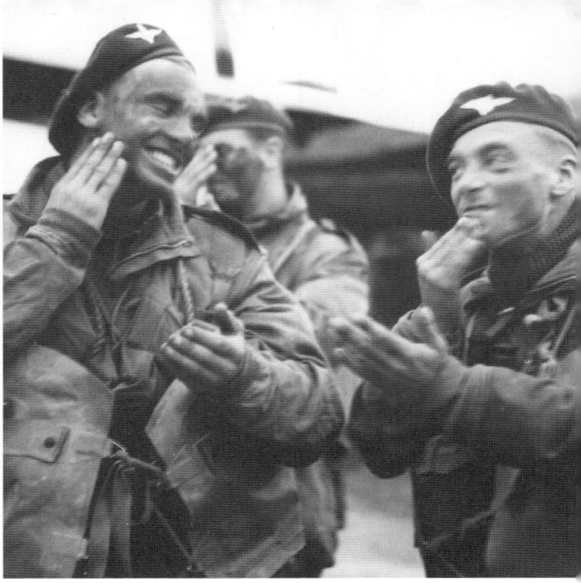

Details of personal camouflage are illustrated below. The steel helmet, because of its shape and position on the body, is the most difficult piece of equipment to hide; to hold the garnish vertical, the cord must be laced round the net in short loops. Some knots of coloured hessian garnish are a good basis to which natural foliage can be added. The end of the helmet net must be tied with a slip-knot which can be quickly released if the net becomes entangled with wire or thick covet while the soldier is crawling. Unless the highest standard of personal camouflage is maintained unnecessary casualties will result. One or two careless men may destroy surprise, jeopardize success, and sacrifice the lives of their comrades.

Above: Personal camouflage was particularly important at night for raiding or parachute operations. Note also the camouflaged Denison smocks worn by the British Paras (**Right**).

Below: British camouflage suggestions. The British helmet, the Brodie Mk II, was more difficult to camouflage than others because of its shape.

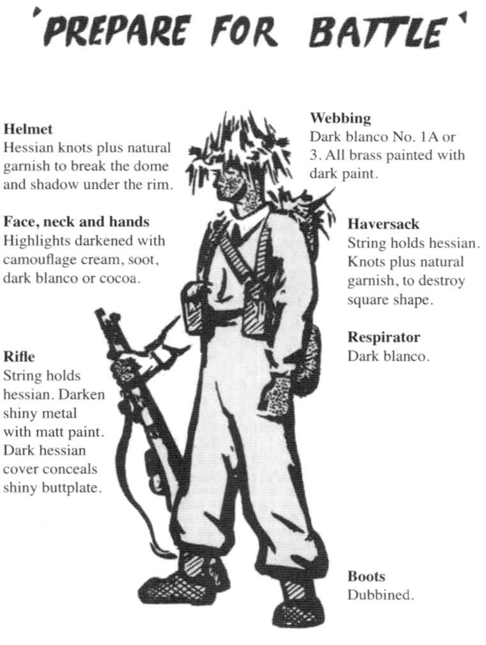
'PREPARE FOR BATTLE'
Helmet
Hessian knots plus natural garnish to break the dome and shadow under the rim.
Face, neck and hands
Highlights darkened with camouflage cream, soot, dark blanco or cocoa.
Rifle
String holds hessian. Darken shiny metal with matt paint. Dark hessian cover conceals shiny buttplate.
Webbing
Dark blanco No. 1A or 3. All brass painted with dark paint.
Haversack
String holds hessian. Knots plus natural garnish, to destroy square shape.
Respirator
Dark blanco.
Boots
Dubbined.

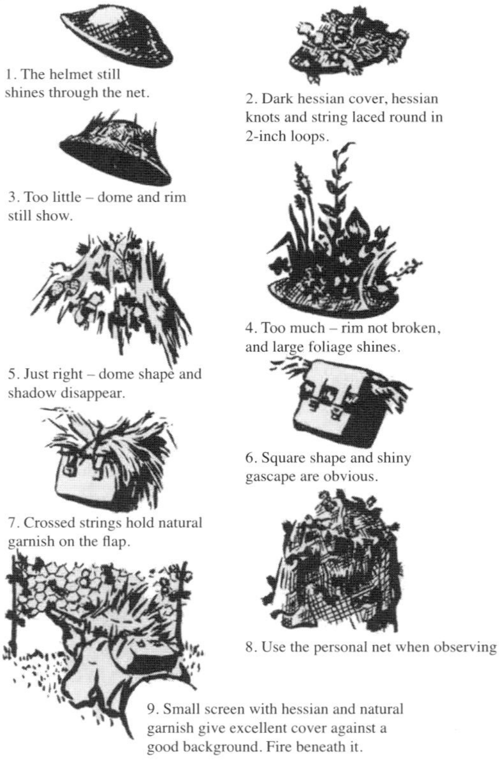
1. The helmet still shines through the net.
2. Dark hessian cover, hessian knots and string laced round in 2-inch loops.
3. Too little – dome and rim still show.
4. Too much – rim not broken, and large foliage shines.
5. Just right – dome shape and shadow disappear.
6. Square shape and shiny gascape are obvious.
7. Crossed strings hold natural garnish on the flap.
8. Use the personal net when observing
9. Small screen with hessian and natural garnish give excellent cover against a good background. Fire beneath it.

Fieldcraft

Behaviour that gives concealment from the enemy on the ground may be of little value against the overhead observer or attacker. It can usually be decided which has the prior claim, or whether both must be considered.

(a) Ground enemy

(i) Shadow is the best protection, keep in it.

(ii) Background. Never be seen against a smooth background such as a green field, dense shadow, or, worst of all, the sky.

(iii) Cover. Observe through or carefully round the side of cover, never over the top. Folds in the ground are excellent, since they are not definite aiming marks for the enemy. Isolated cover draws fire. Cover from view is not cover from fire. If you have been seen getting there. Crawl away at once.

(iv) Water. Keep back from the edge of ponds and streams. The reflection may show up even at night.

(b) Air enemy.

In vertical view, the ground is a carpet, the pattern of which varies with the type of country. Objects which are at variance with the pattern or form an unnatural pattern of their own, are easily seen. Troops must remain under cover as much as possible with air sentries always on the alert. Unless offensive action is to be taken, concealment is best obtained by keeping still, in the correct part of the carpet.

(i) **Movement** catches the eye. So remain still under cover or in shadow.

(ii) Keep to the natural **pattern** and try to imitate it. Move along hedges and never lie in regular lines in the open. The airman admits no dead ground.

(iii) **Shadows** are vivid to the air observer and must be lost in other shadows or broken up. A regular line of straight shadows is an obvious indication to the observer.

(iv) **Grouping**. Amongst gorse or bushes, small groups of men clumped together resemble bushes and pass unnoticed.

(v) White **faces** are conspicuous. Do not look up at aircraft unless the face is darkened or covered.

The Germans had been the first to use printed camouflage in World War I. In the interwar period (1930) they brought in *Splittermuster 31*, which was used on Zeltbahn (tent) sections, in turn these were often used as camouflage ponchos by the troops. In 1941 *Fallschirmjäger* (**Above**) received camouflaged smocks before the invasion of Crete. In 1943 *Sumpftarnmuster* (swamp pattern) was brought in two forms. The Waffen-SS (**Below**) had patterns designed by Johann Schick, used from 1935. Quite often these were reversible with camouflage for two seasons – summer and autumn, or summer and winter (snow). They were: *Platanenmuster* – plane tree pattern (1937–42); *Rauchtarnmuster* – smoke pattern (1939–44); *Palmenmuster* – palm tree pattern (from 1941); *Eichenlaubmuster* – oak leaf pattern (A and B versions 1942–45); *Erbsenmuster* – pea dot pattern (1944–45); *Leibermuster* – body pattern (1945).

3 Mines and Mine-clearing

ENEMY ANTITANK MINEFIELDS AND BOOBY TRAPS

(edited excerpts from *Tactical & Technical Trends* No 6 of 27 August 1942)

The following is a report on an enemy minefield encountered by the British during the fighting in Libya in late 1941.

All the mines were Tellermines – antitank mines shaped like a plate and weighing about 11lb. Many had pull-igniters screwed into the bottom as anti-lifting devices, and occasionally mines were laid upside down to increase the difficulty of disarming the main fuse. The mines were laid at very irregular intervals, but always on or near a desert trail. The mines laid across trails were generally marked with small piles of stones at the corners of the field. Mines were also laid along trails and these were apparently marked by piles of stones at either end of the mined section. In some instances, places where mines were laid showed signs of the earth having been disturbed, but in others there was no such indication. Where trails ran through scrub, loose pieces of scrub, sometimes with booby traps attached, were placed on top of the mines as camouflage. In several places a single strand of wire had been strung on tall stakes marked with warning or notice boards. These boards carry the inscription "Achtung Minen," *or* "Attentions Mena," *or* "Attention Mines." *The wire itself, although attached to booby traps, did not protect live minefields, which were invariably placed to one side of the wire, approximately in prolongation of it.*

Dummy minefields were also encountered; these were completely wired in, and contained tins sunk into the ground with occasional booby traps attached to them. Gaps between dummy minefields were invariably sown with live mines.

A noticeboard with skull and cross bones painted on it always indicated booby traps. (This must not be taken to mean that all German booby traps are marked; the contrary is generally true.) These consisted of small standard charges ignited by standard German pull-igniters. The igniter may be attached by fine binding-wire to stakes in a wire fence, direct to the wire, to trip wires placed a few inches above ground, to stones which support stakes, or to the notice boards themselves. Booby traps also were generally laid in the scrub on either side of the trails. Occasionally a second booby trap was placed underneath the first to make the removal more difficult.

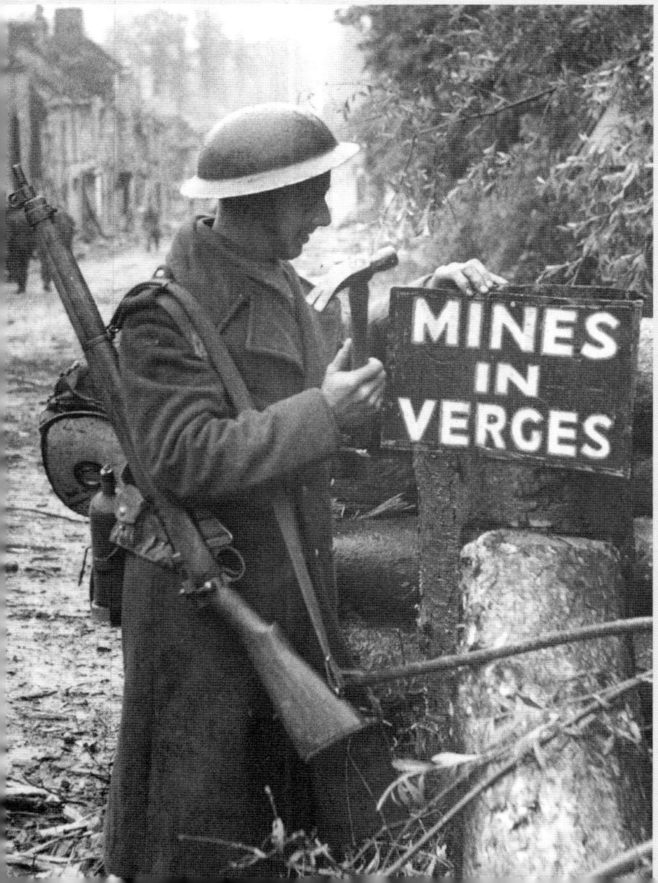
MINES
IN
VERGES

Booby traps could be detected by close scrutiny for anything out of the ordinary, i.e., notice boards facing, or in sight of, the enemy, loose strands of wire, sticks with wire wrapped round them, old explosive wrappings, etc. Stakes with booby traps underneath them were normally dug in, while others were driven in. White wood stakes protruding 6 inches above ground and connected by inconspicuous trip wires were sometimes found. These could usually be identified by the presence nearby of small excavations, containing explosive.

1 Minefields were Rommel's preferred method of slowing down an enemy. He'd used them to great effect in the wastes of the North African desert and ensured the Normandy coast was covered with them including numerous anti-ship mines on stakes that were below the waterline at high tide. Many landing craft were damaged and a number were sunk by these obstacles on D-Day.

2 Ironically, the Germans mined many bridges in the invasion area – this one over the Dives. It's ironic, because one of the tasks allotted to British 6th Airborne Division was the blowing of bridges over the Dives and Divette to ensure that German Panzer counterattacks would be stymied.

3 The Russians trained dogs to sniff out mines. Here, a German Shepherd sapper dog during training.

4 Minefield signage was used for both real and dummy minefields.

5 German defences near Den Helder in the Netherlands mixed dragon's teeth, minefields and bunkers.

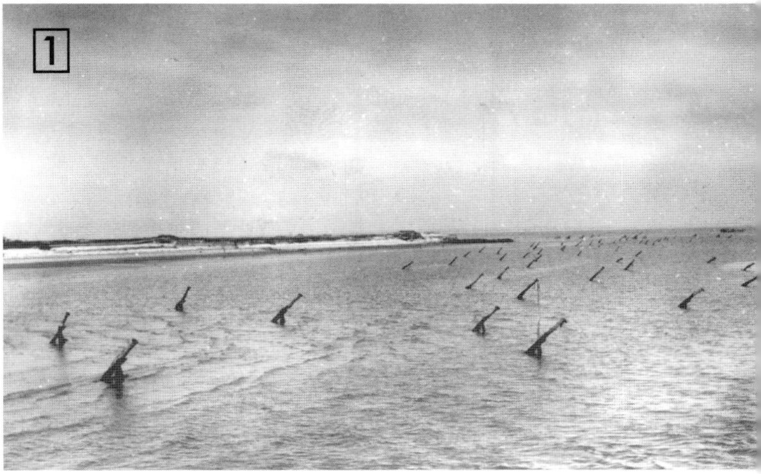
1

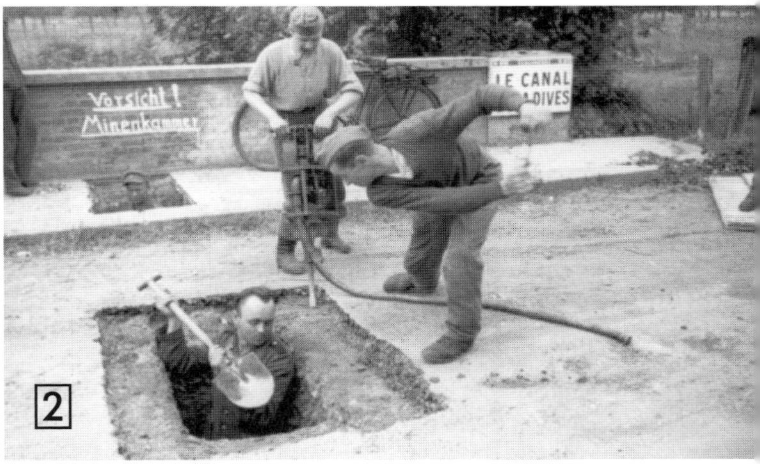
Vorsicht!
Minenkammer
LE CANAL
DIVES
2

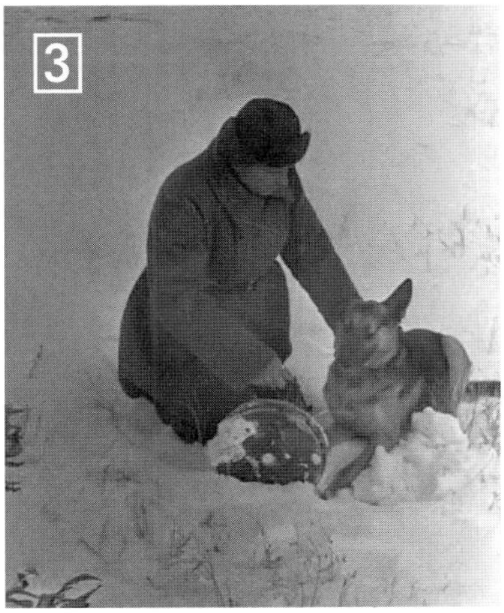
3

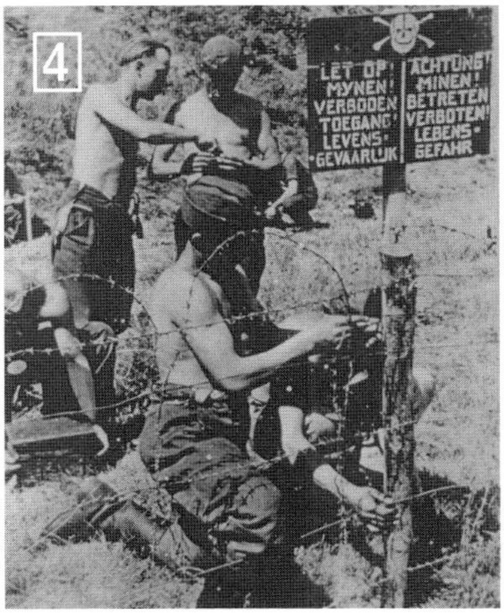
4
LET OP! MYNEN! VERBODEN TOEGANG! LEVENS-GEVAARLIJK
ACHTUNG! MINEN! BETRETEN VERBOTEN! LEBENS-GEFAHR

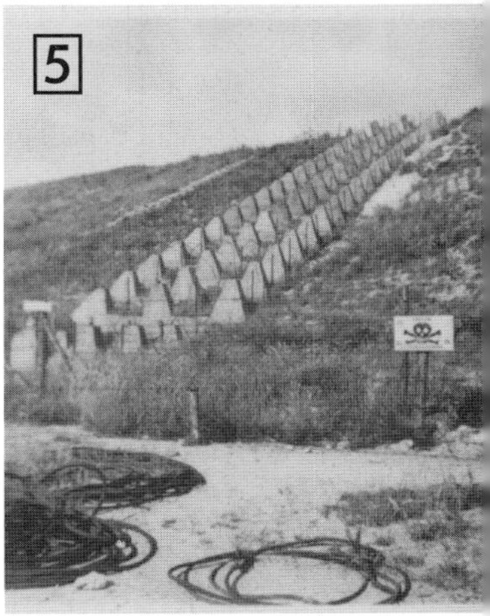
5

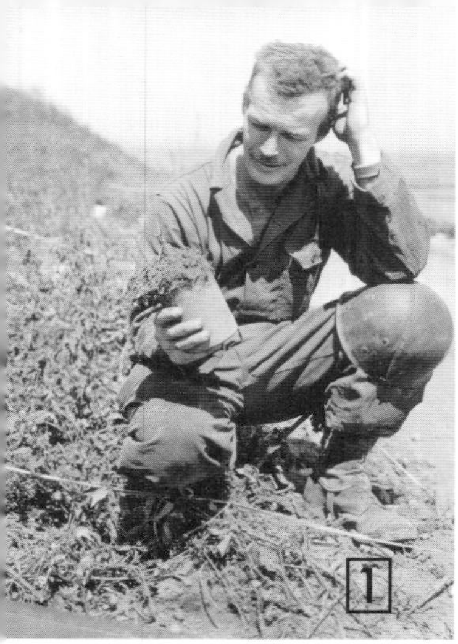
1

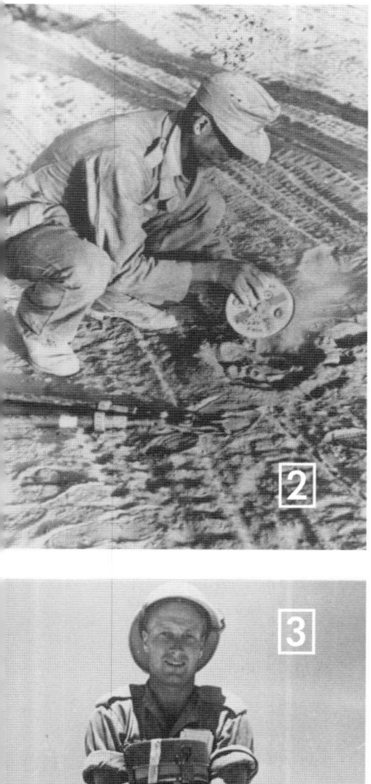
2

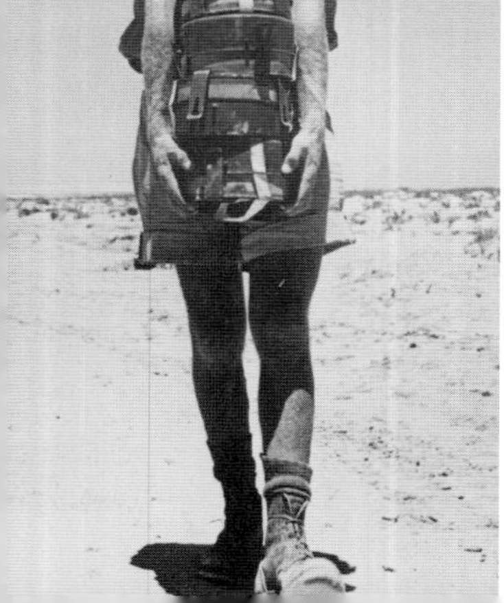
3

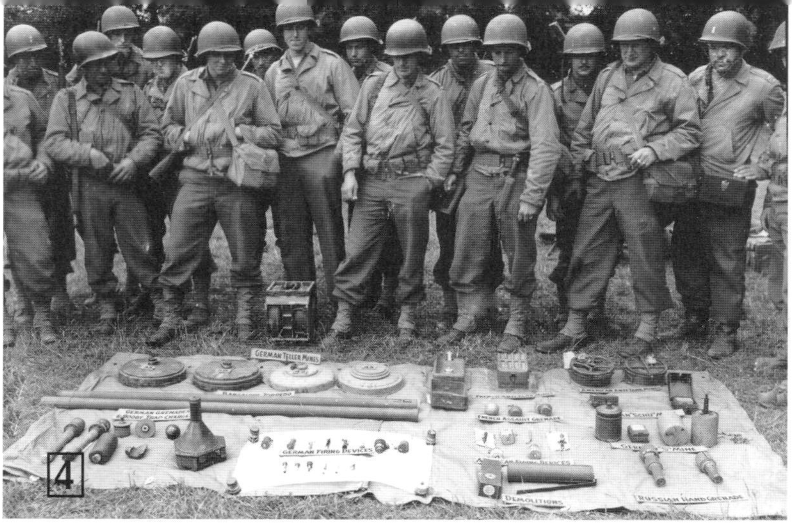
GERMAN TELLER MINES
GERMAN FIRING DEVICES
FRENCH ASSAULT GRENADE
DEMOLITIONS
RUSSIAN HAND GRENADE
4

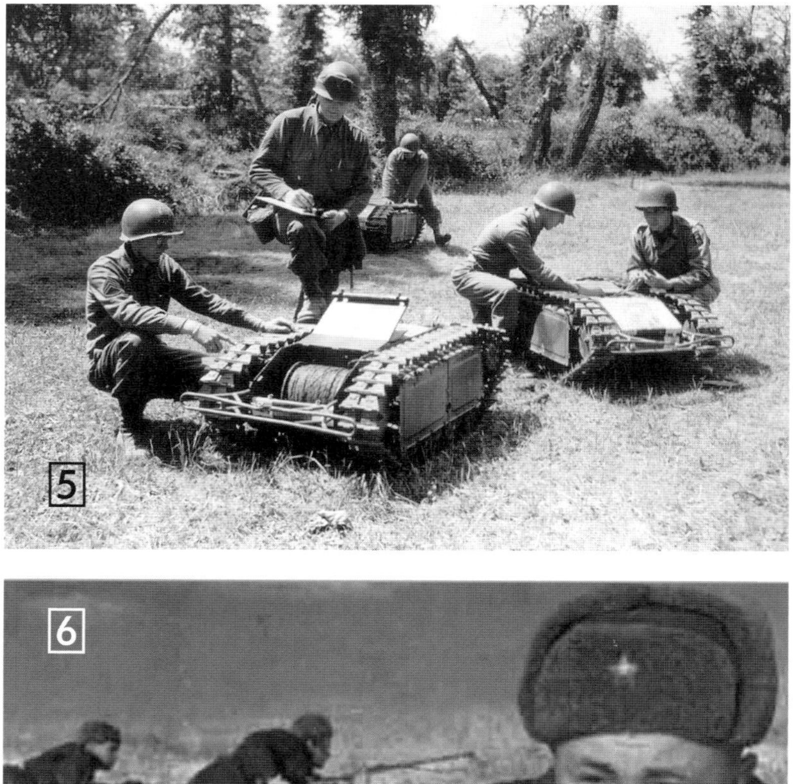
5

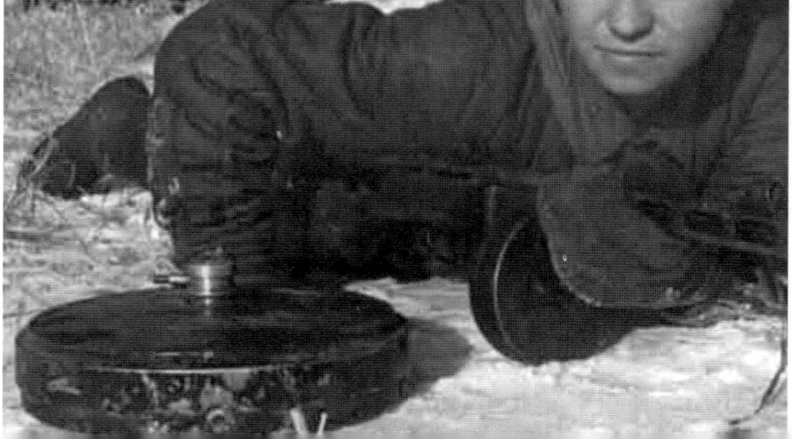
6

One of the most effective anti-personnel weapons, mines could be set off by pressure, tripwire or actively in an ambush. They were a major deterrent, caused significant numbers of casualties to men and vehicles and could be used to channel troops into killing zones. Mines were booby-trapped to make demining difficult. Sometimes they were wired in series and, if the sapper did not investigate after disarming the first mine, he would be blown to bits by the second. Another trick common with the Germans was to plant tin cans, so that the sappers would either become careless or have their attention diverted from the live mines.

1, 7 and 8 The German S-mine – *Schrapnellmine* – better known as the 'Debollocker' or 'Bouncing Betty' was a bounding mine that, three or four seconds after being triggered (pressure on one of the stalks at the top), was ejected to a height of about 3ft. The explosion could cause casualties out to 100m. This was a serious deterrent as the French found out in the Saar in 1939. The only drawbacks were that they were labour-intensive to sow because they had to be dug in, and relatively easy to detect (because they were mainly metal) and deactivate. Later glass versions were even more effective.

2 and 3 In the sandy North African desert, mines were easy to lay. Both sides made extensive use of them – so much so that they are still a hazard today. Here (**2**), a German soldier lifts a British antitank mine – as laid by British sappers such as this one (**3**), a South African.

4 US soldiers in Normandy are given a lesson on mines and grenades from German Teller antitank mines (top left), French mines and grenades (centre) to German S mines and Russian hand grenades (bottom right).

5 The Goliath tracked mine could be powered electrically (SdKfz 302) or by petrol (SdKfz 303). They weren't very effective – although they packed a big punch – because they were slow and their command cables were usually cut by artillery before they reached their target.

6 A Russian engineer with a German Teller mine. Note the padded winter jacket and *shapka-ushanka* artificial fur cap.

RUSSIAN MINEFIELDS
(excerpts from *Peculiarities of Russian Warfare*)

'The Russian made extensive use of mines. As a rule, a protective mine belt was to be found about 8–10m in front of the most forward trench. Terrain particularly favorable for an enemy approach likewise was heavily mined. The Russian preferred to employ wooden box mines, which could not be detected by the standard mine detectors. In the depth of the battle position, mines were laid in unexpected places. In favorable terrain, antitank mines were very numerous. Difficulties in the transport of Teller mines due to lack of transport space were, according to PoW information, solved in a very primitive manner. When marching to the front as relief, every man had to carry two antitank mines. At the front, these mines were laid by the engineers according to a diagrammed mine plan.

'In 1944–45 the Russians, while on the move, also scattered mines around points of main effort in order to block tank attacks. In the Southern Ukraine we saw how the Russians, following a successful tank thrust, immediately protected the terrain they had gained with a belt of antitank mines blocking all roads and approaches. On one day alone, 20,000 such mines were laid. Our counterattacks ground to a halt and collapsed in minefields of that type. The Russian cleared mines in front of our obstacles during the night, and used them for his own purposes. Later on, we laid minefields only behind our own front, at points at which a tank breakthrough or an enemy offensive was to be expected. When the enemy intended to give up a previously defended zone, he used many tricks. He would, for example, attach demolition charges with push-pull igniters to abandoned field kitchens, weapons, corpses, tombstones, etc.; he connected explosive charges to doors, windows, or stoves in the winter; he installed pressure mines under stairs and floors, and booby-trapped abandoned trucks and other equipment.

'When we took Kiev and Vyborg in 1941, and Sevastopol in 1942, the Russian used remote (radio)-controlled mines for blowing up entire blocks of houses as soon as the enemy entered them. The ignition apparatus included a clock, which could be heard with sensitive sound detectors and led to the discovery of the ignition apparatus.'

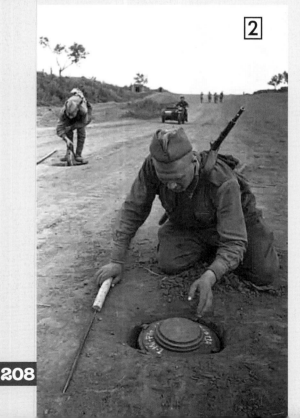

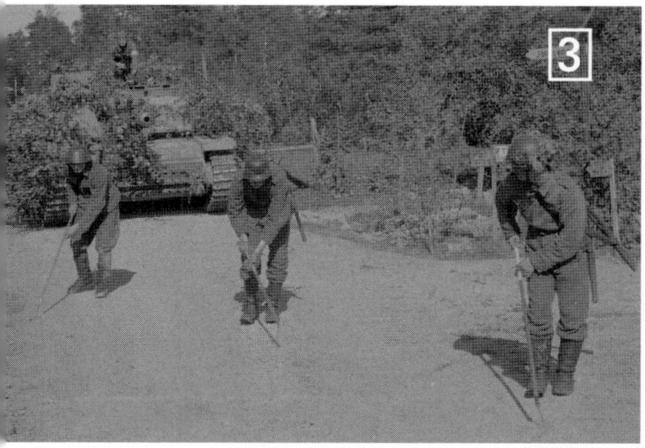
3

Mine detection and clearing is as dangerous a mission as any on the battlefield – particularly when under fire and the path being cleared is essential for the prosecution of an attack as was the case at El Alamein, Kursk or on D-Day. If mine detectors (see pp. 210–211) or, better still, specialised armour – flails, rollers, ploughs or rakes – are available, they will pick up many, but not all, but often the environment doesn't allow these systems or they just aren't there. So, unless you happen to have a penal battalion to hand you have to make your way, slowly and very circumspectly, prodding ahead of you with something pointy – anything from a rifle cleaning rod to a bayonet as these photos show:

1 and 2 Russian sappers in Belgrade wearing camouflage suits (**1**) and unearthing a Tellermine (**2**). The German MS 39 rod was made of two lengths of light metal tubing, one of which, the vibrating tube, has a hardened-steel point, while the other forms an extension piece to be added when the rod is used from an upright position. The rod is to be held lightly 'between fingers and thumb, and inserted vertically into the ground. Should resistance be encountered, the point is to be lifted approximately four inches and dropped. A skilled operator can tell the nature of the object in contact from its "feel," and from the sound emitted by the vibrating tube'; **3** US troops off Utah Beach; **4 and 5** British in the desert and training; **6** Finnish troops ahead of a StuG.

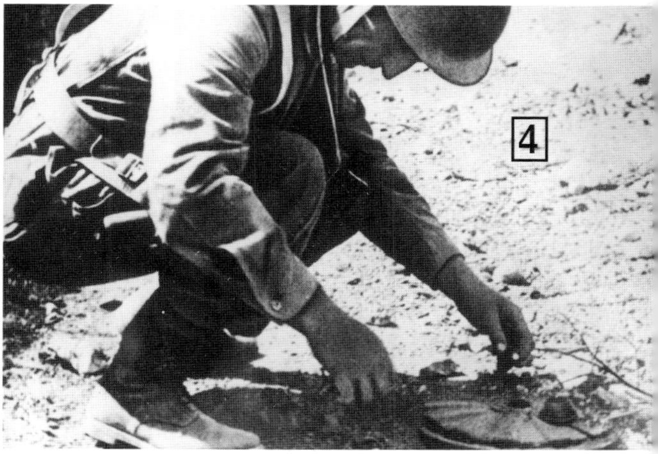
4

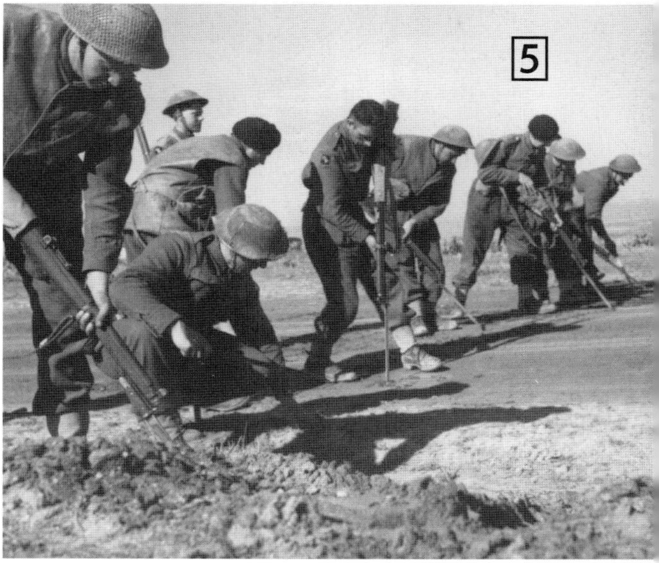
5

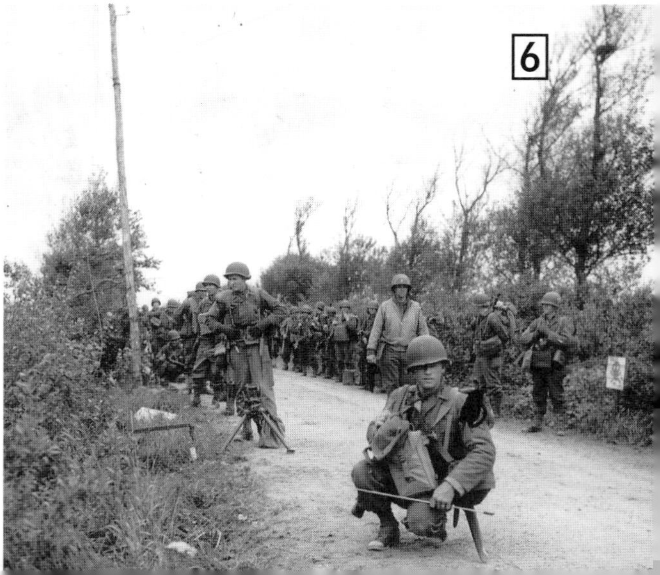
6

Metal detectors have been used since 1942. Designed originally in Poland but delayed by the Nazi invasion, in the end they were the result of work by the brilliant Lt Jozef Kosacki who gave the information to the British MoD. 500 mine detectors were rushed to help Eighth Army at the second battle of El Alamein and contributed materially to its success, as it cut down the time taken to clear German minefields. Pretty soon every army had its own detectors. Illustrated are:
1 A South African engineer in North Africa;
2 A Canadian soldier using a British No 4 light mine detector; **3** The SCR-625 was the American detector – note the canvas haversack containing the batteries. It worked well in Africa but the higher iron content in the Italian soil caused problems – as was the case for all detectors – as did the Germans' use of materials like wood and glass.

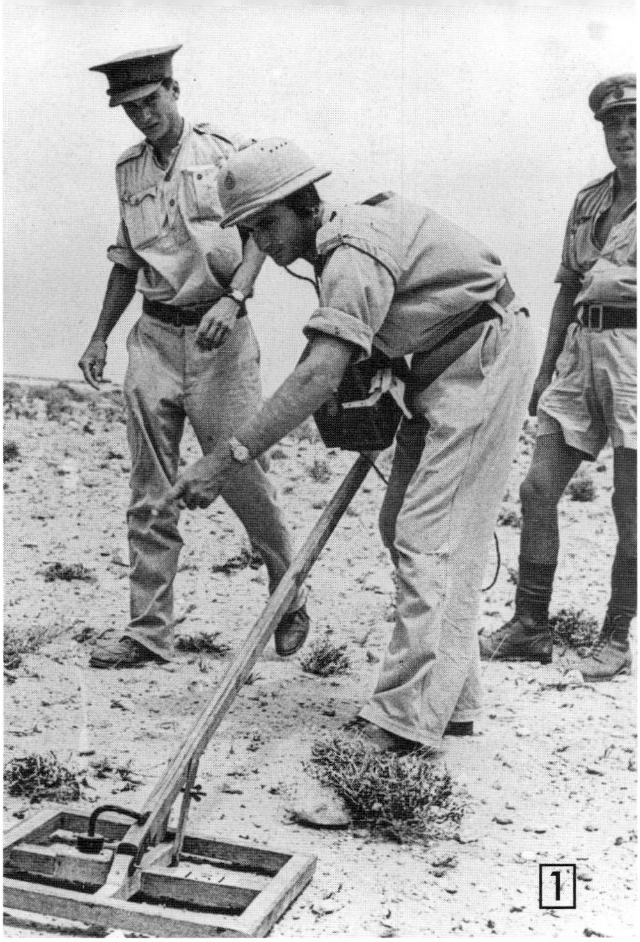
1

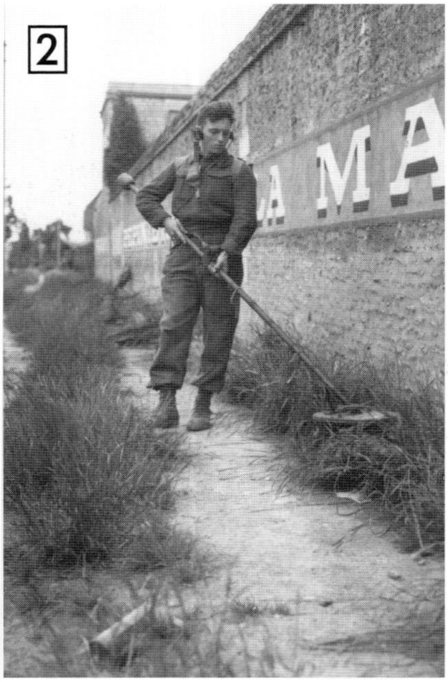
2

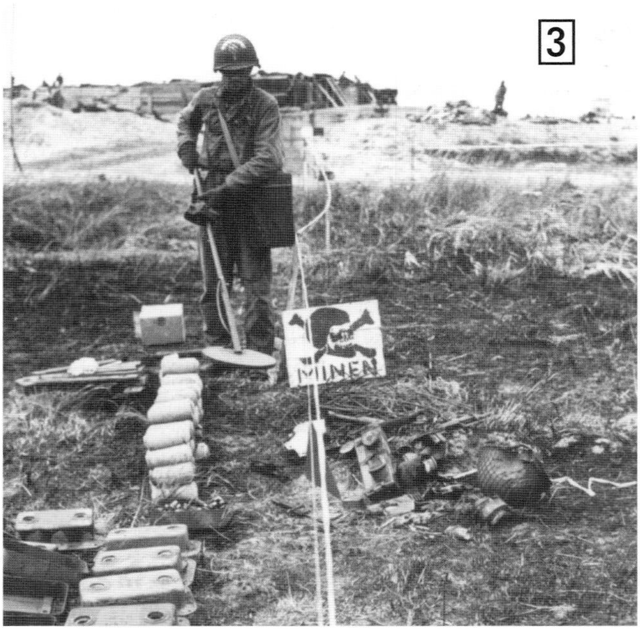
3
MINEN

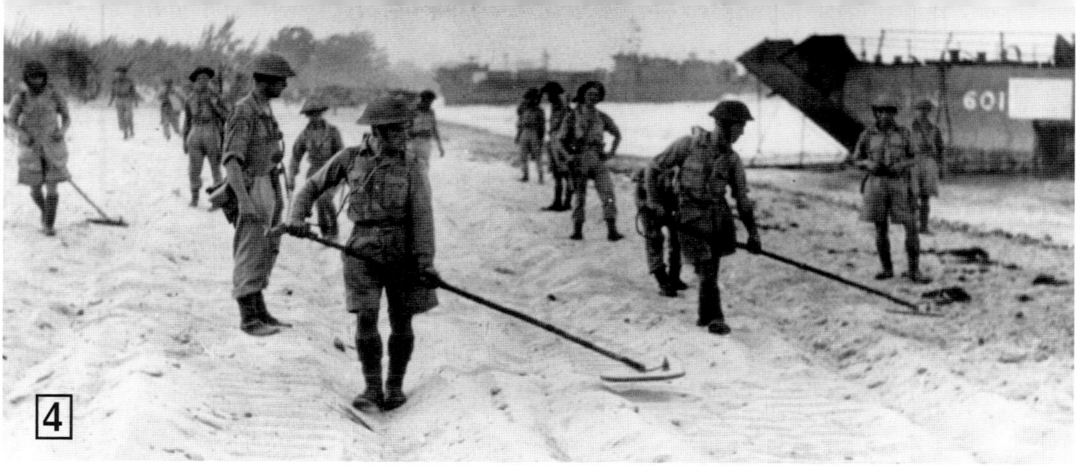
4

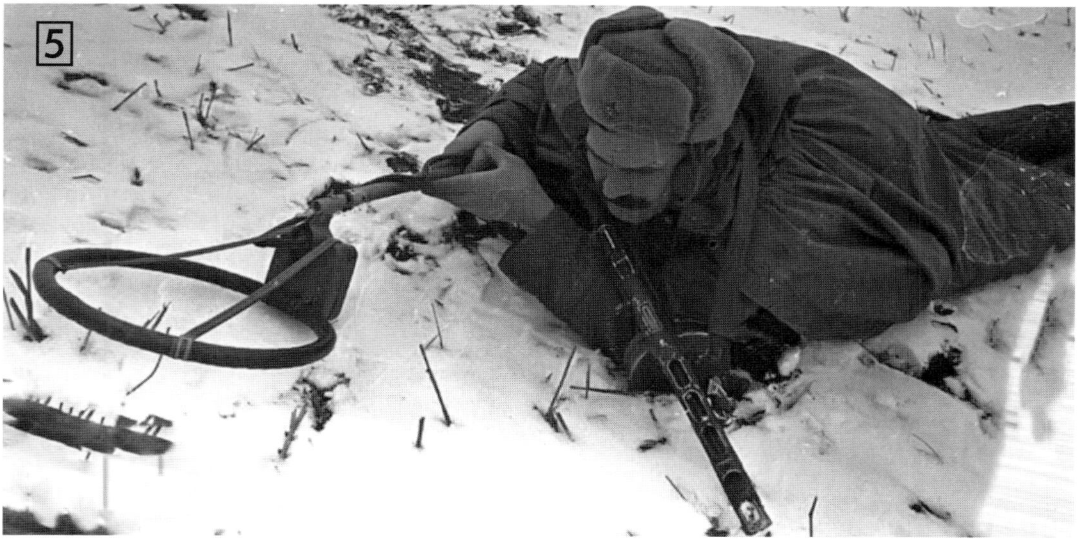
5

4 British detectors at Salerno.

5 The Soviet VIM-203 was used in conjunction with the Mosin rifle or (as here) with a wooden pole. Some 25,000 VIM detectors – VIM-203/210/625/695 – were built 1941–45.

6 The Germans used more mine detectors than most other countries – the Aachen 40 (seen here), Berlin 40, Tempelhof 41, Wien 41, Frankfurt 42, Neptun, Lowedal-Gerät, and the Stuttgart 43 – the latter slightly different in that it measured radioactive material that helped locate nonmetallic Topfmines that were laid with Tarnsand, which was radioactive. Note the tripod-mounted AA MG34 or 42 in the background and the soldier's Combat Engineer arm badge.

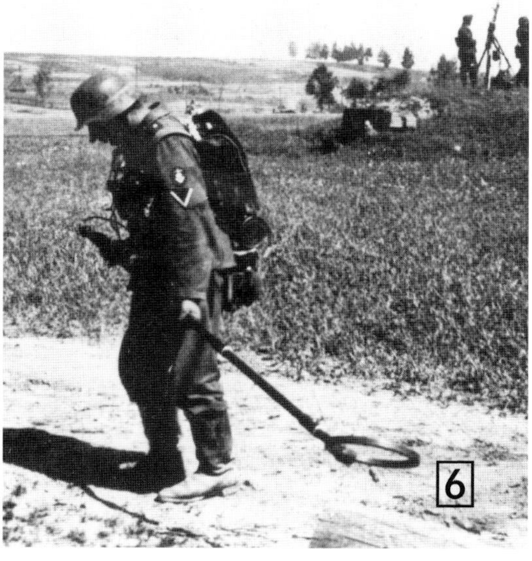
6

4 Grenades

JAPANESE GRENADES

(edited excerpts from *Tactical & Technical Trends* No 5 of 13 August 1942)

5
3
2
6
8
9
1
7
4
10
11
12
13
15
14
17
16

1
2
1.18"
2.60
1.97"

Grenades are particularly useful to the close-in tactics of jungle fighting and the Japanese have used them extensively in their operations in the southwest Pacific and Burma areas, especially with grenade throwers. The following information on Japanese grenades is therefore of interest.

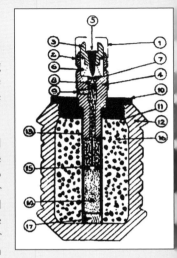

(a) Hand grenade A type 97 grenade examined in Burma is described as follows (see accompanying sketches): The grenade is cylindrical in shape and has a grooved cast-iron body. A plug (10) is screwed into the top of the body through which extends a brass igniter tube (4). The striker (5) with holder (3) creep spring (6) and percussion cap (7) are located in the upper part of the tube while the lower portion contains the fuse and detonator (14). The tube is closed at the top by a light brass cover (1) crimped near the middle to fit into a groove in the tube and held in position by a safety pin (2). The safety pin supports the striker holder and prevents the downward movement of the striker on to the percussion cap. The fuse and detonator are separated by a perforated steel disk (15). The filling (16) is composed of TNT.

The dimensions and weights are:

Maximum diameter	1.97in	Overall length	3.78in
Weight	16.5oz	Weight of filling	2oz

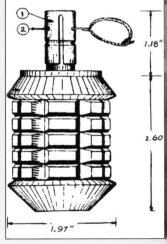

• *Method of arming.* Withdraw the safety pin. The spring is then held at half compression by the brass cover. Give the head of the ignition tube a sharp blow, further compressing the spring and driving the striker on to the percussion cap. The fuse, with a delay of 4–5 seconds, is then ignited and the filling detonated.

• *To disarm grenade.* Remove safety pin and cover. Withdraw striker holder and spring. Unscrew plug at top of grenade and withdraw together with ignition tube. Withdraw copper tube from bottom of plug and remove detonator. Remove filling.

Left: A Spigot-type grenade launcher, grenades, and carrying case.

Right: A Japanese soldier throws a type 91 hand grenade.

• *Variant type*. A grenade examined in England sometime ago was slightly heavier, but otherwise was very similar in appearance and dimensions. A cartridge container, diameter 1.02in, length 1.22in, screwed into the base of the body, contained a propelling charge and percussion cap. This is presumably fitted when the grenade is fired from a discharger, probably the 1.97in grenade thrower, model 89.

(b) Stick grenade A grenade of this type was examined in the Far East (see below). It is similar in design to the German stick grenade 24, the main points of difference being as follows:

	German grenade 24	*Japanese grenade*
Legth of stick	10in	5in
Length of container	4in	3in
Diameter of container	2.75in	2in
Length overall	1ft 2in	8in
Weight	1lb 2oz	1lb 3.5oz (approx)
Weight of filling	6oz (TNT)	2oz (Lyddite)
Thickness of casing	.08in	.25in

Both grenades are operated by a friction-igniter, powder-delay system and have a delay of approximately 4.5 seconds.

The thick cast-iron casing and smaller charge of the Japanese grenade indicate that it is designed for fragmentation, in contrast to the German grenade which relies on blast for its effect.

Method of arming. Remove screwed metal cap from base of stick and take out wire ring. Insert middle finger in ring and retain when throwing grenade. When grenade is thrown, cord attached to ring will be pulled out, igniting fuse which burns for about 4 seconds.

To disarm grenade. Remove the wax around the joint between stick and container and take out three screws located about 0.5in from the base of the container. Hold the grenade by the handle and tap off the container. Remove filling. Remove screwed metal cap from base of stick and cut cord away from ring. With a metal rod, push out igniter, fuse, and detonator complete.

Screw cap
Ring
Pull cord
Wooden handle
Friction primer
Vents, sealed with tinfoil
Delay fuze
Fuze body
Screw securing handle to body
Waxed-paper washers
Grenade body
Waxed-paper cylinder
Detonator
Bursting charge
Waxed-paper cover

Light brass cover
Firing pin
Creep spring
Percussion cap
Fuze
Burster
Rubber pellets (41)
White phosphorus and carbon disulphide filling

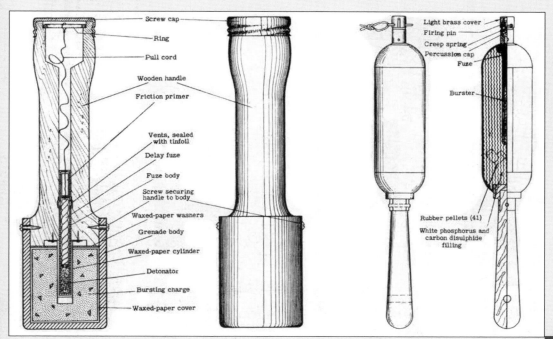

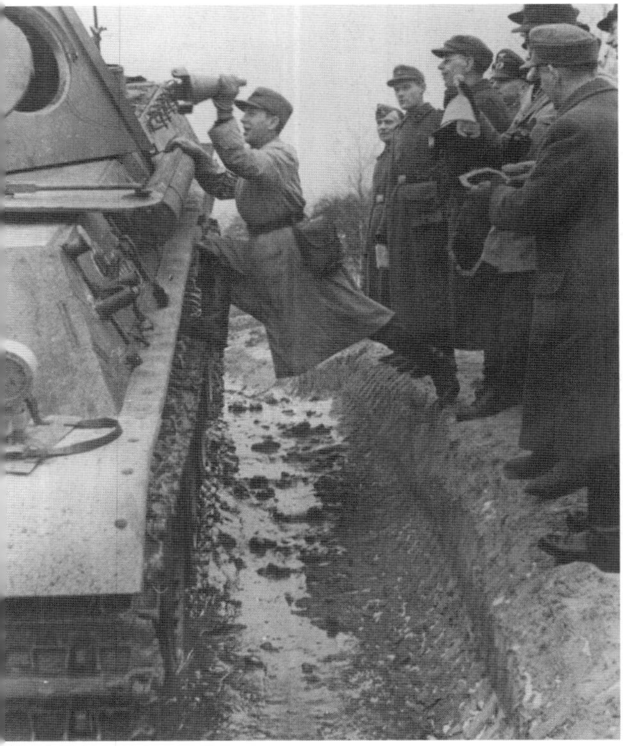

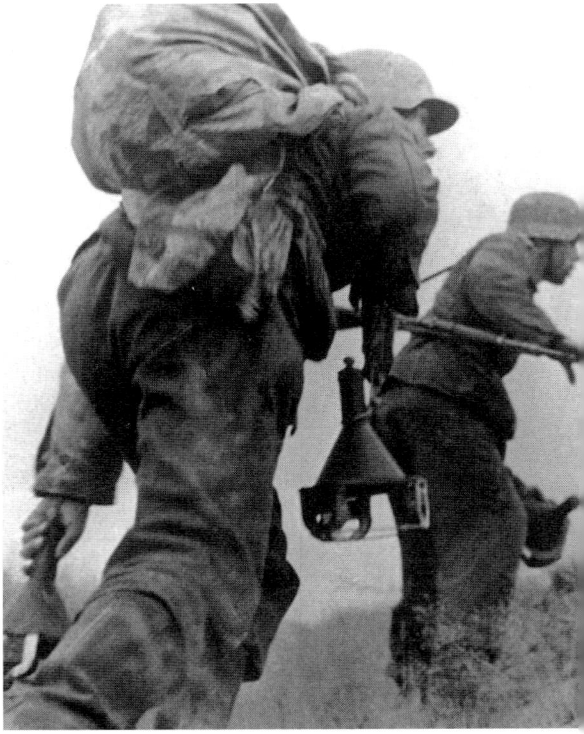

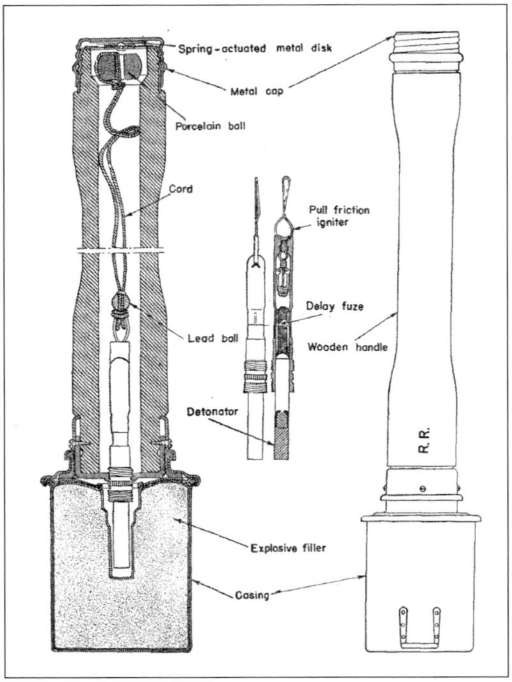
Spring-actuated metal disk
Metal cap
Porcelain ball
Cord
Pull friction igniter
Delay fuze
Lead ball
Wooden handle
Detonator
R.R.
Explosive filler
Casing

GERMAN GRENADES

Above, Left and Right: The *Hafthohlladung* magnetic grenade/mine was a close quarters antitank weapon.

Left: Sketch of a *Stielhandgranate* 24 (stick hand grenade, Model 24), showing outside and cross section of grenade and fuse. The cross section is drawn to a larger scale than the scale of the sketch of the outside view. The Model 24 was an offensive weapon which generated a blast to stun or incapacitate, unlike the Allied grenades which were defensive weapons designed to kill by fragmentation.

Opposite, Above: This MG34 machine-gunner has a range of hand grenades beside him: Model 24s and 39s along with Russian RGD-33s.

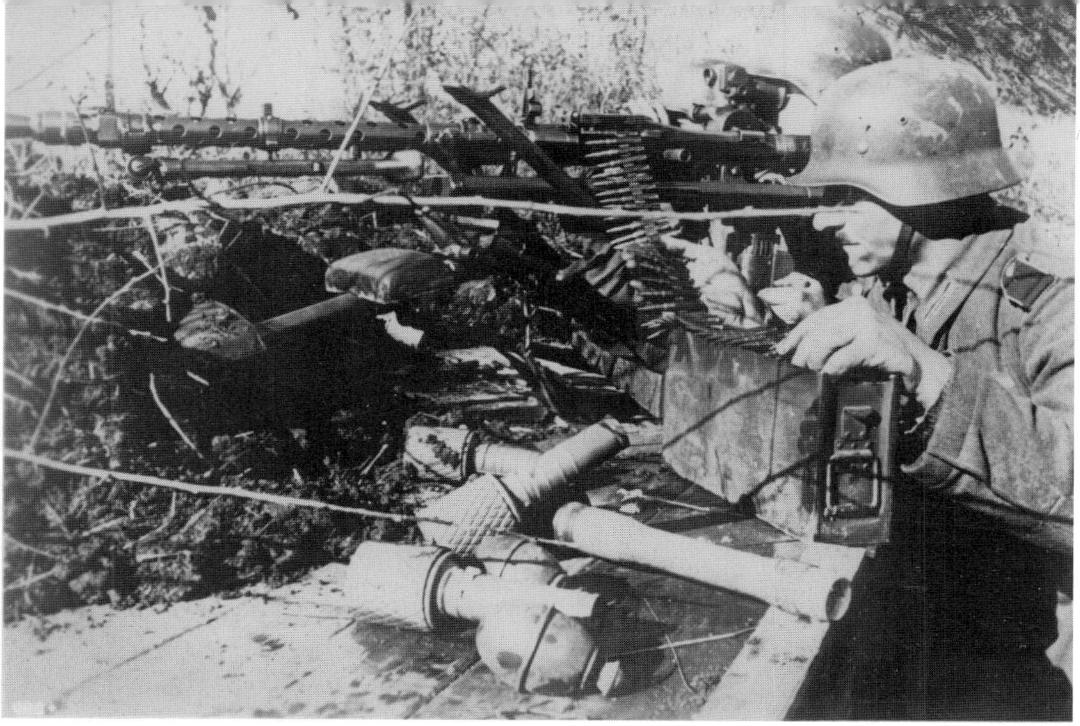

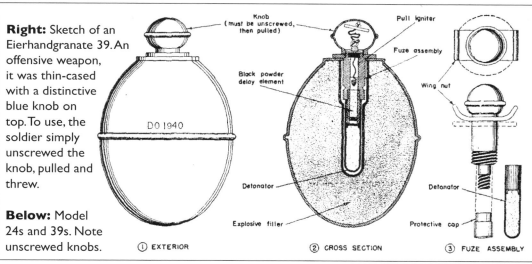

Right: Sketch of an Eierhandgranate 39. An offensive weapon, it was thin-cased with a distinctive blue knob on top. To use, the soldier simply unscrewed the knob, pulled and threw.

Below: Model 24s and 39s. Note unscrewed knobs.

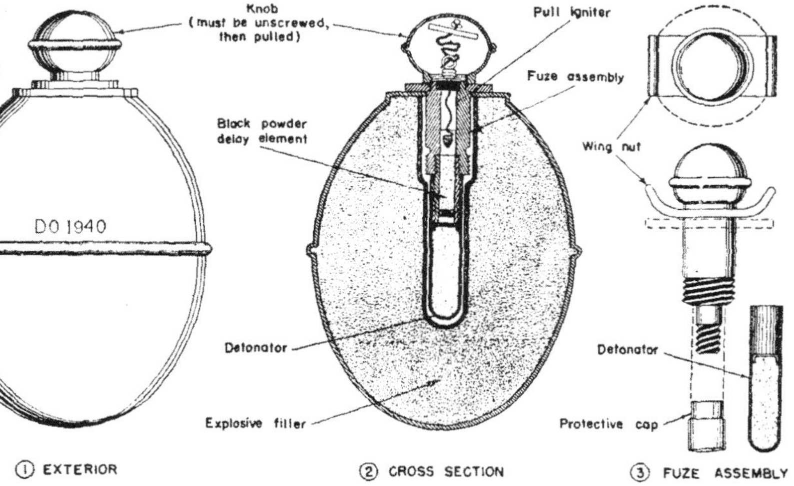
Knob (must be unscrewed, then pulled)
DO 1940
① EXTERIOR
Pull igniter
Fuze assembly
Black powder delay element
Detonator
Explosive filler
② CROSS SECTION
Wing nut
Detonator
Protective cap
③ FUZE ASSEMBLY

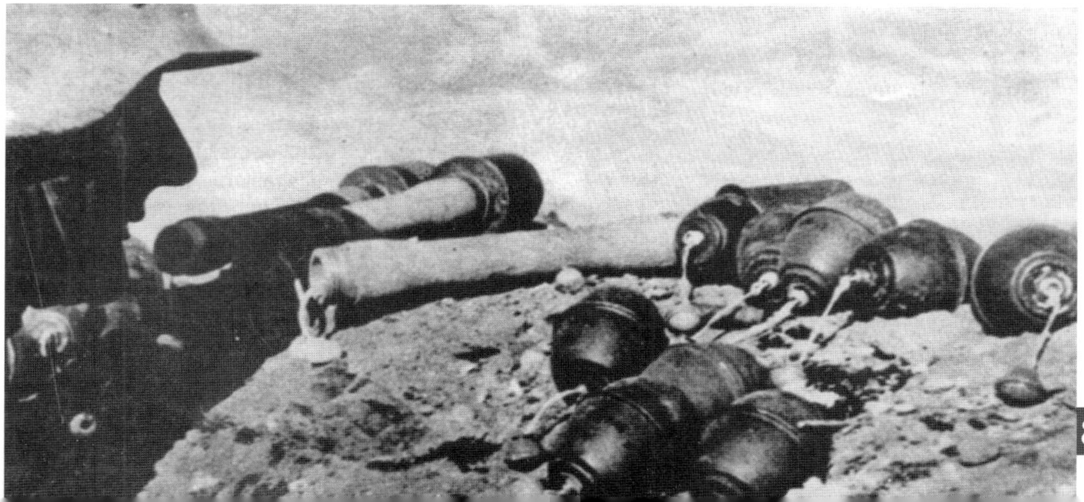

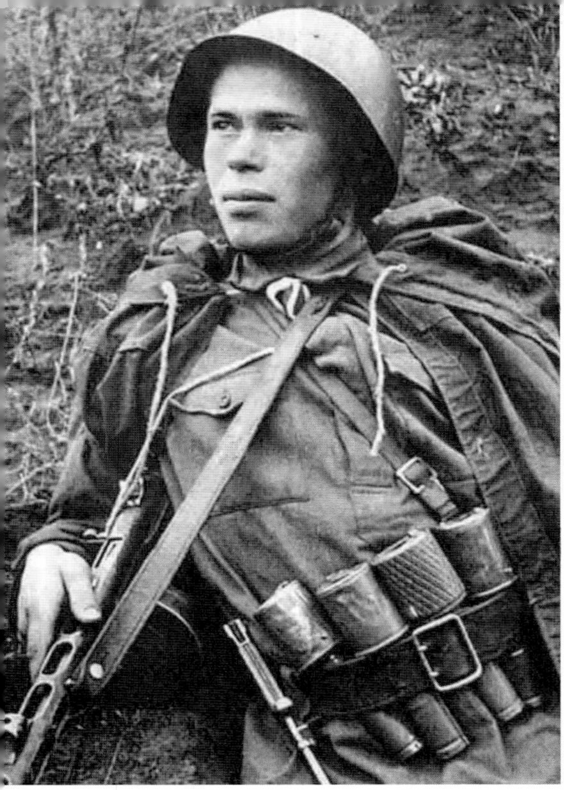

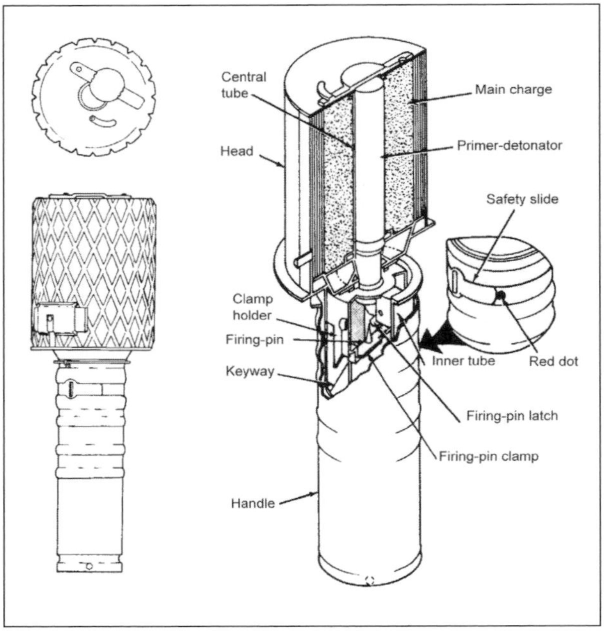

Central tube
Main charge
Head
Primer-detonator
Safety slide
Clamp holder
Firing-pin
Keyway
Inner tube
Red dot
Firing-pin latch
Firing-pin clamp
Handle

ALLIED GRENADES

Above: A Red Army scout armed with PPSH-41SMG and four RGD-33 AP hand grenades. There were three elements to the RGD-33 (**Above Right**) – the warhead and sleeve, spring-loaded handle, and fuze tube. 'To use, the grenade is grasped by the handle with the right hand, and by the head of the grenade with the left hand. The handle is pulled away from the grenade head until it stops, then the handle is turned to the right as far as it will go, and eased down into position. A red mark will then show to the right of the safety slide on the handle, to indicate the grenade is armed. The safety slide is moved to the right until it covers the red mark. The grenade is then safe. The detonator-delay assembly retaining arm on the head of the grenade is then moved aside to uncover the detonator pocket. A detonator-delay assembly is inserted with the tapered (primer) end first and pressed home gently with the thumb. Then the retaining arm is moved back to the closed position, and locked in place under the catch provided. To throw the grenade the safety slide is again moved to the left. The red mark is again visible indicating the grenade is armed, and ready for throwing.' (*IB* June 1946)

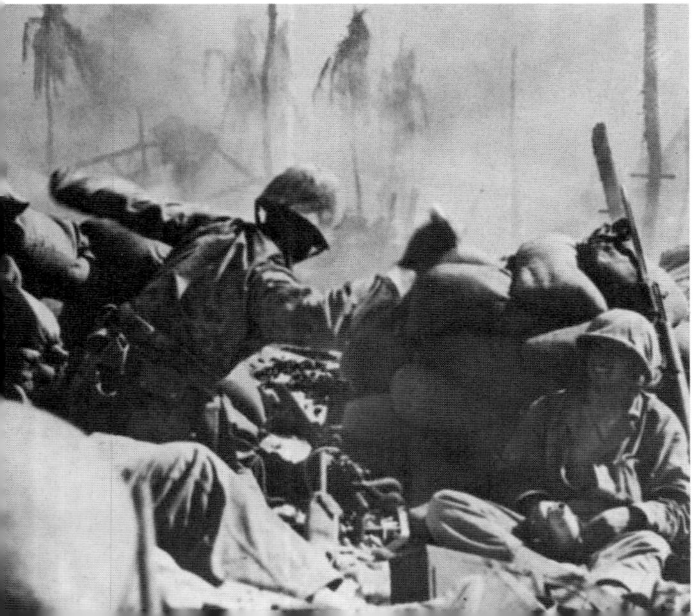

Left: The US Army's Mk II (it became the Mk 2 in 1945) series fragmentation grenade entered service in 1919. Filled with TNT and with a segmented body, it was nicknamed the pineapple for obvious reasons.

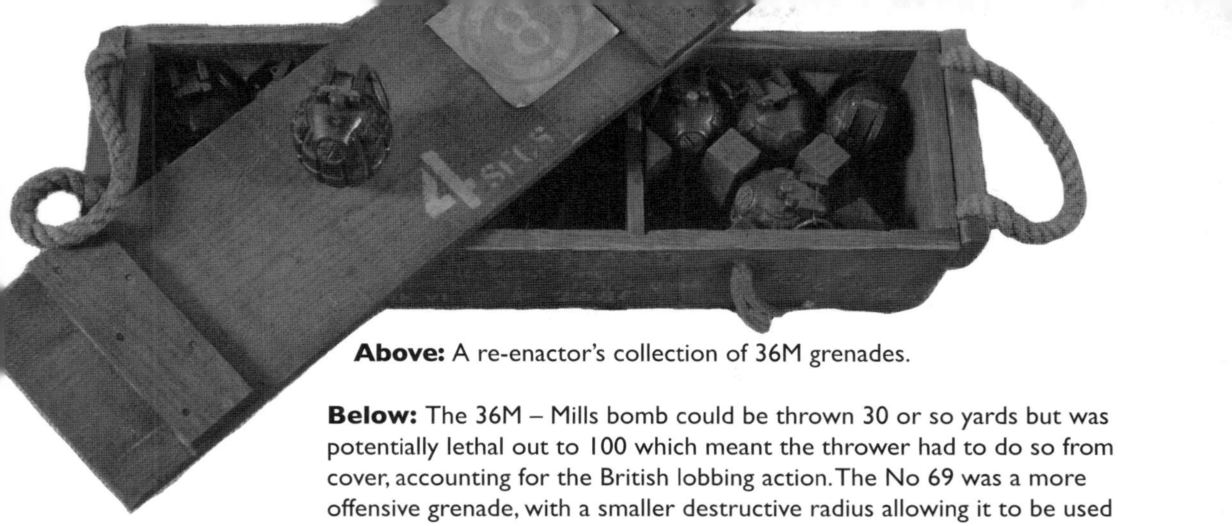

Above: A re-enactor's collection of 36M grenades.

Below: The 36M – Mills bomb could be thrown 30 or so yards but was potentially lethal out to 100 which meant the thrower had to do so from cover, accounting for the British lobbing action. The No 69 was a more offensive grenade, with a smaller destructive radius allowing it to be used without having to take cover.

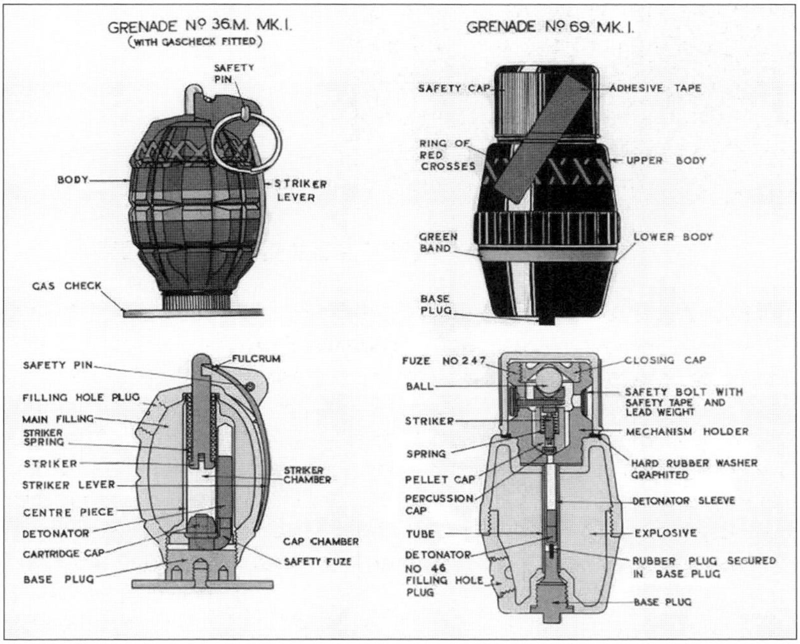
GRENADE Nº 36.M. MK. I.
(WITH GASCHECK FITTED)
SAFETY PIN
BODY
STRIKER LEVER
GAS CHECK
GRENADE Nº 69. MK. I.
SAFETY CAP
ADHESIVE TAPE
RING OF RED CROSSES
UPPER BODY
GREEN BAND
LOWER BODY
BASE PLUG
SAFETY PIN
FULCRUM
FILLING HOLE PLUG
MAIN FILLING
STRIKER SPRING
STRIKER
STRIKER LEVER
STRIKER CHAMBER
CENTRE PIECE
DETONATOR
CARTRIDGE CAP
CAP CHAMBER
SAFETY FUZE
BASE PLUG
FUZE NO 247
CLOSING CAP
BALL
SAFETY BOLT WITH SAFETY TAPE AND LEAD WEIGHT
STRIKER
MECHANISM HOLDER
SPRING
HARD RUBBER WASHER GRAPHITED
PELLET CAP
PERCUSSION CAP
DETONATOR SLEEVE
TUBE
EXPLOSIVE
DETONATOR NO 46
RUBBER PLUG SECURED IN BASE PLUG
FILLING HOLE PLUG
BASE PLUG

Below, Left: L/Cpl George Gagnon, 14th Field Regt, RCA, fuses No 36M hand grenades aboard the LST that will take him to Normandy, 4 June 1944.

Below, Right: Great use was made of rifle grenades, an attachment allowing infantry to fire grenades from an adaptor attached to a rifle barrel. The Germans had their Schiessbecher from World War I attached to the Kar98k. This had a range of 300 yards. Illustrated is a US M7 launcher fitted onto an M1 Garand in use by a French unit during house-to-house fighting in the south of France. It's firing an M9 anti-tank rifle grenade. The range depended on the target, but the blast radius was dangerous to 50 yards.

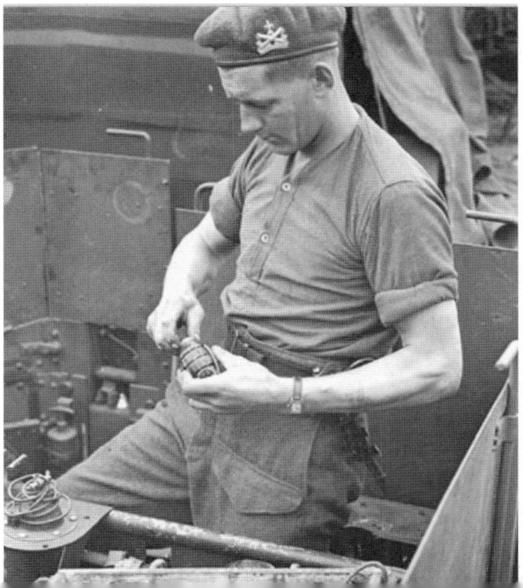

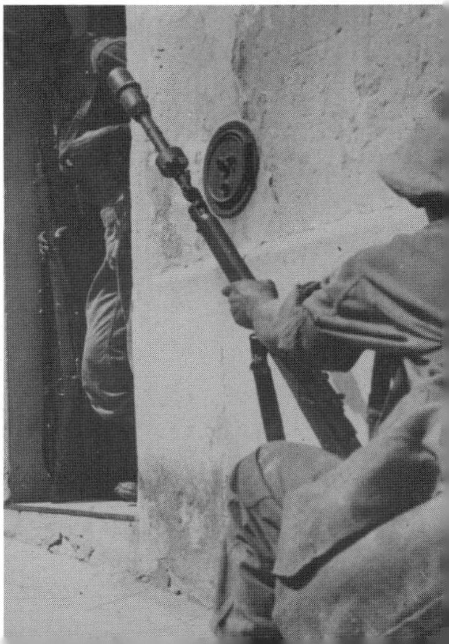

5 Flamethrowers

Flamethrowers were much in evidence during World War II and they were used by every major combatant. The Italians were pioneers of promoting the use of man-portable flamethrowers, using them in Flamethrower units from 1935. Their Lanciaflamme Models 35 and 40 were certainly issued although there are few indications they were used in anger. However, the Axis powers did get the ball rolling – the Germans in Poland in 1939 at the Danzig Post Office on the first day of the war – and then in France and the Low Countries in 1940. The Japanese, too, used flamethrowers in their early battles. However, it was the Allies who would make most use of the vicious weapons as they came up against fixed defences, with their minefields and barbed wire, ranged artillery, concrete bunkers and armoured cupolas. When the Atlantic Wall was breached, flamethrowers were much in evidence but mainly mounted on tanks and carriers. The individual infantryman's backpack version suffered from a very short range, and was bulky and cumbersome. The Germans used the *Flammpanzer*, often on SdKfz 251, PzKpfw II and III chassis; the Western Allies used the Churchill Crab, the Sherman and the LVT4. In the Pacific island-hopping campaign, there was more use for individual flamethrowers because of the restrictive terrain and lack of mobility. The Japanese dug in, using caves and tunnels, and flame was essential to end their resistance.

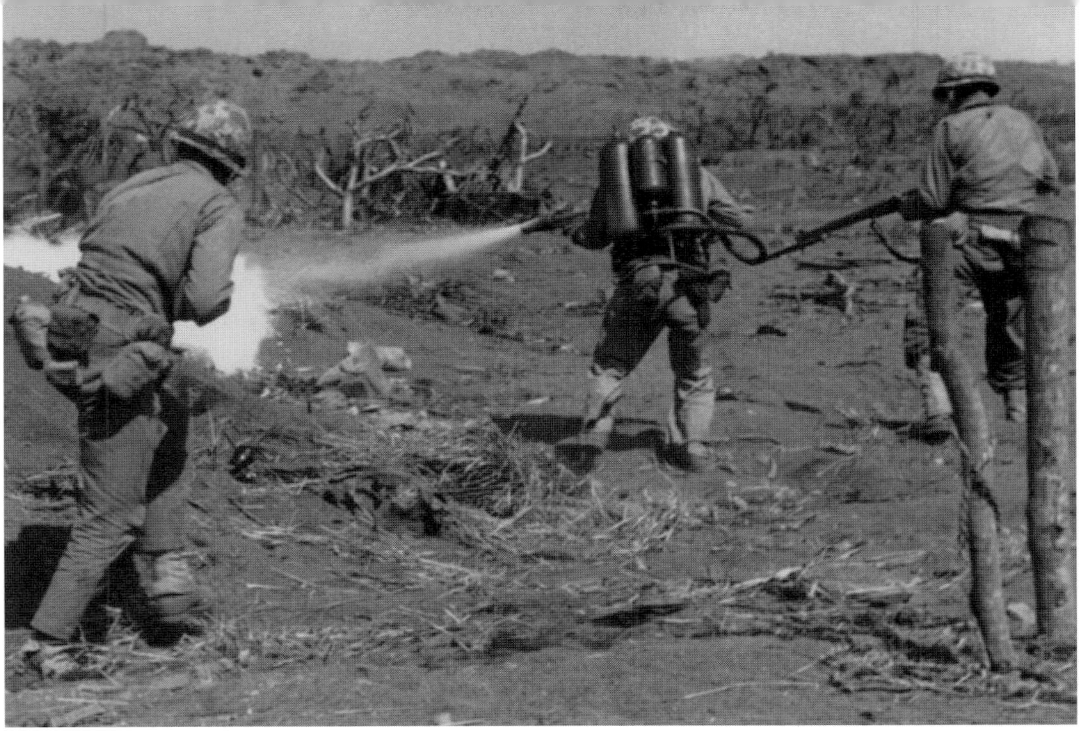

Opposite, Left: The Russian ROKS-2 and ROKS-3 flamethrowers were man-portable with a range of around 45m. The Finns captured a number of them and reemployed them under the designation *liekinheitin M/41-r*. This is a ROKS-3.

Opposite, Right: The ROKS-2 had a knapsack-style outer covering and a rifle-style dispenser to make the bearer a less obvious target for snipers and sharpshooters.

Above and Below: The US Army flamethrowers were developed by the US Chemical Warfare Service. The first, the M1, entered service in early 1942. Improvements to the fuel – the arrival of napalm – and the development of the M1-1 (**Below**) and then, in September 1944, the M2-2 (**Above** in USMC hands), led to a massive increase in use. USMC regiments had over 80 flamethrowers and tactics evolved to make the best use of them. Marines first employed them at Tarawa in November 1943. At Peleliu they used flamethrower-equipped LVT4s, something both services did later in the war.

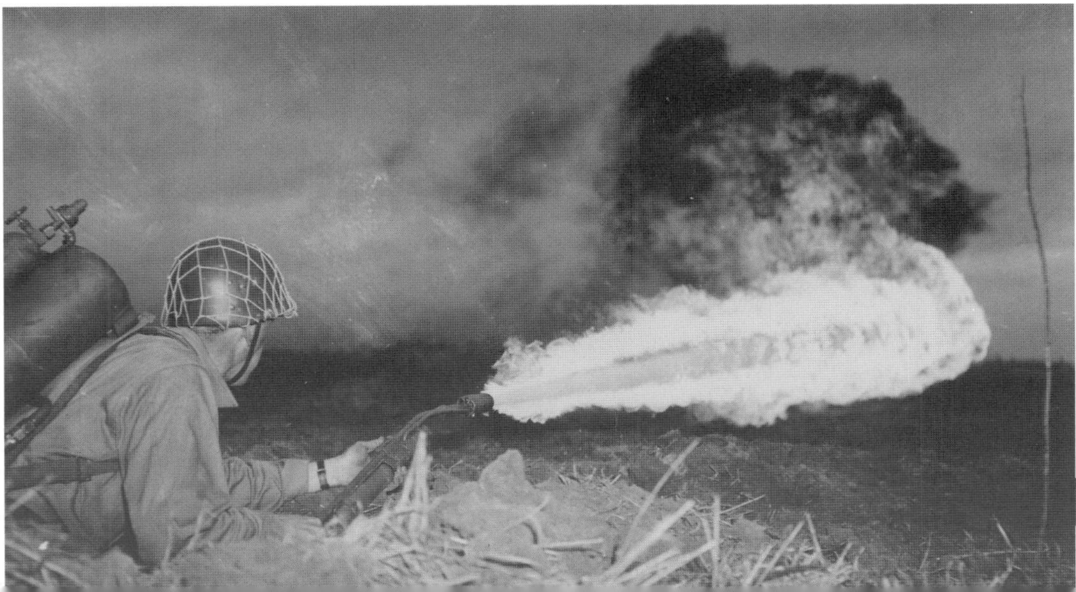

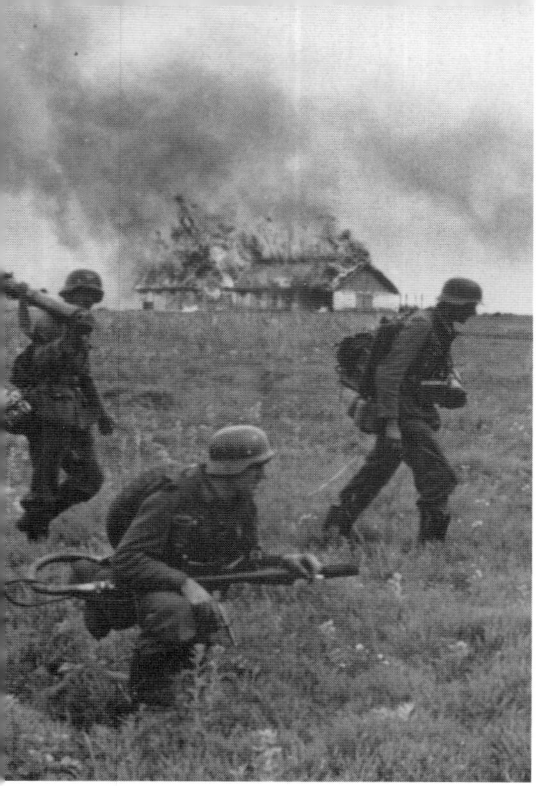

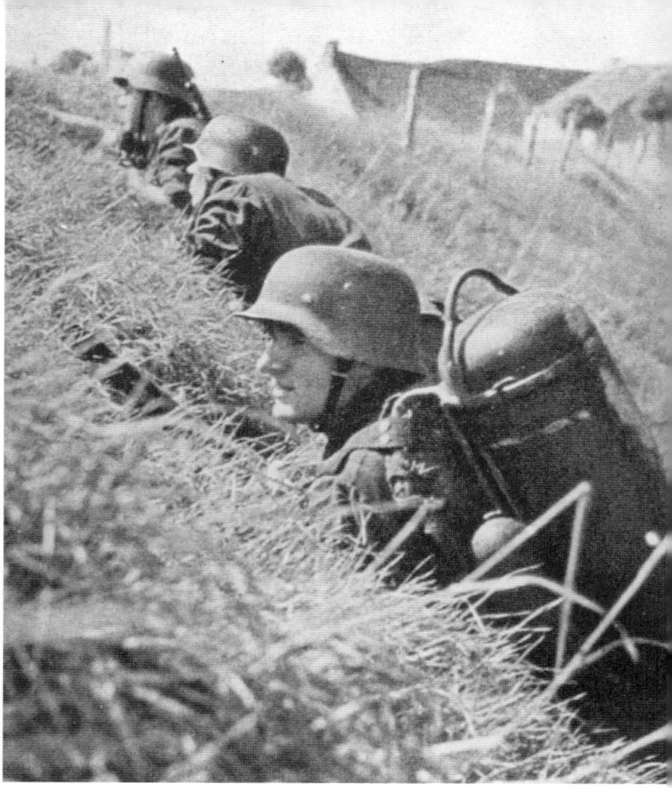

Above left and right: The Germans for all their late war protestations – and murdering of captured flamethrower crews – made heavy use of the Flammenwerfer 35 (**Above right**). Its main drawback was its weight (80lb). A lighter doughnut version (**Above left**), the Model 40, looked more like the British backpack lifebuoy weapon. A lighter version (**Left**), the German Model 41 weighed around 47lb. McKinney (1949): 'Later, in 1942, it was found that the ignition system, under the conditions of extreme cold during the Russian campaign, was unreliable and a new flame gun was developed with a cartridge ignition system. This Model 42 remained the standard German manpack flamethrower until the end of the war. Further developments continued with the view of increasing both the range and fuel capacity without increasing the weight. ... A new design, Model 43, weighing about 53lb when filled with 2gal of fuel, emerged, but only a few samples were made. To meet the demand for greater range, work was begun on Model 44H and Model 44A, the latter of which utilized cordite as a propellant, whereas other models had utilized nitrogen. Models 44 and 44A did not fulfill the requirement underlying their design and their fuel capacity was small, 1gal and 1.5gal, respectively.'

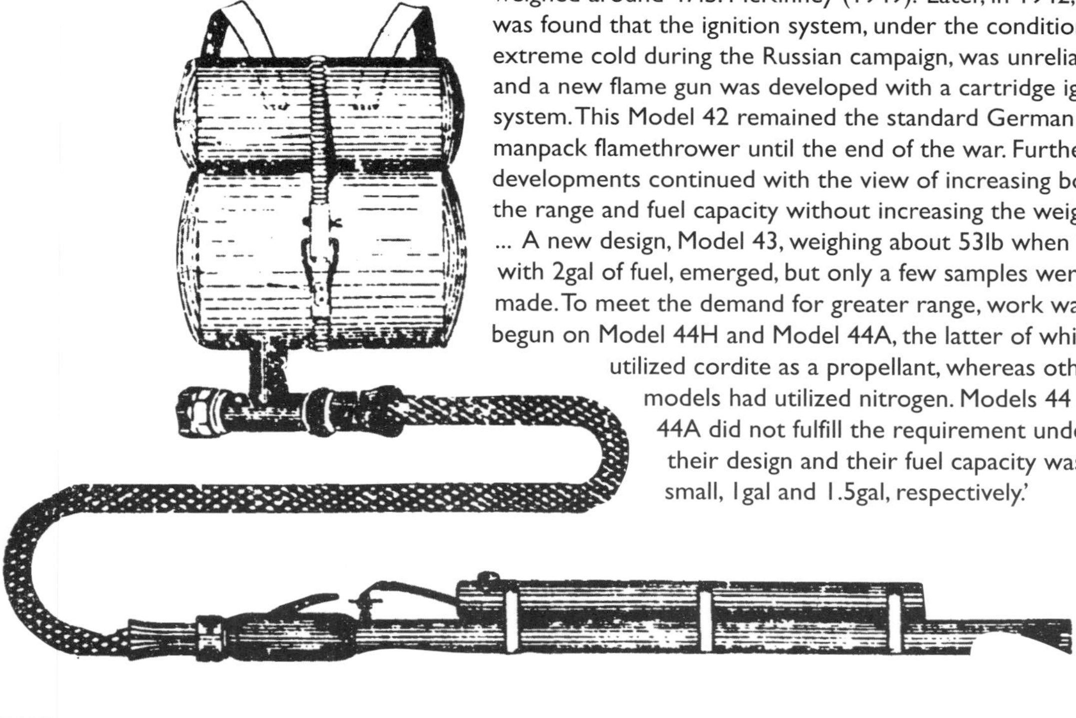

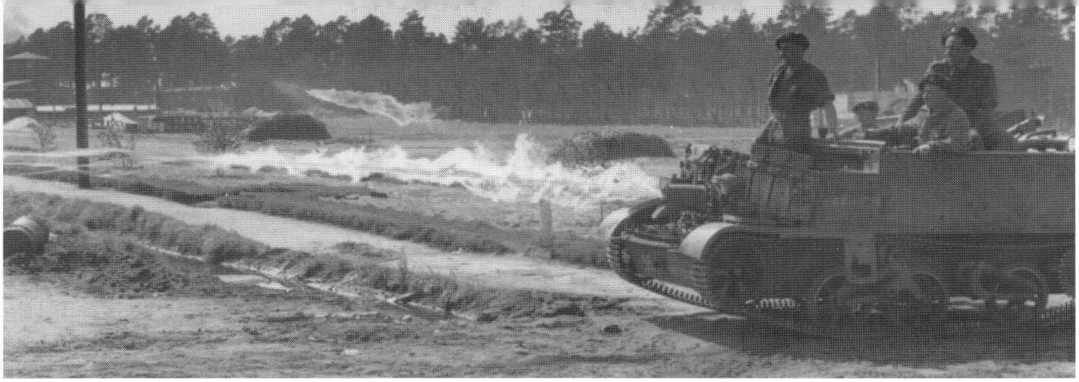

Above: Developed by both British and Canadians (who produced their own first version, the Ronson and went on to convert turretless Ram tanks into flamethrowers), the Wasp came in three versions: the Mk I (thrower fixed at front with 100gal tank), Mk II (flamethrower in co-driver's position) and Mk II* or IIC (Canadian version with fuel tanks on rear of vehicle).

Below: Japanese Type 93. This is modelled on one captured on Bataan. 'The weapon is of excellent design and construction, although considerably heavier than the corresponding American type. The valve of the gun is awkward to operate. The mechanism for positive ignition is a distinct advantage. A desirable feature is that the flame-thrower operator can operate the valve of the pressure cylinder, but the Japanese method of doing this by means of a flexible shaft is considered undesirable as the shaft is heavy and easily kinked.' (*T&TT* No 19, 11 November 1943.)

Below right: US engineers train in the UK with four flamethrowers to the fore. Often flamethrower teams were made up of combat engineer units, later with troops of the chemical warfare service. In the Pacific the flamethrower troops were targeted by the Japanese. The defenders in their 11 miles of deep caves and bunkers were difficult to winkle out on Iwo Jima, but veteran USMC Cpl Raymond Hart remembered that the 'flamethrowers got it done.'

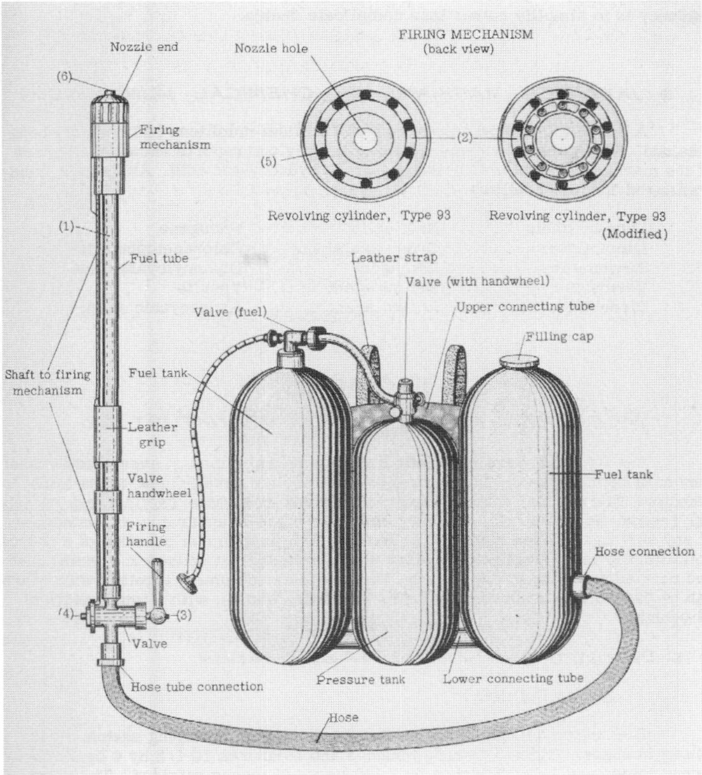

Nozzle end
Nozzle hole
FIRING MECHANISM
(back view)
(6)
Firing mechanism
(5)
(2)
Revolving cylinder, Type 93
Revolving cylinder, Type 93 (Modified)
(1)
Fuel tube
Leather strap
Valve (with handwheel)
Valve (fuel)
Upper connecting tube
Filling cap
Shaft to firing mechanism
Fuel tank
Leather grip
Valve handwheel
Fuel tank
Firing handle
Hose connection
(4)
(3)
Valve
Hose tube connection
Pressure tank
Lower connecting tube
Hose

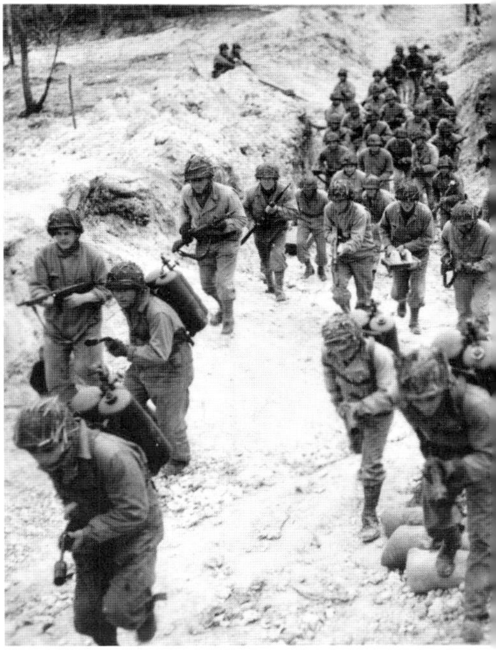

6 Mortars

Developed during World War I by the British and French, taken up by all combatants, mortars were hugely important to the infantrymen of World War II. As with artillery, there were various calibres, each having their own advantages in terms of weight of shot, weight of equipment (and therefore mobility) and availability of ammunition.

Mortars are rugged and relatively easy to construct. In the heavier versions the baseplate anchors the weapon, the smoothbored tube is muzzle-loaded and the tripod or bipod acts as a stabilser. Lighter calibres use a trigger mechanism rather than the primer cap/firing pin used for medium calibres. Sighting is usually rudimentary, and mortars cannot fire direct but the high-angle (usually between about 45° and 80°) gives trajectories that make them perfect for firing over hills and from behind cover. The mortars carried by the infantry have ranges out to around 2,500 (light) to 6,000 (medium) yards. There were heavier mortars (over 100mm) but they tended be treated as artillery being handled by, for example, the Royal Artillery (British) or Chemical Warfare Service (US).

Mortars fire a range of bombs in combat that make them a flexible weapon with a range of tactical roles. HE was, obviously, primarily anti-personnel or soft-skinned vehicles; smoke (two types: bursting – usually white phosphorus – and those that burst into flame on contact) was essential to provide local tactical cover; illumination (such as para illuminating) provided light.

Mortars were not just carried or wheeled. Some were vehicle-mounted for armoured infantry or Panzergrenadiers – such as the US M4/M21 Medium Mortar Carriages – or carried in dedicated vehicles such as the British Universal carrier or German SdKfz 250/7 or 251/2.

Opposite: The American M1 81mm mortar weighed 136lb, each of the three elements (tube/mount/baseplate) weighing around 45lb. With a rate of fire of between 15 and 30 rounds a minute, it had a range out to nearly 2 miles. Here, one crew member sets the sights, another holds a round ready to fire, a third has the next round ready and a fourth is receiving targeting information.

Above right: Pte R.L. Randolf of 1st Bn Canadian Scottish Regiment in a trench with a 2in mortar, 12 June 1944. Note the range of ammunition. The 2in mortar – much like the German 5cm – was usually sighted by eye.

Centre right: Another Canadian mortar, this one a 3in dismounted from a carrier (in the background) of the Support Company, Regina Rifles. Note the distinctive three-round cardboard carrier on the pit side.

Below: US armored infantry units were equipped with mortars in carriers – this is one an M21 MMC. Only 110 of this upgrade of the M4 were built. Most ended up in northwest Europe. With its 81mm mortar facing forward, the line of mines in the side racks and storage bins, its M3 ancestry is obvious.

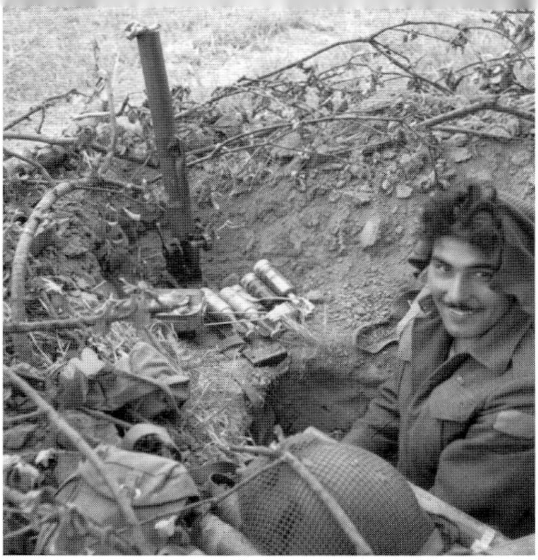

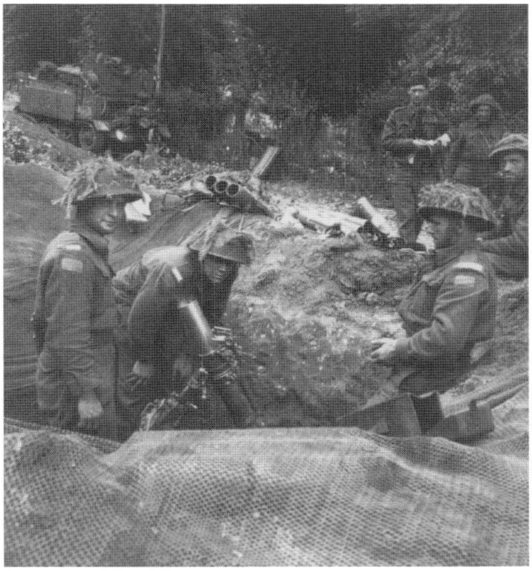

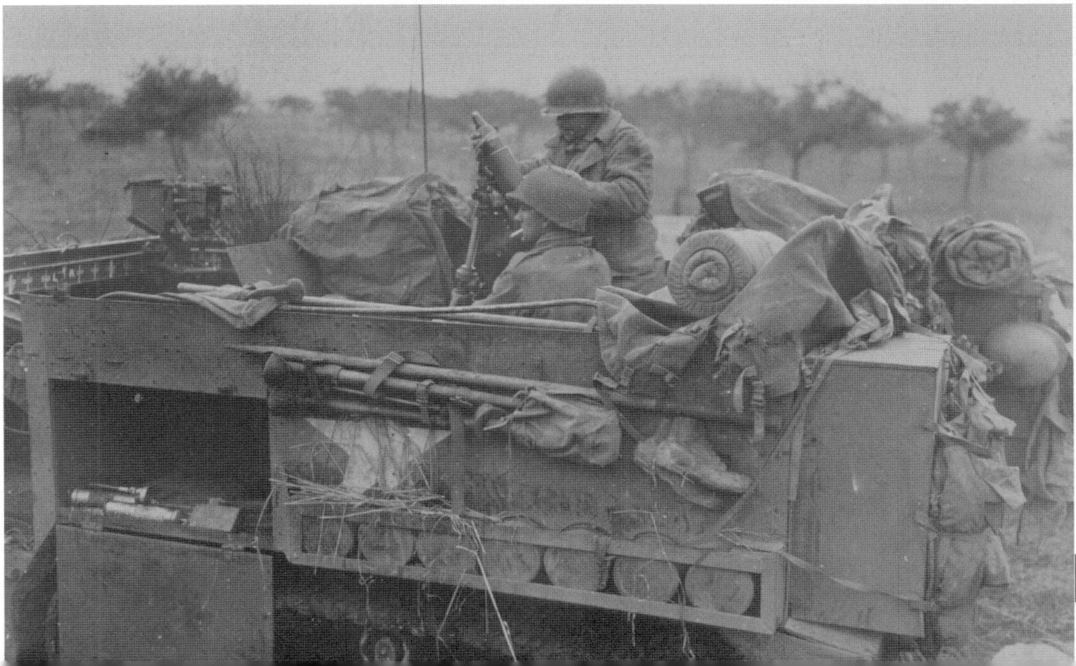

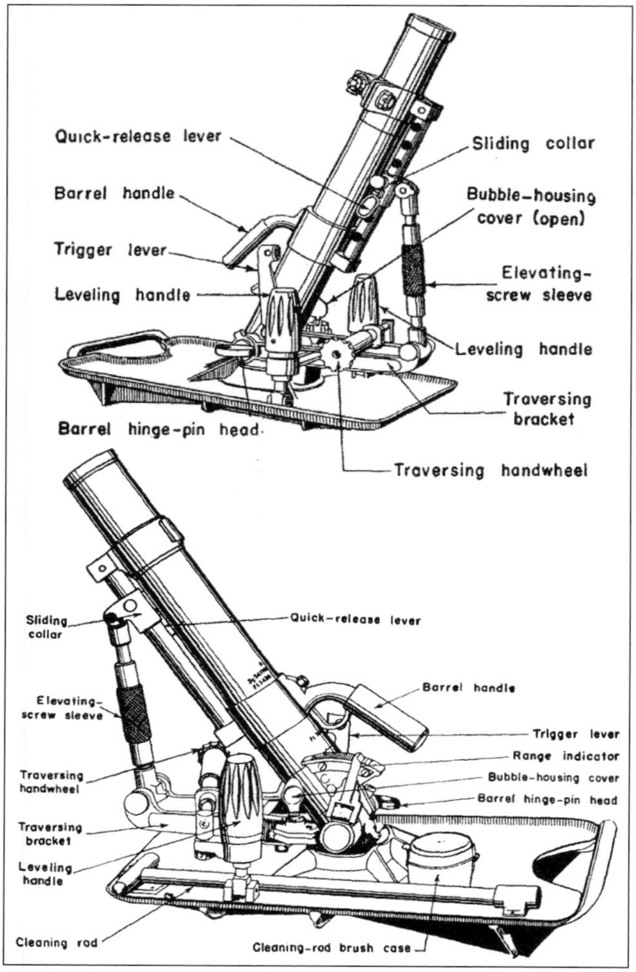
Quick-release lever
Sliding collar
Barrel handle
Bubble-housing cover (open)
Trigger lever
Elevating-screw sleeve
Leveling handle
Leveling handle
Traversing bracket
Barrel hinge-pin head
Traversing handwheel
Sliding collar
Quick-release lever
Barrel handle
Elevating-screw sleeve
Trigger lever
Range indicator
Traversing handwheel
Bubble-housing cover
Barrel hinge-pin head
Traversing bracket
Leveling handle
Cleaning rod
Cleaning-rod brush case

Left and Below left: The German 5cm leichte Granatwerfer 36 (leGrW36) had a three-man crew who carried some 45 rounds with them. It was light enough to be easily portable and therefore provided mobile support out to some 500 yards.

Bottom left: The 8cm schwere Granatwerfer 34 (sGrW34) was the standard medium mortar of German Army. Here a Waffen-SS mortar team in Italy prepares to fire. It was some 125lb in weight and could fire a 15lb projectile over 2,500 yards.

Below: A German 5cm leGrW36 on the Italian front. Note the ammunition case which carried ten rounds. Accurate, if slightly slow to set up, it saw less service as the war progressed.

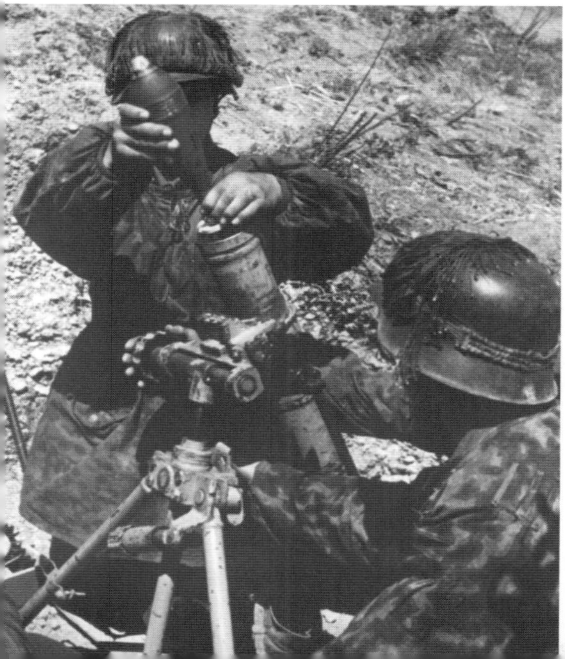

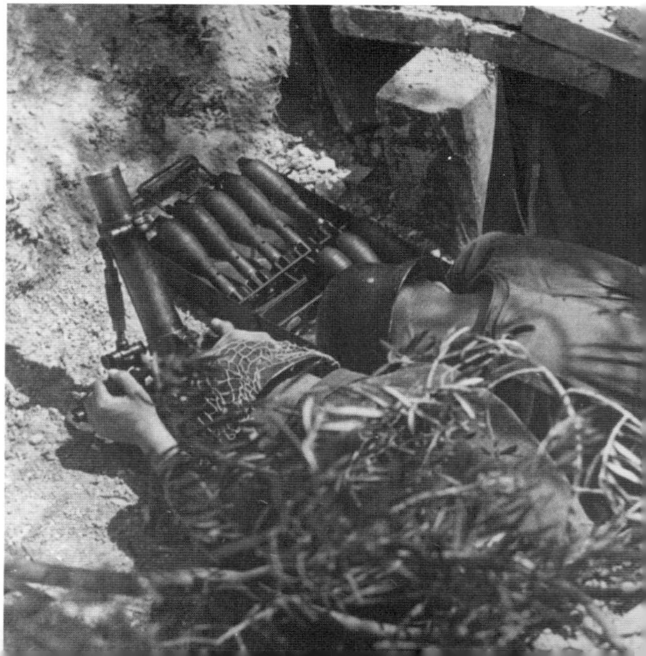

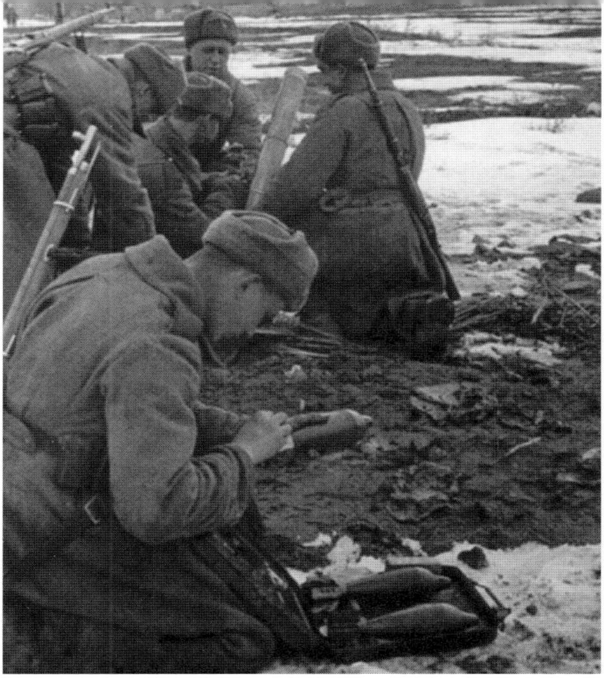

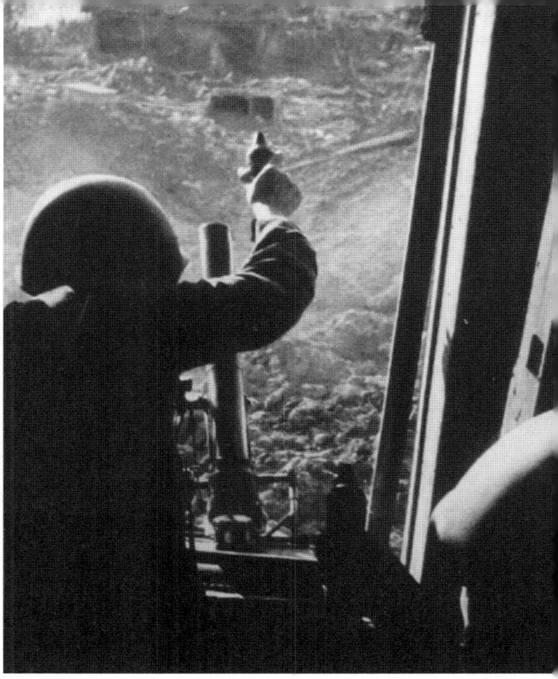

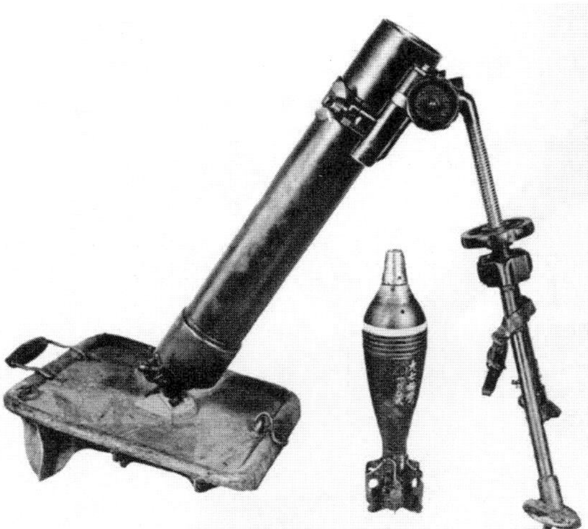

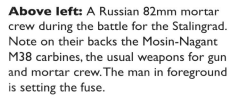

Above left: A Russian 82mm mortar crew during the battle for the Stalingrad. Note on their backs the Mosin-Nagant M38 carbines, the usual weapons for gun and mortar crew. The man in foreground is setting the fuse.

Above: Another Stalingrad view, this Russian 50mm RM 41 was modelled on the leGrW36 and lacked a bipod.

Left: Japanese Model 99 (1939) 81mm mortar.

Below: Australian 3in mortar position on Tarakan Island, May 1945. Man at left is adding extra charges on the fins to increase range.

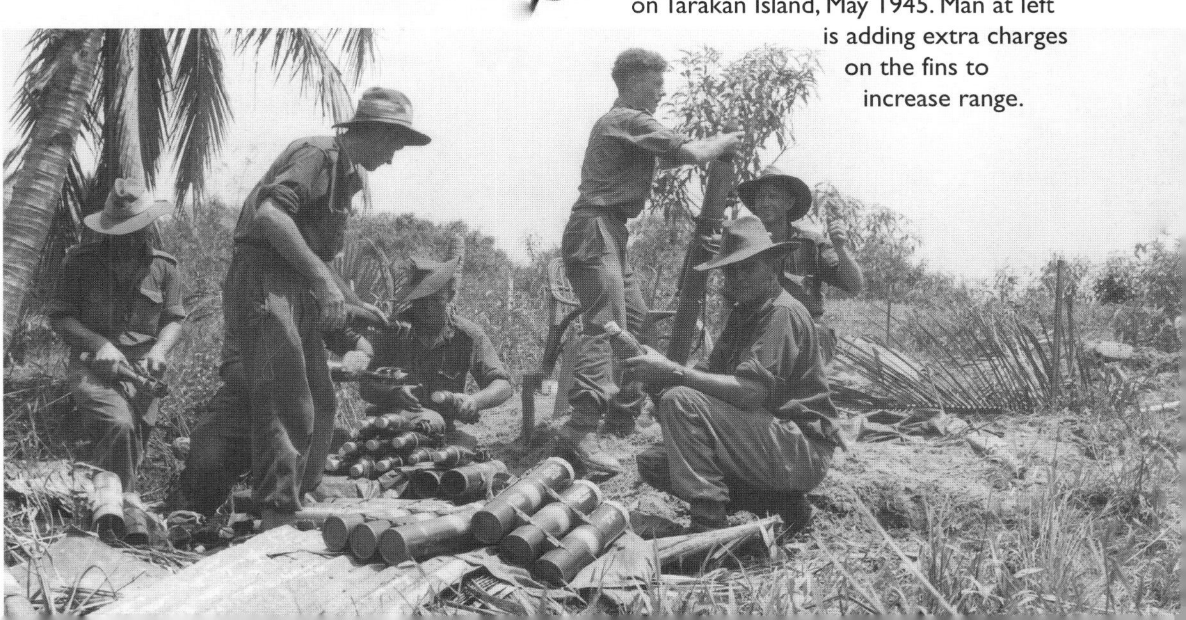

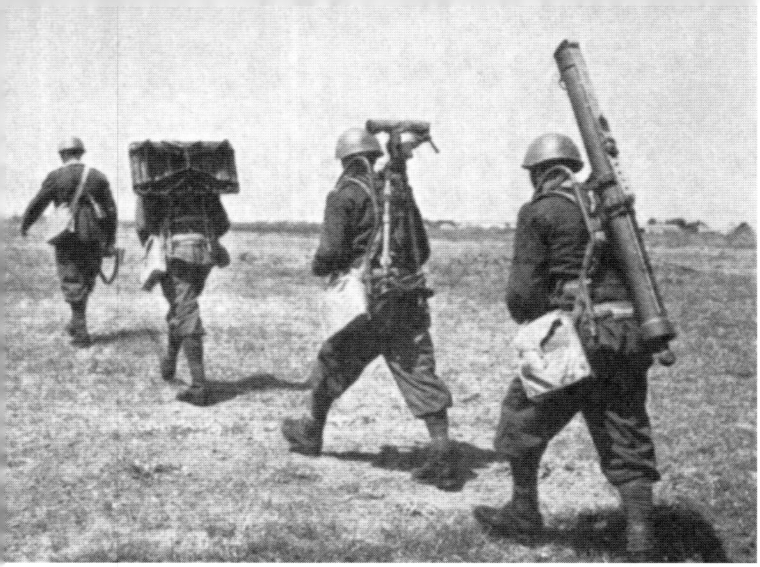

Left: The Italian 81mm mortar weighed 129lb and could be carried by three men. Its bombs weighed between 7.25lb (light) and 15lb (heavy); range between 4,250 yards (light) and 1,640 yards (heavy). If necessary, this mortar could fire sGrW34 bombs to 2,250 yards.

Below: The Italian 45mm Model 35 Brixia light mortar was trigger-fired by a cartridge from a magazine fitted on top of the body.

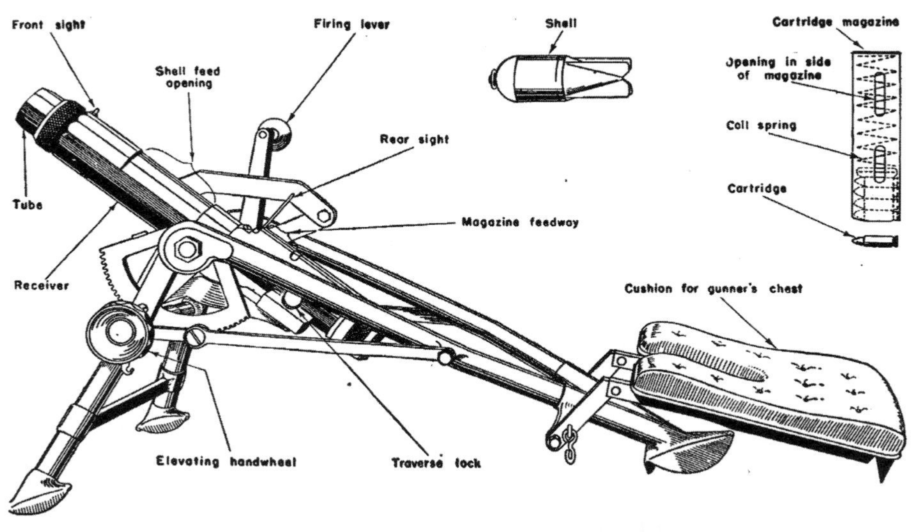
Front sight
Firing lever
Shell
Cartridge magazine
Shell feed opening
Opening in side of magazine
Coil spring
Rear sight
Tube
Cartridge
Magazine feedway
Receiver
Cushion for gunner's chest
Elevating handwheel
Traverse lock

Specifications of Soviet Mortars of WWII

Calibre	*model*	*weight*	*range*	*bomb weight*
37mm	spade	2.4kg	300m	0.5kg
50mm	1938, 1940, 1941	9–12kg	800m	0.85kg
82mm	1936, 1937, 1941, 1943	52–63kg	3,040m	3.1kg
107mm	mountain (1938)	170kg	6,100m	8.0kg
120mm	1938, 1941, 1943	275 kg	5,700m	15.9kg

Left: The Red Army employed a number of 82mm mortars. The 82-PM-41 had built in wheels to help mobility – the only difference between it and the Model 1937.

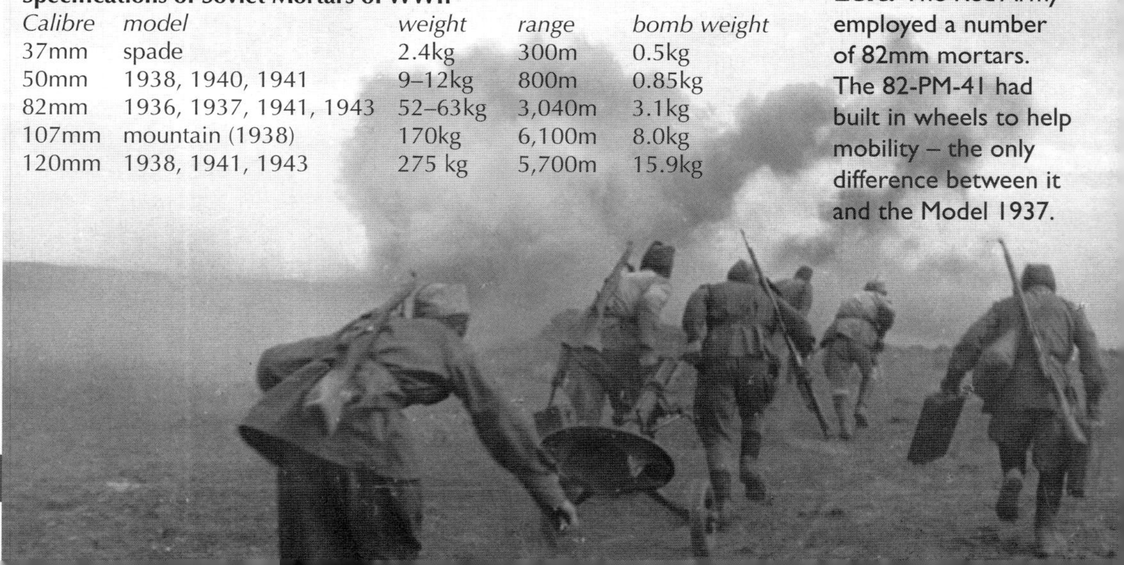

8 Machine Guns

The basic building block of infantry units was the section – eight or ten men, whose tactical function was built around the squad's heavy weapon, usually a machine gun. They came in various forms, usually light, medium, and heavy, and some were able to fight in different ways depending on their mounting. Thus the MG34 was an LMG on a bipod and an MMG on its Lafette 34 tripod. Other than calibre and mounting, there were two other important differences: feed – belt or magazine – and rate of fire. In some cases – again, the MG34 is a good example – the feed could be varied from belt-fed to a drum magazine. A high rate of fire had its drawbacks: barrels overheated and needed replacement. This could be effected quickly, particularly with the MG42, but still caused problems. (Barrel change was the job of the No 2 gunner.)

Tactically, the squad/section split into two, one (with the MG) in support of the other. The MG was there to fix the enemy while the riflemen flanked or manoeuvred. All the men in the squad carried ammunition for the machine-gun team, which usually comprised a minimum of two, the gunner and his No 2, be it boxes of belt-fed 7.92mm for the MG34 or magazines of .30-06 Springfield for the BAR or 7.62mm pan magazines for the DP.

Although less mobile, used on vehicles and in fixed positions, the best HMGs of the war were probably the American Browning M2HB .50cal. and the Soviet DShK Model 1938. Fully 65in long (of which barrel was 45in) and weighing in with tripod at 128lb and accurate at ranges up to 8,000yd, the M2HB was used for air defence, on tanks, aircraft and even naval vessels. The DShK weighed in at 75lb and a whopping 346lb on its wheeled mount. It fired 12.7mm (.50in) rounds to around 2,500 yards.

Below: Luzon, Philippines, June 1945 – an Australian reporter interviews a machine-gunner from US 63rd Inf Div. At the ready, his 30cal Browning M1919A4, a company support weapon.

Below: British squad in the bocage, the section's Bren gun – the other men carry SMLEs. It weighed 20–25lb loaded, as compared to the rifle's 9lb.

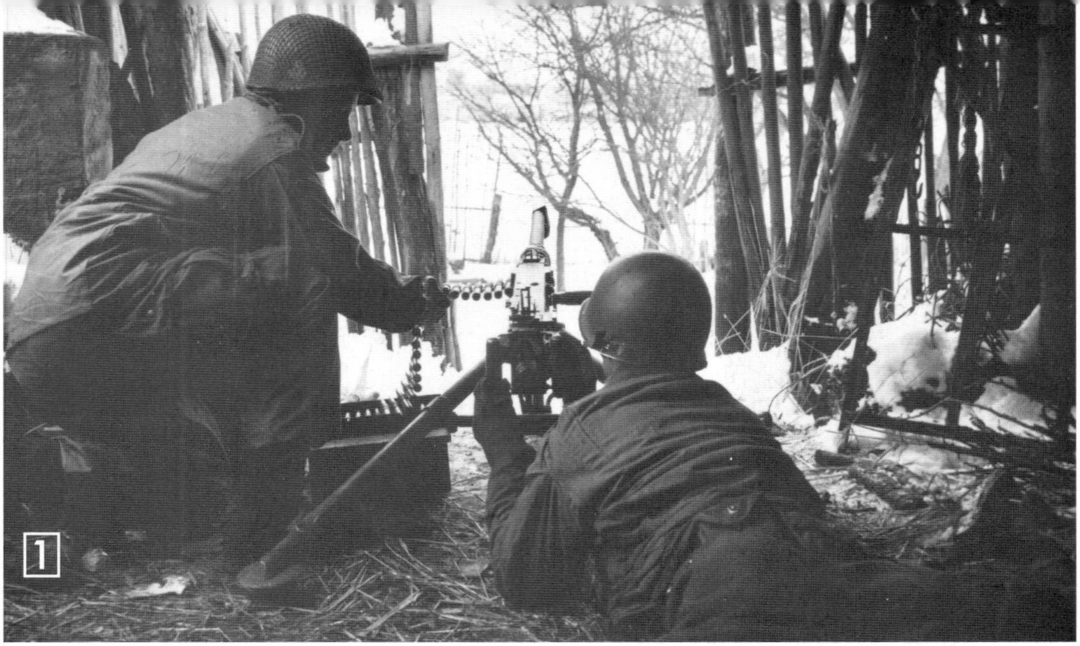
1

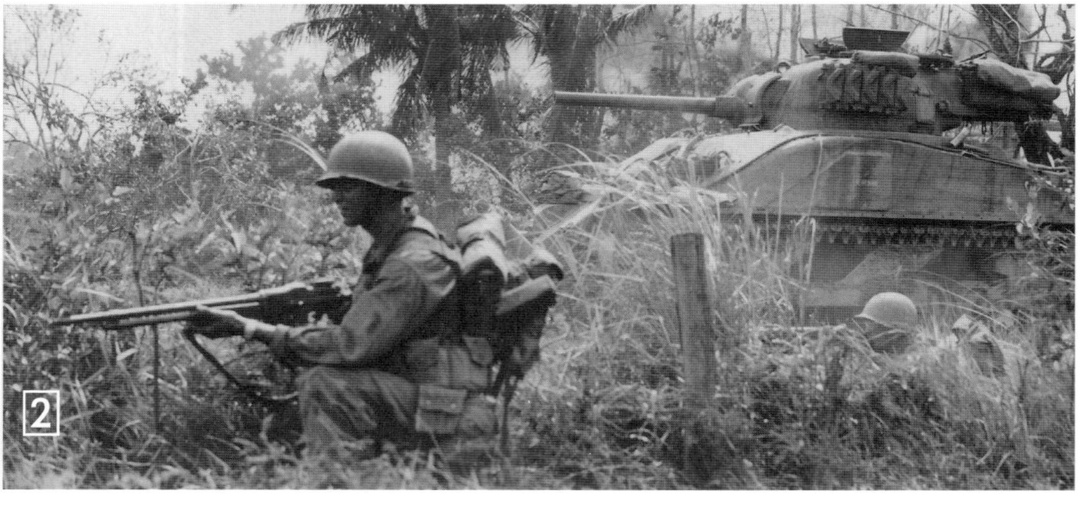
2

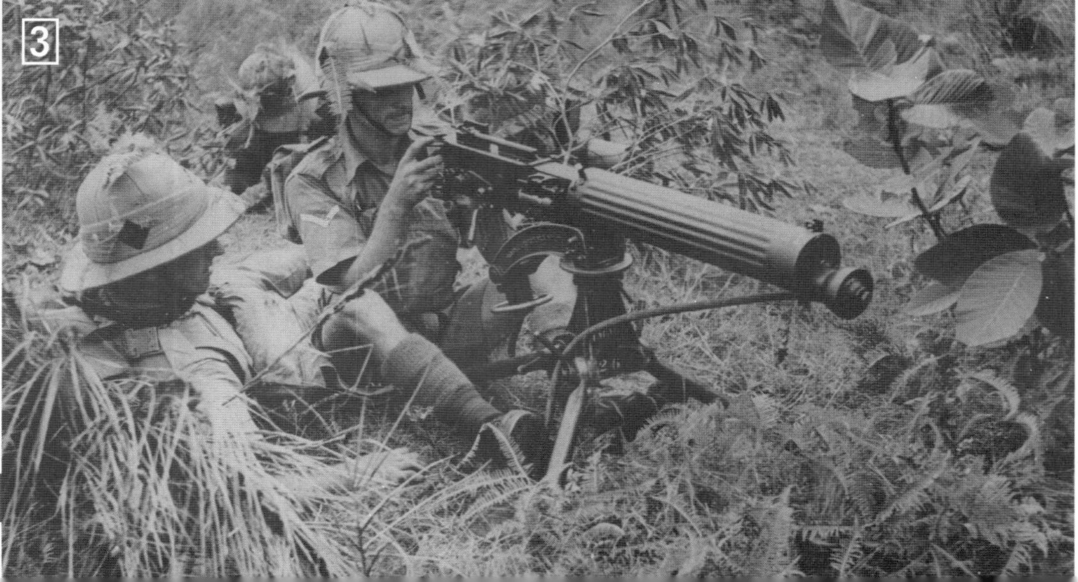
3

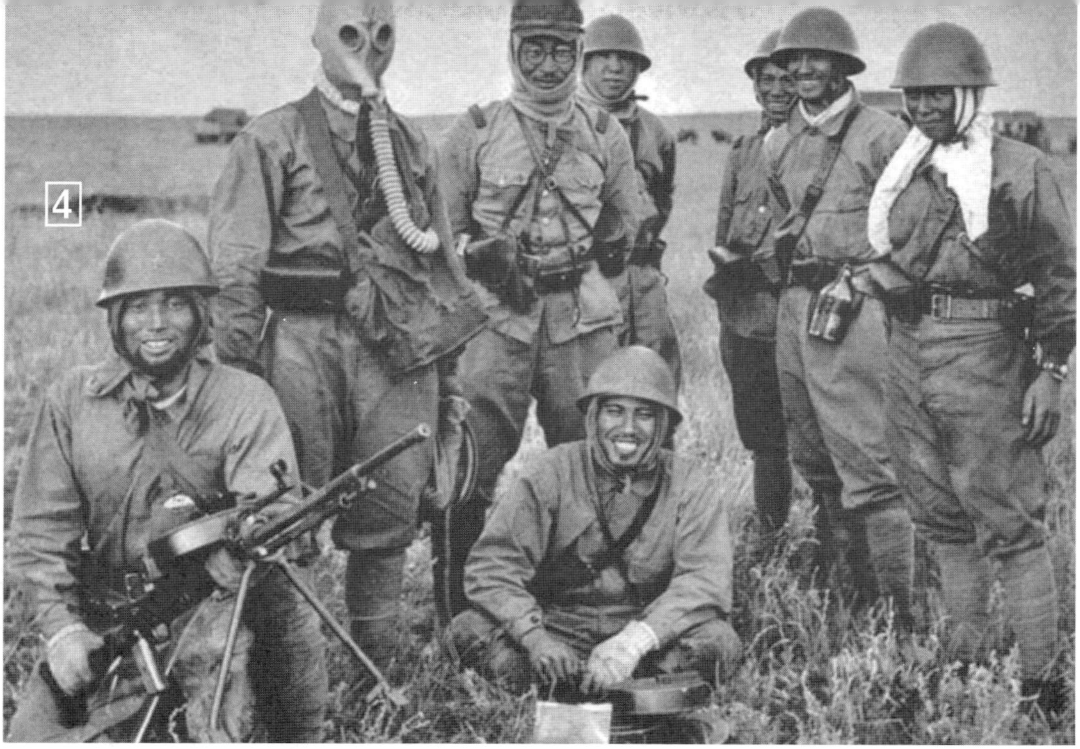
4

1 The US Army's M2HB .50in MG was accurate and could pierce thin armour plate.

2 The US Army made use of the WWI vintage Browning Automatic Rifle as its section weapon. Americans swear by it, in spite of its restricted magazine and accuracy issues, and it continued in service into the 1950s.

3 The water-cooled (note corrugated jacket and water lead) Vickers .303in MMG was as good as or better than other similar weapons.

4 A Japanese group with captured Russian equipment including a DT LMG. These were tank versions of the DP that were modified for use by infantry. They had a larger (60-round) magazine than the usual flat DP 47-round version (see p. 230).

5 Finnish sledge-mounted 7.62mm Maxim M/09-21 (note smooth water jacket). The Finns had around 1,000 of these in 1940 and they saw heavy front line use. The sledge mounting allowed a speedy getaway from an ambush position (see pp. 104–105).

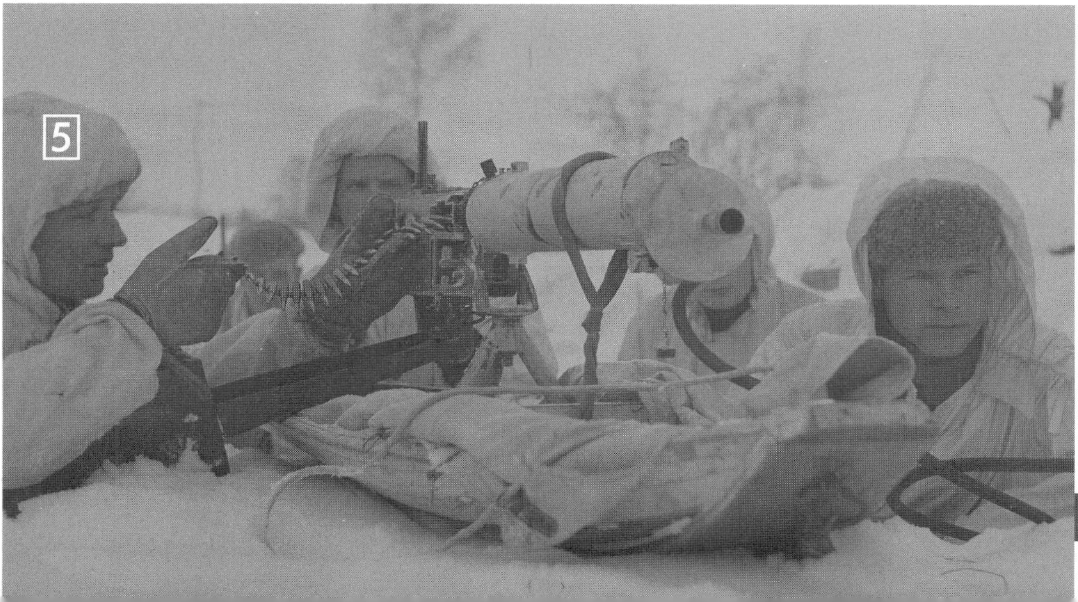
5

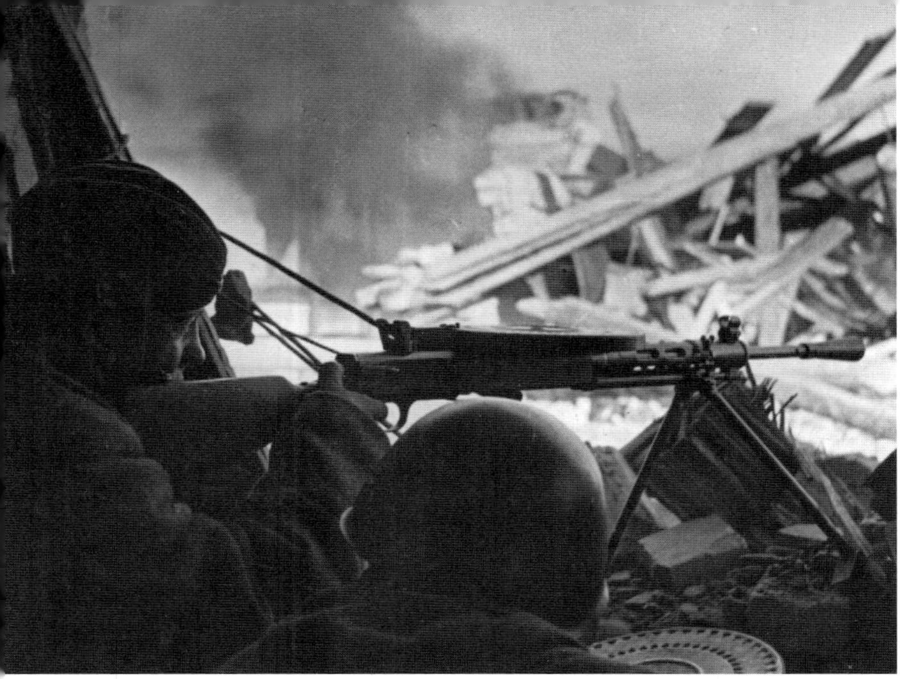

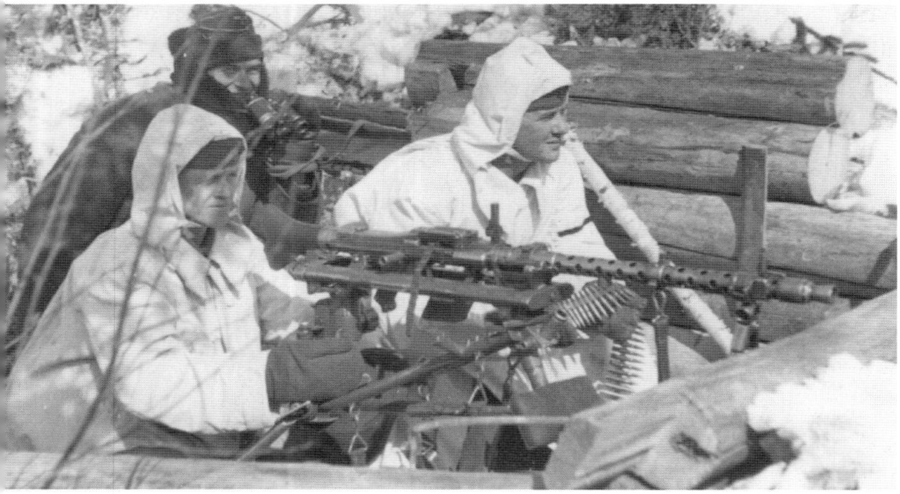

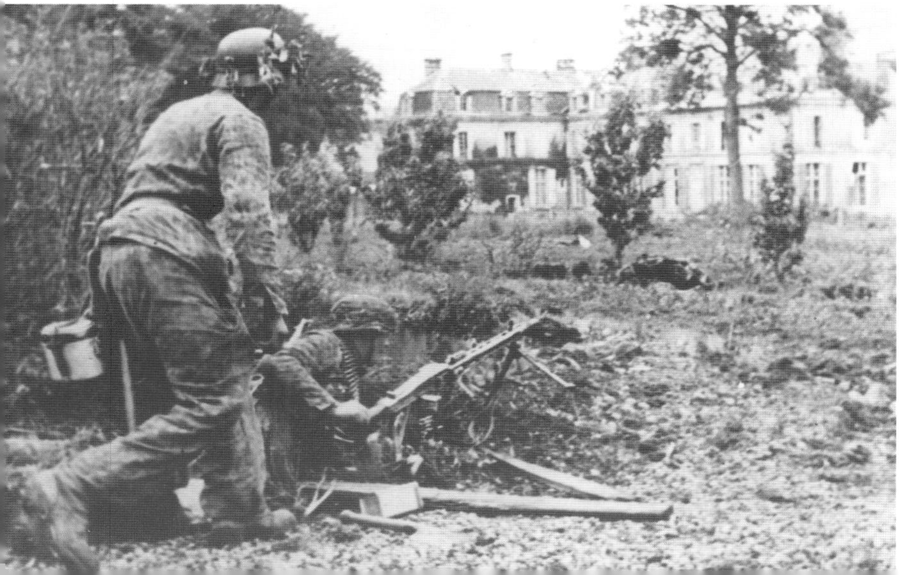

Above left: The classic flat-pan 47-round magazine of the Russian DP LMG saw it given the nickname '*proigryvatel*' – record player.

Centre left: The MG34 had the all-round capabilities that postwar saw the growth of the GPMG – the general-purpose machine gun. Usable with a bipod or – as here – a tripod, with a high rate of fire and an AA capability, it was one of the best machine guns of the war. It had its bad points: it was expensive and complicated to make; barrel heat caused by high rates of fire meant that frequent barrel changes were necessary; and it wasn't the most accurate of weapons.

Below left: The stripped-down MG42 provided an excellent replacement for the MG34. With a high rate of fire, it was reliable and relatively cheap to produce.

7 Ammunition loads

There was much official discussion about what constituted a suitable load for the infantryman. The load had to balance the need for a man to carry his weapons, sufficient ammunition and rations for action, as well as the clothing and accoutrements he needed to survive: haversack, spare clothing, mess tins, water bottle and entrenching tool.

The British 1944 *Infantry Training Pt VIII* notes that each section of 10 men should carry 400 rounds of small arms ammo (for their SMLE rifles and commander's Sten), 10 grenades and 25 Bren gun magazines. In the field, they often carried considerably more than this. Other countries' infantrymen were loaded as follows.

The German loading was: 1,150 rounds of MG ammo (250 rounds carried in 5-belt drums of 50; 900 rounds carried in 3 ammo boxes of 300); 360 rounds of rifle ammo (each rifleman carried 45 rounds on the march; 60 rounds in combat); 16 rounds of pistol ammo; 384 rounds of SMG ammunition (each MP40 gunner carried 6 magazines of 32 rounds, reduced to 28 rounds to stop jamming); 18 stick grenades (2 per man).

Japanese rifle squad had squad leader (rifle), 3 × MG crew (3 × pistol, 1 × LMG), ammo bearer (pistol), and 8 riflemen (rifles) carrying 540 rounds of MG ammo (90 rounds carried in 3 magazines of 30 rounds, 450 rounds carried in 3 boxes of 140 rounds to be loaded into magazines by ammo bearer); 810 rounds of rifle ammo (each rifleman 30 rounds in pouches and 60 in reserve); 24–48 rounds of pistol ammo; 13 hand grenades (2 per man).

The USMC rifle squads were divided into 3 fire teams of 4 men from 1944. Each fire team had a 2-man BAR team (BAR gunner carried 9 magazines, with 8 in the cartridge belt and 1 in the gun; the assistant 12). This brought the squad's BAR magazine count to 63, or 1,260 rounds compared to the Army's 700 rounds. Squad leaders and assistant automatic riflemen were armed with M1 Carbines (5 mags of 15 rounds each).

The US Army rifle squad of 1944 all carried rifles (except the one with the BAR): 1 squad leader, 1 asst, 1 BAR rifleman, 1 asst, 1 ammo bearer, 2 rifle grenadiers (rifle and M7 Grenade Launcher); 5 riflemen. Ammo load was 1,496 rounds of rifle ammunition (assuming 1 cartridge belt, 1 bandolier and 1 clip in the gun for riflemen); 700 rounds of BAR; 15 rifle grenades; 24 frag grenades.

The US Army – and to some extent the USMC – made use of the Thompson and M1 Grease gun SMGs which had 20- and 30-round magazines available. These could be carried in either 3- or 5-pouch belts. A full 5-cell pouch weighed 10lb and held 150 rounds.

The Russian rifle sections were 9-men strong. The heavy sections had a commander armed with a PPSh-41 or PPS-43 SMG, a deputy (Mosin or SVT-40), 2 × DP-27 teams of two (1 × DP, 1 × Mosin), and 3 × riflemen (armed with a Mosin). The light sections had only one DP section and so 5 riflemen. Mosin or SVT-40 rifle ammunition carried would be 70 rounds in clips in pouches on the belt (extras in bandoliers). The DP section would carry four 47-round magazines (1 for commander, 3 for asst). The PPSh-41s had 71- or 35-round magazines, the PPS-43 35-round mags.

8 Communications

Signals were crucial to the infantryman, allowing them to work closely with aircraft, artillery and armour, as well as intercommunication within their own units. General Omar N. Bradley wrote, 'A piece of paper makes you an officer, a radio makes you a commander' and the increasing importance of wireless technology is exemplified by the rise in numbers of signallers: the BEF went to France with 13,000 men of the Royal Signals; the British Liberation Army of 1945 had three times that number and the Royal Signals had expanded to over 150,000 worldwide. Every country's armed forces experienced a similar change and signallers were as indispensible to German troops in Russia as they were to Americans on Guadalcanal.

To cater for this need, technology and industry had to produce equipment that could work in every conceivable weather condition from the Equator to the Arctic Circle. The results were, as could be anticipated for such a relatively moden technology, patchy. While radios were much more prevalent, thousands and thousands of miles of wire were also laid over vast distances: Eighth Army, for example, laid telephone lines from Tripoli to Baghdad – over 2,000 miles. And as well as field telephones, teleprinters were heavily used: the British Army had 181 in 1939 and 11,000 in 1945.

There was even still a place for pigeons! In September 1944 it was a pigeon sent from the bridge at Arnhem that alerted British commanders, otherwise in the dark because of problems with radio reliability, to what was going on. Human messengers – often motorcyclists when the going was good enough – were also much in evidence. Nevertheless, wireless communications blossomed during the war, and most commanders – from sections to army groups – had their radio comms nets. In a mobile war, much of the equipment had to be portable and sturdy. In an age of glass valves and delicate wiring, it is surprising just how resilient the 1940s' technology proved, with man-portable radios becoming an important part of the infantryman's life. However, this meant that, along with the delicate machinery, power sources became as vital a part of military logistics as fuel. Generators worked fine at an army HQ a long way from the front but the infantryman's radio needed batteries and they were cumbersome and heavy. They weren't the easily rechargeable slimline product we see today and it's worth noting that for every transceiver carried by an infantryman, there was usually a bulky battery linked to it.

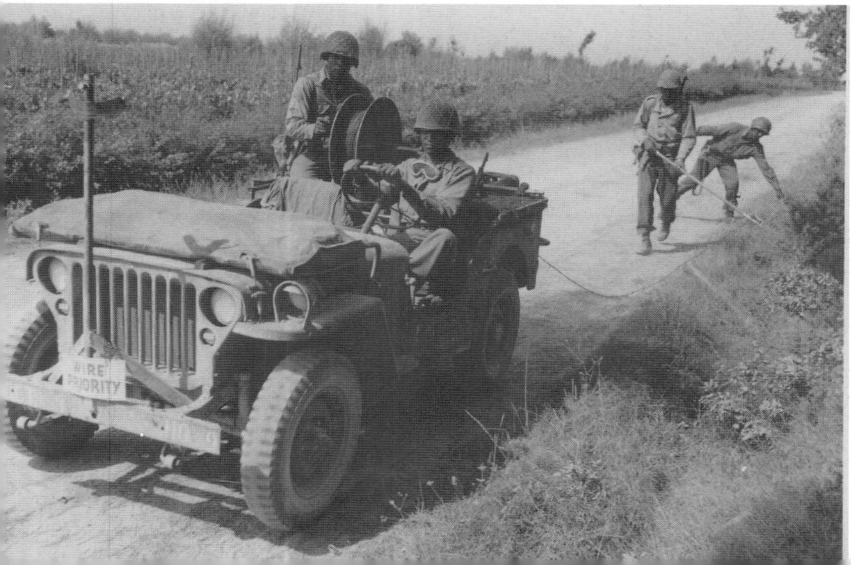
WIRE PRIORITY

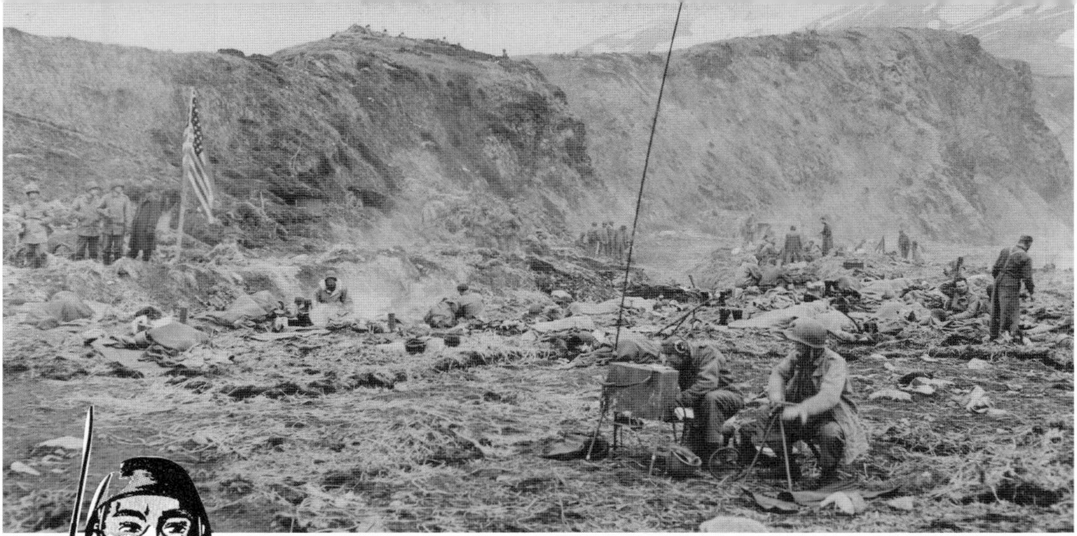

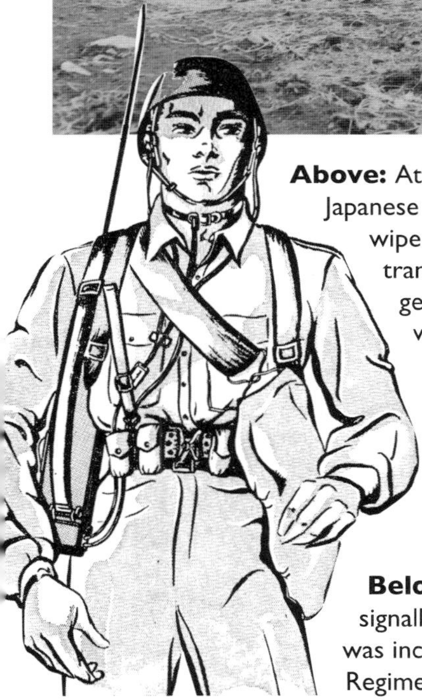

Above: Attu in the Aleutians was the scene of a banzai charge as the last Japanese attacked American troops on 29 May 1943. The Japanese were wiped out. The radio is an SCR-284 set, a combined receiver and transmitter, for which power is being produced by the GN-45 hand generator. Produced in large numbers (some 64,000), the SCR-284 was portable – just – and used from Operation Torch onward.

Left: The SCR-536, as its manual advises, was 'designed for two-way communication over short distances. The outstanding feature of its design is its extreme portability. It is intended primarily as a handietalkie for foot combat troops.' It could be used like this (with a headset) or in hand.

Below: Two of the SCR-536s can be seen in this photo, although the signaller is using wire and an EE-8 handset. Laying and mending wire was incessant. Here (**Opposite**), a wire crew of HQ Company, 370th Regiment (92nd Inf Div) is laying wire in the Ponsacco area, Italy.

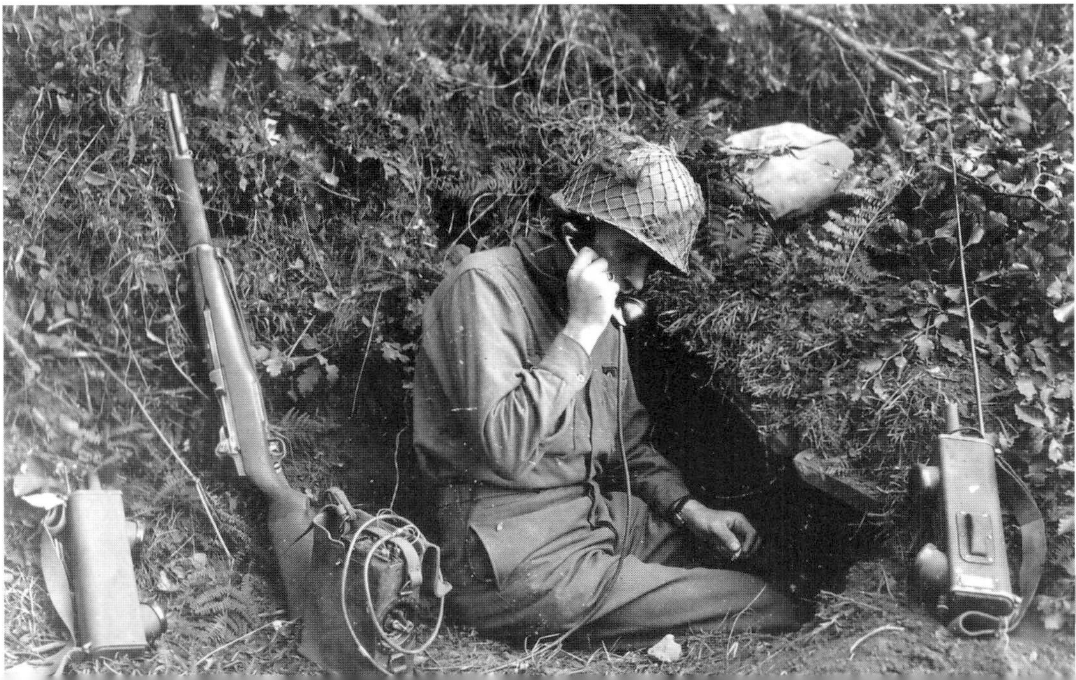

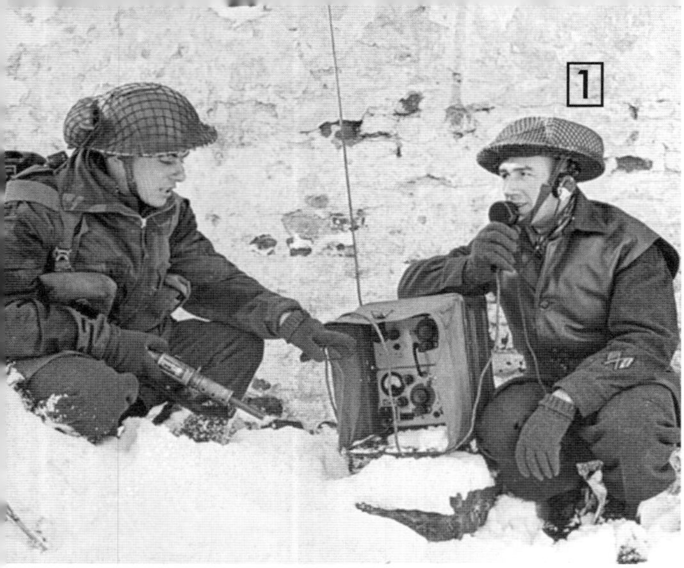

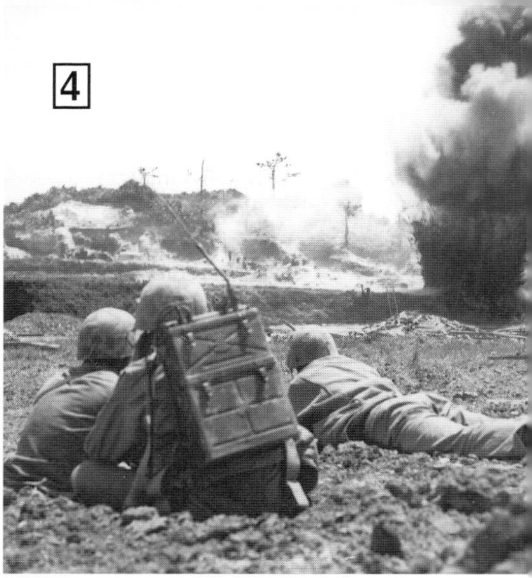

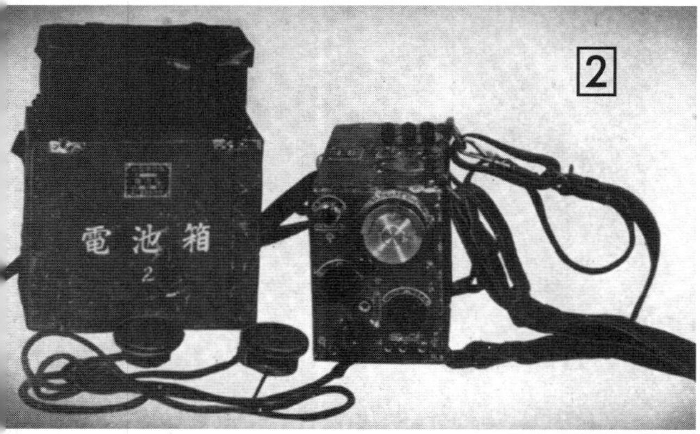
電池箱
2

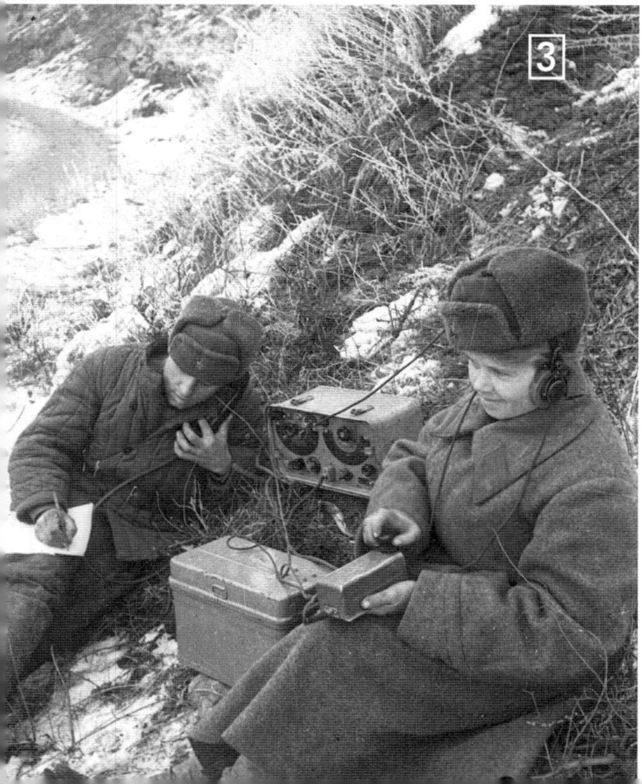

1 The British and Canadian Royal Signals provided communication services in the field down to the headquarters of regiments, batteries and battalions. These are infantrymen of D Coy, Régiment de Maisonneuve with a No 18 wireless set, Cuyk, Netherlands, 23 January 1945. This was the standard portable signals set used for communications between companies in the field and battalion HQs. A smaller and lighter set, the No 38, had a short range and was used within the company. Note crossed flags trades badge at right.

2 *TME30-480 Handbook on Japanese Military Forces* of 1944 said, 'The Japanese place most emphasis on wire communication. However, radio is used initially where communications must be established rapidly or where other means are not practicable. After wire communications have been established, radio assumes a secondary role as a stand-by communication link except where other means cannot be employed. ... Apparatus, to date, is of obsolescent design. Circuits and components are comparable with those used by the Allied Nations between 1935 and 1937. ... A great variety of small transceivers and transmitter-receiver combinations of 1 to 2 watts power are in operation. Such sets are usually man-pack. The transceivers are contained in one case which is carried on the chest; the batteries are carried in another case on the back.' This is one of the manpack sets, the Type 66.

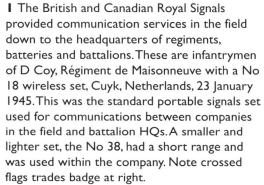

3 The Red Army's RB (3-R) infantry/artillery two-man pack HF radio had separate transceiver and receiver. Most Russian units had three teams: telephone and telegraph, radio and message centre. 'For example, a rifle regiment had a signal company of 50 men organised into two telephone and telegraph platoons, and a radio platoon. The first telephone and telegraph platoon has three squads to establish wire communications with the rifle battalions. The second telegraph and telephone platoon establishes wire communications within the command, staff, and rear area installations of the regiment and maintains the message centre. The radio platoon establishes and operates the radio nets of the regiment.' (*TM30-430*) Their equipment was partly constructed in the USSR, partly from Lend-Lease.

4 The SCR-300 was an American portable radio receiver and transmitter designed for communication over short distances. The manual identifies it as being 'primarily intended as a walkie-talkie for foot combat troops.' The antenna is an AN-130-A, a two-section 33in-long unit; range about 3 miles.

5 Many different vehicles were used as command or radio vehicles. This M3 halftrack is being used by a Royal Artillery commander. Towards the end of the war the British used TCLs (tentacles), as a link between the front line and RAF close support aircraft. These were usually commanded by an artillery officer, crewed by three signallers, who operated and maintained the radios, and a driver mechanic. Housed in a 15cwt truck the wireless had an effective range of about 40km and they could link into the special air support radio network and pass back air support requests to the Joint Battle Room. The artillery officers were able to advise the local ground commander on using air support. They didn't have any radios that could communicate with aircraft. A modified version of the TCL, the visual control posts were introduced for Operation Goodwood on 18 July 1944. They added a fighter-bomber pilot with a VHF radio for communication with overhead aircraft. Observation of targets was an issue, and they were normally positioned in leading divisional or brigade HQ. VCPs consisted of a tank or White Scout car rigged with the required radio sets, and a total of five personnel all ranks.

6 An infantryman from Polish First Armoured Division carries the standard British infantry short-range radio, the No 38 wireless set. Note the long webbing sheath for the antenna.

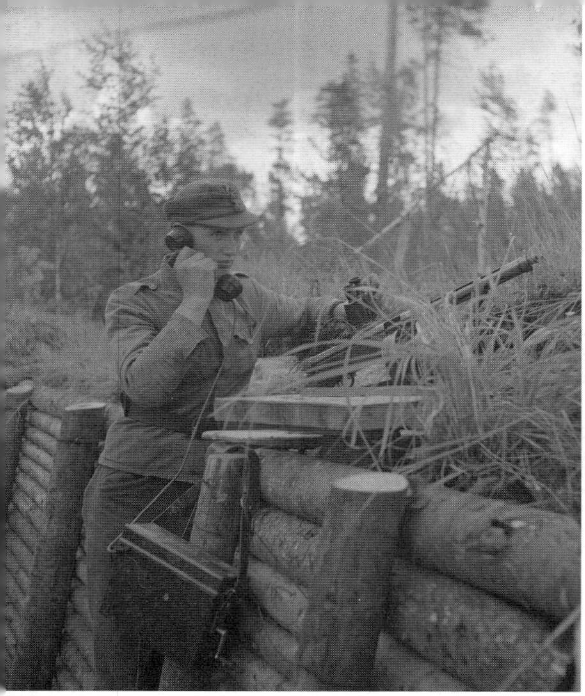

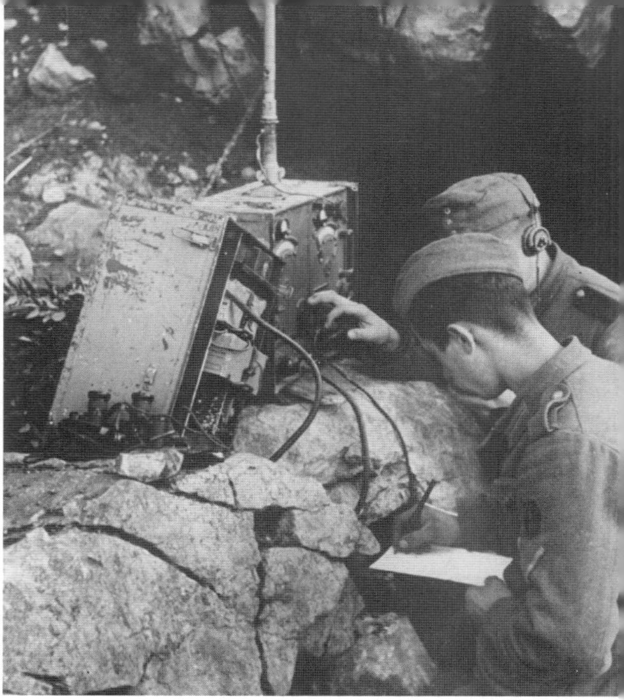

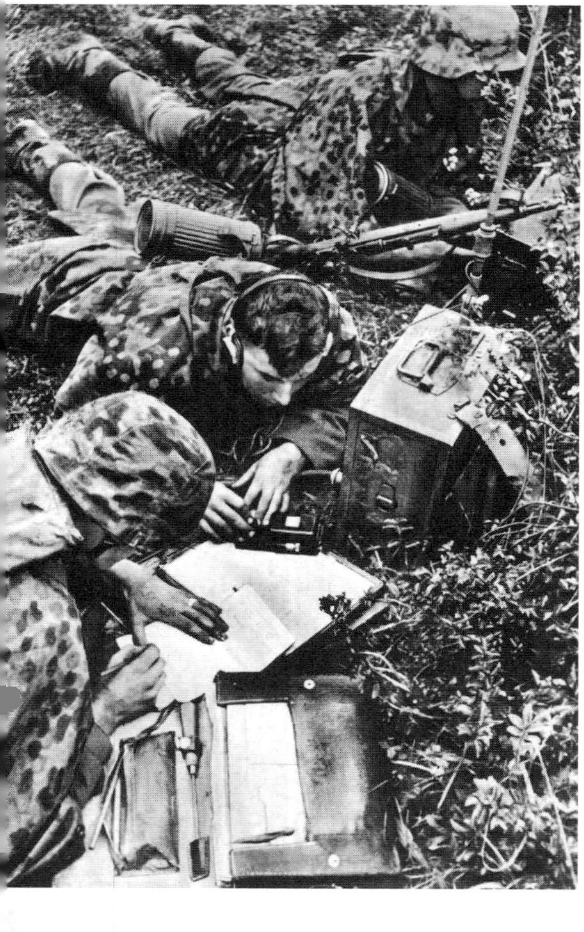

Above left: A Finnish artillery spotter reports back by phone; June 1943.

Above: German short-range communications with other troops – especially mortars or artillery – was by *Feldfunksprecher* (FeldFu) radio. The typical maximum range of the FeldFu.b/b1/b2 was about 1–1.5km. For medium-range coverage, the *Tornisterfunkgerät* (TornFu) was also portable. It had a range of 5–25km (3–15 miles). Messenger dogs, carrier pigeons and rockets (visual or sound) were used to supplement the two basic methods of radio and wire. These two German soldiers are working with a TornFu on the Italian front in February 1944.

Left: Waffen-SS from the Totenkopf Division use a TornFu.d2. German radio operators were taught to restrict radio traffic so as not to give positions away. They were also very careful about radio use having gained importantant intelligence from lax Allied radio procedure in Africa. It was only after capturing Hauptmann Alfred Seebohm's *Nachrichten Fern Aufklärungs Kompanie 621* (a radio intercept unit) that British forces realised quite how much information they were giving away and tightened up accordingly. The problem remained till the end of the war, US forces being particularly prone to chatter.

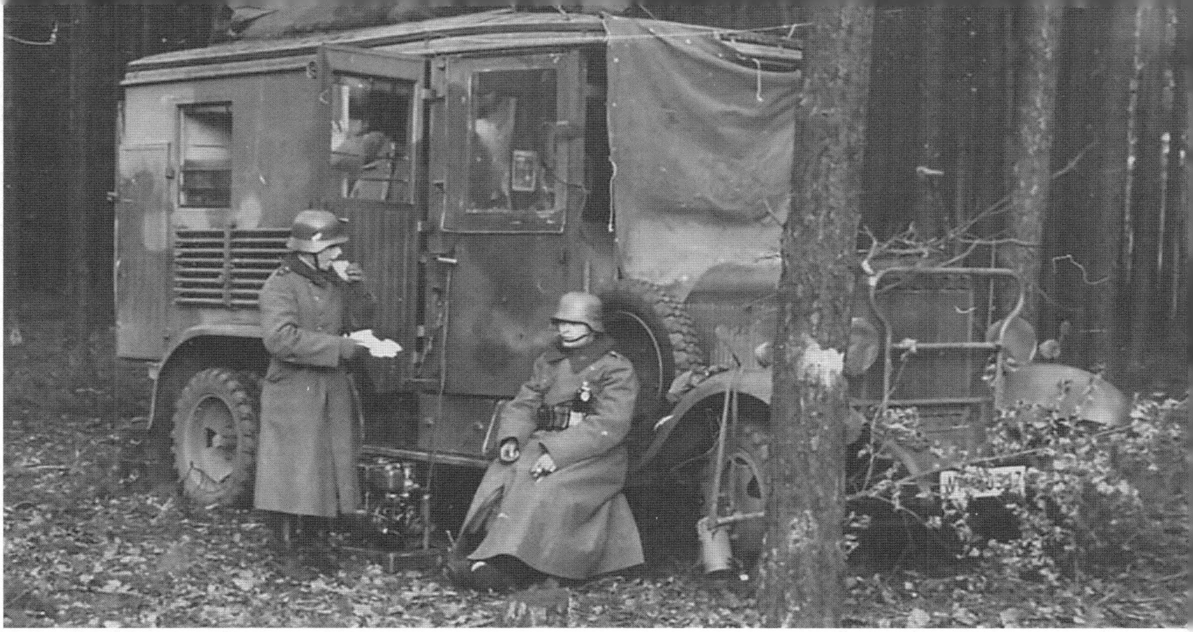

Above and Below: Every country produced a range of radio vehicles – lorries (**Above** a Mercedes-Benz G3A Kfz 72), armoured vehicles (**Below** Guderian in his Sdkfz 251/6 command vehicle. with a FuG 8 radio station) and, of course, Jeeps.

Right and Below right: A German battalion's signals platoon had two light telephone teams in 1939 (with 10km of wire, six handsets and a switchboard), this increasing to three in 1944 with a corresponding increase in wire and handsets. Beside the field telephones, the signallers used *Feldfunksprecher* radios, which were also used in mobile warfare – although only after the enemy had been engaged.

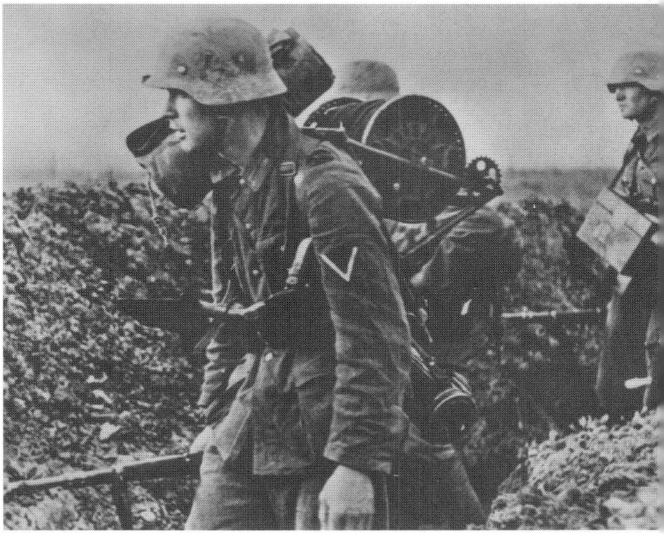

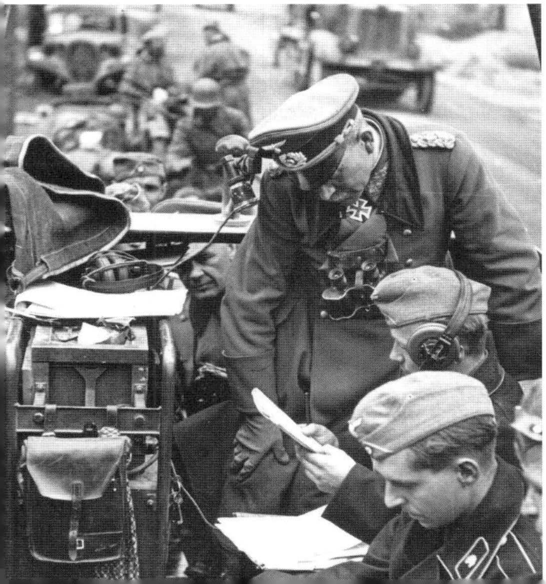

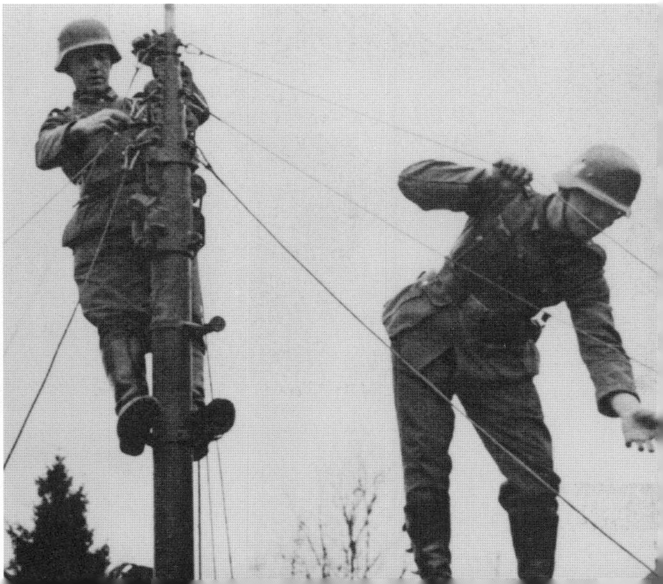

Abbreviations

52 (L) Inf Div — British 52nd (Lowland) Infantry Division

79th Armd Div — Unit that controlled all British specialised armour: Crab anti-mine flails, Crocodile or Wasp flamethrowers, Kangaroo APCs, AVREs, Buffalo LVTs, etc

AFV — armoured fighting vehicle

APC — armoured personnel carrier

AT or A/Tk — anti-tank

AVRE — Armoured Vehicle Royal Engineers – a modified Churchill with a Petard mortar

BAR — Browning automatic rifle

Bty — battery (artillery)

CCA/B/R — Combat Command – a US armored division was usually subdivided into commands

Cdo — Commando, used of the soldier and the units. RAF Cdos protected airfields; RN Cdos beachheads. The Army and RM Cdos were used mainly to spearhead landing operations and were used as such at D-Day and the Rhine crossings

(C)GMC — (Combination) gun motor carriage

CMP — Canadian Military Pattern – range of trucks built in Canada to British inital specs

CP — command post

DD — Duplex Drive – amphibious tanks (usually Shermans)

DLI — Durham Light Infantry (Brit)

DUKW — GMC amphibious haulage vehicle (US)

ETO — European Theatre of Operations

FJR — *Fallschirmjäger* Regiment = German paratrooper. II./FJR6 = second battalion of 6th FJ Regt

GMC — General Motors of Canada

GR — Grenadier Regiment

GS — general service

HBT — herringbone twill – US uniform cloth

JG — Jungle Green – British jungle uniform developed from KD

Kangaroo — APC created by gutting an AFV

KD — Khaki Drill – British hot climate uniform

KIA — killed in action

KOSB — King's Own Scottish Borderers (British regiment)

Kwk — *Kampfwagenkanone* = German tank gun

LC — landing craft types: **A** assault; **G** gun; **I** infantry; **L** large; **R** rocket; **VP** vehicle/personnel. RN contingents brought craft across Europe for use in the major river crossings

le/sGrW — *leichte/schwere Grantwerfer* = light/heavy mortar

LS — landing ship types: **I** infantry; **T** tank

LSSAH Regt — *Leibstandarte-SS Adolf Hitler* bodyguard unit that became 1. SS-Panzer-Division

LVT(A) — landing vehicle tracked (armoured) aka Alligator or Buffalo

MIA — missing in action

MMC — medium mortar carriage

MTO — Mediterranean Theatre of Operations

NF — Royal Northumberland Fusiliers

NKVD — People's Commissariat for Internal Affairs – Russian Secret Police

Pak — *Panzerabwehrkanone* = German anti-tank gun

PIAT — Projector, Infantry Anti Tank – Britain's answer to the *Panzerfaust* looked as if it were designed by Heath Robinson but was effective

PIR/B — Parachute Infantry Regiment/Battalion (US)

PoRW — *Peculiarities of Russian Warfare* (see Bibliography: German Report Series)

PzKpfw — *Panzerkampfwagen* (armoured vehicle)

RAD — *Reichsarbeitsdienst* (Reich labour service)

RB — Rifle Brigade

R(C)AMC — Royal (Canadian) Army Medical Corps

R(C)EME — Royal (Canadian) Electrical and Mechanical Engineers

RTR — Royal Tank Regiment

S/L/M/HMG — sub-/light/medium/heavy machine gun

SBG — small girder bridge (British)

SdKfz — *Sonderkraftfahrzeug* (special motor vehicle)

SP — self-propelled

SSRF — Small Scale Raiding Force

StuG — Sturmgeschütz

SWPA — Southwest Pacific Area

T/O&E — Tables of organisation and equipment (US)

TCL — tentacle (see p. 235)

TOT — time on target (timed artillery shoot)

T&TT — *Tactical & Technical Trends* (see Bibliography)

USMC — US Marine Corps

WIA — wounded in action

Photo Credits

Albumwar2.com 19 (04477), 20 (Evgeni Khaldei), 24T (04999) 24B (03717), 25T (042363), 25B (04029), 26 (02823), 60T (06556), 60C (Semen Fridlyand), 60B (05592), 66B (06246), 72T (02838), 72B (05334), 73T (01909), 81 (08199), 92L (06482), 101TR (Georgiy Zelma), 143C (Valery Faminsky), 148 (Valery Faminsky), 150L (Estonian Historical Museum/ Leonid Velikzhanin), 150R (Anatoly Morozov), 151 (Evgeni Khaldei), 152 (Semen Alperin), 153L (01845), 153R (00750), 154R (Semen Fridland), 154B (Max Alpert), 155 (Mark Markov-Grinberg), 178TR (Natalia Bode), 178BR (02268), 180BR (Arthur Grimm), 182T (01846), 184B (04404), 201 (04424), 201 (02215), 205 (Natalia Bode), 206 (666), 208T (07775), 208B (Natalia Bode), 210C (Natalia Bode), 215B (04959), 216TR (Emmanuel Evzerihin), 225TL (Emmanuel Evzerihin), 225TR (Georgiy Zelma), 226B (06605), 229T (02799), 230T (06666), 234B (Natalia Bode), 236B (05192); **Battlefield Historian** 28B, 42 (insert L), 44B, 48B, 50B, 61T, 61B, 63T, 64B, 80 (C&B), 106, 108 (both), 114 (both), 119B, 122, 128-129, 128(BL&BR), 130 (inset), 172B, 180BL, 195B, 201T, 203T, 204, 205T, 206 (1,2,4,5), 209(6), 221T, 227R; **Bundesarchiv** 76, 197, 205C, 237T&BL; **Richard Charlton-Taylor collection** 16, 31, 69BL, 98B, 142R, 145B, 147C, 178TL, 199TL, 205(4), 230C; **Fortepan Hungarian Archives** 38B (Lissák Tivadar); **HMSO,** 164, 168, 202B; **Library and Archives Canada** 14 (Lt J. Ernest DeGuire, PA-204813), 32 (Lt C.E. Nye, PA-211306), 44C (J.H. Smith, PA-132600), 44B (Lt Donald I. Grant, PA-116536), 53B (Lt Barney J. Gloster, PA-177591), 61C (Alexander M. Stirton, PA-131627), 62T, 63B (Lt Michael M. Dean),68T (Lt Ken Bell, PA-133100), 68BL (PA-136999), 70C (Lt Gilbert Alexander Milne, PA-191182), 144T (Lt Dan Guravich, PA-133165), 145T (Lt Michael M. Dean, PA-131437), 180TL (Lt Strathy E.E. Smith, PA-177347), 210BL, 217BL (Lt Frank L. Dubervill, PA-191017), 223T (Lt Donald I. Grant, PA-131431), 223C (Lt Donald I. Grant, PA-128794), 234T (Lt Michael M. Dean, PA-190099); **Library of Congress** 8, 12-13 (both), 46, 49T, 51B, 80T, 89B, 90T, 116, 139, 186BR, 206(3), 228B; **NARA** 2-3, 4-5, 6, 10, 11 (both), 23, 28T, 29, 37T, 39B, 44T, 47 (both), 48T, 49 (C&B), 51T, 52 (both), 53T, 54T, 55 (C&B), 56, 57 (both), 64(T&C), 65B, 67 (all), 70T, 70B, 71B, 75B, 78-79, 88 (both), 90B, 91 (both), 113T, 117 (all), 118 (both), 119T, 120, 121 (both), 123 (all), 124 (both), 125 (all), 130-131, 132, 136, 137, 140, 141T, 143TL, 143 (TR&BR), 144 (C&B), 146TL, 147T, 156-157 (all), 158, 161, 163 (both), 171, 176, 179B, 180TR, 181 (TL&TR), 182 (C&B), 184TL, 185BL, 186TL, 187 (TR&B), 188 (3&4), 189 (L&BR), 190 (all), 191 (TR&BL), 192 (T&C), 194C, 202 (TL&TR), 207B, 210BR, 211B, 216BL, 217BR, 219 (both), 220TL, 221BR, 222, 223B, 225B, 227L, 228T&C, 230, 231T&B; **Narodowe Archiwum Cyfrowe** 18, 37B, 55T, 66T, 68BR, 71C, 74 (both), 75TL, 75TR, 97, 100T, 105T, 126, 178BR, 179T, 181 (BL&BR), 183, 185BR, 186(TR&BL), 188T, 189TR, 192B, 193, 194T&B, 195T&C, 207T, 209(4), 224BL&BR, 230B, 235B, 236TR; **Nationaal Archief, Dutch archive** 42-43, 205(5); **SA-kuva, Finnish Archives** 35T, 101TL, 103B&T, 104, 141B, 208TL, 218(both), 229B, 236TL; *Tactical and Technical Trends* 196, 198, 200, 221B; **US Army** 84 (all), 86 (both), 87, 96, 99, 100C, 105BR&BL, 135, 160, 212-213, 216, 220B, 225C, 226T&C, 233C, 234T; **WikiCommons** 38T Reinhardphilippi, 50T AlfvanBeem/CC0, 73B Willi Ude/CC BY-SA 3.0, 146BR TwoWings/CC BY-SA 3.0; **World War Photos** 54B

Left: The infantrymen of the Western Allies took a while to come to terms with war, but when they did they proved more than equal to the task.

Bibliography

Documents

Combat Lessons, various.
Battle Experiences 1944–45; HQ US Army ETO, 1945.
British Infantry Training 1944 Part I The Infantry Battalion.
British Infantry Training 1944 Part VI The Anti-Tank Platoon.
British Infantry Training 1944 Part VIII Fieldcraft, Battle Drill, Section And Platoon Tactics.
Field Service Pocket Book.
FM5-20A *Camouflage, Basic Principles*; WD, 1944.
FM5-31 *Land Mines and Booby Traps*, WD, 1943.
FM7-15 *Infantry Field Manual Heavy Weapons Company*, WD, 1942.
FM7-20 *Infantry Battalion*, WD, 1944.
FM72-20 *Jungle Warfare*; WD, 1942.
Foreign Military Studies *Combat in the East*; Historical Division European Command, 1952.
Foreign Military Studies *Mountain Warfare*; Historical Division European Command, 1954.
Foreign Military Studies *Small Unit Tactics: Artillery*; Historical Division European Command, 1954.
German Defense Tactics Against Russian Breakthroughs; CMH, 2000.
German Report Series: Peculiarities of Russian Warfare, 1949.
German Tactical Doctrine; Military Intelligence Service, 1942.
HQ 1st US Infantry Division: *Selected Intelligence Reports vol II December 1944–May 1945.*
Infantry Tactical Manual of the Red Army, 1942.
Intelligence Bulletin, various.
McKinney, Lt Col Leonard L.: *Chemical Corps Historical Studies, No 4: Portable Flame Thrower Operations in World War II*; 1949.
Report on Operation 'Blackcock'
Special Series No 3 German Military Training; Military Intelligence Service, 1942.
Special Series No 14 German Infantry Weapons; Military Intelligence Service, 1942.
Special Series No 18 German Winter Warfare; Military Intelligence Service, 1943.
Special Series No 20 German Ski Training and Tactics; Military Intelligence Service, 1944.
Special Series No 27 Soldier's Guide to the Japanese Army; Military Intelligence Service, 1944.
Special Series No 30 Japanese Mortars and Grenade Dischargers; Military Intelligence Service, 1945.
Tactical & Technical Trends, various.
TME11-227A *Japanese Radio Comms Equipment*, WD, 1944.
TME30-410 *Handbook on the British Army*; WD, 1942.
TME30-480 *Handbook on Japanese Military Forces*; WD, 1944.
TME30-451 *Handbook on German Military Forces*; WD, 1945.
TM11-235 *Radio Sets SCR-536-A, -B, -C, -D, -E, and -F*, WD, 1945.
TM11-242 *Radio Set SCR-300-A*, WD, 1945.
Truppenführung Part I.
War Diary: 9th Battalion The Durham Light Infantry.

Books and articles

Bradley, Omar N.: *A Soldier's Story*; Henry Holt, 1951.
Cox, Maj Alexander A.: *Unit Cohesion and Morale in Combat*:; Fort Leavenworth, 1995–96.
Doubler, Capt Michael J.: *Busting the Bocage*; CSI, 1988.
Ellis, John: *Brute Force*; André Deutsch Ltd, 1990.
Ellis, John: *World War II The Sharp End*; Windrow & Greene, 1990.
Fennell, Jonathan: *Fighting the People's War*; Cambridge, 2019.
Fuschak, K. Graham: *The 43rd Infantry Division: Unit Cohesion and Neuropsychiatric Casualties* Thesis, Fort Leavenworth, 1999.
Glantz, David M.: *Barbarossa*; Tempus, 2001.
Headrick, LCdr Alan C.: *Bicycle Blitzkrieg: The Malayan Campaign and the Fall of Singapore*; Naval War College, 1994.
Holt, Maj Jeffrey P.: *Operational Performance of the U.S. 28th Infantry Division, September to December 1944*; Thesis, Fort Leavenworth, 1994.
Kaplan, Robert: 'Medicine at the Battle of Stalingrad'; *Journal of the Royal Society of Medicine*, Vol 93, February 2000.
Leon, Maj Robert M. Leon: *Battlefield Stress*; Maxwell AFB, 1987.
MacDonald, Charles B.: *The Siegfried Line Campaign*; Washington, 1963.
Rottman, Gordan L.: *Warrior 123 Soviet Rifleman 1941-1945*; Osprey, 2007.
Schlott, Maj John E.: *Culmination In The Moral Domain: Combat Stress*; Fort Leavenworth, 1991–92.
Thompson, Clinton W.: 'Hell in the Snow: The U.S. Army in the Colmar Pocket, January 22–February 9, 1945'; History Theses Paper 9, 2017.
Vigo, Milan: 'The Allied Landing at Anzio-Nettuno, 22 January–4 March 1944: Operation Shingle,' *Naval War College Review*: Vol. 67: No. 4 , Article 8, 2014.
Weest, Lt Col Larry W. : *Annual Report of Medical Department Activities*, 28th Inf Div, 1945.
Willems, Bastiaan: 'Defiant Breakwaters or Desperate Blunders? A Revision of the German Late-War Fortress Strategy'; *The Journal of Slavic Military Studies*, 2015.

Right: The late war British infantrymen with a range of equipment and weapons. They are in action and have dispensed with their packs. They wear leather jerkins and standard webbing, with spades as well as their usual entrenching tools. The two on the left carry Stens, the man in the centre a PIAT and the man on the right an SMLE. He's also got a bandoleer for extra ammunition.